Sustainable Development in the Southeastern Coastal Zone

Rapid population growth in the southeastern coastal zone has had an important influence on both resource management policy at the federal, state, regional, and local levels and the findings of environmental impact studies. This book presents papers from a symposium dealing with the complex problems resulting from the ever-increasing development of the southeastern coastal region. An interdisciplinary approach was taken with a view to developing sustainable development concepts. Twenty-six papers are included by fifty-five contributors representing a variety of disciplines, such as economics, environmental health and sciences, marine science, and statistics. The topics covered include policy in its broadest sense, environmental resources, and population trends.

Sustainable Development in the Southeastern Coastal Zone

THE BELLE W. BARUCH LIBRARY IN MARINE SCIENCE

1   Estuarine Microbial Ecology
2   Symbiosis in the Sea
3   Physiological Ecology of Marine Organisms
4   Biological Rhythms in the Marine Environment
5   The Mechanisms of Mineralization in the Invertebrates and Plants
6   Ecology of Marine Benthos
7   Estuarine Transport Processes
8   Marsh-Estuarine Systems Simulation
9   Reproductive Ecology of Marine Invertebrates
10   Advanced Concepts in Ocean Measurements for Marine Biology
11   Marine Benthic Dynamics
12   Processes in Marine Remote Sensing
13   Marine Pollution and Physiology: Recent Advances
14   Shallow-Water Marine Benthic Macroinvertebrates of South Carolina
15   The Cellular and Molecular Biology of Invertebrate Development
16   Research Data Management in the Ecological Sciences
17   Pollution Physiology of Estuarine Organisms
18   Theory and Application in Fish Feeding Ecology
19   Recent Developments in Fish Otolith Research
20   Sustainable Development in the Southeastern Coastal Zone

THE BELLE W. BARUCH LIBRARY IN MARINE SCIENCE NUMBER 20

Sustainable Development in the Southeastern Coastal Zone

F. John Vernberg
Winona B. Vernberg
Thomas Siewicki
Editors

Published for the Belle W. Baruch Institute for
Marine Biology and Coastal Research
by the UNIVERSITY OF SOUTH CAROLINA PRESS

Library of Congress Cataloging–in–Publication Data

Sustainable development in the southeastern coastal zone / F. John
    Vernberg, Winona B. Vernberg, Thomas Siewicki, editors.
       p.   cm. — (Belle W. Baruch Library in Marine Science ;
  no. 20)
   Papers presented at a symposium held at Myrtle Beach, South
Carolina, March 2–5, 1993.
   "Published for the Belle W. Baruch Institute for Marine Biology
and Coastal Research."
     Includes bibliographical references and index.
     ISBN 1–57003–198–3
     1. Sustainable development—South Atlantic States. 2. South
Atlantic States—Economic policy. 3. Enviromental policy—South
Atlantic States. I. Vernberg, F. John, 1925– . II. Vernberg,
Winona B., 1924– . III. Siewicki, Thomas, 1953– . IV. Belle W.
Baruch Institute for Marine Biology and Coastal Research.
V. Series.
HC107.A13S94   1997   97–9203
338.975—dc21

Contents

Preface   ix

Contributors   xi

Introduction: Sustainable Development   1
   Robert L. Beekman, F. John Vernberg, and Winona B. Vernberg

Policy

Land Settlement, Public Policy, and the Environmental Future of the Southeast Coast   7
   Leonard Shabman

State Perspective in Coastal Zone Management   25
   Christopher L. Brooks

Local Polices to Control Coastal Growth in the Waccamaw Region   31
   Jan S. Davis, Joe W.T. Burch, David M. Essex, Mark H. Hoeweler,
   Mark E. Kinsey, John M. Penney, and William J. Schwartzkopf

Population Trends in the Coastal Area, Concentrating on South Carolina   55
   Walter P. Bailey

Conceptual Models Relevant to Sustaining Coastal Zone Resources   75
   Eugene P. Odum

A Crisis and Opportunity in Coastal Oceans: Coastal Fisheries as a Case Study   81
   John Mark Dean

Geographic Information Systems for Sustainable Development in the   89
Southeastern United States: A Review of Applications and Research Needs
   William K. Michener, David P. Lanter, and Paula F. Houhoulis

Development and the Environment

Coastal Wetlands   111
   Ruth Patrick

Ecology of Southeastern Salt Marshes   117
    F.J. Vernberg

Anthropogenic Impacts on Salt Marshes—A Review   135
    John E. Weinstein

Sustainable Development in the Southeastern Coastal Zone: 171
Environmental Impacts on Fisheries
    Donald E. Hoss and David W. Engel

The Use of Biological Measures in Assessments of Toxicants in the Coastal Zone   187
    Edward R. Long

The Effects of Urbanization on Human and Ecosystem Health   221
    W.B. Vernberg, G.I. Scott, S.H. Strozier, J. Bemiss, and J.W. Daugomah

New Microbiological Approaches for Assessing and Indexing   241
Contamination Loading in Estuaries and Marine Waters
    W.D. Watkins and W. Burkhardt, III

Microbial Biotransformations of Metals: Effects on Altering   265
the Trophic Availability of Metals
    Alan W. Decho

Urbanization Effects on Southeastern Estuaries: Case Studies

Eutrophication in Estuaries and Coastal Systems: Relationships of   285
Physical Alterations, Salinity Stratification, and Hypoxia
    Robert J. Livingston

Long-term Trends in Nutrient Generation by Point and Nonpoint Sources   319
in the Albemarle-Pamlico Estuarine Basin
    Donald W. Stanley

Geographic Information Systems for Sustainable Development: 343
South Carolina's Edisto River Basin Project
    William D. Marshall

Geographic Information Processing Assessment of the Impacts of Urbanization 355
on Localized Coastal Estuaries: A Multidisciplinary Approach
Dwayne E. Porter, William K. Michener, Tom Siewicki, Don Edwards,
and Christopher Corbett

The Effects of Coastal Development on Watershed Hydrography and 389
the Transport of Organic Carbon
Matthew Wahl, H.N. McKellar, Jr., and Thomas M. Williams

Water Quality in Two High-salinity Estuaries: Effects of Watershed Alteration 413
Elizabeth R. Blood and Pauley A. Smith

Polynuclear Aromatic Hydrocarbon and Trace Metal Burdens in Sediment and 445
the Oyster, *Crassostrea virginica* Gmelin, From Two High-salinity
Estuaries in South Carolina
Alan R. Fortner, Marion Sanders, and Sharon W. Lemire

Urbanization Effects on the Fauna of a Southeastern U.S.A. Bar-built Estuary 477
Michael H. Fulton, G. Thomas Chandler, and Geoffrey I. Scott

Summary

Achieving Sustainable Development in the Southeastern Coastal Zone: 505
Roundtable Discussion of Science in Support of Resource Management
Donald Scavia, Robert Boyles, Jr., and Isobel C. Sheifer

Sustainable Development in the Southeastern Coastal Zone: A Summary 509
Carl J. Sindermann

Index 517

Preface

The collected papers in this book are the outcome of the symposium Sustainable Development in the Southeastern Coastal Zone, held at Myrtle Beach, South Carolina, March 2-5, 1993. As this volume reflects, the symposium was interdisciplinary in scope, including papers on policy overviews, environmental resources, and population trends. The discussions of the environmental impacts of urbanization cover eutrophication, toxics, wetlands, fisheries, water resources, public health, and environmental economics. The symposium was sponsored by the National Oceanic and Atmospheric Administration Coastal Ocean Program, the University of South Carolina School of Public Health and the Belle W. Baruch Institute for Marine Biology and Coastal Research, and the National Oceanic and Atmospheric Administration, National Marine Fisheries Service, Charleston Laboratory.

The papers selected for inclusion in this book were reviewed by at least two critical external referees and one or more of the three editors. This volume was supported by the National Oceanic and Atmospheric Administration (grants NA90AADSG672 and NA46RGO336).

The editors would like to thank the University of South Carolina staff whose efforts made the conference a success and Anne B. Miller for editing and production of this volume.

F. John Vernberg
Winona B. Vernberg
Thomas Siewicki

Contributors

Walter P. Bailey
Health and Demographic Statistics
Division of Research and Statistical Services
SC State Budget and Control Board
1000 Assembly Street, Suite 425
Columbia, South Carolina 29201-3117

Robert L. Beekman
Department of Economics
University of South Carolina
Columbia, South Carolina 29208

J. Bemiss
National Marine Fisheries Service
Southeast Fisheries Center
Charleston Laboratory
219 Ft. Johnson Road
Charleston, South Carolina 29412

Elizabeth R. Blood
Joseph W. Jones Ecological Research Center
Route 2, Box 2324
Newton, Georgia 31770

Robert Boyles, Jr.
National Oceanic and
    Atmospheric Administration
Coastal Ocean Office
1315 East-West Highway, Sta. 15140
Silver Spring, Maryland 20910

Christopher L. Brooks
Office of Ocean and Coastal
    Resource Management
South Carolina Department of Health and
    Environmental Control
4130 Faber Place, Suite 300
Charleston, South Carolina 29405

Joe W.T. Burch
Waccamaw Regional Planning and
    Development Council
1230 Highmarket Street
Georgetown, South Carolina 29440

W. Burkhardt, III
United States Food and Drug Administration
Office of Seafood, HFS-407
200 C Street
Washington, D.C. 20204

G. Thomas Chandler
Department of Environmental Health Sciences
University of South Carolina
Columbia, South Carolina 29208

Christopher Corbett
Marine Science Program
University of South Carolina
Columbia, South Carolina 29208

J.W. Daugomah
National Marine Fisheries Service
Southeast Fisheries Center
Charleston Laboratory
219 Ft. Johnson Road
Charleston, South Carolina 29412

Jan S. Davis
Waccamaw Regional Planning and
    Development Council
1230 Highmarket Street
Georgetown, South Carolina 29440

John Mark Dean
Center for Environmental Policy and
Belle W. Baruch Institute for Marine Biology
    and Coastal Research
University of South Carolina
Columbia, South Carolina 29208

Alan W. Decho
Department of Environmental Health Sciences
University of South Carolina
Columbia, South Carolina 29208

Don Edwards
Department of Statistics
University of South Carolina
Columbia, South Carolina 29208

David W. Engel
National Oceanic and
    Atmospheric Administration
National Marine Fisheries Service
Southeast Fisheries Science Center
Beaufort Laboratory
Beaufort, North Carolina 28516-9722

David M. Essex
Waccamaw Regional Planning and
    Development Council
1230 Highmarket Street
Georgetown, South Carolina 29440

Alan R. Fortner
National Marine Fisheries Service
Southeast Fisheries Center
Charleston Laboratory
219 Ft. Johnson Road
Charleston, South Carolina 29412

Michael H. Fulton
National Marine Fisheries Service
Southeast Fisheries Center
Charleston Laboratory
219 Ft. Johnson Road
Charleston, South Carolina 29412

Mark H. Hoeweler
Waccamaw Regional Planning and
    Development Council
1230 Highmarket Street
Georgetown, South Carolina 29440

Donald E. Hoss
National Oceanic and
    Atmospheric Administration
National Marine Fisheries Service
Southeast Fisheries Science Center
Beaufort Laboratory
Beaufort, North Carolina 28516-9722

Paula F. Houhoulis
Joseph W. Jones Ecological Research Center
Route 2, Box 2324
Newton, Georgia 31770

Mark E. Kinsey
Waccamaw Regional Planning and
    Development Council
1230 Highmarket Street
Georgetown, South Carolina 29440

David P. Lanter
Geographic Designs, Inc.
3738 Meru Lane
Santa Barbara, California 93105

Sharon W. Lemire
National Marine Fisheries Service
Southeast Fisheries Center
Charleston Laboratory
219 Ft. Johnson Road
Charleston, South Carolina 29412
Present Address
58 Lake Latimer Drive
Kennesaw, Georgia 30144

Robert J. Livingston
Center for Aquatic Research and
    Resource Management
136b Conradi Building
Florida State University
Tallahassee, Florida 32306

Edward R. Long
National Oceanic and
    Atmospheric Administration
ORCA
Bin C15700
7600 Sand Pt. Way NE
Seattle, Washington 98115

Henry N. McKellar, Jr.
Department of Environmental Health Sciences
University of South Carolina
Columbia, South Carolina 29208

William D. Marshall
South Carolina Department of
    Natural Resources
Water Resources Division
1201 Main Street, Suite 1100
Columbia, South Carolina 29201

William K. Michener
Joseph W. Jones Ecological Research Center
Route 2, Box 2324
Newton, Georgia 31770

Eugene P. Odum
The University of Georgia
Institute of Ecology
Athens, Georgia 30602-2202

Ruth Patrick
The Academy of Natural Sciences
19th and the Parkway
Philadelphia, Pennsylvania 19103

John M. Penney
Waccamaw Regional Planning and
    Development Council
1230 Highmarket Street
Georgetown, South Carolina 29440

Dwayne E. Porter
Belle W. Baruch Institute for Marine Biology
    and Coastal Research
University of South Carolina
Columbia, South Carolina 29208

Marion Sanders
National Marine Fisheries Service
Southeast Fisheries Center
Charleston Laboratory
219 Ft. Johnson Road
Charleston, South Carolina 29412

Donald Scavia
National Oceanic and
    Atmospheric Administration
Coastal Ocean Office
1315 East-West Highway, Sta. 15140
Silver Spring, Maryland 20910

William J. Schwartzkopf
Waccamaw Regional Planning and
    Development Council
1230 Highmarket Street
Georgetown, South Carolina 29440

Geoffrey I. Scott
National Marine Fisheries Service
Southeast Fisheries Center
Charleston Laboratory
219 Ft. Johnson Road
Charleston, South Carolina 29412

Leonard Shabman
Department of Agricultural and
    Applied Economics
Virginia Tech
Blacksburg, Virginia 24061-0401

Isobel C. Sheifer
National Oceanic and
    Atmospheric Administration
Coastal Ocean Office
1315 East-West Highway, Sta. 15140
Silver Spring, Maryland 20910

Tom Siewicki
National Marine Fisheries Service
Southeast Fisheries Center
Charleston Laboratory
219 Ft. Johnson Road
Charleston, South Carolina 29412

Carl J. Sindermann
National Oceanic and
    Atmospheric Administration
National Marine Fisheries Service
Oxford, Maryland 21654

Pauley A. Smith
Environmental Health Sciences
University of South Carolina
Columbia, South Carolina 29208
Present address:
South Carolina Department of Health and
    Environmental Control
Water Pollution Control
2600 Bull Street
Columbia, South Carolina 29201

Donald W. Stanley
Institute for Coastal and Marine Resources and
Department of Biology
East Carolina University
Greenville, North Carolina 27858-4353

S.H. Strozier
School of Public Health
University of South Carolina
Columbia, South Carolina 29208

F. John Vernberg
Belle W. Baruch Institute for Marine Biology
    and Coastal Research
University of South Carolina
Columbia, South Carolina 29208

Winona B. Vernberg
School of Public Health
University of South Carolina
Columbia, South Carolina 29208

Matt Wahl
Department of Environmental Health Sciences
University of South Carolina
Columbia, South Carolina 29208

W. D. Watkins
United States Food and Drug Administration
Office of Seafood, HFS-407
200 C Street
Washington, D.C. 20204

John E. Weinstein
Belle W. Baruch Institute for Marine Biology
    and Coastal Research
University of South Carolina
Columbia, South Carolina 29208
Present address:
Department of Zoology
Miami University
Oxford, Ohio 45056

Thomas Williams
Baruch Forest Science Institute
Clemson University
Georgetown, South Carolina 29440

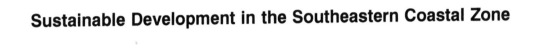

Sustainable Development in the Southeastern Coastal Zone

Sustainable Development

Robert L. Beekman, F. John Vernberg, and Winona B. Vernberg

Defining Sustainable Development

Academics, policymakers, the media and others often use the term sustainable development as a catchall phrase to describe the use of natural resources in some environmentally benign manner. A more polished definition of sustainable development was proposed by the Brundtland Commission (World Commission on Environment and Development 1987, p. 8). According to their definition, sustainable development "meets the needs of the present without compromising the ability of future generations to meet their own needs." The term sustainability has been applied to a wide range of topics, but usually can be categorized into three areas: global sustainability, sustainable yield management, and sustainable development of a system.

Generally the term global sustainability refers to the depletion of less developed countries' resource stock, usually for export to more developed countries. Included are discussions of developed countries' responsibilities to the resources of developing countries. The literature also makes a distinction between sustainable growth and sustainable development. The former being solely a quantitative measure (GNP, for example), while the latter includes qualitative factors such as environmental quality, biodiversity, and public health (Wilcox 1992). These were the issues of the Rio Eco Summit and are the concerns of the World Bank and other development agencies.

The sustainability concept is also employed by managers of fisheries, timber, grazing lands, and other "renewable" resources. Their goal is to actively manage a particular resource to ensure a sustainable yield or use into the future, hence, the term sustainable yield management. This vein of the sustainability literature focuses on one resource or species at a time. Managers strive to control the flow or current use of the resource so as not to cut into the stock (i.e., future flows). A popular analogy is living off the interest without getting into the principal. Note that sustainable yield management is not simply setting harvest limits at an amount equal to the regenerative capacity of a given renewable resource. True management guides technological advances and prescribes harvesting techniques or restrictions that maximize current resource use without threatening future use. For example, timber managers might encourage cutting of mature trees before they succumb to disease and decay. This strategy also allows sunlight to reach younger trees.

The timber management strategy might also foster development of faster growing seedlings in the effort to increase timber yields. It could be argued that the strategy in the preceding example neglects the habitat and biodiversity benefits of old and decaying trees—a symptom of the single resource focus. Sustainable yield management's important lesson though, is that through technological innovations and slight modifications in our use of given resources, the carrying capacity can be increased.

Sustainable development of a system is much like sustainable yield management except that it considers interactions between various species, physical changes, human activities, and established economic incentives present within a given ecological system. Managers must also consider the use of nonrenewable (exhaustible) resources. It is important to note that the "living off of the interest" analogy cannot apply to exhaustible resources. Policymakers wishing to employ this systemwide view of sustainable development face a considerable challenge. The interdisciplinary effort required to simultaneously optimize the use of all resources within a system (or even come close) is a substantial task. Having said that, and with a deep breath, we intend to present a systemwide approach to sustainable development in this manuscript.

Our Focus

We choose as our focus the sustainable development of the coastal zone of the Southeastern United States. Though ecologically diverse, these coastal systems share at least one overwhelming similarity—the significant impact of man's development on their resources. Some of these systems are highly urbanized and others are relatively pristine, but all of the coastal areas within this region are experiencing a growth in human population to some degree. Various estimates of this growth have been cited; Ketchum (1972) stated that approximately 50% of the residents of the United States live within coastal counties, which represent only 10% of the land. By the turn of the century, about 75% of the United States population will live within 50 miles of a coastline: ocean and Great Lakes. In the southeastern region of the United States, the growth in the coastal areas has been particularly rapid, a trend which is expected to continue. Bailey's (1996) detailed analysis of population trends based on census figures substantiates this trend. Although growth is observed in most segments of the population, whites and the elderly are increasing most rapidly. Not included in the census figures, but of paramount importance in the assessment of the potential human impact on environmental resources, is the tremendous influx of tourists. For example, the Myrtle Beach area along the Grand Strand of South Carolina is host to approximately 500,000 visitors per day in the summer. As Bailey (1996) concludes, "it is this population that controls continued development." Clearly, it is important not only to recognize man's impact on the sustainability of these systems but also to develop policies that encourage the most efficient long-term use of resources by this significant component of the ecological system.

The Economics of Sustainable Development

Economic agents (individuals, businesses, organizations, etc.) react to changes in their economic and regulatory environment just as any biological species would react to important environmental changes. If an economic agent does not adapt and respond properly to changes in its economic and regulatory environment, it will not prosper. This economic Darwinism ensures that agents use their resources in the most efficient manner *given the incentives* present in their particular market. Since humans are major players in all of these coastal systems, it behooves policymakers to send the signals, via regulations and the price system, that promote sustainable resource use.

Modern neoclassical economics views natural resources and the environment as commodities (Pearce and Turner 1990). Just as food, clothing, and shelter are efficiently allocated in competitive markets, so should these environmental goods. Having said that, we should recognize some limitations. Namely, environmental commodities often are public goods without clearly defined property rights, and most are difficult to value due to a lack of established private markets for these resources. As a result, we sometimes observe "market failures"—where private competitive markets fail to efficiently allocate resources. Current experimental economics procedures, however, can estimate values for environmental goods by creating hypothetical markets where actual private markets do not exist. The Contingent Valuation Method (CVM), though certainly not perfected, is one of the more widely accepted methodologies in the environmental valuation literature (see Mitchell and Carson 1989 and Cummings and Harrison 1995 for discussions). Public-policy makers can work toward incorporating these values into resource use decisions, correcting market failures so that environmental goods are allocated to their highest and best use.

When we speak of resource "use," it is appropriate to think in the broadest sense of the word. First, the environmental economics literature distinguishes between use and existence (non-use) value. The former represents the value associated with active consumption of the resource now or in the future, and the latter, the value individuals place on the knowledge that a resource exists even if they never plan to actively use the resource. In the context of this chapter when we refer to the value associated with a resource use we mean the sum of use and existence values. Often this sum is termed total value. We do not mean to imply, however, that estimates of total use value could be decomposed into its use and existence value components as it is often (incorrectly) claimed in the valuation literature (see Cummings and Harrison 1992 for a discussion of this debate). Second, we must include the multitude of subtle uses of our environmental resources. For example, fishermen and boaters are not the only agents using a particular estuary. The estuary can also be used by some homeowners and restaurants for its scenic vistas. Others utilize it as a receptor for chemical waste, effluent, and storm water drainage. Chemical spills or septic tank leakages are also uses of the estuary, even if unintentional. Commuters may want to use the estuary as a place to build a new causeway. The many uses of a given resource will each yield a benefit to some segment of the population. Though they need not be consumptive, damaging, or in conflict with each other, any foregone benefits resulting from conflicting uses impose costs on others in society.

Recognition of these costs is crucial in any effective sustainable development plan. The true and total societal cost of a given use is equal to the foregone benefit of the best conflicting use by any agents, now or in the future, who have a property right in that resource. In the case of private goods, with well-established property rights, the owner is motivated to place the asset to its highest and best use. If someone else has a better (conflicting) use for the asset, the established owner can sell for a profit. With public environmental goods (air, water, views, fish stocks, etc.), ownership is either held in the public trust or is simply difficult to establish and maintain. Questions arise as to who owns the fish, who owns the view, and so on. The assignment of rights in public goods is a legal matter, hopefully reflecting existing social norms.

Consider the case of a factory owner who dumps waste into an estuary and does not pay for this use of the resource. We would expect an over exploitation of the estuary because the price the factory owner pays is far below the true societal cost. The environmental economics solution would be to charge the factory owner a dumping fee equal to the true societal cost of the use. If the owner determines that it remains cost-effective to dump when required to incur the true societal cost, then the resource is being put to its highest and best use. The factory owner would then be motivated to investigate any available treatment or production technology that would lower his (and society's) cost of dumping. If, in the end, the benefit to the factory owner of dumping in the most efficient way was greater than any alternative current or future conflicting use of the estuary, he would proceed. If the dumping would preclude a more valuable use of the resource, it would not be profitable for the factory owner. Internalization of true costs into production and consumption decisions will help to correct the aforementioned market failures.

Conflicting future uses should also be considered when determining the true societal cost of current resource use. By definition, future uses must be considered in any sustainable use plan. When we weigh current against future consumption, we are compelled to discount the future benefits to some degree. The higher the discount rate, the more weight society places on current rather than future generations. Lower rates imply more conservation. Though some may object to the idea of discounting future benefits, we must accept the reality that humans have an economic time preference. Most individuals are impatient, and would rather consume now than later. This is why we require positive (real) interest rates on our savings accounts. "If we accept that preferences matter, we are logically obliged to accept that people's preference for the present over the future must be allowed to count as well" (Pearce and Turner 1990, p. 213).

So, if economic agents in a given system are reacting to the correct signals, namely costs that reflect the true value of a resource to current and future generations, then we would expect wise and sustainable resource use. Note that this view does not always guarantee total conservation and zero growth. Conservation itself is a use with benefits and costs in terms of foregone uses. The advantage of conservation, however, is that the benefits continue into perpetuity. Put simply, under any reasonable discount rate assumption, wasteful and overly short-term uses of environmental goods will not be (socially) cost-effective. Consider, for example, fishing activities that would wipe out a certain fish stock within a season or two. As long as *some* weight was placed on the benefits of *all* future harvests, then this nonsustainable activity would most likely be economically unwise.

The Interdisciplinary Effort

As mentioned earlier, a systemwide approach to sustainable development requires a significant interdisciplinary effort. Policymakers need a wide variety of information if they are to design effective sustainable development plans that send proper signals to agents in the system. First, the development plan needs to be politically feasible. It should reflect social norms, achieve community goals, and be practically enforceable. The political and social science disciplines can provide decisionmakers with valuable insight in this arena. Second, the impact of various resource uses within the system must be determined. In terms of our prior discussion, the role of the hard sciences is to identify which uses conflict, and to what extent. In addition, the physical and biological sciences have a role in suggesting or developing new technologies and techniques that limit the impact (cost) of given uses. The role of economics is to estimate dollar values for each of the many environmental resources in the system. These values, in coordination with the impacts determined by the hard sciences, can be used to calculate the true societal cost of particular resource uses.

These costs can then be incorporated into policy recommendations that send proper signals to the individuals and businesses in the system.

Conclusions

Sustainable development can be achieved in economic environments where resources are used in an efficient manner and are allocated according to the preferences of individuals and businesses in the market. At present, battles between opposing interest groups often determine the allocation of our public environmental goods. At stake is the right to use the coastal zone resources either without cost or at a price below true and total societal cost, which leads to resource exploitation. If economic agents incur the true costs of their actions in the coastal zone, then the individuals and businesses themselves will allocate the resources to the highest and best use. As a resource becomes more unique and important to the sustainability of the biotic system, its destruction becomes increasingly costly, and hence is more likely to be protected. On the other hand, more abundant, resilient, or unimportant resources will be used with greater intensity. Individuals and businesses will also be motivated to search for a way to accomplish their consumption and production objectives in a less intrusive (less costly) manner. If all societal costs are internalized, agents will be simultaneously acting in their own and society's best interest to properly manage our stock of coastal zone resources over time.

LITERATURE CITED

Bailey, Walter P. 1996. Population trends in the southeastern coastal area, concentrating on South Carolina, p. 55-74. *In* F.J. Vernberg, W.B. Vernberg, and T. Siewicki (eds.), Sustainable Development in the Southeastern Coastal Zone, Belle W. Baruch Library in Marine Science, no. 20. University of South Carolina Press, Columbia, South Carolina.

Cummings, Ronald G. and Glenn W. Harrison. 1992. Existence Values and Compensatable Damages: Judicial Reliance on Empty Economic Concepts? Economics Working Paper B-92-5, Division of Research, College of Business Administration, University of South Carolina, Columbia, South Carolina.

Cummings, Ronald G. and Glenn W. Harrison. 1995. Measurement and decomposition of non-use values: A critical review. *Environmental and Resource Economics* 4(5): 225-247.

Ketchum, B. H. (ed.). 1972. The Water's Edge: Critical Problems of the Coastal Zone. The Massachusetts Institute of Technology Press, Cambridge, Massachusetts.

Pearce, David W. and R. Kerry Turner. 1988. Economics of Natural Resources and the Environment. Westview Press, Boulder, Colorado.

Wilcox, Bruce A. 1992. Defining sustainable development. *Environmental Science Technology* 26(10): 1902.

World Commission on Environment and Development. 1987. Our Common Future. Oxford University Press, New York.

Land Settlement, Public Policy, and the Environmental Future of the Southeast Coast

Leonard Shabman

For reasons good or ill, owning land is the most effective way in which people keep their distance from each other. Land is the ultimate means of exclusion.

Gibbons 1977, p. 90

Introduction

As the nation's population moves to the coasts, our imaginations, and perhaps fears, about environmental degradation are not focused on pastoral landscapes of farm and forest, although activities associated with those land uses can have adverse effects on coastal resources. The land uses of particular concern are urban activities, that is, the space devoted to residential, commercial, industrial, and public uses, as well as the networks of roads connecting these spaces. It is the pattern of these land uses, more than population density, which is most troubling.[1] A new land-scape is emerging where commercial and residential activity are relocating to the edge, and then beyond, original centers of cities and towns (Garreau 1991).

Our land is being used to separate, or in Gibbons word, to exclude. Land is being used to separate individual homes on large lots in the name of privacy. Land is being used to separate places of residence, places of work, and public facilities in the name of preserving neighborhoods. People separate themselves from the places where they spend their leisure time and call their residences first and second homes. Land is being used to separate racial and socioeconomic classes from each other as images of crime and congestion makes spatial separation appear to be an escape

---

[1] By population settlement I mean the number of people living within a given area, often termed *average population density*. Density is the number of persons per acre living in a state, a county, a city, or a town. However, in computing density, no compensation is made for the nonresidential land uses that must support the area's population. By population settlement I also mean the *pattern*, or spatial arrangement, of different land uses in an area. Two places may have the same population density, but may have a different arrangement of residences, retail and other commercial businesses, farms, open space, and natural areas.

from the pathologies of urban areas and inner suburbs. Linking these separated pockets of land uses is a network of roads making reliance on the automobile, for even the most modest household or business errands, a routine matter.

This land use pattern is commonly, and pejoratively, called sprawl. Concerns over the costs of sprawl have motivated growth management proposals in many southeastern states. Growth management is an umbrella term used to describe public policies and programs intended to contain the limits of the cities and suburbs (Gale 1992). The goals for growth management include reductions in the cost of government and stimulation of economic prosperity. The most powerful motivation for growth management may be the efforts to limit and control pollution of air and water and to minimize the fragmentation and isolation of watershed ecosystems. This belief about the adverse environmental consequences of sprawl explains why, from Maryland to Florida, growth management has become an integral theme of resource management and protection policies of many states (Gale 1992).

In the debate over growth management programs the question often posed is, When should public policy restrict the operation of the private land market? This question fosters an image of a sharp conflict between the market-determined prices and uses for private property and the public policies that limit use and diminish private property prices. Increasingly the focus of this concern is regulations motivated by environmental protection goals (Bailey 1992).

We have recently seen legal arguments made at the United States Supreme Court in the case of *Lucas v. the South Carolina Coastal Council*, where that state's regulations designed to reduce coastal erosion were challenged. At the federal level, the political response to this perceived conflict is illustrated by a bill authored by Congressman J. Hayes of Louisiana, and having over 100 co-sponsors, that requires that compensation be paid to owners of land delineated as wetlands under the federal wetlands regulatory program. More generally, Senator R. Dole of Kansas has promoted legislation to require that all federal regulation assess the impacts on private property values. In my state, Virginia, this theme of a conflict has followed and influenced a legislative study committee which is considering some form of growth management legislation. The committee feels compelled to offer the protection of private property claims as a constraint on policy reforms. At the more general level, the 1993 session of the Virginia General Assembly created a study com-mission to examine the possible effects of state regulation on private property prices. The Virginia General Assembly was one of 35 states where property price legislation had been considered by 1993.

That the price of a parcel of land may be reduced by environmental regulation can not be denied (Fischel 1990), but this is not the only influence of public policy on land settlement and land prices. The land market, the prices created therein, and the population settlement patterns that result are a consequence of federal, state, and local government policy, even if no single policy is intended to alter the way we settle the land. Our nation's land settlement policy and resulting property prices are made by intent, and by accident, at all levels of government. The understanding and redirection of these policies, which include, but are not limited to, energy policy, housing policy and tax policy, are the best hope for an effective long-term environmental protection and restoration program for coastal regions.

Population and Land Settlement in the Southeastern Coastal Zone

Many southeastern coastal areas were populated by the earliest European settlers, and certainly the hospitable environments supported a relatively large population of native people before European settlement. Over time, population in many coastal counties declined as potential income from agricultural and fisheries production became less than the income opportunities in agriculture and manufacturing elsewhere in the nation. Today, there has been a renewed movement back to the coast. What has been the nature of this population movement and what might be the consequences for coastal environments?

COASTAL LAND SETTLEMENT

Commercial development to serve tourism is not considered. Population growth in coastal counties and cities from Delaware to Georgia has been uneven over the past 20 years (Fig. 1).[2] In selected cities, and in a few isolated counties in Virginia and North Carolina, population growth has been negative. In some counties population growth has been below the national average for the past two decades, while in others the growth rate has far exceeded the national average.

Strong population growth has occurred in both rural and metropolitan counties. Metropolitan counties in Fig. 2 are typically, but not always, suburban counties. The United States Bureau of the Census defines a metropolitan statistical area as a geographic area consisting of a large central population nucleus (a census-defined urban area), together with adjacent areas, having a high degree of economic and social integration with that central place.

Rural retirement counties, also shown in Fig. 2, almost filled the area between metropolitan counties along the coast. A retirement county is one with greater than 15% in-migration of people 60 years or older during the preceding decade (Stallmann 1991). A comparison of Figs. 1 and 2 reveals that some of the fastest growing counties were rural retirement counties. This same comparison also reveals that many counties growing at or below the national average were also retirement counties. In those counties, the in-migration of the elderly is what prevented a relative population decline, but the migration certainly changed the counties' age distribution.

How are these new residents of coastal counties settling the land? A recent study by Vesterby and Heimlich (1991) used aerial photography and satellite images to track the use of specific points of land between 1960 and 1970 and between 1970 and 1980. Their study was limited to "fast-growth" counties, which included some from the southeastern coast. Because a fast-growth county was defined using a combination of the percentage increase in population and minimum initial population levels, most study counties were in metropolitan areas at the fringe of large cities.

Vesterby and Heimlich described shifts of land uses to urban uses (residential home sites, commercial sites, and public facilities) as new households were formed in these fast-growth areas. Relating land use shifts to population change, they computed a "marginal urban land-use consumption" coefficient equal to 0.46 acres per household. On a per capita basis, over a two-decade period, each new person required about 0.20 acre of land for *all* "urban uses."

After dividing their study counties into two groups, Vesterby and Heimlich also found that counties that had small initial populations had a larger marginal per capita land-consumption rate. From this finding, one might infer that the rapidly growing, but still sparsely populated, counties on the coast, retirement or otherwise, are devoting significant amounts of land to a lower density and sprawled pattern of development.

---

[2] The following discussion is about land use by and in support of permanent and part-time residents of coastal areas.

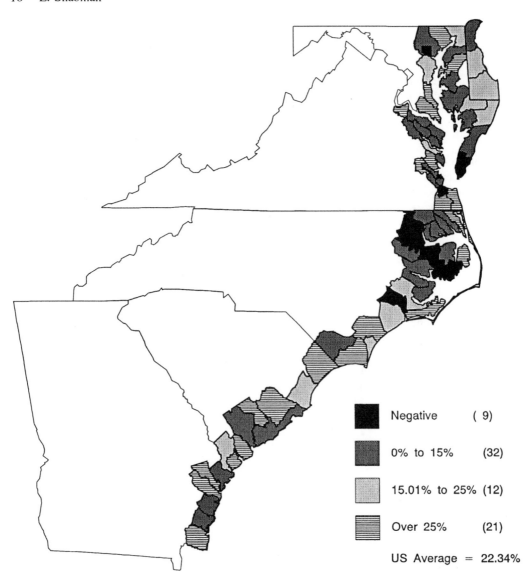

Fig. 1. Population growth, 1970 to 1990, in coastal counties of Delaware to Georgia.

Such a conclusion is partly confirmed by another study of recent home buyers in the Chesapeake Bay region of Maryland (Feitelson unpublished data). This study, which focused only on residential land use, found that waterfront purchases made up almost 25% of all home purchases in Maryland's rural coastal counties. The purchasers of these waterfront lots tended to be retirees, or second home buyers, who bought large lots. One might speculate that this same purchaser profile applies in most coastal rural retirement counties along the southeast coast. If so, then low-density

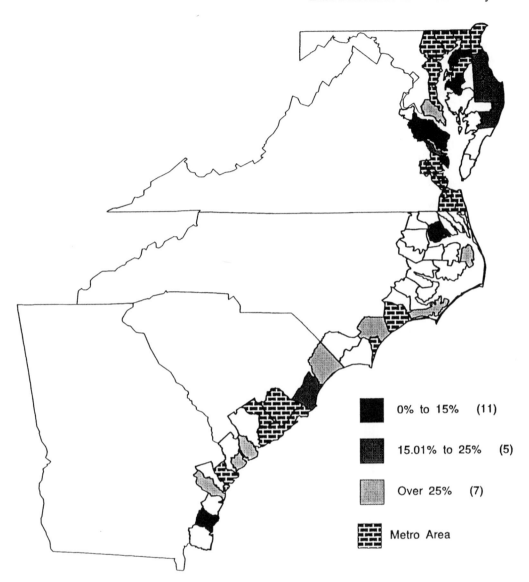

Fig. 2. Population growth, 1970 to 1990, in retirement counties (n = 23) of the coastal zone from Delaware to Georgia. The metropolitan status of the nonretirement counties in 1980 is indicated.

residential use along the shoreline is occurring as small family units of older people having large lots, and second home commuters from the nearby metropolitan areas.

Still more evidence on land settlement patterns and density can be gleaned from a Maryland Office of Planning study (Governor's Commission On Growth in the Chesapeake Bay Region 1991). For the period 1985 to 1990, the study found that of the 144,500 acres of land developed for urban uses in the state, 101,000 were on 0.5- to 5-acre lots. By one computation, 6% of the population growth in the state during the 5-year period consumed 65% of the newly urbanized land. Near the Maryland cities, population growth was rapid, but settlement was compact. Away from the cites, land consumption rates in relation to population were highest (Pressley 1991). And, it was in the coastal retirement counties of Maryland (e.g., Calvert and Charles counties) where the greatest rates of increase in developed land were found (Greer 1991).

It also appears that a land use *pattern* with pockets of urban uses, both high and low density, is occurring. The scattering of these pockets of use over the landscape is often visible to the casual observer, but no formal studies adequately document this occurrence. One piece of evidence can be established by interpreting census data on all United States metropolitan areas (Heimlich and Brooks 1989). Over the past three decades the number of areas classified as metropolitan has increased, but the average density of all the areas has decreased from 365 persons per square mile in 1960 to 315 persons per square mile in 1985. For there to be an increase in the number of counties included in metropolitan areas, while average population densities in those areas decrease, means that the pattern of settlement in metropolitan areas must be spreading out if, as Vesterby and Heimlich suggest, there has been no change in density between 1960 and 1980 where there are urban uses. Other evidence for this spreading out of metropolitan areas is found in the commuting patterns to the Washington, D.C., metropolitan area. According to the 1990 Census, about one-third of the workers in remote rural counties (over a one-hour drive from Washington) commute to the city and inner suburbs for work (Fehr 1993).

This supports the conclusion that fears of being physically consumed by high density development over large areas are unwarranted. On the other hand, in the early stages of urbanization, especially in coastal areas, large per capita consumption of land may be occurring. Even though total population growth numbers may be small relative to the total land base, that land is being settled at low residential densities. And, at the same time this use of land for separation is exaggerated by a land use pattern with pockets of residential, commercial, and public uses spread out from each other.

ENVIRONMENTAL CONSEQUENCES

The environmental effect most often attributed to separated land use is nonpoint source water and air pollution (Alliance for the Chesapeake Bay 1989; 2020 Panel, Council on the Environment 1988; Houlahan et al. 1992). Water quality degradation has been attributed to the organic and inorganic wastes in runoff from lawns, golf courses and other recreation sites, construction sites, streets, and parking lots of urbanized areas.[3] Another consequence of sprawled development is the necessity of individual home septic systems instead of centralized wastewater collection and treatment facilities. Septic systems are designed to control adverse health effects from wastewater (e.g.,. pathogens) and may do that job well. However, septic systems do not (always) remove nutrients, which may find their way into coastal waters. This is especially a matter of concern on

---

[3] Whether these asserted pollutant loadings are always based on sound information is not clear. For example, in Virginia no estimate of the chemical usage on suburban lawns is available. Also, the assertions about nonpoint source pollution do not account for the possible effectiveness of urban best-management practices, such as sediment retention basins, street sweeping, and changed lawn fertilization practices.

coastal soils, which often have high water tables and thus limited ability to "treat" nitrogen residuals.[4]

In metropolitan areas and rural areas of the coastal zone a spread-out land settlement pattern will result in land being dedicated to the support of the automobile. An extreme example of this possibility comes from the most autocentric of places, metropolitan Los Angeles. By one estimate, two-thirds of that area's land is dedicated to the storage or movement of automobiles and other vehicles (Greer 1991). Separation of land uses also may increase the miles driven, resulting in ozone and other air quality problems. Of special note is the problem of nitrogen deposition. In the Chesapeake Bay region there are massive investments have been made and are planned to reduce nitrogen loadings to the estuary. New evidence now suggest that a significant share of the nitrogen load to the estuary is from deposition of air pollutants, which originate, in part, with automobiles. The argument can be made that a more compact pattern and density of settlement might improve air quality as well as water quality, because miles driven and land dedicated to automobiles would decrease.[5]

An environmental consequence of separated land uses that often has not often been considered is the effect on ecosystem function. Landscapes of connected wetlands and uplands provide an array of ecosystem services. It seems reasonable to assert that fragmentation, isolation, and functional degradation of the wetlands and uplands complexes will be one product of a sprawled settlement pattern. Indeed, even our wetlands regulatory programs, which require that development avoid wetlands, may not protect ecosystem functions. Commercial and residential development twisting among so-called protected wetlands is the product of our current regulatory rules. Wetlands isolated in the midst of concrete parking lots will have low ecological value (National Research Council 1992).

The effect of this separated settlement can be to diminish the ecological functions of watersheds not only by inputs of pollutants via runoff but also by changes in hydrologic regimes and by the fragmentation of the landscape, isolating the wetlands from the surrounding uplands, waters, and biological resources of the watershed. When all factors are considered, the most serious consequence for coastal environments of separated land uses may be the fragmentation and isolation of ecosystems.

Population Settlement: Alternative Visions

These possible environmental effects resulting from the emerging land use pattern and associated population density might be avoided if there was an alternative, and attractive, vision for population settlement. This settlement pattern should accommodate and serve the life style aspirations of coastal

---

[4] The arguments about septic tanks must be made on deductive logic, not on empirical studies about septic systems and water quality, of which there are few.

[5] Much driving is discretionary, and total automobile miles traveled is only partly related to distances that must be traveled. Therefore, the number of trips taken may not be simply related to separated land uses. Also, as automobile engine technologies or the formulation of the fuels used are changed, the resulting automobile air pollution might be reduced. This has been the case on a national level as miles traveled has risen, but new engine technologies have reduced NO_x emissions (United States Council on Environmental Quality 1992).

residents and avoid the worst features of sprawling development. That alternative long has been described as "compact and contiguous land settlement" (Subcommittee on the City 1980).

One approach to describing compact and contiguous land settlement is to specify a large area that includes varying densities and mixed land uses (Risse 1989, 1991). Such a landscape is said to exist in Reston, Virginia, a suburban community developed about 20 years ago. Reston includes a mix of land uses and residential housing styles, and within the project boundaries, 40% of the land is open space, although average density for the whole area is 10 persons per acre. This density is twice that computed for rapidly growing, densely settled communities (Vesterby and Heimlich 1991), and it is significantly greater than the densities that are now being realized along the coast. In fact, if the Washington, D.C., suburban area of Fairfax County, Virginia, where Reston is located, were settled in Reston-sized geographic units and at Reston densities, two-thirds of the land area of that county would be vacant (Risse 1991). This would leave large open areas available for "rural," land-extensive economic activities and, of course, for ecologically functioning and resilient watersheds. Risse (1989) defends the Reston vision of land settlement by noting that, "Just about everyone who chooses to live in the suburbs would love Reston. The rest want to live in urbane downtown or on a farm."

The Reston pattern and density of land settlement was the product of *intentional design*, and such design can be applied in both urban and rural coastal areas. In the early 1970s the Rouse Corporation proposed a development on Wye Island, in Kent County, Maryland, which borders the Chesapeake Bay (Gibbons 1977). Wye Island was an area of several hundred acres of wetlands, farms, and forest. For many years, similar undeveloped areas in Kent County had been developed for residential and commercial purposes. Kent County's residential development had been single house lots arrayed in strips along the county's substantial shoreline. Each house had its own water-front access and often its own boat dock. Commercial development was also occurring in strips along highways and away from these residential areas.

It was the vision of the Rouse Corporation to demonstrate a new and more environmentally benign way to develop land on Wye Island. Rouse argued that the future of the island was not preservation or development of the traditional sprawl type, which would carve up the landscape in less desirable ways. Rouse proposed his project as a way to demonstrate that if homes are clustered and if central recreation, water, and sewer facilities are built, that open lands and wetlands in an area can be protected even as a great number of people are housed. He began his plan by first conducting an environmental inventory of the resources of the island and the tidal water circulation and flushing patterns of the nearby rivers and the bay. Only then did he design a pattern of land use for the island that would be in harmony with the area's natural resources.

Rouse's Wye Island project was never approved for development by local officials (a matter discussed later), but the concept recently has been promoted for an area in Virginia along the Chesapeake Bay. The community of Haymont, a 1,600-acre mixed use development, is now under construction (Bacon 1991; Latane 1993). In the development plan, the 3 miles of frontage on the Rappahannock River includes only one boat ramp and a park. Of the total site, 50% is preserved and all houses will be over 0.25 mile from a shoreline buffered by marsh and forest. The Haymont plan will use the remaining land to house up to 12,000 residents in over 4,000 clustered housing units which maintain privacy and offer spacious living quarters. The alternative land use for the Haymont tract would have permitted houses as close as 50 feet to the water and division of the entire frontage into house lots. The Haymont model can accommodate *higher average* density than is currently permitted for the site, while offering more environmental protection. Of equal significance, the site absorbs population growth that might have otherwise spread to many other acres far beyond the Haymont tract.

A compelling discussion of the potential for this design concept is found in a publication from the Center for Rural Massachusetts (Yaro et al. 1990). That publication describes designs for settlement patterns that will accommodate population settlement of the rural landscape and still maintain the open areas along the Connecticut River shoreline. The designs use road layouts and placement of houses and commercial and public buildings to achieve a pattern and density of land use conducive to the protection of the river and to hospitable living. One way to think about this design concept is as a conscious attempt to recreate the traditional American small town, an ideal type that is earning much renewed interest (Duany and Plater-Zyberk 1992).

Explaining Land Settlement Outcomes

Despite the design possibility for, and environmental promise of, compact settlement for the coastal landscape, we are spreading out. Therefore, we must presume that this pervasive land settlement pattern offers benefits to the individuals who choose this living arrangement. This conclusion must be accepted despite our inclination to describe the pattern by the pejorative term sprawl, a term suggesting waste and inefficiency.

THE AMERICAN VISION OF PREFERRED LAND SETTLEMENT

The benefits that might be offered by a sprawled settlement pattern are rooted in our culture and history. Historians have described the "suburbanization" movement (Jackson 1985) as the origin of the sprawl occurring today. Many of the areas that were early suburban enclaves are today viewed as cities. For example, the Yonkers area near New York City and the Chevy Chase area north of Washington, D.C., were suburbs that grew along early public transportation arteries. However, these suburbs used little land in their creation because transportation from a public transit station was by foot or carriage, limiting the spread away from each train or trolley stop.

The association of low population density settlement and separation of land uses with suburbanization is a phenomenon of more recent decades. The trend toward more land-consuming suburbanization arose, according to Anthony Downs (1989), after World War II as a result of a particular vision of how United States metropolitan areas ought to be developed to meet the preferences of the population. And, those preferences called for the dedication of more land to residential, transportation, commercial, and industrial uses and to separation among and between uses. As I will note, our public institutions of zoning, transportation, and tax policy have come together to support these preferences over the last 50 years.

Downs describes a living arrangement aspired to by nearly all American households. The focus is on the ownership of detached, single-family homes on spacious lots. This aspiration is accompanied by the desire to own and use a personal automobile. Indeed, Jackson (1985), describing America's world position in transportation systems, argues we have always had the best personal transportation that technology had to offer. First, it was public transportation which made our cities function and the early suburbs grow. That public transportation system has been replaced by the world's finest system of private transportation as our society devotes vast resources to the "comfort" of the private automobile.

With separated homes and access to the automobile, the ideal workplace could consist of predominantly low-rise office or industrial buildings or shopping centers in attractively landscaped, park-like settings. The access to these places was not the pedestrian walk, but rather the generous, in both size and cost, parking opportunity (Duany and Plater-Zyberk 1992; Fehr 1993). It has been said that one element of the success of WalMart stores has been the hospitality each store's entrance design seems to offer to the automobile (Larimer 1991).

Downs (1989) then concludes that overlying this ideal vision is a governance system with roots going back to the founding of the nation. Americans want to live in small communities (not meaning political units) with governments that are responsive to the wishes of existing residents. Communities are places where people of like mind and social class live. Not surprisingly communities act to keep out those activities deemed incompatible with their goals—be those activities low income housing, racial groups, landfills, recycling centers, or any number of other LULUs (locally unwanted land uses). The NIMBY (not in my backyard) syndrome, where regional and national consequences of local land use decisions are not expected to be a consideration for local communities, has become part of the American vision (Kenyon 1991). In today's America, the concept of community does not have an extended geographic reach.

Downs' (1989) description of this American vision of settlement, transport, and governance applies to people in all regions, rural and urban. Thus, from the small town along a rural South Carolina coast, to the Virginia suburbs of Washington, D.C., on the Chesapeake Bay, patterns of land settlement are emerging that, at first analysis, provide evidence for the existence of the strong demand for separation.

It is even reasonable to see the flight to rural retirement counties as an escape from the city. That escape is made possible by the freedom of time and sometimes generous financial resources that come with retirement. However, rural population growth along the coast is also governed by a desire for the positive features of open spaces and privacy. People are coming to rural coastal areas for the space they offer and for the water access for recreational pursuits. All of these services of space can be obtained at low land prices, and, with new communication systems, without abandoning the virtues of the city cultures they leave behind (Barringer 1991; Vobejda 1991).

POLICY IN SUPPORT OF THE VISION

People may be getting what they want from sprawling land settlement patterns. Separation distance that might allow exclusion of commercial areas from residences, separation of residences from each other (large residential housing lots), or separation of communities from perceived ills of central cities has a positive value. In fact, these benefits of separation yield higher land prices in economic models that control for other factors influencing the land market (Coulson 1991). However, the land market is not a free-standing institution. Market outcomes are influenced and supported by public policies.

Understanding how preferences are realized through the land market and public policy is something we are only beginning to understand. This means that models describing the interaction of the myriad factors controlling land settlement outcomes and buttressing any analysis of the effectiveness of alternative growth management policy tools are poorly developed (Feldman and Goldberg 1987; Porter 1989).

Although complex models of land settlement tend to break down (Randall 1987), the application of simple economic logic offers powerful insights into how numerous public polices create incentives for the current pattern and density of land settlement. This possibility of policy influences can be illustrated with a few selected public policies of significance for coastal areas.

National Mobility Policy

For the individual landowner the price of separation is the cost of travel between an individual's residence, other people's residences, and commercial and employment sites. The cost of travel includes both financial outlays and the value of the time spent traveling. Standard economics (and common sense) tell us that the amount of separation demanded will be inversely related to its price—the cost of travel. Therefore, changes in policy that reduce the cost of travel will increase the demand for distance.

Both the gasoline taxation and transportation infrastructure policies of the United States reduce the cost of travel. Clearly, the time cost of travel can be reduced by highway improvements to reduce traffic congestion and the distance between places. Indeed, it does not take a complicated analysis to predict that continually expanding our road and bridge capacity, extending it away from central places, supports separated land uses (Pauly 1992). However, the highway construction program is a political response to the demand for more driving. That demand, which begins with Downs' (1989) vision about the role of the automobile, is further encouraged by our national energy policy.

Consider how public policy unwittingly has influenced the price of traveling a mile. As a result of federal regulation, the fuel economy of automobiles on the highways has risen from 13.5 miles per gallon of gas in 1971 to about 21.7 miles per gallon in 1991; an increase of 60% (Crandall and Graham 1991). During the same time, the price for gasoline went from $0.43 per gallon in 1971 to $1.00 per gallon in 1991. However, adjusted for inflation, the 1991 gasoline price (in 1971 terms) fell 30% to $0.30 per gallon.

The combination of 60% better gas mileage and a 30% drop in the inflation-adjusted gasoline price lowered the cost of driving and thus the price of separation. In the period from 1971 to 1991, the real fuel cost (1971 base) of driving an average car for 100 miles fell from $3.19 to $1.38, or by 57%. Recognizing how much the fuel price of separation has fallen explains partly why vehicle miles traveled rose by nearly 60% between 1977 and 1990, an amount far greater than the rate of increase in population. The falling cost of travel then helps to explain the increasing demand for separation and the political pressures for highway and bridge capacity expansion.

National Housing Policy

The national vision for home ownership described by Downs (1989) has found its way into our national tax policy toward housing and has indirectly affected our coastal settlement patterns. Consider two illustrations. The federal tax code, and the state codes which follow it, permit deductions for all interest payments on all home mortgages. One purpose of that policy is to make home ownership possible for people who might otherwise not be able to make mortgage payments. A possible side-effect of the full deduction is that it increases the demand for land, in addition to the houses on the land, because interest costs for both the land and the dwelling unit are deductible from taxes. In addition, because the home mortgage deduction also may be taken for second homes along the coast, the demand for those kinds of properties increases.

A recent addition to the tax code was the one-time exemption from capital gains tax liability for homeowners who sell a house after the age of 55. While there are many factors at work, the movement of retired people to the coast, and their subsequent purchase of large waterfront lots, has been at least supported by this tax exemption.

Finally, and particular to coastal areas, is the federal response to disaster aid and flood insurance for coastal storms (Federal Emergency Management Agency 1989). There is at least some evidence that the insurance rates charged for hurricane and flood damage are out of line with the likelihood and consequences of those kinds of storms. As a result, premiums for this insurance are too low (Daly 1993). In addition, when storms strike, the nation has been generous with aid, to the point where coastal residents who locate in storm prone areas may feel that the risks will be partly borne by the general taxpayer through disaster aid.

Planning, Zoning, and Rational Politics

The assertion is frequently made that local zoning is a tool for achieving environmentally sound land settlement. A part of the ideal American vision is control by local communities over their land settlement; local control has made zoning an exclusionary instrument in the service of the idealized vision of land as separation. Zoning is not used to assure compact and contiguous land settlement. This is, in Fischel's (1985) description, a rational community use of zoning. Consider just two examples of this rational behavior.

The first is the use of zoning for social exclusion. Racial, educational, or crime-control policy failures in the cities and close-in suburbs have heightened the demand for separation from those places. In turn, residents who seek to escape these areas then use the zoning tool (or other types of land use control instruments) to exclude groups or types of development from communities where they have now relocated. Fishel (1985, p. 336) concludes that "suburban exclusion of the poor is rooted in a larger social problem whose dimensions transcend the realm of land use control."

The forms of exclusion are especially interesting. There would be no legal basis to discriminate on income or racial factors, and there would be no basis for mandating that houses have a minimum prices. Instead, large-lot zoning or minimum building size requirements are put in place. The justification often given is to protect the environment or to match service availability to the population, but the root cause of these zoning rules is more suspicious.

This exclusionary behavior is not just a suburban phenomena. The Rouse Corporation's effort to put a compact development on Wye Island, Maryland, never was realized. In his book describing that land use decision, Gibbons (1977) reports the vehement opposition from one citizen who was concerned about who might come to the Rouse Corporation's development on Wye Island. In essence, this citizen objected to the development on the grounds that it would not be for the people born on Wye Island, rather it would be for people he considered undesirable based on their race and/or political ideology.

The reasons for using zoning for exclusion may also be more practical. Often property tax is the sole revenue source of local governments. This revenue limitation, when combined with the conventional zoning power of local governments, will increase the community demand for separation. In many areas the perception (whether correct or not) is that property tax revenues from commercial and high-priced residential property exceed the local cost of providing services to those properties. Conversely, property tax revenues are expected to be less than the local cost of services for most other residential property. In areas where this belief is strongly held, there is every reason to expect that the poor will be zoned out of communities, for example, by zoning requirements for large lots. One opponent of the Wye Island project explained it as follows:

> *Blakely did not approve of one-acre lots and the canals because he felt that they would attract too many people and too many boats. But five-acre parcels he could accept:"you get 'the right kind of people'—and not too many—with five-acre lots," he said. That's good land planning. What Blakely disliked was cluster housing. Like Rouse's Wye Island village. To Carl Blakely, cluster housing meant younger people crowding into marinas and families with kids in school, and that implied more taxes for schools and fire protection and police and all that. "If a fellow has five acres, there is just so much land in the county, and the protection to us is that we can know absolutely how many people there will be," he said. Blakely has nothing against people with children, but he wants to see them on five acres and in single-family houses. Not in cluster dwellings.*
>
> Gibbons 1977, p. 140

Indeed, in the suburban setting there is reason to believe that residential development in general will be discouraged and that residential settlement will be displaced to an outlying political jurisdiction, where extensive travel to work and to commercial locations will be required.

That the land settlement consequences of rational zoning behavior can be significant is easily illustrated. Consider 10,000 acres of land in a coastal region. If the land was urbanized at a rate of o.20 acre per person (Vesterby and Heimlich 1991), then the 10,000 acres could accommodate, in all uses, 50,000 people. And, if the "Reston" design model of 10 persons per acre was used, then 100,000 new people could be housed and serviced in that same 10,000 acre space.

Now consider a shift from the Reston pattern to large-lot zoning of 5 acres per house. Using an average household size of 2.5 people, the 100,000 people who might be accommodated on 10,000 acres in a Reston setting would instead need 200,000 acres of land if 5-acre lot zoning was in place. This is the minimum land use because it does not include supporting land uses for roads, public buildings, and commercial establishments. Large-lot zoning practice, which is often advanced as an environmental protection measure or for preservation of the rural landscape, increases the land dedicated to urban uses by over 2,000%.

Achieving an Alternative Vision

Numerous policies quite removed from those typically thought of as land use controls may influence land settlement by increasing the demand for land's service of separation. This paper illustrates this point by describing only a few of the possible policies: deductions for home mortgage interest payments in determining federal and state taxable income will increase the demand for second homes; policies moderating the cost of travel make the demand for separation greater; fiscal policy and crime-control, racial, and education policies all can feedback into rational local zoning decisions, which spread settlement over the landscape.

This observation is not a new one. In his 1979 book, Room and Situation, Jim Hite of Clemson University observed,

> *In any advanced society, land use patterns are an inevitable result of government policies toward...basic social institutions. If those patterns are economically wasteful or environmentally unwise, the remedy lies in institutional reform on a broad scale. Conventional land-use planning and zoning are merely symptomatic prescriptions that fail to correct the underlying institutional flaws responsible for the problem.*
>
> Hite 1979, p. viii

Clearly, in my view, Hite is right. But how are the alternative visions of a more compact landscape to be achieved? The forces of our culture and of public policy are strongly aligned against compact and contiguous settlement. Before succumbing to frustration, advocates of alternative landscapes should recognize that polices which have facilitated the now sprawling land settlement took over 50 years to be established. Neither policy, life style aspirations of the American people, or landscape trends will be reversed overnight. What is needed now is a more direct focus on the way certain policies dictate the pattern and density of settlement. Only then can recommendations to reform those policies be supported analytically. However, many of the influential polices are maintained for reasons other than land settlement (energy policy, local revenue limitations, affordable housing, and so on). In addition, when the environmental consequences of these policies are reviewed, influences on land settlement often are ignored. For example, a recent report to Congress on the environmental effects of gasoline use did not mention landscape fragmentation resulting from emerging land settlement patterns (United States General Accounting Office September 1992).

In this setting, it will be difficult to make the case for redesigning the potentially most significant polices to make them more sensitive to land settlement. However, marginal reforms might be possible. Precedents do exist. National agricultural and tax policies have been reformed not in order to continue to support farm income but to reduce the policy incentive to farm erodible lands and drain wetlands. The Coastal Barrier Island Resources Act has been amended to deny the use of federal funds on roads and bridges that provide access to those areas (United States General Accounting Office July 1992).

Eliminating the deduction for home mortgages may not be possible, but capping its level and denying the deduction opportunity to second homes may be possible. Eliminating flood insurance may not be possible, but charging actuarial rates for flood insurance premiums and more stringency on controlling disaster costs may be possible (Mariano 1993). Eliminating the property tax may not be possible, but expanding local government's access to revenue sources other than the property tax or changing the financial responsibility for provision of some local services may mitigate against "rational" zoning behavior.

An important step would be a higher gasoline tax. If the real cost of moving a mile in the average vehicle on the road in 1991 was made equal to 1971 costs, a gasoline tax of $0.57 per gallon (letting $1.00 per gallon be the current price) would be required. Although the prospects for such a tax may be brighter now than in the recent past, the possibility is low of having an increase of the magnitude that will raise the cost of driving above its level of 20 years ago. But, the longer we wait, the more the settlement patterns get locked in and the more difficult the change will be to make. Indeed, the most persuasive argument against a gas tax is that it places a huge burden on people who have to make long commutes. It is ironic that the need to make long commutes is partly the result of low gas prices of the recent past.

To motivate reform, a more compelling case for concern about the consequences of the pattern and density of land settlement must be built. An important step is to demonstrate the relationship between public policy, land settlement, and statewide and regional environmental goals. This demonstration might be made in the form of required land settlement impact assessments as a part of statewide planning programs. The planning goals for the state should be organized around a critical factor—the pattern and density of land settlement. Then the focal point for state, regional, and municipal planning would be to consider how policies and programs alter land use pattern and density and, in turn, the environmental and other goals of the state.

A state might require such an evaluation for "significant" state, regional, and municipal policies and programs and for changes to these programs. These "impact assessments" could be done for the defined set of significant policies and programs and should be done in accord with particular and carefully defined analytical protocols. The leadership role for a state would include the definition of the actions requiring impact assessment, the development of the assessment protocols, and provision of technical and planning assistance for the use of the analytical protocols. If there is a job for the growth control programs now contemplated or operating from Delaware to Florida, this is it.

IN THE MEANTIME: WHOLE WATERSHED PLANNING

There can be no illusions about simple short-term fixes to the land settlement problem. This said, there is one emerging theme of resource management that will support a move in the desired direction—watershed planning and restoration (National Research Council 1992). This focus on whole watersheds is the next step in the evolution of separate attention to improving the chemical quality of the nation's water and to maintaining particular fish and wildlife populations. While the variety of programs attending to water quality discharges would be maintained in some form, watershed management seeks to restore and maintain functioning ecosystems, in this case—coastal areas. These systems might be protected "reserves" or might be a large expanse of landscape that would include pockets of agricultural, forestry, and urban uses.

The conceptual goal is to reestablish a matrix of chemical, hydrologic, and biological processes, which have been compromised by human alterations. Watershed restoration may mean returning to patterns and timing of water flows that more closely mimic some historical condition. Watershed restoration may mean reestablishing and rehabilitating wetlands and riparian areas, while also reducing the delivery of sediments and chemical contaminants to the water. And, restoration may mean that the biological resources of the waters are reintegrated into the watershed by revegetating upland and riparian areas and reintroducing native species.

Watershed restoration is focused on the selected spaces of the landscape where self-maintaining, evolving ecosystems would be expected to function. Restoration is not a goal for every location, in every watershed of every size, but where the effort is made, a planning process is triggered that identifies lands to be reserved from development, lands to be rehabilitated (e.g., farmlands that might be returned to wetlands status), and lands to be designated for development. The short-term result is that areas for resource protection are identified; long-term pressures from sprawl are not addressed as part of watershed planning.

Designation of a site to be preserved or to be developed carries with it the potential for perceived or anticipated wealth destruction or creation. The effects on property prices of these designations is easily recognized and will generate intense opposition from some landowner-voters and intense support from others. In Oregon, attempts by localities to implement watershed plans have generated landowner opposition. In one instance, this opposition was overcome. In the city of Eugene, a restoration program for Lower Amazon Creek and its associated wetlands was accepted by the community because the local interests were able to secure federal funds from the United States Bureau of Land Management to purchase the areas to be restored or preserved (Gordon 1993). The limitations of this source of funds for fee simple purchase on a national scale are obvious.

One possible alternative to federal funds is being developed. In one area of California, a city government is considering a general environmental impact fee on all development, with the receipts used to purchase and restore lands in designated environmental areas. In effect, this is a program to purchase development rights. Financing this purchase program with fees on development is being accepted by all parties because there has been a general recognition that the public planning for the area, as well as many other public policies, have in large part created the values that are realized by owners of the land available for development. That is, as watershed planning designates certain areas as off-limits to development, it restricts the supply of an available for development, and shifts the development value away from the designated preservation areas to the designated development areas.

Conclusion

The logic behind, and programs for, watershed planning might be a near-term approach to protecting certain coastal landscapes. In the longer term it is compact and contiguous land settlement that offers the best hope for accommodating expanding populations in the coastal zone. To achieve the desired land settlement pattern will require a long-term effort to create a new American vision of desirable land settlement. This will require a change in social values, followed by carefully crafted changes in public policy. That change process should begin by advancing public understanding of the opportunities for alternative settlement patterns and the policy forces that encourage the use of land for separation. This will require creative thinking about the policy linkages that yield our land settlement patterns and creative ideas to reform those polices.

In a recent review of the literature and experience with land-settlement policy, Meeks concludes with a comment that summarizes this paper's themes:

> *Political economists of both the left and the right, with credible documentation, argue that land use and conservation are inextricably tied to American tax law and, in fact, the structure of our economy. Without addressing these fundamental areas, they reason, land use planning laws and regulations will not succeed and may even cause further resource degradation.*
>
> Meeks 1990, p. 42

LITERATURE CITED

2020 Panel, Council on the Environment. 1988. Population Growth and Development in the Chesapeake Bay Watershed to the Year 2020. Council on the Environment, Richmond, Virginia.
Alliance for the Chesapeake Bay. 1989. Managing growth in the Chesapeake Region: A policy perspective. Chesapeake White Paper. Alliance for the Chesapeake Bay, Richmond, Virginia.

Bacon, J.A. 1991. The road to Haymount. *Virginia Business* April 1991: 39-49.

Bailey, S. 1992. Land use regulations and the Takings Clause: Are courts applying a tougher standard to regulators after Nollan? *Natural Resources Journal* 32 (4).

Barringer, F. 1991. Growth industry for Outer Banks: Home for retirees. *Roanoke Times* March 3, 1991. section D5.

Coulson, N.E. August 1991. Really Useful Tests of the Monocentric Model. *Land Economics* 67(3): 299-307.

Crandall, R.W. and J.D. Graham. 1991. New fuel-economy standards? *The American Enterprise* March/April 1991: 68-69.

Daly, C.B. 1993. Federal flood insurance seen by critics as all wet. *The Washington Post* February 18, 1993. section A3.

Downs, A. 1989. The Need for a New Vision for the Development of Large U.S. Metropolitan Areas. Solomon Brothers, New York.

Duany, A. and E. Plater-Zyberk. 1992. The Second Coming of the American Small Town. *Wilson Quarterly* Winter 1992: 19-50.

Federal Emergency Management Agency. 1989. Mandatory Purchase of Flood Insurance Guidelines. Government Printing Office, Washington, D.C. July 13, 1989.

Fehr, S.C. 1992. For many, it pays to drive to work. *The Washington Post* May 25, 1992. section A18.

Fehr, S.C. 1993. Increasingly, workers take the long way home. *The Washington Post* January 14, 1993. section B7.

Feldman, E.J. and M.A. Goldberg (eds.). 1987. Land Rites and Wrongs: The Management, Regulation, and Use of Land in Canada and the United States. The Lincoln Institute of Land Policy, Cambridge, Massachusetts.

Fischel, W.A. 1985. The Economics of Zoning Laws: A Property Rights Approach to American Land Use Controls. John Hopkins University Press, Baltimore, Maryland.

Fischel, W.A. May 1990. Do Growth Controls Matter? The Lincoln Institute of Land Policy, Cambridge, Massachusetts.

Gale, D.E. 1992. Eight State-Sponsored Growth Management Programs. *Journal of the American Planning Association* 58(4): 425-439.

Garreau, J. 1991. Edge Cities: Life on the New Frontier. Doubleday, New York.

Gibbons, B. 1977. Wye Island. John Hopkins University Press, Baltimore, Maryland.

Gordon, S.C. 1993. West Eugene Wetlands Program: A case study in multiple objective water resources management planning. Lane Council of Governments, Eugene, Oregon.

Governor's Commission on Growth in the Chesapeake Bay Region. January 1991. Protecting the Future: A vision for Maryland. Governor's Commission On Growth in the Chesapeake Bay Region, Maryland Office of Planning, Baltimore, Maryland.

Greer, J. 1991. Shaping the Watershed: How Should We Manage Growth? Maryland Sea Grant Program, College Park, Maryland. *Watershed* Spring/Summer 1(1): 2-13.

Heimlich, R.E. and D.H. Brooks. 1989. Metropolitan growth and agriculture: Farming in the city's shadow. Economic Research Service, AER-619. United States Department of Agriculture, Washington, D.C.

Hite, J.C. 1979. Room and Situation: The Political Economy of Land-Use Policy. Nelson-Hall, Inc., Chicago.

Houlahan, J., W. Andrew Marcus, and A. Shirmohammadi. 1992. Estimating Maryland Critical Area Act's impact on future nonpoint pollution along the Rhode River Estuary. *Water Resources Bulletin* 283: 553-567.

Jackson, K. 1985. Crabgrass Frontier: The Suburbanization of the United States. Oxford University Press, New York.

Kenyon, D.A. 1991. The Economics of NIMBYs. Lincoln Institute of Land Policy, Cambridge, Massachusetts.

Larimer, T. 1991. Chain store reaction. *The Washington Post Magazine* December 1, 1991. p. 27.

Latane, L. 1993. Rappahannock change coming. *The Richmond Times-Dispatch* February 15, 1993. section B3.

Mariano, A. 1993. Hill facing new fight over flood insurance. *The Washington Post* April 3, 1993. section E22.

Meeks, G. 1990. A legislator's guide to land conservation and growth management policy. National Conference of State Legislatures, Denver, Colorado.

National Research Council. 1992. Restoration of Aquatic Ecosystems. National Research Council, Washington, D.C.

Pauly, K. 1992. Highways, Sprawl, and... How About a New Approach? Alliance for the Chesapeake Bay, Richmond, Virginia. *Bay Journal* December 2(9).

Pressley, S.A. 1991. Struggling to keep suburbia at bay. *The Washington Post* April 3, 1991. section D1.

Risse, E.M. 1989. Some facts about growth in Virginia. Piedmont Environmental Council, Warrenton, Virginia. *Newsreporter*. October/November 3.

Risse, E.M. 1991. Overzoning, speculation, and fiscal crisis. Piedmont Environmental Council, Warrenton, Virginia. Newsreporter. November 1991.

Stallmann, J. 1991. Rural retirement counties: What do they mean for rural Virginia? *Horizons* January/February 3(1).

House Subcommittee on the City. 1980. Compact cities: Energy saving strategies for the eighties. Committee Print 96-15. July 1980. United States Government Printing Office, Washington, D.C.

United States Council on Environmental Quality. 1992. Environmental Quality: 23rd Annual Report. United States Government Printing Office, Washington, D.C.

United States General Accounting Office. September 1992. Energy Policy: Options to Reduce Environmental and Other Costs of Gasoline Consumption. GAO/RCED-92-260. United States Government Printing Office, Washington, D.C.

United States General Accounting Office. July 1992. Coastal Barriers: Development Occurring Despite Prohibitions Against Federal Assistance. GAO/RCED-92-115. United States Government Printing Office, Washington, D.C.

Vesterby, M. and R. Heimlich. 1991. Land use and demographic change: Results from fast growth counties. *Land Economics* 67 (279).

Vobejda, B. 1991. For the new retirees, out of the way places. *The Washington Post* February 27, 1991. section A2.

Yaro, R.D., R.G. Arendt, H.L. Dodson, and E.A. Brabec. 1990. Dealing with change in the Connecticut River Valley: A design manual for conservation and development. Lincoln Institute of Land Policy and Environmental Law Foundation, Cambridge, Massachusetts.

State Perspective in Coastal Zone Management

Christopher L. Brooks

Introduction

In the Southeast, the strongest coastal zone management programs at the state level have provided a very positive climate for continued growth and development while at the same time protecting the unique resources of the coast. This paper will focus upon some of the programs and activities of federally approved state programs in the Southeast, with primary attention to those of the South Carolina Coastal Council (Council). Although South Carolina does not have an adopted policy per se concerning sustained growth and development, these objectives are an integral part of the mission and functions of the South Carolina Coastal Management Program. To assist in understanding this discussion, a brief look at the federal program and the South Carolina Coastal Council will be presented first.

The Federal Coastal Zone Management Program

The federal coastal zone management programs, which are under the aegis of the United States Department of Commerce, Office of Oceans and Coastal Resources Management (OCRM), promote wise resource utilization and beneficial development of the Nation's coastal areas. Coastal zone management as defined in federal statute encourages long-term growth as opposed to short-term benefit.

The OCRM sets certain standards for program approval as contained in the 1972 federal act and the 1992 reauthorization. Thirty-two state and territorial programs are approved, with three states seeking approval in the near future. While each state program is different, based upon the needs and politics in that state, the programs also contain some common elements such as fresh-water wetlands, beach management, and regulation of salt marsh areas. Many also have interests and concerns founded in jointly managed water bodies, fishery resources, and other resource issues. Sustained growth and development will depend upon how well these different state programs work together to protect shared resources and to address common concerns. Collaborative efforts are made more difficult because some programs are relatively strong and aggressive and others are fairly weak.

The Southeast has some of the country's strongest state coastal management programs with the federally approved programs in Florida, North Carolina, and South Carolina. Other southeastern states participating are Virginia (which has a relatively new program), Alabama, Mississippi, and Louisiana. Both Texas and Georgia are seeking entry to the program and have received program development grants from OCRM.

The South Carolina Coastal Council

The South Carolina Tidelands Act of 1977 established the South Carolina Coastal Council and mandated that the Council conserve and protect coastal resources and promote development and utilization of these resources in a wise manner. In 1979, the Council's management program was adopted by the South Carolina General Assembly and this plan was approved by the Office of Oceans and Coastal Resources Management. The Council is primarily a regulatory agency with jurisdiction throughout the eight-county coastal zone. Its regulatory authority is derived from three provisions. The Council has direct permitting authority over any activity within the tidally influenced critical areas. It also has certification authority over all other state and federal permits issued in the eight-county area. Certification decisions are made according to the policies in the South Carolina Coastal Zone Management Plan. These two authorities result in approximately 1,800 separate regulatory actions each year. The third authority is the federal consistency provision: federal law mandates that direct actions of a federal agency are subject to the review and approval of the state's regulatory agency. This is a very important authority for each of the 32 federally approved state and territorial coastal zone management programs.

Sustaining growth and development in the coastal zone—in the region and in South Carolina—requires that these important resources be utilized but also protected and enhanced if future growth is to be supported. Obviously, this is a balancing act that can be controversial and demanding. The Council has proceeded in this effort with a very open and responsive program, which has as one of its strengths a very high degree of public participation and interaction. In fact, the Council was honored for the performance of its mission by the Department of Commerce, who presented the Council with the first-ever award for long-term achievement given to a state coastal zone management program. This award recognized the Council's program as the best of the federally approved state coastal zone management programs. This award was particularly significant given the diversity of the nominators: environmental, civic, and professional groups as well as local government officials and developers. This demonstrates that the Council is viewed as fair and effective by the public and by the groups whose activities are regulated by the Council—the importance of public confidence in the Council cannot be overstated.

New Federal Provisions

Two new provisions of the 1990 reauthorization of the federal coastal management act strengthened the ability of each state to encourage and promote sustained growth. The provisions are Section 309, which is voluntary, and Section 6217, which is mandatory. Each new section seeks to improve the resource management abilities of the states, which will lead in the long term to problem solution and continued growth.

Under Section 309, states with approved programs can apply for OCRM program enhancement grants to address the following eight issues of national importance: wetlands management; coastal hazards; improved and protected public access; cumulative and secondary impacts on coastal resources; marine debris; special area management planning; use and protection of ocean resources; and energy and government facilities siting and activities. The grants are awarded on a competitive basis. Each state seeking funds produces a guiding document (Assessment), which assesses resource management capabilities and problems, and outlines a plan to address these issues (Strategy).

The Council first applied for funds in 1991. Activities were proposed for each of the eight national concerns and the Council received funding for all areas except ocean resources. Priority was placed upon wetlands management, coastal hazards, cumulative and secondary impacts, and public access protection and improvement. Each of these issues is important to both resource protection and continued wise development of the resource base.

Section 6217, a required provision in the reauthorization, directs all federally approved state programs to produce, implement, and enforce a nonpoint-source pollution management plan for the coastal zone of that state. The program is jointly administered and enforced by the United States Environmental Protection Agency and OCRM. The plan must address five land-use activities: urban development, marinas, hydrologic modifications, agricultural activities, and sivicultural activities. The latter two are the greatest challenge for the states because these activities have heretofore not been regulated but have been subject in most areas only to voluntary best management practices. These activities are exempt from the requirements of Section 404 of the Clean Water Act, which is the most commonly relied upon regulatory means to address land development actions. Section 6217 also requires states to consider expansions of the coastal zone boundary to ensure that activities and their impacts occurring outside of the coastal zone boundary do not impact coastal resources. This provision is very controversial because each state would have to seek legislative authority to expand their coastal zone management area. To avoid this requirement, state programs must be able to demonstrate that the impacts upon coastal resources from activities in adjacent areas are minimal, and/or the problems and impacts are addressed effectively by other state or local programs already in place.

These new provisions in the federal statute correctly tie continued sustainable growth to the protection of environmental quality within the coastal zone. They also correctly recognize impacts from outside this area that could significantly alter coastal resources and ecosystems. Section 6217 therefore provides needed assistance to the states in their efforts to protect the coastal resource base for continued growth.

Over the past two decades, efforts by the states and the United States Environmental Protection Agency have brought most point-source discharges and their impacts under effective management. What remains to be addressed effectively are the nonpoint-source contributions that are threatening to reverse these gains in some areas. For example, in Horry County, South Carolina, even after nearly all point sources have been consolidated into large, well-managed public wastewater treatment plants, monitoring data point to a decline in water quality in some areas of the Intercoastal Waterway. This decline has been attributed to runoff. Uncontrolled runoff can consume the assimilative capacity of receiving waters thus exhausting the future capacity for receiving treated wastewater. State or local permitting agencies may have to prohibit or restrict new building starts and sewer connections. Growth is therefore limited unless the communities resort to expensive advanced treatment or use land treatment systems. Efforts under Section 6217 and by the United States Environmental Protection Agency and its state client agencies to manage nonpoint-source pollution are vitally important to future resource protection and enhancement in the coastal zone and to continued growth and development.

Nonpoint-source pollution originating from activities and sites within the coastal zone and from outside the area can also degrade and eliminate other coastal resources upon which economies and lifestyles may be based. Shellfish resources, commercial and sport fisheries, and recreational opportunities can suffer from pollution to the extent that the impacts jeopardize local economies and growth. Depressed commercial fisheries and declining sport fisheries in many locales are being blamed upon nonpoint-source pollution as well as other factors. According to the South Carolina Department of Health and Environmental Control, over half of South Carolina's shellfish areas are closed to harvesting due to pollution, with nonpoint sources believed to be a significant contributor. Once closed to the harvesting of shellfish because of pollution, these shellfish beds generally remain closed.

The South Carolina Coastal Zone Management Program

The remainder of this discussion will look at the state coastal zone management program in South Carolina and the issues of beach management, freshwater wetlands protection, and water quality management. The South Carolina program has been described by some experts as the strongest coastal zone management program in the country. This program's priorities compare very closely with those of Florida and North Carolina, which also have very progressive and effective programs. Each state has comprehensive beach management and planning authorities based upon a landward retreat of future development and reconstruction away from the hazard- and erosion-prone shoreline. Each state places a strong emphasis upon water quality protection and enhancement, and requires protection of freshwater wetland resources through avoidance.

South Carolina enacted a very far-reaching beach management law in 1988, which has as its primary objective the protection of public beaches and public access. The law is based on a retreat policy requiring a setback from the shoreline (baseline) for all new and rebuilt construction. The setback requirement is the distance equivalent to 40 years times the annual erosion rate. The law also prohibits the construction of new erosion-control structures (e.g., seawalls and revetments) and prohibits the reconstruction of existing walls that have been destroyed. This law is probably the most aggressive of its type in the country. The law applies to all 187 miles of beachfront except for Folly Beach (partial exemption). Impacted by this law are 27.4 miles of existing erosion-control structures, and 1,451 existing habitable structures within the setback area that have an appraised value of $1.15 billion, according to county tax data.

The South Carolina General Assembly, in adopting this law and its 1990 amendments, reacted to what was correctly foreseen as a growing threat to the state's tourism economy, which is based largely upon the high quality beaches possessed by the state. The South Carolina Department of Parks, Recreation, and Tourism has estimated that coastal tourism is a $2-3 billion economy. This business depends upon attractive, accessible beaches. South Carolina was in danger of jeopardizing this resource through the long-term loss of access to the beach, through beach erosion and the resulting armoring of the shoreline, and through encroachment on the beach-dune area by high density development oblivious to the natural forces and risks at play. The law was enacted to protect the coastal economy and beach-dune environment for long-term continued growth and development. Through our tourism economy, the state is literally marketing itself and offering its environment to tourists who have heretofore sought out the South Carolina coastal region over beach areas of other states that possess many of the same amenities. If development is allowed to despoil this resource, the vacationers will go elsewhere. The investment will also go elsewhere.

The State Beach Management Act will result in a long-term, controlled level of shoreline development and redevelopment, which will sustain coastal growth and protect the resource. North Carolina and Florida have taken similar, tough positions on beach management for the same reasons. Each state has also sought to strengthen their respective programs under the enhancement opportunities of Section 309 of the reauthorized federal law, and through support of necessary changes in the federal flood insurance program under the Federal Insurance Administration. The reduction of coastal hazards not only protects lives and property, but it also encourages sound development, which respects the specific development restrictions needed near the coast.

The management of freshwater wetlands is a third common factor among effective coastal zone management agencies which has a definite relationship to long-term sustained growth. Regulation of dredge and fill activities in federally delineated jurisdictional freshwater wetlands under Section 404 of the Clean Water Act is a controversial issue. Much discussion has taken place on the need to strengthen or relax this regulatory program depending upon one's point of view. This issue must first be resolved at the national level to allow the state programs to benefit from some needed stability in this important public policy area. Depending upon the definition of jurisdictional wetlands, the extent of freshwater wetlands in the Southeast is so pervasive that a national policy must be agreed to and supported over the long term if development is to continue without disruption. Investment decisions are made over the long term and uncertain regulatory policies will produce a very poor investment climate. United States Environmental Protection Agency (EPA) has renounced the wetlands initiatives of the Bush Administration, but the national policy guidance is still very much undecided, with the courts now reviewing the appropriateness of the current policies. The 7th Circuit Court of Appeals issued a decision on April 20, 1992, in *Hoffman Homes v. United States Environmental Protection Agency* in which the Court attacks the lack of statutory guidance in defining waters of the United States. The Court also questioned the EPA's authority to impose penalties in such situations

Carol Browner, the Clinton Administration's EPA Administrator, must seek to resolve these policies among a great deal of conflicting interests and pressures. Administrator Browner earned a reputation for dealing effectively with both the business-development community and the environmental community when she served as Secretary of Environmental Regulation of the state of Florida, where freshwater wetlands are vital and are carefully managed by both federal and state controls.

Historically, about 20% of South Carolina's freshwater wetlands have been lost to development according to the United States Department of Agriculture. Inventories by South Carolina's State Heritage Trust Program indicate that less than 200 of the 2,700 identified Carolina Bays have remained relatively undisturbed. Land development is the greatest threat today to the permanent loss of freshwater wetlands. Conversions of wetland areas to agricultural and sivicultural uses, which are largely exempt from Section 404 regulations, are not considered permanent losses in the sense that residential and commercial developments are. The Council reviews and acts upon each permit request under Section 404. Nationwide permit #26, which would allow fill of any freshwater wetland area less than 10 acres, is not in effect due to its noncertification for the South Carolina coastal zone. This permit has not received certification in South Carolina because the Council believes all wetland areas need protection and management.

The Council requires avoidance as the first choice in project planning and land development. Normally less than 100 acres are lost annually as freshwater wetlands are converted for residential, commercial, and road construction purposes, according to Council and United States Army Corps of Engineer's regulatory files. These impacts are generally limited to isolated wetlands of less than one acre. Overall, permit requests to fill wetlands under Section 404 have greatly declined due to the strong policies enforced by the Council and their general acceptance by the development community. Instead, developers have begun preparing plans that largely avoid jurisdictional wetlands, knowing that such requests for fill and disturbance will not likely be approved. Since 1988, when the 1987 freshwater wetlands delineation manual went into effect, the number of requests to fill contiguous wetlands has declined from over 57 total acres in 1988 to less than 4 acres in 1992, according to Council records. This is also attributable to the priority placed upon enforcement by the Council and the United States Army Corps of Engineers, with the Council providing much of the enforcement effort to the Corp's understaffed Charleston District.

Unregulated destruction of freshwater wetlands systems would have serious, long-term consequences for sustained economic growth in the coastal region. These systems serve valuable functions, which we are only now beginning to appreciate. They play a key in role in the coastal ecosystem, which can not be replaced. The long-term sustained use of our land and water resources requires that these wetland resources be protected.

Summary

In summary, sustained development for any coastal area in the Southeast or otherwise will require resource protection and management if development is to continue. The federal coastal zone management program under the Office of Oceans and Coastal Resource Management provides funding and programmatic support to state programs and incentives for program enhancements under sections 309 and 6217 of the 1990 reauthorized federal program. In the Southeast, the strongest coastal zone management programs at the state level have provided a very positive climate for continued growth and development while at the same time protecting the unique resources of the coast. The strongest and most effective state programs—those of Florida, North Carolina, and South Carolina—have definite common authorities and priorities. These program authorities include water quality management, beach management, and freshwater wetlands protection. Each state program enjoys a very strong and vocal level of public support in striking a balance between continued growth and the protection and enhancement of the unique coastal environment, which has attracted that investment and growth.

In June 1994, the state agency known as the South Carolina Coastal Council merged with the South Carolina Department of Health and Environmental Control (SCDHEC). The Coastal Council was renamed Office of Ocean and Coastal Resource Management, a division of SCDHEC. Only the organizational structure has changed; the policies and laws remain the same.

Local Polices to Control Coastal Growth in the Waccamaw Region

Jan S. Davis, Joe W.T. Burch, David M. Essex, Mark H. Hoeweler, Mark E. Kinsey, John M. Penney, and William J. Schwartzkopf

Introduction

The Waccamaw Regional Planning and Development Council is one of the regional Councils of Government established by the South Carolina Legislature in 1969. The councils provide a mechanism for local governments to pool resources and address common problems, such as urban and regional planning, transportation, environmental issues, community and economic development, and job training for economically disadvantaged and older persons. The Waccamaw Region (Fig. 1) comprises Horry, Georgetown, and Williamsburg counties, and has a permanent resident population of 227,170 (Waccamaw Regional Planning and Development Council 1993). The coastal region of Horry and Georgetown counties, known as the Grand Strand, extends 63 miles, from the North Carolina state line and Little River Inlet to the North Santee River at the Charleston County line (shaded area in Fig. 2). The Grand Strand, the primary focus of this paper, is an extremely popular tourist destination.

It is vital that effective planning and various controls are used to protect the fragile resources of the coastal region and accommodate the (inevitable) growth projected for the area. This paper reviews the impact of increased growth on water quality, transportation, stormwater management and golf courses, and discusses some of the management programs or other controls that can be used to minimize the impacts. A comparison of the cost of controlled development with uncontrolled development is made.

Coastal Population

Of the 227,170 permanent residents in the Waccamaw Region in 1990, the greatest concentration is in the south-central and coastal regions of Horry County and the northeastern coast (Waccamaw Neck) of Georgetown County (Fig. 3). The population of this area, which includes

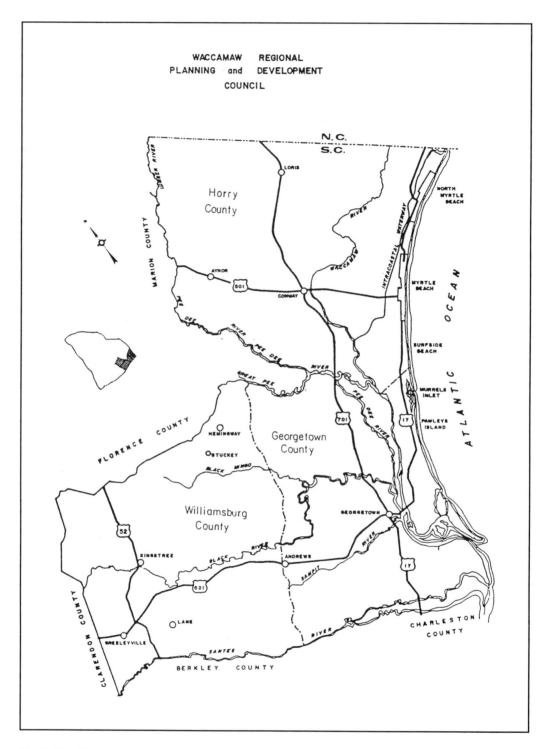

Fig. 1. The Waccamaw region.

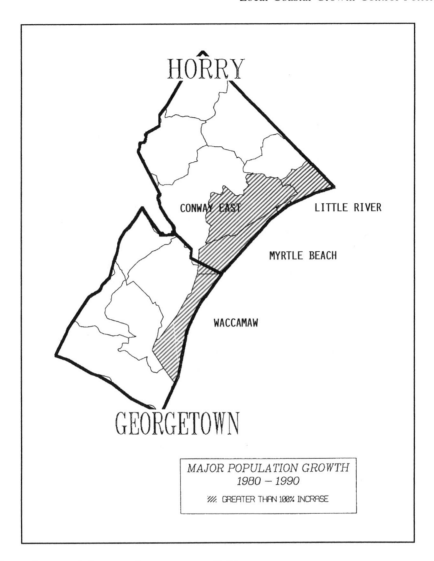

Fig. 2. Population growth for coastal census county divisions.

the Little River, Myrtle Beach, Conway East, and Waccamaw County census divisions, increased by over 100% from 1980 to 1990 (Fig. 2). From 1990 to 2005, the number of permanent residents in this part of Horry County is projected to increase from 93,950 to 174,921 and in the north coastal region of Georgetown County (the Waccamaw Neck) from 9,680 to 17,329 (Waccamaw Regional Planning and Development Council 1993) (Figs. 4 and 5, respectively).

Even more significant is the projected increase in the total peak population, which comprises permanent residents and day and overnight visitors. From 1990 to 2005, the total peak population

Fig. 3. The distribution of permanent resident populations.

in Horry and Georgetown counties is projected to increase from 440,863 to 674,486 and from 60,212 to 98,933, respectively (Waccamaw Regional Planning and Development Council 1993). The large number of day and overnight visitors to the coastal areas of these counties causes many unique problems. They not only place an increased burden on the water, sewer, and roadway infrastructure, but the beaches and other natural resources may also be impacted.

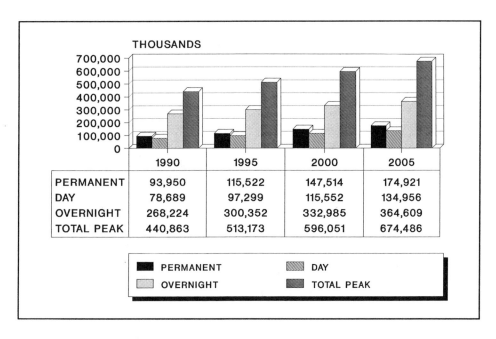

Fig. 4. The peak in the coastal population of Horry County. (Source: 208 Update, Waccamaw Regional Planning and Development Council 1992).

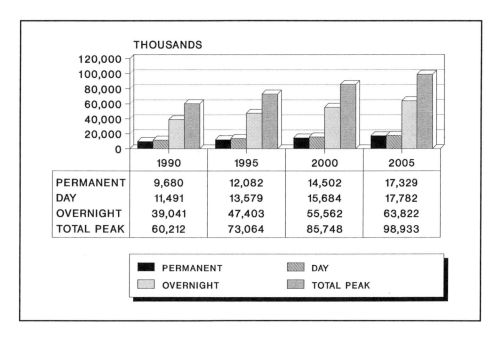

Fig. 5. The peak in the coastal population of Georgetown County. (Source: 208 Update, Waccamaw Regional Planning and Development Council 1992).

Water Quality Management

BACKGROUND

The Federal Water Pollution Control Act (PL92-500) overhauled previous legislation, streamlined procedures, and established a national water pollution control program. The Clean Water Act of 1977 redefined the Federal Water Pollution Control Act and set two basic goals: to attain fishable, swimmable waters, and to eliminate the discharge of pollutants into navigable waters by 1983 (zero discharge). The primary objective of the Clean Water Act was to restore and maintain the chemical, biological, and physical integrity of the nation's waters. Section 208 of the Clean Water Act called for the development of state and areawide water quality planning and management programs to control domestic and industrial wastewaters, stormwater, and other residual wastes to achieve "fishable and swimmable" waters wherever possible. The first objective of 208 plans was to control point sources (discharges through pipes). The second objective was to control pollution caused by nonpoint source discharges, or that which is carried over land by rainwater or melting snow, or which seeps through soil as interflow into waterways (not transmitted through pipes). Examples of nonpoint source pollution are stormwater runoff from agricultural areas, mining or construction sites, urban or developed areas; leachate from landfills or leaking septic tanks; or inadequately treated septic tank effluent due to poor soils or high groundwater tables. Nonpoint source pollution is directly related to land use practices and can be controlled effectively by measures such as zoning, subdivision regulations, stormwater management, erosion and sediment control ordinances, or other similar measures. The Waccamaw Regional Planning and Development Council was designated by the South Carolina Department of Health and Environmental Control to carry out water quality planning for the Waccamaw Region.

WACCAMAW 208 PLAN

The primary objective of the Waccamaw 208 Areawide Water Quality Management Plan, or 208 Plan (Waccamaw Regional Planning and Development Council 1978), is to maintain and improve water quality and provide the sewer infrastructure to meet demands of the rapidly developing region. Planning areas for wastewater collection and treatment facilities to meet 20-yr needs (to 1997) in the Waccamaw Region are shown in Fig. 6. These areas are also referred to as 201 planning areas, after Section 201 of the Clean Water Act, which lists extensive requirements that all wastewater facility plans must address, including
- planning area boundaries for sewer service;
- 20-yr needs for sewer service, based on population and economic projections, land use, and other local or regional factors;
- an evaluation of technically feasible treatment options to meet required effluent limits;
- a cost-effective and environmental analysis of the most viable alternatives; and
- identification and implementation of the selected alternative.

The 208 Designated Management Agencies in the Waccamaw Region are shown in Fig. 7. Point-source agencies are public entities, such as municipalities or sewer districts, that have permitted authority over wastewater treatment plants. Nonpoint source agencies are local governments that have the legal authority to implement land use controls (e.g., zoning) to minimize the impact of nonpoint source pollution on the water quality of surface waters or groundwaters. Many

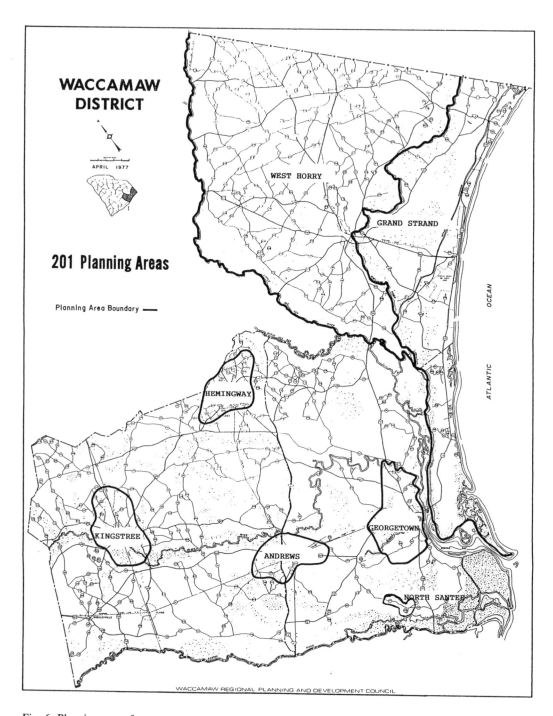

Fig. 6. Planning areas for wastewater treatment facilities.

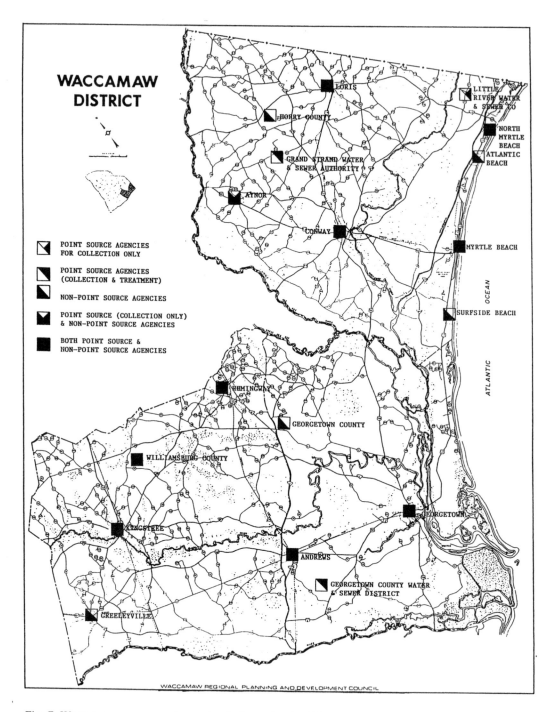

Fig. 7. Wastewater management agencies designated under 208.

Many municipalities are designated as both point source and nonpoint source management agencies. Most municipalities have implemented zoning regulations to control growth, but only Georgetown County and the cities of Myrtle Beach, North Myrtle Beach, and Surfside Beach had implemented stormwater management ordinances prior to the statewide stormwater management and erosion and sediment reduction law in 1991.

208 ACCOMPLISHMENTS

When the Waccamaw 208 Plan was prepared in 1977, all municipal, private, and industrial wastewater treatment facilities were inventoried and evaluated to determine if they were adequate to operate throughout the 20-yr planning period. As shown in Fig. 8, the coastal region was covered with numerous private wastewater treatment facilities which served mobile home parks, campgrounds, small subdivisions, or multi-family developments; many of these discharged directly into the ocean. Typically, most of these facilities were operated by part-time operators and were subject to frequent operational upsets (or failures) that could result in partially treated wastewater being discharged to the receiving waters. A primary goal of the 208 program, therefore, was to eliminate most of these small, inefficiently operated wastewater treatment facilities, and transfer their flow to regional municipal treatment facilities operated by certified full-time operators.

Since the implementation of the Waccamaw 208 Plan, this goal has almost been met (Fig. 9); most of the remaining private facilities will be eliminated as soon as regional treatment facilities are available. Under the current 208 Plan, a private facility cannot be upgraded to a higher design flow unless it is operated and maintained by the 208 designated management agency having jurisdiction for that planning area. Finally, under a memorandum of agreement with the South Carolina Department of Health and Environmental Control, any proposed wastewater construction project, new or reissued NPDES permit, or 201 plan or update must be certified to be in conformance with the Waccamaw Regional Planning and Development Council's 208 Plan before it can be approved by South Carolina Department of Health and Environmental Control.

SPECIAL 208 PROJECTS

In an on-going cooperative project with the United States Geological Survey, the 208 program is coordinating a study to develop a new hydrodynamic water quality model for the Pee Dee River-Waccamaw River-Atlantic Intracoastal Waterway system (Fig. 10). The new model will be used to determine the waste assimilative capacity of the system over a complete tidal cycle. A network of water quality and flow monitoring stations will be maintained at the boundaries of the study area to keep the model calibrated even after the study is completed.

South Carolina Department of Health and Environmental Control will use the model to determine the total maximum daily loads for the system and to evaluate proposed wasteloads for new and existing treated wastewater discharges to the system. The evaluation of proposed wastewater discharge locations is even more critical now, since most municipalities in Horry County have switched to the surface waters in this same system as a source of drinking water.

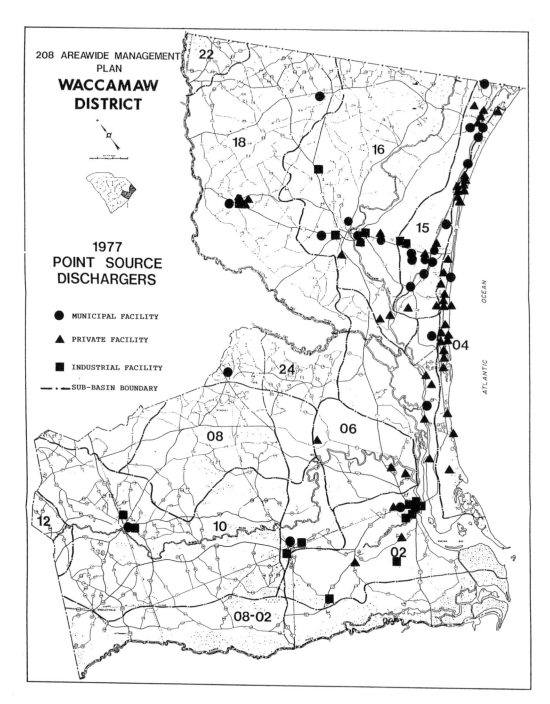

Fig. 8. Inventory of wastewater treatment plant discharges in 1977.

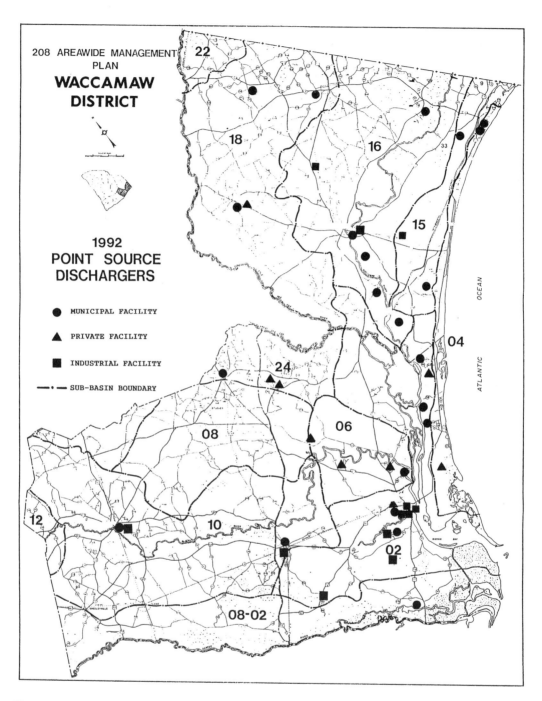

Fig. 9. Inventory of wastewater treatment plant discharges in 1992.

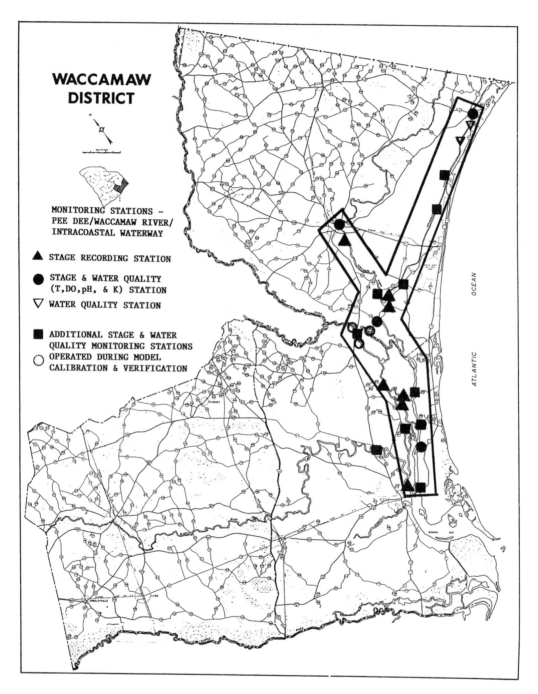

Fig. 10. Study for the development of the new hydrodynamic water quality model.

Stormwater Drainage

For years, the stormwater drainage problem was an "out of sight, out of mind" issue. Beginning in the late 1970s, several branches of the federal government began to identify "new" methods of managing stormwater. These methods began to be implemented at the state and local levels during the 1980s. Very little guidance has been provided to local governments by state or the federal governments regarding implementation. In the early 1990s, regulations were promulgated by the State of South Carolina and the federal government. What have these regulations meant to the local governments and, in this particular case, to Georgetown County and developers in the coastal zone?

The coastal zone has many unique natural and manmade features affecting stormwater drainage and its management. These features sometimes present problems, solutions, or in some cases, both problems and solutions in the design or operation of stormwater management systems. The natural features are flat terrain, poor soils, vast amounts of wetlands, the convergence of rivers and bays, high groundwater tables, and high volumes of rainfall. The manmade features and issues are old and new development (whether by necessity or waste), which grew out of human desire to enjoy the coastal environment.

In the past, local governments largely ignored the issue of stormwater drainage. This was because no problem was perceived; because it was considered a small problem or one which has always been present, so why worry with it; or because regulating and managing it would be too costly or would hurt development. However, the problems associated with ignoring this issue continued to worsen and eventually reached a crisis. Examples are the degradation of wetlands and/or rivers and bays; erosion of the soil and/or beaches; an increase in the groundwater table; flooding; a decline in the quality of the community potable water supply; the destruction of public and private property; decreased aesthetics; an increase in the insect population; or any combination of the above. Such problems eventually lessen the quality of life and create an atmosphere that discourages quality development. The results of ignoring the issue of stormwater drainage are very costly in the long term, and are paid by governments (local, state, and federal), businesses, and individuals within the community.

Local governments that have approached the issue of stormwater drainage have done so through stormwater management—usually through the adoption of local ordinances and/or regulations. Ordinances usually have required the developer to design and install a system to manage the development's stormwater such that adverse impacts are negated or minimized. Some local governments have required developers and the community in their respective watershed basin(s) to pay fees for the design and installation of the required stormwater management system. In both cases, the result is abating, eliminating, or preventing the problem(s).

Georgetown County addressed the issue by adopting the Georgetown County Stormwater Management Ordinance in early 1984. This ordinance required any development, except that which qualifies for an exemption, to have an approved stormwater management plan before construction can begin. The requirements and standards of the ordinance dealt with the design criteria, runoff volume and rate, waterbody, watercourse and wetland protection measures, sediment and erosion control, and system maintenance. The ordinance required a professional engineer, registered in the state of South Carolina, to certify that the plan met the standards. In early 1988, the ordinance was amended to include additional requirements and standards, which made it the strictest county stormwater ordinance in South Carolina. The amendments, initiated by Georgetown County, included input from citizens and developers prior to adoption. The ordinance allowed the County to use the majority of its drainage budget to solve old, existing stormwater drainage problems, and experience quality development and growth, while minimizing or avoiding new stormwater drainage problems.

As noted in the beginning of this section, both the state and federal government began addressing the issues of stormwater drainage and management in the 1970s. During the 1980s, local governments were required to meet additional guidelines and regulations. In 1977, the South Carolina Legislature created the South Carolina Coastal Council[1], to manage the natural resources of the eight coastal counties of the state. These natural resources are faced with the same basic issues as other natural resources with respect to stormwater drainage and management. The South Carolina Coastal Council adopted Storm Water Management Guidelines in 1985. These guidelines were the first step in establishing uniform standards for stormwater management in the coastal zone. In late 1988, the guidelines were amended to include additional requirements and standards. Ninety-eight percent of stormwater management standards and requirements of the Georgetown County ordinance are stricter than the South Carolina Coastal Council's guidelines. These differences have required a dual review of stormwater management plans for all development projects in Georgetown County, increasing the time, resources, and costs for the agencies involved (the County and the South Carolina Coastal Council) and the developer.

In 1991 legislation was passed by the South Carolina Legislature requiring each county to adopt a stormwater management and sediment control ordinance. This legislation required, as a minimum, each county to use the same standards and requirements for stormwater management. Jurisdiction over the counties was given to the South Carolina Land Resources Conservation Commission; an exception was made for the eight coastal counties, which remain accountable to the South Carolina Coastal Council. This action was instituted to avoid a possible triple review, approval, and inspection of stormwater management plans in coastal zone counties. Regulations were finalized and implemented in 1992. Under the regulations, each local government may request delegation of the stormwater management program within its jurisdiction from the appropriate parent agency. As a minimum, a delegated local government must implement the regulations by means of a local ordinance, and the program must be reviewed and recertified every three years. Georgetown County initially requested interim delegation of the county's stormwater management program to permit the County to administer a program, using the stricter standards and requirements of either the county ordinance or state regulations, until the county ordinance could be amended. However, the Georgetown County ordinance was rescinded in June 1996, to avoid having stricter requirements than the state law and to eliminate duplicate reviews and inspections.

As a result of the 1987 amendments to the Federal Clean Water Act, the United States Environmental Protection Agency began developing stormwater management regulations and permitting requirements. In late 1992, the United States Environmental Protection Agency finalized its permitting regulations and delegated the authority to administer the federal regulations in South Carolina to the South Carolina Department of Health and Environmental Control. The department developed a general permit for construction activities on nonindustrial sites of five or more acres.

---

[1] In June 1994, the South Carolina Coastal Council merged with the South Carolina Department of Health and Environmental Control (DHEC). The Council is now known as the Office of Ocean and Coastal Resource Management, a division of DHEC.

In most cases, the requirements of the State's general permit will be fulfilled in the submission of a stormwater management plan prepared in accordance with South Carolina Land Resources Conservation Commission regulations or any delegated local government ordinance. South Carolina Department of Health and Environmental Control can require additional requirements, however, in cases where the proposed activity could adversely impact the water quality of surface or ground waters. This should eliminate at least 90% of the duplication of efforts in the review process.

In conclusion, it is now evident that stormwater drainage and its management is no longer a forgotten issue. Many governmental agencies (federal, state, and local) are now involved in regulating stormwater drainage. Unlike in the past, the state and federal governments have developed mechanisms to delegate the administration of stormwater management regulations almost exclusively to local governments. This trend will allow local governments to manage a program to protect their community which requires less time in review and approval, and smaller state and federal staffs. Developers within their jurisdiction will therefore save time and money. Hopefully, the local government staffs will provide the desired level of administration that stormwater management requires and deserves. This will give local governments the opportunity to control an important utility and continue quality development and growth while protecting coastal resources. By managing stormwater, local governments can protect, maintain, enhance, and/or improve the area's aesthetics and quality of life, and foster quality development with minimum financial impact to their citizens.

Transportation

LOCAL ISSUES AFFECTING NEW ROADS

A key issue for sustainable development in the southeastern coastal zone is roads. Are new roads needed, or should existing roads be expanded to increase capacity? If new roads are needed, where should they be located? Does the road network allow for convenient access, which is the lifeblood of an area dependent on tourism for the growth of its economy? And finally, how are the needed improvements funded?

Whether new roads are needed or existing roads need to be expanded, there are certain geographic constraints that must be considered in both Horry and Georgetown counties. Naturally, the ocean provides a distinct boundary that reduces the options in locating roads to service the linear development in coastal counties. The numerous wetlands in both counties represent another constraint. Wetlands issues—both economic and environmental—must be addressed in almost all instances in which a new road is proposed to serve coastal development in the southeastern states. There is a multiplying effect on the overall cost associated with building a road through a wetland area if the wetlands have to be bridged. There are also additional costs associated with construction in an environmentally sensitive area. Due to either economic or environmental considerations, certain road projects are not feasible.

Another physically limiting factor particular to the Georgetown area is the location of the Intracoastal Waterway (Fig. 11). Winyah Bay and the Waccamaw River create a water barrier paralleling the Atlantic Ocean; the land area between the two is called the Waccamaw Neck. This is the fastest growing area in Georgetown County. In order to connect the Waccamaw Neck with the rest of Georgetown County, the Intracoastal Waterway (which traverses the Waccamaw River

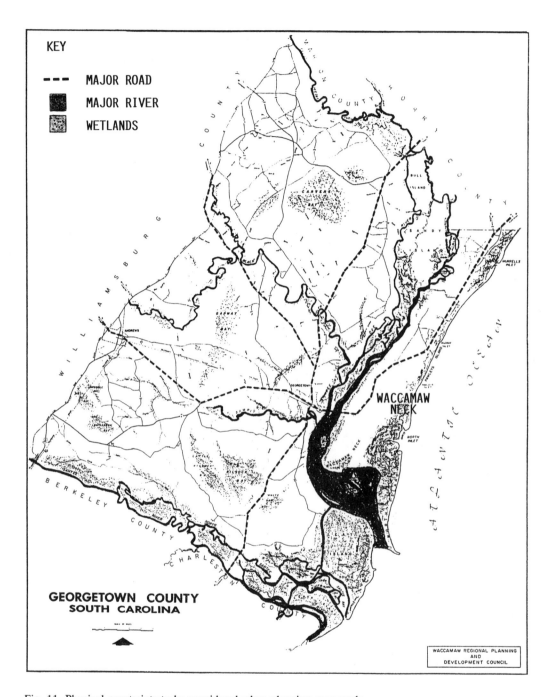

Fig. 11. Physical constraints to be considered when planning new roads.

and Winyah Bay) must be bridged, and it must be bridged to maintain a clearance of 65 ft from mean high water to allow passage of large (or tall) vessels. These factors add heavily to the cost of construction.

The effects of tourism upon the area's infrastructure are considerable and are difficult to quantify. Roads cannot be designed solely to handle the traffic generated by the year-round permanent population. To satisfy the demands of both a growing population and the influx of tourists, the tourist population must be identified and monitored separately from the permanent population.

Tourism is a vital component of the local economy, and a primary factor in the growth of the region as a whole. There must be a balance in the manner in which new road projects are funded. The permanent population cannot be expected to assume the burden of tourism-generated demand. A funding alternative would be to implement some type of special tax targeted at the tourists but which would not affect the area's appeal as a tourist destination. In an effort to quantify the tourist population and evaluate the demand for roads, Georgetown County, Horry County, and the Wilbur Smith Agency are participating in a cooperative effort to model the traffic patterns within the urbanized portion of Georgetown County. Georgetown County has also made transporta-tion one of the elements of its comprehensive plan. The traffic model will allow for more accurate planning and updates to the plans.

Another variable that must be considered in Horry and Georgetown counties, with regard to road system performance, is the possibility of tropical storms or hurricanes which would necessitate the evacuation of the entire population along the coast. These situations impose severe demands on the road system as a whole. While no system is capable of efficiently dealing with a large-scale evacuation, it should be able to accomplish the task given a reasonable amount of advanced warning. Decreased warning time or the reversing of the storm's path could result in a panic situation if the roads clog at key locations.

Many variables must be considered when contemplating the expansion of the existing road system. All variables must be balanced in order to effect the desired result—a system of roads that balances the demands of a growing population and the demands of tourist access against the desire for harmony with environmental interests, and that is also fiscally responsible.

COST OF DEVELOPMENT

Once demands have been established and location issues have been settled, the questions remaining to be resolved are who will fund a project and by what method. Should the private sector pay for all or part of the costs involved in road improvements or new roads necessitated by new development? Should the public sector, in general, be asked to pay for additional roadways that may only serve a select portion of the local population?

Private interest must assume the burden of the initial demands and costs of new development, whether it is the interior road network of a new subdivision or the impacts associated with new development on existing systems. After the initial cost of development has been met, however, it should be the responsibility of the public sector to maintain the road system. It is also in the public sector's interest to infill certain areas of the road network or to upgrade the system as conditions may determine in the future.

If development is not controlled, there is the potential for haphazard or piecemeal growth. The public sector would have to bear the burden of this inefficient type of growth on its own. The cost involved with uncontrolled development can be severe. Development needs to be controlled to ensure that precious public resources are not wasted and that public sector dollars are used efficiently.

LOCAL PROBLEMS, LOCAL SOLUTIONS

Several problems are encountered on the local level that affect the ability to provide an expanded road system. If there is no clear definition of goals, no plan for future needs, and no vision established by the community, it will be difficult, if not impossible, to build a consensus of public opinion for new roads. There may be a portion of the community that does not want new roads or does not care where the new roads will be located. This can especially be true if traffic is to be diverted around an existing commercial corridor.

These local problems can be resolved by having a comprehensive plan that is a living document: one that can be adapted and updated as conditions and situations demand, that is in the public domain, and that has had input from the public prior to its implementation.

Another solution to problems on the local level is to have a set of rules and guidelines in place to regulate and control development within its jurisdiction. Georgetown County uses the County Subdivision Regulations. This document delineates the requirements for new development, as well as requirements for platting new roads and the standards for designing them. Clear articulation of what is required from a new development can reduce the friction between the developer and the permitting agency. Another problem on the local level is the sometimes com-peting interests of a community that is both rural and urban. How can the interests of both be served? The solution to this problem is again, controlled development. Both rural and urban segments of the population can best be served by ordered and controlled growth.

Problems on the state level are the generation and allocation of tax dollars for new roads. If the funds for new roads are not available from the state, then efforts should be made on the local level to fund projects.

There are several problems that exist when dealing with the federal government. Among these are the status of South Carolina as a donor state, which means that it receives less than its share of funds back from the federal government based on contributions. Another related problem is the federal formula used for the allocation of funding for roads. This formula is based upon permanent population figures generated by the census and does not account for tourism.

To receive federal funding, it is necessary to demonstrate a legitimate need for new roads. The Grand Strand Area Transportation Study (GSATS) Area Traffic Model is an instrument that will be able to demonstrate the need for new roads in the present and in the future. Efforts must also be made to take advantage of existing federal legislation. The Intermodal Surface Transportation Efficiency Act (ISTEA) allows for the funding of new roads based on several criteria, but it primarily funds projects that link two or more different modes of transportation. All efforts should be made to propose projects that fit the funding criteria to ensure a greater chance for receiving federal funding.

There are many issues and special considerations to be addressed when providing new roads to a growth area. Those considerations are increased when the factors unique to a coastal zone are included in the mix. It is vital that these issues be met directly to insure that communities are able to sustain development and growth.

Golf Courses

In Georgetown County, it is common practice to require environmental studies as a part of the development plans for a golf course. The basis for the requirement is the catchall statement, "other studies as required by the planning staff," which is included in the planning commission approval process. One of the prime examples of an environmentally sensitive golf course development plan is the DeBordieu course.

DeBordieu Colony is a 2,706-acre site stretching 4 miles from U.S. Highway 17 to the Atlantic Ocean, and located 4.5 miles north of Georgetown. Environmental regimes at the site range from maritime forest to marsh and beach. The site was developed in 1969 into a nine-hole golf course with 340 associated properties.

When the site changed ownership in 1984, the new owners inherited several existing limitations and/or environmental problems. These included a sewage treatment plant permitted for spray irrigation of tertiarily treated effluent on the golf course (ND permit), which did not have enough capacity for the proposed new development plan; an altered wetland environment; and a golf course in the lowlands of the property.

The new owners included an upgrade of the wastewater treatment facility to a higher design flow as a part of their development plan. Secondarily treated effluent would be filtered, aerated, and chlorinated before being mixed with fresh well-water prior to being spray irrigated on the golf course. The existing golf course was elevated, and the new nine holes were also placed on elevated ground. Restratification procedures were followed on golf course soil during construction in order to enhance infiltration rates. Stormwater detention was designed to hold water on site for 72 h, three times the County requirement of 24 h. For this, an interconnected system of more than 70 acres of 6-ft deep lakes was designed for the site. The course was designed so that none of the sprayed wastewater effluent would sheet flow into the wetlands but would instead be stored until allowed to filter offsite.

But, the most useful accomplishment of the development was the return of the wetlands and marine environment to a condition similar to that which existed prior to the 1969 construction. A more natural water flow was reintroduced to the wetlands, and some of the marine canals were deepened to promote flushing and avoid eutrophication and fish kills.

Planning staff required that water quality testing sites be included in the plan so that environmental conditions before and after development could be evaluated. Both groundwater monitoring wells and creek testing sites were employed for this determination. Much of the water received from offsite was low in dissolved oxygen and high in fecal coliform bacteria and nitrates. Based on monitoring reports submitted to Waccamaw Regional Planning and Development Council, the overall water quality was improved by the on-site collection and filtering system.

Some of the best examples of environmentally sensitive golf courses incorporate natural sand and vegetation into the design of the course. Use of the existing natural environment in golf course design can protect the environment, cut down on maintenance, and provide for a more unique golfing experience. Another activity that lowers maintenance and protects the environment is the careful selection of grasses which require less fertilizers, pesticides, and fungicides.

Most golf courses have 100-150 acres of Bermuda grass, which is very high in maintenance, requiring large amounts of fertilizers and pesticides. DeBordieu, which uses only 36 acres of Bermuda grass for its fairways and tees, is an example of a low maintenance course. Greens are constructed using Bentgrass, a moderate-maintenance grass. Roughs, and other areas utilize centipede grass, love grass, natural straw, ryegrass, wildflowers, and fescue. All of these grasses require little or no maintenance.

A trained agronomist was hired for the golf course, as well as individuals trained in fertilizer and pesticide application. Application schedules were designed for the soil additives, and mowing is kept to a minimum. Grass clippings are also left on the fairways, limiting waste. All of these activities were part of the "Best Management Practices Plan" submitted as part of the approval process for the DeBordieu PUD. Computerized irrigation systems that water the course based on feedback from tensiometers, and modern maintenance facilities are also important components of an environmentally sensitive golf course.

The most modern golf maintenance facility planned for Georgetown County is the new facility at Willbrook. The chemical storage facilities and the mixing and loading pad with associated wash rack are state-of-the-art. Waste chemicals washed from equipment and off of employees are collected and stored for proper offsite disposal. All efforts are made to ensure that chemicals do not wash off the pad or work area and enter the groundwater as they would in an uncontrolled site. The procedures follow the guidelines set forth in a publication of the Alliance for a Clean Rural Environment (ACRE fact sheet 14). (This publication is distributed through the Cooperative Extension Service of Clemson University.)

Both DeBordieu Colony and Willbrook serve as excellent case examples of environmentally sensitive golf courses, which provide Georgetown County with precedents for future golf course development. Using a tool such as the "Best Management Plan" allows for controlled development, which serves to focus attention on protecting the environment and saving money in golf course maintenance.

Comparing the Cost of Controlled Development with Uncontrolled Development

It is difficult, if not impossible, to quantify the dollar savings realized under a controlled development scheme versus an uncontrolled situation. However, few would dispute the fact that development controls are cost-effective if they are properly implemented. Georgetown County implemented zoning restrictions, building codes, and a flood damage prevention ordinance over 20 yr ago; subdivision regulations have been in effect for almost 12 yr; stormwater management regulations were adopted in 1984; and within the last 2 yr, the County instituted tree protection regulations into the zoning code. A land use plan was prepared for the entire county in 1976. An updated plan for the rapidly developing beach area was completed in 1985. County leaders had the foresight and fortitude to establish development controls before growth pressures were exerted, and today Georgetown County is reaping the benefits. The issues of protecting open space, preserving prime farmland, protecting wetlands and endangered species habitat, historical preservation, and energy efficiency in the land planning process can all be addressed in a controlled development format. The following is a comparison of specific development issues in a controlled and uncontrolled environment.

ACCESSIBILITY

Rapid, unplanned growth produces a random pattern of residential subdivisions and commercial shopping areas, unrelated to public services and utilities and without consideration of the landscape. Without control, important considerations such as reservation of areas for public access to beaches and rivers are neglected. In controlled growth, a site's accessibility is a major factor in determining the appropriate land use(s) for the area. In rural communities, residential areas should not be located more than 30-40 min travel time from places of employment; more than 4 miles from major shopping centers; ¾ mile from neighborhood shopping facilities; 1 mile from a grade school; 2½ miles from a high school; and 3½ miles from cultural and recreational facilities (Hoyt 1968).

DRAINAGE

A random approach to drainage is not cost-effective and may even be foolhardy in the flat terrain of the lowcountry. Careful site planning and drainage consideration can save money for both the developer and the County. Poorly drained sites are often better left undisturbed as the short- and long-term cost of installing and maintaining a drainage system can exceed the value of the "improved" property.

VEGETATION

The cost of locating and saving trees prior to development is repaid many times by the value added to each house or storefront. Developers have found that saving good, large trees is no more expensive than the cost to plant a sapling. The value of vegetation's functions: providing shade, acting as air and water filters, storing groundwater, and providing wildlife habitat, have been quantified in various publications of the American Forestry Association. The value exceeds $30,000 over the life of some large urban trees.

UTILITY SERVICES

Thankfully, the days of construction without consideration of available water, sewer, and electrical services are on the wane, since these factors represent some of the most important factors in the site-selection process. The main problem facing land planners today is accurately predicting the necessary line sizes, pump stations, transformer locations, etc., that will be needed to serve the area adequately when build-out occurs. The expenses associated with running parallel lines and upgrading existing systems are extremely high and represent a wasteful allocation of resources. The regulation of land subdivision for residential and other uses is widely recognized as an efficient method of insuring sound community growth and safeguarding the interests of the homeowner, the land developer, and county government.

LAND USE

Incompatible land uses create nightmares, such as depressed land values for the developer; noise, glare (from automobile headlights), and traffic for the land owner; and a reduced tax base for the county. Proper groupings and intermingling of certain land uses achieve superior living arrangements. Physical buffers such as parks, golf courses, wetlands, and even cemeteries can minimize adverse effects. The Georgetown County Land Use Plan contains development policies for low-density residential, high-density residential, commercial, industrial, and institutional uses and utilities. These policies set forth recommended locational requirements that should be considered in the siting process. A feature of the Georgetown County Plan is the nodal commercial growth recommended for U.S. Highway 17 through the beach area, as opposed to the creation of a strip commercial corridor. This allows for commercial development around major intersections along the highway, which preserves the volume capacity of the roadway and provides a safer and more pleasing route to the motorist.

TRANSPORTATION

Freedom of neighborhoods from the adverse effects of through traffic is highly important. New developments should be coordinated to insure that their respective locations will complement the thoroughfare plan for the area. Uncontrolled development such as strip commercial uses can quickly devour the carrying capacity of the highway that serves it with numerous curb cuts and lack of an interconnecting access road. This translates into a tremendous financial burden on the public as the need for new roads continues.

FLOODING

The need for affordable flood insurance was one of the factors that encouraged Georgetown County to adopt land use controls over 20 yr ago. The amount of land in the county that lies within floodplains is enormous and the potential effects of flooding of any new development must be considered prior to construction. Building elevation requirements and special building codes help to minimize the flood damage potential of property and therefore, indirectly result in savings to federal taxpayers.

FIRE PROTECTION

Any new development within the county is required to submit development plans to a technical review committee, made up of many agency representatives, including fire inspectors. The plans are carefully reviewed to insure that forethought was given to fire safety and emergency access by fire department personnel. Uncontrolled development does not benefit from this level of review and increases the possibility of the loss of property or human life.

SCHOOLS

The presence of elementary schools is one of the greatest drawing cards in new residential developments. The prudent developer considers existing and future school sites as a part of the site-selection process. As mentioned previously, the recommended maximum travel distance to a grade school is 1 mile. Greater distances result in costly transit facilities, which are publicly funded.

AIRPORTS

Any community without land use controls places the long-term viability of their airport in jeopardy. No other public facility is as sensitive to the adverse effects of incompatible land uses. Rigid regulations, such as zoning, are necessary to protect the airport from encroachment of incompatible land uses and also to protect the developed areas around the airport from airport hazards, such as noise, vibration, and crash potentials.

SOLID WASTE DISPOSAL

The ability of a community to control the location of various types of development results in savings of the county's expenditures to collect and dispose of solid waste. Given the lack of adequate landfill sites in the lowcountry, restricting development in areas suitable for new or expanded landfills also results in savings.

COMMUNITY FACILITIES

In an uncontrolled development scenario, there is no overseer monitoring the cumulative effect of a small development upon existing community facilities such as churches, hospitals, recreation centers, etc. As a result, problems are not prevented and when they become evident, amelioration is usually quite expensive and inefficient. Controlled development typically has strategic reservations of land for future community facilities, resulting in a better living arrangement and a more complete community.

LITERATURE CITED

Hoyt, Homer. 1968. Future highways and urban growth, p. 33. *In* J. Ross McKeever (ed.), The Community Builders Handbook, Urban Land Institute, Washington, D.C.

Waccamaw Regional Planning and Development Council. 1993. Population and Economy Study. Waccamaw Regional Planning and Development Council, Georgetown, South Carolina.

Waccamaw Regional Planning and Development Council. 1978. Waccamaw 208 Areawide Water Quality Management Plan. Waccamaw Regional Planning and Development Council, Georgetown, South Carolina.

Population Trends in the Coastal Area, Concentrating on South Carolina

Walter P. Bailey

Introduction

Changes in population occur over time, and society must respond to these changes in terms of what is needed and what is "best" for the populace. There are two issues in terms of population growth and the environment. The first is preserving the natural beauty and environment of a particular geographic area; the second is economic development, providing jobs and overall economic improvement of the people. Frequently, these issues are in competition, although they do not have to be.

Census data provide solid information regarding the population, not merely the density of persons in a geographic area but also the age distribution, racial composition, economic status, migration rates, etc., and how these have changed over time. Prior to the 1990 census of the United States population, the Census Bureau tabulated data at the block and enumeration district (EDs) levels. Blocks are the smallest type of census area, averaging about 70 people and most commonly small rectangular areas bounded by four streets. Prior to the 1990 census, block statistics were published for urbanized areas, and enumeration districts were used for areas where census blocks were not defined. EDs vary in population size, but average about 600 people. The population census in 1990 was the first time the *entire* United States was blocked. The number of blocks increased from 2.5 million in 1980 to 7 million in 1990 for the United States (South Carolina increased from 28,000 blocks to 127,000 blocks), which gave tremendous capability to measure changes in population at the smallest geographic level.

Most often population change is expressed in terms of the percent change in population from one decade to another. Growth may occur as a result of a higher birth rate than death rate and/or through migration. To understand the real story behind population change, one must look at migration. Migration is defined as the difference in actual population size and the expected population size, based on a previous population count (e.g., census) adjusted for the number of births and deaths in the time period. The migration rate is then calculated as the number migrated divided by the total population.

Because the census counts people at their place of residence, temporary populations such as summer populations are not included. This is unfortunate because in coastal areas the population that promotes development and environmental changes is not the year-round resident population but the summer population. Thus, for coastal planning, efforts should be made to collect and make available to policymakers and planners information concerning this temporary population group.

The United States and the Southeast

In order to consider population trends in the Southeast, one must consider where population growth in the United States has occurred. A comparison of the 1980 United States census with the 1990 census shows that overall the United States population increased 9.8%. Strong growth was apparent in the coastal states, with the exception of Massachusetts, Rhode Island, Connecticut, and New Jersey in the Northeast and Louisiana, Mississippi, and Alabama along the Gulf Coast (Fig. 1). Despite low growth for Alabama and Kentucky and negative growth for West Virginia, the Southeast had an overall growth rate of 14.8% (Fig. 2). For the United States as a whole and particularly for the coastal states, county census divisions show that growth rates were higher in resort areas and bedroom communities (Fig. 3), and the population is concentrated in a narrow strip that parallels the coast (Fig. 4). However, the bedroom community growth may not be true growth for the large urban areas as a whole, but simply the population moving from one area to another for better schools or better neighborhoods. As seen in Fig. 5, the migration rates within the United States are also greatest for the coastal areas, again, particularly for the resort areas and bedroom communities. While the population may increase or decrease as a whole as a result of migration, different rates for segments of the population may also occur.

For planning purposes, it would be beneficial to know the types of persons who composed this population growth. Thus, examination of the persons in terms of age and job status who made up the growth between 1980 and 1990 was done. The percent changes within the age group under age 60 and the group age 65 and over in the Southeast are similar to the United States as a whole. Stronger growth appears to be occurring in the age group 65 and over. However, comparison of age-specific growth rates across decades must be interpreted cautiously since calculated change is based on different populations (e.g., the number in the 15 to 24 age group in 1980 compared to the number in this same age group in 1990). Some of this growth is certainly due to an aging population, but for some areas, in-migration of retirees may be significant.

Current projections for population change in the United States between 1990 and 2010 (Fig. 6) are similar to the actual population growth that occurred between 1980 and 1990. These projections show increasing population growth in the coastal regions, particularly the southeastern coastal regions.

South Carolina

As was true for the nation and the Southeast, the percent population change from 1980 to 1990 for South Carolina shows a larger percent growth in resort areas and bedroom communities, especially those with better school systems (Fig. 7). The largest growth rates occurred in counties

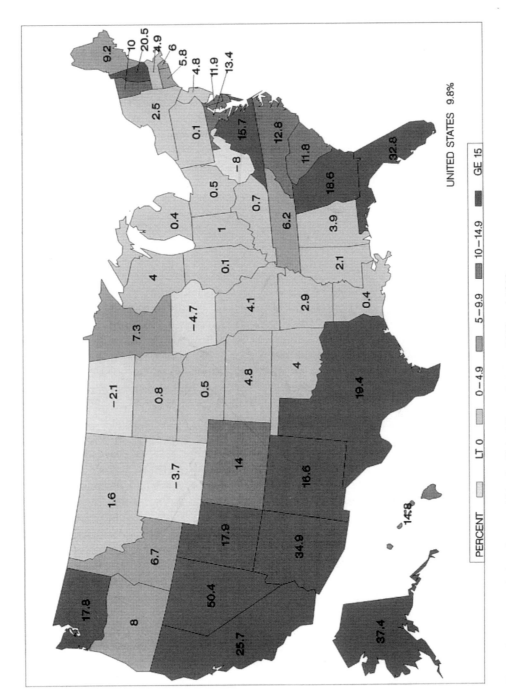

Fig. 1. Percent population change within the United States between 1980 and 1990.

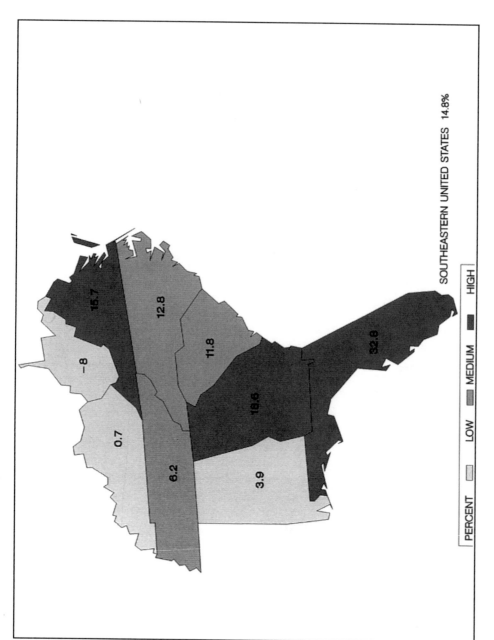

SOUTHEASTERN UNITED STATES 14.8%

PERCENT LOW MEDIUM HIGH

Fig. 2. Percent population change within the Southeast United States between 1980 and 1990.

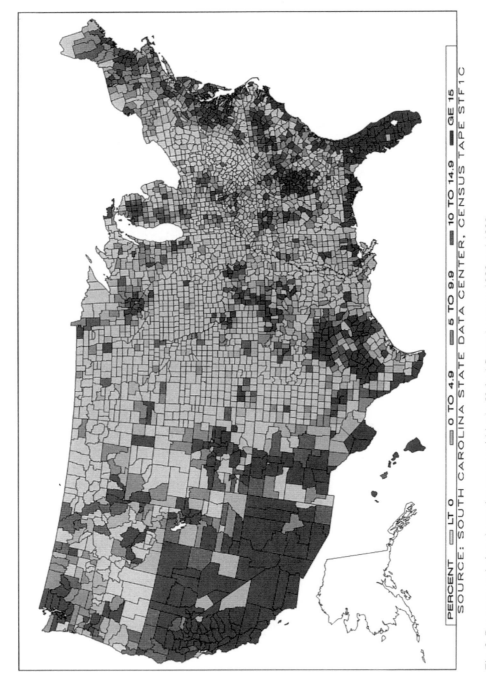

PERCENT ☐ LT 0 ☐ 0 TO 4.9 ☐ 5 TO 9.9 ■ 10 TO 14.9 ■ GE 15

SOURCE: SOUTH CAROLINA STATE DATA CENTER, CENSUS TAPE STF1C

Fig. 3. Percent population change by county within the United States between 1980 and 1990.

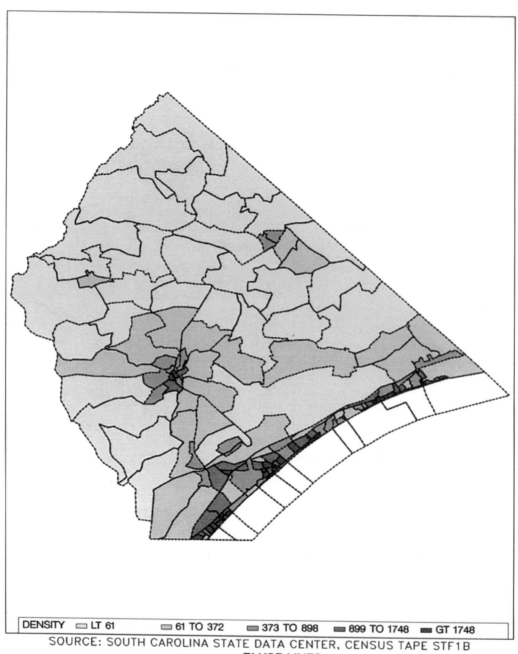

DENSITY ⬜ LT 61   ⬜ 61 TO 372   ▨ 373 TO 898   ▨ 899 TO 1748   ▧ GT 1748

SOURCE: SOUTH CAROLINA STATE DATA CENTER, CENSUS TAPE STF1B

_ _ _ _ BLKGP LINES

Fig. 4. Population density for Horry County, South Carolina, from the 1990 census. Density is number per square mile and is shown at the county census block level.

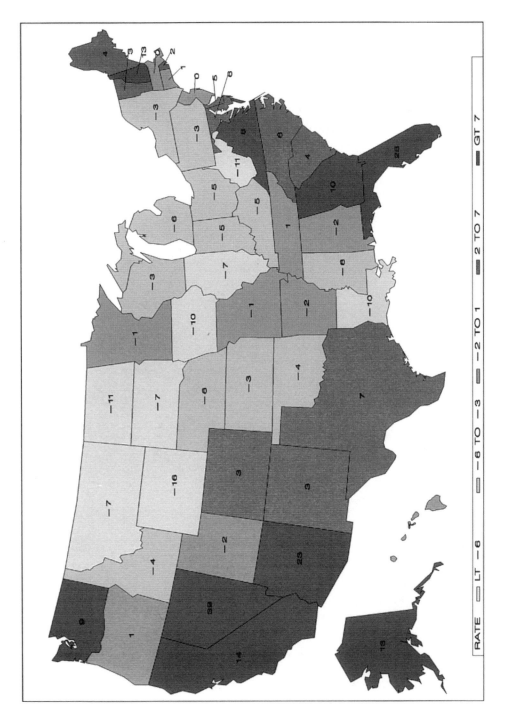

Fig. 5. Migration rates within the United States between 1980 and 1990.

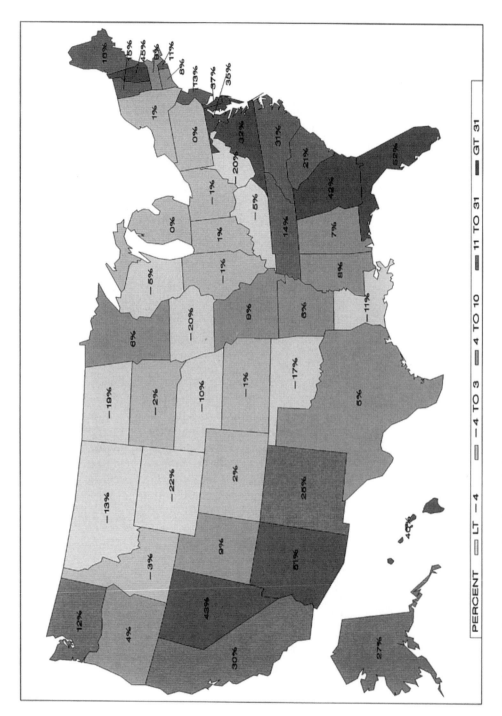

Fig. 6. Projected percent population change within the United States between 1990 and 2010.

PERCENT   LT −4   −4 TO 3   4 TO 10   11 TO 31   GT 31

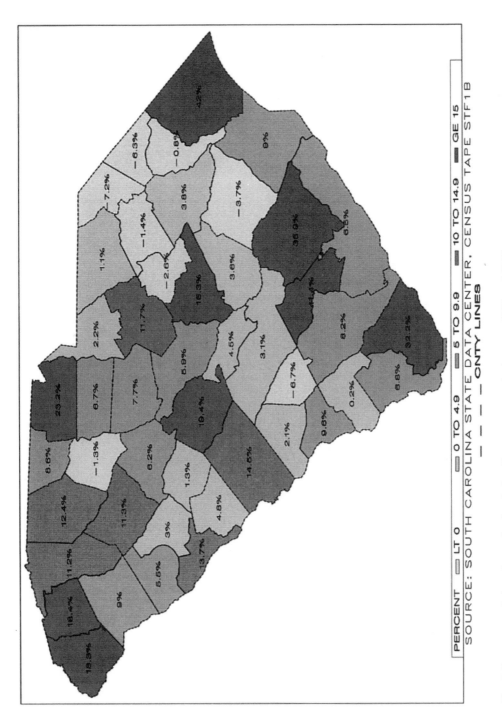

Fig. 7. Percent population change for South Carolina census counties between 1980 and 1990.

Table 1. Calculation of population migration and migration rate of South Carolina.

Births 1980-1990	526,388	
Deaths 1980-1990	-271,724	
Natural Increase	254,664	
1980 Population		3,121,820
Natural Increase 1980-1990		+254,664
Expected population for 1990		3,376,484
Actual population for 1990	3,486,703	
Expected population for 1990	-3,376,484	
Migration	110,219	
Total Growth 1980-1990		364,883
(Natural Increase + Migration)		
% Natural Increase		68%
% Migration		32%

either having large urban areas or adjacent to such areas and thus having bedroom communities; these counties were Lexington (19%), York (23%), Pickens (18%), Berkeley (36%), and Dorchester (41%). The resort counties having strong growth were Horry (42%), Beaufort (32%), and Oconee (18%). The 16% population growth in Sumter County may be due to military buildup. Among the coastal counties, the most growth can be seen in Horry and Beaufort counties and in the bedroom community around the city of Charleston (Fig. 8).

These growth patterns are similar for both the white and nonwhite populations in South Carolina (Figs. 9 and 10). However, the white population had stronger growth in the resort areas and in certain bedroom counties such as York and Kershaw. A decrease in the white population is evident in the "black belt" counties of South Carolina. Strong population growth occurred for the black population in urban counties such as Richland County and in the Greenville-Spartanburg area.

The total migration rate for South Carolina from 1980 to 1990 was 32% (Fig. 11 and Table 1). However, for whites the migration rate was 49% and for nonwhites 0%, a distinct difference in migration between the two race groups. Figures 12 and 13 illustrate the difference in migration rates for the white and nonwhite populations of South Carolina at the county level; much of the positive migration is due to the movement of whites, with the exceptions of Pickens, Lexington, Berkley, and Dorchester counties.

Table 2. Migration and migration rates by age group, South Carolina, 1980-1990.

Age Group	Number	Rate	Percent
< 5	-8,575	-3.2	-7.8
5-14	-6,367	-1.2	-5.8
15-24	43,773	6.9	37.9
25-34	-39,624	-6.3	-35.9
35-44	17,481	5.0	15.9
45-54	20,738	6.9	18.8
55-64	24,798	8.9	22.5
65-74	26,131	13.8	23.7
75-84	2,084	2.7	1.9
Total	110,219	3.5	100

The migration rates by age group for the South Carolina population are shown in Table 2. Rates were higher and positive (in-migration) for those age 55 to 64 (8.9%) and for those age 65 to 74 (13.8%) compared to the lower, negative rates (out-migration) of -1.2% for those age 5 to 14 and -6.3% for those age 25 to 34.

ECONOMIC AND ENVIRONMENTAL EFFECTS OF POPULATION CHANGE

Figure 14 shows the percent change in jobs between 1980 and 1990. The counties that had the greatest gains in jobs also typically had the largest growth in population. Again, these counties were the resort counties and the bedroom counties. In analyzing the growth in jobs for the coastal area, the issues of maintaining a natural environment versus economic development were examined. A continuing issue for almost any state is the improvement of the social and economic well-being of its citizens. Closer analysis of this issue showed an awareness that the greatest movement of population that brings about massive economic development in resort areas especially along the coast shows up very little in censuses. Economic development in terms of the building of hotels, condominiums, entertainment parks, eating establishments, and associated infrastructure does not occur just for the year-round residents of the coastal areas but for the summer population. The effect on wetlands, wildlife, and marine resources and the demand on water and sewage resources from massive development is due to the summer growth of people visiting coastal areas. Little information is available concerning this population movement, yet it is this summer population that controls continued development.

What the analysis of census data and other information has shown is interesting. One such fact is that even with the development in coastal areas such as Horry County, the coastal areas are still not in the top ranking by such measures as median family income. The number of people

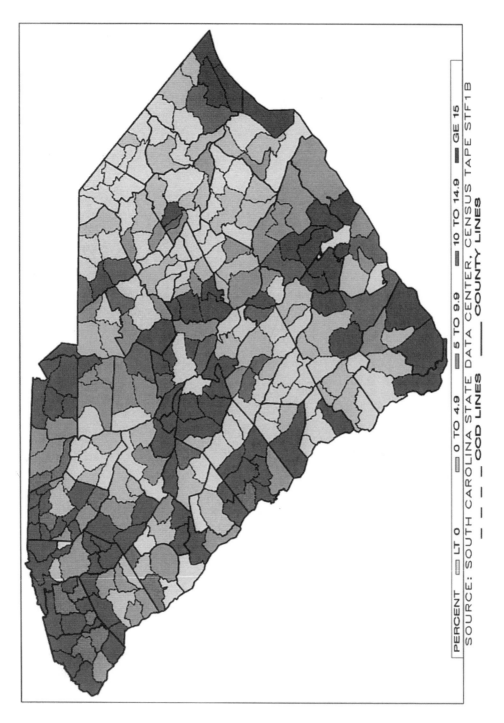

PERCENT ▨ LT 0 ▨ 0 TO 4.9 ▨ 5 TO 9.9 ▨ 10 TO 14.9 ▨ GE 15

SOURCE: SOUTH CAROLINA STATE DATA CENTER, CENSUS TAPE STF1B

– – – CCD LINES ———— COUNTY LINES

Fig. 8. Percent population change in county census divisions of South Carolina between 1980 and 1990.

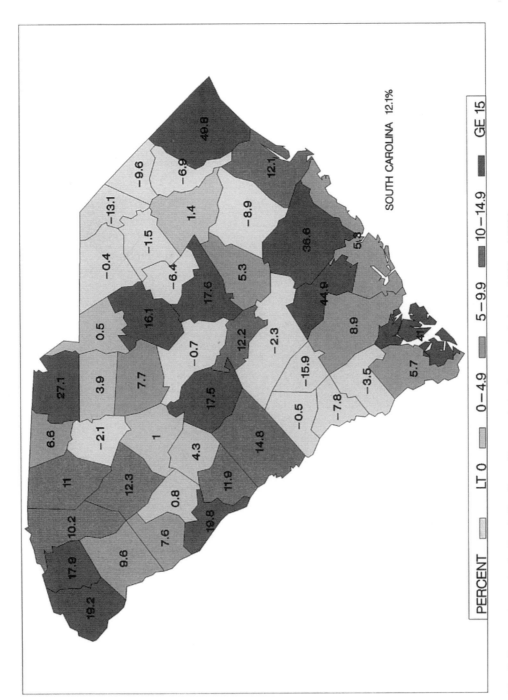

Fig. 9. Percent change in the South Carolina white population by county between 1980 and 1990.

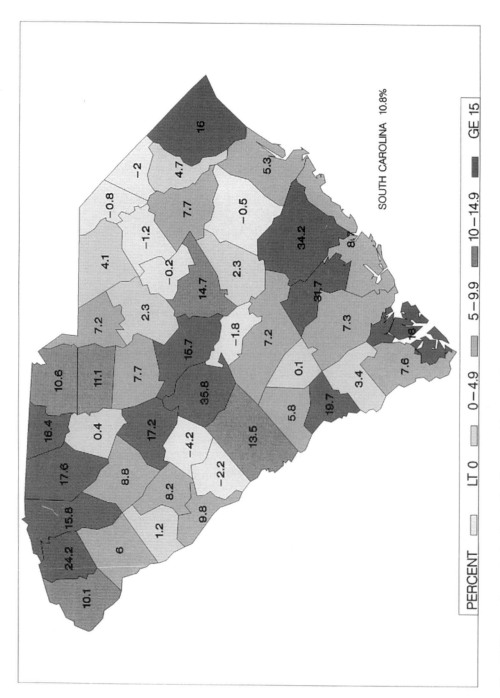

PERCENT   LT 0   0 – 4.9   5 – 9.9   10 – 14.9   GE 15

SOUTH CAROLINA   10.8%

Fig. 10. Percent change in the South Carolina nonwhite population by county between 1980 and 1990.

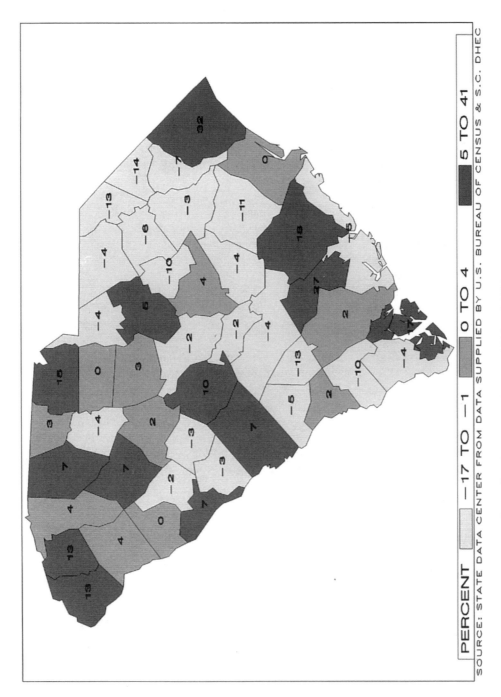

Fig. 11. Total migration rate for South Carolina counties between 1980 and 1990.

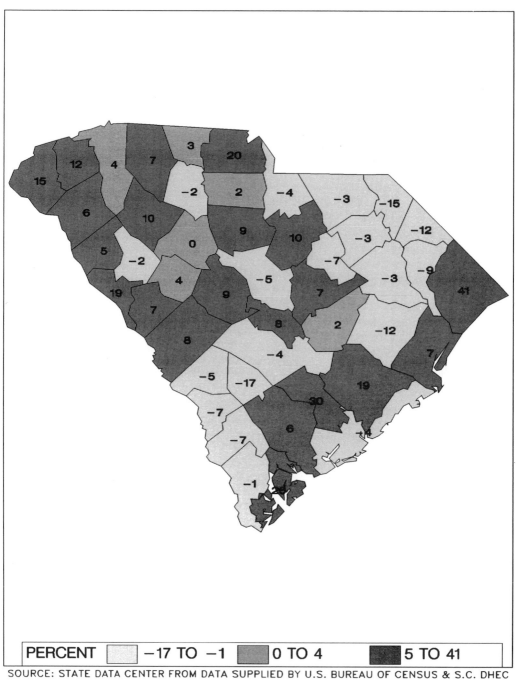

Fig. 12. Migration rate by county of the South Carolina white population between 1980 and 1990.

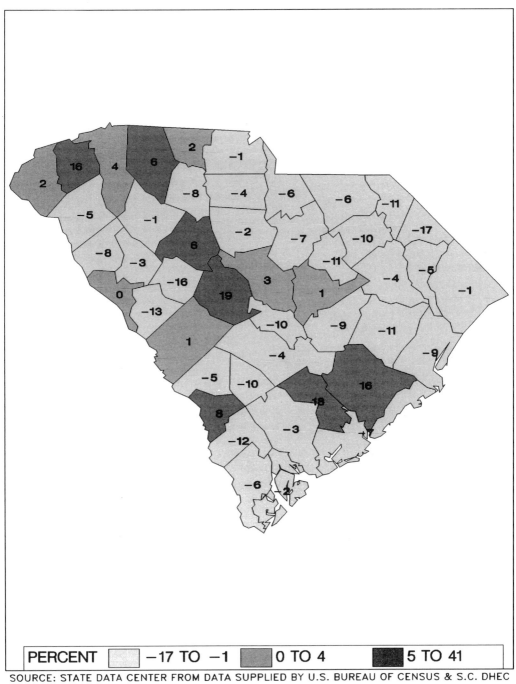

Fig. 13. Migration rate by county of the South Carolina nonwhite population between 1980 and 1990.

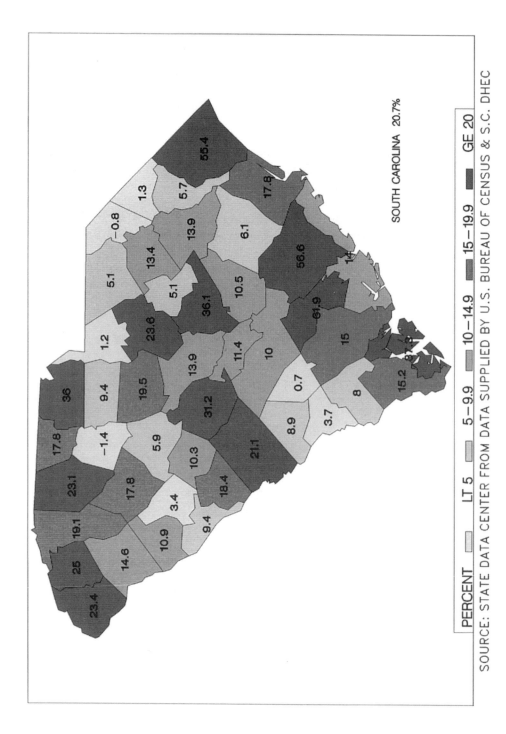

Fig. 14. Percent change in jobs in South Carolina counties between 1980 and 1990.

in poverty and the number of unemployed actually has grown when comparing the 1980 census with the 1990 census. This fact is true even at the county census division level where most development has occurred. When the income distribution of families in the resort county of Horry are compared with a non-resort county such as Greenville County, Horry has a much higher percentage of families earning less than $30,000 per year (53.3%) versus Greenville (41.7%). On the higher income side ($60,000 or more), Horry County has a smaller percentage, 11.89%, than Greenville at 18.6%. The poverty of these counties is further evidence that the economic development is not for the year-round residents, who should gain from economic development, but rather for the summer population which is overlooked when income levels are assessed by the census.

Summary

The impact of coastal growth in the United States must be considered in long-range planning. To maintain the environment while not hindering economic development is the challenge. However, to achieve the proper balance between the environment and economic development it is important to know not only who makes up this population but also to understanding the changes taking place in the population. Census data are an important tool for planners; however, for coastal areas, information on the summer population is essential. Further research into the summer population is needed.

Conceptual Models Relevant to Sustaining Coastal Zone Resources

Eugene P. Odum

Introduction

Conceptual models, as presented in this paper, are concise statements, with or without simplified diagrams, that outline and illustrate unifying concepts or paradigms. For a popular book in preparation I am including a series of such models in the form of "ecological vignettes" that direct attention to what we learn from ecology that can help us understand and deal with human predicaments in the crowded world of the future.

For this paper I have selected several of these conceptual models that are especially relevant to sustaining mutual quality of life for humans and the environment in current and future development of the Southeastern coastal zone. Sustainability as a goal can be envisioned in terms of "intergenerational equity," that is, providing for today while retaining resources and options for tomorrow. The challenge is to manage so that the scale and intensity of resource use and economic development now and in the near future does not endanger environmental life-support systems, and thereby the quality of life for future generations. To do this will require some major changes in the way we think, behave, and do business.

Model 1. The Market-Nonmarket Dichotomy

In this model (Fig. 1), the free market economy deals primarily with human-made goods and services, while nature's goods and services that provide our physiological needs for breathing, drinking and eating are external to the market for the most part. True, we buy and sell water and food, but we don't pay for the solar-driven hydrological cycle or the soil and water maintenance work of nature. Currently we rely on political and legal means to protect our nonmarket life-support resources, but these market corrections, so to speak, are often either too little or to late. It is encouraging that both economists and ecologists are seeking ways to incorporate the nonmarket

Market   Nonmarket
Goods & Services   versus   Goods & Services
(Human made)   (Life support)

When nonmarket goods and services are not properly valued, then there is *market failure*.

"Earlier studies of environmental limits to growth *emphasized source limits* (depletion of petroleum, copper, etc). Experience has shown, however, that *sink* constraints (air and water pollution, greenhouse, ozone depletion, etc) are more stringent. Because sink functions are common property to a greater extent that source functions, this overuse is less correctable by automatic market adjustment" (UNESCO 1991).

Fig. 1. Model 1, the nonmarket problem.

values more directly into the economic system (see, for example, Costanza 1991, and the new journal *Ecological Economics*). One thing is certain: unless life-support resources, including, wetlands, soils, forests, atmosphere, rivers, oceans, groundwater, good farmland, and so on, are properly valued and protected as vital parts of the total landscape the quality of human life will decline as the human population increases, and sustainable development can not be achieved. Including environmental values and futures in economic accounting is especially urgent on the coast since coastal zones worldwide are currently sites of accelerated human population growth.

Model 2. How Things Grow; The Extremes in Growth Forms

Very fast exponential or "boom and bust" growth as one extreme, and slower sigmoid or "self-regulating" growth as the other extreme are shown in Fig. 2. Overshooting some basic limits (e.g., resources, space, pollution, or maintenance costs) is almost inevitable if growth continues to accelerate exponentially. On the other hand, with sigmoid growth the growth rate is progressively slowed as limits are approached. Only when growth is managed in this way can sustainability be achieved. To avoid the "boom and bust" not only must the nonmarket values be sustained but serious land-use planning at the regional level must be begun early in development before real estate prices become inflated. Ecological economists Goodland et al. (1991) suggest that quantitative growth (or the biblical metaphor of taking dominion) should shift to qualitative growth (or stewardship) as density and complexity increases. In other words, the time has come for promoting better not just bigger development in terms of maintaining a high quality of life for both humans and our life-supporting environment.

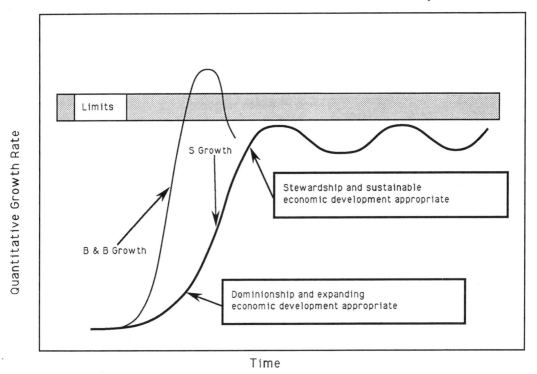

Fig. 2. Model 2, how things grow.

Model 3. The Pulsing Paradigm

A statement of nature's pulsing paradigm is presented in Model 3 (Fig. 3). Just about every-thing in the coastal zone environment is pulsed (Odum et al. 1995). There are, of course, the tides and the seasonal flooding of the low country. And there are the periodic fires, natural and human-made, that sustain pine forests, and the fluctuations in rainfall and the groundwater and periodic violent storms. In general, attempts to stabilize these pulses with dikes, dams, sea walls, and so on have had decidedly mixed benefits. Experience with sea walls, for example, has shown that while the barrier may protect the house or other structure built too close to the shore for the time being, the beach itself is eventually lost because the energy of the waves and storms is concentrated at the barrier and reflected back on the strand instead of being dissipated gradually over the dune system (Kaufman and Pilkey 1983). Also, the source of sand that would naturally renourish the beach after storms is cut off by the barrier with the result that very expensive artificial renourish-ment may be required to restore the strand. The challenge in the future is to design our human-made structures to accommodate these pulses (including hurricanes). For example, requiring that beach houses be build on tall poles that allow storm water to flow underneath is an alternative to sea walls. We need more environmental engineering, less mechanical engineering. Or, to put it more broadly, we can

---

NATURE'S PULSING PARADIGM

"While the steady state is often seen as a final result of self-organization of nature and society there may be a more realistic concept that nature pulses regularly to make a pulsing steady state, a new paradigm gaining acceptance in ecology and many other fields." (Odum et al. 1995)

Fig. 3. Model 3, the pulsed environment.

extend Ian McHarg's famous 1969 pronouncement "design with nature" by promoting the concept of "design with the energy flow." After all, tides and other pulses are what makes the coastal zone so interesting, exciting, and beautiful!

Model 4. The Network "Law"

A diagram and the formula for the network or complexity "law" is shown in Model 4 (Fig. 4). As size and complexity of a system increases, the cost of maintenance increases at some power function (see Pippenger 1978). In other words, when a forest or city doubles in size, the cost of maintaining the expanded infrastructure more than doubles. Planners, decision-makers, and people in general seem strangely unaware of the fact that increasing per capita taxes or other revenue are required to meet the increasing demands for services required to "pump out the disorder" inherent in large, complex systems like cities. In other words, there are not only increasing returns of scale (the economists "article of faith") but decreasing returns of scale as development becomes intense. At least people ought to be told the truth that unrestrained economic development of the coastal fringe, for example, can become costly (higher taxes for everybody) and concurrently generate a lot of other negative returns such as resource depletion, pollution, and crime. The challenge is to determine when diminishing returns begin to exceed increasing returns of scale.

Model 5. The Hierarchical Nature of Sustainable Development

The problems of scale can be approached by thinking in terms of hierarchies since just about everything in nature and in human affairs exhibits a hierarchical organization (Allen and Starr 1982; Urban et al. 1987). Thus, in government we have the successive rank orders of local, state, and federal agencies. In ecology we have the population to ecosystem to biosphere sequence. In agriculture we have the crop field (agronomic level), the farm (microeconomic level), the watershed (ecological level), and the region or nation (macroeconomic level) (Lowrance et al. 1986). No matter how well managed the crop field, it is not sustainable if the farm of which it is a part is not sustainable, and so on up the line.

Network "law": cost of maintenance (C) increases as a power function, roughly as a square of the number of network services (N). As a city doubles in size, cost of maintenance quadruples.

$$C = N(N-1)/2 \text{ or approximately } N^2$$

A. In early development the major flow of energy must be directed to growth

B. In later development an increasing proportion of available energy must be directed to maintenance and control of disorder

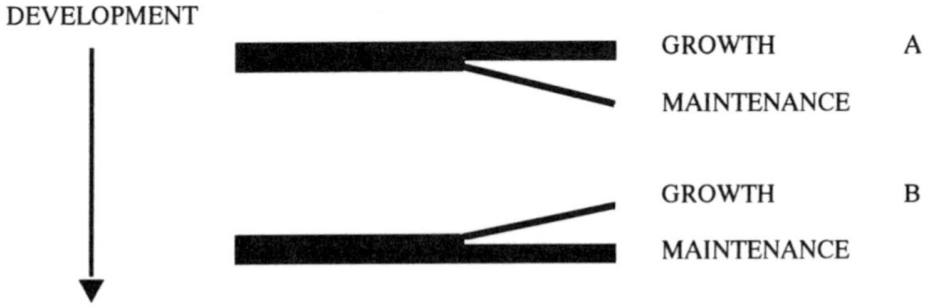

DEVELOPMENT

GROWTH   A

MAINTENANCE

GROWTH   B

MAINTENANCE

Fig. 4. Model 4, costs of development.

The successive levels of organization influencing the sustainability of the coastal zone are shown in Fig. 5. Maintaining salt marshes in good shape, for example, depends on sustaining the estuary, which in turn depends on the unpolluted inflows from the rivers and riverine wetlands, which in turn are influenced by the upcountry terrestrial watersheds. Current unsustainable agricultural practices that erode the soil and allow huge outflows of fertilizers and pesticides into the rivers can produce major stresses on marshes, estuaries, beaches, and even the sea. Accordingly, local land-use decisions ultimately must consider the welfare of the region as whole.

Summary

Anything even approaching sustainability can not be achieved unless (among other things) the nonmarket goods and services are valued and preserved, unless sigmoid growth can be promoted, unless we can learn to design *with* rather than against environmental pulses, unless we recognize

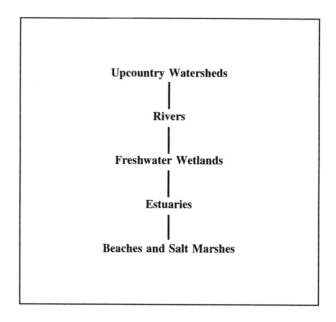

Fig. 5. Model 5, the hierarchical arrangement of landscapes.

when diminishing returns of scale adversely affect quality of life, and, most of all, unless we recognize the hierarchical nature of resources, and coordinate and plan at the landscape and regional levels.

LITERATURE CITED

Allen, T.F.H. and T.B. Starr. 1982. Hierarchy: Perspectives for Ecological Complexity. University of Chicago Press, Chicago, Illinois.

Costanza, R. (ed.) 1991. Ecological Economics: The Science and Management of Sustainability. Columbia University Press, New York.

Goodland, R.H., S.E. Daly, Serafy and B. von Droste (eds.). 1991. Environmentally Sustainable Economic Development: Building on Brundtland. United Nations Educational, Scientific, and Cultural Organization (UNESCO), Paris.

Kaufman, W. and O.H. Pilkey. 1983. The Beaches are Moving. Duke University Press, Durham, North Carolina.

Lowrance, R., P.F. Hendrix, and E.P. Odum. 1986. A hierarchical approach to sustainable agriculture. *Journal of Alternate Agriculture* 1: 169-173.

McHarg, I.L. 1969. Design With Nature. Natural History Press, Garden City, New York (revised edition, 1992, Wiley, New York).

Odum, W.E., E.P. Odum, and H.T. Odum. 1995. The pulsing paradigm. *Estuaries* 18(4): 547-555.

Pippenger, N. 1978. Complexity theory. *Scientific American* 238 (6): 114-124.

Urban, D.L., R.V. O'Neill, and H.H. Shugart. 1987. Landscape ecology. *Bioscience* 37: 119-127.

A Crisis and Opportunity in Coastal Oceans: Coastal Fisheries as a Case Study

John Mark Dean

> *Content without method leads to fantasy, method without content to empty sophistry; matter without form to unwieldy erudition, form without matter to hollow speculation.*
>
> Goethe, *Maximen und Reflexionen no. 435*

The coastline, that jigsaw puzzle interface of the coastal ocean and the terrestrial margin, is clearly under great stress. From the Atlantic, Gulf, and the Pacific coasts of the United States come increasingly frequent reports of closed bathing beaches, restricted shellfish beds, garbage washing up on shorelines, contaminated water and sediments, oil spills, declining marine environmental quality, and ailing fisheries. The coastal ocean contains extraordinarily productive natural ecosystems, and the totality of its physical, chemical, geological, and biological processes are not well understood. In addition, the natural causes of change in this environment are complex, highly variable, and occur over different spatial and temporal scales. Moreover, the impacts we generate can alter those processes at scales and rates far exceeding anything we thought possible.

We have an opportunity in the United States to correct this situation before it reaches the level it has in other seas and oceans of the world. As bad as it appears to us with our parochial vision, you only have to visit or read of the situation in the Mediterranean, Baltic, Caspian, Black, South China and Yellow seas to realize the opportunity that is within our grasp. Those used and abused marine resources are the visions of the future. Examine what has and is occurring in those coastal environments (Platt 1995) and you cannot help but be concerned. We should be fully aware that we are not required to follow that same pathway.

The thin blue-green line of the coast seems to act as a magnetic field, and people respond like iron filings. Fifty percent of the world's population lives within 50 miles of coastlines. While that region is only 8% of the planet's surface, it is the source of 26% of its primary production capacity. The result is that the impact on the ecosystems, which are roughly twice as productive as other systems, is nine times more severe because of the population load. And, we know that populations are increasing, and increasing more rapidly in the coastal zone than other regions of the globe. The economic values associated with the region are staggering. Of the world's 10 largest cities, 9 are in the coastal zone and, to carry it further, so are 33 of the top 50. That is readily understood when we realize that 80% of the world's commerce travels by ship. In addition, of the $1.9 trillion spent annually on tourism worldwide, a significant percentage of that is in the coastal zone. All of that incredible commercial activity creates a great deal of economic benefit, but it also demands a great deal from the natural resources of the coastal zone, site of the world's major fisheries, of the nursery grounds for those fisheries, and of one of the most diverse ecosystems, coral reefs.

Alteration in the coastal zone habitat can occur in several ways. One of the major impacts is the loading of the estuarine and coastal ocean with nutrients that are transported by riverine systems (Varanasi 1992). Cole et al. (1993) described the immense contribution of riverine systems to coastal pollution. Their studies showed that the level of pollution is linearly correlated with the level of human activity in the watershed. For example, even though the Mississippi drains an area 14 times as large as the Rhine and contains one of the most intensive and highly productive agricultural regions on the planet, the Rhine has 10 times the population density of the Mississippi and dumps 10 times more nutrients into the sea. For many years Turner (1977, 1979, 1992; Boesch and Turner 1984; Turner and Boesch 1988) has studied the relationship between coastal habitats and fisheries production. He has argued that the relationship between loss or modification of wetland habitats and their effect on fisheries production is not as rigorously documented as critical scientists should expect. However, the overwhelming accumulation of indirect as well as direct evidence is that habitat alterations play a significant role in the decline of fishery resources (Stroud 1992). The evidence of specific case studies on a global scale does provide evidence for the loss or decline of fisheries. However, there are confounding effects that are not always taken into account. These factors include climatic variation, fishing effort, and coincidental factors that vary as the coastal habitat changes. Very large economic issues and public policy decisions are at stake, and the larger the stakes, the more serious are the players.

The print and electronic media regularly report on the declining state of the coastal fisheries of the United States and the other nations of this water planet. Pick up any magazine and newspaper, listen to radio stations that do in-depth reporting, or watch the information television channels and you find numerous reports bemoaning the decline in fisheries. *U.S. News and World Report* (Rape of the Seas, June 22, 1992), *Congressional Quarterly* (October 5, 1992), *The Boston Globe* (April 12, 1993), *The Seattle Times* (June 17, 1992 and May 23, 1993), *The Raleigh News and Observer* (Fishing for Trouble, August 28, 1994), *The Charlotte Observer* (Our Disappearing Fish, August 28, 1994), and *Science* magazine (May 27, 1994) are just a few examples of those that have done feature articles or a series on the topic. There are also extremely vigorous concerns expressed in almost every issue of magazines and trade journals such as *Salt Water Sportsman, Florida Sportsman, Commercial Fishing News, National Fisherman,* and Times-Mirror magazines. The Audubon Society, Center for Marine Conservation, World Wildlife Fund, and other conservation organizations regularly report on the decline in fishery resources. One cannot avoid the coverage of the New England groundfish issue, salmon in Oregon and Washington, pollack in Alaska, or the Atlantic bluefin tuna. However, they are just the most visible fisheries in the very complex and difficult arena of management of a public resource that has essentially no limitations on who can and will pursue a fish.

It is relatively easy to produce horror stories about this issue (*U.S. News and World Report*, June 22, 1992). It is relatively easy to get media attention on a real or perceived crisis. Photographs of dead fish on boat decks or in gill nets are in abundance which makes commercial fisheries vulnerable to targeting by special interest groups. Recreational anglers raise a hue and cry when a management agency proposes regulations reducing the number of fish they can take or impose size limits that the anglers consider outrageous. Attempts to cut the landings of commercial fishers are met with aggressive resistance because the economically depressed industry cannot afford to cut back its current catch. Such responses are typical of all the user groups that depend upon coastal fishery resources. The response depends upon the characteristics of the user group and the client species of fish.

Marine fisheries are, in almost all instances, the only resource managed by state and federal agencies that are not routinely limited as far as who can use the resource for private economic gain. The consensus among fishery managers is that uncontrolled access in fisheries, overcapitalization, and controversial allocation decisions among various fishing groups, rather than scientific information, drive decision-making (Davis and Robb 1992; National Oceanic and Atmospheric Administration 1993). For example, it is well documented that the Atlantic bluefin tuna that is captured along the East Coast of the United States is at a stock level that is about 20% of its 1970 level. It would seem reasonable that a management agency might limit the number of anglers that could capture bluefin. In fact, there are bag limits for anglers, and there are landing limits for individual commercial fishing boats, but there are no limits to the number of fishers of any user group that can get a permit, and there is no charge for the permit. Of all the coastal fisheries of the United States, only about 1/3 have any access controls, and those are only for those species that have management plans developed by the regional fishery management councils under the Magnuson Act. Fisheries are virtually the only federally managed natural resource with unlimited access to harvest; as contrasted with national forests, grazing lands, and continental shelf oil.

What is orders of magnitude more difficult than documenting the crisis is to develop an agenda and implement a plan of action (National Marine Fisheries Service 1991; Stroud 1992; National Oceanic and Atmospheric Administration 1993). It is essential to provide support for the agenda and the plan of action, with implementation of the plan to correct the problem. However, doing so is extremely contentious, which makes it very time-consuming, with the result that it is very expensive. Why is this so? Simply put, it is because the implementation will cost money and it will interfere with many different individuals and organizations that do not want to be inconvenienced, do not want to pay for the action, or think that it is not in their economic self-interest to have the plan imple-mented. Ludwig et al. (1993) have argued that the history of natural resource management is not replete with success stories and other alternatives should be considered. That is quite possibly so, on a case-by-case basis, as it relates to client species intervention. An alternative view for natural resource management is presented by Lee (1993).

A comprehensive view of the United States fishery resources is presented by Sissenwine and Rosenberg (1993) and Our Living Oceans (National Marine Fisheries Service 1992). Both documents give quantitative evidence of the decline in landings of many species of fishes. The National Marine Fisheries Service estimates that nearly 90% of United States fish stocks are overused or below the level needed to sustain long-term potential yield. The 236 groups of fish considered by the National Marine Fisheries Service, including finfish and shellfish, made up about 450 species. The total recent annual yield, globally, for these fisheries of interest to the United States is about 6.6 million metric tons (mmt) of which the United States' share is about 5.0 mmt. The long-term potential yield (LTPY) of those fisheries of interest to the United States is estimated to be about 9.5 mmt, which is about 40% higher than the recent average yield. Groundfish account for about 48% of the LTPY, highly migratory and pelagic species make up 43%, and nearshore fish, shellfish, and anadromous fish constitute the other 9%. It is estimated that the Southeast has about 33% of the overutilized stocks, which is second only to the Northeast with 45%. In economic terms, it is estimated that the potential increase in net value of United States fisheries is about $2.9 billion annually. The impact on the gross domestic product of increasing the yield to achieve LTPY would be about $8 billion and 300,000 jobs. It is acknowledged that these are rough estimates, but it does clearly show the seriousness of the situation and the potential that exists for the benefits of fishery management.

What is the status of the coastal fishery stocks of the southeastern United States? As previously stated, the Southeast does have many seriously overfished stocks and others for which there are concerns (National Marine Fisheries Service 1992). In a recent analysis of fishery landings from North Carolina, summer flounder (*Paralichthys lethostigma*) had a peak in landings of 16.1 million pounds (MP) in 1979 but since has shown an almost annual decline in landings to 3.1 MP in 1993. Spot (*Leiostomus xanthurus*) declined from a peak of 8.3 MP in 1975 to 2.7 MP in 1993. Similarly, Atlantic croaker (*Micropogonias undualatus*) declined from 21.1 MP in 1980 to its current level of 3.3 MP and the weakfish or gray trout (*Cynoscion regalis*) went from 20.3 MP in 1980 to 4.3 MP in 1993.

The red drum (*Sciaenops ocellatus*) has always been a most prized recreational angling fish. In the 1980s, blackened redfish became a popular menu item for the seafood restaurant industry. Due to the demands made upon the resource by both the recreational and commercial industries, it has been designated as an overfished species, designated as a "game fish," and has a no sale provision in most southeastern states, with very severe bag and size limits. The critical point to remember in this discussion of these different fishes is that they are the most important recreational and commercial finfishes of the southeast coast. And, every single one of them is absolutely dependent upon estuaries and the nearshore environment for critical larval, postlarval, or juvenile stages of development. A similar picture can be drawn for the shellfish fisheries, which are experiencing an increase in the acreage of beds closed annually. An outbreak of neurological shellfish poisoning in North Carolina had a negative economic impact of $25 million in 1988-1989. Such economic consequences are considered conservative estimates because the decline in consumer confidence in seafood affects all other fisheries as well as seafood restaurants. These examples are representative and consistent with the situation for other southeastern states.

It is important to recognize that species such as these are managed by three administrative entities. They are the state natural resource agency, which has the authority from the coast to 3 miles offshore, the regional fishery management council (in this case the Southeast Council), with authority from 3 miles to 200 miles offshore, and the Atlantic States Marine Fisheries Commission, which coordinates among states for those species that move up and down the coast. This administrative dilemma was vigorously debated in a special section of the symposium sponsored by the National Coalition for Marine Conservation (Stroud 1994, p. 227-251).

Some species of the southeastern coastal waters are not in crisis and support viable and extremely economically valuable commercial and recreational fishing industries. Stock assessments show that the Atlantic menhaden (*Brevoortia tyrannus*), southern flounder (*Paralichtyhys dentatus*), king mackerel (*Scomberomorus cavalla*), Spanish mackerel (*Scomberomorus maculatus*), and the complex of species that make up the shrimp fishery are presently not considered overfished. Important fishes whose status is unclear include the striped mullet (*Mugil cephalus*) and the spotted sea trout (*Cynoscion nebulosus*). King and Spanish mackerel were in a critical situation and stock assessments showed those species had suffered a precipitous decline in the stocks since early 1970 and were overfished. The management plan implemented by the South Atlantic Fishery Management Council has apparently halted the decline in those fisheries and they show signs of recovery (Williams 1994), and the South Atlantic stock has been removed from the overfished category. This has had significant economic benefits for the recreational industry that had some of its most productive seasons eliminated by closures in the late 1980s, with negative impacts on major tournaments. The tournaments and charter fisheries are flourishing under the existing regulations and there is greatly reduced conflict with the commercial industry.

There is an abundance of evidence that shows that many fisheries are heavily overcapitalized. We simply have too many recreational and commercial boats with equipment and technology that can overwhelm the fish. If you examine the records obtained by the fishery management councils when they take proposed management plan amendments through the public comment process, those records clearly show that virtually all who use that fishery resource hold someone else responsible for the decline in fishery resources. It is a massive finger-pointing exercise and, to hear them tell it, they could not possibly be responsible. On an individual basis, that is quite possibly correct. What is lacking is an understanding of the cumulative impact of their activities (Costanza 1987; Gosselink and Lee 1989). A lack of understanding is not limited to those capturing fish for personal pleasure, consumption, or feeding the increased appetite of United States consumers for fishery products. The commercial and recreational fishing industries regularly accuse the coastal develop-ment industry of being responsible for the decline in coastal fishery resources due to habitat loss (*National Fisherman*, October 1994). But, is recreational angling and commercial fishing the sole or even principal reason for the decline in fisheries? What other possibilities are there to account for the decline in fishery resources?

Extraordinary changes have occurred in nation's coastal regions over the last 30 years. The development that has taken place in the coastal zone has altered the way society views, values, and manages coastal resources. Despite societal attitudes and desires to support measures to protect habitats, degradation is occurring at an alarming rate. Marine habitats are altered by natural processes such as erosion and subsidence. They are also directly or indirectly threatened by human activity, including acceleration of natural phenomena associated with human alteration of physical processes. The prodigious cumulative losses of marine habitat within the coastal zone are alarming, because marine habitats are critical to the production and replenishment of living marine resources that support the commercial and recreational fishing industries as well as the growing economic value of tourism, and the understanding of the processes and interactions needed to maintain the functioning of a natural system is incomplete.

The incredible migration and occupation of the coastal zone by the people of the United States is well documented (Culliton et al. 1990). The results of the demands of those people on coastal resources is manifested in the decline in the quality of the coastal environment. In a recent report, the National Research Council (1994b) clearly identified a number of coincidental developments that have contributed to this situation. They include the concentration and continuing growth of human populations in the coastal zone; the proliferation of industrial and residential shoreline development; human activities that degrade water quality; the increasing commercial and recrea-tional use of marine and estuarine areas; the development of natural resources in the coastal zone; physical changes in the environment, including subsidence, elevation and sea-level changes; and the construction and maintenance of port and waterways systems and operation of associated commercial vessels.

They concluded that, if current trends continue and degradation of the coastal environment is to be halted or reversed, significant institutional policies, regulations, and procedures need to be changed. Specifically, we currently offer disincentives, rather than incentives, to invest in marine habitat protection and restoration. A case in point is the Federal Flood Insurance Act, which subsidizes the construction of commercial and residential development in the coastal zone. Restoration technologies exist that can make significant contributions to the enhancement of the coastal environment, but implementation is difficult due to structural impediments from management agencies. In addition, there is a lack of fundamental knowledge of many of the processes and no coherent plan to gain the information.

In an attempt to address the lack of basic information, the National Science and Technology Council asked the National Research Council to provide an integrated assessment of research priorities based on previous National Research Council studies. Their report, Priorities for Coastal Ecosystem Science (National Research Council 1994a), identified the most significant threats to the integrity of coastal ecosystems and then developed priorities for science activities to address coastal environmental issues. The threats are eutrophication, habitat modification, hydrologic and hydrodynamic disruption, exploitation of resources, toxic effects, introduction on nonindigenous species, global climate change and variability, shoreline erosion and hazardous storms, and pathogens and toxins affecting human health. It is important to state the research priorities as they clearly and unambiguously relate to fishery resources. These are integrated monitoring; water availability and flow; water quality and aquatic ecosystem functions; ecological restoration and rehabilitation; and predictive systems management.

One of the most astonishing gaps in our database for fishery resources is our lack of knowledge of their basic reproductive biology. We have little understanding of the interannual variability of fishery populations (National Research Council 1994a). What are the factors regulating and controlling the production of successful year classes of populations? Those are critical issues when you make public policy decisions by implementation of management regimes. It is stated that we often manage one fishery that is a prey species of another managed fishery, and yet we manage them as though they were independent of one another. If that is so, then we should consider our situation when we have fisheries that are not yet developed, and lack the most basic information on them. A case study was the explosive development of the red drum fishery in the Gulf of Mexico in the late 1980s. Only now have we acquired the fundamental information that is essential for the development of policies necessary for the management of that resource (Ross et al. 1995).

The Southeast has suffered from a lack of resources committed to the development of essential information, as well as the funding necessary to study the structure and function of coastal ecosystems as they relate to fishery resources (Hinman and Safina 1992). It is now clear that it is essential that we study entire watersheds if we are to truly understand the factors that affect our coastal fisheries (National research Council 1994a). Fishery resources in the Southeast are essentially no different than anywhere else. They are threatened by overfishing from the highly technologically sophisticated and overcapitalized commercial and recreational industries, and their nurseries and spawning environments are threatened by habitat alteration from development interests and the runoff from the rivers that ultimately form our estuaries. The problems and issues have been created by our own consumptive life style. The question is, will we alter our behaviors in a manner that will enable the coastal ecosystem to function in the sustainable manner of which it is capable?

> *The world we have created today as a result of our thinking thus far, has problems which cannot be solved by thinking the way we thought when we created them.*
> Albert Einstein

LITERATURE CITED

Boesch, D.F. and R.E Turner. 1984. Dependence of fisheries species on salt marshes: A question of food or refuge. *Estuaries* 7: 460-68.

Cole, J.J., B.L. Peierls, N.F. Caraco, and M.L. Pace. 1993. Nitrogen loading of rivers as a human-driven process, p. xx-xx. *In* M.D. McDonnel and S.T.A. Pickett (eds.), Humans as Components of Ecosystems: The Ecology of Subtle Human Effects and Population Areas. Springer-Verlag, New York.

Costanza, R. 1987., Social traps and environmental policy. *BioScience* 37(6): 407-412.

Culliton, T.J., M.A. Warren, R.R. Goodspeed, D.G. Remer, C. M. Blackwell, and J. J. McDonough, III. 1990. 50 Years of population change along the nation's coasts, 1960-2010. National Oceanic and Atmospheric Administration, Department of Commerce, Washington, D.C.

Davis, D.G. and D.M. Robb. 1992. Agency interface in the coastal zone, p. 175-178. *In* R. Stroud (ed.), National Coalition for Marine Conservation. Stemming the Tide of Coastal Fish Habitat Loss. MRF 14. Savannah, Georgia.

Gosselink, J.C. and L.C. Lee. 1989. Cumulative impact assessment in bottomland hardwood forests. *Wetlands: The Journal of the Society of Wetland Scientists.* Vol. 9. Special Issue.

Hinman, K. and C. Safina. 1992. Summary and Recommendations, p 245-249. *In* R.H. Stroud (ed.), Stemming the Tide of Coastal Fish Habitat Loss. National Coalition for Marine Conservation, Savannah, Georgia.

Lee, K.N. 1993. Compass and Gyroscope: Integrating Science and Politics for the Environment. Island Press, Washington, D.C.

Ludwig, D., R. Hilborn, and C. Walters. 1993. Uncertainty, resource exploitation and conservation: Lessons from history. *Science* 260(17): 36.

Stroud, R.H. (ed.). 1992. Stemming the Tide of Coastal Fish Habitat Loss. National Coalition for Marine Conservation. MRF 14. Savannah, Georgia.

Stroud, R.H. (ed.). 1994.Conserving America's Fisheries. National Coalition for Marine Conservation. MRF 15. Savannah, Georgia.

National Marine Fisheries Service. 1991. Strategic Plan of the National Marine Fisheries Service: Goals and Objectives. National Marine Fisheries Service, Silver Spring, Maryland.

National Marine Fisheries Service (NMFS). 1992. Our Living Oceans: Report on the Status of U.S. Living Marine Resources. NOAA Tech. Mem. NMFS-F/SPO-2, Silver Spring, Maryland.

National Oceanic and Atmospheric Administration. 1993. National Oceanic and Atmospheric Administration 1995-2005 Strategic Plan. Department of Commerce, Washington, D.C.

National Research Council 1994a. Priorities for Coastal Ecosystem Science. National Academy Press, Washington, D.C.

National Research Council. 1994b. Restoring and Protecting Marine Habitat: The Role of Engineering and Technology. National Academy Press, Washington, D.C.

Platt, A.E. 1995. Dying Seas. *World Watch* 8(1): 10-19.

Ross, J.L., T.M. Stevens, and D. S. Vaugh. 1995. Age, growth, mortality, and reproductive biology of red drums in North Carolina waters. *Transactions of the American Fisheries Society* 124(1): 37-54.

Sissenwine, M.P. and A.A. Rosenberg. 1993. Marine Fisheries at a Critical Juncture. *Fisheries* 18(10): 6-14.

Turner, R.E. 1977. Intertidal vegetation and commercial yields of penaeid shrimp. *Transactions of the American Fisheries Society* 106: 411-416.

Turner, R.E. 1979. Louisiana's fisheries and changing environmental condition, p. 363-370. *In* J.W. Day, D.D. Culley, R.E. Turner, and A.J. Mumphrey (eds.), Proceedings of the Third Coastal Marsh and Estuary Management Symposium. Center for Continuing Education, Louisiana State University, Baton Rouge, Louisiana.

Turner, R.E. 1992. Coastal wetlands and penaeid shrimp habitat, p. 97-104. *In* R.H. Stroud (ed.), Stemming the Tide of Coastal Fish Habitat Loss. National Coalition for Marine Conservation. Savannah, Georgia.

Turner, R.E. and D.F. Boesch. 1988. Aquatic animal production and wetland relationships: Insights gleaned following wetland loss or gain, p. 25-39. *In* D.D. Hooks, W.H. McKee, Jr., H.K. Smith, J. Gregory, V.G. Burrell, Jr., M.R. DeVoe, R. E. Sojka, S. Gilbert, R. Banks, L. H. Stolzy, C. Brooks, T.D. Matthews, and T. H. Shear (eds.), The Ecology and Management of Wetlands. Timber Press, Portland, Oregon.

Varanasi, U., 1992. Chemical contaminants and their effects on living marine resources, p. 59-71. *In* R. Stroud (ed.), Stemming the Tide of Coastal Fish Habitat Loss. National Coalition for Marine Conservation. Savannah, Georgia.

Williams, R.O. 1994. A case history of king and Spanish mackerel management under the Magnuson Act, p. 99-107. *In* R. Stroud (ed.), Conserving America's Fisheries. National Coalition for Marine Conservation, Savannah, Georgia.

Geographic Information Systems for Sustainable Development in the Southeastern United States: A Review of Applications and Research Needs

William K. Michener, David P. Lanter, and Paula F. Houhoulis

ABSTRACT: Geographic Information Systems (GIS) have evolved as a significant technology in the understanding of environmental problems at local, regional, and global scales. Recent environmental GIS applications illustrate the power and promise of GIS for facilitating sustainable development research and management. However, as environmental scientists and managers increasingly direct their attention to broader spatial scales, issues related to geospatial data acquisition and analysis will increase in complexity. Addressing regional and global questions, for example, may entail acquisition of hundreds of geospatial datasets from dozens of different sources (having variable quality and currency) as well as the use of up-to-date, high resolution satellite imagery. Many constraints associated with utilizing GIS technology for sustainable development research and management have been removed during the past decade due to the availability of a larger number of environmental geospatial databases, new user interfaces that facilitate use of computer-driven applications, improvements in network technology, and decreasing costs and increasing power of computer hardware and software. Concerns in the future will need to focus on how to best identify, acquire, manage, and analyze geospatial data that are timely, relevant to a specific problem, and of sufficient quality to support prudent scientific and management decisions. In this chapter, we discuss three relevant issues and some potential technical solutions: data identification and acquisition, metadata (including source documentation and data lineage), and data quality documentation. Technology alone, however, will not entirely solve all relevant problems. We, therefore, present a stepwise approach that can be followed in the design and implementation of a GIS project for supporting sustainable development research and management. The approach highlights the importance of metadata and lineage tracking throughout all phases of research and resource management projects.

Introduction

Humans are transforming the earth's environment at an unprecedented scale and magnitude. Examples include the rapid global decrease in biodiversity; air, water, and soil pollution; and broad-scale land-use changes that prevent us from identifying any large areas that may still be classified as "relatively pristine" (Brown 1994). A more detailed examination of direct and indirect effects of human activities on coastal wetlands illustrates the magnitude of changes that have occurred over broad geographic areas during a relatively short period.

Coastal wetlands comprise less than 5% of the world's terrestrial land mass (cf. Tiner 1984). They include a complex and diverse assemblage of freshwater swamps and marshes, mangrove swamps, salt marshes, mud flats, sandbars, hypersaline lagoons, sandy beaches, rocky shorelines, and seagrass beds. The combination of high secondary productivity (Mitsch and Gosselink 1986) and easy access has made coastal wetlands attractive sites for human settlement for millennia (Bildstein et al. 1991). As a result, many of the world's largest cities are located in coastal areas (Day et al. 1989). Fifty-two percent of the United States population resides within 80 km of the United States coast (Southworth 1989), and some estimates place 70% of the world's human population in the coastal zone (cf. Cherfas 1990).

Coastal wetlands have been directly modified by humans in numerous ways, including alterations of the physical structure of wetlands, the introduction of toxic materials, enrichment with excessive levels of nutrients, sediments, and heat, the harvest of native species, and the introduction of exotic ones (cf. Day et al. 1989). Since 1900, approximately 50% of the world's wetlands have been converted to other uses (Tiner 1984). Increased urbanization is likely to exacerbate impacts projected to accompany global climate change (Tiner 1984) and wetlands will continue to be affected by increased resource exploitation, pollution, and water use. One recent estimate suggests that more than 75% of the human population will live within 60 km of the coast by the year 2000 (Bernal and Holligan 1992).

Indirect effects of human populations on coastal wetlands are also important. Many of the watersheds surrounding remaining wetlands bear little or no resemblance to those existing prior to human modification. For example, longleaf pine (*Pinus palustris* Mill.) savannas dominated the Coastal Plain of the Southeastern United States, occupying nearly 25 million ha of land prior to European settlement, but logging, naval stores production, agricultural clearing, fire suppression, and plantation-oriented silviculture have since eliminated longleaf pine from more than 98% of its former range (Ware et al. 1993). Furthermore, the remaining 2% of this vegetation type has been altered by several factors: fire regimes that do not adequately simulate those found in nature, landscape fragmentation, extirpation of ecologically important species, and invasion of exotic organisms.

Sustainable development entails "deriving needed resources from the environment, and for making use of it in other ways, without compromising the ability of future generations to maintain themselves and to sustain their quality of life" (Lubchenco et al. 1991). Sustainability further implies that areas adjacent to exploited systems will not be adversely affected by human activities (Turner 1988). Sharitz et al. (1992) emphasize the need for multiple use management whereby a balance is struck between natural resource commodity production and protection of noncommodity values (e.g., biodiversity, aesthetics, etc.).

Environmental scientists have recognized the need to acquire, communicate, and incorporate necessary ecological knowledge into policy and management for the responsible use of the earth's resources and for the maintenance of earth's life-support systems (Lubchenco et al. 1991). Attention is increasingly being focused on broader spatial scale processes, acknowledging that project-specific research data collection procedures, assessment criteria, and management strategies may not be directly transferable or relevant to appropriate geographical-ecological units (e.g., ecosystem, region, etc.) (Kelly et al. 1987; Becker and Armstrong 1988; Schaeffer et al. 1988).

Objectives of this chapter are to provide a brief review of current GIS applications in research and resource management that can facilitate meeting sustainable development objectives. Issues and potential technological solutions associated with the identification and acquisition of relevant geospatial data, developing adequate source documentation, utilization of data lineage for tracking data manipulations within complex analyses, and dealing with uncertainty in GIS analyses are presented. Finally, we present a stepwise approach for design and implementation of a GIS project that can facilitate prudent scientific and management decision-making.

Relevance of GIS to Sustainable Development

Geographic Information Systems (GIS) are tools that can be used to further our understanding of environmental problems at local, regional, and global scales. GIS is a technology designed to capture, store, manipulate, analyze, and visualize the diverse set of georeferenced data required to support accurate modeling of the earth's environmental processes (Goodchild et al. 1993). A GIS comprises computer hardware, computer software, data, and personnel (Maguire 1991). GIS can interface with many other technologies such as CAD, remote sensing, DBMS, photogrammetry, video, word processing, address information systems, and terrain modeling systems (Dangermond 1988a).

Due to the availability of low-cost computer hardware and software, and the need for more efficient data management strategies, the popularity of GIS has grown, expanding rapidly to become one of the most dynamic computer-related businesses of the 1990s (Maguire 1991). For example, in three years the European GIS market nearly doubled: from $322 million in 1989 to $546 million in 1991 (Maguire 1991). In addition, hundreds of GIS software packages have been developed over the last decade (GIS World 1990). GIS technology has moved from the mainframe to smaller machines with increased power and decreased costs (Juhl 1989). Consequently, GIS and remote-sensing technologies now provide us with the capabilities to monitor and manage natural resources across scales ranging from soil mycorrhizal mats (Griffiths et al. unpublished data) to large regions (Burke et al. 1991).

Numerous characteristics distinguish GIS as a powerful tool for environmental and other applications, including the ability to easily update or modify existing geospatial databases, the rapid synthesis of information contained in multiple data layers, and a wide range of analytical algorithms for supporting complex spatial analyses (Burrough 1986; Cowen 1988). Analytical operations routinely performed in GIS-based environmental applications and relevant examples are included in Table 1. In addition, GIS is being linked increasingly with simulation models for examining biogeochemical cycling and primary productivity as well as the potential effects of sea-level rise, nonpoint source pollution, and global climate change.

GIS has been used by a heterogeneous group of individuals and organizations for a wide variety of applications (Maguire 1991). For example, GIS has been used to evaluate environmental impacts, economic implications, land use changes, and resource conflicts (Parker 1988). Other environmental GIS applications include monitoring aquatic macrophytes (Welch et al. 1986; Remillard and Welch 1992, 1993), modeling land-use change (Chuvieco 1993), natural resource management (Bildstein et al. 1991; Constanza et al. 1993; Ward and Weigle 1993; Lachowski et al. 1994), cumulative impact assessment (Green et al. 1993; Johnston 1994), pest management (Rykiel et al. 1984), waste disposal site assessment (Buckley and Hendrix 1986; Smith 1993), estimating seagrass biomass (Long et al.

Table 1. Generic GIS data management and analytical operations with relevant environmental examples (also see Burrough 1986; Johnson 1990; Star and Estes 1990).

Operation	Example
Renaming/Reclassification	Reclassify soil classes into hydric, mesic, or xeric based on hydrogeological characteristics
Geometric (rotation, translation, scaling, rectification, registration)	Convert data layer from latitude-longitude to Universal Transverse Mercator
Boolean (AND, OR, NOT, etc.)	Combine low-elevation hydric areas with areas vegetated by *Spartina* to produce a new "vegetated salt marsh" class
Overlay	Overlay soils and vegetation data layers
Spatial Coincidence	Show all oyster beds that are located in polluted waters
Proximity	Show all oyster beds that are located within 200 m of a marina
Measurement (length or distance, area, perimeter, fractal dimension, etc.)	Calculate area of a salt marsh vegetated by *Spartina*
Statistical	Calculate mean area and standard deviation of oyster reefs located within an estuary; correlate reef size and creek flow velocity

1994), water-quality monitoring (Rifai et al. 1993), shoreline mapping (Thieler and Danforth 1994), modeling sea-level rise (Chmura et al. 1992), habitat evaluation (Sader et al. 1991; Friel and Haddad 1992), pollution studies (Bendoricchio et al. 1993; Laughlin et al. 1993), and assessing the impacts of large natural disturbances, especially hurricanes and tropical storms (Gardner et al. 1991, 1993; GIS World 1992; Michener 1992; Cablk et al. 1994).

GIS Issues, Research Needs, and Facilitating Technologies

Environmental scientists and natural resource managers historically have been closely tied to that portion of the landscape for which they are attempting to understand and manage specific populations, ecosystems, and other ecological patterns and processes. The complex issues associated with sustainable development have, however, necessitated that environmental scientists cross traditional academic and geographic boundaries. Consequently, environmental scientists and resource managers must rely heavily upon data that were collected by other disciplinary specialists.

As environmental scientists and managers direct their attention to broader spatial scales, it becomes apparent that issues related to geospatial data acquisition and analysis will only increase in complexity. Addressing regional and global questions, for example, may entail acquisition of hundreds of geospatial datasets from dozens of different sources, which have variable accuracy, precision, and update history, as well as acquisition of up-to-date, high-resolution satellite imagery. New satellite data acquisition programs will likely add more than a terabyte of data each day to national and commercial data repositories (Marshall 1989). As environmental scientists access these databases and attempt to assemble views of entire ecosystems, regions, increasing in scale to the entire biosphere, the situation may prove to "be analogous to attempting to obtain a drink of water from the jetstream of an eight-inch fire hose" (Gosz 1994). Thus, concerns in the future will need to focus on how to best identify, acquire, manage, and analyze geospatial data that are timely, relevant to a specific problem, and of sufficient quality to support prudent scientific and management decisions. In the remainder of this section, we focus discussion on relevant issues or problem areas, and some potential technical solutions: data identification and acquisition, metadata, data lineage, and uncertainty.

IDENTIFICATION AND ACQUISITION OF RELEVANT DATA

Often we cannot find or access existing GIS databases because their contents and the meaning of those contents are unknown. One reason for this is that the meaning of data is exogenous and not found in the data (Tobler 1979). In many situations, potential users are not aware that data they require already exist. Consequently, important studies are postponed until additional data are captured or created.

Software tools are needed for visualizing, interacting with, and learning about the contents of environmental databases (Geographic Designs Inc. 1994a). These tools would facilitate understanding by providing users with abilities to interact with visualizations of the thematic, spatial, and temporal dimensions of a database's contents. Simultaneous interactive views of what data were collected, where they were collected, and when they were collected obviates which specific information requirements are met by available datasets and which ones remain to be filled.

One such software system design (Lanter and Essinger 1994) is based on the principle that geographic facts can be well specified within three general dimensions: theme, space, and time (Berry 1964; Sinton 1978). Interactions with representations of how the data vary among these dimensions enables researchers to:

- view the arrangement of locations within the context of a set of thematic attributes,
- view the set of thematic attributes available at a particular location,
- compare sets of thematic attributes as they vary across locations,
- compare locations in terms of the thematic attributes they are characterized by,
- study a set of attributes at a set(s) of locations involving some or all of the above with the additional ability to study spatial association to enrich understanding of areal differentiation in terms of thematic characteristics of various sets of locations,
- compare locations through time in terms of the changing spatial distributions of collected thematic attributes,
- compare the set of thematic attributes collected at a location over time,

- compare changing spatial associations between thematic attributes,
- study changing areal differentiation (e.g., change in the nature of a habitat),
- compare a set(s) of locations and the associated thematic attributes over time, and examine the interplay of the preceding approaches.

These capabilities can support researchers and analysts working to understand interrelationships among diverse geographically referenced data.

Lanter and Essinger implemented their design in a system that stores each observation (i.e., data sample) as a composite object assembled from spatial, thematic, and temporal components (Geographic Designs Inc. 1994a). A visualization of an environmental database is presented to the user within windows for each of the three components (Fig. 1). Thematic classes and associated attributes and values, locations, and time periods are each shaded to display the nature of the database that covers them. The result is a portrayal of the covariation in the contents of the database.

User selections made in one spatial, thematic, or temporal dimension are immediately reflected in all three dimensions. For example, a user selection of an attribute in the thematic window reflects in the other two, showing when and where it was measured. Selection of a place results in display of what was collected there and at which times. Selection of a time displays what was collected then and at which locations. These capabilities enable the user to dynamically explore collections of datasets by manipulating theme, space, and time individually, or in concert, as they

- select data by specifying what is needed, where and when,
- explore covariation among different thematic variables, locations, and times,
- find places and times where data with chosen criteria coincide,
- determine what additional data are available at the same time and place as a selected subset of data, within user-specified space and time constraints.

METADATA

Metadata describe "the content, quality, condition, and other characteristics of data" and represent higher level information about geospatial data that facilitate: (1) identification of available data for a particular geographic location; (2) determination of fitness for use of data for meeting a specific objective; (3) data acquisition; and (4) data processing and analysis (Federal Geographic Data Committee 1994). There have been numerous attempts over the past decade at developing standards for geospatial data transfer that incorporate a metadata component, including the Spatial Data Transfer Standard (National Institute of Standards and Technology 1992), Digital Geographic Exchange Standard (Digital Geographic Information Working Group 1991), and the Vector Product Format (Defense Mapping Agency 1992). Recently, a comprehensive set of Content Standards for Digital Geospatial Metadata has been released (Federal Geographic Data Committee 1994). The goal of physically integrating metadata and data within GIS has not yet been fully realized, although numerous vendors are devoting research and development funds to this activity, and the United States Geological Survey has developed DOCUMENT.AML, an ARC Macro Language program that facilitates manual documentation for ARC/INFO coverages.

Despite the significant progress in the area of metadata standards, Chrisman (1994) asserted that "all the standardized procedures in the world cannot ensure that the product actually satisfies the user's needs." He emphasized the joint responsibilities of users and providers in relation to geospatial data use and documentation, the need to incorporate spatial statistics more fully into GIS, research leading to a better understanding of error propagation in GIS and, importantly, the critical

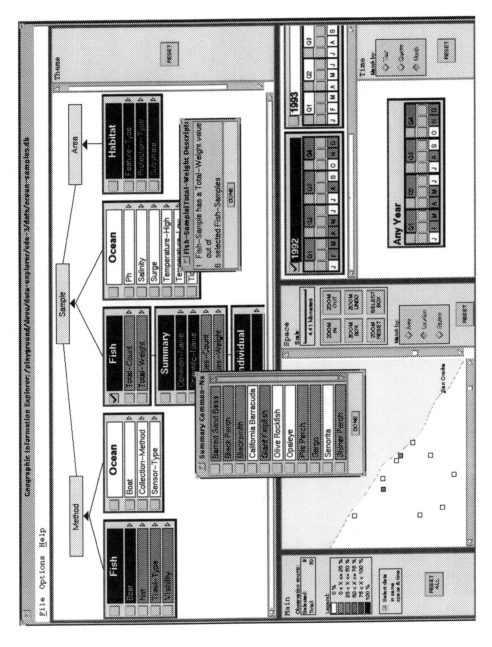

Fig. 1. Exploration of a coastal fisheries GIS database illustrating the thematic (upper), spatial (lower left), and temporal (lower right) windows.

need to develop "procedures that can handle large differences in resolution, accuracy and other key properties."

DATA LINEAGE

Geospatial data are often decentralized and partitioned across distributed networked computer systems. Most partitioning of data, however, is done randomly in response to project needs and available software and hardware. These fragmented data are often stored redundantly in different locations, on different databases, and in different data structures. They are typically named inconsistently, defined poorly, and documented incompletely. As a result, their meaning may have been lost and their quality unknown. Such data are difficult to understand, identify, and access, and expensive to maintain. As a result many databases contain massive quantities of disparate data that are poorly understood and cannot be reused (see Brackett 1994).

If data within existing GIS databases are going to be of use to those outside the immediate user community, the data will have to be examined and defined element by element. This implies that each map within the GIS database must be understood. The data must be analyzed to determine what the originators intended the maps to mean when they were created. This meaning, exogenous to the data itself, must be determined from available metadata. Lineage metadata (Lanter 1994a) is a formal basis for determining the meaning of GIS-derived geospatial data. It consists of specific documentation pertaining to data sources, processing history, and product use (Lanter 1991). The National Committee for Digital Cartographic Data Standards' (1988) Spatial Data Transfer Standard (also see National Institute of Standards and Technology 1992) recommends that source documentation include name, feature content, dates, responsible agency, scale, projection, and accuracy elements.

Lineage metadata provides a basis for uniquely identifying and defining data and specifying how GIS-derived maps relate to other relevant maps in the database. Automation of lineage metadata makes it possible to optimize the contents of the geospatial database (Lanter 1993), model errors propagating within spatial analyses (Lanter and Veregin 1992), identify and remove redundancy and propagate updates through a distributed geospatial database (Lanter 1994a), and generalize spatial analytic logic used within GIS applications (Lanter 1994b).

Figure 2 illustrates a lineage metadata-based graphical user interface that supports GIS users in understanding, documenting, updating, and managing geospatial databases (Lanter 1992; Geographic Designs Inc. 1994b). Lanter and Surbey (1994) pioneered the use of lineage metadata as a data discovery tool for assessing the quality of disparate data derived within prior GIS applications databases. As Lanter and Surbey's metadata analysis illustrated, reverse engineering data quality documentation requires thought, analysis, intuition, and consensus by knowledgeable people to identify the true content and meaning of disparate data. An automated tool, based on lineage metadata, can support people in the data engineering process, but it cannot create missing documentation or clearly define unknown prior data.

DEALING WITH UNCERTAINTY

Increased use of GIS for research and management and the creation of multiple use, widely-shared geographic databases require that data quality and the data entry process be closely examined and well documented (Dangermond 1988b). Geospatial data are prone to uncertainty and

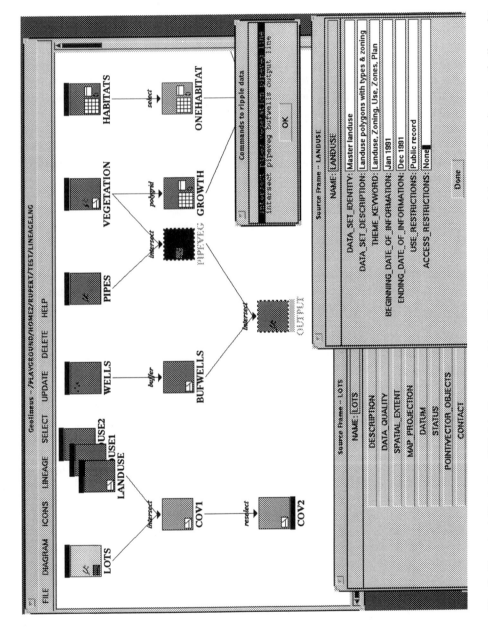

Fig. 2. Flowchart illustrating GIS data lineage tracking. Note: "ripple" command (small window) automatically updates all coverages in a complex series of GIS analyses.

inaccuracy, and the reliability of any computer-based analysis will be constrained by data quality (Goodchild et al. 1993). There is a natural tendency to ignore the fact that maps are only approximations of the truth, representing subjective interpretations of real spatial variability. Burrough (1986), for example, asserts that "many soil scientists and geographers know from field experience that carefully drawn boundaries and contour lines on maps are elegant misrepresentations of changes that are often gradual, vague, or fuzzy. People have been so conditioned to seeing the variation of the earth's surface portrayed either by the stepped functions of choropleth maps or by smoothly varying mathematical surfaces that they find it difficult to conceive that reality is otherwise." Consequently, the ease of access and manipulation provided by GIS, and its inherent precision, encourages users to see geospatial data as accurate and to lose touch with the uncertainties of the measurement and capture process (Goodchild and Gopal 1989; Goodchild et al. 1993).

Many of the "environmental" geospatial datasets currently available in digital form (e.g., soils, wetland inventory data, etc.) were originally derived from digitization of cartographic maps based on interpreted aerial photography. Thus, these data are subject to various primary and secondary data collection errors (Thapa and Bossler 1992). Primary data collection errors include personal, instrument, and environmental errors. Secondary data collection errors are attributable to numerous aspects of cartographic and GIS processing, including: plotting control points, compilation error, drawing or plotting, map generalization, map reproduction, color registration, material deformation (humidity changes, etc.), changing scales, uncertainty in feature definition, feature exaggeration, digitization or scanning, labeling and feature coding, etc.

Cartographic standards have been relatively stable for several decades. For example, if 90% of "well-defined" points fall within 0.5 mm of their true position, then the map can be certified as complying with the United States National Map Accuracy Standard (NMAS) (Bureau of the Budget 1947). The effective resolution of some common map scales assuming 0.5-mm resolution is shown in Fig. 3 (adapted from Goodchild 1993). Although very effective for roads, utilities, and other easily defined features, the NMAS is not as easily translated to many environmental features that are, by nature, fuzzy and nonlinear.

Additional errors may be incorporated into GIS analyses when data layers are based on processed satellite imagery. For example, although Jensen et al. (1993) were able to classify coastal wetland and upland habitats with 86% to 92% overall accuracy, efforts to differentiate among some classes (bare soil, cultivated land, herbaceous) and among the various wetland types (estuarine, riverine, marine) were not feasible. Errors may be further compounded when satellite data at the pixel scale are aggregated into larger units. For example, land-cover classification accuracy was 57% and 43% for Multispectral Scanner data aggregated to 100 m^2 and 200 m^2, respectively, and errors in the categorization of slope angle and aspect were consistently over 50% for digital elevation models summarized at 100 m^2 and 200 m^2 (Walsh et al. 1987).

Various GIS procedures lead to nonlinear and often counter-intuitive propagation of errors. For example, addition of data layers of fixed accuracy results in a negative exponential error rate (Veregin 1989), whereas the buffer operation can actually lead to increases in overall accuracy for the final product (Veregin 1994). Finally, GIS may be leading to uses for which the data were never intended when they were collected and mapped (Goodchild 1993). It is important, therefore, to have well-documented metadata and known sources or contacts, in order to determine "fitness for use."

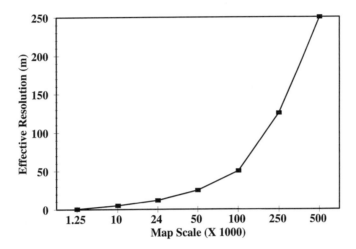

Fig. 3. Effective resolution of some common map scales assuming 0.5-mm resolution (adapted from Goodchild 1993).

A Conceptual Model for GIS Design and Implementation

Despite database and technological improvements, several impediments remain to effective integration of GIS into sustainable development research and management activities. First, how do we identify and acquire data of appropriate scale (spatial, temporal, thematic) and quality that are required for a particular project? Second, how can we be assured that the cartographic products resulting from a series of GIS and modeling operations are both geographically and statistically significant and environmentally meaningful?

Technology alone may ameliorate the problems but will not entirely solve them. We suggest that what is needed is a major change in how we go about designing and performing GIS-based sustainable development research and management. The approach which we propose (Fig. 4) highlights the importance of data and metadata-based data-quality assessments (hexagons), and metadata development and lineage tracking (rounded rectangles) throughout all phases of research and resource management projects. Each step in the process is discussed more fully below.

(1) Project Needs Assessment. The project needs assessment includes consideration of all aspects associated with design and implementation of a project. The first and most important step entails specifying overall project objectives and fully defining the questions and/or hypotheses that are to be addressed. Second, requisite data layers and their optimal spatial, temporal, and thematic scales are explicitly identified. Third, all project-specific GIS operations, analyses, and modeling steps are outlined. Fourth, project deliverables and their desired level of accuracy are specified. Finally, project needs and implementation constraints are assessed, including budgeting, staffing, hardware and software, performance milestones, and final project deadlines for deliverables.

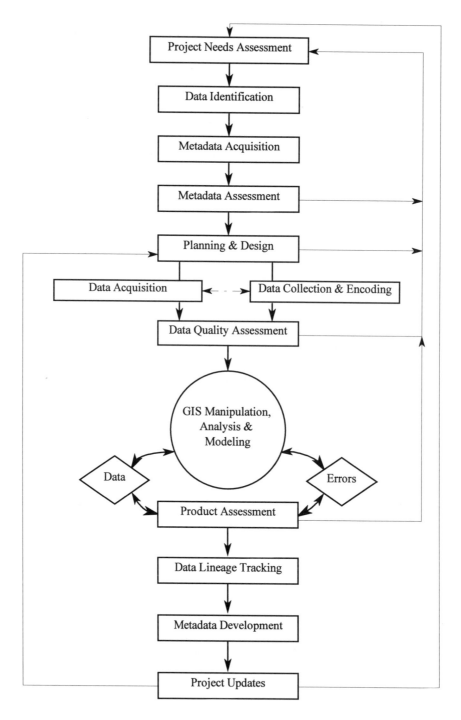

Fig. 4. GIS design and implementation strategy for sustainable development research and resource management.

(2) Data Identification. Data availability, sources, costs, etc. are identified. If the desired pro-duct has been previously completed and is available, then the project can conclude at this step.

(3) Metadata Acquisition. If metadata are available separately from the data they describe, then metadata should be initially acquired and compiled.

(4) Metadata Assessment. Metadata assessment entails thorough examination of all aspects of the data that are necessary for determining "fitness for use," especially information pertaining to data quality. Frequently, direct consultation with contact personnel listed in the metadata or relevant disciplinary experts is appropriate and necessary. "Acceptable" existing data and data development needs should be identified. Results of the metadata assessment should then be directly related to project objectives and requirements as outlined in the project needs assessment (Step 1).

(5) Project Implementation Planning and Design. After data needs are assessed, project design and implementation schedules are reevaluated, and activities, budgeting, personnel allocation, and project milestones are revised accordingly.

(6) Data Acquisition. Data collection, encoding, acquisition of existing data, and compilation proceed according to schedule outlined in Step 5. Ideally, for large projects, data acquisition for some smaller portion of the full spatial extent would be initially prioritized for inclusion in a "pilot project." This data subset would be processed through Step 11, and a decision could be made at that time as to whether to proceed with the full project.

(7) Source Metadata Creation. Comprehensive metadata are developed for any newly created geospatial datasets.

(8) Data Quality Assessment. Once the requisite data are acquired and compiled, it is useful to reexamine the data in relation to requirements outlined in the Project Needs Assessment (Step 1). Results of the data quality assessment are also incorporated into the source metadata (Step 7).

(9) GIS Management, Analysis, and Modeling. Data manipulations, GIS operations, and model-ing proceed as planned. As illustrated, the analytical process will result in two types of products: one representing the desired end-product that is derived from the various data sources; and one characterizing the variability associated with that end-product.

(10) Data Lineage Tracking. Data lineage should be tracked through all data management, GIS, and modeling operations. Ideally, all or, at least, major portions of this process would be automated (Lanter 1992).

(11) Product Assessment. Suitability of the product for meeting project objectives is evaluated. An informed determination must be made as to whether results are both geographically significant and ecologically meaningful. This assessment may lead to a reevaluation of questions, hypotheses, and project objectives.

(12) Product Metadata Development. Unless the project is disbanded prior to completion, significant effort should be planned for and devoted to developing comprehensive metadata for the products (final data layers), and possibly for many of the intermediate data layers as well. Attention should focus on metadata development for those data layers that are likely to be used in other projects.

(13) Product Updates. In many cases, data layers will be updated prior to completion of the full project or a decision will be made to continue the project for some indefinite period. Thus, it will likely be necessary that data layers be updated and that processing and analysis steps be repeated. All or portions of this process could be automated (Lanter 1994a).

Ideally, errors associated with each of the data layers would be propagated through the series of analyses to evaluate uncertainty associated with the final product(s) (Fig. 4, Step 9). The process

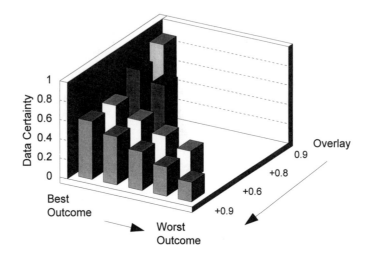

Fig. 5. Uncertainty associated with overlaying coverages of variable accuracy (0.9, 0.8, 0.6, and 0.9, respectively).

of tracking error within GIS has been automated (Lanter and Veregin 1992). Although much basic research remains to be done in this area, new understanding is emerging of how errors are affected by some specific GIS operations (e.g., AND/OR operations [Veregin 1989; Lanter and Veregin 1992] and buffering [Veregin 1994]). Thus, it is currently possible to overlay coverages of known accuracy and examine the magnitude and range of errors that may result in final products. For example, Fig. 5 illustrates the potential range of uncertainty (expressed as probability of certainty) associated with overlaying coverages of variable accuracy (0.9, 0.8, 0.6, and 0.9, respectively). In this case, accuracy of the final product may range from 0.6 to 0.2. Such analyses can prove critical for determining whether available geospatial data are adequate for meeting project objectives or what level of accuracy is required in new data layers. Figure 6, for example, illustrates different scenarios of how position errors may be propagated in overlaying soils data and wetlands data with variable levels of accuracy.

Conclusions and Recommendations

Many constraints associated with utilizing GIS technology for sustainable development research and management have been removed during the past decade. Computer hardware and software costs have decreased dramatically and processing power and ease-of-use have increased (Stafford et al. 1994). The volume of data available for environmental and sustainable development studies is increasing exponentially; approximately doubling every 20 months (Frawley et al. 1992). The Earth Observing System will produce one terabyte of data every day, generating the equivalent of 17 years worth of Landsat data every two weeks (Marshall 1989). In the near future, GIS and network technology will be able to support transparent access of geospatial data from areas around the world for support of sustainable development research and resource management (Stafford et al. 1994).

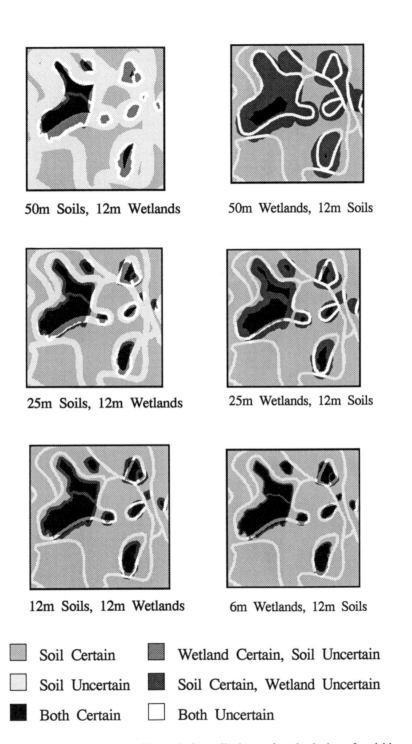

50m Soils, 12m Wetlands

50m Wetlands, 12m Soils

25m Soils, 12m Wetlands

25m Wetlands, 12m Soils

12m Soils, 12m Wetlands

6m Wetlands, 12m Soils

Soil Certain

Wetland Certain, Soil Uncertain

Soil Uncertain

Soil Certain, Wetland Uncertain

Both Certain

Both Uncertain

Fig. 6. Propagation of errors associated with overlaying soils data and wetlands data of variable accuracy.

A brief review of pertinent applications illustrates that GIS has tremendous potential to support research and resource management, which can facilitate meeting sustainable development objectives. As environmental geospatial databases continue to increase in size and diversity, and as more organizations adopt GIS as a research and management tool, concerns will increasingly focus on how best to acquire relevant, up-to-date data of sufficient quality for supporting wise scientific and management decisions. Technological support for identification of "appropriate" data, acquiring adequate metadata, tracking data lineage, and modeling error propagation are, therefore, identified as critical emerging needs. Several existing technologies can facilitate these activities. The proposed stepwise approach for GIS design and implementation highlights the importance of data and metadata-based quality assessments, developing and maintaining comprehensive metadata for new geospatial coverages, tracking data lineage, and modeling error propagation. Ultimately, GIS-based sustainable development research and resource management depends upon the quality of available data. If a priori consideration is paid to metadata and data quality issues, then organizations can focus valuable time and effort on performing appropriate analyses with the requisite high-quality data. As data lineage tracking and metadata maintenance programs are formally incorporated into project planning and implementation, organizations can further benefit by being able to re-use data developed for other applications.

ACKNOWLEDGMENTS

Funding for portions of the research described in this chapter was provided by Geographic Designs, Inc. ARC/INFO is a trademark of Environmental Systems Research Institute, Inc.; Geolineus is a trademark of Geographic Designs, Inc.

LITERATURE CITED

Becker, D.S. and J.W. Armstrong. 1988. Development of regionally standardized protocols for marine environmental studies. *Marine Pollution Bulletin* 19(7): 310-313.

Bendoricchio, G., M. Luzio, P. Baschieri, and A. Capodaglio. 1993. Diffuse pollution in the lagoon of Venice. *Water Science Technology* 28(3-5): 69-78.

Bernal, P. and P.M. Holligan. 1992. Marine and coastal systems, p. 157-172. *In* J.C.I. Dooge, G.T. Goodman, J.W.M. la Rivière, J. Marton-Lefèvre, T. O'Riordan, and F. Praderie (eds.), An Agenda of Science for Environment and Development into the 21st Century. Cambridge University Press, Cambridge.

Berry, B. 1964. Approaches to regional geography: A synthesis. *Annals of the American Association of Geographers* 54: 2-11.

Bildstein, K., G. Bancroft, P. Dugan, D. Gordon, R. Erwin, E. Nol, L. Payne, and S. Senner. 1991. Approaches to the conservation of coastal wetlands in the western hemisphere. *Wilson Bulletin* 103(2): 218-254.

Brackett, M.H. 1994. Data Sharing - Using a Common Data Architecture. John Wiley & Sons, Inc., New York.

Brown, J.H. 1994. Grand challenges in scaling up environmental research. Pages 21-26 *In* W. K. Michener, J. W. Brunt, and S. G. Stafford (eds.), Environmental Information Management and Analysis: Ecosystem to Global Scales. Taylor & Francis, London.

Buckley, D. and W. Hendrix. 1986. Use of geographic information systems in assessment of site suitability for land application of waste, p. xx-xx. *In* Proceedings: Geographic Information Systems in Government. United States Army Engineer Topographic Laboratory, Ft. Belvoir, Virginia.

Bureau of the Budget. 1947. National Map Accuracy Standards. United States Government Printing Office, Washington, D.C.

Burke, I.C., T.G.F. Kittel, W.K. Lauenroth, P. Snook, C.M. Yonker, and W.J. Parton. 1991. Regional analysis of the Central Great Plains. *BioScience* 14(10): 685-692.

Burrough, P.A. 1986. Principles of Geographic Information Systems for Land Resource Assessment. Clarendon, Oxford.

Cablk, M.E., B. Kjerfve, W.K. Michener, and J.R. Jensen. 1994. Impacts of Hurricane Hugo on a coastal forest: Assessment using Landsat TM data. *Geocarto International* 9(2): 15-24.

Cherfas, J. 1990. The fringe of the ocean-under siege from the land. *Science* 248: 163-165.

Chmura, G., R. Constanza, and E. Kosters. 1992. Modeling coastal marsh stability in response to sea level rise: A case study in coastal Louisiana, USA. *Ecological Modeling* 64: 47-64.

Chrisman, N.R. 1994. Metadata required to determine the fitness of spatial data for use in environmental analysis, p. 177-190. *In* W. K. Michener, J. W. Brunt, and S. G. Stafford (eds.), Environmental Information Management and Analysis: Ecosystem to Global Scales. Taylor & Francis, London.

Chuvieco, E. 1993. Integration of linear programming and GIS for land-use modelling. *International Journal of Geographical Information Systems* 7(1): 71-83.

Constanza, R., W. Kemp, and W. Boynton. 1993. Predictability, scale, and biodiversity in coastal and estuarine ecosystems: Implications for management. *Ambio* 22(2-3): 88-96.

Cowen, D.J. 1988. GIS versus CAD versus DBMS: What are the differences? *Photogrammetric Engineering and Remote Sensing* 54: 1551-1554.

Dangermond, J. 1988a. A review of digital data commonly available and some of the practical problems of entering them into a GIS. Environmental Systems Research Institute, Redlands, California.

Dangermond, J. 1988b. GIS trends and comments. *ARC News* Summer/Fall Issue, p. 13-17.

Day, J.W. Jr., C.A.S. Hall, W.M. Kemp, and A. Yanez-Arancibia. 1989. Estuarine Ecology. John Wiley & Sons, Inc., New York.

Defense Mapping Agency (DMA). 1992. Vector Product Format, Military Standard 600006. United States Department of Defense, Washington, D.C.

Digital Geographic Information Working Group (DGIWG). 1991. DIGEST: A Digital Geographic Exchange Standard. United States Defense Mapping Agency, Washington, D.C.

Federal Geographic Data Committee (FGDC). 1994. Content standards for digital geospatial metadata (June 8). Federal Geographic Data Committee, Washington, D.C.:

Frawley, W.J., G. Piatetsky-Shapiro, and C.J. Mathews. 1992. Knowledge discovery in databases: An overview. *AI Magazine* Fall: 57-70.

Friel, C. and K. Haddad. 1992. GIS brings new outlook to Florida Keys marine resources management. *GIS World* 5(9): 32-36.

Gardner, L.R., W.K. Michener, B. Kjerfve, and D.A. Karinshak. 1991. The geomorphic effects of Hurricane Hugo on an undeveloped coastal landscape at North Inlet, South Carolina. *Journal of Coastal Research* 8: 181-186.

Gardner, L.R., W.K. Michener, T.M. Williams, E.R. Blood, B. Kjerfve, L.A. Smock, D.J. Lipscomb, and C. Gresham. 1993. Disturbance effects of Hurricane Hugo on a pristine coastal landscape: North Inlet, South Carolina, USA. *Netherlands Journal of Sea Research* 30: 1-12.

Geographic Designs, Inc. 1994a. Geographic Information Explorer Version 2.02. Santa Barbara, California.

Geographic Designs, Inc. 1994b. Geolineus 3.0 User Manual. Santa Barbara, California.

GIS World. 1990. Gis Technology '90: Results of the 1990 Gis World Geographic Information Systems Survey. *GIS World*, Fort Collins, Colorado.

GIS World. 1992. Hurricane Andrew: A story of what could have been. *GIS World* 5(9): 13-15.

Goodchild, M. 1993. Data models and data quality: Problems and prospects, p. 94-103. *In* M.F. Goodchild, B.O. Parks, and L.T. Stayaert (eds.), Environmental Modeling with GIS. Oxford, New York.

Goodchild, M. and S. Gopal. 1989. Accuracy of Spatial Databases. Taylor & Francis, New York.

Goodchild, M.F., B.O. Parks, and L.T. Stayaert. 1993. Environmental Modeling with GIS. Oxford, New York.

Gosz, J.R. 1994. Sustainable biosphere initiative: Data management challenges, p. 27-39. *In* W.K. Michener, J.W. Brunt, and S.G. Stafford (eds.), Environmental Information Management and Analysis: Ecosystem to Global Scales. Taylor & Francis, London.

Green, K., S. Bernath, L. Lackey, M. Brunengo, and S. Smith. 1993. Analyzing the cumulative effects of forest practices: Where do we start? *Geo Info Systems* 3(2): 30-41.

Jensen, J.R., D.J. Cowen, J.D. Althausen, S. Narumalani, and O. Weatherbee. 1993. An evaluation of the CoastWatch change detection protocol in South Carolina. *Photogrammetric Engineering and Remote Sensing* 59(6): 1039-1046.

Johnson, L.B. 1990. Analyzing spatial and temporal phenomena using geographic information systems. *Landscape Ecology* 4(1): 31-43.

Johnston, C. 1994. Cumulative impacts to wetlands. *Wetlands* 14(1): 49-55.

Juhl, G. 1989. GIS technology coming of age. *American City and County* April: 50-54.

Kelly, D.R., R.P. Cote, B. Nicholls, and P. Ricketts. 1987. Developing a strategic assessment and planning framework for the marine environment. *Journal of Environmental Management* 25: 219-230.

Lachowski, H., T. Wirth, P. Maus, and P. Avers. 1994. Remote sensing and GIS: Their role in ecosystem management. *Journal of Forestry* 92(8): 39-40.

Lanter, D.P. 1991. Design of a Lineage-Based Meta-Database for GIS. Cartography and *Geographic Information Systems* 18(4): 255-261.

Lanter, D.P. 1992. GEOLINEUS: Data management and flowcharting for ARC/INFO. Technical Software Series S-92-2, National Center for Geographic Information and Analysis, Santa Barbara, California.

Lanter, D.P. 1993. A lineage meta-database approach towards spatial analytic database optimization. *Cartography and Geographic Information Systems* 20(2): 112-121.

Lanter, D.P. 1994a. A lineage metadata approach to removing redundancy and propagating updates in a GIS database. *Cartography and Geographic Information Systems* 21(2): 91-98.

Lanter, D.P. 1994b. Comparison of spatial analytic applications of GIS. Pages 413-425 *In* W. K. Michener, J.W. Brunt, and S. G. Stafford (eds.), Environmental Information Management and Analysis: Ecosystem to Global Scales. Taylor & Francis, London.

Lanter, D.P. and R. Essinger. 1994. The Environmental Data Explorer, An intelligent interface for exploring unfamiliar environmental data sets. Geographic Designs Inc., Santa Barbara, California.

Lanter, D.P. and C. Surbey. 1994. Metadata analysis of GIS data processing: A case study, p. 314-324. *In* T. C. Waugh and R.G. Healey (eds.), Advances in GIS Research. Proceedings of the Sixth International Symposium on Spatial Data Handling. Taylor & Francis, London.

Lanter, D.P. and H. Veregin. 1992. A research paradigm for propagating error in layer-based GIS. *Photogrammetric Engineering and Remote Sensing* 58(6): 825-833.

Laughlin, G., M. Hutchinson, and B. Mackey. 1993. An intuitive approach to analyzing small point-source spatial data sets. *International Journal of Geographical Information Systems* 7(1): 21-38.

Long, B., T. Skewes, and I. Poiner. 1994. An efficient method for estimating seagrass biomass. *Aquatic Botany* 47: 277-291.

Lubchenco, J., A.M. Olson, L.B. Brubaker, S.R. Carpenter, M.M. Holland, S.P. Hubbell, S.A. Levin, J.A. MacMahon, P.A. Matson, J.M. Melillo, H.A. Mooney, C.H. Peterson, H.R. Pulliam, L.A. Real, P.J. Regal, and P.G. Risser. 1991. The sustainable biosphere initiative: An ecological research agenda. *Ecology* 72: 371-412.

Maguire, D.J. 1991. An overview and definition of GIS, p. *19-20. In* D.J. Maguire, M.F. Goodchild, and D. Rhind (eds.), Geographical Information Systems: Principles and Applications. John Wiley & Sons, Inc., New York.

Marshall, E. 1989. Bringing NASA down to earth. *Science* 244: 1248-1251.

Michener, W.K. 1992. GPS support vital to long-term ecological research program. *GIS World* 3(2): 58-63.

Mitsch, W.J. and J.G. Gosselink. 1986. Wetlands. Van Nostrand Reinhold, New York.

National Institute of Standards and Technology. 1992. Spatial Data Transfer Standard. Federal Information Processing Standard 173. National Institute of Standards and Technology, Gaithersburg, Maryland.

National Committee for Digital Cartographic Data Standards (NCDCDS). 1988. The proposed standard for digital cartographic data. *The American Cartographer* 15(1): 9-140.

Parker, H.D. 1988. The unique qualities of a geographic information system: A commentary. *Photogrammetric Engineering and Remote Sensing* 54(11): 1547-1549.

Remillard, M.M. and R.A. Welch. 1992. GIS technologies for aquatic macrophyte studies: I. Database development and changes in the aquatic environment. *Landscape Ecology* 7(3): 151-162.

Remillard, M.M. and R.A. Welch. 1993. GIS technologies for aquatic macrophyte studies: Modeling applications. *Landscape Ecology* 8(3): 163-175.

Rifai, H., C. Newell, and P. Bedient. 1993. GIS enhances water quality monitoring. *GIS World* 6(8): 52-55.

Rykiel, E., M. Saunders, T. Wagner, D. Loh, R. Turnbow, L. Hu, P. Pulley, and R. Coulson. 1984. Computer-aided decision making and information accessing in pest management systems, with emphasis on the southern pine beetle (Coleoptera: Scolytidae). *FORUM: Journal of Economic Entomology* 77: 1073-1082.

Sader, S., G. Powell, and J. Rappole. 1991. Migratory bird habitat monitoring through remote sensing. *International Journal of Remote Sensing* 12(3): 363-372.

Schaeffer, D.J., E.E. Herricks, and H.W. Kerster. 1988. Ecosystem health: I. Measuring ecosystem health. *Environmental Management* 12(4): 445-455.

SDTS. 1992. ASTM Section D18.01.05 Draft Specification for Meta-Data Support in Geographic Information Systems. Information Exchange Forum on Spatial Metadata. Federal Geographic Data Committee, United States Geological Survey, Reston, Virginia.

Sharitz, R. R., L.R. Boring, D.H. Van Lear, and J.E. Pinder, III. 1992. Integrating ecological concepts with natural resource management of southern forests. *Ecological Applications* 2(3): 226-237.

Sinton, D. 1978. The inherent structure of information as a constraint to analysis: Mapped thematic data as a case study. *In* G. Dutton (ed.), Proceedings of First International Advanced Study Symposium on Topological Data Structures for Geographic Information Systems, Volume 7. Harvard Papers on Geographic Information Systems, Laboratory for Computer Graphics and Spatial Analysis, Graduate School of Design, Harvard University, Cambridge, Massachusetts.

Smith, L. 1993. Wastewater management project provides timely revenues. *GISWorld* 6(8): 38-41.

Southworth, A.D. 1989. Conserving southeastern coastal wetlands, p. 223-257. *In* W. J. Chandler (ed.), Audubon Wildlife Report 1989/1990. Academic Press, New York.

Stafford, S.G., J.W. Brunt, and W.K. Michener. 1994. Integration of scientific information management and environmental research, p. 3-19. *In* W.K. Michener, J.W. Brunt, and S.G. Stafford (eds.), Environmental Information Management and Analysis: Ecosystem to Global Scales. Taylor & Francis, London.

Star, J. and J. Estes. 1990. Geographic Information Systems: An Introduction. Prentice-Hall, Inc. Englewood Cliffs, New Jersey.

Thapa, K. and J. Bossler. 1992. Accuracy of spatial data used in geographic information systems. *Photogrammetric Engineering and Remote Sensing* 58(6): 835-841.

Thieler, E.R. and W.W. Danforth. 1994. Historical shoreline mapping (II): Applications of the digital shoreline mapping and analysis systems (DSMS/DSAS) to shoreline change mapping in Puerto Rico. *Journal of Coastal Research* 10(3): 600-620.

Tiner, R.W. 1984. Wetlands of the United States: Current status and recent trends. United States Environmental Protection Agency, Washington, D.C.

Tobler, W.R. 1979. A transformational view of cartography. *The American Cartographer* 6(2): 101-106.

Turner, R.K. (ed.). 1988. Sustainable Environmental Management. Principles and Practice, Westview, Colorado.

Veregin, H. 1989. Error modeling for the map overlay operation, p. 3-18. *In* M. Goodchild and S. Gopal (eds.), The Accuracy of Spatial Databases. Taylor & Francis, New York.

Veregin, H. 1994. Integration of simulation modeling and error propagation for the buffer operation in GIS. *Photogrammetric Engineering and Remote Sensing* 60(4): 427-435.

Walsh, S.J., D.R. Lightfoot, and D.R. Butler. 1987. Recognition and assessment of error in geographic information systems. *Photogrammetric Engineering and Remote Sensing* 53(10): 1423-1430.

Ward, L. and B. Weigle. 1993. To save a species: GIS for manatee research and management. *GIS World* 6(8): 34-37.

Ware, S., C. Frost, and P.D. Doerr. 1993. Southern mixed hardwood forest: The former longleaf pine forest, p. 447-493. *In* W.H. Martin, S.G. Boyce, and A.C. Echternacht (eds.), Biodiversity of the Southeastern United States. John Wiley & Sons, Inc., New York.

Welch, R., M.M. Remillard, and S.S. Fung. 1986. Monitoring aquatic vegetation and water quality with a geographic information system. Proceedings of the Geographic Information Systems Workshop. American Society of Photogrammetry and Remote Sensing, Atlanta, Georgia.

Coastal Wetlands

Ruth Patrick

The United States is fortunate in having many very productive, protected wetlands; the majority of which are usually associated with estuaries. According to Pritchard (1967) estuaries can be subclassed based on geomorphology as fjord-type estuaries, estuaries produced by tectonic processes, bar-built estuaries, and drowned river valleys. In New England and along the northern West Coast are fjords. Fjords differ from other types of estuaries in having a sill across their mouth, which prevents the escape of water in the lower depths of the estuary. These sills are formed by geological action. The water below the sill often does not circulate or circulates very little over long periods of time, whereas there is free exchange of water in the upper part of the estuary. While the best known fjord in the United States is Puget Sound, there are also several small fjords along the coast of Maine. These fjords are typically formed below the mouths of relatively small streams. Grass wetlands are usually associated with them. Also on the West Coast are estuaries formed by the slippage of tectonic plates, San Francisco Bay is an example. The San Francisco Bay—San Joaquin Estuary is a combination of riverine estuary and the slippage of the tectonic plates.

A common type of wetland occurs behind barrier islands. These barrier islands are natural reefs formed across estuaries of small rivers where the flow of the river is not strong enough to maintain an open mouth. As a result, over time, barrier islands build up, channels are cut across or around these barrier islands that drain the estuary behind them. These barrier islands are very protective to the grass marshlands and mangrove swamps. Sometimes there are, on these barrier islands, large brackish water pools, and in a few cases, these barrier islands are inundated by groundwater, but this is relatively rare. This type of wetland is very common along the East Coast and Gulf Coast. They are being rapidly destroyed by civilization, because they are very favorable habitats for development.

The most common type of wetland in the United States is a grassland wetland. These extend from Maine, along the eastern and southeastern coasts of North America, around the Gulf of Mexico, and to some extent are present on the Pacific Coast. They typically have a mud flat, which is always submerged at high tide and often is a few inches below water at low tide. On these mud flats algae grow, and many invertebrates live within the sediments in these areas. I refer particularly to crustacea and some of the clams. Behind the mud flats are the grasslands. In the northern New England states and Middle Atlantic states grasslands are dominated by *Spartina*, whereas along the Southeast and Gulf coasts, *Spartina* is often intermixed with *Juncus* and other plants. Behind

111

the area of these grass marshlands, which are regularly inundated at high tide, are the high marsh areas that are inundated a few times a year. This part of the grassland marsh is often in communication with groundwater, and fairly fresh water or low salinity ponds will often exist in the high marsh. Thus we see ecological conditions favorable to the supporting of fresh, low brackish, high brackish, and marine organisms. One of the most important factors in these wetlands are the small channels which are inundated via tidal action. Often the water from the tides is supplemented by seepage from groundwater. As a result, there is a distinct salinity pattern in many of these channels that is favorable to a variety of invertebrates and fish at various developmental stages (Mitsch and Gosselink 1986).

Coastal wetlands play a very important role in protecting and stabilizing the dry areas of the continent. They absorb the force and energy of storms, including the storm surge produced by high wind and tidal action. Vegetation of these wetlands is usually very stable. For example, in the grass wetlands, *Spartina* spp. have extensive rhizome systems which hold the sediments in place and thus stabilize the structure of the marsh. In the mangrove estuaries, it is the roots of the mangrove trees that stabilize the marsh.

A relatively rare type of wetland is that occurring around the tip of the Florida coast. This wetland is usually completely submerged; however, at water over these wetlands is very shallow at low tides and at extreme low tides they may be exposed. They are mainly dominated by *Thallasosira* sp., which forms a habitat for many invertebrates and fish. They are easily destroyed by dredging, by boat activity, and other anthropogenic activities.

Wetlands are very important in removing pollutants that arise in coastal rivers before they enter the sea. Studies by Grant and Patrick (1970) were the first to show that approximately 512 acres of Tinicum Marsh, a wetland in the Delaware Estuary, produced about 20 tons of oxygen and removed 4.3 tons of $N-NO_3$ and 4.9 tons $P-PO_4$ in a day.

Most marine organisms prefer very low concentrations of nitrogen and phosphorus and if it were not for these processes in the many marshlands that occur up and down our coast, the effects of manmade pollution would be much greater in our coastal waters. These marshlands also function in the removal of heavy metals.

The nitrogen and phosphorus removed by these wetlands is utilized in the production of the grasses or the mangroves that form their vegetation. Whereas relatively few organisms eat living *Spartina*, the detritus, which is formed in the cooler months, enters the sea and is a very important food for fish and invertebrates when other sources of nutrients are relatively scarce.

A function of wetlands that has been recognized largely in the latter part of this century is their role in denitrification. Long ago Delwitche (1970) pointed out that our civilization is fixing much more nitrogen than is being denitrified by the natural world. Before the advent of large human populations, the denitrification and nitrification processes were in balance. Now they are rapidly getting out of balance, and, indeed, are out of balance to some extent. The recent work of Seitzinger and others has clearly shown the role of these wetlands in denitrification. The soils of wetlands are stratified with sand and gravel intermixed with layers of organic matter. This organic matter is often anaerobic, and it is in these anaerobic areas that denitrification takes place. Many of the sediments deposited in these wetlands are acted on by microorganisms and the nitrogen is removed by this process, thus reducing the excess amount of nitrogen available in the estuary. As stated previously, most of the organisms, particularly the algae which are the primary producers of the aquatic world, prefer relatively low nitrogen and phosphorus concentrations for their best growth.

Wetlands are important for many species of aquatic life. Many species of fish and invertebrates breed and have their nursery grounds in estuarine waters. Thus the salinity gradients that are naturally found in these wetlands is very important to their development. When the young fish or shrimp eggs are first hatched the pre-larval and early larval stages need water of relatively low salinity. As they mature, they prefer higher salinity waters. The gradient of salt from fresh to salt water is a very important attribute of estuaries.

The importance of estuaries for commercial fisheries is emphasized by the fact that most of the shrimp harvests are produced in a relatively few estuaries on our Gulf and Florida coasts. If these are destroyed by pollution, then the shrimp industry and the crab industry will be destroyed. Likewise many fish, such as the striped bass and the sturgeon, depend upon these almost fresh estuarine waters as breeding grounds and nursery grounds in the early stages of development of the larvae.

For many years, civilization considered wetlands as wastelands and as breeders of mosquitos and hence the production of malaria. They were often drained in order to make sure that they were not the habitat for malaria-carrying mosquitos. Because they were considered to be of little value, they were often used as depositories for dredge materials and thus destroyed. It is only relatively recently that we have realized their importance. Thus the many marinas, industrial docks, and trading areas have become hazards, rather than benefactors to the natural functioning of the estuary.

Another great value of the estuary has been for recreation. It is estimated, by the middle of the next century about 70% of the population of our country will live within 50 miles of the coast. Such a movement of population did not occur when people worked from sun-to-sun. It is the shorter work week and other factors that have enabled people to get away from their place of business and to recreate on the sea or in the estuary. Also many businesses have tended to move to the coast.

Often one does not know the harm that is being created when one thoughtlessly tries to change the characteristic of an estuary and its associated wetlands. Such changes are usually done for the benefit of a single industry, such as shipping, which is very important to the development of the commerce of the country, but, in so doing, many other deleterious effects occur whose costs far outweigh the benefits of improving the shipping of an estuary. An example of this is the Savannah River Estuary. The Savannah River Port is very old and has been dredged moderately for a long time. But only recently has the estuary been greatly altered to accommodate the shipments from South America of vegetables and fruits as well as other products. The desire to enlarge the port has resulted in the deepening and widening of the channel; and construction of turning basins. As a result the volume of the estuary has been greatly increased. This was done without consideration of the size of the tidal prism. It is the force of the freshwater flow and the size of the tidal prism that determines the flushing time of the estuary. It is the flushing of the estuary that scours it and keeps the channel open. Also it is the fairly rapid flushing time that removes organic materials produced in the upstream river from the estuary, and into the open sea. By increasing the volume without increasing the tidal prism the flushing time is lengthened. As a result, the banks of the estuary slump, and the oxygen utilized by the bacteria, in metabolizing any organic matter that is present, increases. Thus the estuary's suitability for wildlife is harmed.

As a result of longer flushing time, the banks of the channel were slumping. This demanded more dredging to increase the flow in the Front Channel. The United States Army Corps of Engineers decided to build a curtain on the Back Channel which would close when the high tide started to decrease. By increasing the volume in the upper estuary in the Back Channel, they hoped to increase the flushing time in the Front Channel and thus have more scouring and a removal of the sediment from the channel.

The water did not move from the Back Channel to the Front Channel as fast as they anticipated so they cut channels in the island that divided the Back and Front channels. The result was that the salinity of the Back Channel was greatly increased and the gradient of salinity in the marshes of the upper estuary was destroyed. This had a very deleterious effect on the fish and invertebrates that used this area as a spawning ground.

By altering the natural flow conditions and salinity gradients of the Back Channel they destroyed the fisheries of that area and also the suitability of the area for wildlife. The oxygen in the Front Channel decreased and industry was charged with creating a high BOD load in the waters of the Front Channel. This was proven not to be the case. It was the slower flushing time that produced a higher oxygen demand of the organic matter that came from upstream into the estuary as well as from the organic matter produced in the estuary. This was the reason why the oxygen decreased in the Front Channel.

Realizing the error of their actions, the United States Army Corps of Engineers has now removed the curtain, and is closing the channels across the island that separates the Back from the Front Channel. But it will take a long while to restore the fisheries that have been severely harmed.

Another effect of man's alterations on natural estuaries and wetlands is that they tend to widen channels by deep cuts without preserving the shallow edges. It is the shallow water of the estuary—that is, that area in which the photosynthetic zone is present—that is the most important for algal production, and this is the area in which many organisms feed and breed. By destroying these shallow water areas, the in-situ productivity of the estuary is greatly reduced.

It is clear that the time has come when we must take a holistic approach that considers all factors, before we start to alter a natural system, because the price that is paid by alteration may be greater than the benefit gained in many cases.

The recent law of the Bush Administration of "no net loss of wetlands" has placed a great emphasis on the creation of wetlands. Unfortunately, it is very difficult to reproduce a natural wetland with all of its functions and its stability. Certain functions can be reproduced, but the complexity of our coastal wetlands with their intricate flow regimes, nutrient cycling, and the great diversity of species, many of which are often endangered, makes it extremely hard to reproduce a natural wetland. In fact, it is almost impossible. It is true that one can reproduce wetland functions in restored areas, but to reproduce the complexity of a natural estuary takes a long time. A natural environment has a certain carrying capacity and it is very difficult to impact it with the anthropogenic activities of people without serious damage.

The manipulations of the Savannah Estuary are only one example of the many taking place along our coast. I refer to the building of piers, of loading stations, of marinas, and their associated pollution. We must plan and control how society uses these coastal areas.

Literature Cited

Delwiche, C.C. 1970. The Nitrogen Cycle. *Scientific American* 223(3): 136-170.

Grant, R.R., Jr., and R. Patrick. 1970. Tinicum Marsh as a water purifier, p. 105-123. *In* Two Studies of Tinicum Marsh, Delaware and Philadelphia counties, PA. The Conservation Foundation, Washington, D.C.

Mitsch, W.J. and J.G. Gosselink. 1986. Wetlands. Van Nostrand Reinhold, New York.

Patrick, R. 1994. Rivers of the United States. Vol. I. Estuaries. John Wiley and Sons, Inc., New York.

Pritchard, D.W. 1967. What is an estuary: Physical viewpoint, p. 3-5. *In* G.H. Lauff (ed.), Estuaries. American Association for the Advancement of Science, Washington, D.C.

Ecology of Southeastern Salt Marshes

F.J. Vernberg

Introduction

One of the predominant coastal habitats in the southeastern United States is marshes bordering estuaries and riverine systems. Dardeau et al. (1992) reported that 34 large-size estuaries or estuarine environments in the Southeast encompass 30,605 km^2: 18 estuaries occur from Albemarle Sound in North Carolina to Biscayne Bay, Florida, and 16 estuaries are located on the Gulf Coast from the Texas-Louisiana border to southern Florida. In addition more than 320 small, high-salinity creeks, inlets, and estuaries exist between Cape Fear, North Carolina, and Cape Canaveral, Florida, (Vernberg et al. 1992). The coastal intertidal emergent wetlands, located between aquatic and terrestrial habitats, comprise approximately 4.4 million acres. Gosselink and Baumann (1980) estimated that southeastern tidal wetlands represent 78% of the total coastal marshes in the United States. Because marshes dominate the coastal zone landscape, any plan to manage coastal resources on a sustainable development basis must incorporate an understanding of the strategic ecological role(s) marshes play in the functioning of this dynamic ecosystem. An overview of United States coastal wetlands is presented in the preceding chapter by Patrick, and the following chapter by Weinstein describes the major anthropogenic impacts on salt marshes. The present chapter focuses on the ecology of undisturbed salt marshes, with specific examples provided by the North Inlet estuary in South Carolina.

Along temperate zone estuaries, wetlands extend from the sublittoral zone to the spring high tide mark. In the tropics, salt marshes are typically confined to salt flats landward of mangroves (Chapman 1974). In general, marshes have several characteristics in common: 1) Seaward of the marsh exists a bare mud or sand flat and landward is an area of low-growing vegetation that abuts upland vegetation (Fig. 1). 2) Characteristically, few plant genera dominate North American salt marshes (*Spartina, Juncus, Salicornia,* and *Plantago*); however, extending up the salinity gradient from the ocean to rivers, the salt marsh vegetation changes and the transition to freshwater swamps is characterized by macrophytes of the genus *Typha, Scirpus,* and *Phragmites* (Chapman 1974). 3) Numerous drainage creeks and subunits of river systems bisect salt marshes. 4) Survival and growth of marshes are dependent on the availability of silt, and protection from erosion by high-energy waves is necessary to permit sedimentation. Sediment accretion must occur at a rate compatible with colonization by salt marsh vegetation for growth to occur. If sedimentation is too rapid, an area may emerge from the intertidal area and be flooded less frequently, receiving less sediment. By contrast, regions experiencing subsidence or sea-level rise may be flooded more frequently and receive more

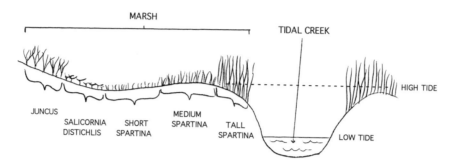

Fig. 1. A diagrammatic cross section of a southeastern salt marsh.

sediment. An example of the imbalance between sedimentation rate and marsh growth is seen in parts of the marshlands along the Gulf Coast of the United States where subsidence is resulting in marsh degradation.

Marshes are a dynamic ecosystem alternately subjected to environmental factors characteristic of both aquatic and terrestrial habitats. Although the following sections deal with discrete aspects of the ecology of salt marshes, it must be kept in mind that all abiotic and biotic components of the salt marsh interact as one holocoenocytic system.

Geological Factors

In geologic time, a given estuary exists for a relatively short period: thousands to a few tens of thousand years. Various factors acting over time contribute to the life and death of estuarine systems (e.g., sea-level change, subsidence, and sedimentation changes). In addition to these longer term geological changes, human perturbations (Weinstein 1996) can have profound effects within a rather short time frame (days to years).

Estuaries of the world are formed in various ways: submerged river systems, plate tectonic movements, bar built systems, and fjords (Pritchard 1967). Knowledge of the method of estuarine formation is important in explaining how a specific estuary functions. For example, soil types of marshes from different geographic areas may vary and the soil type can influence the affinity of various chemicals to sediments. Sedimentation dynamics are not only important to the existence of marshes, but the type of sediment influences the distribution and occurrence of the biota. For example, fine sediments tend to be more anoxic than large-grained sediments and represent a hostile environment to anoxic-sensitive biota. In turn, not only does sediment type influence the biota, but burrowing benthic organisms influence sediments by transporting deeper sediments to the surface and influencing such processes as biogeochemical cycling and resuspension of pollutants.

As indicated earlier, sedimentation rates must be equal to or exceed sea-level rise for salt marshes to persist. Estimates for various East Coast marshes indicate active accretion rates between 1.5 mm yr^{-1} and 51.8 mm yr^{-1}, exceeding local sea-level rise in some estuaries (Redfield 1972; Fleesa et al. 1977; Kjerfve et al. 1978; Sharma et al. 1987). The annual accretion of coastal marshes must be accounted for by the net sediment transport per tidal cycle between the vegetated marsh and the adjacent tidal creek integrated over a yearly cycle. To estimate the net transport per tidal cycle, transport during tidal inundation and export from the marsh via runoff during low tide exposure must be known.

Detailed studies in the North Inlet estuary, Georgetown, South Carolina, provide insights into sedimentation dynamics. As part of an extensive study to determine the role of vegetated marshes and oyster reef subsystems in sediment transport within and through a marsh-estuarine basin, Wolaver et al. (1988), measured the net inorganic suspended sediment (ISS) and organic suspended sediment (OSS) transport between an euhaline salt marsh and an adjacent tidal creek for 34 tidal cycles over a year. In general, the marsh was a sink for suspended sediments throughout the year but the largest imports occurred during the summer months. Based on annual flux estimates, ISS and OSS import to the vegetated marsh occurred during tidal inundation. Export values of ISS and OSS from the marsh via runoff during low-tide exposure were about 35% of respective import values during tidal inundation. The net flux values of sediments between the vegetated marsh and the adjacent tidal creek suggested the marsh was a sink for both constituents. The inorganic sediment input approximated the amount needed for the marsh surface to keep pace with the recent sea-level rise. Wolaver et al. (1988) suggested that the marsh keeps pace with sea-level rise by a dynamic interaction of deposition and resuspension processes that are controlled by differences in marsh and mean sea-level height, sediment load, and climatic events. The marsh platform tends to adjust itself to an elevation equivalent to the local near high tide. At this elevation, the net sedimentation rate approaches zero.

Gardner et al. (1989) analyzed a nearly continuous time series of organic and inorganic suspended sediment measurements taken daily over a period of about 5 yr at three sites in the North Inlet estuary. To assist in the interpretation of these data, they examined synchronous daily measurements of particulate organic carbon, water temperature, salinity, tide height, Secchi disk, air temperature, wind speed and direction, and rainfall. Using power spectrum analysis of these data, they found most of the explainable variance in the inorganic suspended sediment, particulate organic carbon, and Secchi disk data were related to a yearly cycle that was strongly coherent with water temperature such that high turbidity is associated with high water temperature. Only a small fraction of the explainable variance was associated with frequencies related to the semidiurnal tide. Simple correlation analysis indicated turbidity is more closely associated with water temperature than with tide height or salinity. From their results, Gardner et al. (1989) hypothesized that temperature-regulated bioturbation is the main factor controlling turbidity variations in the system. The lack of a strong inverse correlation between turbidity and salinity suggests river runoff has little immediate impact on the suspended sediment of nearshore coastal waters in ecological systems similar to North Inlet. They speculated this marsh-estuarine system acts like a lung, exhaling suspended sediment into the coastal ocean during the summer and inhaling it during the winter.

The significant variables controlling sediment concentration and transport were variability of freshwater discharge at the upstream boundary (Uncles 1983; Sharp et al. 1986; Williams 1989) and tidal forcing at the downstream boundary (Uncles 1983; Abraham 1988). These two factors produce gravitational circulation and salinity stratification within estuaries and can be related to the distribution of total suspended sediments (TSS) and the location of the turbidity maximum zone (TMZ). Recently Althausen and Kjerfve (1992), studying the turbidity maximum zone for the river-influenced Charleston Harbor and the Cooper River, South Carolina, reported a well-correlated relationship between TSS and light transmissivity. Based on this correlation, they found that the TMZ shifted upstream-downstream in response to tidal amplitude, tidal stage, and the phase of the moon. Net downstream transport of suspended sediment is largely a function of freshwater discharge. Over the tidal cycle, the TMZ shifts downstream during the ebb and upstream during the flood, suggesting that sediment particles from both marine and freshwater sources compose the TMZ.

For marshes to persist over time, given rising sea level, sediment deposition is important. However, as pointed out by Pillay et al. (1992), it is not easy to estimate deposition because certain problems exist in comparing results of various investigators. In general, along the East Coast, data support the observation that the relative rate of sea level is rising (Dardeau et al. 1992). In marshes without input from a river source, inorganic sediments would have to be deposited on marshes via tidal creeks from the ocean source; however, some measurements of net transport of suspended sediment have indicated export of sediment rather than import. These researchers suggest that this dilemma may result from the difficulty of measuring small residual transportal rates in tidal systems characterized by substantial spatial and temporal variation in velocity and concentration. Also, Chrzanowski et al. (1981) suggested that, in general, differences in material transport rates found in the literature may result from different techniques of sampling and/or standardized measurements. Using the extensive database for the Outwelling Project in North Inlet, South Carolina (Dame et al. 1986) and data from an intensive study at Kiawah Island (ward 1981), South Carolina, Pillay et al. (1992) compared three methods of computing sediment transport rates in tidal creeks: Method 1 calculated rates based on the area-integrated product of sediment concentration, velocity, and sample subarea (this is the most accurate method); Method 2 used the product of instantaneous channel cross-sectional area, cross-sectionally averaged velocity, and cross-sectionally averaged concentration; and Method 3 computed rates as the product of instantaneous discharge and sediment concentration at a single, near-surface, mid-channel sample location. At times logistical and financial constraints prohibit the use of the more rigorous Method 1. The difference between transport rates determined by methods 2 and 3 compared with those of Method 1 can be as large as 120%. Because these large differences occur at times of low Method 1 transport, linear regressions of Method 1 transport rates on those of Methods 2 or 3 yield correlation coefficients > 0.9. Hence, it may be possible to calculate tidal residual suspended sediment transport rates by correcting results obtained by methods 2 or 3 by regression analysis to give reliable estimates of the Method 1 transport rate.

Geological processes may also be altered by natural catastrophic events (hurricanes) or anthropogenic activities (dredge and fill). These alterations may profoundly influence salt marshes, often in unpredictable ways.

Physical Factors

Of vital importance to understanding the functioning of salt marshes is knowledge of the complex interactions of physical factors with the chemical, geological, and biotic components. The rhythmic pulsating action resulting from tidal changes represents an important energy subsidy to the salt marshes. Water alternately flows over the marsh and then ebbs, typically leaving the marsh surface exposed to an aerial environment. Sedimentation, chemical transport, temperature, salinity, light, and biotic distribution are just a few of the environmental factors influenced by water movement.

Circulation patterns in an estuarine-salt marsh system are influenced by wind, tidal action, freshwater input, and geomorphology. Depending on variations in the factors controlling circulation pattern, an estuary may exhibit all types of salinity regimes at some time. The type of salinity profile—vertically stratified, partially mixed, or homogeneous, in turn influences the vertical distribution of the biotic component, nutrients, and temperature, as well as the flux rate of materials between the ocean and an estuary.

Tidal amplitude varies temporally between neap and spring tides with the greatest amplitude between spring low tide and spring high tides. In addition, increased wind velocity can result in greater tidal changes depending on the wind direction in reference to the orientation of an estuary. Kjerfve et al. (1978) reported that water level changes can occur on time scales of weeks to seasons. The biotic impact of these anomalies in mean sea level (MSL) can influence ecosystem dynamics as demonstrated by Morris et al. (1990). They found that, if this transitory elevation in MSL occurs during the growing season, the annual aboveground productivity of *Spartina* increased by a factor of two and that the commercial landings of two estuarine-dependent species (shrimp and menhaden) were positively correlated with sea-level anomalies. These investigators postulated that the increased MSL caused more of the marsh to be covered by tidal waters and the pore-water salinity to be lowered in the higher elevations of the marsh. The decrease in salinity stimulated primary production of *Spartina* and the increased amount of submerged marsh vegetation provided more habitat area for organisms dependent on marsh for food and predator avoidance.

Physical factors influence the salinity of water bathing salt marshes. The salinity of surface and soil water varies depending on a number of factors, including rainfall; freshwater inputs from surface runoff from adjacent uplands, groundwater influx, and rivers and streams; extent and frequency of tidal flooding; evapotranspiration; soil type; and vegetation. If the salinity remains below 5‰, the salt marsh vegetation is typically replaced by freshwater species. High temperatures can increase evaporation of water from shallow water pools and upper portions of the intertidal zone, resulting in salinities higher than that of seawater. These fluctuations in salinity have influenced markedly estuarine biota. Some species are tolerant of a wide range of salinity (euryhalinic) while others have a narrow salinity range (stenohalinic) and die if subjected to a changed salinity for too long. Organisms sensitive to hyposaline or hypersaline waters avoid these conditions by behavioral mechanisms. Mobile species swim away while sessile organisms avoid direct contact with adverse conditions by walling themselves away from the external environment (i.e., clams, oysters, and barnacles close their shells).

Temperature not only directly affects the physiological mechanism of the biota but also interacts with other abiotic factors. It differentially influences the density of seawater, the concentration of dissolved oxygen, hydraulic conductivity, and the rate of chemical reactions.

Chemical Factors

Salt marshes and the overlaying water column represent a complex chemical environment influencing the associated biota. The chemical composition of the water column and the salt marsh varies temporally over intervals ranging from seconds to years depending on the chemical compounds and the processes under study. Tidal cycles, atmospheric deposition, and riverine inputs of fresh water greatly influence chemical dynamics. Various investigators have studied the dynamics of chemical changes in the water column and in salt marsh soils, as well as the exchange of materials between the water column and the salt marsh surface. Recently the importance of atmospheric exchanges with salt marshes-estuaries has been emphasized (Morris 1991). Previously this type of exchange was poorly understood and exchanges between the water and the marsh were thought to be the major (only) exchange pathway. In addition, the extensive vegetation associated with salt marshes plays an integral role in changes in chemical substances (Morris 1988).

Oxygen concentrations of the water column associated with salt marshes vary greatly, ranging from anoxic to supersaturated. The photosynthetic activity of the vegetation results in the addition of oxygen, and to a lesser extent, oxygen is added by diffusion from the atmosphere, tidal exchanges, and turbulence of the water.

Typically surface waters are saturated with oxygen throughout the year while oxygen concentrations at various depths depends on vertical mixing. In many regions, one of the indicators of water quality is oxygen concentration, low values indicate waters of poor quality and subject to regulatory action. However, even in salt marshes unaffected by human perturbation, oxygen concentrations may drop below acceptable limits, especially at low tide and periods of low photosynthetic activity. This suggests that low oxygen concentration is a normal phenomenon in certain salt marsh areas and may not be a good indicator of human degrading of water quality (Vernberg et al. 1992).

Important to the functioning of the salt marsh-estuarine ecosystem is the availability of nutrients. The sources of nutrients are from runoff from terrestrial systems to river systems and adjacent highlands and from oceanic waters. Nutrients occur both as organic compounds—dissolved organic matter (DOM), dissolved organic carbon (DOC), particulate organic matter (POM), and particulate organic carbon (POC)—and as inorganic compounds and/or elements—nitrites, nitrates, ammonia, phosphates, and other substances. These nutrients are utilized and chemically altered by the salt marsh-estuarine biota, resulting in a very dynamic system. The dynamics of biogeochemical cycling are discussed in more detail later in this paper.

The quantity of available nutrients, especially carbon, phosphorous, and nitrogen influence various biotic components of the ecosystem. In general, nitrogen is important as a potential nutrient-limiting factor, phosphorous is limiting sometimes, and carbon is almost never limiting. On the other hand, excess nutrient concentrations alter system dynamics by stimulating biomass production, especially primary producers, a process known as eutrophication.

By virtue of their location where the ocean meets large river systems, salt marshes-estuaries are exposed to other chemical substances (many are toxic), such as effluents and storm water inputs, carried by upland runoff into rivers or introduced directly into estuaries from human activities associated with estuaries.

Biological Components of Salt Marshes

The biology of salt marshes has been extensively studied using various approaches. Taxonomic studies have focused on describing the interrelationship of the various biotic groups in marshes. Several of these studies include a listing of various species found in southeastern estuaries and their habitat preferences (Zingmark 1978; Gosselink 1984; Kneib 1984; Fox and Ruppert 1985; Ogburn et al. 1988; Ruppert and Fox 1988; Eleuterius 1990). Another approach is to study the ecology and life history of a single species. The literature on this subject is too voluminous to be included in the present paper; however, in addition to the references on southeastern estuaries listed above, Remane and Schlieper (1971), Vernberg and Vernberg (1972), McLusky (1981), and Hackney et al. (1992) summarize a representative number of species-oriented studies. A third approach is to study the functional adaptations of the biota to the environmentally stressful life encountered in the marsh-estuarine system. A few references which summarize adaptation studies follow: Newell (1970),

Schlieper (1971), Vernberg and Vernberg (1972), Vernberg (1975), Gilles (1979), Vernberg and Vernberg (1981), and Pandian and Vernberg (1987).

Rather than emphasizing the ecology, physiology, or taxonomy of one or a few species, another approach is to view the salt marsh-estuary as an ecosystem and group the various species into broader functional and structural units, such as primary producers, secondary producers, and decomposers. Obviously there is overlap among these different approaches. For example, a study of the control of primary production of *Spartina alterniflora* could be classified as a study of a single species but since this species is so dominant in southeastern salt marshes the results are important to understanding ecosystem dynamics. Because of the interaction and the interconnectiveness of the various salt marsh-estuarine species with the abiotic environment, any attempt to develop sustainable development models must consider the results of the various approaches used to study this dynamic coastal environment. The following overview briefly highlights the results of some ecosystem level studies involving primary production, secondary production, decomposition, and biochemical cycling.

Primary Production

Within the marsh-estuarine system, total primary production is the sum of the production of several groups of organisms: phytoplankton, epibenthic algae, attached macrophytes, and vascular plants. Table 1, representing the contributions of these various components to the annual net primary production of an extensively studied estuary, the North Inlet estuary system, South Carolina, illustrates this point. Reviews of estuarine primary production summarize much of the literature on this subject (Keefe 1972; Turner 1976; Pomeroy et al. 1981; Dardeau et al. 1992; Vernberg 1993).

The contribution to the primary production of marshes by *Spartina alterniflora*, a dominant plant species in the marshes of the southeastern United States, has been extensively studied (see reviews cited above for details) and seasonal, interannual, and geographical differences have been reported. For example, Dame and Kenny (1986) determined total primary production (aboveground and belowground production) of *Spartina* in the North Inlet estuarine system from different sites over a 4-yr period. Aboveground live biomass was most abundant in late summer and early fall. The creekside site exhibited the highest aboveground primary production, the next highest values were recorded for *Spartina* in the high marsh, and the lowest values for plants in the mid marsh.

Interannual variation was observed with the creekside plants showing the greatest degree of variability, a response which appears to be correlated with increased rainfall. Other environmental factors have been shown to influence *Spartina* primary production, including salinity, nutrient availability, temperature, light, frequency of flooding, species competition, and environmental perturbations by humans (pollutants, dredging, habitat modification).

The different values found for *Spartina* primary production from estuaries ranging from North Carolina to Louisiana have been compared (Dardeau et al. 1992). However, Dame and Kenny (1986) and Kaswadji et al. (1990) stress the difficulty in comparing production values of estuaries because of the differences in sampling techniques and differences in local environmental conditions. In spite of variation in production numbers, salt marshes are considered one of the most productive habitats in the world.

The epibenthic microalgae, composed primarily of motile pennate diatoms inhabiting the upper few millimeters of sediments, also contribute significantly to the primary production of salt marshes. Earlier Pomeroy et al. (1981) reported that these organisms accounted for 25-33% of aboveground

Table 1. North Inlet estuarine system estimated net annual primary production showing the contributions by the various producers (Vernberg 1989).

	Annual net primary production (g C m^{-2} yr^{-1})	Percentage of net primary production
Spartina plant community	400	40
Macroalgae	200	20
Microphytobenthos	200	20
Phytoplankton	100	10
Epiphytes and neuston	100	10
Totals	1,000	100

macrophyte productivity in East Coast estuaries. Sullivan and Moncreiff (1988a,b), working in an estuary in Mississippi, identified 155 diatom taxa in 30 genera and determined values for both species diversity and distribution in a marsh. Using canonical correlation analysis, these researchers collapsed the complex database into two interpretable, orthogonal dimensions and identified edaphic algal production, chlorophyll *a*, and soil moisture as potentially related to the distribution of diatoms within the marsh. They were also able to highlight the importance of edaphic algae using carbon, sulfur, and nitrogen stable isotope ratios to compare the relative importance of vascular plants and algae in estuarine food webs (Sullivan and Moncreiff 1990). Pinckney and Zingmark (1991) found that benthic diatoms exhibited vertical migration which was influenced by tidal and light cycles. Microalgal production at low tide was twice that at high tide and was significantly correlated with diurnal and tidal periodicities.

Although not uniformly found in salt marshes throughout the world, Durako and Dawes (1980), Coutinho et al. (1982), Coutinho and Zingmark (1985), and Pregnall and Rudy (1985) have emphasized the role of macroalgae in the annual productivity of estuaries. However, compared with phytoplankton and epibenthic microalgae, attached macrophytes have not been extensively studied. Of the more detailed studies, the work of Coutinho (1987) and Coutinho and Zingmark (1987, 1993) provides data highlighting the energetic importance of macroalgae in systems dynamics. They developed a model to calculate annual macroalgae production based on relationships of photosynthesis versus irradiance, tidal variability, light attenuation, and distribution of algal biomass by depth. They found that most of the macroalga production occurred between December and April. The amount of production was about the same as the annual phytoplankton production in the study estuary, North Inlet. Macroalgae represent the most important source of carbon for herbivores in this estuary during winter, when other plant productivity is seasonally depressed.

Although well represented in marsh-estuarine systems in terms of high species diversity but low biomass, the significance of phytoplankton in the annual production budget of this system is not well known. Based on values for a number of estuaries, phytoplankton production is low compared to other primary producers: 6% of the total production in the Duplin River estuary and in Daboy Sound, Georgia (Whitney et al. 1981) and 10% in North Inlet, South Carolina (Vernberg 1993).

Although primary production is important in systems dynamics of southeastern marsh-estuaries, bacterially rich detritus is believed to be the principal food source for many of the animals found here. However, having multiple sources of food available has resulted in a variety of feeding preferences and mechanisms by marsh animals and in complex food webs. This could be of particular significance since detritus tends to be available throughout the year while the primary production values generally decline during colder seasons. This diversity in food availability and abundance of food could explain why marshes provide an excellent habitat for the many oceanic species which invade marshes on a temporary basis as well as an ideal habitat for resident animals.

Secondary Producers

PRIMARY CONSUMERS

A variety of feeding mechanisms allow many organisms to feed directly on primary producers. Suspension feeding is common in zooplankton and benthic species, especially sessile macroinvertebrates such as oysters. Dame and his co-workers (1984) reported that an oyster reef not only functions as a biological filter removing materials from the water but also is important in processing some materials by transforming them. Herbivorous insects particularly feed on marsh vascular plants. For example, Davis (1978) listed over 600 species of insects expected to occur in maritime environments in the southeastern United States. Deposit-feeding bivalves feed on microalgae and have been shown to create patchiness in microalgae distribution (Page et al. 1992). In general, it appears that the high levels of production for primary consumers supports a high level of secondary producers.

SECONDARY CONSUMERS

Conspicuous in marsh-estuarine systems are the numerous and varied types of secondary consumers. To the general public it is this group of animals which attract their attention for recreational, esthetic, and commercial reasons. For example, about 90% of the fishery landings on the Southeast and Gulf coasts involve species that spend some portion of their lives in an estuary (Gunter et al. 1974). However, as pointed out earlier, without sufficient representation of the other components of an ecosystem, the population levels of secondary consumers would be greatly diminished. The literature on secondary production in estuaries is too voluminous to review in this paper; however, some general comments are in order.

With numerous transient and resident species utilizing the marshes, complex food webs have evolved which attempt to maximize the utilization of available food sources. There is not only intraspecific but complex interspecific interactions for space and food. All sizes of food particles are used by carnivores, omnivores, and detritivores. The food preferences for a given species may vary with its body size: the young of a species may be a filter feeder, utilizing small-sized particles, while the adult may be carnivorous, feeding on large-size prey. Trophic dynamics are not only governed by biotic factors (competition, body size, physiological needs) but by abiotic factors such as temperature, salinity, oxygen concentration, water currents, tidal flooding, light (see *Animal Energetics* by Pandian and Vernberg 1987, for a detailed review of primary and secondary consumer production).

DECOMPOSERS

To utilize detritus as a food source, it must be broken down (decomposed) into smaller-sized particles. This process is accomplished by mechanical means by animals and by functional activity of bacteria, fungi, and protozoa. Microorganisms not only process detrital material but they serve as vital links to higher trophic levels. A variety of mechanical techniques have evolved to assist in the decomposition process. For example, gastropods use a radula to rasp and shred detritus, crustaceans use gastric mills, and fish have gizzard-like organs. Various studies have investigated decomposition of marsh vegetation (see reviews by Pomeroy and Wiegert 1981; Mitsch and Gosselink 1986; Vernberg 1993).

Some recent studies demonstrate the importance of decomposition processes to the functioning of estuarine systems. Newell and Barlocher (1993) reported that a marsh snail, *Littorina irrorata*, ingested dead shoot particles of *Spartina* and enzymatically broke down these particles and associated fungi. Using litter bags placed on the surface and some placed 10 cm below ground, Pozo and Colino (1992) found higher breakdown rates of *Spartina* in those samples that were maintained at the surface. They suggested that low faunal richness and densities below ground reflected the unfavorable life conditions existing there. After 10 mo of decomposition in seawater, fragments of fresh or dead *Spartina* yielded appreciable amounts of humic substances (Filip and Alberts 1989). These authors calculated a potential annual input similar to 330 kg of fresh *Spartina*-related humic substances per hectare of salt marsh. Moran and Hodson (1990) reported that the bulk DOC pool in salt marsh environments increased as *Spartina* lignocellulose degrades. DOC accounted for 50% to 60% of the total degradation products of the lignin fraction of lignocellulose when determined using radiolabeled *Spartina* lignocellulose during an initial 6 mo of decomposition. By contrast, only 20% to 30% of the polysaccharide portion of *Spartina* lignocellulose accumulated as DOC during decomposition.

Biogeochemical Cycling

Biogeochemical cycling of such important nutrients as phosphorus, nitrogen, carbon, and sulfur has been studied extensively. Nutrients are in a constant state of flux, being changed from one form to another and being located in different components of the ecosystem. Nutrients may be translocated from one area of an estuary to another. For example, Whiting and Childers (1989) reported that important amounts of inorganic nutrients (NH_4 and PO_4) were added to the overlying creek water by the process of advective movement of interstitial water from subtidal creek sediments. In addition, Spurrier and Kjerfve (1988) estimated that on an annual basis the marsh was a statistically significant sink for nitrogen from adjacent tidal creeks. The biochemical processes in transformation of various nutrients demonstrate the complexity of these various chemical reactions. Because nutrients are imported to estuaries from riverine systems and terrestrial runoff, the dynamics of increased nutrient inputs on the productivity of marsh-estuaries is of concern (see Valiela 1992; Weinstein 1996). Input can also come from oceanic water (Dame et al. 1986). Biogeochemical cycles can vary in complexity for different nutrients. For example, Whitney et al. (1981) reported that the nitrogen cycle is more complex than for phosphorus. A review by Morris (1991) synthesized the results in the literature of the consequences of nitrogen loading on marshes, especially the importance of atmospheric deposition. Cycling activity associated with one chemical substance can influence other nutrient cycles. For example, Webb (1981) found that sulfur dynamics can mobilize sediment phosphate to diffuse from anoxic sediments to oxic sediments and the water column. A detailed paper by Gardner and Lerche (1990) reviewed the extensive literature on sulfur diagenesis in marine sediments and proposed a simulation model. The cycling of carbon is important to the energetics of a marsh and is influenced by biotic and abiotic factors. To interpret some of these interactions, Gardner (1990) developed a steady-state numerical model for simulating vertical profile of the concentration of organic matter, pyritic sulfur, dissolved oxygen, and the carbon isotope composition of organic matter in marsh sediments. Morris (1988) presented a review paper on the pathways and controls of the carbon cycles in salt marshes, a topic of importance when considering management of coastal regions.

Modeling

In recent years an increasing interest in developing models of salt marsh processes, ranging in scale from microbes to landscapes, has taken place. Earlier Teal (1962) and Weigert et al. (1981), respectively, proposed an energy flow model and a simulation model. Major ecological modeling efforts have focused on Louisiana marshes (Hopkinson and Day 1977; Scaife et al. 1983; Deegan et al. 1984; Hopkinson and Day 1988; Boumans and Sklar 1990).

Along the Southeast coast, modeling of the dynamics of North Inlet estuary, South Carolina, started in 1974 (Vernberg et al. 1977, 1978) with the development of conceptual models. Since then various models of the entire system and subsystems have been published: subsystem coupling and carbon exchange (Summers and McKellar 1979; Summers et al. 1980; Summers and McKellar 1981a,b); intertidal oyster reef (Dame and Patten 1981; Dame et al 1984); water-column dynamics (Childers and McKellar 1987); and the geohydrologic continuum theory for the spatial and temporal evolution of marsh-estuarine ecosystems, including North Inlet (Dame et al. 1992). An example of a model, energy flow in the salt-marsh ecosystem, is shown in Fig. 2.

Summary

Saltwater marshes are a dominant feature of the southeastern coastal landscape. Not only is the areal extent of these marshes great, but they play a significant role in the ecology of estuaries and coastal waters. Due to the dominant vascular plant, *Spartina*, and the attendant other plants, salt marshes are one of the most productive habitats in the world. Associated with the richness and abundance of food found in marsh-estuarine system are the many animal species utilize this system on either a temporary or permanent basis. About 90% of the commercial fishery landings in the Southeast include species that spend a portion of their life cycle in estuaries.

Salt marshes are exposed to marked fluctuations in biotic and abiotic factors since they are exposed alternately to aerial and aquatic conditions depending upon such factors as tides, winds, and rainfall. The biotic structure of this habitat fluctuates and represents a complex series of food webs and biogeochemical cycles.

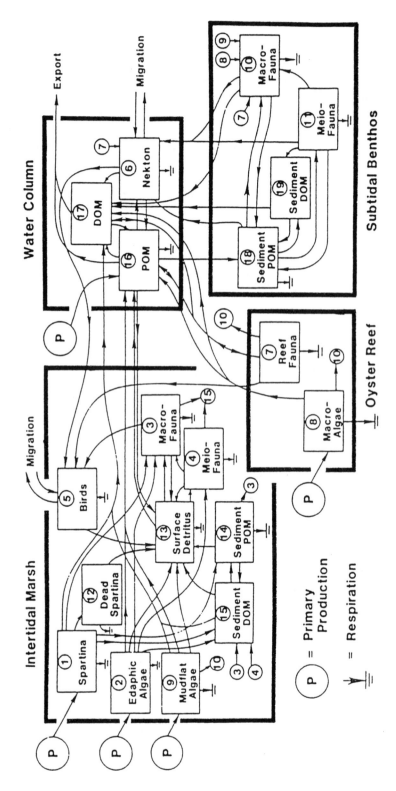

Fig. 2. Energy flow in the North Inlet salt marsh ecosystem (figure from Asmus and McKellar 1990, reprinted with permission).

Because of their close association with estuarine and riverine water, which are subjected to human perturbations, salt marshes are subjected to various activities by human populations. To understand how unperturbed marshes function is imperative in order to develop environmentally sensitive management plans that are compatible with sustainable development.

LITERATURE CITED

Althausen, J.D., Jr. and B. Kjerfve. 1992. Distribution of suspended sediment in a partially mixed estuary, Charleston Harbor, South Carolina. *Estuarine, Coastal and Shelf Science* 35: 517-531.

Asmus, M.L. and H.N. McKellar, Jr. 1990. Network analysis of the North Inlet salt marsh ecosystem, p. 206-219. *In* J. Wulff, J.G. Field, and K.H. Mann (eds.), Network Analysis in Marine Ecology. Methods and Applications. Coastal and Estuarine Studies Series, Springer-Verlag, Berlin.

Boumans, R.M.J. and F.H. Sklar. 1990. A polygon-based spatial (PBS) model for simulating landscape change. *Landscape Ecology* 4: 83-97.

Chapman, V.J. 1974. Salt marshes and salt deserts of the world, p 3-19. *In* R.J. Reimold and W.H. Queen (eds.), Ecology of Halophytes. Academic Press, New York.

Childers, D.L. and H.N. McKellar, Jr. 1987. A simulation of salt marsh water column dynamics. *Ecological Modeling* 36: 211-238.

Chrzanowski, T.H., L.H. Stevenson, and B. Kjerfve. 1981. Variability in total microbial biomass measurements made in cross sections of salt marsh creeks. *Marine Geology* 40: 155-170.

Coutinho, R. and R. Zingmark. 1985. Macroalgal productivity in a salt marsh estuarine system. Second International Phycological Congress, Copenhagen, Abs.

Coutinho, R., N.B. Baptista, and U. Seeliger. 1982. Field and culture studies on selected green algae of the Patos Lagoon Estuary. International Symposium of Coastal Ecosystem: Planning, Pollution and Productivity. Rio Grande, Brazil, Abstract

Coutinho, R. 1987. Ecology of macroalgae in North Inlet estuary, SC. Ph.D. dissertation, University of South Carolina, Columbia, South Carolina.

Coutinho, R. and R. Zingmark. 1987. Diurnal photosynthetic response to light by macroalgae. *Journal of Phycology* 23: 336-343.

Coutinho, R. and R.G. Zingmark. 1993. Interactions of light and nitrogen on photosynthesis and growth of the marine macroalga *Ulva curvata* (Kutzing) De Toni. *Journal of Experimental Marine Biology and Ecology* 167:11-20.

Dame, R., D. Childers, and E. Koepfler. 1992. A geohydrologic continuum theory for the spatial and temporal evolution of marsh-estuarine ecosystems. *Netherlands Journal of Sea Research.* 30: 63-72.

Dame, R.T., T. Chrzanowski, K. Bildstein, B. Kjerfve, H. McKellar, D. Nelson, J. Spurrier, S. Stancyk, H. Stevenson, F. Vernberg, and R. Zingmark. 1986. The outwelling hypothesis and North Inlet, South Carolina. *Marine Ecology Progress Series* 33: 217-229.

Dame, R.F. and P.D. Kenny. 1986. Variability of *Spartina alterniflora* primary production in the euhaline North Inlet estuary. *Marine Ecology Progress Series* 32: 70-80.

Dame, R. and B. Patten. 1981. Analysis of energy flows in an intertidal oyster reef. *Marine Ecology Progress Series* 5: 115-124.

Dame, R.F., R.G. Zingmark, and E. Haskin. 1984. Oyster reefs as processors of estuarine materials. *Journal of Experimental Marine Biology and Ecology* 83: 239-247.

Dardeau, M.R., R.F. Modlin, W.W. Schroeder, and J.P. Stout. 1992. Estuaries, p. 615-744. *In* C.T. Hackney, S., M. Adams, and W.H. Martin (eds.), Biodiversity of the Southeastern United States. John Wiley and Sons, Inc., New York.

Davis, L.V. 1978. Class Insecta, p. 186-220. *In* R.G. Zingmark (ed.), An Annotated Checklist of the Biota of the Coastal Zone of South Carolina. University of South Carolina, Columbia, South Carolina.

Deegan, L.A., W.H. Kennedy, and C. Neill. 1984. Natural factors and human modification contributing to marsh loss in Louisiana's Mississippi River deltaic plain. *Environmental Management* 8: 519-528.

Durako, M.J. and C.J. Dawes. 1980. A comparative study of two populations of *Hypnea musciformis* from the east and west coasts of Florida, USA. II. Photosynthetic and respiratory rates. *Marine Biology* (Berlin) 59:157-162.

Eleuterius, L.N. (ed.). 1990. Tidal Marsh Plants. Pelican Publishing Company, Gretna, Louisiana.

Filip, Z. and J.J. Alberts. 1989. Humic substances isolated from *Spartina alterniflora* (Loisel) following long-term decomposition in sea water. *Science of the Total Environment* 83: 273-285.

Fleesa, K.W., K.J. Constantine, and M.K. Kushman. 1977. Sedimentation rates in a coastal marsh determined from historical records. *Chesapeake Science* 18: 172-176.

Fox, R.S. and E.E. Ruppert (eds). 1985. Shallow-Water Marine Benthic Macroinvertebrates of South Carolina: Species Identification, Community Composition and Symbiotic Associations. Belle W. Baruch Library in Marine Science, No. 14. University of South Carolina Press, Columbia, South Carolina.

Gardner, R.G. 1990. Simulation of the diagenesis of carbon, sulfur, and dissolved oxygen in salt marsh sediments. *Ecological Monographs* 60: 91-111.

Gardner, L.R., L. Thombs, D. Edwards, and D. Nelson. 1989. Time series analyses of suspended sediment concentrations at North Inlet, South Carolina. *Estuaries* 12: 211-221.

Gardner, L.R. and I. Lerche. 1990. Simulation of sulfur diagenesis in anoxic marine sediments using Rickard kinetics for FeS and FeS_2 formation. *Computers and Geosciences* 16: 441-460.

Gilles, R. (ed). 1979. Mechanisms of Osmoregulation in Animals. John Wiley & Sons, New York.

Gosselink, J.G. 1984. The ecology of delta marshes of coastal Louisiana: A community profile. United States Fish and Wildlife Service Office, Technical Report FWS/OBS/84-09:1-134.

Gosselink, J.G. and R.H. Baumann. 1980. Wetland inventories: Wetland loss along the United States coast. *Geomorphology* Suppl. (N.S.) 34: 173-187.

Gunter, G., B.S. Ballard, and A. Venkataramiah. 1974. A review of salinity problems of organisms in United States coastal areas subject to the effects of engineering works. *Gulf Research Report* 4: 380-475.

Hackney, C.T., S.M. Adams, and W.H. Martin (eds.). 1992. Biodiversity of the Southeastern United States. Aquatic Communities. John Wiley & Sons, Inc.

Hopkinson, C.S. and J.W. Day, Jr. 1977. A model of the Barataria Bay salt marsh ecosystem, p. 235-266. *In* C.A.S. Hall and J.W. Day, (eds.), Ecosystem Modeling in Theory and Practice. Wiley (Interscience), New York.

Hopkinson, C.S. and J.W. Day, Jr. 1988. Models of coastal wetland and estuarine systems, p. 235-266. *In* W. Mitsch, M. Straskraba, and S. Jorgensen (eds.), Wetland Modeling. Elsevier, New York.

Kaswadji, R.F., J.G. Gosselink, and R.E. Turner. 1990. Estimation of primary production using five different methods in a *Spartina alterniflora* salt marsh. *Wetlands Ecological Management* 1: 57-64.

Keefe, W. 1972. Marsh production: A summary of the literature. *Contributions in Marine Sci*ence 16: 163-181.

Kjerfve, B., J.E. Greer, and L.R. Crout. 1978. Low frequency response of estuarine sea level to non-local forcing. *In* M.L. Wiley (ed.), Estuarine Interactions. Academic Press, New York,

Kneib. R.T. 1984. Patterns of invertebrate distribution and abundance in the intertidal salt marsh: causes and questions. *Estuaries* 7: 392-412.

Mitsch, W.J. and J.G. Gosselink (eds.). 1986. Wetlands. Van Nostrand Reinhold Company Inc., New York.

Moran, M.A. and R.E. Hodson. 1990. Contributions of degrading *Spartina alterniflora* lignocellulose to the dissolved organic carbon pool of a salt marsh. *Marine Ecology Progress Series* 62(1-2): 161-168.

Morris, J.T. 1988. Pathways and controls of the carbon cycle in salt marshes, p. 497-510. *In* D.D. Hook, W.H. McKee, Jr., H.K. Smith, J. Gregory, V.G. Burrell, Jr., M.R. DeVoe, R.E. Sojka, S. Gilbert, R. Banks, L.H. Stolzy, C. Brooks, T.D. Matthews, and T.H. Shear (eds.), The Ecology and Management of Wetlands, Vol. 1: Ecology of Wetlands. Croom Helm, London.

Morris, J.T. 1991. Effects of nitrogen loading on wetland ecosystems with particular reference to atmospheric deposition. *Annual Review of Ecology and Syst*ematics 22: 257-79.

Morris, J.T., B. Kjerfve, and J.M. Dean. 1990. Dependence of estuarine productivity on anomalies in mean sea level. *Limnology and Oceanography* 35(4): 926-930.

McLusky, D.S. (ed.). 1981. Tertiary Level Biology. The Estuarine Ecosystem. Halsted Press, New York.

Newell, R.C. (ed.). 1970. Biology of Intertidal Animals. American Elsevier Publishing Company, Inc., New York.

Newell, S.Y. and F. Barlocher. 1993. Removal of fungal and total organic matter from decaying cordgrass leaves by shredder snails. *Journal of Experimental Marine Biology and Ecology* 171: 39-49.

Ogburn, M.V., D.M. Allen, and W.K. Michener (eds.). 1988. Fishes, Shrimps, and Crabs of the North Inlet Estuary, SC: A Four-Year Seine and Trawl Survey. Baruch Institute Technical Report No. 88-1. Belle W. Baruch Institute, University of South Carolina, Columbia.

Page, H.M., J.E. Dugan, and D.M. Hubbard. 1992. Comparative effects of infaunal bivalves on an epibenthic microalgal community. *Journal of Experimental Marine Biology and Ecology* 157: 247-262.

Pandian, T.J. and F.J. Vernberg (eds.). 1987. Animal Energetics. Vol. 1. Protozoa through Insecta. Vol. 2. Bivalvia through Reptilia. Academic Press, New York.

Pillay, S., L.R. Gardner, and B. Kjerfve. 1992. The effect of cross-sectional velocity and concentration variations on suspended sediment transport rates in tidal creeks. *Estuarine, Coastal and Shelf Science* 35: 331-345.

Pinckney, J. and R.G. Zingmark. 1991. Effects of tidal stage and sun angles on intertidal benthic microalgal productivity. *Marine Ecology Progress Series* 76: 81-89.

Pomeroy, L.R., W.M. Darley, E.L. Dunn, J.L. Gallagher, E.B. Haines, and D.M. Whitney. 1981. Primary production, p. 39-67. *In* L.R. Pomeroy and R.G. Wiegert (eds.), The Ecology of a Salt Marsh. Springer-Verlag, New York.

Pomeroy, L.R. and R.G. Wiegert (eds.). 1981. The Ecology of a Salt Marsh. Springer Verlag, New York.

Pozo, J. and R. Colino. 1992. Decomposition processes of *Spartina maritima* in a salt marsh of the Basque Country. *Hydrobiologia* 231: 165-175.

Pregnall, A.M. and P.P. Rudy. 1985. Contribution of green macroalgal mats (*Enteromorpha* sp.) to seasonal production in an estuary. *Marine Ecology Progress Series* 24: 167-76.

Pritchard, D.W. 1967. What is an estuary: Physical viewpoint, p. 3-5. *In* G.H. Lauff (ed.), Estuaries. A.A.A.S. Publ. No. 83, Washington, D.C.

Redfield, A.C. 1972. Development of a New England salt marsh. *Ecological Monographs*. 42: 201-237.

Remane, A. and C. Schlieper (eds.). 1971. Biology of Brackish Water. Wiley Interscience Division, John Wiley & Sons, Inc., New York.

Ruppert, E.E. and R.S. Fox (eds.). 1988. Seashore Animals of the Southeast. University of South Carolina Press, Columbia, South Carolina.

Scaife, W.W., R.E. Turner, and R. Costanza. 1983. Coastal Louisiana recent land loss and canal impacts. *Environmental Management* 7(5): 433-442.

Schlieper, C. 1991. Physiology of brackish water, p. 211-323. *In* A. Remane and C. Schlieper (eds.), Biology of Brackish Water. University of South Carolina Press, Columbia, South Carolina.

Sharma, P., L.T. Gardner, W.S. Moore, and M.S. Bollinger. 1987. Sedimentation and bioturbation in a salt marsh as revealed by ^{210}Pb, ^{137}Cs and ^{7}Bi studies. *Limnology and Oceanography* 32: 313-326.

Sharp, J.H., L.A. Cifuentes, R.B. Coffin, J.R. Pennock, and K.C. Wong. 1986. The influence of river variability on the circulation, chemistry and microbiology of the Delaware estuary. *Estuaries* 9: 271-282.

Spurrier, J.D. and B. Kjerfve. 1988. Estimating the net flux of nutrients between a salt marsh and a tidal creek. *Estuaries* 11: 10-14.

Sullivan, M.J. and C.A. Moncreiff. 1988. Primary production of edaphic algal communities in a Mississippi salt marsh. *Journal of Phycology* 24: 49-58.

Sullivan, M.J. and C.A. Moncreiff. 1988. A multivariate analysis of diatom community structure and distribution in a Mississippi salt marsh. *Botanica Marina* 31: 93-99.

Summers, J.K. and H.N. McKellar, Jr. 1979. A simulation model of estuarine subsystem coupling and carbon exchange with the sea. I. Model structure, p. 323-366. *In* S.E. Jorgensen (eds.), State-of-the-art-in Ecological Modelling. International Society for Ecological Modelling, Copenhagen.

Summers, J.K. and H.N. McKellar, Jr. 1981a. The role of physical forcing functions in an estuarine model of carbon exchange with the sea. *ISEM Journal* 3:71-101.

Summers, J.K. and H.N. McKellar, Jr. 1981b. A sensitivity analysis of an ecosystem model of estuarine carbon flow. *Ecological Modeling* 13: 282-301.

Summers, J.K, H.N. McKellar, Jr., R.F. Dame, and W.M. Kitchens. 1980. A simulation model of estuarine subsystem coupling and carbon exchange with the sea. II. North Inlet model structure, output and validation. *Ecological Modeling* 11: 101-140.

Teal, J.M. 1962. Energy flow in the salt marsh ecosystem of Georgia. *Ecology* 43: 614-624.

Turner, R.E. 1976. Geographic variations in salt marsh macrophyte production: A review. *Contributions in Marine Science* 20: 47-68.

Uncles, R.J. 1983. Modeling tidal stress, circulation and mixing in the Bristol Channel as a prerequisite for ecosystem studies. *Canadian Journal of Fisheries and Aquatic Sciences* 40: 8-19.

Valiela, I. (ed.). 1992. Couplings Between Watersheds and Coastal Waters. Fifth International Congress of Ecology (NTECOL). *Estuaries* 15(4).

Vernberg, F.J. (ed.). 1975. Physiological Ecology of Estuarine Organisms. Belle W. Baruch Library in Marine Science, No 3. University of South Carolina Press, Columbia, South Carolina.

Vernberg, F.J. 1989. Long-term ecological research on the North Inlet forest–wetlands–marine landscape, Georgetown, SC, p. 53-76. *In* Barrier Island/Salt marsh Estuaries, Southeast Atlantic Coast: Issues, Resources, Status, and Management. NOAA Estuary-of-the-Month Seminar Series No. 12. U.S. Department of Commerce, Washington, D.C.

Vernberg, F.J. 1993. Salt marsh processes: A review. *Environmental Toxicology and Chemistry* 12(12): 2167-2195.

Vernberg, F.J., R. Bonnell, B.C. Coull, R.F. Dame. P. DeCoursey, W. Kitchens, B. Kjerfve, L.H. Stevenson, W.B. Vernberg and R. Zingmark. 1977. The Dynamics of an Estuary as a Natural Ecosystem. Part I. United States Environmental Protection Agency Technical Report EPA-600/3077-016. Gulf Breeze, Florida.

Vernberg, F.J., W. Kitchens, H.N. McKellar, Jr., J.K. Summers, and R. Bonnell. 1978. The Dynamics of an Estuary as a Natural Ecosystem, Part II. United States Environmental Protection Agency Technical Report EPA-600/3-78-092.

Vernberg, F.J. and W.B. Vernberg (eds.). 1981. Functional Adaptations of Marine Organisms. Academic Press, New York.

Vernberg, F.J., W.B. Vernberg, E. Blood, A. Fortner, M. Fulton, H. McKellar, W. Michener, G. Scott, T. Siewicki, and K. El-Figi. 1992. Impact of Urbanization on high salinity estuaries in the southeastern United States. *Netherlands Journal of Sea Research*. Vol. 30, pp. 239-248.

Vernberg, W.B. and F.J. Vernberg (eds.). 1972. Environmental Physiology of Marine Animals. Springer-Verlag, New York.

Ward, L.G. 1981. Suspended material transport in marsh tidal channels, Kiawah Island, South Carolina. *Marine Geology*. 40: 139-154.

Webb, K.L. 1981. Conceptual models and processes of nutrient cycling in estuaries, p. 25-46. *In* B.J. Nielson and L.E. Cronin (eds.), Estuaries and Nutrients. Humana Press, Clifton, New Jersey.

Weinstein, J.E. 1996. Anthropogenic Impacts on Salt Marshes—A Review, p. 135-170. *In* Vernberg, F.J., W.B. Vernberg, and T. Siewicki (eds.), Urbanization of Southeastern Estuaries. University of South Carolina Press, Columbia, South Carolina.

Whiting, G.J. and D.L. Childers. 1989. Subtidal advective water flux as a potentially important nutrient input to southeastern U.S.A. salt marsh estuaries. *Estuarine, Coastal and Shelf Science*. 28: 417-431.

Whitney, D.M., A.G. Chalmers, E.G. Haines, R.B. Hanson, L.R. Pomeroy, and B. Sherr. 1981. The cycles of nitrogen and phosphorus, p. 164-181. *In* L.R. Pomeroy and R.G. Wiegert (eds.), The Ecology of a Salt Marsh. Springer-Verlag, New York.

Wiegert, R.G., R.R. Christian, and R.L. Wetzel. 1981. A model view of the marsh, p. 164-181. *In* L.R. Pomeroy and R.G. Wiegert (eds.), The Ecology of a Salt Marsh. Springer-Verlag, New York.

Williams, G.P. 1989. Sediment concentration vs. water discharge during single hydrologic events in rivers. *Journal of Hydrology* 111: 89-106.

Wolaver, T.G., R.F. Dame, J.D. Spurrier, and A.B. Miller. 1988. Sediment exchange between a euhaline salt marsh in South Carolina and the adjacent tidal creek. *Journal of Coastal Research* 4: 17-26.

Zingmark, R.G. (ed.). 1978. An Annotated Checklist of the Biota of the Coastal Zone of South Carolina. University of South Carolina Press, Columbia, South Carolina.

Anthropogenic Impacts on Salt Marshes—A Review

John E. Weinstein

ABSTRACT: The inherent resilience of salt marshes to stressors and their capacity to absorb anthropogenic impacts have been strained by human uses—both present and past. Anthropogenic activities in salt marshes have included dredging, oil spills, marina development and recreational boating, and point- and nonpoint-source inputs of contaminants and nutrients. The cumulative impacts from these activities have resulted in the destruction of countless acres of tidal marshes, eutrophication and pathogenic contamination, alterations in community structure and functional processes, and reductions in productivity and overall habitat quality. Despite current (and possible future) legislation protecting salt marshes, the potential for anthropogenic alteration of marshes will always exist. Where it does, salt marsh mitigation, restoration, and/or creation should be attempted. In the case of created marsh, full ecosystem functioning is not guaranteed and will only occur following several decades.

Introduction

Salt marshes are extremely productive ecologically and serve a number of important functions, among which are the catchment of fertile sediments; biogeochemical transformations of C, H, S, and N; the exchange of chemicals, nutrients, and organic matter with associated ecosystems; and the provision of nursery grounds and habitat for many species of wildlife, including many commercially important species (such as peneid shrimp, blue crabs, oysters, red drum, spotted seatrout, and spot; Stender and Martore 1990). In addition, salt marshes and their adjacent tidal creeks have inherent artistic and aesthetic values, serve as preferred recreational fishing and boating areas, provide natural flood mitigation (by acting as a sponge), and naturally purify runoff and wastewater (Reimold et al. 1980; Tiner 1984; Daiber 1986; Weigert and Freeman 1990).

Historically, coastal regions have been favored sites of colonization, commerce, and industry. As these areas became colonized, economic and strategic concerns were the motivation to heavily modify salt marshes. These alterations have included the filling in and drainage of marshes, the diversion and control of water resources, and the discharge of waste into adjacent tidal creeks. For example, during the 19th Century, marshes at the mouths of major rivers in the Southeast United States were extensively diked for growing rice. During the peak of the rice cultivation period (1850-

1860), Georgia alone had 9,300 ha of salt marsh diked (Johnson et al. 1974). As a direct result of these and other human modifications, less than 50% of the marshes that existed when the nation was first settled still remains (Tiner 1984).

Today, coastal regions in the United States are experiencing their highest rates of population growth and industrial expansion. Already, nearly half of the country's population resides in coastal counties. By the year 2010, the coastal population is expected to increase to 127 million—a 60% increase over the 1960 coastal population (Culliton et al. 1990). As coastal population growth continues to accelerate, the ability of salt marshes to sustain myriad activities and conflicting uses will increasingly become impaired. In no other environment are the multiple uses and demands so great as those seen in salt marshes and their immediately surrounding areas (Chabreck 1988). Multiple uses in these regions include urban and tourism development, transportation (highways, railroads, airports), dredging, agriculture, industry, forestry, oil and gas operations, marinas, and waste disposal.

Until recently, the cumulative impacts of human pressures and development have not been considered a serious problem, because, for the most part, impacts have not significantly overtaxed the marsh ecosystem. Salt marshes are quite resilient and have a great capacity to absorb anthropogenic impacts (Stickney 1984). However, as coastal populations continue to grow, the long-term, cumulative impacts of these multiple uses will become more evident. These cumulative impacts can be extremely significant, since they can interfere with the natural processes of the marsh system and prevent the ecosystem as a whole from maintaining an equilibrium.

In the past, human society has not utilized salt marshes and their resources in sustainable ways. Currently, human activity is taxing the ecosystem's capacity to absorb these impacts without further degradation. It has been suggested that the only way to preserve these regions for future generations is to develop a framework for sustainable development that includes local, state, and federal legislation and cooperation (Beatley et al. 1994). To define the limits of sustainable development in the coastal zone, it is necessary to understand how humankind's various activities impact salt marsh processes.

Dredging

Salt marsh canals are dredged for a variety of reasons, the most common being the maintenance of sufficient water depth for recreational and commercial boating activities, pipelines, and flood control. Dredging activities cause a direct loss of ecologically valuable marsh habitat in two important ways (Chabreck 1988): excavation changes the site from marshland to open water, converting intertidal habitat to subtidal; and, dredge spoils are typically deposited on adjacent marshland, converting intertidal habitat to upland.

The most acute biotic impact of dredging and dredge spoil disposal is to benthic organisms (Kennish 1992). In most cases dredging results in the complete removal of the benthic community from the marsh and its translocation to the spoil disposal area (Stickney 1984). Mechanical damage to the organism and smothering can result in a mortality rate approaching 100%, especially when the spoils are deposited on marshland or terrestrial habitats. Less mortality may result from the subaqueous disposal of spoils (Van Dolah et al. 1984); however, these mortality rates are dependent upon the organism type and physical factors associated with their new benthic habitat (i.e., salinity, turbidity, current velocity, grain size, depth, etc.).

In general, it has been found that recolonization and eventual recovery of the benthic community does occur at dredge-impacted sites. However, the rate of recovery is variable depending upon the types of organisms composing the benthic community (Bonvincini Pagliai et al. 1985). In most benthic estuarine communities, recovery occurs slowly (within 12-18 mo) with opportunistic species (such as *Capitella* spp.) appearing first, followed by equilibrium assemblages of organisms in a successional pattern (Pfitzenmeyer 1969; Rhoads and Boyer 1982). In the shallow Dawho River estuary, South Carolina, recolonization of a dredged shoal occurred within 3 mo following dredging (Van Dolah et al. 1984). This rapid recovery was attributed to immigration of macrofauna through slumping of channel wall sediments into the dredged area. Similar results were observed by Stickney and Perlmutter (1975) along the Atlantic Intracoastal Waterway in Ossabaw Sound, Georgia. Within 1 mo of dredging, polychaete species (primarily *Paraprionospio pinnata*) were abundant in the dredged area. Recovery appeared to be complete within 3 mo. These authors also attributed the rapid recovery to immigration of macrofauna through slumping of the channel walls (Stickney and Perlmutter 1975). Recolonization with the same species can be expected as long as sediment type and hydromorphology of the intertidal habitat has not been dramatically altered (Windom 1976).

The effects of dredging on motile species are more difficult to assess. It has been generally assumed that motile animals (such as fish and shrimp) merely leave the area being dredged, and return when the environment is once again suitable for habitation (Windom 1976; Stickney 1984). Bybee (1969) observed that peneid shrimp return to impacted areas as early as 3-4 wk following dredging. Although the acute effects of dredging may be minimal for motile species, the long-term ecological consequences may be severe. For example, Holland et al. (1993) suggested that dredging activities in Charleston Harbor, South Carolina, could impact the commercially important white shrimp (*Peneus setiferus*) by destroying important marsh habitat, increasing siltation which would adversely affect juveniles, impairing egg and larval development, and interfering with important migration routes. Such impacts could lead to decreased productivity of the fishery.

Plant communities can be equally devastated by dredging activities. The disposal of dredge spoils in salt marshes can eradicate significant biomasses of vegetation, and modify sediment-type, elevation, and water movement patterns of the marsh. These alterations in the environmental conditions of disposal areas do not favor reestablishment of smooth cordgrass (*Spartina alterniflora*) (Holland et al. 1993). Additionally, the newly created environment has a much reduced role in material and nutrient cycling, and no longer provides a habitat that can function as a nursery for commercially and recreationally important species.

Less devastating to plant communities is thin-layer disposal of dredge spoils. Studies have shown recovery of plant communities following thin-layer disposal, but the rate of recovery depends on the depth of applied sediment. Burger and Shisler (1983) found that areas of a Barnegat Bay, New Jersey, salt marsh receiving less that 5 cm spoil had 60-90% cover after 1 yr. The addition of more than 5 cm spoil resulted in only about 5% cover after 1 yr, and changes in species composition during later years.

Few studies have been conducted to determine the impacts of dredging on phytoplankton or benthic algae communities (Stickney 1984). Corliss and Trent (1971) compared phytoplankton production in dredged and undredged (reference) marshes of Galveston Bay, Texas. In that study, the dredged marsh had undergone a considerable amount of modification including channelization, bulkheading, and filling. Average gross phytoplankton production (mg C l^{-1} d^{-1}) in the dredged marsh was 8% higher than the reference marsh. Dredging does not seem to adversely impact marsh phytoplankton; however, more conclusive studies are necessary.

Salt marsh biota can also be impacted by dredging activities occurring off-site. The dredging of a navigational inlet in an estuary can modify local circulation and sediment transport processes, leading to an increased degree of salinity intrusion and increased tidal range in the upper portion of the estuary (National Research Council 1985a). These modifications can result in the exposure of shellfish beds, the elimination of benthic invertebrates, and changes in vegetation patterns. Consideration should also be given to dredging impacts that may extend beyond the initial event. Wave wash from boats is a major cause of erosion in some areas, and the rate of canal erosion has been found to be proportional to the amount of boat traffic (Chabreck 1988). Dredging to maintain or provide sufficient depth for boat traffic not only leads to further losses of marshland via erosion, but sediments settle in the canal bed, requiring additional dredging. The width of some canals has been observed to double after a decade due to erosion (Craig et al. 1979).

Another concern related to dredging activities is the potential environmental impacts attributed to the release of previously sequestered pollutants (Kennish 1992), which may include pesticides, hydrocarbons, and heavy metals. Release of these contaminants may pose a threat to marsh biota and/or human health. For example, dredging of the James River estuary, Virginia, resulted in significantly elevated levels of the organochlorine insecticide kepone in wedge clams, *Rangia cuneata* (Lunsford et al. 1987). Engler (1976) found that sediments contaminated with heavy metals generally do not release them water column during dredging.

Since the late 1960s the disposal of dredged material on salt marshes has been discouraged because these systems have been recognized as an important habitat for many organisms (Stickney 1984). Concern over dredging activities have primarily focused on the direct and indirect impacts related to the physical and chemical alterations of the marsh, which can severely impact the indigenous flora and fauna.

Out of these concerns, more environmentally sound dredging practices have been developed. For example, dredge spoils are now typically deposited on land and capped rather than dumped in the open water, thus minimizing the impact of the dredge spoils on the aquatic biota. Another trend has been to use dredge spoils to create dredge spoil islands (Kirby et al. 1975). On one such island in Winyah Bay, South Carolina, an approximately 35-ha *S. alterniflora* marsh has developed over a 14-yr period (LaSalle et al. 1991). Interestingly, the density of flora and fauna on this island was similar to nearby natural salt marshes. These management practices represent more sound environmental alternatives than the practice of dumping dredge spoils on valuable marshland.

Contaminants

The introduction of contaminants has become an increasingly serious problem in estuaries adjacent to urban, industrial, and agricultural regions (Dardeau et al. 1992; Kennish 1992). Depending on location, the sediments and biota of these salt marshes are exposed to a variety of contaminants, for example, insecticides, herbicides, heavy metals, trace elements, dioxin, polycyclic aromatic hydrocarbons (PAHs), and polychlorinated biphenyls (PCBs). Many of these contaminants are persistent in the intertidal sediments and have the ability to bioaccumulate in food chains (Barron 1995).

Pollutants enter salt marshes through point and nonpoint sources, and by fluvial transport to the marsh from inland areas. Other routes of entry include dry and wet deposition of atmospheric particulates and aerosols; direct disposal of dredge spoils; and direct introduction through commercial and recreational boating activities, highways, landfills, and marinas (reviewed by Kennish 1992; Catallo 1993).

One major class of chronically toxic, carcinogenic, and mutagenic contaminants found in the sediments and biota of salt marshes are PAHs. An estimated 2.3×10^5 metric tons of PAHs enter aquatic and estuarine environments every year, primarily through routine and accidental petroleum spills and atmospheric deposition (Eisler 1987). Other major sources of PAHs are urban runoff, wastewaters, and biosynthesis. In heavily industrialized regions, atmospheric deposition has been found to be the primary source of PAHs to estuarine systems (Jensen 1984); studies elsewhere have found urban runoff to be the principal contributor of PAHs (Hoffman et al. 1984). PAHs also enter coastal environments through the combustion of fossil fuels, forest and brush fires, creosote oil leachates, recreational boating activities, and street dusts containing exhaust particulates and residues from lubricating oils and gasoline (Lake et al. 1979; Takata et al. 1990).

Although commercial production of PCBs ceased in 1977, they continue to be a major pollutant concern in salt marshes due to their persistence in sediments and very high biomagnification potential. Before PCB manufacturing was banned, an estimated 540 million kg of these compounds had been produced in the United States, primarily for the insulation of electrochemical capacitors and transformers (Kennish 1992). Other products containing PCBs include adhesives, caulking compounds, additives to hydraulic oils, paints, varnishes, and plastics (Hutzinger et al. 1974). PCBs can reach salt marshes either as runoff or leachate from adjacent landfills and industrial areas or via long-range transport by rivers emptying into estuarine systems (Hobbie and Copeland 1980).

Heavy metals also pose a significant threat to salt marsh biota due to their persistence in sediments, toxicity at high levels, and tendency to bioaccumulate. Those heavy metals of particular concern in salt marshes are cadmium, chromium, mercury, lead, selenium, arsenic, and antimony. Kennish (1992) has identified these metals as contributing to severe pollution problems in various estuaries throughout the United States. The major source of heavy metals to coastal marshes is direct anthropogenic inputs from domestic and industrial processes. Substantial quantities of copper, lead, and zinc are released from pipes and tanks in domestic wastewater systems. Large amounts of metal are also derived from the mining and processing of phosphate and other metal ores; finishing and plating of metals; manufacturing of dyes, paints, and textiles; and the leaching of metals from antifouling paints used in recreational boating (Abel 1989). Other sources of heavy metals to marshes are riverine input, urban runoff, and atmospheric deposition.

Pesticides have also become a major contaminant concern in coastal marshes. Salt marshes are the primary repository for agricultural pesticides that originate in upland regions and are transported via runoff to streams and rivers (Clark et al. 1993). Pimentel and Edwards (1982) have estimated that as much as 5% of surface- and soil-applied pesticides leave agricultural fields and are eventually deposited in estuarine sediments. Pesticides from agricultural operations can reach salt marshes more directly through aerial drift during application (Glotfelty et al. 1990). As coastal populations grow, the use of pesticides is becoming even more prevalent: insecticides are used to control flies and mosquitoes out of public health concerns and to lessen public annoyance, and herbicides are used to control weeds on residential lawns and golf courses.

In general, the introduction of pollutants into ecosystems is accompanied by alterations in an interrelated series of processes that can operate long after the initial introduction of contaminants (Moriarty 1983; Day et al. 1989). This is particularly true in salt marshes, where the organically-enriched sediments can sequester hydrophobic contaminants, such as PCBs, PAHs, and metals for very long periods. Therefore, salt marshes have a very high potential to manifest chronic degradation over long periods of time (Kennish 1992). Moreover, the intimate chemical and biological coupling between the marsh and other systems (e.g., coastal oceans or upland forests) may allow for impacts to be manifested outside of the marsh (Harris 1988; Chambers 1991). For example, commercial landings of fish and shellfish along the Southeast Atlantic and Gulf of Mexico coasts have decreased by 42% since 1982 (Chambers 1991). Virtually all landings are composed of estuarine-dependent species, and Chambers (1991) has primarily attributed their decline to salt marsh destruction and degradation, and current commercial and recreational fishing practices.

A wide variety of factors influence the magnitude and type of toxicant responses in salt marsh systems, and these have previously been reviewed in Catallo (1993). Briefly, these factors include the identity of the pollutant mixture; the exposure concentration and toxicities of individual components of the mixture; exposure time, duration, and route of entry; contaminant partitioning, speciation, and bioavailability under ambient marsh conditions; life stage, physiological resilience, and previous exposure history of the exposed populations; the degree of interaction between populations; the presence of external physical forces on the system (e.g., tidal flushing, weathering processes, and natural and anthropogenic stresses); and the types and diversity of energy and functional linkages between populations (Cairns and Buikema 1984; Sheenan et al. 1984).

The major fates of pollutants in salt marshes are adsorption to organic matter and sediment, biodegradation, and weathering. Resuspension of sediments and detrital material during tidal exchanges may serve as another mechanism by which contaminants are flushed from the salt marsh. Some hydrophobic contaminants, such as PCBs and DDT, are rapidly accumulated in the lipids of marsh organisms, passed up the food chain, and may eventually leave the system in motile predators, including fish, crabs, and birds (Kennish 1992). Other hydrophobic contaminants, such as PAHs, are more vulnerable to bacterial degradation and eukaryotic metabolic processes (e.g., the mixed-function oxygenase system) (McElroy et al. 1989). The eventual recovery of a salt marsh following contamination is primarily the function of chemical processes (sequestration and weathering), and the introduction of new marsh through the accretion of sediments and detritus (Catallo 1993).

CONTAMINANT EFFECTS ON PRIMARY PRODUCTION

The soft-bottomed intertidal salt marsh is subject to rapid changes in water level, temperature, and salinity. Accordingly, the plants found in marshes are extremely hardy. These plants, such as smooth cordgrass (*Spartina alterniflora*), have developed several means of coping with natural stressors, including mechanisms to exclude substances from their subsurface rhizomes, the ability to pump substances out through their leaves, and metabolic pathways to convert them to less toxic forms (Lee et al. 1976; McGovern et al. 1979; Kraus et al. 1986; Alberts et al. 1990).

Spartina alterniflora generates an oxidized rhizosphere (root zone) by the diffusion or advection of molecular oxygen from its leaves to its root system. The oxidized rhizosphere allows for soluble materials in pore water (such as Fe^{2+} and Mn^{2+}) to be converted to insoluble oxides and oxyhydroxides, which subsequently are precipitated as solid or colloidal matrices adjacent to the root surface (DeLaune and Pezeshki 1991). These matrices have the ability to limit the diffusion of metallic and organic contaminants by coprecipitating them before they reach the root surface, preventing them from making direct contact with the root surface (Catallo 1993).

Alberts et al. (1990) surveyed the sediment and *S. alterniflora* tissue concentrations of a suite of metals (including Al, Cu, Fe, Mg, Mn, and Zn) in marshes located in Savannah and Brunswick,

Georgia. Although sedimentary metal concentrations in the port cities were higher by a factor of 10 compared with the reference site, these authors found no differences with regard to plant tissue concentrations. However, results of other studies are in disagreement. For example, marsh grasses (*S. alterniflora*, *S. patens*, and *Phragmites communis*) exposed to dredge spoil in a Virginia marsh accumulated significant levels of Zn and Pb compared to plants in a control marsh (Drifmeyer and Odum 1975). In that study, lead was 2.5 times and 10 times higher in *S. alterniflora* and *S. patens*, respectively, compared to control plants. Other studies have found that Hg can be assimilated and accumulated by *Spartina* spp. (Gardner et al. 1978).

The discrepancies between studies may be related to the physical and/or chemical properties of the sediment (Catallo 1993). In undisturbed marshes, it is unlikely that *S. alterniflora* actively accumulates metals from the sediments due to the effective barrier created by the rhizosphere. However, when the integrity of the rhizosphere is breached through activities such as dredging, the susceptibility of *Spartina* spp. to metal uptake, and thus toxic effects, increases. This was demonstrated in a study conducted by Gambrell et al. (1987). Under natural, anaerobic sediment conditions, *S. alterniflora* exhibited no adverse effects to cadmium exposure, since it was largely unavailable for uptake. Under oxidized sediment conditions, the bioavailability of Cd increased and the growth of *S. alterniflora* was significantly inhibited.

Dunstan and Windom (1975) examined the potential toxicity of lead, cadmium, and copper to *S. alterniflora* seedlings growing in nutrient solutions containing 100 ppm of metal. Copper was the most toxic metal and resulted in 100% mortality. Lead exposure resulted in 62% mortality, and surviving plants attained less than half the height of controls. Cadmium had no toxic effects, but it was accumulated in plant tissues as high as 150 times those of controls. Although these levels were considerably higher than levels normally observed in estuarine sediments, these results suggest that some metals can pose a serious risk to plants as a result of activities that physically disrupt the integrity of the rhizosphere.

Sediment-bound organic compounds are generally not available for uptake by species of *Spartina*; however, those contaminants dissolved in pore water can be accumulated. PCBs in pore water have been reported to bioaccumulate in *S. alterniflora* at levels several orders of magnitude greater than ambient concentrations (United States Army Corps of Engineers 1987). DDT has also been found to bioaccumulate in marsh grasses. Woodwell et al. (1967) found DDT levels in a Long Island (New York) salt marsh ranged from 5.0×10^{-5} ppm in water to 0.33 ppm and 2.80 ppm in the shoots and roots, respectively, of salt-meadow cordgrass, *Spartina patens*. Detrital material from *S. patens* had as high as 50 times the amount of DDT found in living shoots. Evidence of DDT biomagnification to higher trophic levels was also reported; ring-billed gulls in these marshes had DDT levels of 75 ppm (Woodwell et al. 1967).

Herbicides are commonly used for weed control in agricultural and urban areas adjacent to marshes; however, few studies have investigated the potential impacts on primary production from these applications. The application of large amounts of herbicides, including fenuron, paraquat, and dalapon, directly to marsh grasses results in 100% mortality (reviewed by Edwards and Davis 1974). In fact, prior to the 1970s, these herbicides were commonly used for the widespread eradication of *Spartina* spp. for the economic and agricultural development of marshland. More recently, the use of dalapon has proved to be beneficial to shorebirds by controlling the encroachment of *Spartina* spp. on intertidal mudflats (Evans 1986).

The herbicide atrazine is commonly applied to sugar cane, corn, and sorghum fields for selective weed control throughout the Southeast United States. Wu et al. (1977) estimated that 1.2%

of the atrazine applied in a Maryland corn field was lost in runoff. Downstream, weekly weighted concentrations of atrazine were as high as 0.05 ppm. These stream concentrations are approximately half the concentration reported to significantly reduce dry weight biomass of *S. alterniflora* stems and roots (Pillai et al. 1977). Although the stream concentrations reported in this study were measured prior to dilution by estuarine water, these results suggest that herbicides in nonpoint-source runoff from heavily farmed regions may pose as a significant risk to salt-marsh primary production.

CONTAMINANT EFFECTS ON SALT MARSH MICROBES

Few studies have examined the effects of pollutants on salt-marsh microbial communities; however, it can be expected that these communities would manifest changes similar to those observed in freshwater wetlands (reviewed by Catallo 1993). These community changes have included decreased species diversity; dominance of adapted, generalist, or resilient populations; and alterations in biomass (McKinley et al. 1982; Sayler et al. 1982). The microbial community structure of salt marshes has been observed to change in response to petroleum hydrocarbons. In an experimental salt-marsh plot contaminated with crude oil, the biomass of indigenous hydrocarbon-degrading bacteria increased relative to the biomass of other aerobic heterotrophs, such as chitin- and cellulose-degrading bacteria (Hood et al. 1975).

A variety of alterations in microbial metabolic processes have been documented in response to contaminant exposure in salt marshes. The application of sewage sludge has been observed to depress oxygen uptake by heterotrophic microorganisms in the aerobic zone of the sediment (Giblin et al. 1983), and depress denitrification by microorganisms in the anaerobic zone of the sediment (Sherr and Payne 1981). In both cases, the decreased metabolic functions were attributed to the high levels of heavy metals in the sludge. Interestingly, Giblin et al. (1983) reported that the aerobic heterotrophic organisms were able to develop a tolerance to chromium and copper within 1 mo. Following exposure to PCBs, bacteria involved in *S. alterniflora* detritus formation decreased their CO_2 output, but the overall quality of the detritus was unaffected (Marinucci and Bartha 1982). In addition, these bacteria bioaccumulated the PCBs at levels three to four times higher than the abiotic controls. These findings strongly suggest that detrital bioaccumulation of PCBs can be an important means of entry for this pollutant into the food web.

CONTAMINANT EFFECTS ON SALT MARSH MEIOFAUNA

Of all the organisms found in salt marshes, perhaps the benthic meiofauna are the most susceptible to anthropogenic contaminants. These organisms, typically found in the top 5 cm of the sediment profile, are constantly exposed to both dissolved and adsorbed contaminants through contact with pore water and sediments. Meiofauna have been defined as those sediment invertebrates passing through a 500-μm sieve but retained on a 63-μm sieve (Fenchel and Jorgensen 1977). Major taxonomic groups of meiofauna include crustaceans (e.g., copepods and ostracods), nematodes, turbellarians, rotifers, gastrotrichs, and annelids (e.g., some oligochaetes and polychaetes). Benthic meiofauna are ecologically important in salt marshes because they serve as an important link in the food web: they graze on detrital aerobic and anaerobic bacteria, and in turn, are preyed upon by shrimp and juvenile fish (Coull and Bell 1979; Montagna et al. 1983).

Following exposure to anthropogenic contaminants, salt marsh meiofauna have been reported to experience alterations in community structure and biomass, mortality of the most sensitive species, and increased body burdens of contaminants (Catallo 1993). Spilled petroleum has been observed to result in decreased meiofauna (Hampson and Moul 1978), and increased diversity and biomass of species more resistant to the insult (Chandler and Fleeger 1983). Other hydrophobic contaminants, such as DDT and PCBs, are available for uptake by salt marsh meiofauna, and have been shown to be bioaccumulated (Nathans and Bechtel 1977; Wirth et al. 1994).

Research has demonstrated that meiofauna are sensitive to most contaminants found in salt marshes (reviewed by Coull and Chandler 1992). Fenvalerate, a pyrethroid insecticide, is extremely toxic in the aqueous phase to the estuarine harpacticoid copepod, *Nitocra spinipes* (96-h LC_{50} = 1.9 ppb) (Linden et al. 1979); however, sediment-bound phase concentrations of up to 100 ppb caused no mortality to the copepods *Microarthridian littorale, Paronychocamptus wilsoni*, and *Enhydosoma propinquum* (Chandler 1990). Apparently, the bioavailability of the pesticide is greatly reduced once it becomes bound to the sediment (Coull and Chandler 1992). Despite the lack of acute mortality of the sediment-bound phase, concentrations as low as 25 ppb caused a depression of egg production and mean clutch size of *M. littorale* and *P. wilsoni* (Chandler 1990). Field-collected sediments contaminated with the organochloride insecticide endosulfan at 50 ppb significantly inhibited colonization by larvae of the polychaete *Streblospio benedicti*, and at 200 ppb caused significant mortality in the copepod *Nannopus palustris* (Chandler and Scott 1991). By contrast, the common benthic copepod *Pseudobradya pulchella* demonstrated no significant mortality or depressed reproduction at the highest endosulfan concentrations (Chandler and Scott 1991). Very low concentrations (4 ppm) of sediment-bound PCBs have also been reported to depress fecundity of the copepod *M. littorale* (DiPinto et al. 1993).

Meiobenthic nematodes have also been reported to be sensitive to in situ levels of contaminants. Reproductive rates of *Chromadorina germanica* and *Diplolaimella punicea* were significantly reduced following exposure to sediments from the Hudson-Raritan estuary which contain high levels of PCBs, PAHs, and heavy metals (Tietjen and Lee 1984). Critical life stages and behaviors of salt marsh meiofauna are highly sensitive to certain contaminants; strongly suggesting that even low levels of contaminants could result in population declines and alterations in the ecological balance of the marsh.

Oil Impacts

Among the most serious threats to salt marshes is oil pollution, which can impact the biota either directly by the toxic effects of the water-soluble components of the petroleum, or indirectly via the degradation of critical habitat. Although salt marshes along the Gulf Coast of the United States are at the highest risk of oil pollution due to intense drilling and refining activities, all salt marshes are at some risk, as evidenced by major spills in Nova Scotia and Massachusetts over the last 30 yr (Table 1).

In estuaries, the major sources of oil are from upland river runoff, urban runoff, routine transportation activities, and municipal and industrial wastes (Kennish 1992). While major oil spills and accidents are perceived by the public as the principal danger, these sources account for only 12% of the oil entering the environment each year (Clark 1989). Perhaps an even greater threat to salt marshes is derived from the chronic oil pollution associated with routine operations of coastal

Table 1. Oil spills reported to have impacted salt marsh biota.

Tanker/Date	Location	Oil Type	Reported Impacts	References
Torrey Canyon March 1967	English Channel	Kuwait Crude Oil	Salt marsh plant species survived all but the heaviest contamination; chlorotic symptoms in some plants. Recovery apparent within 10 mo.	Stebbings 1970
Florida September 1969	Buzzards Bay, Massachusetts	No. 2 Fuel Oil	Plants, crustaceans, fish and birds suffered high mortality immediately after spill. Recovery not complete after 7 yr. After 20 yr, traces of bio-degraded oil were still evident at some sites, resulting in cytochrome P4501A induction in *Fundulus*.	Burns and Teal 1979; Sanders et al. 1980; Teal et al. 1992
Arrow February 1970	Chedabucto Bay, Nova Scotia	Bunker C Fuel Oil	Initial effects of oil included smothering of fauna and extensive mortality of *Spartina alterniflora*. After 5 yr, intertidal oil not static, but continu-ously released. After 20 yr, a full range of weathered oil residues persist.	Thomas 1973; Vander-meulen and Gordon 1976; Singh 1994
Brouchard 65 October 1974	Buzzards Bay, Massachusetts	No. 2 Fuel Oil	After 3 yr, marsh grass unable to be reestablished in lower intertidal. Reduced numbers and species of interstitial fauna. Affected areas had higher erosion rates.	Hampson and Moul 1978
Exxon Refinery Spill January 1990	Arthur Kill, New Jersey	No. 2 Fuel Oil	Fiddler crabs (*U. pugnax*) from contaminated salt marshes demonstrated abnormal behavioral responses.	Burger et al. 1991

oil refineries and installations, which account for 30-50% of the total oil released into the environment every year (National Research Council 1989).

Salt marshes are especially vulnerable to oil pollution. Being intertidal, they are often the final repository of oil since it can be dispersed no further, and their thick deposits of fine sediments and organic material are capable of sequestering oil for long periods of time (Hall et al. 1978; Kennish 1992). Once the oil has penetrated the sediments, normal breakdown processes, such as microbial degradation and weathering, are impaired. This allows the oil to accumulate and persist for years, hindering the recovery of the marsh biota. In addition, the oil is not necessarily restricted to a particular location but can be translocated over time. For example, immediately following the No. 2 fuel oil spill of the barge *Florida* off of West Falmouth, Massachusetts, in September 1969, the greatest concentrations of petroleum hydrocarbons were found in the intertidal and shallow subtidal regions of the Wild Harbor River (Sanders et al. 1980). After 5 yr, the oiled sediments had moved, and the highest concentrations occurred in the deeper subtidal regions of the river. This translocation of oil over time can prolong the spill's impact by exposing organisms previously unexposed.

Also, oil trapped in bottom sediments can slowly leach back into the overlying water column protracting the impacts of a spill by providing a chronic source of oil to the marsh. Following the Bunker C fuel oil spill from the tanker *Olympia Arrow* in Chedabucto Bay, Nova Scotia, in February 1970, oil was found to re-enter the overlying water column for at least 5 yr (Vandermeulen and Gordon 1976). Based on flow experiments, Vandermeulen and Gordon (1976) estimated that oil was released from the sediments at an average rate of 630 μg oil h^{-1}; at this rate the oil would have a residence time in the sediments of 150 yr. Twenty years following the spill, a full range of oil residues were still evident in intertidal sediments (Vandermeulen and Singh 1994).

The overall susceptibility of a salt marsh to damage from oiling is related to two factors. Hall et al. (1978) suggested that the amount of weathering the oil undergoes prior to washing ashore is important in determining the severity of damage. Perhaps a more important factor is the sediment depth to which the oil penetrates (Hall et al. 1978). In both the Bunker C oil spill in Nova Scotia and the No. 2 fuel oil spill off of West Falmouth, Massachusetts, oil penetrated deeply into the sediments (up to 115 cm), and the damage to the biota was extensive (Vandermeulen and Gordon 1976, Burns and Teal 1979). However, the oil that washed up onto the French salt marshes following the *Torrey Canyon* spill in March 1967 only penetrated 3-10 cm into the sediment, resulting in considerably less damage (Stebbings 1970). Apparently, if oil sinks deep enough into the sediment to reach the rhizomes of the marsh grass, then the damage is extensive and recovery very slow. But, if oil penetration is slight and the rhizomes remain undamaged, recovery can be rapid (Stebbings 1970). Along the East Coast of the United States, penetration of oil into salt marsh sediments may be facilitated by bioturbating infauna, such as fiddler crabs (Hall et al. 1978).

The rate of recovery of a salt marsh following an oil spill is also related to the rate of sedimentation. Following the *Torrey Canyon* oil spill, Stebbings (1970) reported that within 16 mo up to 20 cm of new sediment had overlain the oiled sediments. This very high rate of sedimentation facilitated the rapid colonization by salt marsh grasses by preventing their rhizomes from reaching the oiled sediments.

EFFECTS ON BIOTA

A considerable amount of research has been performed to determine the effects of petroleum on salt marsh biota. The severity of impact on marsh biota is primarily a function of the chemical composition of the petroleum (Kuwait crude oil, South Louisiana crude oil, No. 2 fuel oil, etc.), the amount spilled, and the form that eventually reaches the marsh (degree of weathering, emulsification) (Kennish 1992). Other factors involved in determining the severity of impact include occurrence of the oil (solution, suspension, dispersion, or adsorbed to particulates), duration of exposure, life stage of the organism exposed (larvae, juvenile, adult), previous history of oil impacts on the marsh, season of exposure, natural environmental stressors (temperature, salinity, etc.), and restoration efforts (chemical dispersants, cutting, burning, etc.) (Evans and Rice 1974).

Salt marsh microbes appear to be rather resistant to petroleum impacts. In fact, many groups of microorganisms can use polluting oil as a source of carbon and energy (National Research Council 1985b). Thus, oil spills typically result in an increase in the biomass of microbial populations (Kator and Herwig 1977). Long-term, chronic exposure of a salt marsh to South Louisiana crude oil resulted in an increased biomass of indigenous hydrocarbon-degrading bacteria compared with a pristine marsh (Hood et al. 1975). Interestingly, no differences were observed with respect to the indigenous chitin- and cellulose-degrading bacteria. Salt marsh microcosm studies have also demonstrated that chronic, low-level (3.33 g C m^{-2} d^{-1}) hydrocarbon additions stimulate soil microbial activities, including CO_2 production, methanogenesis, N_2 fixation, and denitrification; however, microbial activities were inhibited at higher levels (33.3 g C m^{-2} d^{-1}) of hydrocarbon addition (Li et al. 1990). Most recently, nitrogen- and phosphorous-containing fertilizers have been applied to spilled oil to enhance microbial degradative activities. This bioremediation technique increased microbial degradation of oil twofold to threefold following the March 1989 *Exxon Valdez* spill in Prince William Sound, Alaska (Pritchard 1991).

Likewise, phytoplankton communities due to their patchy distribution and high rate of proliferation appear to be resistant to oil spills. Typically, phytoplankton populations quickly recover following oil spills, even catastrophic ones (Nelson-Smith 1972). Photosynthesis by algae can be either enhanced or depressed depending on oil concentrations: below 50 ng g^{-1} photosynthesis is enhanced, above 50 ng g^{-1} photosynthesis is depressed (GESAMP 1977).

Following exposure to oil, salt marsh macroflora have been reported to exhibit a wide variety of responses. These responses appear to be dependent upon the type of petroleum, manner of application, and season of exposure (Stickney 1984). In a Louisiana salt marsh, the application of crude oil to the sediments in summer had no effect on *Spartina alterniflora* production, probably because the low tidal amplitudes (0.3 m) did not distribute the oil on the leaves. Autumn application of various crude and refined petroleum over the entire leaf surface of *S. alterniflora* resulted in plant mortality in salt marshes in Georgia (Lee et al. 1981) and Texas (Webb et al. 1985). Chronic low levels (3.33 g C m^{-2} d^{-1}) of hydrocarbon application to salt marsh microcosms resulted in increased aboveground and belowground biomass of *S. alterniflora* probably due to the increased nitrogen fixation and/or nitrogen mineralization; however, higher levels (33.3 g C m^{-2} d^{-1}) resulted in reduced biomass (Li et al. 1990). Following the No. 2 fuel oil spill of the *Florida* in Massachusetts, mortality of *S. alterniflora* was reported in those sediments containing 1-2 mg oil g^{-1} sediment (Burns and Teal 1979). Similar observations have been reported following a No. 2 fuel oil spill in the Chesapeake Bay (Hershner and Lake 1980). *Spartina alterniflora* receiving the most oil became chlorotic and died, while plants receiving a sublethal dose exhibited delayed spring development, increased stem density, and reduced stem weight. No. 2 fuel oil appears to be the most toxic petroleum type to *Spartina* spp., since it damages both aboveground and belowground plant parts (Webb et al. 1985). According to Webb et al. (1985), it is the belowground damage that hinders the recovery of *Spartina*, which can take up to several years. Other salt marsh plants, such as

Salicornia spp., are very sensitive to oil pollution and die following one application of Kuwait crude oil, whereas some, such as *Oenanthe lachenalii*, can withstand 12 successive monthly applications (Baker 1979). Baker (1979) found that these highly resistant species are able to gain a competitive advantage over more sensitive species following oil exposure.

Petroleum exposure has also been shown to inhibit metabolic processes, such as photosynthesis and respiration, in salt marsh plants (Baker 1979). Pezeshki and DeLaune (1993) observed complete cessation of photosynthetic activity when the entire leaf of *S. alterniflora* and black needlerush, *Juncus roemarianus*, were coated with oil, and significantly decreased activity upon partial coating. Although no mortality was observed in this study, photosynthetic processes took up to 4 wk to improve (Pezeshki and DeLaune 1993).

In general, meiofaunal diversity and biomass decline in response to exposure to petroleum; however, the meiofauna are among the quickest to recover (Coull and Chandler 1992; Catallo 1993). Controlled field exposures to South Louisiana crude oil have demonstrated that nematodes are highly resistant to petroleum, and only at the highest levels of exposure do they exhibit lower densities and depressed colonization rates (3.8 g oil kg^{-1} sediment) (Decker and Fleeger 1984). Even when nematodes have been acutely impacted by oil pollution, they have demonstrated rapid density recoveries within 3 mo (Giere 1979). Meiobenthic copepods are generally much more sensitive to petroleum exposure than nematodes (Catallo 1993); however, Fleeger and Chandler (1983) reported increased copepod densities after exposure to very high sediment concentrations of crude oil (2-44 mg oil kg^{-1} sediment). This positive effect was attributed to the disproportionate increase in abundance of one species (*Enhydrosoma woodini*), which probably was the result of either an increased food source (oil-degrading bacteria) or an oil-induced inhibition of predation (Fleeger and Chandler 1983).

In contrast to these controlled exposures of crude oil, accidental spills of refined petroleum have produced catastrophic damage to salt marsh meiofauna. Following the No. 2 fuel oil spill of the barge *Brouchard 65* in Buzzards Bay, Massachusetts, in October 1974, Hampson and Moul (1978) reported numerous dead and moribund invertebrates in the marsh. Three years after the spill, densities of interstitial meiofauna, including nematodes, harpacticoid copepods, and oligochaetes, were still significantly reduced.

Salt marsh macrofauna have exhibited a wide range of responses to petroleum exposure, including no effect, sublethal effects (such as histological lesions, impaired reproductive capabilities, and altered behavior), and acute mortality. In general, these studies have demonstrated that crude oil and lightly refined products have considerably less impact than the more intensely refined petroleum products. For instance, Lee et al. (1981) found few negative effects on the epifauna of a Georgia salt marsh in response to exposure to heavy fuel oil. Fiddler crabs, oysters, and mussels exhibited no changes, and densities of the mud snail (*Nassarius obsoleta*) increased due to the immigration of adults from uncontaminated regions. Periwinkles (*Littorina irrorata*) were killed in large numbers immediately following exposure but quickly recolonized the area within 3 mo (Lee et al. 1981). Similar findings were reported in a Louisiana salt marsh following exposure to South Louisiana crude oil; the only exception was that *L. irrorata* populations did not experience reduced densities (DeLaune et al. 1984).

By contrast, widespread mortality of salt marsh macrofauna was observed following the No. 2 fuel oil spill of the *Florida* in Massachusetts (Sanders et al. 1980). This immediate die-off was followed by a temporary invasion by the opportunistic polychaete *Capitella capitata*, which was able to obtain relatively high densities. Despite the rapid colonization of *C. capitata*, Sanders et al. (1980) reported that macrofaunal recovery was still not complete 5 yr after the spill. Twenty years after the oil spill, elevated petroleum hydrocarbons were still present in intertidal sediments and believed to be responsible for cytochrome P4501A induction in the marsh fish *Fundulus heteroclitus* (Teal et al. 1992).

Other sublethal effects have been reported in salt marsh macrofauna in response to petroleum spills. Behavioral alterations in fiddler crabs (*Uca pugnax*) were observed following a No. 2 fuel oil spill in the Arthur Kill between New Jersey and New York (Burger et al. 1991). Aberrant behaviors included an increased presence on the oiled marsh surface (despite winter temperatures), inability to right themselves, and less intense defensive behaviors. Oysters (*Ostrea edulis*) exhibited necrosis, inflammation, and atrophy of gonadal cells up to 7 yr following the *Amoco Cadiz* oil spill off the coast of Brittany (France) (Berthou et al. 1987). The presence of oil has also been reported to significantly reduce spat settlement in oysters (*Crassostrea virginica*) (Smith and Hackney 1989). Sublethal effects are generally subtle and may predispose an organism to a greater long-term risk for death. For example, aberrant behaviors could increase the susceptibility of an organism to predation.

MITIGATION

Various methods have been used to mitigate the aesthetic and ecological impacts of oil pollution in salt marshes. These techniques have included containment by barriers, physical removal of the oil, chemical dispersal, and burning and/or cutting of the affected vegetation. For the most part, these techniques have not been very effective. Several studies have reported that marsh cleaning methods such as burning and cutting often result in poor regrowth and do not necessarily increase the rate of marsh recovery (Westree 1977; DeLaune et al. 1979; Baker 1979). In fact, the mixing of oil and sediment during cutting often creates more damage (Westree 1977). The use of dispersants also has not been very effective, and, on occasion, may have accelerated damage to salt marsh biota. In a British salt marsh, the use of dispersant nearly doubled the mortality rate of *Spartina* spp. following exposure to Kuwait crude oil (Cowell 1969). Lane et al. (1987) reported that creek-edge and mid-marsh plants in an Atlantic Coast salt marsh exhibited the greatest sensitivity to an oil-dispersant mixture. In that study, oil alone had the less impact on the plant community. DeLaune et al. (1984) exposed a Gulf Coast salt marsh to high concentrations of South Louisiana crude oil to assess salt marsh restoration techniques following oil exposure. Application of dispersant to the oil-exposed *S. alterniflora* resulted in reduced biomass compared to oil-only exposed plants, and cutting of the affected marsh grass resulted in significantly poorer regrowth for two growing seasons. Based on these results, DeLaune et al. (1984) concluded that in many salt marshes, especially those with low sensitivity to oil pollution, the best response to an oil spill is no action at all.

Marina and Recreational Boating Impacts

The tremendous influx of people to the coastal areas of the United States has been accompanied by a growing number of recreational boaters. This is especially true in the Southeast United States, where states such as South Carolina, Georgia, and North Carolina now rank high (ninth, thirteenth, and fourteenth, respectively) in the total number of boats registered (United States Department of

Transportation 1993). Marinas have proliferated in response to the increasing demand for boating facilities. Designed to provide safe, protected moorings for boats, marinas need to be situated in calm waters with protected shorelines. Based on this criteria, estuaries with extensive salt marshes are considered excellent sites (United States Environmental Protection Agency 1985). In addition, these areas make good marina sites because they are low, give easy access to the ocean and upland rivers, and serve as a natural barrier against storm floods and hurricanes. Salt marsh vegetation and the low gradient of the marsh act to dissipate wave energy and serve as a receptacle for storm-tide waters.

The construction and operation of a marina can affect the ecology of a salt marsh through the destruction of critical habitat during dredging and construction of shoreline structures, the introduction of various pollutants via stormwater runoff and direct boat operation, and the alteration of hydrographic regimes. Although most individual marina projects result in relatively small impacts on the salt marsh ecosystem, the cumulative effect of many marinas has destroyed and degraded vast areas of salt marsh.

Several studies have documented elevated levels of various pollutants, such as heavy metals, in close proximity to marinas. Elevated levels of copper and zinc have been reported in oysters (*C. virginica*) collected from South Carolina and North Carolina marinas (Marcus and Thompson 1986; Adair 1987; Byers 1993). Marina activities have also been linked to elevated copper levels in other marsh biota, including benthic algae (Nixon et al. 1973) and the mud snail, *Ilyanasa obsoleta* (Byers 1993).

Copper and zinc can enter estuarine waters through a variety of sources associated with marina operations and boating activities (United States Environmental Protection Agency 1985). High levels of copper (600 μg l^{-1}) in the form of copper oxide are found in antifouling paints used on the bottom of boats and channel markers. Zinc is added to steel structures and steel boat bottoms to prevent rusting. Both copper and zinc can enter the water column through dissolution or through surface runoff containing debris from sandblasting and painting.

Although lead and cadmium have generally not been found to be elevated in the sediments or biota near marinas (Adair 1987; Byers 1993), elevated levels of organotin, primarily in the form of tributlytin, have been reported (Espourteille et al. 1993; Kure and Depledge 1994). Like copper, tributlytin is used as the active ingredient in antifouling paints, and it has recently gained favor over the copper oxide-containing paints (Kennish 1992). The effective action of copper oxide-based paints depends on the slow release of copper ions. Since this type of paint is only effective as long as copper is being released, its life expectancy is very limited. By contrast, tributlytin-based paints last considerably longer than copper oxide paints due to their "self-polishing" nature. As the layers of paint wear off, they are continually replaced by new layers of tributlytin-containing paint. Tributlytin, like copper, tends to leach into the water column.

Because tributlytin is a potential threat to estuarine organisms, research concerning its effects has accelerated in recent years. Both oysters (*C. virginica*) and periwinkles (*L. littorea*) accumulate tributlytin to very high levels; *L. littorea* concentrates tributlytin at levels 500 to 10,000 greater than water concentrations (Esporteille et al. 1993; Kure and Depledge 1994). Tributyltin has been reported to induce abnormal shell growth in oyster spat (*C. gigas*) and alter behavioral patterns in fiddler crabs (*Uca pugilator*) at very low levels (0.15 μg l^{-1} and 0.50 μg l^{-1}, respectively) (Waldock and Thain 1983; Weis and Perlmutter 1987). Certainly, further research is warranted concerning the potential impacts of tributyltin on salt marsh biota.

PAHs are another contaminant linked to marina and recreational boating activities. Recreational boating can contribute PAHs to estuaries through engine exhausts, fuel spills, and sources directly related to marinas, such as creosote-treated wood pilings and bulkheads, lubricating oils, and surface runoff from marina parking lots and boat ramps. High levels of PAHs were found in sediments (Voudrias and Smith 1986; Marcus et al. 1988) and oysters (*C. virginica*) (Marcus and Stokes 1985) in close proximity to marinas.

In general, PAHs are only acutely toxic at very high levels; however, a wide variety of sublethal effects to salt marsh biota have been reported at environmentally realistic levels. Bottom-feeding fish, including the hogchoker (*Trinectes maculatus*) and spot (*Leiostomus xanthurus*), were reported to have higher incidences of integumental lesions, cataracts, gill hyperplasia, and liver necrosis in areas with high PAH contamination (Weeks and Warriner 1984; Roberts et al. 1989). Hydrocarbon exposure has been reported to induce histological changes in the mantle, gill epithelium, and gonads of adult oysters (*C. virginica*) (Barszcz et al. 1978). Renzoni (1975) reported depressed fertilization in oysters as well as hampered swimming activity of larvae.

Studies have shown oysters can be adversely impacted by marina construction and operation through the degradation of water quality and destruction of critical habitat (United States Environmental Protection Agency 1985); however, few studies have examined the possible physiological and ecological impacts of marinas on oysters. Van Dolah et al. (1992) assessed oysters collected from shellfish beds in close proximity to four South Carolina marinas and found no major differences in oyster condition or stage of gametogenesis compared to reference oysters. However, spat settlement was significantly lower at two of the four marinas studied; this was probably the result of reduced flushing rates and lower oyster densities in the nearby creeks, rather than contaminant effects associated with marina proximity. In fact, spat settlement was enhanced in the immediate vicinity of some marinas by the presence of pilings, docks, and other structures that may have reduced wave energy (Van Dolah et al. 1992). Oyster spat settle preferentially in areas where water motion is lowest (Bushek 1988).

Other ecological impacts related to the presence of a marina have also been documented. Wendt et al. (1990) examined the benthic macrofaunal community of a South Carolina marina and three sites (reference) located in a nearby undeveloped salt marsh. Some of the community changes these researchers observed were consistent with known community responses to organic enrichment and PAH contamination. These changes included a slightly lower overall species diversity, lower abundances of pollution-sensitive tubiculous polychaetes and crustaceans, and higher abundances of pollution-tolerant capitellid polychaetes. Other community changes appeared to be related to the altered hydrography and increased complexity of the microhabitat resulting from the floating docks and shell hash. These changes included higher abundances of deposit-feeding oligochaetes and ophiuroids, and the presence of a sessile "fouling" community (Wendt et al. 1990). Although the presence of a fouling community may be beneficial in attracting fish to the marina, potential adverse effects include lowered dissolved oxygen and the bioaccumulation of potentially toxic contaminants in successively higher levels of the food chain (Nixon et al. 1973). Nevertheless, the high species abundance at the marina suggests that metals (copper, zinc, and organotin) were not present in sufficient levels to seriously impact the benthic community (Wendt et al. 1990).

Other impacts to salt marshes have been attributed to marina and recreational boating activities. The operation of boats in tidal creeks can create turbulence and wakes, subsequently accelerating shoreline erosion. Oysters can be disturbed by the increased wave action, which can both damage the fragile shells of spat and remove fine-grained substrate suitable for larval settlement. In fact, wake turbulence from boating traffic was found to be the limiting factor in oyster production along the Intracoastal Waterway in Brunswick County, North Carolina (Godwin 1977). Aesthetically, the presence of a marina and the operation of boats can adversely alter the sights, sounds, and smells of a previously unaltered salt marsh (Chmura and Ross 1978).

Based on the actual and potential adverse impacts on sensitive salt marshes, the United States Environmental Protection Agency (1985) has made several recommendations to minimize the impacts of marina construction and operation, including siting marinas to minimize habitat destruction, designing basins to promote flushing, using effective spill, runoff, and erosion control measures, making pumpout facilities and slipside wastewater collection mandatory, scheduling dredging and other construction activities to avoid spawning, migration, and critical life stages of the biota, and using dredge spoils to create new salt marsh habitat. Based on criteria established by the United States Environmental Protection Agency, the United States Army Corps of Engineers issues permits for and enforces the regulations pertaining to marina construction and operation. Numerous states also issue their own permits for marina construction (United States Environmental Protection Agency 1985).

Eutrophication

Eutrophication is to the progressive organic enrichment of waters due to the addition of large amounts of nutrients. Nitrogen, phosphorous, and silicon are the key macronutrients with respect to autotrophic growth in estuaries; however, nitrogen is generally the chief limiting element to primary production in coastal waters (Boynton et al. 1982). Whereas the addition of inorganic nutrients in some ecosystems can maintain species diversity and high productivity, excessive nutrients in estuaries results in an overproduction of phytoplankton, increased biological oxygen demand and oxygen depletion in bottom waters, and mortality of the biota (Kennish 1992). Shallow estuaries with restricted freshwater inflow and tidal ranges tend to be the most susceptible to the impacts of eutrophication; however, larger estuarine systems, such as the Chesapeake Bay, are experiencing increased anoxic events (Correll 1987).

Human activities in coastal areas are the major sources of nutrients entering estuarine systems. Surface water (rivers, streams, and direct runoff during rain events) and groundwater are the major routes of nutrient entry in most areas. In large metropolitan areas, wastewater from sewage treatment plants contributes large amounts of nutrients to estuaries; however, in areas without centralized sewage systems, overflowing and malfunctioning septic tanks are an important source of nutrients, especially in the Southeast United States (Stickney 1984; Lapointe and Clark 1992). Agricultural lands can contribute significant nutrient loads to estuaries via nutrient-rich runoff containing fertilizers and manure.

Urbanization of coastal regions often involves deforestation, which increases the loading rates of nutrients to coastal waters since forests naturally intercept, store, and utilize nutrients. For example, hardwood deciduous forests can remove up to 80% of the nitrate and total phosphorous in surface flows to estuaries, and about 85% of the nitrate in shallow groundwater drainage form agricultural croplands (Correll et al. 1992). In areas without much development, natural sources of nutrients (e.g., atmospheric deposition, wildlife and waterfowl, and organic mineralization) can be significant (Dardeau et al. 1992).

In some regions, significant amounts of nitrogen, primarily as nitrate (NO_3^-), ammonium (NH_4^+), and organic nitrogen, can enter estuaries in bulk atmospheric deposition (both wet and dry deposition) (Morris 1991). In the Rhode River estuary, a subestuary of the Chesapeake Bay, atmospheric deposition accounted for 31% of the total nitrogen influx to the watershed (Correll et al. 1992). When hydrologic factors are taken into account, Correll (1987) estimated that atmospheric deposition and land runoff were of about equal importance as an average annual source of readily available nitrogen to the estuary. By contrast, little phosphorous or available silicate enters the Chesapeake Bay through bulk atmospheric deposition.

The ecological effects of eutrophication can be devastating. The general chain of events begins with excessive nutrient enrichment, which brings about undesirably heavy growth of phytoplankton. Decay of the accumulated dead phytoplankton consumes large amounts of dissolved oxygen, resulting in lowered dissolved oxygen concentrations in bottom waters. Extended periods of anoxia can alter the benthic community and change the dynamics of the estuarine community. For example, extended periods of anoxia have resulted in numerous fish kills and the loss of valuable oyster grounds in the Chesapeake Bay (Correll 1987). In urbanized regions of the Waquoit Bay, Massachusetts, the increased frequency of anoxic events has led to decreased abundance of both eelgrass and the commercially important bay scallop, *Argopectin irradians* (Valiela et al. 1992). Increased nutrient loading from the widespread use of septic tanks was reported to increase algal blooms, seagrass epiphytization and die-off, and the loss of coral cover in the Florida Keys (Lapointe and Clark 1992). Not only does eutrophication impact the benthic community, but it can also impact higher trophic levels. For instance, the disappearance of the estuarine bivalve *Cerastoderma edule* and the proliferation of the opportunistic polychaete *Pygospio elegans* in response to eutrophication in the Bay of Somme (France) has led to a localized redistribution of and dietary changes in birds, particularly the oystercatcher (*Haematopus ostralegus*) and the common gull (*Larus canus*) (Desperez et al. 1992)

Excessive nutrient enrichment of estuaries can also effect the salt marsh macroflora (see Morris 1991 for a review). Fertilization experiments in *Spartina alterniflora*-dominated salt marshes have demonstrated that primary production is stimulated by the addition of nitrogen but not phosphorous (Buresh et al. 1980; Morris 1984). The magnitude of the response of primary production to nitrogen addition is dependent upon several variables: in situ availability of nitrogen, availability of other nutrients, and influence of exogenous factors on nutrient uptake. For instance, the greatest absolute and relative increases in the standing biomass of nitrogen-fertilized *S. alterniflora* occurred where the control biomass was low. In contrast, where the control biomass was high, nitrogen fertilization had little effect on the standing biomass. Based on these observations, Morris (1991) concluded the nitrogen availability in some marsh systems has already reached a threshold, and other factors, such as phosphorous availability, have become secondarily limiting.

The magnitude of the response of *Spartina alterniflora* to nutrient enrichment is also dependent upon the form of nitrogen. In *Spartina*-dominated salt marshes, ammonium tends to be the predominant form of inorganic nitrogen (Maye 1972). Compared to nitrate, application of ammonium to a North Carolina salt marsh significantly increased the standing crop of the short form of *S. alterniflora* sometimes by as much as 24% (Mendelssohn 1979). Thus, *S. alterniflora* is able to assimilate ammonium, the predominant form of nitrogen, better than nitrate, which generally is in poor supply. Excessive nitrate in salt marsh systems is probably lost through denitrification by bacteria, soil leaching, and/or tidal export. Interestingly, Mendelssohn (1979) observed no changes in the standing crop of the tall form of *S. alterniflora* to either ammonium or nitrate. Apparently, the tall form of *S. alterniflora* was not nitrogen limited in that study.

In salt marshes, plant biomass serves as a sink for excess nitrogen, and in the absence of vegetation, the major fate is nitrification-denitrification by bacteria, incorporation into sediment organic pools, and diffusion into the water column. A study of the fate of $^{15}NH_4^+$–N applied to a *Spartina*-dominated Louisiana salt marsh found 28% of the added ^{15}N was recovered in the aboveground biomass and 65% in the sediments and belowground biomass after one growing season (DeLaune et al. 1983). After the second and third growing seasons, the added ^{15}N declined to 50% and 43%, respectively, in the sediment and belowground biomass. Aboveground biomass only accounted for 9.8% and 1.2% of the ^{15}N following the second and third growing season, respectively. DeLaune et al. (1983) postulated that the annual decline of ^{15}N was due to the loss of nitrogen from the leaves, either by physical transport of the plant material off-site or by decomposition of leaf material at the sediment surface, followed by nitrification-denitrification reactions.

By contrast, the addition of $^{15}NH_4^+$ to Louisiana estuarine sediments in the absence of vegetation resulted in ^{15}N rapidly being converted to sediment organic nitrogen within 15 d, this fraction remained stable for the remaining 337 d of the study (Smith and DeLaune 1985). The amount of $^{15}NH_4^+$ in the sediment decreased exponentially to a undetectable levels by day 185. Denitrification by bacteria and diffusion into the water column accounted for the loss of 80% of $^{15}NH_4^+$ from the sediment. The results from these salt marsh studies suggest that *S. alterniflora* does successfully compete with bacteria for excessive nitrogen, especially in the ammonium form (Morris 1991). These studies also underscore the ecological importance of *Spartina* in the estuarine nitrogen cycle, especially its role as a sink for excess nitrogen. In its absence, more nitrogen would consequently be available to fuel phytoplankton blooms, which are known to produce eutrophic conditions.

Microbial degradation processes in salt marshes are sensitive to the nitrogen concentration of the decomposing tissues and the surrounding environment. Plant tissues with elevated nitrogen concentrations have been observed to decompose at faster rates than control tissues (Marinucci et al. 1983; Neely and Davis 1985). Marinucci et al. (1983) found the decomposition rate of nitrogen-fertilized *S. alterniflora* litter was 50% faster than unfertilized litter. Increased litter decomposition rates, and the subsequent increase in detrital material, could potentially alter the trophic dynamics of salt marshes as detritus is thought to support much of the secondary production in salt marsh food webs (Mann 1988).

Because of the diffuse sources of nutrients in estuaries, regional approaches have been undertaken to prepare and implement coordinated plans to control nutrient inputs and improve overall water quality. One such effort has been the Chesapeake Bay Program, a United States Environmental Protection Agency-coordinated effort involving numerous federal and state agencies, which was initiated in 1987 (Spooner 1987). Nutrient inputs into the Chesapeake Bay have been curtailed as a result of the many projects associated with this program. For example, the State of Maryland in 1985 allocated $7 million for agricultural best management practices to control nutrient and pesticide runoff (Garreis 1987). These practices included use of herbacious buffer strips, no-till farming, proper fertilizer applications, and proper storage of manure. Stronger laws and regulations have also been adopted by the State of Maryland. The most significant of these was banning the sale of laundry detergents containing phosphates in excess of 0.5% by weight. Another law requires postdevelopment runoff rates and characteristics to be similar to predevelopment rates in order to control erosion, nutrients, and local flooding (Garreis 1987). Such coordinated efforts are proving beneficial to the improvement of water quality.

Pathogen Contamination

A major concern in coastal regions of the Southeast United States is the closure of commercial and recreational shellfish areas. In 1989, 42% of South Carolina's 140,000 acres of shellfish grounds were closed or restricted from harvesting primarily due to bacterial pollution (Low 1991). The primary criterion used to limit shellfish harvest is contamination of the water by coliform bacteria, which is associated with fecal material. Human coliform bacteria can enter estuaries through overflowing or neglected septic tanks, sewage plant discharges, and municipal and industrial runoff. In some areas, natural sources of coliform bacteria, especially from wildlife populations, can be significant (Dardeau et al. 1992). Consumption of shellfish contaminated by sewage has led to numerous outbreaks of hepatitis A, Norwalk illness, and nonspecific viral gastroenteritis. Between 1973 and 1987, the Centers for Disease Control reported the following cases of shellfish-borne (involved oysters, clams, mussels, and scallops) illness: 335 cases of hepatitis A, 42 cases of other viral origin, and 3,524 cases of unknown etiology (Jaykus et al. 1995).

Elevated nutrient levels in estuaries have been linked to increased frequency, duration, and geographic range of intense dinoflagellate blooms known as red tides. Dinoflagellates associated with red tides, including *Protogonyaulax catenella*, *P. tamarensis*, and *Pyrodinium bahamense*, concentrate in shellfish (e.g., mussels, clams, and oysters). These organisms produce a neurotoxin (saxitoxin) which causes paralytic shellfish poisoning (PSP) in humans when contaminated shellfish are ingested. PSP is an acute illness typified by numbness of the lips, tongue, and fingertips, and in the most severe cases, it can result in death (Hall et al. 1990).

Although the incidence of PSP is low (only 600 reported cases between 1793 and 1966), there has been a growing concern over the increased frequency and greater geographical ranges of the dinoflagellate blooms (Kao 1966; Kennish 1992). For example, a massive bloom of *P. tamarensis* affected the coasts of Maine, New Hampshire, and Massachusetts in 1972, closing numerous shellfish beds. Previous to this bloom, *P. tamarensis* was thought to be restricted to the east coast of Canada. More recently, *P. tamarensis* cysts have been reported in Connecticut and Long Island (Anderson et al. 1982).

In November 1987, a bloom of the dinoflagellate *Ptychodiscus brevis* occurred in North Carolina, forcing the closure of over 300,000 acres of shellfish grounds. Prior to this event, the presence of *Ptychodiscus brevis* had never been documented north of Jacksonville, Florida. Within the first 2 mo of this red tide, it was estimated that commercial oyster and clam fishermen in North Carolina lost $1.7 million (Hearing Before the Committee on Small Business 1988). In addition, this outbreak caused a virtual failure in larval recruitment of the bay scallop, *Argopectin irradians* (Summerson and Peterson 1990). Thus, not only do these intense dinoflagellate blooms put the public at risk for PSP, but they also cause severe economic and ecological impacts.

Salt Marsh Creation, Restoration, and Mitigation

Although salt marshes are now legally protected in most states, previous anthropogenic activities, such as dredging, filling, urban development, and pollution, have resulted in the destruction and degradation of countless acres of ecologically valuable marshes. Recognition of the importance of this loss by scientists and the general public has led to an interest in the restoration and creation of salt marshes. The development of techniques for creation, mitigation, and restoration was originally undertaken by the United States Army Corps of Engineers (the Coastal Engineering Research Center) in order to facilitate habitat development and stabilization of dredge spoils areas (Newling and Landin 1983). The development of techniques to vegetate dredge spoil areas has prompted environmental managers to recommend increasingly the creation of new marshes as mitigation for the loss of natural marshes from development activities. However, these recommendations have been largely unjustified, since the functional level of these created marshes compared to natural marshes has been largely uninvestigated (Race and Christie 1982).

The primary objective in these marsh creation and restoration projects has been to establish the dominant native angiosperm species of the specific region. Once the plants are established, the assumption has been that the animal component and other native plants will soon invade, become established, and the marsh will eventually approximate the structure and function of natural marshes (Broome et al. 1988). Along the East and Gulf coasts of the United States, smooth cordgrass, *Spartina alterniflora*, is the dominant angiosperm in regularly flooded marshes, and it is the principal species used in marsh restoration projects (Woodhouse and Knutson 1982). Along the Pacific Coast of the United States, *S. foliosa* occupies the lower intertidal zone, and it has been used successfully in marsh restoration (Faber 1991). In the United Kingdom, the vigorous and aggressive *S. anglica* has been successfully planted intertidally, and it has been reported to accelerate the recovery of a chronically oiled marsh (Dicks and Iball 1981).

S. alterniflora has probably received more study and can be planted with better chance of success than any other coastal marsh species native to the United States (Woodhouse and Knutson 1982). It is relatively easy to propagate and quick to establish and spread. The propagation of *S. alterniflora* to establish salt marshes has occurred through seeds, vegetative material harvested from natural stands, and vegetative material produced in nurseries. All of these methods have proven successful under certain conditions. These techniques have been described by Woodhouse and Knutson (1982) and Broome et al. (1988).

Direct seeding is usually the most economical method of marsh establishment; however, results of seeding experiments have indicated that this method is only feasible in the upper half of the intertidal zone (Woodhouse and Knutson 1982). When seeding is successful, complete vegetative cover can be established by the end of the first growing season (Seneca et al. 1975). Transplanting sprigs (single stem plants), plugs (15 cm diameter cores of roots, substrate, and stems), and nursery seedlings can be more successful than seeding, especially in the lower half of the intertidal zone and in areas exposed to waves and currents. However, these methods are considerably more expensive and labor intensive than direct seeding (Woodhouse and Knutson 1982). Furthermore, the amount of protective cover after one growing season is usually less than that of direct seeding (Broome et al. 1974). Typically, it takes at least two growing seasons to establish full protective cover of a transplanted marsh. Plugs and sprigs can be transplanted either manually or mechanically depending on size of the marsh and its accessibility (Seneca et al. 1975). Nursery-grown seedlings offer the best chance of success because they suffer less root damage than plants dug from the field and are able to resume growth quicker following transplantation. This allows the plant to become anchored in the marsh sediments at a faster rate (Woodhouse and Knutson 1982).

A number of factors influence the success of establishing vegetation on salt marshes. The severity of the wave climate is a major determinant of the probability for success. Seedlings and transplants require stability and protection from erosion for several weeks in order to become anchored within the sediment. Woodhouse and Knutson (1982) suggested three useful indicators of wave climate severity: fetch, shoreline configuration, and grain size. Fetch has been found to be inversely related to successful marsh establishment. Following numerous planting trials, Wood-house (1979) advised that seeds can be successfully used to establish vegetation at sites with < 1 km of fetch, but at sites with > 1 km of fetch transplants are more successful. A shoreline's configuration determines its vulnerability to wave attack, for example, a cove is relatively sheltered, whereas a headland is subject to wave attack from a variety of directions. Grain size is also related to wave energy; fine-grained sands usually indicate high-energy shorelines.

Estuarine depth and boat traffic were also considered by Woodhouse and Knutson (1982) as useful indicators of wave climate. Marshes in close proximity to boat traffic will be subject to increased wave action. Shallow estuarine depths impede the growth and development of large waves. Based on all of the factors determining wave climate severity, Knutson et al. (1981) developed a Vegetative Stabilization Site Evaluation method to determine the potential for planting success. In areas subject to severe wave impact, wave stilling devices, such as rubber tires and sandbag breakwaters, have been successfully used to protect plants through the critical establishment period (Woodhouse and Knutson 1982).

Slope is another important factor in determining the success of establishing marsh vegetation (Broome et al. 1988). Within limits, gentle slopes provide a greater area of tidal submergence, and thus, a greater area on which marsh vegetation can become established. Furthermore, gentle slopes offer a wider area to dissipate wave energy, which increases the likelihood of establishing vegeta-tion. However, the slope must be sufficient enough to allow for good surface drainage in order to prevent ponding, and the consequential salinity increases due to evaporation. Marshes have been established on slopes from 10% to < 1%, but slopes of 1-3% have been the most successful (Broome et al. 1988).

Other factors controlling the success of establishing vegetation on a marsh are soil type and salinity. Marsh plants will grow on a wide variety of substrates, ranging from coarse sands to fine clays with both high and low concentrations of organic matter (Broome et al. 1988). Sandy substrates are usually the easiest to plant because they provide adequate bearing strength for manual or machine manipulations; however, they often have insufficient amounts of nutrients necessary for vigorous and rapid growth. The addition of fertilizers to sandy substrates will accelerate growth, thus shortening the time that plants are most vulnerable to waves and currents (Garbisch et al. 1975). Conventional fertilizers using ammonium as the form of nitrogen are the most effective and economical. However, Woodhouse and Knutson (1982) warn that fertilization should be a one-time event using slow release materials to prevent acceleration of eutrophic processes.

Salinity variation affects all salt marsh plants. Owing to substrate characteristics, season, seepage, and frequency of inundation, salinity of salt marsh sediments can range from fresh water to more than twice that of seawater. Although salt marsh plants exhibit some degree of salt tolerance, under certain conditions, salinity levels may be too high for successful establishment of vegetation, especially since seedlings are more salt sensitive than established plants (Broome et al. 1988). Although *S. alterniflora* is fairly tolerant of elevated salt concentrations, sediment concentrations greater than 45‰ may prevent its establishment on a marsh (Broome et al. 1988). Sediments of marshes experiencing regular tidal regimes usually do not develop high salt concentrations. High concentrations may occur as a result of evaporation in the high marsh during periods of unusually low rainfall and warm temperatures, and in marshes located in areas subject to wind-driven tides when the prevailing wind patterns result in extended periods of low water. In these cases, Broome et al. (1988) has suggested that the construction of sandy domes adjacent to and above the marsh can reduce substrate salinities. These domes reduce salinity by slowly seeping accumulated precipitation out over the marsh.

Although a considerable amount of research has been directed toward developing techniques for establishing marsh vegetation in intertidal areas, comparatively fewer studies have addressed whether or not these artificial salt marshes are functionally equivalent to natural salt marshes. Unfortunately, there continues to be an underlying assumption in most of the literature that the establishment and persistence of salt marsh vegetation on a site over several years automatically constitutes a level of functioning equivalent to that of natural marshes (reviewed by Race and Christie 1982). The mere presence of vegetation does not indicate that the salt marsh is performing its many inherent ecologically important functions. With this in mind, the degree of functional equivalency between created and natural marshes can be evaluated by reviewing the literature concerning measurements of primary production, faunal community structure, physical-chemical characteristics of the sediment, and utilization of created marshes by fish.

Most research on manmade marshes has focused on the primary production of the newly established vegetation. In general, these studies have determined that aboveground biomass of manmade marshes can equal or exceed that of natural marshes in two or three growing seasons; however, belowground biomass may take up to 4 yr or 5 yr to equal natural marshes. For example, Broome et al. (1986) conducted a long-term (10 yr) study on the vegetative biomass of a *Spartina alterniflora* transplanted marsh along a shoreline of Bogue Banks, North Carolina. Aboveground and belowground biomass was equal to that of ecologically similar natural marshes after two and four growing seasons, respectively. Following the fourth growing season, belowground biomass in the transplanted marsh exceeded that of the natural marsh (Broome et al. 1986). Similar results have been observed on a naturally established *Spartina alterniflora* marsh occurring on unconfined dredge spoils in Winyah Bay, South Carolina (LaSalle et al. 1991). Other, short-term (2 or 3 yr) studies concerning the transplantation of vegetation on dredge spoils in North Carolina (Cammen 1976a) and Texas (Webb and Newling 1985) have reported aboveground biomass equal to that of natural marshes, but the belowground biomass was significantly less than that of natural marshes. Based on the results of long-term studies, it appears that belowground biomass takes about twice as long as aboveground biomass to resemble that of natural marshes. Therefore, these short-term studies were probably not of sufficient duration to detect the complete establishment of the belowground biomass.

Fewer studies have investigated the faunal composition of artificially created salt marshes. In general, these studies indicate that macrofaunal community development takes considerably longer than the establishment of vegetation. Cammen (1976a,b) monitored the macrofauna composition of two transplanted *S. alterniflora* dredge spoil marshes in North Carolina (Drum Inlet and Snow Cut) and found lower abundances, lower biomass, and different community compositions compared to nearby natural marshes, even after three growing seasons. The faunal affinity between the transplanted and natural marshes was only 40% and 10%, respectively, at Drum Inlet and Snow Cut. The dominant fauna of the natural marshes were polychaetes, which composed up to 65% of the total biomass. By contrast, the dominant fauna at the transplanted marshes were insects and amphipods, which composed 64% and 77% of the total biomass at Drum Inlet and Snow Cut, respectively (Cammen 1976b). Total biomass at the natural marshes was sixfold greater (7.7 g m^{-2} yr^{-1} versus 1.2 g m^{-2} yr^{-1}) than the transplanted marsh at Drum Inlet and tenfold greater (5.7 g m^{-2} yr^{-1} versus 0.5 g m^{-2} yr^{-1}) than the transplanted marsh at Snow Cut (Cammen 1976a).

Qualitative observations concerning the faunal composition of transplanted *S. alterniflora* marshes on dredge spoils have also been documented. Blair (1991) reported lower densities of macroinvertebrates in a Chesapeake Bay transplanted marsh compared to a nearby natural marsh 4 yr after the establishment of the marsh. The natural marsh was dominated by nematodes and fiddler crabs, whereas the transplanted had comparatively higher densities of clams and lower densities of fiddler crabs. Lower densities of fiddler crabs have also been reported in an artificially created marsh in Georgia (Reimold et al. 1978). Results from these short-term studies strongly suggest the community structure of transplanted marshes is considerably different from that of natural marshes.

Several authors, including Cammen (1976a) and Blair (1991), have suggested that these differences stem from the lower organic content of artificially created marshes compared to that of natural, mature salt marshes. For example, the organic matter content of the Drum Inlet and Snow Cut transplanted marshes was only 15% and 6%, respectively, of the natural marshes (Cammen 1976a). Other studies also have found manmade marshes have considerably less organic matter in the soil. In a survey of soils from five manmade North Carolina salt marshes ranging in age from 1 yr to 15 yr, the macroorganic matter was generally lower in the transplanted marshes compared with nearby natural marshes; however, there was a trend toward increasing macroorganic matter with the age of the marsh (Craft et al. 1988). At the 15-yr-old site, levels of macroorganic matter were approximately equal. Based on these results, Craft et al. (1988) estimated that the macroorganic matter of transplanted marshes would approximate those levels observed in mature, natural marshes in 15-30 yr. If the organic content of artificial marsh sediments needs to be similar to that of mature marshes in order to develop a detritus-based food web, as suggested by Race and Christie (1982), then it can be expected that it will also take at least 15-30 yr for the faunal composition and abundance of these marshes to approximate that of natural marshes.

With respect to the hydrologic and nutrient cycling functions, studies conducted by Craft et al. (1989, 1991) suggest that created marshes do not duplicate natural tidal marshes, at least not initially. For example, pore water collected from a 5-yr-old transplanted marsh in North Carolina had a significantly higher redox potential (Eh), dissolved O_2, Fe, Mn, and NO_3–N, and significantly lower dissolved organic carbon and nitrogen, NH_4–N, PO_4–P, and pH compared to natural marshes (Craft et al. 1991). Likewise, total nitrogen and organic carbon nutrient pools are lower in these created marshes than in natural marshes; however, little difference in total phosphorous pools was observed (Craft et al. 1988).

The fluxes of nutrients between the marsh and estuarine waters also differ between created and natural marshes (Craft et al. 1989). Unlike natural marshes, which act as a source of NH_4–N to adjoining estuarine waters (Whiting et al. 1987), transplanted marshes removed NH_4–N and PO_4–P from the water, probably due to uptake of NH_4–N by the vegetation and PO_4–P by the soil. The export of dissolved organic carbon and nitrogen by these transplanted marshes was evidence that these marshes were performing at least some of the normal functions of a salt marsh (Craft et al. 1989). Salt marshes typically provide dissolved organic carbon to estuarine waters, which subsequently supports the food web (Wolaver and Spurrier 1988). Craft et al. (1989) suggested that these created marshes will continue to remove NH_4–N and PO_4–P from the estuarine water until sufficient nutrient pools are established to support the marsh community. Although the macroorganic matter in transplanted marshes can approximate that of natural marshes in 15-30 yr, Craft et al. (1988) have estimated that soil nitrogen and carbon levels will take considerably longer.

Utilization of transplanted marshes by finfish has also received some attention. In general, transplanted marshes should not exactly replicate the fishery habitat functions of natural marshes due to the reduced marsh-water interface in most transplanted marshes. Under the assumption that access to the marsh surface is regulated by the amount of marsh-water interface, Minnello and Zimmerman (1990) created two experimental channels in a previously established *S. alterniflora* marsh in Galveston Bay, Texas. The effects of the channelization were an increased density of both finfish and crustaceans in the marsh. In addition, the stem density and biomass of *S. alterniflora* increased adjacent to the channels (Minnello and Zimmerman 1990).

Finfish utilization of newly created marshes has also been studied in North Carolina (Rulifson 1991). These marshes were built to mitigate the impacts of phosphate mining activities, and were intentionally constructed to simulate the meandering and channelized nature of the surrounding natural creeks. In general, the abundance of fish, including the bay anchovy, Atlantic menhaden, spot, and southern flounder, was equal to or greater than that of nearby control creeks within 4 yr of construction. The only exception was Atlantic croaker, which was less abundant in the mitigation creeks (Rulifson 1991). Based on these results, it appears that the overall value of created marshes as a fishery habitat can approximate that of natural marshes if they are channelized to allow for greater marsh-water interface.

In summary, created marshes may eventually approach the functional equivalency of natural marshes; however, the duration of this process probably occurs over several decades. Aboveground and belowground biomass of *Spartina alterniflora* can rapidly approach that of natural marshes within 5 yr. Likewise, colonization of the marsh sediments by macroinvertebrates occurs rapidly. But, the total biomass, abundance, and species composition generally differs from that of natural marshes. These differences appear to be the result of lower organic matter and altered physical and/or chemical properties of the sediments. In order to establish a more typical detritus-based marsh food web, the following events need to occur in the sediments: accumulation of organic matter, establishment of nutrient pools of carbon and nitrogen, and formation of an anaerobic decomposition zone, characterized by reduction processes. Levels of organic matter in created marshes can approximate that of natural marshes in 15-30 yr; however, the nutrient pools will take considerably longer (Craft et al. 1988). Although the abundance of benthic infauna and the taxa present may influence the utilization of a created marsh by finfish, research has demonstrated that the amount of marsh-water interface is also an important factor. Provided with proper channelization, finfish will rapidly utilize the marsh habitat.

Conclusions

Although salt marshes are inherently resilient to stressors and have a great capacity to absorb anthropogenic impacts, historically human society has not utilized salt marshes and their resources in ways that have been sustainable. These past practices have resulted in the destruction of countless acres of valuable tidal marshes. Fortunately, legislation developed during the 1970s, such as the Coastal Zone Management Act and Clean Water Act, currently regulate many activities directly impacting marshes, including marina development and point-source pollutant discharges. However, the cumulative effects of various indirect impacts (e.g., nonpoint-source pollutants and nutrient inputs) continue to be manifested as decreased species diversity and abundance, alterations in community structure and functional processes, and reductions in productivity and overall habitat quality.

As coastal populations in the United States continue to increase, the management of this growth, its ancillary urban development, and the utilization of resources will become even more critical. To preserve the aesthetic and ecological values associated with salt marshes for future generations, a collective framework for sustainable development involving local, state, and federal cooperation needs to developed.

Despite current legislation protecting salt marshes, there will always be the potential for possible disturbance, especially when national security or energy concerns are involved. When salt marsh disturbance and destruction are *absolutely unavoidable*, the creation of new marshes should be required, especially since the technology for marsh restoration exists and the costs are reasonable compared to a marsh's estimated value as a natural resource (Broome et al. 1988). In these situations, marsh creation can be an effective tool to minimize on-site damage, control shoreline erosion, and return degraded wetlands to tidal influence (Race and Christie 1982). However, it should be understood prior to any marsh creation effort that full ecosystem functioning of the marsh is not guaranteed, and may only occur following several decades. Therefore, environmental managers need to be cautious in the widespread adoption of marsh creation as an acceptable mitigation strategy. Based on the paucity of data that exists, it is also apparent that more long-term research is necessary to investigate the functional equivalency of created marshes.

LITERATURE CITED

Abel, P.D. 1989. Water Pollution Biology. Ellis Horwood, Chichester, United Kingdom.

Adair, J. 1987. Assessment of heavy metal contamination in *C. virginica* from marina facilities. *Northeast Gulf Science* 9: 135-142.

Alberts, J.J., M.T. Price, and M. Dania. 1990. Metal concentrations in tissues of *Spartina alterniflora* (Loisel.) and sediments of Georgia salt marshes. *Estuarine Coastal and Shelf Science* 30: 47-58.

Anderson, D.M., D.M. Kulis, J.A. Orphanos, and A.R. Ceurvels. 1982. Distribution of the toxic dinoflagellate, *Gonyaulax tamarensis* in Southern New England region. *Estuarine Coastal and Shelf Science* 14: 447-458.

Baker, J.M. 1979. Responses of salt marsh vegetation to oil spills and refinery effluents, p. 529-542. *In* R.L. Jeffries and A.J. Davy (eds.), Ecological Processes in Coastal Environments. Blackwell Scientific Publishing, London.

Barron, M.G. 1995. Bioaccumulation and bioconcentration in aquatic organisms, p. 652-666. *In* D.J. Hoffman, B.A. Rattner, G.A. Burton, Jr., J. Cairnes, Jr. (eds.), Handbook of Ecotoxicology. Lewis Publishers, Boca Raton, Florida.

Barszcz, C., P.O. Yenich, L.R. Brown, J.D. Yarbrough, and C.D. Minchew. 1978. Chronic effects of three crude oils on oysters suspended in estuarine ponds. *Journal of Environmental Pathology, Toxicology and Oncology* 1: 879-896.

Beatley, T.D., J. Brower, and A.K. Schwab. 1994. An Introduction to Coastal Zone Management. Island Press, Washington, DC.

Berthou, F., G. Balouët, G. Bodennec, and M. Marchang. 1987. The occurrence of hydrocarbons and histopathological abnormalities in oysters for seven years following the wreck of the *Amoco Cadiz* in Brittany (France). *Marine Environmental Research* 23: 103-110.

Blair, C. 1991. Successful tidal wetland mitigation in Norfolk, Virginia, p. 463-476. *In* H.S. Bolton (ed.), Coastal Wetlands. American Society of Civil Engineers, New York.

Bonvincini Pagliai, A.M., A.M. Cognetti Varriale, R. Crema, M. Curini Galletti, and R. Vandini Zunarelli. 1985. Environmental impact of extensive dredging in a coastal marine area. *Marine Pollution Bulletin* 16: 483-488.

Boynton, W.R., W.M. Kemp, and C.W. Keefe. 1982. A comparative analysis of nutrients and other factors influencing estuarine phytoplankton production, p. 69-90. *In* V.S. Kennedy (ed.), Estuarine Comparisons. Academic Press, New York.

Broome, S.W., E.D. Seneca, and W.W. Woodhouse, Jr. 1986. Long-term growth and development of transplants of the salt marsh grass *Spartina alterniflora*. *Estuaries* 9: 63-74.

Broome, S.W., E.D. Seneca, and W.W. Woodhouse, Jr. 1988. Tidal salt marsh restoration. *Aquatic Botany* 32: 1-22.

Broome, S.W., W.W. Woodhouse, Jr., and E.D. Seneca. 1974. Propagation of smooth cordgrass, *Spartina alterniflora*, from seed in North Carolina. *Chesapeake Science* 15: 214-221.

Buresh, R.J., M.E. Casselman, and W.H. Patrick, Jr. 1980. Nitrogen and phosphorus distribution and utilization by *Spartina alterniflora* in a Louisiana Gulf Coast marsh. *Estuaries* 3: 111-121.

Burger, J., J. Brzorad, and M. Gochfeld. 1991. Immediate effects of an oil spill on behavior of fiddler crabs (*Uca pugnax*). *Archives of Environmental Contamination and Toxicology* 20: 404-409.

Burger, J. and J. Shisler. 1983. Succession and productivity on perturbed and natural *Spartina* salt marsh areas in New Jersey. *Estuaries* 6: 50-56.

Burns, K.A. and J.M. Teal. 1979. The West Falmouth oil spill: Hydrocarbons in the salt marsh ecosystem. *Estuarine and Coastal Marine Science* 8: 349-360.

Bushek, D. 1988. Settlement as a major determinant of intertidal oyster and barnacle distributions along a horizontal gradient. *Journal of Experimental Marine Biology and Ecology* 122: 1-18.

Bybee, J.R. 1969. Effects of hydraulic pumping operations on the fauna of Tijuana Slough. *California Fish and Game* 55: 213-220.

Byers, J.E. 1993. Variations in the bioaccumulation of zinc, copper, and lead in *Crassostrea virginica* and *Ilyanassa obseleta* in marinas and open water environments. *Journal of the Elisha Mitchell Scientific Society* 109: 163-170.

Cairns, J., Jr. and A.L. Buikema. 1984. Restoration of Habitat Impacted by Oil Spills. Butterworth, Boston, Massachusetts.

Cammen, L.M. 1976a. Macroinvertebrate colonization of *Spartina* marshes artificially established on dredge spoil. *Estuarine and Coastal Marine Science* 4: 357-372.

Cammen, L.M. 1976b. Abundance and production of macroinvertebrates from natural and artificially established salt marshes in North Carolina. *American Midland Naturalist* 96: 487-493.

Catallo, W.J. 1993. Ecotoxicology and wetland ecosystems: Current understanding and future needs. *Environmental Toxicology and Chemistry* 12: 2209-2224.

Chabreck, R.A. 1988. Coastal Marshes: Ecology and Wildlife Management. University of Minnesota Press, Minneapolis, Minnesota.

Chambers, J.R. 1991. Habitat degradation and fishery declines in the United States, p. 46-60. *In* S. Bolton (ed.), Coastal Wetlands. American Society of Civil Engineers, New York.

Chandler, G.T. 1990. Effects of sediment-bound residues of the pyrethroid insecticide fenvalerate on survival and reproduction of meiobenthic copepods. *Marine Environmental Research* 29: 65-76.

Chandler, G.T. and J.W. Fleeger. 1983. Facilitative and inhibitory interactions among estuarine meiobenthic harpacticoid copepods. *Ecology* 68: 1906-1919.

Chandler, G.T. and G.I. Scott. 1991. Effects of sediment-bound endosulfan on survival, reproduction and larval settlement of meiobenthic polychaetes and copepods. *Environmental Toxicology and Chemistry* 10: 375-382.

Chmura, G.L. and N.W. Ross. 1978. The environmental impacts of marinas and their boats: A literature review with management considerations. Memorandum 45, University of Rhode Island, Marine Advisory Service, Narragansett, Rhode Island.

Clark, J.R., M.A. Lewis, and A.S. Pait. 1993. Pesticide inputs and risks in coastal wetlands. *Environmental Toxicology and Chemistry* 12: 2225-2233.

Clark, R.B. 1989. Marine Pollution, 2nd edition. Clarendon Press, Oxford.

Corliss, J. and L. Trent. 1971. Comparison of phytoplankton production between natural and altered areas in West Bay, Texas. *Fisheries Bulletin* 69: 829-832.

Correll, D.L. 1987. Nutrients in Chesapeake Bay, p. 298-320. *In* S.K. Majumdar, L.W. Hall, and H.M. Austin (eds.), Contaminant Problems and Management of Living Chesapeake Bay Resources. Typehouse of Easton, Phillipsburg, New Jersey.

Correll, D.L., T.E. Jordan, and D.E. Weller. 1992. Nutrient flux in a landscape: Effects of coastal land use and terrestrial community mosaic on nutrient transport to coastal waters. *Estuaries* 15: 431-442.

Coull, B.C. and S.S. Bell. 1979. Perspectives of marine meiofaunal ecology, p. 189-216. *In* R.J. Livingston (ed.), Processes in Coastal and Marine Ecosystems. Plenum Press, New York.

Coull, B.C. and G.T. Chandler. 1992. Pollution and meiofauna: Field, laboratory, and mesocosm studies. *Oceanography and Marine Biology Annual Review* 30: 191-271.

Cowell, E.B. 1969. The effects of oil pollution on salt marsh communities in Pembrokeshire and Cornwall. *Journal of Applied Ecology* 6: 133-142.

Craft, C.B., S.W. Broome, and E.D. Seneca. 1988. Nitrogen phosphorus, and organic carbon pools in natural and transplanted marsh soils. *Estuaries* 11: 272-280.

Craft, C.B., S.W. Broome, and E.D. Seneca. 1989. Exchange of nitrogen, phosphorus, and organic carbon between transplanted marshes and estuarine waters. *Journal of Environmental Quality* 18: 206-211.

Craft, C.B., E.D. Seneca, and S.W. Broome. 1991. Porewater chemistry of natural and created marsh soils. *Journal of Experimental Marine Biology and Ecology* 152: 187-200.

Craig, N.J., R.E. Turner, and J.W. Day, Jr. 1979. Land loss in coastal Louisiana (USA). *Environmental Management* 3: 133-144.

Culliton, T.J., M.A. Warren, T.R. Goodspeed, D.G. Remer, C.M. Blackwell, and J.J. McDonough. 1990. Fifty years of population change along the nation's coast, 1960-2010. Strategic Environmental Assessments Division, ORCA/NOS/NOAA. Silver Spring, Maryland.

Daiber, F.C. 1986. Conservation of Tidal Marshes. Van Nostrand Reinhold Company Inc., New York.

Dardeau, M.R., R.F. Modlin, W.W. Schroeder, and J.P. Stout. 1992. Estuaries, p. 615-744. *In* C.T. Hackney, S.M. Adams, and W.H. Martin (eds.), Biodiversity of the Southeastern United States: Aquatic Communities. John Wiley & Sons, Inc., New York.

Day, J.W., C.A.S. Hall, W.M. Kemp, and A. Yanez-Arancibia. 1989. Estuarine Ecology. Wiley Interscience, New York.

Decker, C.J. and J.W. Fleeger. 1984. The effect of crude oil on the colonization of meiofauna into salt marsh sediment. *Hydrobiologia* 118: 49-58.

DeLaune, R.D., W.H. Patrick, and R.J. Buresh. 1979. Effect of crude oil on a Louisiana *Spartina alterniflora* salt marsh. *Environmental Pollution, Series A* 20: 21-31.

DeLaune, R.D., and S.R. Pezeshki. 1991. Role of soil chemistry in vegetative ecology of wetlands. *Trends in Soil Science* 1: 101-113.

DeLaune, R.D., C.J. Smith, and W.H. Patrick, Jr. 1983. Nitrogen losses from a Louisiana gulf coast salt marsh. *Estuarine Coastal and Shelf Science* 17: 133-141.

DeLaune, R.D., C.J. Smith, W.H. Patrick, Jr., J.W. Fleeger, and M.D. Tolley. 1984. Effect of oil on salt marsh biota: methods for restoration. *Environmental Pollution, Series A* 36: 207-227.

Desperez, M., H. Rybarczyk, J.G. Wilson, J.P. Ducrotoy, F. Sueur, R. Olivesi and B. Elkaim. 1992. Biological impact of eutrophication in the Bay of Somme and the induction and impact of anoxia. *Netherlands Journal of Sea Research* 30: 149-159.

Dicks, B. and K. Iball. 1981. Ten years of salt marsh monitoring of the case history of a Southampton Water salt marsh and a changing refinery effluent discharge, p. 362-374. *In* Proceedings of the 1981 World Oil Spill Conference, API/EPA/USCG, Washington, DC.

DiPinto, L.M., B.C. Coull, and G.T. Chandler. 1993. Lethal and sublethal effects of the sediment-associated PCP aroclor 1254 on a meiobenthic copepod. *Environmental Toxicology and Chemistry* 12: 1909-1918.

Drifmeyer, J.E. and W.E. Odum. 1975. Lead, zinc, and manganese in dredge-spoil pond ecosystems. *Environmental Conservation* 2: 39-45.

Dunstan, W.M. and H.L. Windom. 1975. The influence of environmental changes in heavy metal concentrations on *Spartina alterniflora*, p. 393-404. *In* L.E. Cronin (ed.), Estuarine Research, Vol. II. Geology and Engineering. Academic Press, New York.

Edwards, A.C. and D.E. Davis. 1974. Effects of herbicides on the *Spartina* salt marsh, p. 531-546. *In* R.J. Reimold and W.H. Queen (ed.), Ecology of Halophytes. Academic Press, New York.

Eisler, R. 1987. Polycyclic aromatic hydrocarbon hazards to fish, wildlife, and invertebrates: A synoptic review. United States Fish and Wildlife Service, Biological Report 85, Washington, DC.

Engler, R.M. 1976. Environmental impacts of the aquatic disposal of dredge material: Fact and fancy, p. 220-235. *In* Proceedings of the Eighth Dredging Seminar. Texas A&M University Sea Grant Publication, TAMU-SG-77-102. College Station, Texas

Espourteille, F.A., J. Greaves, and R.J. Huggett. 1993. Measurement of tributyltin contamination of sediments and *Crassostrea virginica* in the southern Chesapeake Bay. *Environmental Toxicology and Chemistry* 12: 305-314.

Evans, P.R. 1986. Use of the herbicide "Dalapon" for control of *Spartina* encroaching on intertidal mudflats: beneficial effects on shorebirds. *Colonial Waterbirds* 9: 171-175.

Evans, D.R. and S.D. Rice. 1974. Effects of oil on marine ecosystems: A review for administrators and policy makers. *Fishery Bulletin, United States* 72: 625-638.

Faber, P.M. 1991. The Muzzi marsh, Corte Madera, California, long-term observations of a restored marsh in San Francisco Bay, p. 424-438. *In* H.S. Bolton (ed.), Coastal Wetlands. American Society of Civil Engineers, New York.

Fenchel, T.M. and B.B. Jorgensen. 1977. Detritus food chains of aquatic systems. *Advances in Environmental Microbiology* 45: 71-78.

Fleeger, J.W. and G.T. Chandler. 1983. Meiofauna responses to an experimental oil spill in a Louisiana salt marsh. *Marine Ecology Progress Series* 11: 257-264.

Gambrell, R.P., V. Collard, and W.H. Patrick, Jr. 1987. Cadmium uptake by marsh plants as affected by sediment physiochemical conditions, p. 425-443. *In* R.A. Baker (ed.), Contaminants and Sediments, Vol. 2. Ann Arbor Science, Ann Arbor, Michigan.

Garbisch, E.W., Jr., P.B. Woller, W.J. Bostian, and R.J. McCallum. 1975. Biotic techniques for shore stabilization, p. 405-437. *In* L.E. Cronin (ed.), Estuarine Research, Vol. II. Geology and Engineering. Academic Press, New York.

Gardner, W.S., D.R. Kendall, R.R. Odom, H.L. Windom, and J.A. Stephens. 1978. The distribution of methyl mercury in a contaminated salt marsh ecosystem. *Environmental Pollution* 15: 243-251.

Garreis, M.J. 1987. The State of Maryland's response to Chesapeake Bay ecological problems, p. 498-511. *In* S.K. Majumdar, L.W. Hall, and H.M. Austin (eds.), Contaminant Problems and Management of Living Chesapeake Bay Resources. Typehouse of Easton, Phillipsburg, New Jersey.

GESAMP (IMCO/FAO/UNESCO/WMO/WHO/IAEA/UN Joint Group of Experts on the Scientific Aspects of Marine Pollution). 1977. Impact of oil on the marine environment. Reports and Studies No. 6, Food and Agricultural Organization, Rome.

Giblin, A.E., M. Piotrowski, B. Leighty, I. Valiela, and J.M. Teal. 1983. Responses of a salt marsh microbial community to inputs of heavy metals: Aerobic heterotrophic metabolism. *Environmental Toxicology and Chemistry* 2: 343-351.

Giere, O. 1979. The impact of oil pollution on intertidal meiofauna. Field studies after the La Coruna-spill, May 1976. *Cahiers de Biologie Marine* 21: 51-60.

Glotfelty, S.E., G.H. Williams, H.P. Freeman, and M.M. Leach. 1990. Regional atmospheric transport and deposition of pesticides in Maryland, p. 191-221. *In* D.A. Duntz (ed.), Long Range Transport of Pesticides. Lewis, Chelsea, Michigan.

Godwin, W.F. 1977. A survey of closed shellfish waters in western Brunswick County, North Carolina. North Carolina Division of Marine Fisheries. Morehead City, North Carolina.

Hall, C.A.S., R. Howarth, B. Moore, and C.J. Vorosmorthy. 1978. Environmental impacts of industrial energy systems in the coastal zone. *Annual Review of Energy* 3: 395-475.

Hall, S., G. Strichartz, E. Moczydlowski, A. Ravindran, and P.B. Rerchardt. 1990. The saxotoxins: sources, chemistry, and pharmacology, p. 29-65. *In* S. Hall and G. Strichartz (eds.), Marine Toxins: Origin, Structure, and Molecular Pharmacology. American Chemical Society, Washington, DC.

Hampson, G.R., and E.T. Moul. 1978. No. 2 fuel oil spill in Bourne, Massachusetts: immediate assessment of the effects on marine invertebrates and a 3-year study of growth and recovery of a salt marsh. *Journal of the Fisheries Research Board of Canada* 35: 731-744.

Harris, L.D. 1988. The nature of cumulative impacts on biotic diversity of wetland vertebrates. *Environmental Management* 12: 675-693.

Hearing Before the Committee on Small Business (House of Representatives). 1988. Impact of red tide infestation on North Carolina small businesses and the response of the United States Small Business Administration. Serial No. 100-3, United States Government Printing Office, Washington, D.C.

Hershner, C. and J. Lake. 1980. Effects of chronic oil pollution on a salt marsh grass community. *Marine Biology* 56: 163-173.

Hobbie, J.E. and B.J. Copeland. 1980. Estuarine ecosystems, p. 186-197. *In* F.E. Guthrie and J.J. Perry (eds.), Introduction to Environmental Toxicology. Elsevier Publishing Corporation, New York.

Hoffman, E.J., G.L. Mills, J.S. Latimer, and J.G. Quinn. 1984. Urban runoff as a source of polycyclic aromatic hydrocarbons to coastal waters. *Environmental Science and Technology* 18: 580-587.

Holland, A.F., D.E. Porter, R.F. Van Dolah, R.H. Dunlap, G.H. Steel, and S.M. Upchurch. 1993. Environmental assessment for alternative dredged material disposal sites in Charleston Harbor. South Carolina Wildlife and Marine Resources Department, Marine Resources Division, Technical Report Number 82. Charleston, South Carolina.

Hood, H. W. Bishop, F. Bishop, S. Meyers, and T. Whelan. 1975. Microbial indicators of oil-rich salt marsh sediments. *Applied Microbiology* 30: 982-987.

Hutzinger, O., S. Safe, and V. Zitko. 1974. The Chemistry of PCBs. CRC Press, Cleveland, Ohio.

Jaykus, L.A., M.T. Hemard, and M.S. Sobsey. 1995. Human enteric pathogenic viruses, p. 92-171. *In* C.R. Hackney and M.D. Pierson (eds.), Environmental Indicators and Shellfish Safety. Chapman and Hall, New York.

Jensen, K. 1984. Benzo(a)pyrene input and occurrence in a marine area affected by refinery effluent. *Water Air and Soil Pollution* 22: 57-65.

Johnson, A.S., H.O. Hillestad, S.F. Shanholzer, and G.G. Shanholzer. 1974. An ecological survey of the coastal region of Georgia, Scientific Monograph Series No. 3, National Park Service, Washington, D.C.

Kao, C.Y. 1966. Tetrodoxin, saxitoxin, and their significance in the study of excitation phenomena. *Pharmacological Review* 18: 997-1049.

Kator, H. and R. Herwig. 1977. Microbial responses after two experimental oil spills in an eastern coastal plain estuarine ecosystem, p. 517-522. *In* Proceedings of the 1977 Oil Spill Conference, American Petroleum Institute, Washington, D.C.

Kennish, M.J. 1992. Ecology of Estuaries: Anthropogenic Effects. CRC Press, Boca Raton, Florida.

Kirby, C.J., J.W. Keeley, and J. Harrison. 1975. An overview of the technical aspects of the corps of engineers national dredged-material research program, p. 523-535. *In* L. Cronin (ed.), Estuarine Research, Vol. 2. Geology and Engineering, Academic Press, New York.

Knutson, P.L., J.C. Ford, M.R. Inskeep, and J. Ozler. 1981. National survey of planted salt marshes (vegetative stabilization and wave stress). *Wetlands* 1: 129-157.

Kraus, M.L., P. Weis, and J.H. Crow. 1986. The excretion of heavy metals by the salt marsh cord grass, *Spartina alterniflora*, and *Spartina's* role in mercury cycling. *Marine Environmental Research* 20: 307-316.

Kure, L.K., and M.H. Depledge. 1994. Accumulation of organotin in *Littorina littorea* and *Mya arenaria* from Danish coastal waters. *Environmental Pollution* 84: 149-157.

Lake, J.L., C. Norwood, C. Dimock, and R. Bowen. 1979. Origins of polycyclic aromatic hydrocarbons in estuarine sediments. *Geochimica et Cosmochimica Acta* 43: 1847-1855.

Lane, P.A., J.H. Vandermeulen, M.J. Crowell, and D.G. Patriquin. 1987. Impact of experimentally dispersed crude oil on vegetation in a northwestern Atlantic salt marsh-preliminary observations, p. 509-517. *In* Proceedings of the 1987 Oil Spill Conference, API/EPA/USGC, Washington, D.C.

LaSalle, M.W., M.C. Landin and J.G. Sims. 1991. Evaluation of the flora and fauna of a *Spartina alterniflora* marsh established on dredged material in Winyah Bay, South Carolina. *Wetlands* 11: 191-208.

Lapointe, B.E. and M.W. Clark. 1992. Nutrient inputs from the watershed and coastal eutrophication in the Florida Keys. *Estuaries* 15: 465-476.

Lee, C.R., R.E. Hoeppel, P.G. Hunt, and C.A. Carlson. 1976. Feasibility of the functional use of vegetation to filter, dewater, and remove contaminants from dredged material. United States Army Corps of Engineers, Waterways Experiment Station, Technical Report D-76-4. Vicksburg, Mississippi.

Lee, R.F., B. Dornseif, F. Gonsoulin, K. Tenore, and R. Hanson. 1981. Fate and effects of a heavy oil spill on a Georgia salt marsh. *Marine Environmental Research* 5: 125-143.

Li, Y., J.T. Morris, and D.C. Yoch. 1990. Chronic low level hydrocarbon amendments stimulate plant growth and microbial activity in salt marsh microcosms. *Journal of Applied Ecology* 27: 159-171.

Linden, E. B.E. Bengtsson, O. Svanberg, and B. Sundstrom. 1979. The acute toxicity of 78 chemicals and pesticide formulations against two brackish water organisms, the bleak (*Alburnus alburnus*) and the harpacticoid *Nitocra spinipes*. *Chemosphere* 11/12: 843-851.

Low, R.A. 1991. South Carolina Marine Fisheries, 1989. South Carolina Wildlife and Marine Resources Department, Office of Fisheries Management, Data Report 7. Charleston, South Carolina.

Lunsford, C.A., M.P. Weinstein, and L. Scott. 1987. Uptake of Kepone by the estuarine bivalve, *Rangia cuneata*, during the dredging of contaminated sediments in the James River, Virginia. *Water Research* 21: 411-416.

Mann, K.H. 1988. Production and use of detritus in various freshwater, estuarine and coastal marine systems. *Limnology and Oceanography* 33: 910-930.

Marcus, J.M., and T.P. Stokes. 1985. Polynuclear aromatic hydrocarbons in oyster tissue around three coastal marinas. *Bulletin of Environmental Contamination and Toxicology* 35: 835-844.

Marcus, J.M. and A.M. Thompson. 1986. Heavy metals in oyster tissue around three coastal marinas. *Bulletin of Environmental Contamination and Toxicology* 36: 587-594.

Marcus, J.M., G.R. Swearingen, A.D. Williams, and D.D. Heizer. 1988. Polynuclear aromatic hydrocarbon and heavy metal concentrations in sediments at coastal South Carolina marinas. *Archives of Environmental Contamination and Toxicology* 17: 103-113.

Marinucci, A.C., and R. Bartha. 1982. Biomagnification of Aroclor 1242 in decomposing *Spartina* litter. *Applied and Environmental Microbiology* 44: 669-677.

Marinucci, A.C., J.E. Hobbie, J.V.K. Helfrich. 1983. Effect of litter nitrogen on decomposition and microbial biomass in *Spartina alterniflora*. *Microbial Ecology* 9: 27-40.

Maye, P.R. 1972. Some important inorganic and organic nitrogen and phosphorous species in Georgia salt marshes. Environmental Resources Center. Georgia Institute of Technology. Report No. 272. Atlanta, Georgia.

McElroy, A.E., J.W. Farrington, and J.M. Teal. 1989. Bioavailability of PAH in the aquatic environment, p. 1-39. *In* U. Varanasi (ed.), Metabolism of Polycyclic Aromatic Hydrocarbons in the Aquatic Environment. CRC Press, Boca Raton, Florida.

McGovern, T.A., L.J. Laber, and B.C. Gram. 1979. Characteristics of the salt secreted by *Spartina alterniflora* and their relation to estuarine production. *Estuarine and Coastal Marine Science* 9: 351-356.

McKinley, V.L., T.W. Federle, and J.R. Vestal. 1982. Effects of petroleum hydrocarbons on plant litter microbiota in an Arctic Lake. *Applied and Environmental Microbiology* 43: 129-135.

Mendelssohn, I.A. 1979. The influence of nitrogen level, form, and application method on the growth response of *Spartina alterniflora* in North Carolina. *Estuaries* 2: 106-112.

Minnello, T.J. and R.J. Zimmerman. 1990. Creation of salt marshes for fishery organisms. *In* R.L. Lazor (ed.), Beneficial Uses of Dredged Material. United States Army Corps of Engineers, Waterways Experiment Station, Technical Report D-90-3. Vicksburg, Mississippi.

Montagna, P.A., B.C. Coull, T.R. Herring, and B.W. Dudley. 1983. The relationship between abundances of meiofauna and their suspected microbial food (diatoms and bacteria). *Estuarine, Coastal and Shelf Science* 17: 381-394.

Moriarty, F. 1983. Ecotoxicology: The Study of Pollutants in Ecosystems. Academic Press, New York.

Morris, J.T. 1984. Effects of oxygen and salinity on ammonium uptake by *Spartina alterniflora* Loisel. and *Spartina patens* (Aiton) Muhl. *Journal of Experimental Marine Biology and Ecology* 78: 87-98.

Morris, J.T. 1991. Effects of nitrogen loading on wetland ecosystems with particular reference to atmospheric deposition. *Annual Review of Ecology and Systematics* 22: 257-279.

Nathans, M.W. and T.J. Bechtel. 1977. Availability of sediment-adsorbed selected pesticides to benthos with particular emphasis on deposit-feeding infauna. United States Army Corps of Engineers, Waterways Experimental Station, Technical Report D-77-34. Vicksburg, Mississippi.

National Research Council. 1985a. Dredging Coastal Ports: An Assessment of the Issues. National Academy Press, Washington, D.C.

National Research Council. 1985b. Oil in the Sea: Inputs, Fates, and Effects, National Academy Press, Washington, D.C.

National Research Council. 1989. Using Oil Spill Dispersants on the Sea. National Academy Press, Washington, D.C.

Neely, R.K. and C.B. Davis. 1985. Nitrogen and phosphorus fertilization of *Sparganium eurycarum* Engelm. and *Typha glauca* Godr. stands. II. Emergent plant decompostion. *Aquatic Botany* 22: 363-375.

Nelson-Smith, A. 1972. Oil Pollution and Marine Ecology, Paul Elek Scientific Book, London.

Newling, C.J. and M.C. Landin. 1983. Long-term monitoring of habitat development at upland and wetland dredged material disposal sites, 1974-1982. United States Army Corps of Engineers, Waterways Experiment Station, Environmental Laboratory, Technical Report D-83. Vicksburg, Mississippi.

Nixon, S.W., C.A. Oviatt, and S.L. Northby. 1973. Ecology of small boat marinas. University of Rhode Island, Marine Technical Report Series No. 5. Kingston, Rhode Island.

Pezeshki, S.R. and R.D. DeLaune. 1993. Effect of crude oil on gas exchange functions of *Juncus roemerianus* and *Spartina alterniflora*. *Water, Air and Soil Pollution* 68: 461-468.

Pfitzenmeyer, H.T. 1969. The effects of spoil disposal on the benthos of the upper Chesapeake Bay. *Proceedings of the National Shellfish Association* 60: 9-10.

Pillai, C.G.P., J.D. Weete, and D.E. Davis. 1977. Metabolism of atrazine by *Spartina alterniflora* 1. Chloroform-soluble metabolites. *Journal of Agricultural Food and Chemistry* 25: 852-855.

Pimentel, D. and C.A. Edwards. 1982. Pesticides and ecosystems. *Bioscience* 32: 595-600.

Pritchard, P.H. 1991. Bioremediation as a technology: Experience with the *Exxon Valdez* oil spill. *Journal of Hazardous Materials* 28: 115-130.

Race, M.S. and D.R. Christie. 1982. Coastal zone development: Mitigation, marsh creation, and decision making. *Environmental Management* 6: 317-328.

Reimold, R.J., M.A. Hardisky, and P.C. Adams. 1978. Habitat development field investigations. Buttermilk Sound marsh development site, Atlantic Intracoastal Waterway, Georgia. United States Army Corps of Engineers, Waterways Experiment Station, Technical Report D-78-26. Vicksburg, Mississippi.

Reimold, R.J., J.H. Phillips, and M.A. Hardisky. 1980. Sociocultural values of wetlands, p. 79-89. *In* V.S. Kennedy (ed.), Estuarine Perspectives, Academic Press, New York.

Renzoni, A. 1975. Toxicity of three oils to bivalve gametes and larvae. *Marine Pollution Bulletin* 6: 125-128.

Rhoads, D.C. and L.F. Boyer. 1982. The effects of marine benthos on physical properties of sediments: A successional perspective, p. 3-52. *In* P.L. McCall and M.J.S. Tevesz (eds.), Animal-Sediment Relations: The Biogenic Alteration of Sediments. Plenum Press, New York.

Roberts, M.H., Jr., W.J. Hargis, Jr., C.J. Strobel, and P.F. Delisle, 1989. Acute toxicity of PAH contaminated sediments to the estuarine fish, *Leiostomus xanthurus*. *Bulletin of Environmental Contamination and Toxicology* 42: 142-149.

Rulifson, R.A. 1991. Finfish utilization of man-initiated and adjacent natural creeks of South Creek Estuary, North Carolina, using multiple gear types. *Estuaries* 14: 447-464.

Sanders, H.L., J.F. Grassle, G.R. Hampson, L.S. Morse, S. Garner-Price, and C.C. Jones. 1980. Anatomy of an oil spill: Long-term effects from the grounding of the barge *Florida* off West Falmouth, Massachusetts. *Journal of Marine Research* 38: 265-280.

Sayler, G.S., T.W. Sherrill, R.E. Perkins, L.M. Mallory, M.P. Shiaris, and D. Pederson. 1982. Impact of coal-coking effluent on sediment microbial communities: A multivariate approach. *Applied and Environmental Microbiology* 44: 1118-1129.

Seneca, E.D., W.W. Woodhouse, Jr., and S.W. Broome. 1975. Salt-Water Marsh Creation, p. 427-437. *In* L.E. Cronin (ed.), Estuarine Research, Vol. II. Geology and Engineering. Academic Press, New York.

Sheehan, P.J., D.R. Miller, G.C. Butler, and P. Bourdeau. 1984. Effects of Pollutants at the Ecosystem Level. Scope 22. John Wiley & Sons, New York.

Sherr, B.F. and W.J. Payne. 1981. The effect of sewage sludge on salt marsh denitrifying bacteria. *Estuaries* 4: 146-149.

Smith, C.J. and R.D. DeLaune. 1985. Recovery of added ^{15}N-labelled ammonium-N from Louisiana Gulf Coast estuarine sediment. *Estuarine Coastal and Shelf Science* 21: 225-233.

Smith, C.M., and C.T. Hackney. 1989. The effects of hydrocarbons on the setting of the American oyster, *Crassostrea virginica*, in intertidal habitats of southeastern North Carolina. *Estuaries* 12: 42-48.

Stebbings, R.E. 1970. Recovery of a salt marsh in Brittany 16 months after heavy pollution by oil. *Environmental Pollution* 1: 163-167.

Stender, B.W. and R.M. Martore. 1990. Finfish and invertebrate communities, p. 241-287. *In* R.F. Van Dolah, P.H. Wendt, and E.L. Wenner (eds.), A Physical and Ecological Characterization of the Charleston Harbor Estuarine System. South Carolina Wildlife and Marine Resources Department, Marine Resources Division. Charleston, South Carolina.

Stickney, R.R. 1984. Estuarine Ecology of the Southeastern United States and Gulf of Mexico. Texas A&M University Press, College Station, Texas.

Stickney, R.R. and D. Perlmutter. 1975. Impact of intracoastal waterway dredging on a mud bottom benthos community. *Biological Conservation* 7: 211-226.

Spooner, C.S. 1987. The restoration of living Chesapeake Bay resources, p. 541-554. *In* S.K. Majumdar, L.W. Hall, and H.M. Austin (eds.), Contaminant Problems and Management of Living Chesapeake Bay Resources. Typehouse of Easton, Phillipsburg, New Jersey.

Summerson, H.C. and C.H. Peterson. 1990. Recruitment failure of the bay scallop, *Argopectin irradians concentricus*, during the first red tide, *Ptychodiscus brevis*, outbreak recorded in North Carolina. *Estuaries* 13: 322-331.

Takata, H., T. Onda, and N. Ogura. 1990. Determination of polycyclic aromatic hydrocarbons in urban street dusts and their source materials by capillary gas chromatography. *Environmental Science and Technology* 8: 1175-1185.

Teal, J.M., J.W. Farrington, K.A. Burns, J.J. Stegeman, B.W. Tripp, B. Woodin, and C. Phinney. 1992. The West Falmouth oil spill after 20 years: Fate of fuel oil compounds and effects on animals. *Marine Pollution Bulletin* 24: 607-614.

Thomas, M.L.H. 1973. Effects of bunker C oil on intertidal biota in Chedabucto Bay, Nova Scotia. *Journal of the Fisheries Research Board of Canada* 30: 83-90.

Tietjen, J.H. and J.J. Lee. 1984. The use of free-living nematodes as a bioassay for estuarine sediments. *Marine Environmental Research* 11: 233-251.

Tiner, R.W., Jr. 1984. Wetlands of the United States: Current Status and Recent Trends. United States Fish and Wildlife Service, National Wetlands Inventory, Washington, D.C.

United States Army Corps of Engineers. 1987. Ranking potential contaminants in the lower Mississippi River delta. DACW 29-82-D-0187, Vicksburg, Mississippi.

United States Department of Transportation. 1993. Boating Statistics, 1992. United States Coast Guard, CMDTPUB P16754.6. Washington, DC.

United States Environmental Protection Agency. 1985. Coastal Marinas Assessment Handbook. United States Environmental Protection Agency, EPA 904/6-85-132, Atlanta, Georgia.

Valiela, I. D. Foreman, M. LaMontagne, D. Hersh, J. Costa, P. Peckol, B. DeMeo-Anderson, C. D'Avanzo, M. Babione, C. H. Sham, J. Brawley, and K. Lajtha. 1992. Couplings of watersheds and coastal waters: Sources and consequences of nutrient enrichment in Waquoit Bay, Massachusetts. *Estuaries* 15: 443-457.

Vandermeulen, J.H. and D.C. Gordon, Jr. 1976. Reentry of 5-year old stranded Bunder C fuel oil from a low energy beach into the water, sediments, and biota of Chedabucto Bay, Nova Scotia. *Journal of the Fisheries Research Board of Canada* 33: 2002-2010.

Vandermeulen, J.H. and J.G. Singh. 1994. *Arrow* oil spill, 1970-90: Persistence of 20-yr weathered Bunker C fuel oil. *Canadian Journal of Fisheries and Aquatic Sciences* 51: 845-855.

Van Dolah, R.F., M.Y. Bobo, V.V. Levisen, P.H. Wendt, and J.J. Manzi. 1992. Effects of marina proximity on the physiological condition, reproduction, and settlement of oyster populations. *Journal of Shellfish Research* 11: 41-48.

Van Dolah, R.F., D.R. Calder, and D.M. Knott. 1984. Effects of dredging and open-water disposal on benthic macroinvertebrates in a South Carolina estuary. *Estuaries* 7: 28-37.

Voudrias, E.A., and C.L. Smith. 1986. Hydrocarbon pollution from marinas in estuarine sediments. *Estuarine Coastal and Shelf Science* 22: 271-284.

Waldock, M.J. and J.E. Thain. 1983. Shell thickening in *Crassostrea gigas*: Organotin antifouling or sediment induced. *Marine Pollution Bulletin* 14: 411-415.

Webb, J.M., S.K. Alexander, and J.K. Winters. 1985. Effects of autumn application of oil on *Spartina alterniflora* in a Texas salt marsh. *Environmental Pollution,* Series A 38: 321-337.

Webb, J.M. and C.J. Newling. 1985. Comparison of natural and man-made salt marshes in Galveston Bay Complex, Texas. *Wetlands* 4: 75-86.

Weeks, B.A. and E. Warriner. 1984. Effects of toxic chemicals on macrophage phagocytosis in two estuarine fishes. *Marine Environmental Research* 14: 327-334.

Weigert, R.G. and B.J. Freeman. 1990. Tidal Salt Marshes of the Southeast Atlantic Coast: A Community Profile. United States Fish and Wildlife Service, Biological Report 85(7.29). Washington, D.C.

Weis, J.S. and J. Perlmutter. 1987. Effects of tributyltin on activity and burrowing behavior of the fiddler crab, *Uca pugilator. Estuaries* 10: 342-346.

Wendt, P.H., R.F. Van Dolah, M.Y. Bobo, and J.J. Manzi. 1990. Effects of marina proximity on certain aspects of the biology of oysters and other benthic macrofauna in a South Carolina estuary. South Carolina Wildlife and Marine Resources Department, Marine Resources Center, Technical Report No. 74, Charleston, South Carolina.

Westree, B. 1977. Biological criteria for the selection of clean-up techniques in salt marshes, p. 231-235. *In* Proceeding of the 1977 Oil Spill Conference, American Petroleum Institute, Washington, D.C.

Whiting, G.J., H.N. McKellar, B. Kjerfve, and J.D. Spurrier. 1987. Nitrogen exchange between a southeastern USA. salt marsh ecosystem and the coastal ocean. *Marine Biology* 95: 173-182.

Windom, H.L. 1976. Environmental aspects of dredging in the coastal zone. *Critical Reviews in Environmental Control* 6: 91-109.

Wirth, E.F., G.T. Chandler, L.M. DiPinto, and T.F. Bidleman. 1994. Assay of PCB accumulation from sediments by marine benthic copepods using a novel microextraction technique. *Environmental Science and Toxicology* 28: 1609-1614.

Wolaver, T.G. and J.D. Spurrier. 1988. Carbon transport between a euhaline vegetated marsh in South Carolina and the adjacent tidal creek—Contributions via tidal inundation, runoff, and seepage. *Marine Ecology Progress Series* 42: 53-62.

Woodhouse, W.W., Jr. 1979. Building salt marshes along the coasts of the continental United States. United States Army, Coastal Engineering Research Center, Special Report 4. Fort Belvoir, Virginia.

Woodhouse, W.W., Jr. and P.L. Knutson. 1982. Atlantic coast marshes. *In* R.R. Lewis (ed.), Creation and Restoration of Coastal Plant Communities. CRC Press, Boca Raton, Florida.

Woodwell, G.M., C.F. Wurster, and P.A. Isaacson. 1967. DDT residues in an east coast estuary: A case of biological concentration of a persistent insecticide. *Science* 156: 821-824.

Wu, T.L., N.J. Mick, and B.M. Fox. 1977. Runoff studies of the agricultural herbicides alachlor and atrazine form the Rhode River watershed during the 1976 growing season, p. 707-726. *In* D.L. Correll (ed.), Watershed Research in Eastern North America. Chesapeake Bay Center for Environmental Studies, Smithsonian Institution, Edgewater, Maryland.

Sustainable Development in the Southeastern Coastal Zone: Environmental Impacts on Fisheries

Donald E. Hoss and David W. Engel

ABSTRACT: Coastal zone development is increasing at an alarming rate, with adverse affects on our fisheries resources. If we are to conserve the habitat that makes the coastal zone valuable for these fisheries, immediate steps must be taken. In this paper we discuss the various types of impacts that can result from inappropriate development and land use practices. We suggest that to correct these situations it is essential to 1) coordinate and enforce municipal, county, and state land use plans; 2) demonstrate to the public the importance of coastal wetland habitat to fisheries; 3) support local, state, and federal efforts to limit nonpoint-source runoff; 4) encourage the prudent and safe use of pesticides, herbicides, and fertilizers; and 5) reinforce the concept that people are the source of the fishing, pollution, and habitat degradation problems, and that each of us must be environmentally responsible.

Introduction

Commercial and residential development and associated demographic changes in the coastal zone and their associated costs (e.g., increased fishing pressure, waste disposal, and nonpoint-source runoff) may be the greatest threat to the health and well-being of coastal fisheries of the United States from North Carolina to Florida. Commercial and recreational fishery resources in the United States are being jeopardized by human activities in the coastal zone. From 1980 to the year 2000, coastal development and human population along the Atlantic Coast will increase by about 73% (Chambers 1992). Along the southeast coast, from North Carolina to Florida, the population is expected to increase 27% by 2010. This would be an increase of 181% between 1960 and 2010 (Culliton et al. 1990). It is estimated that over 50% of the population of the United States lives within 50 miles of the coast. This immigration to the coast caused the director of the National Marine Fisheries Service (NMFS) to highlight nearshore ocean and estuarine fishery habitat loss as the greatest threats to marine fishery productivity throughout the United States (Fox 1992). If coastal development is to be sustained, without adverse environmental impacts, it must be managed well, in order to protect important and sensitive coastal habitats necessary for the survival and growth of fishery populations. Such management must combine responsible developmental practices at the local and state levels with scientific oversight of environmental conditions in the coastal zone. This can only be accomplished through long-term ecological research and education programs, thus providing the basis for assessing the combined impacts of exploitation of fishery stocks and habitat degradation and informing the public of the importance of a healthy and productive coastal habitat.

Unfortunately, despite years of research, the specific relationships between development and impacts on fisheries production are not well documented. Fishery biologists, therefore, have been unable or reluctant, due to information gaps, to provide resource managers adequate guidelines that will provide a "sustained yield" in conjunction with escalating coastal development. In this case we use sustained yield to mean maintaining a constant harvest without depleting the breeding stock necessary to replenish what is removed (D'Elia 1992).

The scientific literature is replete with evidence showing that coastal and estuarine environments are necessary for the production of commercially and recreationally important fishery organisms (Peters and Schaaf 1991; Hoss and Thayer 1993). It is estimated that in excess of 90% of the fish and shellfish caught commercially in the Southeast Atlantic are dependent on estuaries for survival at some time during their life cycle (Lindall and Thayer 1982). Circumstantial evidence supports the hypothesis that uncontrolled development adversely affects the sustained production of coastal fisheries. Examples of decreases in fisheries exist, but cause and effect relationships linking coastal development to reduced fisheries production have been difficult to quantify. The problem in determining cause and effect is the result of difficulties in assessing the importance of natural fishery mortality relative to pollution-related or habitat-related mortalities (Peters and Cross 1992). Two examples, one from the East Coast and one from the West Coast, show correlations with development and increased population. On the East Coast, in Chesapeake Bay, submerged aquatic vegetation decreased drastically between 1965 and 1980. Associated with this habitat change were declines in several estuarine-dependent species, including American shad, alewife, blueback herring, blue crab, and oysters. On the West Coast, at least 106 populations of salmon and steelhead are extinct, and 214 are facing extinction due to fishing and modification of stream flow for hydropower, agriculture, and logging. In both cases the changes are associated with population growth but can not be directly attributed to it.

The objective of this paper is to provide evidence of the importance of the coastal zone to southeast fisheries, and to discuss the possible ways that development and demographic changes can impact fisheries. We will cite examples of how development, or processes associated with development, may have caused changes in the coastal environment that could be detrimental to fishery organisms. The basic question is: What evidence is there that improperly managed coastal development will affect fisheries? This question is complex and emotionally charged and, therefore, not easily answered. To address the question it is first necessary to understand the structure of the fisheries along the Southeast Coast.

Fisheries in the Southeast Coastal Zone

On a national basis, United States commercial and recreational fisheries contribute about $30 billion annually to the United States gross national product, and 70% of these fisheries are made up of species which are estuarine dependent at some life history stage (Fox 1992). In the coastal zone between Virginia and Florida, estuarine dependency (Table 1) is even higher (> 90%).

Table 1. Listing of some of the important estuarine dependent finfish and shellfish utilized by the commercial and recreational fisheries in the Southeastern United States.

FINFISH
Blue fish   *Pomatomus saltatrix*
Spotted seatrout   *Cynoscion nebulosus*
Weakfish   *Cynoscion regalis*
Atlantic croaker   *Micropogonias undulatus*
Spot   *Leiostomus xanthurus*
Red drum   *Sciaenops ocellatus*
Black drum   *Pogonias cromis*
Atlantic menhaden   *Brevoortia tyrannus*
Tarpon   *Megalops atlanticus*
Summer flounder   *Paralichthys dentatus*
Southern flounder   *Paralichthys lethostigma*
Striped mullet   *Mugil cephalus*
Gag   *Mycteroperca microlepis*
Black seabass   *Centropristis striata*
Cobia   *Rachycentron canadum*
Spanish mackerel   *Scomberomorus maculatus*
Snook   *Centropomus undecimalis*

SHELLFISH
American oyster   *Crassostrea virginica*
Quahog   *Mercenaria mercenaria*
Blue crab   *Callinectes sapidus*
Stone crab   *Menippe mercenaria*
Pink shrimp   *Penaeus duorarum*
White shrimp   *Penaeus setiferus*
Brown shrimp   *Penaeus aztecus*
Bay scallop   *Argopecten irradians*
Spiny lobster   *Panulirus argus*

Estuarine nursery grounds in the coastal zone of the Southeast and Gulf provide protection and food for menhaden (second largest United States fishery by poundage), shrimp (most valuable United States fishery), flounder, spot, Atlantic croaker, spotted seatrout, redfish, crabs, oysters, scallops, clams, and a host of other important species (Hoss and Thayer 1993). All of these species, except oysters and scallops, spawn in coastal waters. After the eggs hatch, the larval and juvenile stages are transported across the shelf and through inlets into coastal embayments and estuaries by ocean currents (Nelson et al. 1977; Miller et al. 1984; Checkley et al. 1988). The importance of specific areas in estuaries as habitat for fishery species varies both with the species of organism and life stage. Hoss and Thayer (1993) recently reviewed the habitat requirements of the early life

Table 2. National Marine Fisheries Service priority issues concerning fisheries in the United States territorial waters.

Coastal Habitat Modification and Loss

Freshwater Diversion

Coastal Eutrophication

Chemical Loading

Pathogen Introduction

Marine Debris

Mitigation Techniques

Exploitation of Fishery Resources

Cumulative Effects

stages of fish. In the Southeast, seagrass beds and emergent coastal marshes appear to be the best habitats for providing food and cover for the youngest juveniles, while sand or mud bottoms in open bays may be more effectively exploited by older juveniles. Passes or inlets may have short term but essential value as migratory routes or places of spawning activity. Late-stage juveniles and adults move out of estuaries into the open coastal waters where they compete and grow and also become major food items for coastal pelagic fishes (e.g., mackerel and bluefish).

The importance of coastal zone habitats to the survival and growth of fishery organisms cannot be minimized, but the specific mechanisms of the utilization of habitat resources for any given species or group of species are not well understood (Peters and Cross 1992). In most instances, even in habitats identified as critical (e.g., primary nursery habitats in North Carolina) the components that make such habitats especially valuable have not been clearly identified. Elimination of a habitat component critical to any life stage, however, will cause adverse effects on survival. It is important, therefore, to identify the structure, components, and function of coastal ecosystems that are critical to fisheries production so they can be protected from alteration.

The National Marine Fisheries Service has developed a list of priority issues that apply to coastal environments of the East Coast (Table 2). Each issue is either directly or indirectly associated with developmental activity and demographic changes underway in the southeastern United States. The consequences of each of these activities will affect coastal fishery resources to varying degrees. The discussion examines each issue from the perspective of its impact on fishery resources.

COASTAL HABITAT MODIFICATION AND LOSS

The majority of species important to commercial and recreational fisheries along the Southeast Coast of the United States are dependent upon nearshore coastal and estuarine habitats for the

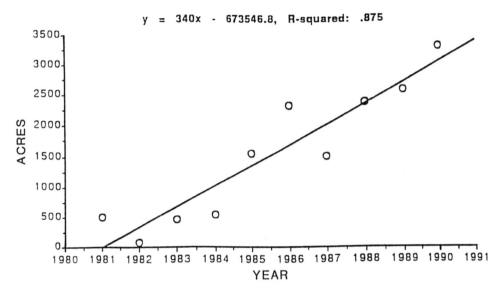

Fig. 1. The number of acres of coastal wetlands proposed to United States Army Corps of Engineers for alteration in North Carolina in the years 1981-1990. The data was collected by the National Marine Fisheries Service, Habitat Conservation Division, Beaufort, North Carolina office (figure taken from Wheeler and Hardy in press).

completion of their early life histories. Habitats (salt marshes, seagrass meadows, oyster reefs, etc.) utilized by juveniles provide abundant food resources, protection from predators, and low competition with adults. It follows, therefore, that modification of these estuarine or coastal habitats can be deleterious to the production and recruitment to fishable stocks with a subsequent negative change in fishery yield (Hoss and Thayer 1993). These nursery habitats are presently being lost along the Southeast and Gulf coasts at an alarming rate. These losses are due to a combination of changes in land use, canals, ports, marinas and urban development.

One measure of development activity in the region is the number of applications submitted to the United States Army Corps of Engineers and received by the NMFS Habitat Conservation Division. The number of requests received annually by the NMFS regional and area offices averages about 10,000 nationwide. There are more permit requests in the Southeast Region than in any other NMFS region (Mager and Thayer 1986). Although the numbers of requests have not increased greatly on an annual basis, the total acreage proposed for modification is increasing. In North Carolina, acres proposed for alteration increased from 500 in 1981 to in excess of 3000 in 1990 (Fig. 1). A model developed for North Carolina predicts that under the present permitting system, wetland loss will increase (Wheeler and Hardy in press).

Many of these modifications have the probability of causing deleterious effects to fishery habitats, and evidence is building to support this contention. Nixon (1980), in an extensive review of the importance of marsh to fishery productivity, plotted the catch of estuarine-dependent species per unit-area as a function of marsh. There was a strong positive linear relationship between catch and an increased ratio of marsh to open water. The Gulf of Mexico and the Southeast Atlantic coasts have the largest amount of marsh acreage, and estuarine-dependent fishery landings are higher here than for the northeast, southwest, or northwest coasts.

Boesch and Turner (1984) report that habitat composition and quality affect fishery recruitment and utilization. More specifically, they showed a strong positive correlation between the penaeid shrimp catch in the Gulf of Mexico and the total area of coastal marsh. In their discussion it was noted that fish with life histories and habitat requirements similar to shrimp also may have their recruitment limited by the quality and quantity of wetland habitat. In Chesapeake Bay, the catch of a number of fish species has declined drastically due to disease, habitat degradation, and over-fishing. Rothschild et al. (1994) also showed that in Chesapeake Bay 100 years of intensive and increasingly mechanized fishing practices altered oyster habitat. This oyster habitat modification may have been the most important cause for the decline of the fishery.

In nearshore coastal waters, we have less information concerning the possible effects of development on fishery habitat. Although the coastal habitat of the Southeast United States is not yet overly contaminated or developed in the same sense as many estuarine habitats, nearshore waters do have the potential for being degraded by offshore dump sites, oil exploration and production, mining and energy production, and riverine inputs.

ALTERATIONS OF FRESHWATER INFLOW

The quality and quantity of freshwater inflow into the coastal zone is a major factor main-taining wetland and estuarine productivity, and contributes to the nearshore productivity of fishery spawning zones on the continental shelf. Large-scale agricultural projects, irrigation, water diver-sions, upland canal development, deforestation, residential development, and road construction are among the activities that can alter freshwater inflow patterns. Modifying either the flow or the timing of freshwater inflow can affect the species composition and productivity of both plant and animal populations present in estuaries (Ley 1992). Inflow-related fishery problems exist throughout the southeast and range from reduced inflow to excessive inflow. For example, about 400,000 acres in eastern North Carolina have been ditched and drained to provide land for agriculture, thereby altering the capacity of the land to absorb and retain water. By altering the rate and quantity of freshwater runoff there also is an increased probability that there will be increased nutrient loading and suspended solid inputs into estuaries.

It has been suggested that these agricultural practices are responsible for the closure of important shellfish beds. For example, between 1980 and 1990 the acreage closed to shellfishing in the South River area of Carteret County, North Carolina, increased from 160 acres to 560 acres—a 250% increase in closed acreage. The South River area is dominated by a > 40,000 acre super farm that has ditched and drained forested wetlands. While it has not been shown conclusively that the farm caused the closing, it almost certainly contributed to the problem along with agricul-ture practices and increased residential development in the South River community.

In Louisiana, oil exploration canals in marshes have resulted in an increased flushing rate, and deep water barge canals have allowed salinity intrusions to occur in the low-salinity marshes. These changes in salinity may adversely affect shrimp populations. When these physical changes are added to the current rate of subsidence along the Gulf Coast, the effects on marsh acreage is dramatic.

In Florida there are a number of documented cases where changes in freshwater inflow have affected the ecological structure and productivity of coastal embayments. Colby et al. (1985)

documented the effects of excessive freshwater inflow from the channelization of runoff from a residential development on a mangrove-dominated embayment in southwest Florida. The result of increased freshwater inflow was a decrease in the numerical abundance of juvenile fish and shrimp relative to control areas removed from the site of impact. In the Everglades, water diversion projects for flood control and agriculture are thought to be a major cause of habitat changes and may be related to the seagrass dieoff in the Everglades National Park. In addition, the water that does reach the Everglades is contaminated with pesticides and fertilizers from agricultural and residential sources. Seagrass die-off in western Florida Bay has been occurring since the summer of 1987, with resultant shifts in plant communities from monospecific turtle grass to mixed habitat with large denuded areas. The current hypothesis is that turtle grass has become weakened from environmental stress, including decreased freshwater inflow, making it vulnerable to disease (Thayer et al. 1994). Changes in resident fishery community structure is occurring (Thayer and Sheridan, NMFS, personal communication). Also symptomatic of a stressed system are occurrences of blue-green algal blooms, deaths of loggerhead sponges (lobster habitat), and the die-back of some mangroves in the bay.

COASTAL EUTROPHICATION

A consequence of increased human populations and intensive agricultural development is an elevation in inorganic and organic nutrient loading in estuarine and coastal waters. This process can result in transient increased productivity and standing crop of phytoplankton, decreased levels of dissolved oxygen, and shifts in species composition. Higher phytoplankton production and biomass, although potentially beneficial as a food source, may cause decreases in light penetration, which will affect the productivity of benthic algae, submerged aquatic vegetation, and subsequently benthic animals. Increased nutrients also can lead to shifts in the species composition of the phytoplankton community to fewer and less desirable organisms. Algal blooms, should they occur, can result in decreases in dissolved oxygen that can be detrimental to survival and production of both finfish and shellfish. Noxious algal and dinoflagellate blooms, which produce toxins that can be harmful to both aquatic organisms and humans, also can result from nutrient loading. Eutrophication during the past 30 years in the upper Chesapeake Bay has been identified as a major contributing factor to the decline of submerged aquatic vegetation due to increased turbidity, and also to large reductions in crab and fish populations due to decreases in dissolved oxygen. The large geographic area in the southeast and the dependency of fisheries on estuarine habitat makes it potentially vulnerable to eutrophication. If not managed properly, the current and projected rate of population growth and agricultural activity could result in eutrophication events that may have large-scale effects on fishery production.

CHEMICAL LOADING

Despite recent pollution control measures and stricter environmental laws, toxic organic and inorganic chemicals are still introduced into the marine environment. Some of the important sources in the southeast are agricultural practices, combustion of fossil fuel, sewage, urban runoff, boating and golf course runoff. Recent court decisions also increase the likelihood that ocean disposal of municipal and industrial wastes will increase substantially in the near future. Ocean outfalls for disposal of sewage are viable alternatives to estuarine and nearshore disposal but should not be used in lieu of adequate treatment of the waste prior to disposal. The long-term impact of chemicals (e.g., petroleum hydrocarbons, halogenated hydrocarbons, metals, etc.) on populations of marine organisms is not well documented for marine species, but there is a probability that in the long term, toxic contaminants will have an impact on fish populations (Schaaf, et al. 1987). In some cases the impact on fisheries is through the marketability of fish and shellfish: accumulation and retention of certain toxic and/or noxious chemicals cause tainting of edible tissues.

Increased boating activity may be a meaningful source of petroleum hydrocarbons to coastal waters in the southeast. This particular input of petroleum hydrocarbons from the exhaust and leakage of outboard motors is often overlooked or ignored. All outboard engines require that oil be mixed with gasoline either directly in the tank or by injection, and a portion of the oil that does not burn is ejected with the exhaust gases into the water. In coastal North Carolina there were 52,030 boats registered in 1990 (North Carolina Wildlife Resources Commission personal communication). Assuming that all of these use outboard engines and each boat was operated 65 days over the period of a year (i.e., assume 1.25 trips per week) for an average of 4 hours per trip, a total of 13,527,800 trip-hours would be made. An average gasoline tank on a boat holds about 6 gallons, and one pint (i.e., 0.125 gal) of oil is used per tank, a 50:1 mix. We also assume that the average 60 hp engine is two cycle and consumes fuel at a rate of 1.5 gal h^{-1}. If the efficiency of combustion of the oil is 95%, then we estimate that 84,549 gal of oil will be put into coastal North Carolina waters per year based on 1990 boat registrations in coastal counties. Over the long term this type of input could be significant, and a meaningful addition to the other hydrocarbon inputs. If a comparison is made between the estimated hydrocarbon input from urban runoff from coastal North Carolina counties in 1982 to possible boating inputs in 1982, the estimated values are 2270 tons $year^{-1}$ versus 470 tons $year^{-1}$ of petroleum hydrocarbons (National Oceanic and Atmospheric Administration's National Coastal Pollutant Discharge Inventory unpublished data). While the effects of such hydrocarbon inputs may be open to question, some of the most serious contamination problems have been the result of small, seemingly negligible, inputs of contaminants into the environment. This is particularly true of oil where only the catastrophic spills get press notices.

PATHOGENS IN SHELLFISH

Residential, industrial and agricultural growth in the southeastern United States has increased the amount of nonpoint-source runoff into coastal waters that contain untreated or marginally treated human and animal wastes. Siting of sewage disposal facilities in estuarine areas has resulted, in some cases, in the closing of shellfish beds; in other cases, construction of sewage treatment facilities has reduced septic runoff and allowed reopening of shellfish beds. The fact is, however, that increased development invariably results in more acres of shellfish waters being closed. The shellfish that have been most affected are oysters and clams. These species inhabit portions of coastal embayments and estuaries that receive most of the sewage discharges and agricultural runoff. In the past 10 years proliferation of marinas in coastal areas has been blamed for the increased number of closures. In some southeastern states the waters within a given radius of a marina are closed by regulation regardless of coliform count.

Coliform bacteria counts in the water and in shellfish are used to close shellfish beds. While coliform bacteria are not directly harmful to human health, their presence is considered an indicator of pathogenic viruses. Since these pathogens are not harmful to the bivalves, the organisms themselves are not affected, but since the shellfish cannot be harvested, the stock has been lost for all practical purposes. However, cleaning up the discharges will allow the beds to depurate and once again become productive.

In addition to pathogens that are harmful to humans, there are those that are harmful to molluscan shellfish themselves. Two of the most common diseases are MSX (*Haplosporidium nelsoni*) and Dermo (*Parkinsus marinus*) both of which are caused by protozoan parasites. These diseases have devastated the oyster populations in Delaware and Chesapeake bays and are currently increasing in intensity southward. In 1990 a survey of oyster disease prevalence indicated that both MSX and Dermo were widely distributed in North Carolina: MSX was found at 30% of the sampling sites and Dermo at 70-80% (Albermarle-Pamlico Estuarine Study 1994). The incidences of these diseases are on the increase, resulting in substantial mortalities among the oyster stocks in North Carolina (North Carolina Division of Marine Fisheries, Shellfish Sanitation, personal communication). While appropriate salinity and temperature conditions are necessary for the spread of infections, there is a persistent, nonquantifiable correlation with increased population growth in coastal areas.

MARINE DEBRIS

One of the most obvious byproducts of human activity is the presence of marine debris or "trash" in coastal waters and on the beaches and intertidal areas. The debris ranges is size from microscopic plastic particles in the water (Carpenter et al. 1972) to mile-long pieces of drift net, discarded plastic bottles and bags, and aluminum cans. In laboratory studies Hoss and Settle (1990) were able to show that larvae of estuarine-dependent fishes, Atlantic menhaden, spot, mullet, pinfish and flounder, would feed on polystyrene microspheres. A number of investigations have also demonstrated that adult fish, such as tuna, striped bass, and dolphin, have plastic debris in their guts (Manooch 1973; Manooch and Mason 1983). Hoss and Settle (1990) reviewed the literature on the ingestion of plastics by marine fish and found the problem pervasive.

Most of the media attention has been given to incidences where marine debris is associated with the deaths of endangered and threatened marine mammals and turtles. In these cases, the animals become entangled in netting or fishing line or ingest plastic bags or other materials. Recently, a 35 ft sperm whale stranded and died in North Carolina because it had ingested a plastic float, plastic jugs, large piece of rubber, 50 ft nylon rope, and a large plastic bag (Bowen and Engel personal communication). All of these materials were from human activities at sea or in coastal waters. These types of incidences occur because of a general lack of concern and the feeling by the public that "one plastic bag won't make a difference."

MITIGATION TECHNIQUES

Mitigation is a technique that is being used a great deal in the Southeast for the development of coastal areas where wetland habitat is destroyed through the permitting process. Mitigation generally is considered to be the actual restoration, creation, or enhancement of wetlands to compensate for permitted wetland loss. To compensate for the loss of wetland habitat, new habitat ideally is created either on 1 : 1 or > 1 : 1 basis. Because of frequent lack of success or only partial success and because of the interim loss of habitat during the developmental process, resource agencies attempt to obtain > 1 : 1 compensation. In practice the mechanistic techniques for the transplanting and creation of seagrass beds, salt marsh, or wetland hardwoods exist and have been proven generally to be successful from the standpoint of the plant community. While it is possible to transplant marsh plants as well as other plant species, there has been concern expressed that these created habitats do not have the same value to fishery organisms as the one that was destroyed. Minello and Zimmerman (1993) showed that 3-5 years after the creation of new marsh habitat, it still was not as productive as a natural marsh in the same area. Similar results have been noted in three restored marshes in North Carolina (Meyer et al. 1993). An additional difficulty with mitigation is that for the technique to be useful for the creation or restoration of useful fishery habitat there needs to be procedural and legislated mechanisms for verifying the compliance of the mitigation agreement by the developer. Detailed discussions on successes of habitat restoration approaches are provided in a review by Thayer (1992). The fact is, while mitigation may be useful, it should not be viewed as a methodology acceptable in justifying the destruction of existing wetlands. From the standpoint of fishery production, existing submerged and emergent vegetation should continue to be protected and all alterations minimized.

Exploitation of Fishery Resources

Continuing demographic changes are increasing fishing pressure on selected fish species, which in turn is having a significant effect on maintaining sustainable fisheries in the Southeast. It has been suggested that the primary anthropogenic cause of fish mortality may not be from pollution or habitat changes, but from commercial and recreational fishing. The aforementioned environmental conditions play an important role in recruitment and production of fish, but the increases in the number and efficiency of commercial and sport fishing methods are exacerbating the effects of environmental alterations on fish populations along the southeast coast. Species such as king and Spanish mackerel, Atlantic weakfish, and red drum have been target species for both recreational and commercial fishermen in the Southeast for many years. The Atlantic weakfish catches have decreased drastically since 1980 due to a combination of factors, not the least of which is overfishing (Vaughan et al. 1991).

One of the major problems confronting fishery scientists is demonstrating how natural variability in fish populations and fishing interact with other environmental alterations. While it is possible to measure fish catch or numbers killed in a pollution event, it is very difficult to differentiate between mortalities induced by human perturbations and natural variability. In other words, our database is not sufficient to show such differences. A case in point is the Atlantic menhaden population along the Atlantic Coast where there exists an extensive database from 1954 to the present. From this database, Vaughan et al. (1986) estimated that there is only a 50% chance of detecting a 71% decline in recruitment of age-1 fish from a catastrophic pollution event. Regulations setting catch quotas for fish are often promulgated without taking into account this lack of sensitivity, but the alternative is to allow the fishing pressure to continue on fish stocks until they collapse, which is unacceptable. It is necessary, therefore, to go forward with research programs that are designed to demonstrate how the interactions between human activities, including fishing, and natural processes affect fish stocks, and provide education programs that will make the public aware of the potential impacts of human activities.

CUMULATIVE EFFECTS

Generally, regulations and guidelines to protect environmental quality and fish stocks are designed to only look at specific chemicals, specific physical changes, eutrophication, weather, or fishing as causative agents for the reduction or loss of fishery populations or cohorts. In reality, most often the effect or change that we are trying to assess is caused by a combination of stressors or environmental factors, not just a single factor or perturbation. Increased human population densities associated with development may not be detrimental in and of themselves if appropriate management strategies are used to minimize impacts to the environment. There are, however, associated environmental costs that go along with even the best managed projects, and in most cases those changes result in reduced environmental quality and possible detrimental effects on fishery production.

The assessment of possible impacts to fishery populations due to the continued development of the coastal zone is a complex and perplexing problem. Fishery populations should be considered as integrators of environmental conditions. Interactions between and among insults are the norm, and the resulting cumulative effects will probably exact a greater impact on coastal ecosystems than any single change in an environmental factor. As stated earlier, guidelines and regulations of federal and state agencies to control environmental impacts are considered individually. The integrating capacity of fishery population makes it unlikely that we will be afforded the luxury of assessing the impact of a single stressor but rather will have to evaluate multiple insults (e.g. Vaughan et al. 1984). Therefore, risk/hazard assessment techniques, similar to those used in evaluating contaminant-associated impacts, should be developed for fisheries to predict the probabilities of interactive processes and activities affecting fish stocks.

Areas that have had a history of contaminant inputs and degraded water quality seem to have increased incidences of pathological conditions among the endemic species, for example, liver tumors in winter flounder from Boston Harbor (Johnson et al. 1993), extensive shell degenerative disease among blue crabs from the Pamlico River, North Carolina (Noga et al. 1990, 1994), shell disease in lobsters from the New York Bight (Sindermann et al. 1989), and the spread of MSX and Dermo among the oysters along the east coast (United States Environmental Protection Agency 1994). As in human populations some disease processes (e.g., the induction of malignant tumors) cannot always be traced to a single causative agent. Liver tumors in fish appear to be well correlated with chemical contamination, chlorinated pesticides, and PAHs, but not all species of fish from the same environments are equally affected. Other factors, environmental or genetic, probably play an important role in the development of the disease process. In the case of shell disease among the blue crabs of the Pamlico River, North Carolina, a first assumption would be that the disease is related to a large phosphate mining operation, but there is a high probability that other factors such as low oxygen concentrations may play a major role (Engel et al. 1993), and may not be connected with the mining operation. Effects of other activities like increased residential development, extensive agricultural activity, and deforestation of the flood plain are more subtle. This conclusion is based on the fact that the same type of shell lesions are seen in crabs collected from the Alligator River, North Carolina, St. Johns River, Florida, and Biscayne Bay, Florida. These locations range from rural to heavily developed. In other words, direct cause and effect relationships are hard to show under normal environmental conditions and cumulative effects of multiple stressors on fishery populations are difficult to demonstrate until a population or cohort crashes, but even then relationships between specific stressors and effects to individuals are difficult to document.

Conclusions

Throughout this paper our approach may have appeared to be totally negative, but when confronted with problems that have more questions than answers, it is easy to be negative. The bottom line in the consideration of the effects of development on fisheries in the Southeastern United States, however, is "There is no free lunch." To achieve sustainable development there will be a cost that will have to be borne by both those groups that are interested in pursuing development, both commercial and residential, and those who are trying preserve the coastal and estuarine environments for fisheries and wildlife. Neither group can have it entirely their own way, but that should not stifle efforts to communicate and negotiate. The quality of life for all of those individuals that reside in or utilize the coastal and estuarine areas of the Southeast will be determined by the effort that is made to work together.

This discussion has concentrated on the potential and real impacts on fishery resources of residential and industrial development and demographic changes in the coastal zone. While cause and effect relationships between development and fishery production can be difficult to demonstrate, there are well-documented cases of how the pressures of human activities can cause serious damage to fishery populations. Striped bass, summer flounder, red drum, and weakfish populations have been impacted seriously by a combination of exploitation and deleterious habitat changes. As the coastal human population increases, there are increased pressures on fish populations due to recreational and commercial fishing. If in conjunction with increased fishing pressure there are destructive habitat changes, either physical or chemical, the effects on fish behavior and/or reduction of egg and larval survival, the cumulative impact on the fishable stocks could be devastating (Schaaf et al. 1987). For example, the near collapse of the striped bass population in Chesapeake Bay is the result of a combination of factors, including changes in water quality, stream flow, and overfishing. Inadequate aeration of the water due to reduced flow caused reduced egg hatch and poor water quality did not provide adequate food for the first feeding larvae. The overriding problem, however, was overexploitation of the stock. In the Gulf of Mexico, the spawning assemblages of red drum were seriously reduced because of increased fishing pressure due to the popularity of redfish (Goodyear 1993). It seems reasonable, therefore, to promulgate regulations that address both fishing pressures and environmental requirements of species of concern.

Theoretically, increasing development of coastal areas can be managed so that the more important and sensitive areas will be protected. Unfortunately, the relative importance of various estuarine habitats to fishery production is poorly known, so that managers cannot provide adequate guidelines to assure continued high fishery yields as coastal development continues. The needed guidance for protecting fisheries cannot be provided without additional information on processes and environmental factors that influence fish production in specific habitats.

Probably the most effective way to manage estuarine and coastal fisheries and coastal development is to educate people that are using fishery resources and are involved in coastal development. Through education it should be possible to show user groups that effective management of both fisheries and development is in their best interest. To accomplish such a goal we suggest that immediate action be taken to implement the following objectives: 1) Encourage the enactment, coordination, and enforcement of municipal, county, and state land use plans, so that development can be planned and orderly; 2) Increase efforts by the scientific community to demonstrate in an understandable manner the importance of coastal wetland habitat to fisheries; 3) Work actively to promote and encourage local, state, and federal efforts to control and limit non-point-source runoff; 4) Encourage contributors (homeowners, farmers, municipal governments, and managers of golf courses) of inputs of pesticides, herbicides, and fertilizers to use them in a prudent manner; and 5) Reinforce the fact that we all contribute to contamination problems presently affecting the environment in the Southeast and that each of us must be environmentally responsible. This rationale should be a useful way to preserve aesthetic values and allow for a reasonable financial return. Such an approach may be idyllic, but it is probably the only way to limit the conflicts that are bound to arise without massive amounts of regulation at the federal and state levels. It also should be remembered that most of the people relocating to the coastal areas of the Southeast are doing so because it is a desirable, or even preferred, human "habitat." If we are to protect the structure that make this habitat desirable, we must manage the natural resources better than we have in the past. We can do this so that we can have both sustained fishery production and continued quality development, if we develop a better understanding of the "niche" or status of humans as a component of coastal and estuarine ecosystems.

ACKNOWLEDGMENTS

We thank Drs. Ford Cross and Gordon Thayer for their critical review of the manuscript. We also thank all of the staff of the Division of Estuarine and Coastal Ecology and the Habitat Conservation Field Office, National Oceanic and Atmospheric Administration, National Marine Fisheries Service, Beaufort Laboratory, who have freely provided much of the information used in this paper.

LITERATURE CITED

Albermarle-Pamlico Estuarine Study (APES). 1994. Comprehensive Conservation Management Plan. United States Environmental Protection Agency, Raleigh, North Carolina.

Boesch, D.F. and R.E. Turner. 1984. Dependence of fishery species on salt marshes: The role of food and refuge. *Estuaries* 7: 460-468.

Carpenter, E.J., S.J. Anderson, G.R. Harvey, H.P. Milkas, and B.B. Peck. 1972. Polystyrene spherules in coastal waters. *Science* 178: 749-750.

Chambers, J.R. 1992. Coastal degradation and fish population losses. p. 45-51. *In* Richard H. Stroud (ed.), Stemming the Tide of Coastal Fish Habitat Loss. National Coalition for Marine Conservation, Savannah, Georgia.

Chambers, J.R. 1991. Coastal degradation and fish population loss. p. 1-11. *In* Proceedings of the National Symposium on Fish Habitat Conservation, Baltimore, Maryland.

Checkley, D.M., S. Raman, Jr., G.L. Maillet, and K.L. Mason. 1988. Winter storm effects on the spawning and larval drift of a pelagic fish. *Nature* 335: 346-348.

Colby, D.R., G.W. Thayer, W.F. Hettler, and D.S. Peters. 1985. A comparison of forage fish communities in relation to habitat parameters in Faka Union Bay, Florida and eight collateral bays during the wet season. National Oceanic and Atmospheric Administration Technical Memorandum. NMFS-SEFC-162. Beaufort, North Carolina.

Culliton, T.J., M.A. Winer, T.R. Goodspeed, D.G. Remer, C.M. Blackwell, and J.J. McDonough, III. 1990. 50 years of population change along the nations coasts 1960-2010. United States Department of Commerce, National Oceanic and Atmospheric Administration, National Ocean Service, Rockville, Maryland.

D'Elia, C.F. 1992. Sustainable development and the Chesapeake Bay: A case study. Invited Paper, United Nations University, International Conference on the Definition and Measurement of Sustainability: the Biophysical Foundations. The World Bank, Washington, D.C.

Engel, D.W., M. Brouwer, and S. McKenna. 1993. Hemocyanin concentrations in marine crustaceans as a function of environmental conditions. *Marine Ecology Progress Series* 93: 235-244.

Fox, William W., Jr. 1992. Stemming the tide: Challenges for conserving the nations coastal fish habitats. P. 9-13 *In* Richard H. Stroud (ed.), Stemming the tide of coastal fish habitat loss. National Coalition for Marine Conservation, Savannah, Georgia.

Goodyear, C.P. 1993. Status of the red drum stocks in the Gulf of Mexico. Miami Laboratory Contribution MIA-92/93-47. Miami, Florida.

Hoss, D.E. and L.R. Settle. 1990. Ingestion of plastics by teleost fishes, p. 693-709. *In* R.S. Shomura and M.L. Godfrey (eds.), Proceedings of the Second International Conference on Marine Debris. NOAA Technical Memorandum NOAA-TM-NMFS-SWFSC-154. Miami, Florida.

Hoss, D.E. and G.W. Thayer. 1993. The importance of habitat to the early life history of estuarine dependent fish, p. 147-158. *In* L.A. Fuiman (ed.), Water Quality and the Early Life Stages of Fishes. American Fisheries Society Symposium Series. American Fisheries Society, Bethesda, Maryland.

Johnson, L.L., C.M. Stehr, O.P. Olson, M.S. Myers, S.M. Pierce, C.A. Wigren, B.B. McCain, and U. Varanasi. 1993. Chemical contaminants and hepatic lesions in winter flounder (*Pleuronectes americanus*) from the northeast coast of the United States. *Environmental Science and Technology* 27: 2759-2771.

Ley, L.A. 1992. Influence of changes in freshwater flow on the use of mangrove prop root habitat by fishes. Ph.D. Dissertation. University of Florida, Tallahassee, Florida.

Lindall, W.N., Jr. and G.W. Thayer. 1982. Quantification of National Marine Fisheries Service habitat conservation efforts in the southeast region of the United States. *Marine Fisheries Review* 44:18-22.

Mager, A., Jr. and G.W. Thayer. 1986. National Marine Fisheries Service habitat conservation efforts in the southeast region of the United States from 1981-1985. Marine Fisheries Review 48:1-8.

Manooch, C.S., III. 1973. Food habits of yearling and adult striped bass, *Morone saxatalis* (Walbaum), from Albemarle Sound, North Carolina. *Chesapeake Science* 14: 73-86.

Manooch, C.S., III and D.L. Mason. 1983. Comparative food studies of yellowfin tuna, *Thunnus atlanticus* (Pisces: Scrombridae) from the southeastern and gulf coasts of the United States. *Brimleyana* 9: 33-52.

Meyer, D.L., M.S. Fonseca, D.R. Colby, W.J. Kenworthy and G.W. Thayer. 1993. An examination of created marsh and seagrass utilization by living marine resources, p. 1-6. *In* O.T. Magoon, H. Converse, D. Miner, L.T. Tobin, and D. Clark (eds.), Coastal Zone 93. Proceedings of the

Seventh Symposium on Coastal Ocean Management. American Society of Civil Engineers, New York.

Miller, J.M., J.P. Reed, and L.J. Pietrafesa. 1984. Patterns, mechanisms and approaches to the study of migration of estuarine-dependent fish larvae and juveniles. p. 209-225. *In* J.B. McCleave, G.R. Arnold, J.J. Dodson and W.H. Neill (eds.), Mechanisms of migrations in fishes. Plenum Press, New York.

Minello, T.J. and R.J. Zimmerman. 1993. Utilization of natural and transplanted Texas saltmarshes by fish and decapod crustaceans. *Marine Ecology Progress Series* 90: 273-285.

Nelson, W.R., M.C. Ingham, and W.E. Schaaf. 1977. Larval transport and year-class strength of Atlantic menhaden, *Brevoortia tyrannus*. *Fishery Bulletin* 75: 23-41.

Nixon, S.W. 1980. Between coastal marshes and coastal waters-A review of twenty years of speculation and research on the role of salt marshes in estuarine productivity and water chemistry, p. 437-525. *In* P. Hamilton and K.B. Macdonald (eds.), Estuarine and Wetland Processes: With Emphasis on Modeling, Volume 11. Plenum Publishing Corporation, New York.

Noga, E.J., D.W. Engel, and T.W. Arroll. 1990. Shell disease in blue crabs, *Callinectes sapidus*, from the Albemarle-Pamlico estuary. Final Report to the Albemarle/Pamlico Estuarine Study, Project No. 90-22. Raleigh, North Carolina.

Noga, E.J., D.W. Engel, T.W. Arroll, S. McKenna, and M. Davidian. 1994. Low serum antibacterial activity coincides with increased prevalence of shell disease in blue crabs *Callinectes sapidus*. *Diseases of Aquatic Organisms* 19: 121-128.

Peters, D.S. and F.A. Cross. 1992. What is coastal fish habitat? p. 17-22. *In* Richard H. Stroud (ed.), Stemming the tide of coastal fish habitat loss. National Coalition for Marine Conservation, Savannah, Georgia.

Peters, D.S. and W.E. Schaaf. 1991. Empirical model of the trophic basis for fishery yield in coastal waters of the eastern USA. *Transactions of the American Fisheries Society,* 120: 459-473.

Rothschild, B.J., J.S. Ault, P. Goulletquer, and M. Heral. 1994. Decline of the Chesapeake Bay oyster population: A century of habitat destruction and overfishing. *Marine Ecology Progress Series* 111: 29-39.

Schaaf, W.E., D.S. Peters, D.S. Vaughan, L. Coston-Clements, and C.W. Krouse. 1987. Fish population responses to chronic and acute pollution: The influence of life history strategies. *Estuaries* 10: 267-275.

Sindermann, C.J., F. Csulak, T.K. Sawyer, R.A. Bullis, D.W. Engel, B.T. Estrella, E. J. Noga, J. B. Pearce, J. C. Rugg, R. Runyon, J. A. Tiedemann, and R. R. Young. 1989. Shell Disease of Crustaceans of the New York Bight. National Oceanic and Atmospheric Administration Technical Memorandum NMFS-F/NEC-74. Woods Hole, Massachusetts.

Thayer, G.W., P.L. Murphey, and M.W. LaCroix. 1994. Responses of plant communities in the western Florida Bay to the die-off of seagrass. *Bulletin of Marine Science* 54: 718-726.

Thayer, G.W. 1992. Restoring the nation's marine environment. Maryland Sea Grant, College Park, Maryland.

Vaughan, D.S., R.J. Seagrave, and K. West. 1991. An assessment of the status of the Atlantic weakfish stock, 1982-1988. Atlantic States Marine Fisheries Commission. Special Report No. 21.

Vaughan, D.S., J.V. Merriner, and W.E. Schaaf. 1986. Detectability of a reduction in a single year class of a fish population. *Journal of the Elisha Mitchell Society* 102: 122-128.

Vaughan, D.S., R.M. Yoshiyama, J.E. Beck, and D.L. DeAngelis. 1984. Modeling approaches for assessing the effects of stress on fish populations, p. 260-276. *In* V.M. Cairns, P.V. Hodson, and J.O. Nriagu (eds.). Contaminant Effects On Fisheries. John Wiley, New York, New York.

Wheeler, T. L. and L. H. Hardy. In press. National Marine Fisheries Service habitat conservation efforts in North Carolina from 1987 through 1989. *In* Proceedings of the 17th Annual Conference of the National Association of Environmental Professionals, May 1992. Seattle, Washington.

The Use of Biological Measures in Assessments of Toxicants in the Coastal Zone

Edward R. Long

ABSTRACT: Potentially toxic substances occur throughout many estuaries in different mixtures and in varying concentrations. Although the concentrations of these substances can be compared with available criteria or guidelines, direct measures of adverse biological effects are needed to assess the significance of chemical contamination. As a part of its National Status and Trends Program, the National Oceanic and Atmospheric Administration (NOAA) conducts intensive regional assessments of the biological effects of toxicants, which include analyses of sediments, bivalve molluscs, and demersal fish. These measures are used to estimate the spatial patterns and extent of toxicity, the prevalence and severity of biological impacts, and the relationships between the measures of effects and the concentrations of chemicals within each survey area. Also, these data are used to compare the severity and magnitude of impacts among survey areas nationwide. The tests and data from selected areas are presented to illustrate the use of biological measures in toxicant assessment, and the kinds of results and their use by NOAA.

Introduction

Potentially toxic chemicals that enter coastal waters, estuaries, and bays can accumulate in sediments and resident biota. A number of national monitoring and survey programs have established that toxicants occur in these media throughout most coastal areas of the United States (e.g., Butler 1973; Farrington et al. 1983; O'Connor 1991; Paul et al. 1992). The data on chemical concentrations are useful to identify areas with the most severe contamination, to describe the mixtures of substances in each area, to identify spatial patterns of contamination within estuaries and among estuaries, and to estimate the potential ecological risks posed by the chemicals. Occasionally, the chemical mixtures in the receiving waters can be linked to the mixtures found in specific sources. However, the chemical data, alone, do not provide information on the biological significance of the contamination.

The biological significance of the contamination can be estimated by applying effects-based numerical standards or can be measured directly by using a battery of biological assays. Some means of estimating or directly measuring biological effects (bioeffects) are needed to answer and quantify the proverbial "So what?" question (Boesch 1984). Recently, some marine environmental quality programs have begun using biological measures as components of their assessments. Included among these are the National Status and Trends (NS&T) Program administered by the National Oceanic and Atmospheric Administration (NOAA) (Wolfe et al. 1993) and the Environmental Monitoring and Assessment Program (EMAP) administered by the Environmental Protection Agency (Paul et al. 1992). The objectives of the NS&T Program surveys are to determine (1) the spatial patterns and extent of bioeffects, (2) the severity of bioeffects, and (3) the relationships between the measures of effects and the concentrations of contaminants in the samples. The surveys are not intended to identify temporal trends in contamination or effects, nor are they intended to identify the sources of contamination. The purpose of this paper is to briefly describe the biological assessment tools currently employed by the NS&T Program as an example of the use of measures of toxicant bioeffects in monitoring.

The data from the measurements of bioeffects can provide evidence that toxic substances in the environment are not benign; rather, they are bioavailable and represent a real hazard to valuable living resources. These data can establish exposure of living resources to these substances, and the occurrence of adverse impacts as a result of the chemical exposure. They can be used to identify areas in which development of the coastal zone has resulted in unacceptable pollution, and to target efforts to clean up the most contaminated areas. Land-use and/or wastewater treatment practices can be adjusted accordingly to provide better protection for the resources.

The ideal bioeffects assessment tools are those that are ecologically meaningful; responsive to multiple toxicants; insensitive to natural (or "nuisance") variables; effective surrogates for other measures of effects; easily performed, interpreted, and understood; and relatively inexpensive (Wolfe 1992). Since no single biological assay meets all of these criteria, a battery of tests must be used. There are many choices available; all with advantages and disadvantages (MacDonald et al. 1992). Generally, as the specificity of the measures increases, the ecological relevance decreases and vice versa. For example, the data from benthic and fish community surveys have high ecological relevance, but these communities are sensitive to a vast array of natural factors, such as habitat types, as well as toxicants. Some biochemical assays are highly toxicant-specific, but their ecological relevance as a measure of the size and health of a population is relatively poor.

In the NS&T Program surveys, analyses are performed to estimate the severity of chemical contamination to which the biota are exposed. These measures of exposure include quantification of parent compounds and their metabolites. Also, assays are performed to determine if the biota have responded to the exposure to the chemicals. Assays of exposure include biochemical tests in fish, immuno-response and heat-stress protein response assays in bivalves, and sublethal toxicity tests performed with sediments. Finally, a battery of tests are performed to measure adverse biological effects. These include the quantification of sediment toxicity in acute tests, quantification of cyto-genetic and histopathological disorders in bivalves, and the prevalence of histopathological disorders and impaired reproductive success in demersal fish.

Complementary measures of exposure, response, and effects are used to develop a weight of evidence regarding the spatial patterns and severity of bioeffects within each study area. The three media tested are sediments, bivalve molluscs, and demersal fish. Depositional sediments represent a relatively ubiquitous and stable medium within which toxicants can accumulate. They can be collected in relatively dense sampling designs, and, therefore, can provide information on biological impacts with the finest spatial resolution. Because bivalve molluscs are sessile, measures of bio-accumulation and bioeffects can be attributed to the conditions at the specific sampling or transplant locations. Also, filter-feeding bivalves can provide information on contamination in areas where toxic substances may not accumulate in the sediments. Demersal fishes range over large areas and integrate exposures to toxicants from different sources. Fish are highly valued resources and often represent higher trophic levels than molluscs. A variety of well-developed biomarkers of exposure, response, and effects are available for fish.

Existing data were compiled and reviewed either before or during the planning for the surveys in San Francisco Bay (Long et al. 1988); the Hudson River-Raritan Bay estuary (Ayers et al. 1988; Squibb et al. 1991); Long Island Sound (Bricker et al. 1993); Tampa Bay (Long et al. 1991); Boston Harbor (MacDonald 1991); and southern California (Mearns et al. 1991). Often, these data indicated that the industrial harbors and channels that constitute the periphery or the inland portion of the study areas were more contaminated than the open-water basins.

In the following discussions the types of bioeffects assays used in the NS&T Program surveys will be described. Examples of the results from selected surveys will be provided to illustrate the types of data generated. The severity of effects among samples will be compared in selected survey areas and results of some tests will be compared among selected bays.

Sediment Toxicity Tests

Surveys of sediment toxicity have been performed, thus far, in San Francisco Bay, numerous bays and lagoons in southern California, four areas in the Northeast, five estuaries in Georgia and South Carolina, Tampa Bay, and four bays in the northern Florida panhandle (Fig. 1). Additional surveys were initiated in 1995 in Biscayne Bay near Miami and in Sabine Lake, Texas.

SELECTION OF TESTS

Toxicity tests of sediments provide a means of determining if sediment-bound chemicals are bioavailable and if they are of toxicological significance. The tests are performed under controlled laboratory conditions to minimize the effects of "nuisance" variables, such as salinity (Chapman and Long 1983). Although sediment toxicity tests commonly are performed during evaluations of prospective dredged material (United States Army Corps of Engineers and United States Environmental Protection Agency 1991), they, also, have proved useful in surveys of large study areas (e.g., Swartz et al. 1982, 1986). Sediment quality surveys based upon the use of multiple tests are recommended (Burton 1992) since different taxa have different sensitivities to toxicants. A variety of different tests has been developed (Burton 1992); five of which were evaluated for possible use in the NS&T Program (Long et al. 1990). Each of the candidate tests was evaluated according to its sensitivity to field-collected samples, within-sample variance, total range in response, and concordance with chemical concentrations. Following that evaluation and other comparisons among candidate tests (e.g., Pastorok and Becker 1989; Carr and Chapman 1992), a "core" battery of tests was adopted.

Currently, the core battery of tests consists of (1) a solid-phase (bulk) sediment test performed with an amphipod; (2) a porewater test performed with the larvae or gametes of an invertebrate; and (3) an organic solvent extract test performed with a bioluminescent bacteria (the Microtox™ test). All three types of tests have been performed in most of the NS&T Program surveys thus far. Similarly, three tests performed with amphipods, mollusc larvae, and Microtox™ were used to prioritize areas for remediation in a hazardous waste site investigation (Williams et al. 1986). They

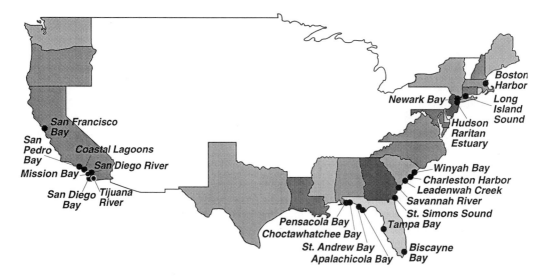

Fig. 1. Bays and estuaries of the United States in which sediment toxicity surveys have been performed or are under way by the National Oceanic and Atmospheric Administration.

provided overlapping, but not duplicative, patterns and responses in toxicity. Collectively, by using this battery of tests, three phases of the sediments are tested, data are acquired from three species that have different sensitivities, and a number of both acute and sublethal endpoints are measured. The data from each test individually and from the battery of tests collectively are used to rank and compare sampling stations and to determine the spatial patterns in toxicity within each study area.

In the 10-d amphipod tests, percent survival is determined following the protocols of the American Society for Testing Materials (1992). In the Microtox™ tests, the concentrations of an organic extract that causes a 50% reduction in bioluminescence is determined after 5-min exposures (United States Environmental Protection Agency 1990). Various tests of the toxicity of liquid-phase extracts (elutriates) and pore waters of sediments has been performed. In a survey of San Francisco Bay (Long and Markel 1992), sediment-water elutriates were prepared, following the methods of the United States Army Corps of Engineers and United States Environmental Protection Agency (1991) and the percent survival and percent normal development of bivalve embryos were determined after 48-h exposures (United States Environmental Protection Agency 1990). Similar tests were performed by NOAA in surveys of the Hudson-Raritan estuary (Wolfe et al. in press) and Long Island Sound (Bricker et al. 1993), following centrifugation of the elutriates.

In more recent surveys (Tampa Bay, southern California bays, Boston Harbor, coastal South Carolina-Georgia bays, western Florida bays), toxicity tests were performed with the sediment pore-waters. In these tests the sediments were "squeezed" in a sealed chamber and the interstitial (pore) waters were retained (Carr et al. 1989). Usually, the tests were performed with the gametes and/or embryos of sea urchins (*Arbacia punctulata* or *Strongylocentrotus purpuratus*) in which percent fertilization of the eggs (Dinnel et al. 1987) and/or percent normal morphological development of the embryos (Oshida et al. 1981) were measured. However, sea urchins were not available for the first phase of the southern California surveys, and 48-h tests of the survival and normal development of mollusc larvae (*Haliotis rufescens*) were performed (Hunt and Anderson 1989).

SPATIAL PATTERNS IN TOXICITY

The data from these surveys have proven useful in identifying the spatial patterns in toxicity (Long et al. 1994). Regions within each study area in which toxicity was highest, lowest, and intermediate were determined. Thus far, the toxicity data have shown three types of distribution patterns. In some survey areas (e.g., Newark Bay) toxicity was pervasive, occurring in the majority of the samples throughout the entire area and no major spatial patterns were evident among stations. In other areas (e.g., Pensacola and St. Andrew bays) toxicity was restricted to small, highly industrialized portions of the bays. Finally, in some estuaries (e.g., Boston Harbor) toxic samples were widely scattered throughout the system.

In a survey of the bays adjoining Long Island Sound, four toxicity tests were performed: survival of amphipods (*Ampelisca abdita*) exposed to solid-phase sediments; survival and morphological development of bivalve embryos (*Mulinia lateralis*) exposed to liquid-phase elutriates; and microbial bioluminescence (Microtox™) in exposures to organic solvent extracts (Wolfe et al. 1994). The samples having a statistically significant response in all four tests were assumed to be the most toxic; those samples having no significant response in all four tests were the least toxic. Generally, the samples from the bays of western Long Island Sound (Fig. 2) were more toxic (causing significant responses in two to four tests) than those from the bays along eastern Long Island Sound (Bricker et al. 1993). Based upon the data from 60 sampling stations, toxicity was highest in sediments collected in Bridgeport Harbor (Connecticut), Little Neck Inlet (New York), Manhasset Bay (New York), Cold Spring Harbor (New York), Eastchester Bay (New York), Oyster Bay (New York), and Larchmont Harbor (New York). The sediments from one station in Bridgeport Harbor had significant toxicity to all four toxicity endpoints. Only five of the 60 samples were nontoxic for all of the four test endpoints.

In Tampa Bay, toxicity tests were performed on 165 sediment samples collected throughout this estuary (Long et al. 1994). Based upon the combined results of the amphipod survival (*A. abdita*) tests, the microbial bioluminescence tests, and the sea urchin (*Arbacia punctulata*) egg fertilization tests, toxicity was highest in the portion of the estuary known as northern Hillsborough Bay. The data from the sea urchin tests exemplified the spatial pattern in toxicity within northern Hillsborough Bay (Fig. 3). Usually, fertilization success in the 100% porewater samples from upper Ybor Channel and the mouth of the Hillsborough River was very low, often zero. The sea urchin data indicated that toxicity diminished slightly down the Ybor and Sparkman channels into Hillsborough Bay. Also, toxicity measured by sea urchin fertilization success was high in the samples from nearby McKay Bay and East Bay. Toxicity continued to diminish southward down Hillsborough Bay toward the mouth of the estuary, indicating a relatively clear gradient in toxicity (Long et al. 1994).

None of the samples from Charleston Harbor, South Carolina, caused a significant decrease in amphipod (*A. abdita*) survival relative to controls. However, some of the samples were toxic as measured by the sea urchin (*A. punctulata*) and Microtox™ tests. The Microtox™ tests indicated that many samples from the lower Cooper River, along with a few from the lower Wando River and Charleston Harbor were toxic (Fig. 4). None of the samples from the lower Ashley River were toxic in this test. The sea urchin tests performed with 100% pore water were more sensitive than the Microtox™ tests; that is, toxicity was apparent in considerably more samples (Fig. 5). Most of

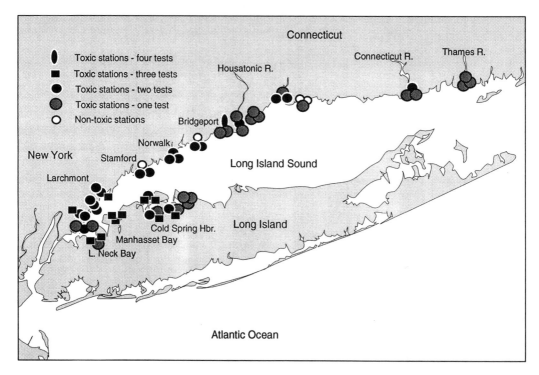

Fig. 2. Sampling stations in the bays adjoining Long Island Sound, New York, in which sediments were not toxic (p > 0.05) in any test or were significantly toxic (p < 0.05) in one, two, three, or four of the toxicity tests. The toxicity tests were amphipod survival, bivalve embryo survival and development, and microbial bioluminescence.

the samples from the lower Ashley, Cooper, and Wando rivers and two samples from the lower Charleston Harbor were toxic in this test.

As observed in Charleston Harbor, none of the samples from St. Andrew Bay in western Florida was toxic to amphipod (*A. abdita*) survival. Most of the samples that caused a significant reduction in sea urchin (*A. punctulata*) fertilization success were collected in or near a relatively small area, Watson's Bayou, near the urbanized area of Panama City (Fig. 6). Samples collected near the mouth of the estuary and in the rural areas of East Bay and West Bay were not toxic in this test.

The data from these tests provide complementary, but different, information on the relative quality of the sediments (Long et al. 1995a). The test of microbial bioluminescence is indicative of a microbial response to the chemicals extracted from the sediment matrix with an organic solvent, not a test of effects. The organic solvent elutes primarily organic contaminants from the sediment matrix regardless of their actual bioavailability. Therefore, this is a test of the potential exposure to sediment-bound compounds. The sea urchin tests are performed using the pore waters of the sediments, the phase in which dissolved and, therefore, highly bioavailable toxicants are thought to reside (Zarba 1992). Also, since they are performed with the highly sensitive gametes or embryos of invertebrates, these tests often are highly sensitive. The relative severity or degree of toxicity in test samples can

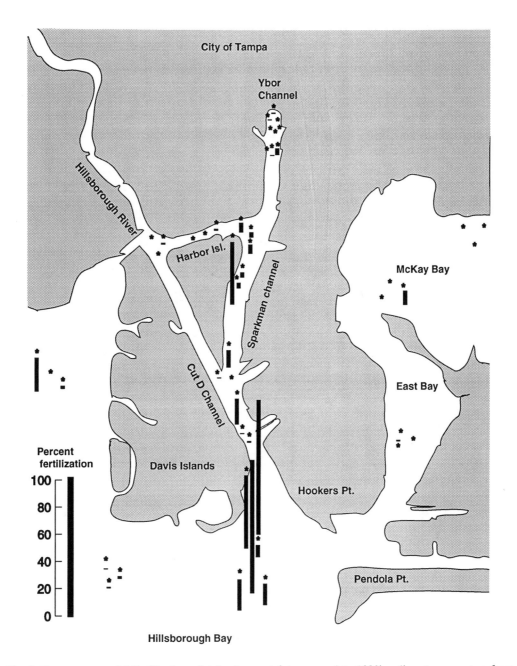

Fig. 3. Percent successful fertilization of *Arbacia punctulata* exposed to 100% sediment pore-waters from sampling stations in northern Hillsborough Bay, Florida. Stations in which fertilization success was significantly lower (p < 0.05) than controls are shown with asterisks.

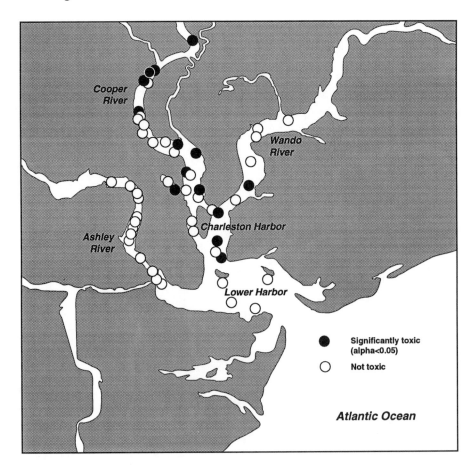

Fig. 4. Sampling stations in Charleston Harbor, South Carolina, in which sediments were toxic or not toxic in microbial bioluminescence tests of organic extracts ($\alpha < 0.05$).

be described with the results of iterative sample dilutions. These tests are direct assays of the pore waters in which a sublethal endpoint is measured with a highly sensitive life stage. Perhaps they are indicative of conditions in sediment pore-waters that invertebrate larvae encounter during attempts to colonize sediments. The amphipod tests are performed with adult benthic organisms exposed to relatively unaltered sediments, and are commonly interpreted as laboratory tests of toxic effects often indicative of in situ toxicity (American Society for Testing Materials 1992). They have been the least sensitive of the three tests used in these surveys. Data from several studies have indicated that highly significant amphipod mortality in laboratory tests often is associated with alterations in resident benthic populations and communities (Swartz et al. 1982, 1986, 1994; Chapman et al. 1987).

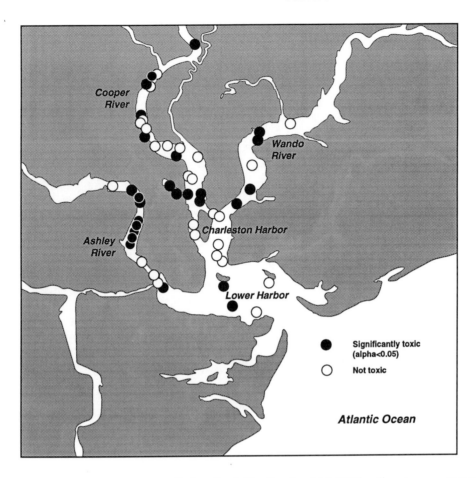

Fig. 5. Sampling stations in Charleston Harbor, South Carolina, in which 100% sediment pore-waters were toxic or not toxic in sea urchin (*Arbacia punctulata*) fertilization tests ($\alpha < 0.05$).

SPATIAL EXTENT OF TOXICITY

The spatial scales of biological effects can differ by many orders of magnitude among different areas and as a function of the type of biological impact measured (O'Connor et al. 1987). Sediment toxicity surveys conducted by the NS&T Program are designed to identify spatial patterns in toxicity within each study area. Regions are sampled that are suspected to be relatively contaminated, transitional, and relatively clean. The incidence of toxicity in each of the tests is calculated and compared among the tests and among survey areas. However, by stratifying the study area and collecting samples at randomly-chosen locations within each stratum, the toxicity data can be weighted to the size of each stratum (Paul et al. 1992), and the spatial extent of toxicity (expressed as km^2) can be

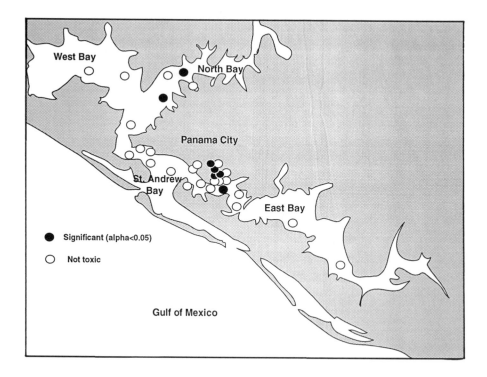

Fig. 6. Sampling stations in St. Andrew Bay, Florida, in which 100% sediment pore-waters were toxic or not toxic in sea urchin (*Arbacia punctulata*) fertilization tests ($\alpha < 0.05$).

estimated for each of the tests. Therefore, the NS&T Program has also estimated the spatial extent of sediment toxicity for each survey area (Long et al. 1994).

Following the stratification of the survey area, the sizes of the strata were determined on navigation charts with a planimeter. The sizes of each stratum (weighted to the number of samples collected within each) that were identified as toxic were summed to provide the estimates of the spatial extent of toxicity. For all toxicity tests, the results for each station were compared with those from the nontoxic controls, and stations were identified as "toxic" when the results were less than 80% of the control values (Schimmel et al. 1994).

The estimates of the spatial extent of toxicity in Charleston Harbor, South Carolina, are provided to illustrate this type of information (Table 1). In the Charleston Harbor survey area, 17.6 km^2 were estimated to be toxic to microbial bioluminescence, representing approximately 43% of the survey area. Approximately 11.3 km^2 (27.6%) were toxic to sea urchin fertilization determined in the 100% porewater tests. None of the samples was toxic in the amphipod tests. The Microtox™ and sea urchin fertilization tests suggested overlapping, but not duplicative, patterns in toxicity. Only 2.4 km^2 (5.8%) of the study area were toxic in both tests. Furthermore, approximately 0.8 km^2 (2.0%) were toxic in both the Microtox™ test and the porewater tests performed at all dilutions.

Table 1. Estimated spatial extent (km^2 and percent total area) of sediment toxicity in Charleston Harbor, South Carolina, based upon the results of three laboratory tests weighted to the size of each sampling stratum. Critical values in each category were < 80% of controls. Total area = 41.0 km^2.

Toxicity Test	Area (km^2)	Percent of Area
Microbial bioluminescence (Microtox™)	17.6	42.9
Sea urchin fertilization		
in 100% porewater	11.3	27.6
in 50% porewater	9.4	22.9
in 25% porewater	6.2	15.1
Amphipod survival	0.0	0.0
Microtox™		
+ urchin @ 100% porewater	2.4	5.8
+ urchin @ 100% + 50% porewater	0.8	2.0
+ urchin @ 100% + 50% + 25% porewater	0.8	2.0
+ urchin @ 25% porewater + amphipod survival	0.0	0.0

In contrast to the results from Charleston Harbor, the data from Tampa Bay, Florida, suggested that approximately 84.3% of the total survey area (550 km^2) was toxic in the sea urchin fertilization tests of 100% pore water (Long et al. 1994). However, in Tampa Bay only approximately 0.1% of the bay was toxic in the sea urchin tests at all three porewater concentrations, in the amphipod tests, and in the Microtox™ tests. In the survey of the Hudson-Raritan estuary (total area of 350 km^2), approximately 133 km^2 (38%) were toxic in the amphipod tests and approximately 136 km^2 (39%) were toxic in the Microtox™ tests (Long et al. 1995b).

In the NS&T Program surveys performed thus far, the incidence of samples that were significantly different from controls (p < 0.05) has differed considerably among the survey areas. In the amphipod tests, the incidence of toxic samples ranged from 84% (48 of 57 samples) in Newark Bay, New Jersey, and 83.3% (50 of 60 samples) in the bays of Long Island Sound, New York-Connecticut, to 0.0% in 40 samples from Pensacola Bay, 31 samples from St. Andrew Bay, Florida, and 63 samples from Charleston Harbor, South Carolina. In the Microtox™ tests, the incidence of toxic samples ranged from 100% in St. Andrew Bay to 26.7% in Tampa Bay and 9.5% in Charleston Harbor. In the sea urchin fertilization tests of 100% pore waters, the incidence of toxicity ranged from 89% (8 of 9 samples) in Winyah Bay, South Carolina, to 54% (34 of 63 samples) in Charleston Harbor to 22.6% (7 of 31 samples) in St. Andrew Bay.

These survey areas ranged from approximately 7 km^2 to 550 km^2, therefore, the magnitude of the toxicity differed considerably among areas. In Fig. 7 the sizes of some of the survey areas and the percent of those areas that were "toxic" (critical value of < 80% of controls) in the amphipod survival tests are compared. Although Tampa Bay was by far the largest survey area, only a tiny

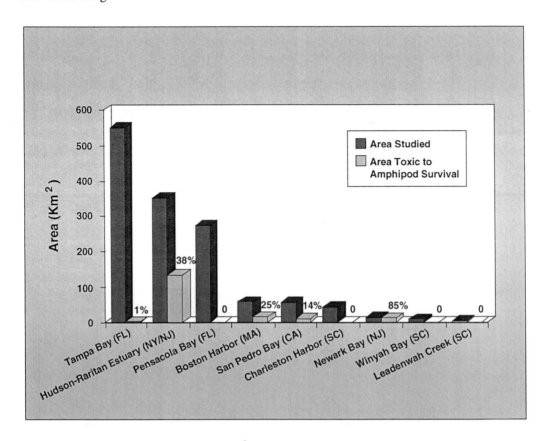

Fig. 7. A comparison of the spatial extent (km^2 and percent of total area surveyed) of sediment toxicity in nine survey areas. Sediment toxicity was determined using the amphipod survival test. Tests were performed with *Ampelisca abdita* in all areas except San Pedro Bay, California, in which *Rhepoxynius abronius* was used.

portion of it (< 1%) was toxic in the amphipod survival tests. The Hudson-Raritan estuary was relatively large and over one-third of it was toxic in these tests. In adjoining Newark Bay, 85% of the area was toxic in the amphipod survival test, but the survey covered only approximately 13 km^2. The survey areas were similar in size in Boston Harbor, Massachusetts, and San Pedro Bay, California, and 25% and 14% of these areas, respectively, were toxic in tests performed with *A. abdita* and *Rhepoxynius abronius*, respectively. Toxicity was not apparent in these tests with the samples collected in Charleston Harbor, Winyah Bay, and Leadenwah Creek, South Carolina.

Toxicity–Contaminant Relationships

The test species used in sediment toxicity tests generally are sensitive to many different toxicants. The utility of toxicity tests in accurately identifying anthropogenically-contaminated sediments has been debated (Spies 1989; Chapman et al. 1991). In some cases, they can be sensitive to naturally occurring physical and/or chemical properties of sediments as well as toxic substances. DeWitt et al. (1988) developed a numerical model that accounts for the contribution of high levels of fine-grained particles to reduced survival of the amphipod *R. abronius*. High concentrations of un-ionized ammonia in anoxic, subsurface sediments may contribute to toxicity in laboratory tests (Kohn et al. 1994).

In the NS&T Program surveys, the toxicity data have been compared to the chemistry data to identify which substances may have contributed to the toxicity observed. The measures of toxicity consistently have correlated strongly with the concentrations of toxicants in the sediments and relatively poorly with natural environmental variables (Long and Markel 1992; Bricker et al. 1993; Long et al. 1994; Sapudar et al. 1994; Wolfe et al. in press). However, the specific chemicals or classes of substances that most likely contributed to toxicity have differed among the survey areas.

In San Francisco Bay, toxicity to the normal morphological development of bivalve embryos exposed to sediment elutriates was strongly correlated with the concentrations of total high-molecular-weight and total low-molecular-weight polynuclear aromatic hydrocarbons (PAHs) ($R^2 = 0.556$ and 0.574, respectively, $p < 0.0001$). Also, toxicity was correlated with the concentrations of total tin ($R^2 = 0.434$, $p < 0.0005$), and tributyl tin ($R^2 = 0.289$, $p < 0.03$) but not with percent silt and clay ($R^2 = 0.040$, $p > 0.05$) (Long and Markel 1992).

Percent amphipod survival was highly correlated with the concentrations of numerous PAHs, lead, zinc, and other trace elements in samples from San Pedro Bay (Sapudar et al. 1994). Results of abalone embryo development tests performed with the pore waters were correlated with the concentrations of lead, copper, and tin in the sediments. The concentrations of PAHs, DDT, and several trace metals exceeded sediment guideline values in samples that were toxic.

In 17 of the 20 Long Island Sound bays sampled, the stations were arranged in a transect from the upper to the lower reaches of the bays (Bricker et al. 1993). There was a trend of significantly decreasing concentrations of inorganic and organic contaminants, percent total organic carbon (TOC), grain size, and total acid-volatile sulfides (AVS) from the head to the mouth of each of these bays. Toxicity indicated by the Microtox™ test showed an identical pattern in these bays (i.e., high toxicity in the upper portions of the bays, decreasing toward the mouth). However, the amphipod and bivalve larvae tests showed reversed patterns in toxicity with greatest toxicity generally observed near the mouth of each bay. The Microtox™ test was performed with an organic solvent extract of the sediment, whereas the amphipod and bivalve embryo tests were performed with solid-phase sediments and a seawater elutriate of the sediments, respectively. The relatively high TOC content of the upper bay stations may have modulated and reduced the availability of the contaminants in the invertebrate tests, whereas those contaminants were made available artificially via the organic solvent elution in the Microtox™ tests. Complex mixtures of trace metals, PAHs, chlorinated pesticides, PCBs, organic carbon, and fine-grained sediment were strongly correlated with toxicity in the amphipod and Microtox™ tests.

In the Tampa Bay survey, toxicity in the amphipod, sea urchin, and Microtox™ tests was strongly correlated with the concentrations of lead, zinc, many individual PAHs, total high-molecular-weight PAHs, total PCBs, total DDT isomers, and endrin (Long et al. 1994). In addition, the average concentrations of these substances were higher in the toxic samples than in the nontoxic samples and generally exceeded respective sediment quality guidelines or criteria. Other substances were correlated with the toxicity results but failed to exceed the respective guideline values.

Percent sea urchin fertilization was highly correlated with the concentrations of total PCBs (Spearman-rank, rho = −0.678, $p < 0.0001$, n = 61) in the Tampa Bay samples (Fig. 8). Also, sea

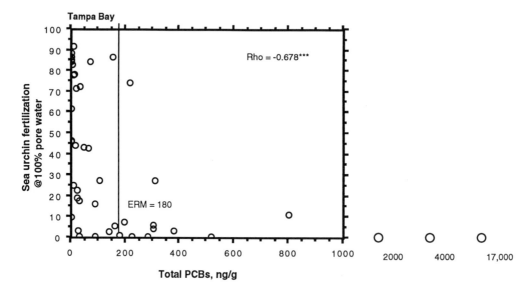

Fig. 8. Relationship between the percent fertilization of sea urchins (*Arbacia punctulata*) in 100% sediment pore-water from Tampa Bay and the concentrations of total PCBs in the bulk sediment. Effects Range-Median (ERM) value from Long et al. (1995c) and the Spearman-rank correlation coefficient are shown.

urchin fertilization success was highly variable at PCB concentrations below the Effects Range-Median (ERM) guideline of 180 ng g^{-1} (Long et al. 1995c). In samples with PCB concentrations above the ERM value, percent fertilization was invariably low. The average PCB concentrations in the samples that were significantly toxic in tests of 25% pore water (920 ng g^{-1}) exceeded the average concentrations in samples that were not toxic in the 100% pore water (13 ng g^{-1}) by a factor of 34.6, and, also exceeded the ERM value by a factor of 5.1. These correlative data do not demonstrate that PCBs caused the toxicity; however, they do suggest that PCBs occurred in sufficiently high concentrations, along with other substances, to have contributed to toxicity in the samples.

In the survey of the Hudson-Raritan estuary, the results of the amphipod and Microtox™ tests were correlated very strongly with many different substances in the samples (Wolfe et al. in press). Notably, the concentrations of the PAHs were highly correlated with toxicity (Fig. 9). Amphipod survival was relatively high in samples with PAH concentrations less than the Effects Range-Low (ERL) value of Long et al. (1995c). Survival began to decrease in samples with PAH concentrations above the ERL value, and was invariably low (< 40%) in all samples with PAH concentrations above the ERM value. One sample that had over 1 million ng g^{-1} total PAH caused 100% amphipod mortality. The average concentration of PAHs in samples that were toxic to amphipods (80,270 ng g^{-1}) exceeded the average concentration in nontoxic samples (5,427 ng g^{-1}) by a factor of 14.8 and also exceeded the ERM value (44,792 ng g^{-1}, Long et al. 1995c) by a factor of 1.8. Numerous individual PAHs and classes of these compounds were highly concentrated in the toxic samples and were highly correlated with toxicity, indicating that they probably co-varied with each other.

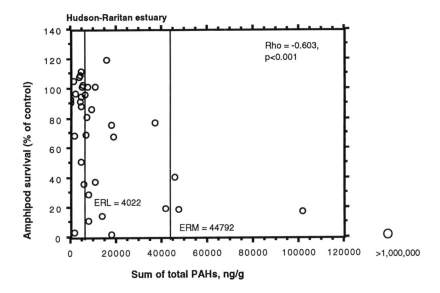

Fig. 9. Relationship between percent survival of the amphipod *Ampelisca abdita* and the concentration of total PAHs in sediment samples from the Hudson-Raritan estuary. Effects Range-Low (ERL) and Effects Range-Median (ERM) values from Long et al. (1995c) and Spearman-rank correlation coefficient are shown.

Bivalve Biomarkers

Biomarkers are commonly used as molecular, biochemical, or cellular measurements of an animal's exposure to chemical contamination and the magnitude of the animal's response to the contamination (McCarthy and Shugart 1990). Since many measures of adverse effects, such as liver lesions in fish, can be triggered or exacerbated by natural factors, it is important to establish that the animal was actually exposed to toxicants and was required to respond to the exposure. The battery of biomarkers that have been developed assist in providing this linkage.

SELECTION OF BIOMARKERS

Bivalve molluscs have been used frequently in national and regional programs as bioindicators of toxicant uptake and accumulation (Mearns et al. 1988). Chemical analyses of these animals have been useful in identifying contamination patterns and establishing the bioavailability of toxicants. A major component of the NS&T Program consists of the National Mussel Watch Project, in which chemical analyses are performed on tissues of oysters and mussels from hundreds of locations nationwide (O'Connor 1991). However, most of the programs, including the NS&T Program, testing for contamination have rarely, if ever, included assays of toxicant bioeffects to estimate the significance of bioaccumulated toxicants to the bivalves (Butler 1973; Farrington et al. 1983; O'Connor 1991; Paul et al. 1992).

Unlike fish, data from assays of bivalves can be attributed to the collection site, since the recent history and whereabouts of the animals are known. Since they are filter feeders, information may be obtainable from bivalves in nondepositional areas in which analyses of sediments are not useful. Bivalves can be caged and transplanted to sites in which suitable habitat for them does not occur naturally, thereby ensuring information from most areas (Salazar and Salazar 1995). However, considerably less effort has been expended on the development and interpretation of biomarkers in bivalves than in fish (Bayne et al. 1988).

Historically, the most commonly used measure of bivalve health has been the condition index. A number of different condition indices have been used (Crosby and Gale 1990); all of which are based upon the percentage of the internal shell volume occupied by the oyster's soft body tissue. These indices were initially developed as a gauge of the meat content of commercially grown oysters, but they also have been used as an indicator of effects in pollution studies. These indices are not toxicant-specific. That is, they are highly influenced by the amount and availability of food, and stresses caused by natural environmental factors such as parasite burden, salinity changes, and temperature. Scope for growth, a measure of the energetic balance of molluscs, has been used effectively in biomarker studies (Widdows and Johnson 1988) but is subject to the same natural factors as condition indices.

Biomarkers that are more toxicant-specific, such as cytochrome P-450 activity, have been measured in molluscs, but these enzymatic systems are poorly developed and poorly understood in molluscs (Livingstone et al. 1989). Also, a number of hydrocarbon-metabolizing enzymes in mussels were relatively insensitive to large doses of diesel oil and other hydrocarbons (Suteau et al. 1988).

Biomarkers that are biologically relevant and responsive mainly to toxic chemicals were needed by the NS&T Program to properly assess the significance of the exposure to these stressors. Thus, experimental work and surveys were initiated by the NS&T Program in the Boston Harbor– Buzzards Bay area, Tampa Bay, and San Diego Bay to develop such biomarkers. In each study, resident animals were collected in highly contaminated, transitional, and relatively clean areas. In Boston Harbor, the biochemical mechanisms of the impairment of gametogenesis and spawning in mussels (*Mytilus edulis*) were being evaluated (J. McDowell Capuzzo, Woods Hole Oceanographic Institution, Woods Hole, Massachusetts). In San Diego Bay, both resident and transplanted mussels (*M. edulis*) were being examined for organism condition indices, gonadal condition indices, levels of heat stress proteins in gill and mantle tissues (Sanders et al. 1992), and DNA integrity in hemocytes (B. Sanders, University of California, Long Beach, California). In addition, the growth rates of transplanted adult mussels were being measured (Salazar and Salazar 1991).

In Tampa Bay, numerous assays were performed on resident oysters, *Crassostrea virginica* (W. Fisher, United States Environmental Protection Agency, Gulf Breeze, Florida). The assays included a large battery of histolopathological disorders, condition indices, gonadal indices, cellular and subcellular disorders, and measures of the immuno-competence of hemocytes (Table 2). The growth rates of transplanted juvenile oysters were measured, using technology and methods previously applied to mussels (Salazar and Salazar 1991). Many of the assays under evaluation in Tampa Bay have shown dose-responses in laboratory exposures to toxic substances, whereas others have not been so tested (Fisher and Long in review). For example, several measures of the immuno-competence of the hemocytes of oysters have been developed and evaluated in laboratory tests (Fisher et al. 1989, 1990). Their performance in complex field conditions is being evaluated in Tampa Bay.

Table 2. Biomarker assays performed on oysters, *Crassostrea virginica*, sampled in Tampa Bay, Florida (from Fisher and Long in review).

Toxicant Exposure	Tissue chemical analyses
Response to Toxicants	Heat-stress protein activity
Physical, Morphological, Metabolic	Organism size
	Morphological index
	Shell density
	Condition index
	Gender and gender ratio
	Gonadal maturity index
	Gonadal condition
	Population gonadal index
	Tissue elemental composition
	Hemolymph biochemistry
	Digestive gland structure index
	Connective tissue structure index
Immuno-competence and Status	Hemocyte morphology
	Hemocyte mobility and locomotion
	Phagocytic index
	Superoxide production
	Serum lysozyme content
Parasite, Disease, and Microbial Burden	Total parasites in tissue sections
	Intensity of *Perkinsus marinus* in hemolymph
	Bacterial levels in hemolymph
Cytogenetic Disorders	Hemic neoplasia
	Organ neoplasia
	Gill epithelial cell micronuclei
	Gill cell DNA damage
Organism Growth	Comparative growth rates of transplanted juveniles

TAMPA BAY OYSTERS

The assays listed in Table 2 were performed with resident oysters collected from six locations in Tampa Bay that, based upon the data from the sediment toxicity survey (Long et al. 1994), were expected to represent a wide range of toxicant levels. Each assay or suite of complementary assays

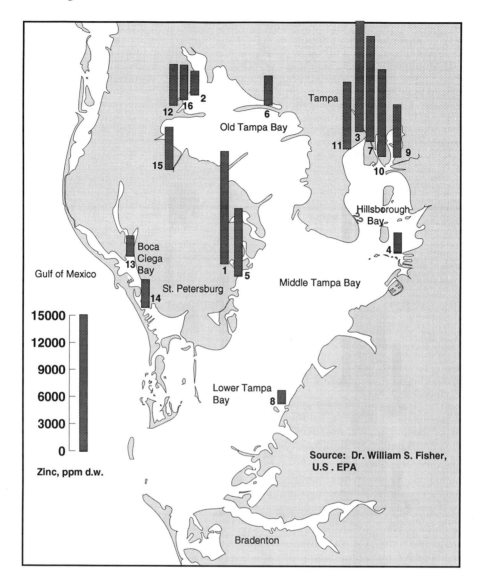

Fig. 10. Zinc concentrations in the tissues of oysters (*Crassostrea virginica*) collected at 16 locations within Tampa Bay, Florida.

was evaluated to: (1) identify those that were sufficiently sensitive to indicate between-site differences, (2) determine concordance with chemical concentrations in the tissues, and (3) estimate the discriminatory power (Long and Buchman 1990) of the tests. Several of the assays indicated patterns in response that corresponded with the expected pollution gradients, others indicated no statistically-significant between-site differences, and some indicated patterns reversed from what was expected.

Following evaluation of the data from this first field trial, some assays were deleted, other prospective tests were added, and the methods for some assays were modified for use in a subsequent survey of additional sites in Tampa Bay. During the second phase of the study, samples were collected at 16 sites throughout Tampa Bay. As exemplified by zinc (Fig. 10), the concentrations of most trace metals were highest in the oysters collected in northern Hillsborough Bay (sites 3, 7, and 10) and inner Bayboro Harbor (site 1). Detectable concentrations of DDT isomers and PCBs were found in oysters from the same locations. Concentrations of all substances were relatively low or nondetectable elsewhere in the estuary, including sites 2, 12, and 16 in Cooper's Bayou and site 8 at Piney Point, which were expected to represent background or reference conditions.

The biological assays that were performed on these oysters showed different patterns in response and concordance with the chemical concentrations (Fisher and Long in review). Many of the assays, however, showed a pattern in response consistent with the chemical concentrations in the tissues. For example, two measures of the immune response of the oysters, hemocyte cell density and hemocyte rate of locomotion, were significantly elevated in samples from sites 1, 3, and 7 relative to oysters collected at other, less contaminated sites (Fig. 11). Phagocytosis, the ingestion and destruction of foreign materials by the hemocytes (blood cells), is considered the principal mechanism of defense in oysters and progresses in several steps (Fisher 1988). Increases in hemocyte densities may occur in response to exposures to trace metals (Cheng 1988) as well as exposures to other foreign materials such as parasites or to elevated temperatures. Also, changes in the rate of mobilization of hemocytes may occur in response to foreign materials, such as parasites or toxic substances (Fisher et al. 1990).

The data from Tampa Bay, exemplified by the assays of immune response, suggest that the oysters from the sites in which tissue concentrations of toxicants were highest, may have been adversely affected by stressors, including toxic chemicals. The spatial pattern in the tissue concentrations of toxicants and in many of the biological assays corresponded with the patterns in sediment contamination and toxicity. Taken together, the data from the tests of sediments and oysters indicated that potentially toxic chemicals found in the sediments also were accumulating in oysters. Also, toxicity observed in the laboratory tests of sediments was accompanied by some measures of response and effects in resident biota (oysters).

Fish Biomarkers

SELECTION OF BIOMARKERS

A wide variety of biomarkers in marine and estuarine fish has been developed in laboratory experiments and applied to differing degrees in field surveys (Stegeman and Heath 1984; White 1984; McCarthy and Shugart 1990; Huggett et al. 1992; Peakall 1992). Compared with toxicant bioeffects surveys using bivalve molluscs, surveys using fish have many more biomarkers available for use, the cause-effects mechanisms are better understood, and the availability of laboratory expertise is much greater. Many biomarkers (e.g., biochemical responses to organic toxicants) are responsive in many species of fish, thus allowing applications among biogeographic zones. Some biomarkers are responsive only to specific toxicants, or even specific classes of toxicants, thus aiding in their utility. Some biomarkers (e.g., incidence of micronuclei) were developed initially as human clinical techniques, and, therefore, benefit from the legacy of that usage.

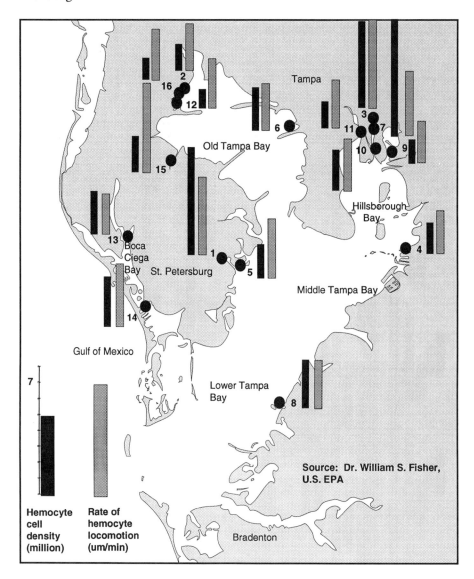

Fig. 11. Hemocyte cell densities and rates of hemocyte locomotion in resident oysters (*Crassostrea virginica*) from 16 sampling locations in Tampa Bay, Florida.

In 1987 the NS&T Program evaluated and compared the relative performance of a number of candidate fish biomarkers in a field experiment conducted in San Francisco Bay (Long and Buchman 1990). Starry flounder (*Platichthys stellatus*) were collected at sites within and outside San Francisco Bay that represented large differences in chemical contamination. The incidence of micronuclei in erythrocytes and a suite of measures of catalyzing and metabolizing enzyme activities in the livers proved to be useful assays. As a biomarker of toxicant effects, the incidence of micronucleated erythrocytes indicated significant differences among sampling sites, was applicable to numerous species, and was highly correlated with the concentrations of organic compounds in the fish tissues; however, it showed relatively high variability among fish from individual sampling locations. The suite of enzymatic assays included measures of total cytochrome P-450 content, P-450E content, ethoxyresorufin-o-deethylase (EROD) activity, and aryl hydrocarbon hydroxylase (AHH) activity in livers. All of these measures, except the AHH activity assay, proved to be very sensitive, indicated significant differences among sites, were correlated with contaminant concentrations, and showed relatively low within-site variability.

Based upon the previous years of experience (Johnson et al. 1992a,b; Varanasi 1992; Wolfe 1992), the NS&T Program has developed a battery of biological and chemical tests to assess exposure of fish to toxicants, to determine if the animals responded to the exposure, and to quantify adverse effects (Table 3). In each survey area, fish are captured in relatively contaminated, transitional, and relatively clean areas. The concentrations of selected toxicants in the fish tissues, the metabolites of aromatic hydrocarbons in the bile, and toxicant-DNA adducts in the liver provide indications that the animals were exposed to xenobiotics. Data from assays of xenobiotic-metabolizing enzymes in the fish tissues indicate that the animals were induced to respond to the chemical exposure. Elevated prevalences of adverse effects (i.e., impaired reproductive success, histopathological disorders) suggest that the fish were unsuccessful in their defensive response to the toxicants. As part of NOAA's bioeffects surveys, these tests have been performed on fish from Puget Sound, San Diego Bay, San Francisco Bay, Boston Harbor, the Hudson-Raritan estuary, and Long Island Sound (Malins et al. 1984; McCain et al. 1988, 1992; Spies et al. 1990; Gronlund et al. 1991; Johnson et al. 1992a). Recently, these tests were performed on fish collected in Tampa Bay, Pensacola Bay, Charleston Harbor, and Biscayne Bay within the same areas where sediment samples were collected for toxicity testing. The results of the tests of the fish will be published in the near future (B. McCain, National Marine Fisheries Service, personal communication).

MEASURES OF TOXICANT EXPOSURE

In Puget Sound, correlations between the prevalence of idiopathic liver lesions and numerous chemicals in sediments from the sites where fish were captured often were significant (Malins et al. 1984). However, chemical analyses of the fish tissues were confounded by the realization that some potentially toxic contaminants were readily metabolized and excreted by fish, and thus were not detectable with traditional analytical methods. Therefore, techniques that were developed to quantify the concentrations of these metabolites in the bile of the fish (Krahn et al. 1984) were incorporated into the assessments (McCain et al. 1988, 1992; Collier and Varanasi 1991). The correlations (Table 4) between the concentrations of hydrocarbon metabolites in the bile and the incidence of several idiopathic liver lesions in English sole *(Parophrys vetulus)* from Puget Sound were highly significant (Krahn et al. 1986).

The modification of DNA by exposure to xenobiotics or their metabolites may trigger the onset of carcinogenesis. Therefore, the quantification of toxicant-DNA adducts can be a powerful interpretive tool when coupled with measures of the incidence of liver lesions in the same fish. Techniques for quantifying toxicant-DNA adducts in fish have been developed with very low detection limits (Varanasi et al. 1989); these have been applied in a number of study areas. For example, the levels of hepatic DNA adducts showed a nearly fourfold, statistically-significant difference between winter flounder from a reference site and a contaminated site in Long Island

Table 3. Biological assays and chemical analyses performed with demersal fish sampled in the National Status and Trends Program (from Johnson et al. 1992a).

Fish Condition	Age, gender, length, weight Condition index Gonadosomatic index
Toxicant Exposure	Levels of fluorescent aromatic compounds in the bile PCB concentrations in the brain, ovaries, and liver Xenobiotic-DNA adducts in the liver
Responses to Toxicants	Aromatic hydrocarbon hydroxylase activity in the liver
Pathology	Incidence of hepatic lesions, including neoplasms
Impairment of Reproductive Success	Ovarian development, recrudescence, atresia, lesions Plasma estradiol concentrations Fecundity and egg weight

Sound (Gronlund et al. 1991). The prevalence of proliferative liver lesions and the levels of DNA adducts in winter flounder from northeastern estuaries were significantly correlated (rho = 0.717) (Johnson et al. 1992a).

MEASURES OF TOXICANT RESPONSE

While the chemical analyses of sediments and tissues provide information on the kinds and concentrations of toxicants to which fish have been exposed, toxicant-specific biochemical assays can indicate that the fish actually responded to the chemicals. Many assays have been developed (Stegeman and Heath 1984) that can indicate biochemical responses to toxicant classes. They include a group of xenobiotic metabolizing enzymes (XMEs) that function primarily in the livers of fish (Collier and Varanasi 1991). The XME assays include those for microsomal cytochrome P-450 content, EROD activity, and AHH activity. All three of these assays have been shown to be highly responsive in some species of fish in some studies.

Although AHH activity was responsive in winter flounder (*Pleuronectes americanus*) in one study (Bend and Foureman 1984), it showed a weak response in another study (Johnson et al. 1992). Also, AHH activity responded weakly in starry flounder (Long and Buchman 1990). The cytochrome P-450 content and EROD activity assays responded strongly to exposures to hydrocarbons (Stegeman et al. 1988; Long and Buchman 1990). These and other related assays have been incorporated into the battery of tests performed on fish (Collier and Varanasi 1991).

Table 4. Spearman's rank correlations (r_s) between benzo(a)pyrene wavelength metabolites and the incidence of hepatic lesions in English sole from Puget Sound (from Krahn et al. 1986).

	r_s	p
Neoplasia	0.853	< 0.002
Hyperplasia, foci of altered cells	0.773	< 0.01
Megalocytic hepatosis	0.891	< 0.001

MEASURES OF EFFECTS

The prevalence of histopathological disorders, such as liver lesions, has been used as a monitoring tool in the NS&T Program on a nationwide scale (National Oceanic and Atmospheric Administration 1987; Johnson et al. 1992b; Varanasi 1992). Annually, selected fish species from the Atlantic, Gulf, and Pacific coasts have been collected, examined for histopathological disorders, and analyzed for chemical concentrations. Also, lesion prevalence have been the keystone biomarker in the regional bioeffects assessments.

Initial surveys in the early 1980s of histopathological disorders and tissue contamination in English sole were used to determine that some of the urban-industrial waterways of Puget Sound were degraded (Malins et al. 1984; Becker et al. 1987). Fish collected in these areas demonstrated high prevalence of histopathological disorders, including liver neoplasms, that were associated with mixtures of toxicants in the sediments and tissues. Compared to the fish from rural bays (e.g., Case Inlet, Port Madison), fish from the urban-industrial waterways (e.g., Hylebos Waterway at Tacoma, in the Duwamish River, and near Harbor Island at Seattle) had significantly higher prevalences of several types of idiopathic liver lesions (Table 5).

Because the prevalence of liver lesions is an age-dependent measurement, between-station comparisons of prevalence must take into account the age distribution of the fish. For example, Becker et al. (1987) reported highly significant correlations between the age of English sole and the prevalence of liver neoplasms and foci of altered cells (r_s = 0.90 and 1.00, respectively, p < 0.005, n = 702).

Similar to fish from Puget Sound, fish collected in some parts of San Diego Bay demonstrated relatively high prevalence of certain lesions (McCain et al. 1992). Black croaker (*Cheilotrema saturnum*) collected in the Harbor Island and Shelter Island yacht basins had significantly more idiopathic liver lesions and fin erosion than fish collected near Mission Bay (Table 6).

In the southeastern region (Pamlico Sound, North Carolina, to Biscayne Bay, Florida, and the Gulf Coast), sediments and fish were sampled from up to 19 estuaries as a part of the NS&T Program (Hansen and Evans 1989, 1991). Organic and trace metal concentrations in sediments and fish tissues, hydrocarbon metabolites in fish bile, and the prevalence of pathological disorders in fish were compared among the estuaries. Atlantic croaker (*Micropogonias undulatus*) and spot (*Leiostomus xanthurus*) were collected from most of the locations. The data suggested no clear

Table 5. Prevalence of idiopathic liver lesions in English sole *(Parophrys vetulus)* from Puget Sound (n = 2,190) (from Malins et al. 1984).

	Case Inlet	Alki Point	Port Madison	Hylebos Waterway	Harbor Island	Duwamish River
Neoplasia	0.0	0.0	0.0	3.4	5.5	16.2
Hyperplasia, foci of altered cells	0.0	0.0	0.0	8.4	10.2	24.3
Megalocytic hepatosis	0.0	0.0	2.6	8.4	16.5	21.3

and consistent patterns in contamination or biological measures. That is, fish from some estuaries had high concentrations of some compounds and high prevalence of some pathological disorders, but, had low levels of others. Relative to fish from other regions of the United States, those from the southeastern region had relatively low prevalences of lesions. For example, the prevalence of liver hyperplasia ranged from 2.0% in Sapelo Sound, Georgia, and 4.0% in Charleston Harbor, South Carolina, to 17% in St. Johns estuary, Florida. The correlations between the incidence of pathological conditions and chemical concentrations often were significant. However, many of the lesions observed were not toxicant-specific and could have been caused by natural factors (Hansen and Evans 1989).

In female winter flounder from Boston Harbor, Raritan Bay, and adjoining areas, the prevalence of foci of altered cells ranged from 0.0% in several areas to 22% in inner Boston Harbor and 54% in Sandy Hook Bay. The prevalence of toxicopathic liver lesions generally was highest in fish with the highest concentrations of most classes of contaminants (Johnson et al. 1992b). However, the relationships between chemical concentrations and lesion prevalence were much weaker than those observed in English sole from Puget Sound. In addition, lesion prevalence was greatest in fish from stations with the oldest fish. Also, there were no between-station differences in fecundity or egg weight. English sole exposed to Puget Sound contaminants demonstrated reduced reproductive success (Johnson et al. 1989), whereas the winter flounder in the Northeast did not demonstrate such marked effects.

Similar to the results obtained in the sediment toxicity and oyster biomarker studies performed in Tampa Bay, chemical concentrations in several species of demersal fishes were elevated in Hillsborough Bay compared to fish from other portions of the Tampa Bay estuary (McCain et al. in press). Also, the levels of hepatic cytochrome P4501A and hepatic DNA adducts were elevated in fish from Hillsborough Bay. Finally, the prevalences of liver lesions commonly associated with chemical contamination often were highest in the fish from Hillsborough Bay.

Table 6. Incidence of idiopathic liver lesions in black croaker from San Diego Bay, California (from McCain et al. 1992).

	Outside of Mission Bay (n = 23)	Shelter Island (n = 59)	East Harbor Island (n = 88)
Neoplasia	0.0	3.4	10.2
Hyperplasia, foci of altered cells	0.0	2.2	4.5
Fin erosion	0.0	3.1	18.2

Conclusions

The sediment toxicity tests have proven to be effective assessment tools in surveys of toxicant effects (Swartz et al. 1982, 1986, 1994). Performed under controlled laboratory conditions, the influences of natural factors in the test results are reduced. The tests can demonstrate the bioavailability and toxicity of toxicant mixtures. Data are easily interpreted, can be attributed to the specific sampling locations, and can be generated relatively quickly to portray both large-scale and small-scale patterns in toxicity. A battery of tests can be performed with each sample, thereby forming a weight of evidence as regards the toxicity of the study area. However, because these tests are performed in worst-case exposure conditions, their ecological significance is limited unless they are accompanied by measures of benthic population or community alterations. Several studies have demonstrated that benthic populations of sensitive taxa were depauperate or absent in areas in which toxicity to amphipods was significantly elevated in laboratory tests (Swartz et al. 1982, 1986, 1994; Chapman et al. 1987).

Bivalve molluscs are used widely as bioindicators of chemical contamination. Toxicant biomarkers will provide powerful tools for interpreting the biological significance of chemical contamination of the tissues of these animals. A large and diverse array of candidate assays are being developed, some of which should prove to be effective tools. Since oysters and mussels are sessile, data collected from assays of their tissues can be attributed to the specific sampling locations. Also, these animals generally are plentiful and easy to collect, thereby facilitating their use in environmental assessments. In addition, they can be transplanted readily to portions of survey areas in which suitable habitat for them is lacking. Significant reductions in the growth rates of transplanted mussels have been demonstrated and correlated with exposures to toxic substances in the water and bivalve tissues (Salazar and Salazar 1991, 1995). However, bivalves commonly are relatively insensitive to the effects of toxicants and other stressors, which may frustrate efforts to demonstrate adverse effects.

The development of biomarkers for fish has progressed much farther than it has for bivalve molluscs. Many methods have been developed for defining the degree of toxicant exposure, response, and adverse effects, and these have been applied to many different species. The data generated by these analyses have been effective in identifying biologically significant contamination, and, therefore, have been useful in prioritizing areas in need of source control and remediation. However, because of their mobility, fish are not always available when and where they are needed and data cannot be necessarily attributed to conditions at the sampling station. Also, each species of fish can respond differently to xenobiotics, therefore, interspecific comparisons in data over large spatial scales are not always feasible. In addition, some histopathological disorders, condition indices, and measures of fecundity are age-dependent; confounding the interpretation of the data if the age distribution of fish differs among sampling stations (Becker et al. 1987; Johnson et al. 1992a).

The measures of biological effects in sediments, bivalves, and fish used by the NS&T Program provide a broad representation of the kinds of effects and their severity in the study areas. Collectively, they provide information on the level of contamination to which living resources are exposed, the biochemical responses of biota to toxicants, and measures of lethality and chronic sublethal effects of the toxicants. They provide information on distribution and severity of toxicant bioeffects over large and small areas. They provide information that is ecologically relevant and toxicant-specific.

Currently (1995), the interpretation of bioeffects data from the coastal estuaries of the Southeastern United States are underway. These include data from samples collected throughout the entire region (the Carolinian biogeographical province) as a part of the Environmental Monitoring and Assessment Program (EMAP) and from specific urbanized estuaries targeted in the NS&T Program surveys. The data from the tests of sediments, bivalves (oysters and clams), and demersal fishes will be analyzed to determine spatial patterns in contamination and effects, the spatial extent of effects, the severity of effects, and the relationships between estimates of exposure, response, and effects.

Collectively, the data from these surveys should be useful in determining whether or not contamination in Southeastern estuaries has elevated to the point of causing biological damage to living resources. If adverse effects are observed, the data will be useful in comparing the severity and extent of effects among the different estuaries. The regions within each estuary in which effects were observed can be identified, and with the use of the sediment toxicity data, pinpointed to small-scale portions of the estuaries. The chemical composition of the toxicant mixtures will be identified and those chemicals that pose the greatest potential threat to resident biota will be determined.

These data will be available to local managers in setting priorities for further environmental characterization and/or clean-up strategies and remediation. As demonstrated in similar research performed in Puget Sound (Puget Sound Water Quality Authority 1987), high-quality, contaminant bioeffects data can be very powerful tools in the initiation of action plans to restore environmental quality.

ACKNOWLEDGMENTS

Much of the assessment work described herein was support by funding from the National Oceanic and Atmospheric Administration's Coastal Ocean Program. Douglas A. Wolfe and Jo C. Linse (National Oceanic and Atmospheric Administration) contributed to the manuscript. William S. Fisher (United States Environmental Protection Agency, Gulf Breeze, Florida) provided data on oysters from Tampa Bay. K. John Scott and Glen B. Thursby (Science Applications International Corporation, Narragansett, Rhode Island) provided data on sediment toxicity to amphipods. R. Scott Carr (National Biological Service, Corpus Christi, Texas) provided data on sediment pore-water toxicity to sea urchins. Geoffrey Scott (National Oceanic and Atmospheric Administration, National Marine Fisheries Service, Charleston, South Carolina) provided data from the Microtox™ tests of samples from Charleston Harbor. Data from analyses of fish were provided by Bruce McCain (National Oceanic and Atmospheric Administration, National Marine Fisheries Service, Seattle, Washington). Chemical analyses of sediment samples from the Hudson-Raritan Estuary were performed by Carol Peven (Battelle Ocean Sciences, Duxbury, Massachusetts). Chemical analyses of sediment samples from Tampa Bay were performed by Herbert Windom (Skidaway Institute of Ocean Sciences, Savannah, Georgia).

LITERATURE CITED

American Society for Testing Materials. 1992. Standard guide for conducting 10-day static sediment toxicity tests with marine and estuarine amphipods. Designation E 1367-90. American Society for Testing Materials, Philadelphia, Pennsylvania

Ayers, R. U., L. W. Ayers, J. A. Tarr, and R. C. Widgery. 1988. An historical reconstruction of major pollutant levels in the Hudson-Raritan Basin, 1880-1980. Volume 1. Summary. National Oceanic and Atmospheric Administration Technical Memorandum, NOS OMA 43. National Oceanic and Atmospheric Administration, Rockville, Maryland.

Bayne, B. L., K. R. Clarke, and J. S. Gray (eds.). 1988. MEPS Special Biological Effects of Pollutants. Results of a Practical Workshop. *Marine Ecology Progress Series* 46(1-3): 278 p.

Becker, D. S., T. C. Ginn, M. L. Landolt, and D. B. Powell. 1987. Hepatic lesions in English sole (*Parophrys vetulus*) from Commencement Bay, Washington (USA). *Marine Environmental Research* 23(1987): 153-173.

Bend, J. R. and G. L. Foureman. 1984. Variation of hepatic aryl hydrocarbon hydroxylase (AHH) and 7-ethoxyresorufin O-deethylase (7-ERD) activities in marine fish from Maine: Evidence that mono-oxygenase activities of only a few species are induced by environmental exposure to polycyclic aromatic hydrocarbon (PAH)-type compounds, p. 405-407. *In* J. J. Stegeman and G. W. Heath (eds.), Responses of Marine Organisms to Pollutants. Elsevier Applied Science Publishers, London.

Boesch, D. F. 1984. Introduction. Field assessment of marine pollution effects: The agony and the ecstasy, p. 643-646. *In* H.H. White (ed.), Concepts in Marine Pollution Measurements, University of Maryland Sea Grant, College Park, Maryland.

Bricker, S.B., D.A. Wolfe, K.J. Scott, G. Thursby, E.R. Long, and A. Robertson. 1993. Sediment toxicity in Long Island Sound embayments, p. 181-189. *In* Proceedings, Long Island Sound Research Conference, October 23-24, 1992, University of Connecticut, Groton, Connecticut. Publication no. CT-SG-93-03.

Burton, G.A., Jr. (ed.). 1992. Sediment Toxicity Assessment. Lewis Publishers, Boca Raton, Florida.

Butler, P.A. 1973. Residues in fish, wildlife, and estuaries. Organochlorine residues in estuarine mollusks, 1965-1972, National Pesticide Monitoring Program. *Pesticides Monitoring Journal* 6(4): 238-362.

Carr, R.S. and D.C. Chapman. 1992. Comparison of solid-phase and pore-water approaches for assessing the quality of marine and estuarine sediments. *Chemical Ecology* 7: 19-30.

Carr, R.S., J.D. Williams, and C.T.B. Fragata. 1989. Development and evaluation of a novel marine sediment pore water toxicity test with the polychaete *Dinophilus gyrociliatus*. *Environmental Toxicology and Chemistry* 8: 533-543.

Chapman, P.M. and E.R. Long. 1983. The use of bioassays as part of a comprehensive approach to marine pollution assessment. *Marine Pollution Bulletin* 14: 81-84.

Chapman, P.M., R.N. Dexter, and E.R. Long. 1987. Synoptic measures of sediment contamination, toxicity and infaunal community composition (the Sediment Quality Triad) in San Francisco Bay. *Marine Ecology Progress Series* 37: 75-96.

Chapman, P.M., E.R. Long, R.C. Swartz, T.H. DeWitt, and R. Pastorok. 1991. Sediment toxicity tests, sediment chemistry and benthic ecology do provide new insights into the significance and management of contaminated sediments—A reply to Robert Spies. *Environmental Toxicology and Chemistry* 10: 1-4.

Cheng, T.C. 1988. In vivo effects of heavy metals on cellular defense mechanisms of *Crassostrea virginica*; phagocytic and endocytotic indices. *Journal of Invertebrate Pathology* 51: 207-214.

Collier, T.K. and U. Varanasi. 1991. Hepatic activities of xenobiotic-metabolizing enzymes and biliary levels of xenobiotics in English sole (*Parophrys vetulus*) exposed to environmental contaminants. *Archives of Environmental Contamination and Toxicology* 20: 462-473.

Crosby, M.P. and L.D. Gale. 1990. A review and evaluation of bivalve condition index methodologies with a suggested standard method. *Journal of Shellfish Research* 9 (1): 233-237.

De Witt, T.H., G.R. Ditsworth, and R.C. Swartz. 1988. Effects of natural sediment features on survival of the phoxocephalid amphipod, *Rhepoxynius abronius*. *Marine Environmental Research* 25: 99-124.

Dinnel, P.A., J.M. Link and Q.J. Stober. 1987. Improved methodology for a sea urchin sperm cell bioassay for marine waters. *Archives of Environmental Contamination and Toxicology* 16: 23-32.

Farrington, J.W., E.D. Goldberg, R.W. Riseborough, J.H. Martin, and V.T. Bowen. 1983. U.S. "Mussel Watch" 1976-1978: An overview of the trace-metal, DDE, PCB, hydrocarbon, and artificial radionuclide data. *Environmental Science and Technology* 17(8): 490-496.

Fisher, W.S. 1988. Environmental influence on bivalve hemocyte function. *American Fisheries Society* 18: 225-237.

Fisher, W.S., M.M. Chintala, and M.A. Moline. 1989. Annual variation of estuarine and oceanic oyster *Crassostrea virginica* Gmelin hemocyte capacity. *Journal of Experimental Marine Biology and Ecology* 127: 105-120.

Fisher, W. S., A. Wishovsky, and F.E. Chu. 1990. Effects of tributyltin on defense-related activities of oyster hemocytes. *Archives of Environmental Contamination and Toxicology* 19: 354-360.

Gronlund, W.D., S. Chan, B.B. McCain, R.C. Clark, Jr., M.S. Myers, J.E. Stein, D.W. Brown, J.T. Landahl, M.M. Krahn, and U. Varanasi. 1991. Multidisciplinary assessment of pollution at three sites in Long Island Sound. *Estuaries* 14(3): 299-305.

Hansen, P.J. and D.W. Evans. 1989. Contaminant assessment for the Southeast Atlantic and Gulf of Mexico coasts: 1984 (cycle 1) and 1985 (cycle 2) results of the National Benthic Surveillance Project. National Marine Fisheries Service, National Oceanic and Atmospheric Administration, Beaufort, North Carolina.

Hansen, P.J. and D.W. Evans. 1991. Metal contaminant assessment for the Southeast Atlantic and Gulf of Mexico Coasts: Results of the National Benthic Surveillance Project over the first four years 1984-87. National Oceanic and Atmospheric Administration Technical Memorandum

NMFS-SEFSC 284. National Oceanic and Atmospheric Administration, Beaufort, North Carolina.

Huggett, R.J., R.A. Kimerle, P.M. Mehrle, Jr., H.L. Bergman (eds.). 1992. Biomarkers. Biochemical, physiological, and histological markers of anthropogenic stress. Lewis Publishers, Boca Raton, Florida.

Hunt, J.W. and B.S. Anderson. 1989. Sublethal effects of zinc and municipal effluents on larvae of the red abalone, *Haliotis rufescens*. *Marine Biology* 101: 545-552.

Johnson, L.L., E. Casillas, D. Misitano, T.K. Collier, J.E. Stein, B.B. McCain, and U. Varanasi. 1989. Bioindicators of reproductive impairment in female English sole (*Parophrys vetulus*) exposed to environmental contaminants, p. 391-396. *In* Proceedings of Oceans '89. IEEE, Washington, D.C.

Johnson, L.L., J.E. Stein, T.K. Collier, E. Casillas, B. McCain, and U. Varanasi. 1992a. Bioindicators of contaminant exposure, liver pathology, and reproductive development in pre-spawning female winter flounder (*Pleuronectes americanus*) from urban and nonurban estuaries on the Northeast Atlantic Coast. National Oceanic and Atmospheric Administration Technical Memorandum NMFS-NWFSC-1. National Marine Fisheries Service, Seattle, Washington.

Johnson, L.L., C. Stehr, O.P. Olson, M.S. Myers, S.M. Pierce, B.B. McCain, and U. Varanasi. 1992b. National Benthic Surveillance Project: Northeast Coast. Fish histopathology and relationships between lesions and chemical contaminants (1987-89). National Oceanic and Atmospheric Administration Technical Memorandum. NMFS-NWFSC-4. National Oceanic and Atmospheric Administration, Seattle, Washington.

Kohn, N.P., J.Q. Word, D.K. Niyogi, L.T. Ross, T. Dillon, and D.W. Moore. 1994. Acute toxicity of ammonia to four species of marine amphipod. *Marine Environmental Research* 38: 1-15.

Krahn, M.M., M.S. Myers, D.G. Burrows, and D.C. Malins. 1984. Determination of metabolites of xenobiotics in bile of fish from polluted waterways. *Xenobiotica* 14: 633-646.

Krahn, M.M., L.D. Rhodes, M.S. Myers, L.K. Moore, W.D. MacLeod, Jr., and D.C. Malins. 1986. Associations between metabolites of aromatic compounds in bile and the occurrence of hepatic lesions in English sole (*Parophrys vetulus*) from Puget Sound, Washington. *Archives for Environmental Contamination and Toxicology* 15: 61-67.

Livingstone, D.R., M.A. Kirchin and A. Wiseman. 1989. Cytochrome P-450 and oxidative metabolism in molluscs. *Xenobiotica* 19(10): 1041-1062.

Long, E.R., D. MacDonald, M.B. Matta, K. VanNess, M. Buchman, and H. Harris. 1988. Status and trends in concentrations of contaminants and measures of biological stress in San Francisco Bay. National Oceanic and Atmospheric Administration Technical Memorandum NOS OMA 41. National Oceanic and Atmospheric Administration, Seattle, Washington.

Long, E.R. and M.F. Buchman. 1990. A comparative evaluation of selected measures of biological effects of exposure of marine organisms to toxic chemicals, Chapter 20, p. 355-394. *In* J. F. McCarthy and L.R. Shugart (eds.), Biomarkers of Environmental Contamination. Lewis Publishers, Boca Raton, Florida.

Long, E.R., M.F. Buchman, S.M. Bay, R.J. Breteler, R.S. Carr, P.M. Chapman, J.E. Hose, A.L. Lissner, J. Scott, and D.A. Wolfe. 1990. Comparative evaluation of five toxicity tests with sediments from San Francisco Bay and Tomales Bay, California. *Environmental Toxicology and Chemistry* 9: 1193-1214.

Long, E.R. and L.G. Morgan. 1990. The potential for biological effects of sediment-sorbed contaminants tested in the National Status and Trends Program. National Oceanic and Atmospheric

Administration Technical Memorandum NOS OMA 52. National Oceanic and Atmospheric Administration, Seattle, Washington.

Long, E.R., D. MacDonald, and C. Cairncross. 1991. Status and trends in toxicants and the potential for their biological effects in Tampa Bay, Florida. National Oceanic and Atmospheric Administration Technical Memorandum NOS OMA 58. National Oceanic and Atmospheric Administration, Seattle, Washington.

Long, E.R. and R. Markel. 1992. An evaluation of the extent and magnitude of biological effects associated with chemical contaminants in San Francisco Bay, California. National Oceanic and Atmospheric Administration Technical Memorandum NOS ORCA 64. National Oceanic and Atmospheric Administration, Seattle, Washington.

Long, E.R., D.A. Wolfe, R.S. Carr, K.J. Scott, G.B. Thursby, H.L. Windom, R. Lee, F.D. Calder, G.M. Sloane, and T. Seal. 1994. Magnitude and extent of sediment toxicity in Tampa Bay, Florida. National Oceanic and Atmospheric Administration Technical Memorandum NOS ORCA 78. National Oceanic and Atmospheric Administration, Silver Spring, Maryland.

Long, E.R., D.D. MacDonald, S.L. Smith, and F.D. Calder. 1995c. Incidence of adverse biological effects within ranges of chemical concentrations in marine and estuarine sediments. *Environmental Management* 19(1): 81-97.

Long, E.R., R.S. Scott, G.B. Thursby, and D.A. Wolfe. 1995a. Sediment toxicity in Tampa Bay: Incidence, severity, and spatial distribution. *Florida Scientist* 58(2): 163-178.

Long, E.R., D.A. Wolfe, K.J. Scott, G.B. Thursby, E.A. Stern, C. Peven, and T. Schwartz. 1995b. Magnitude and extent of sediment toxicity in the Hudson-Raritan estuary. National Oceanic and Atmospheric Administration, Silver Spring, Maryland. Technical Memorandum NOS ORCA 88.

MacDonald, D.A. 1991. Status and trends in concentrations of selected contaminants in Boston Harbor sediments and biota. National Oceanic and Atmospheric Administration Technical Memorandum NOS ORCA 62. National Oceanic and Atmospheric Administration. Seattle, Washington.

MacDonald, D.A., M.B. Matta, L.J. Field, C. Cairncross, and M.D. Munn. 1992. The coastal resource coordinator's bioassessment manual. National Oceanic and Atmospheric Administration Technical Report No. HAZMAT 93-1. National Oceanic and Atmospheric Administration, Seattle, Washington.

McCain, B.B., D.W. Brown, M.M. Krahn, M.S. Myers, R.C. Clark, Jr., S-L. Chan, and D.C. Malins. 1988. Marine pollution problems, North American West Coast. *Aquatic Toxicology* 11: 143-162.

McCain, B.B., S-L. Chan, M.M. Krahn, D.W. Brown, M.S. Myers, J.T. Landahl, S. Pierce, R.C. Clark, Jr., and U. Varanasi. 1992. Chemical contamination and associated fish diseases in San Diego Bay. *Environmental Science and Technology* 26(4): 725-733.

McCain, B.B., D.W. Brown, T. Hom, M.S. Myers, S.M. Pierce, T.K. Collier, J.E. Stein, S-L. Chan, and U. Varanasi. In press. Chemical contaminant exposure and effects in four fish species from Tampa Bay. *Estuaries*

McCarthy, J.F. and L.R. Shugart (eds.). 1990. Biomarkers of Environmental Contamination. Lewis Publishers, Boca Raton, Florida.

Malins, D.C., B.B. McCain, D.W. Brown, S-L. Chan, M.S. Myers, J.T. Landahl, P.G. Prohaska, A.J. Friedman, L.D. Rhodes, D.G. Burrows, W.D. Gronlund, and H.D. Hodgins. 1984.

Chemical pollutants in sediments and diseases in bottom-dwelling fish in Puget Sound, Washington. *Environmental Science and Technology* 18: 705-713.

Mearns, A.J., M.B. Matta, D. Simecek-Beatty, M.F. Buchman, G. Shigenaka, and W.A. Wert. 1988. PCB and chlorinated pesticide contamination in U.S. fish and shellfish: A historical assessment report. National Oceanic and Atmospheric Administration Technical Memorandum NOS OMA 39. National Oceanic and Atmospheric Administration, Seattle, Washington.

Mearns, A.J., M. Matta, G. Shigenaka, D. MacDonald, M. Buchman, H. Harris, J. Golas, and G. Lauenstein. 1991. Contaminant trends in the Southern California Bight: Inventory and assessment. National Oceanic and Atmospheric Administration Technical Memorandum NOS ORCA 62. National Oceanic and Atmospheric Administration, Seattle, Washington.

National Oceanic and Atmospheric Administration. 1987. National Status and Trends Program for marine environmental quality. Progress Report and Preliminary Assessment of Findings of the Benthic Surveillance Project–1984. National Oceanic and Atmospheric Administration, Rockville, Maryland.

O'Connor, T.P., M.G. Norton, A.J. Mearns, D.A. Wolfe, and I.W. Duedall. 1987. Scales of biological effects, p. 1-7. *In* T.P. O'Connor, W.V. Burt, and I.W. Duedall (eds.), Oceanic Processes in Marine Pollution. Vol. 2. Robert E. Krieger Publishing Co., Malabar, Florida.

O'Connor, T.P. 1991. Concentrations of organic contaminants in mollusks and sediments at NOAA National Status and Trends sites in the coastal and estuarine United States. *Environmental Health Perspectives* 90: 69-73.

Oshida, P.S., J.M. Link, and Q.J. Stober. 1981. Effects of municipal wastewater on fertilization, survival, and development of the sea urchin, *Strongylocentrotus purpuratus*, p. 389-402. *In* F.J. Vernberg, A. Calabrese, F.P. Thurberg, and W.B. Vernberg (eds.), Biological Monitoring of Marine Pollutants. Academic Press, New York.

Pastorok, R.A. and D.S. Becker. 1989. Comparison of bioassays for assessing sediment toxicity in Puget Sound. EPA 910/9-89-004. United States Environmental Protection Agency, Region 10, Seattle, Washington.

Paul, J.F., K.J. Scott, A.F. Holland, S.B. Weisber, J.K. Summers, and A. Robertson. 1992. The estuarine component of the U.S. EPA's Environmental Monitoring and Assessment Program. *Chemistry and Ecology* 7: 93-116.

Peakall, D. 1992. Animal biomarkers as pollution indicators. Chapman & Hall, London, England.

Puget Sound Water Quality Authority. 1987. Final Environmental Impact Statement and Revised Preferred Plan for the 1987 Puget Sound Water Quality Management Plan. Puget Sound Water Quality Authority, Seattle, Washington.

Salazar, M.H. and S.M. Salazar. 1991. Assessing site-specific effects of TBT contamination with mussel growth rates. *Marine Environmental Research* 32 (1991): 131-150.

Salazar, M.H. and S.M. Salazar. 1995. In situ bioassays using transplanted mussels: I. Estimating chemical exposure and bioeffects with bioaccumulation and growth, p. 216-241. *In* J.S. Hughes, G.R. Biddinger, and E. Mones (eds.), Third Symposium on Environmental Toxicology and Risk Assessment. ASTM STP 1218. American Society for Testing and Materials. Philadelphia, Pennsylvania.

Sanders, B.M., V.M. Pascoe, P.A. Nakagawa, and L.S. Martin. 1992. Persistence of the heat-shock response over time in a common *Mytilus* mussel. *Molecular Marine Biology & Biotechnology* 1(2): 147-154.

Sapudar, R.A., C.J. Wilson, M.L. Reid, E.R. Long, M. Stephenson, M. Puckett, R. Fairey, J. Hunt, B. Anderson, D. Holstad, J. Newman, and S. Birosik. 1994. Sediment chemistry and toxicity in the vicinity of the Los Angeles and Long Beach Harbors. Project Report. California State Water Resources Control Board. Sacramento, California.

Schimmel, S.C., B.D. Melzian, D.E. Campbell, C.J. Strobel, S.J. Benyi, J.S. Rosen, and H.W. Buffum. 1994. Statistical Summary EMAP-estuaries. Virginian Province-1991. EPA/620/R-94/005. United States Environmental Protection Agency, Washington, D.C.

Spies, R.B. 1989. Sediment bioassays, chemical contaminants and benthic ecology: New insights or just muddy water? *Marine Environmental Research* 27: 73-75.

Spies, R.B., J.J. Stegeman, D.W. Rice, Jr., B. Woodin, P. Thomas, J.E. Hose, J.N. Cross, and M. Prieto. 1990. Sublethal responses of *Platichthys stellatus* to organic contamination in San Francisco Bay with emphasis on reproduction, p. 87-122. *In* J.F. McCarthy and L.R. Shugart (eds.), Biomarkers of Environmental Contamination, Lewis Publishers, Boca Raton, Florida.

Squibb, K.S., J.M. O'Connor, and T.J. Kneip. 1991. New York/New Jersey Harbor Estuary Program. Module 3.1: Toxics Characterization Report. Prepared by Institute of Environmental Medicine, New York University Medical Center for the United States Environmental Protection Agency, Region 2, New York City, New York.

Stegeman, J.J. and G.W. Heath (eds.). 1984. Responses of Marine Organisms to Pollutants. Elsevier Applied Science Publishers, London, England.

Stegeman, J.J., B.R. Woodin, and A. Goksoyr. 1988. Cytochrome P-450 induction in flounder, p. 55-60. *In* B.L. Bayne, K.R. Clarke, and J.S. Gray (eds.), Biological Effects of Pollutants. *Marine Ecology Progress Series* Spec. Vol. 46.

Suteau, P., M. Daubeze, M.L. Migaud, and J.F. Narbonne. 1988. PAH-metabolizing enzymes in whole mussels as biochemical tests for chemical pollution monitoring. *Marine Ecology Progress Series* 46(1-3): 45-49.

Swartz, R.C., W.A. Deben, K.A. Sercu, and J.O. Lamberson. 1982. Sediment toxicity and the distribution of amphipods in Commencement Bay, Washington, USA. *Marine Pollution Bulletin* 13(10): 359-364.

Swartz, R.C., F.A. Cole, D.W. Schults, and W.A. Deben. 1986. Ecological changes in the Southern California Bight near a large sewage outfall: Benthic conditions in 1980 and 1983. *Marine Ecology Progress Series* 31: 1-13.

Swartz, R.D., F.A. Cole, J.O. Lamberson, S.P. Ferraro, D.W. Shults, W.A. Deben, H. Lee II, and R.J. Ozretich. 1994. Sediment toxicity, contamination and amphipod abundance at a DDT- and dieldrin-contaminated site in San Francisco Bay. *Environmental Toxicology and Chemistry* 13(6): 949-962.

United States Army Corps of Engineers-United States Environmental Protection Agency. 1991. Evaluation of dredged material proposed for ocean disposal. Testing Manual. EPA 503/8-91/001. United States Department of the Army–United States Environmental Protection Agency, Washington, D.C.

United States Environmental Protection Agency. 1990. Recommended protocols for conducting laboratory bioassays on Puget Sound sediments. Puget Sound Estuary Program, United States Environmental Protection Agency, Region 10, Seattle, Washington.

Varanasi, U. 1992. Chemical contaminants and their effects on living marine resources, p. 59-72. *In* R. H. Stroud (ed.), Stemming the Tide of Coastal Fish Habitat Loss. Proceedings of a

Symposium on Conservation of Coastal Fish Habitat. National Coalition for Marine Conservation, Inc. Savannah, Georgia

Varanasi, U., W.L. Reichert, and J.E. Stein. 1989. 32P-postlabelling analysis of DNA adducts in liver of wild English sole (*Parophrys vetulus*) and winter flounder (*Pseudopleuronectes americanus*). *Cancer Research* 49: 1171-1177.

White, H.H. (ed.). 1984. Concepts in Marine Pollution Measurements. University of Maryland Sea Grant, College Park, Maryland.

Widdows, J. and D. Johnson. 1988. Physiological energetics of *Mytilus edulis*: Scope for Growth. *Marine Ecology Progress Series* 46 (1-3): 113-121.

Williams, L.G., P.M. Chapman, and T.C. Ginn. 1986. A comparative evaluation of marine sediment toxicity using bacterial luminescence, oyster embryo, and amphipod sediment bioassays. *Marine Environmental Research* 19: 225-249.

Wolfe, D.A. 1992. Selection of bioindicators of pollution for marine monitoring programmes. *Chemistry and Ecology* 6: 149-167.

Wolfe, D.A., S.B. Bricker, E.R. Long, K.J. Scott, and G.B. Thursby. 1994. Biological effects of toxic contaminants in sediment from Long Island Sound and environs. National Oceanic and Atmospheric Administration, Silver Spring, Maryland. Technical memorandum NOS OCRA 80.

Wolfe, D.A., E.R. Long, and A. Robertson. 1993. The NS&T bioeffects surveys: Design strategies and preliminary results, p. 298-312. *In* O. T. Magoon, W. S. Wilson, H. Converse, and L. T. Tobin (eds.), Coastal Zone '93: Proceedings of the 8th Symposium on Coastal and Ocean Management. Vol .1. American Society of Civil Engineers, New York.

Wolfe, D.A., E.R. Long, and G.B. Thursby. In press. Sediment toxicity in the Hudson-Raritan Estuary: Distribution and correlations with chemical contamination. *Estuaries*

Zarba, C.S. 1992. Equilibrium partitioning approach. Chapter 6. *In* Sediment Classification Methods Compendium. EPA 823-R-92-006. United States Environmental Protection Agency, Washington, D.C.

The Effects of Urbanization on Human and Ecosystem Health

W.B. Vernberg, G.I. Scott, S.H. Strozier, J. Bemiss, and J.W. Daugomah

Introduction

In C.E.A. Winslow's discussion of the evolution of modern public health, he noted that its development began in the nineteenth century with the recognition of clear linkages between lack of proper sanitation and communicable diseases (Winslow 1923). Today, of course, we have a better understanding of the enormous impact of the environment on health, although the negative outcomes of human activities are often ignored or in some cases entirely overlooked. In the United States Environmental Protection Agency document *Reducing Risk* (1990), the tie between the environment and health was clearly acknowledged when it was noted that "Over the long term, ecological degradation either directly or indirectly degrades human health and the economy—human health and welfare ultimately rely upon the life support systems and natural resources provided by healthy ecosystems." Surprisingly, it has taken many years for this concept of linking ecosystem and human health to be widely recognized. But as world population increases and becomes more and more urbanized, there must be a reconciliation between the perceived need to modify natural systems and the outcomes of such modifications. The focus of this paper is primarily on the impact of environmental manipulations on water quality, and ultimately health, recognizing that this is only one of many negative outcomes that can be documented.

It is human nature to want to change the environment to meet some perceived need. Some of the more common human activities that have unintended negative ecosystem impacts are shown in Fig. 1 (Lutchenco et al. 1991). For example, land clearing is often involved in many activities in industrialized and urbanized areas, and usually the objective is to improve the quality of life, increase food production, provide recreational opportunities, construct housing, or build industries. Except in rare instances, unintended negative results are often inevitable with development. Deforestation, soil degradation often accompanied by pollution, eutrophication or the destruction of natural ponds and lakes, are a few examples.

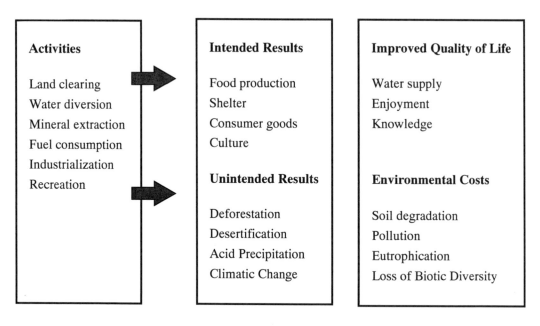

Fig. 1. Human activities with unintended ecosystems impacts (after Lutchenco et al. 1991).

Thus, while many ecosystem modifications may be viewed as having positive economic and quality of life impacts, more often than not, damaging, unintended results and environmental costs are the outcome. One of the most frequently overlooked outcomes is the negative health consequences of such actions, making human costs at least as great as environmental ones.

Two activities, industrialization and urbanization, generate a number of negative unintentional impacts to both human and ecosystem health. Both activities are linked, since industrialization spurs urban development. Urbanization is increasing worldwide, especially in industrialized countries and in Latin America (Fig. 2). It is projected that 83% of the population in Latin America will be living in urban areas by 2020, compared with 81% in industrialized countries and 62% worldwide (United Nations Report 1991). An interesting aspect of the urbanization trends is that the population concentrations are increasing most rapidly in coastal areas. Human populations have always been attracted to coastal areas, where the seas provided not only food but also the main avenue of transportation. It is, therefore, not surprising that the earliest cities developed in these regions. Even today, eight of the ten most populous cities in the world are located in coastal and estuarine areas (United Nations Report 1991). In the United States, over half the population now lives within 50 miles of a coastline, which represents only 10% of the land mass. Projections are that by the turn of the century, the population in these areas will increase to 75% (Vernberg et al. 1992).

Let us consider some of the results of urbanization and industrialization on health and the ecosystem. Much of the impact results in marked changes in the landscape—natural forested areas

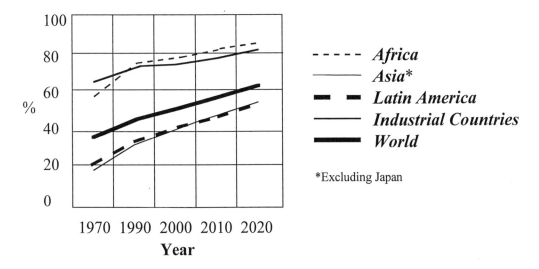

Fig. 2. Worldwide view of urbanization in industrialized countries and Latin America.

are destroyed and other natural land cover is removed to make way for housing and industry, streets and pathways are cleared and/or paved, and the whole watershed of the area is altered. This is illustrated in Fig. 3. In an undisturbed watershed, run-off is decreased since the trees and other plants absorb rain and the flow of water from the uplands. Rain water continually replaces the groundwater and eventually flows into rivers or streams, which because they are in an undisturbed watershed tend to be of high quality. In contrast, urbanized areas are plagued with water pollution, floods, and soil erosion. A watershed that has been cleared leaves no areas to filter out heavy rainfall, resulting in excessive run-off, erosion, flooding, and, often, mud slides. Because of the excessive runoff of the rainwater, the groundwater is not recharged and is often depleted. River or stream channels are clogged with sediment, reservoirs become silted, and water quality in general is affected.

Urbanization of upland areas adjacent to estuarine ecosystems has resulted in significant inputs of bacterial and chemical contaminants in salt marsh ecosystems of the southeastern United States (Vernberg et al. 1992). During the pioneering stages of urban development, human waste disposal needs were met by use of septic-tank-based technology. As urban development proceeds, a critical carrying capacity (i.e., human population density) is reached, and significant inputs of bacterial pollution from septic tank discharges into estuarine ecosystems may result (El-Figi 1990), often causing closure of shellfish harvesting waters due to the presence of pathogenic bacterial and/or viral pollution (Leonard 1993). The normal solution to this problem is to construct a central sewer collection system to reduce estuarine inputs from individual septic tank systems. This may result in point-source discharge of secondary treated sewage into coastal waters (Jolley et al. 1975).

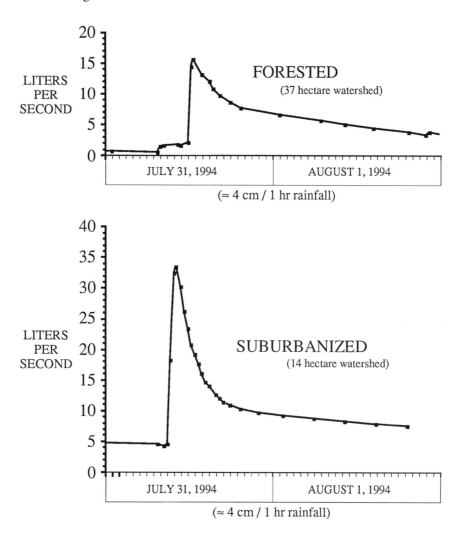

Fig. 3. Impact of urbanization on nonpoint source (NPS) runoff. Note the increase in NPS runoff in urban areas due to the loss of active infiltration surfaces as areas are developed.

Case Study of Urbanization

A good example of how destruction of undeveloped land can have an impact on an area can be found in the comparative study of two coastal estuarine areas along the South Carolina coast, North Inlet and Murrells Inlet (Vernberg et al. 1992). These two regions are about 25 km apart geographically (Fig. 4). Both are bar-built estuaries and have similar geological histories. Both

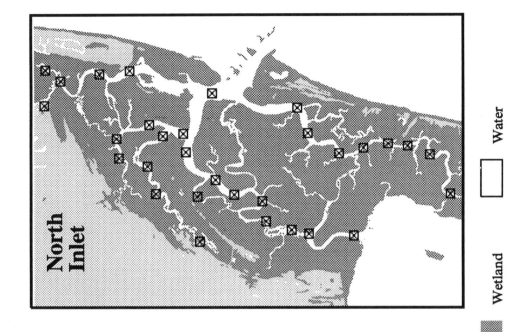

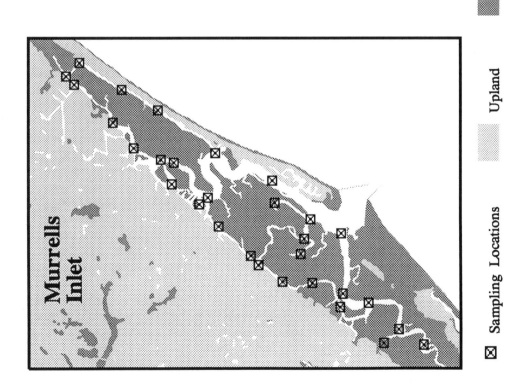

⊠ Sampling Locations

⊠ Wetland   □ Water

[:::] Upland

Fig. 4. Map of North Inlet and Murrells Inlet study sites.

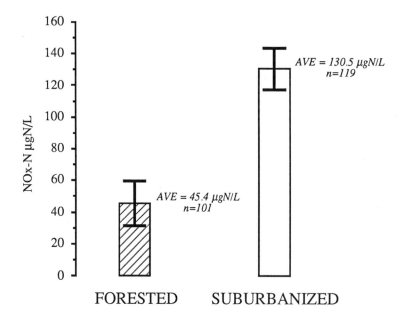

Fig. 5. Effects of urbanization on nitrate and nitrite concentrations in surface waters of Murrells Inlet. Bars are mean annual NO_x-N concentration.

are approximately the same size and are dominated by extensive strands of marsh grasses, primarily *Spartina alterniflora*. The primary difference between these two estuaries is that the North Inlet area is virtually undeveloped and is surrounded by heavily forested uplands areas with no urban development. In contrast, Murrells Inlet has been highly developed to meet urban and tourist demands. This area has been subjected to many man-induced stresses resulting from extensive development: restaurants, strip malls, high-rise condominiums and single family dwellings, roads, marinas, and the manipulation of the waterways by dredging, filling, and jetty construction.

The difference in these two areas following a moderate 1-hour rainfall is shown in Fig. 3. In the undeveloped North Inlet area, the rainwater is absorbed by the soil and absorbed and filtered through the forested uplands area. Except under highly abnormal conditions (such as a hurricane), flooding does not occur. On the other hand, the initial flow rate following the same 1-hour rainfall is twice as high in the urbanized area. There is nothing to stop the rainwater from washing through the watershed with little or no absorption since the natural covering has been replaced by housing, roads, golf courses, and other development.

The heavy concentration of human activity in a coastal watershed has an enormous impact on the coastal ecosystem and brings in polluted runoff from city streets, farms, lawns, golf courses, residential development, and storm water runoff (Wahl et al. 1993). An example of the amount of pollution discharge can be demonstrated in a comparison of nitrates and nitrites discharged in the two areas. The amount of nitrates and nitrites discharged was three times greater in the coastal waters of the urbanized areas as in those of the forested area (Fig. 5). If nitrates end up in the drinking water, the nitrates can be reduced to nitrites and, once absorbed by living animals, combine with hemoglobin to form methemoglobin. When this occurs it is then impossible for the oxygen to bind and transport oxygen from the lungs to other tissues. This result is particularly critical in young infants. Nitrites, formed through the production of nitrates, can also combine with other substances to produce nitrosamines, which can form powerful carcinogenic compounds (Conway and Pretty 1991).

In the ecosystem, nitrates and nitrites also contribute substantially to the eutrophication of bodies of water. Eutrophication degrades water quality by enriching bodies of water with plant nutrients, causing algal blooms. The waters become clouded, often with long filamentous algae, and fish cannot survive because the algae respire and utilize all the available oxygen, leaving none for the fish. Thus, with excessive nitrate and nitrite production, both human and ecosystem health are potentially damaged.

Increased population growth and urbanization also creates significant demands for water for treatment of human wastes. In the Chesapeake Bay, > 1,335 million gallons of treated sewage is discharged into the watershed per day (Horton and Eichbaum 1991), which may result in significant degradation of estuarine water quality, leading to the closure of shellfish harvesting areas (Leonard et al. 1991). In the Southeastern United States, the number of shellfish harvesting areas closed due to bacterial pollution from urban runoff has increased almost annually (Leonard et al. 1991).

Studies conducted throughout the United States have clearly indicated that inputs from urbanization may result in significant loading of bacterial pathogens into estuarine waters which may be taken up by estuarine shellfish (Turner 1978; Scott et al. 1982; Greunhagen 1985). Significant bacterial contamination of shallow groundwater and adjacent estuarine waters and oysters has been observed. Urbanization of many coastal areas has led to closure of shellfish harvesting areas due to bacterial contamination from urban inputs. Over 30% of South Carolina shellfish harvesting areas are listed as SB waters, which means they are unsafe for harvest of molluscan shellfish (Scott 1976; Marcus 1988). In the state of North Carolina, a similar portion of state waters are classified as unsafe for shellfish harvesting. These findings clearly underscore the need for better management of bacterial inputs into the estuarine ecosystem in the Southeastern United States. Vernberg et al. (1992) and El-Figi (1990) reported that the largest source of bacterial pollution occurs at the land-estuarine interface.

Results of spatial and temporal sampling of fecal coliform bacterial densities in surface water and oysters, using the MPN five-tube dilution method (American Public Health Association et al. 1985), clearly indicated significant contamination of estuarine surface waters in highly urbanized regions of Murrells Inlet. Greatest differences between North Inlet and Murrells Inlet were observed during the summer and fall sampling, peak periods of urban habitat utilization (Fig. 6). Greatest coliform densities occurred at the inner and outer stations of Murrells Inlet. This included the highly urbanized areas of Murrells Inlet (inner stations) and Garden City Beach (outer stations). Numerous studies have implicated failing septic tanks as the primary source of bacterial contamination of surface waters (Viraghaven and Warnock 1976; Dewalle and Schaff 1980; Scott et al. 1982; Yates et al. 1985). Most of these studies found clear linkages between septic tanks and groundwater pollution. Scott et al. (1982) found significantly greater bacterial pollution in salt waters rated A (SA) of Santa Rosa Sound, an area serviced by septic tanks, than in SB waters adjacent to a secondary sewage treatment plant. Dudda and Cromartie (1983) reported that septic tanks in highly

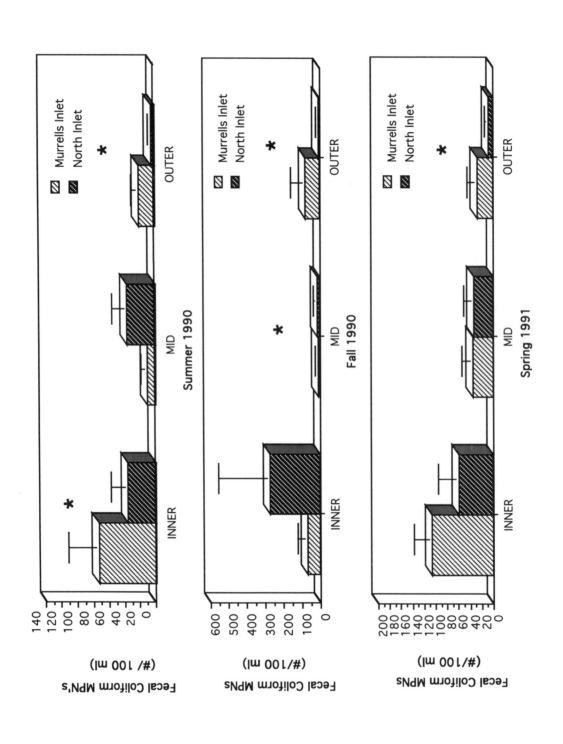

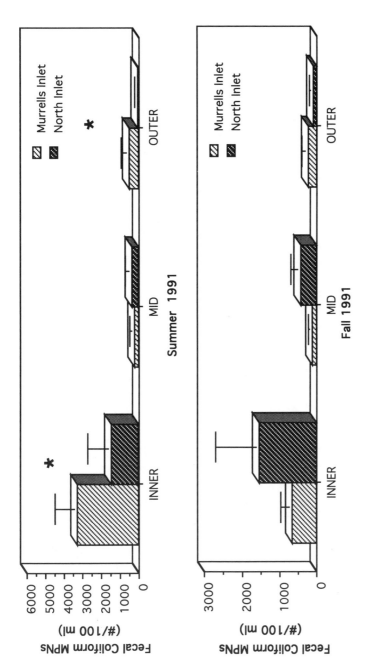

Fig. 6. Spatial differences in fecal coliform densities in surface waters of Murrells Inlet and North Inlet. Asterisks (*) indicated estuarine regions where fecal coliform densities were significantly ($p \leq 0.05$) different in inter-estuarine comparisons. Significantly ($p \leq 0.05$) elevated fecal coliform densities were found at the land-estuarine inner sites at Murrells Inlet and the outer station at Garden City Beach. Elevated fecal coliform densities at North Inlet were from wildlife residing in upland area. Note the differences in Y-axis scales for the individual graphs.

populated coastal areas of North Carolina may have an impact on estuarine surface waters. They also found significant correlations between septic tank drain field densities and fecal coliform bacterial densities. While the majority of Murrells Inlet is served by a central sewage system, there are isolated areas still served by septic tanks, which impact adjacent surface waters (Newall 1991). Another source of bacterial pollution are the several marinas located in the inner and outer stations of Murrells Inlet. Marcus (1988) has reported significantly higher coliform densities in surface waters around several coastal marinas in South Carolina. The percentage of water sampling stations exceeding the Water Quality Criteria Standard for fecal coliform bacteria was much higher in Murrells Inlet (67%) than North Inlet (37%). These results agreed quite well with results by Newall (1991), who reported that 65% of the state monitoring stations in Murrells Inlet exceeded the water quality standard for fecal coliform contamination.

Figure 7 depicts annual summaries for fecal coliform bacterial biotyping of surface waters in North Inlet and Murrells Inlet. There were significant differences in the speciation of coliform positive species in surface waters of Murrells Inlet and North Inlet. In urbanized Murrells Inlet, there was a greater occurrence of *E. coli* bacteria, fewer stations that were coliform negative, and a reduced number of species composing the coliform group, particularly soil-sorbed microbes of the Pseudomonid family. In pristine North Inlet, surface waters had a greater number of coliform negative stations, a reduced occurrence of *E. coli* bacteria, and an increased number of species composing the coliform group, with an increased occurrence of soil-sorbed microbes in the Pseudomonid family. The greater diversity and species richness in the coliform group members in North Inlet resulted from the availability of bacteria from the deciduous hardwood forest when compared with upland watersheds in urbanized Murrells Inlet, which contain more monoculture (i.e., lawns with grass and ornamental plants).

Spatial sampling of oysters indicated there were no significant differences in fecal coliform densities in comparisons between North Inlet and Murrells Inlet (Fig. 8). Figure 9 depicts annual summaries for fecal coliform bacterial biotyping of oysters in North Inlet and Murrells Inlet. Unlike results for surface waters, there were no significant differences in the speciation of coliform-positive species in oysters from Murrells Inlet and North Inlet. One factor related to this observation may have been that the high levels of fecal coliform bacteria measured in surface waters, which were measured at ebb tide, may have been diluted to comparable densities at flood tide, and these were then bioconcentrated equivalently by oysters in each estuary.

These results indicated that the percentage of stations where oyster fecal coliform densities exceeded the Interstate Shellfish Sanitation Conference oyster meat depuration standard (230 /100 g) was 52% in Murrells Inlet versus 55% in North Inlet. While results from surface water coliform serotyping indicated that there were greater potential risks of oyster exposure to *E. coli* and other pathogenic coliform members in urbanized Murrells Inlet than in pristine North Inlet, oyster results indicated that the greater potential human health risks measured in surface waters were not translated into greater actual or realized human health risk in terms of oyster bioconcentration potential. These results suggest that while there are clearly greater inputs of fecal coliform bacteria from human waste sources in urbanized areas, the process of tidal dilution and dispersion resulted in no net discernible differences in oyster bioconcentration of these pathogens. Indeed the fecal coliform "fingerprints" based upon oyster bioconcentration were not significantly different nor were there quantifiable differences in coliform densities in oysters between the two estuaries. This suggests that the current Interstate Shellfish Sanitation Conference method of regulating shellfish

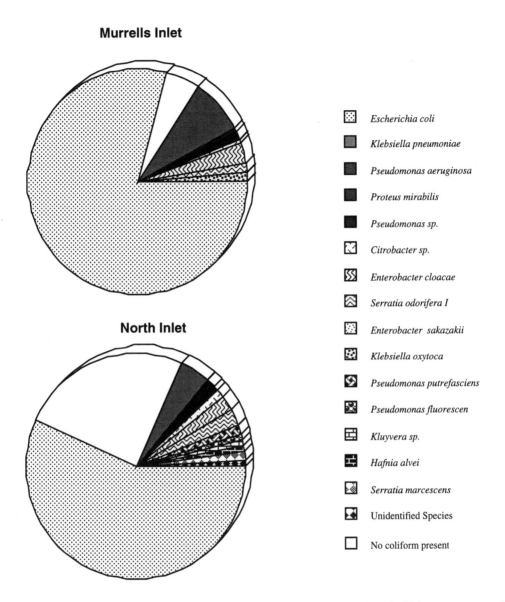

Fig. 7. Biotyping of fecal coliform bacteria in North Inlet and Murrells Inlet. Note the higher occurrences of *E. coli* positive fecal coliform in Murrells Inlet and the smaller proportion of stations testing negative for fecal coliform in urbanized Murrells Inlet.

harvesting, which is based on surface water quality, provides a margin of safety but may be some what over protective, as there were no actual differences in fecal coliform levels accumulated by oysters between the two estuaries. With recent international agreements reached on trade, North

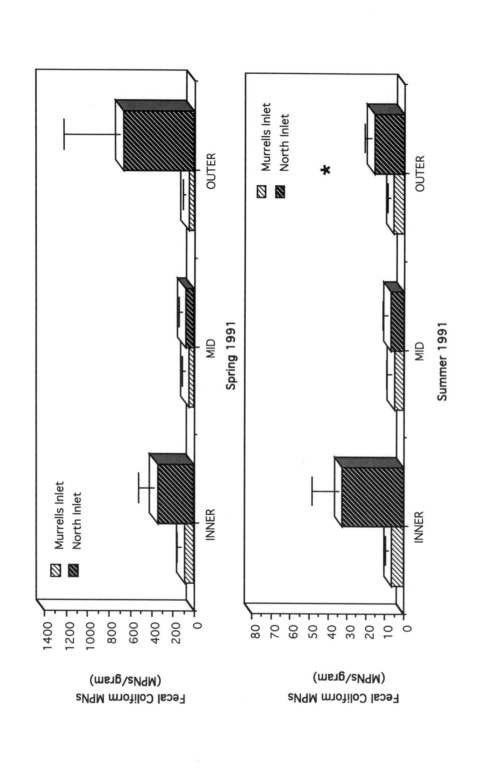

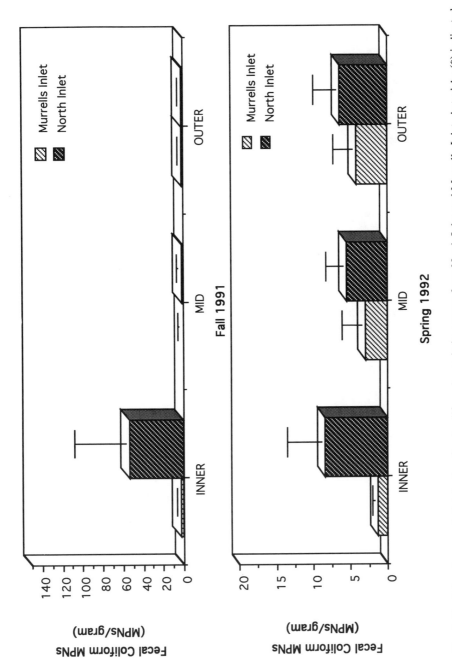

Fig. 8. Spatial and seasonal distribution fecal coliform bacteria in oysters from North Inlet and Murrells Inlet. Asterisks (*) indicated estuarine regions where fecal coliform densities were significantly ($p \leq 0.05$) different in inter-estuarine comparisons. Note the Y-axis scales are different for the individual graphs.

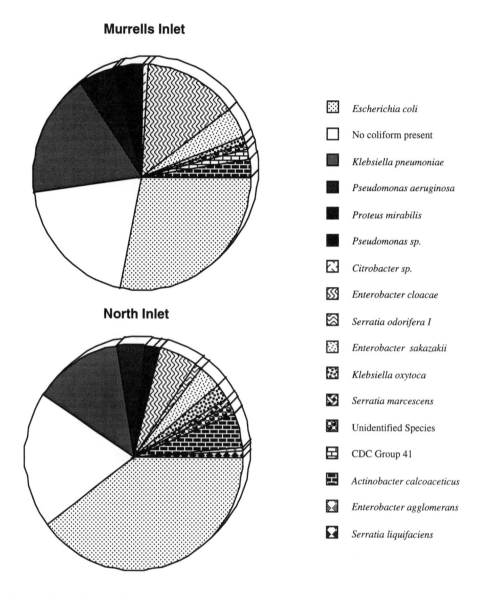

Fig. 9. Biotyping of fecal coliform bacteria in North Inlet and Murrells Inlet. Note the similar fecal coliform "fingerprints" in oysters from each estuary.

American Free Trade Agreement (NAFTA) and General Agreement on Tariffs and Trade (GATT), there may be increased pressures for the United States to adopt a new policy on oyster meat standards in addition to our current surface waters standard for shellfish harvesting.

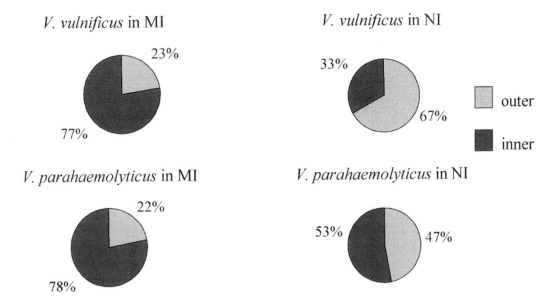

Fig. 10. Tissue distribution of *Vibrio* bacteria in oysters from Murrells Inlet and North Inlet. Note the high prevalence of *Vibrio vulnificus* in internal tissues of oysters from urbanized Murrells Inlet, which were heavily infected with the parasite *Perkinsus marinus*. Inner tissues were gonad, digestive diverticulum, and adductor muscle. Outer tissues were mantle, gill and labial palps.

In addition to *E. coli*, many naturally occurring marine bacterial pathogens may pose significant risks to humans via consumption of raw oysters. In particular, members of the genus *Vibrio* have been responsible for deaths and morbidity in healthy individuals (*V. cholerae* and *V. parahaemolyticus*) as well as susceptible individuals (*V. vulnificus*). Strozier (1996) has found significant correlation between high incidences of *Vibrio* and high incidence of parasitism in oysters from urbanized areas.

The oyster parasite *Perkinsus marinus* has severely affected oyster populations throughout the southeastern United States. Of particular concern is the effect of this parasite on the physiology of the American oyster, *Crassostrea virginica*. Alterations in the physiology of the oyster may ultimately affect the uptake and feeding response of the oyster. Scott et al. (1982) reported significant effects of *P. marinus* infections on the respiration rate and condition index of *C. virginica* exposed to low salinity and chlorine-produced oxidants. This parasite may adversely affect the oyster by catabolizing amino acid reserves, which are important in ion and water balance and in opsonin and agglutination reactions, important processes that the oyster uses to depurate harmful bacterial pathogens. From June 1991 to December 1992, oyster and surface water samples were collected monthly from North Inlet (CH2 = Oyster Landing) and Murrells Inlet (MC5) and analyzed for fecal coliform bacteria, *V. vulnificus*, and *V. parahaemolyticus* along with a suite of oyster physiological indices (condition index, gonadal index, and survival) using techniques described

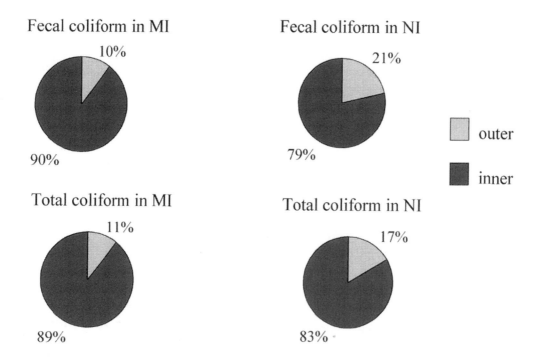

Fig. 11. Tissue distribution differences of coliform bacteria in oysters from North Inlet and Murrells Inlet. Note that unlike *Vibrio* bacteria, fecal coliform tissues distribution were similar in both estuaries. Inner tissues were gonad, digestive diverticulum, and adductor muscle. Outer tissues were mantle, gill, and labial palps.

by Scott et al. (1982). Oyster samples were also dissected and the distribution of fecal coliform and *Vibrio* measured and enumerated in outer (gills, mantle, and labial palps) and inner (digestive diverticula, and adductor muscle) tissues using methods described by American Public Health Association et al. (1985) and Tamplin and Fisher (1989).

Figures 10 and 11 depict the annual distribution of fecal and total coliform bacteria, *V. vulnificus*, and *V. parahaemolyticus* in oysters from North Inlet and Murrells Inlet. Note that in Murrells Inlet oysters, which were more heavily parasitized by *P. marinus* as a result of the high salinity waters within the estuary, there was a greater portion of *V. vulnificus* (Murrells Inlet = 77.3%, North Inlet = 34.1%) and *V. parahaemolyticus* (Murrells Inlet = 77.6%, North Inlet = 53.2%) in internal tissues (gonad, digestive diverticulum, and adductor muscle) than in external tissues (gills, mantle, and labial palps) (Fig. 10). The greater occurrence of *V. vulnificus* within inner tissues suggests that oyster immune functions (opsonin and/or agglutination) have been suppressed by increased parasitism rates by *P. marinas* in urbanized Murrells Inlet. There were no significant differences between fecal and total coliform distributions in North Inlet and Murrells Inlet oysters as the majority of the bacterial burden was found in internal tissues (Murrells Inlet = 89.4-89.7%, North Inlet = 78.6-83.4%) (Fig. 11).

The greater occurrence of *V. vulnificus* in more internal tissues of heavily parasitized oysters suggests that *P. marinus* may indeed adversely affect the immune response of oysters. The depletion of n-hydrin positive amino acids, such as taurine and glycine, which may occur following heavy *P. marinus* infections, is important in opsonin and agglutination responses by the oyster dealing with *Vibrio* exposures. These results suggest that one indirect effect of urbanization may be increased high salinity conditions, which may result from reduced freshwater inflows into estuarine areas with modified surface drainage systems (e.g., impounded watersheds). Results from this study indicate that the higher salinity conditions and accompanying increased *Perkinsus* infection intensity may predispose oysters in urbanized areas, so affected, to have greater accumulation of *V. vulnificus* in more internalized tissues which in turn may increase risks to susceptible human consumers.

Conclusions

The evidence that human and ecosystem health are linked is undisputable. It is also clear that uncontrolled development cannot continue without serious consequences to human and ecosystem health and also to economic health. Until these problems associated with uncontrolled and unplanned development are addressed, both human and ecosystem health will continue to degrade and, in turn, badly needed economic development will not occur. Development of appropriate environmental and public health management techniques are sorely needed to address these issues in terms of urbanization. Only with appropriate data and development of new analytical techniques to discern pollution sources from naturally occurring sources (e.g., wildlife versus human) will managers be able to appropriately identify and manage pollution sources and accompanying human health risks.

Literature Cited

American Public Health Association, American Water Works Association, and Water Pollution Control Federation. 1985. Standard Methods for the Examination of Water and Waste Water, 16th Edition. American Public Health Association, American Water Works Association, and Water Pollution Control Federation, Washington, D.C.

Conway, G.R. and J.N. Pretty. 1991. Unwelcome harvest: Agriculture and pollution. Earthscan, London, Great Britain.

DeWalle, F.B. and R.M. Schaffe. 1980. Groundwater pollution by septic tank drain fields. *Journal of Environmental Engineering*, Div of Proc. American Society of Civil Engineers 106 (EE3): 631-646.

Duda, A.M. and K.D. Cromartie. 1983. Coastal pollution from septic tank drain fields. *Journal of Environmental Engineering*, Div of Proc. American Society of Civil Engineers 108 (EE6): 1265-1279.

El-Figi, K.A. 1990. Epidemiological and microbiological evaluation of enteric bacterial water-borne diseases in coastal areas of South Carolina. Ph.D. Dissertation, University of South Carolina, Columbia, South Carolina.

Gruenhagen, K. 1985. Physiological responses of the eastern or American oyster, *Crassostrea virginica*, exposed to combined pollutants from a marina in a developed coastal estuary. M.S. Thesis, University of South Carolina, Columbia, South Carolina.

Horton, T. and W.M. Eichbaum. 1991. Turning the Tide: Saving the Chesapeake Bay. The Chesapeake Bay Foundation, Island Press, Washington, D.C.

Jolley, R.L. , G. Jones, W.W. Potts, and J.E. Thompson. 1975. Chlorination of organics in cooling waters and process effluents, p. 105-139. *In* R.L. Jolley (ed.), Water Chlorination: Environmental Impacts and Health Effects. Vol. 1. Ann Arbor Science Press Inc., Ann Arbor, Michigan.

Leonard, D.L. 1993. Turning the tide on water quality and declines in shellfish resources. *World Aquaculture* 24 (4): 57-64.

Leonard, D.L., E.A. Slaughter, P.V. Genovase, S.L. Adamany, and C.G. Clement. 1991. The 1990 National Shellfish Register of Classified Estuarine Waters. National Oceanic and Atmospheric Administration, NOS/SAB, Rockville, Maryland.

Lutchenco, J., A.M. Olson, L.B. Brubaker, S.R. Carpenter, M.M. Holland, S.P. Hubbell, S.A. Levin, J.A. MacMahon, P.A. Matson, J.M. Melillo, H.A. Mooey, C.H. Peterson, H.R. Pulliam, L.A. Real, P.J. Regal, and P.G. Risser. 1991. The sustainable biosphere initiative: An ecological research agenda. *Ecology* 72: 371-412.

Marcus, J.M. 1988. The impacts of selected land-use activities on the American oyster, *Crassostrea virginica* (Gmelin). Ph.D. Dissertation, University of South Carolina, Columbia, SC.

Newall, C. L. 1991. Shellfish sanitary survey reappraisal, area IV (Murrells Inlet/Pawleys Island) —October 1988 to May 1991. South Carolina Department of Health and Environmental Control, Columbia, South Carolina.

Scott, G.I. 1976. Oyster condition index as a monitor of biological pollution in South Carolina coastal waters: A pilot study. Masters Thesis, University of South Carolina, Columbia, South Carolina.

Scott, G.I., T.I. Sammons, D.P. Middaugh, and M.J. Hemmer. 1982. Impacts of water chlorination and coliform bacteria on the American oyster, *Crassostrea virginica* (Gmelin), p. 505-529. *In* W.B. Vernberg, A. Calabrese, F.P. Thurberg, and F.J. Vernberg (eds.), Physiological Mechanisms of Marine Pollutant Toxicity, Academic Press, New York.

Strozier, S.H. 1996. Effects of urbanization on the American oyster, *Crassostrea virginica*, in terms of bacterial and parasitic infections and physiological condition. Ph.D. Dissertation, University of South Carolina, Columbia, South Carolina.

Tamplin, M.L and W.S. Fisher. 1989. Occurrence and characteristics of agglutination of *Vibrio cholerae* by serum from the eastern oyster, *Crassostrea virginica*. *Applied Environmental Microbiology* 53: 2882-2887.

Turner, L.E. 1978. The effects of intermittent, low level water chlorination upon the American oyster, *Crassostrea virginica*: A field study. M.S. Thesis, University of South Carolina, Columbia, South Carolina.

United Nations, Development of International Economic and Social Affairs. 1991. World urbanization prospects 1990. United Nations, New York.

United States Environmental Protection Agency, Science Advisory Board. 1990. Reducing risks: Setting priorities and strategies for environmental protection. United States Environmental Protection Agency, Washington, D.C.

Vernberg, F.J., W. B. Vernberg, E. R. Blood, A. Fortner, M. Fulton, H. McKellar, W. Mitchener, G. I. Scott, T. Siewicki, and K. El-Figi. 1992. Impacts of urbanization on high salinity estuaries in the southeastern United States. *Netherlands Journal of Sea Research* 30: 239-248.

Viraraghavan, T. and R.G. Warnock. 1976. Ground water quality adjacent to septic tank systems. *American Water Works Association* 68: 611-614.

Wahl, M., H.N. McKellar, Jr., and T.M. Williams. 1993. The effects of coastal development on watershed hydrography and the transport of organic carbon, p. 389-411. *In* F.J. Vernberg, W.B. Vernberg, and T. Siewicki (eds.), Urbanization in Southeastern Estuaries. Belle W. Baruch Library in Marine Science, no. 20. University of South Carolina Press, Columbia, SC.

Winslow. C.E.A. 1923. The evolution and significance of the modern public health campaign. Yale University Press, New Haven, Connecticut. Reprint with an introduction by M. Terris, 1984. Journal of Public Health Policy, South Burlington, Vermont.

Yates, M.V., C.P. Gerba, and L.M. Kelley. 1985. Virus persistence in groundwater. *Applied Environmental Microbiology* 49: 778-781.

New Microbiological Approaches for Assessing and Indexing Contamination Loading in Estuaries and Marine Waters

W.D. Watkins and W. Burkhardt, III

ABSTRACT: Human intrusion on the aquatic environment continues to increase, and with it associated pollutants and contamination, which frequently require assessment, either for abatement or safety purposes. Traditional microbial indicators of contamination—total and fecal coliforms—have poor survival in many of the circumstances encountered in estuarine and marine environments. However, certain pathogenic microorganisms, particularly human enteric viruses, can be viable and present in the absence of bacterial indicators. Also, traditional indicators do not distinguish human from animal fecal contamination. Several recent studies by the United States Food and Drug Administration have employed alternative microbial indicators and methods in attempts to distinguish relative amounts of contamination in estuarine and marine environments. The results from coastal and offshore projects show that sediments, rather than water samples, often provide a more reliable determination of contamination loading, and that certain of these alternative indicators provide a more sensitive indication of such contamination. Comparative findings from estuarine areas receiving contamination from mixed sources, including both treated and untreated wastewater discharges, show that relative contaminant loading is better determined by *Clostridium perfringens* densities than fecal coliforms. Areas impacted by nonpoint-source pollution, but essentially devoid of human input, were not found to harbor hazardous levels of infectious agents. The utility of alternative indicators is described in these studies.

Introduction

Historically, the indicators and standards of sanitation used in the United States have been exceptionally successful. This country enjoys the safest drinking water and food supplies in the world. It is not surprising, therefore, that there exists substantial reluctance among regulators to make changes in bacterial indicators used as indexes of sanitation, even though scientists and sanitarians have long known that the standards are based on imperfect indicators.

During the last three decades, fecal coliforms have been widely accepted as indicators of fecal contamination. This group of indicator bacteria are used in the United States for indexing the sanitary quality of drinking water supplies (American Public Health Association 1992), foods (American Public Health Association 1984), and environmental waters (American Public Health Association 1970). However, there exist certain situations where these indicator bacteria do not provide a reliable measure of either the amount of contamination present, or the implied, inherent health threat to humans. For example, treated and chlorinated wastewater effluents frequently show little if any contamination present based on fecal coliform content, whereas fecal coliform levels found in untreated, undisinfected wastewater discharges are generally very large indeed (Rippey and Watkins 1992). In actuality, the levels of viable, infectious viruses (both human viral pathogens and indicator viruses) from two such dissimilar wastewaters can be, and often are, nearly equivalent (Rippey and Watkins 1992). Moreover, in waters around offshore wastewater discharges, fecal coliforms generally fail to survive and, thus, may not provide an accurate measure of either contaminant loading or viable infectious agents (Burkhardt and Watkins 1992). In terms of indexing potential human health threats, many remote, relatively unpolluted areas exhibit persistent fecal coliform levels where no proportionate sources of either indicators or pathogens can be identified (United States Food and Drug Administration and Texas Department of Health 1990). It is understandable, therefore, that sanitary standards based on fecal coliforms have been criticized for their inability to index fecal contamination. Critics of existing control measures for shellfish-borne illness have claimed that fecal coliform standards are not always protective enough, citing numerous outbreaks of suspected viral-caused illness annually among shellfish consumers (Rippey 1992). In contrast, commercial interests have claimed that existing fecal coliform standards are needlessly restrictive and serve to overstate actual health risks, citing many instances where no human sources are impacting certain environments that are nonetheless classified as prohibited or restricted for the harvesting of shellfish. In light of such criticisms, and cognizant of future human population projections for coastal regions, new approaches to our often complex contamination problems are needed, particularly those concerned with environmental water quality and human health risks posed by microbial pathogens.

Indicators and Sanitation Standards

The merits of the indicator concept are as valid as ever, even with certain inherent limitations. Numerous problems associated with monitoring for disease-causing agents (pathogens) preclude direct pathogen measurement as a means for routinely protecting public health (Table 1). Analyses for disease-causing organisms instead of for indicators provides very little predictability since the presence or absence of pathogens at any given time does not reliably forecast the likelihood of future occurrences. Indicators, on the other hand, indicate the presence of fecal contamination in our foods and waters, usually before there are public health consequences, thereby alerting officials to potential health threats before they become manifest. Quantified, indicators may also provide a measure of the amount of contamination present and, thus, a relative indication of risk. Thus, indicators ordinarily provide both a degree of predictability and a margin of safety that are essential to reliable public health protection.

The key to effective public health protection has been the predictability afforded by indicators, and the relatively low cost of analyses. It is not possible to measure every portion of food or water

Table 1. Monitoring enteric pathogens to protect public health versus monitoring indicators of sanitation.

Pathogens	Indicators
Too many types to measure	One or a few groups to measure
Present only intermittently	Sewage and/or feces associated
Pathogens not indexed to each other	Indicators index the presence of sewage and/or fecal contamination
Analytical methods for many pathogens are costly and laborious	Methods for indicators are inexpensive, facile
Hazardous levels (infectious doses) not always known	Protective indicators standards established
Avirulent biotypes exist for many pathogens	Indicators easily identified
New pathogens can emerge	Standard indicators exist
Pathogen data not predictive	Indicators show contamination
Many analyses are too costly	Assays relatively inexpensive

we consume, every small volume of waste discharged, or all waters in recreational areas. At best, only spot checks or periodic monitoring can be performed. Consequently, the results determined must provide as much meaningful information as practical about the current and future safety of the commodities we examine today. That is precisely why, for example, the National Shellfish Sanitation Program (United States Food and Drug Administration 1992) relies most heavily on determining the water quality of shellfish harvest areas, and far less on the shellfish meats, themselves.

The standards employed for determining the potability of drinking waters and the relative suitability of shellfishing areas have evolved from original estimates of safety based on experience, practice, and pragmatic modifications. These empirical processes have occasionally been supplemented by information derived from clinical trials and prospective epidemiology. Important infectious dose data for some enteric pathogens is available from volunteer experiments. The United States Environmental Protection Agency recently revised recreational water quality standards (United States Environmental Protection Agency 1984) based on a "new" microbial indicator identified during epidemiological studies. Establishment of standards based on health risk is highly desirable. The recently initiated National Indicator Study also proposes to identify a more scientifically valid indicator of health risks associated with raw shellfish consumption by conducting feeding trials with clinical follow-up.

There are situations, however, where prospective epidemiological investigations relating health consequences to levels of indicators present can not be directly employed to establish sanitation standards. In particular, environments that receive varying amounts of contamination loading and

Table 2. Major obstacles to establishing new indicators and standards.

Universal utility
Body of evidence (databases)
Relatedness
Governing bodies

ordinarily have only indirect interaction with humans, such as marine sediments, must be assessed in light of other risk information.

In summary, the indicator groups (total and fecal coliforms) we use, and the sanitary standards based on these, provide significant protection in spite of certain imperfections. Shortcomings are generally true for most indicators, including virtually all proposed alternative indicators. The question remains, what better means for determining the amount of fecal contamination and associated risks can be employed in situations where existing indicators fail to provide reliable information?

New Indicators and Standards

Numerous microbial organisms and biological chemicals have been proposed at various times as alternatives to traditional indicator bacteria. In recent decades, related research efforts have focused on correlating indicators with measurable human health effects. Thus, studies have attempted to define health effects indicators using prospective epidemiological approaches. The United States Environmental Protection Agency recommends enterococci as the indicator correlating best with swimming-associated gastrointestinal illnesses (Cabelli 1981; Dufour 1983). Other studies conducted jointly by the United States Environmental Protection Agency and National Oceanic and Atmospheric Administration have suggested that male-specific bacteriophage (MSB) may provide a more reliable indication of risk to consumers of raw molluscan shellfish (oysters and clams) for gastrointestinal illness (Harris White, National Oceanic and Atmospheric Administration, Washington, D.C., personal communication). As previously stated, the recently initiated National Indicator Study also proposes to identify a more scientifically valid indicator of the health risks associated with raw shellfish consumption.

With the exception of enterococci for recreational waters, none of the proposed alternative indicators have gained the support necessary from public health organizations for establishment of new standards in the United States. The principal reason for this that the dependabilities of new or alternative indicators of contamination and of new systems and standards for determining water quality have been extremely difficult to assess. Probably the principal impediment, among others (Table 2), has been the magnitude of studies required to define new indicators, where both the costs and scope of effort have generally exceeded available resources. In essence, the amount of evidence (data) needed to validate a new indicator and derive new standards simply has been too large for any one research group to address effectively. Even the wide-reaching effort of the National Indicator

Study has encountered difficulties and confusion in developing suitable study parameters. These problems relate to a another major obstacle to establishing new indicators and standards, that being the concept of universal utility. Among the public health community there remains a residual notion that dependable indicators need be universally useful. Limitations on the utility of a given indicator (i.e., exceptions to its usefulness) invariably generate serious scientific criticisms about reliability. And, these criticisms generally have served to deter further development and consideration of new standards or indexes.

Aside from the existing indicators and standards employed, there is a general lack of meaningful criteria against which to assess new indicators. A key question generally asked of new indicators is, How does its applicability compare to the current indicator system used nationwide? This applicability criterion obviously requires direct comparison with the current indicator system. Also, the relatedness of proposed new indicators and standards refers to the type of indicator and level of sensitivity, specifically, Will it serve the intended purpose? Traditionally, for foods and waters the purpose has been public health protection against transmissible enteric diseases. Fecal coliforms alone do not always attain this purpose.

To what, then, must an alternative indicator be related? Several obvious public health choices are (1) the general source of contamination (i.e., feces and sewage); (2) the specific source (i.e., human feces and sewage); (3) the most prevalent enteric pathogens of concern (i.e., human enteric viruses); (4) the specific illnesses of concern; and (5) naturally occurring pathogens. Though this may sound simple, these relationships are difficult to define scientifically, and few solid, alternative public health indices have been sufficiently characterized to date.

It seems reasonable to assume that no single new indicator or standard will be found universally applicable. Alternative indicators may have merit, even though their use may be limited. A list of alternative indicators proposed, compared, and partially investigated over recent years is provided in Table 3. Moreover, in aquatic environments, densities of traditional and alternative indicators usually can not be meaningfully compared to hazards or risks without further knowledge about initial (source) densities, distance and time of travel from a common source, as well as dilution and relative decay rates. Differential effects on indicators from environmental, seasonal, physical, and geographical factors must also be weighed. Once determined, significant differences found between alternative and traditional indicator levels may serve to enhance rather than diminish the reliability and acceptance of the former. The two factors of utility and comparability, perhaps more than any of the other obstacles, have frustrated the promotion and implementation of new indicators and new standards.

Ultimately, there also remains the challenge of gaining official acceptance and adoption of new indicators and standards by governing bodies. In the case of the National Shellfish Sanitation Program, these sanctioning authorities include the American Public Health Association (APHA), the Association of Official Analytical Chemists, the United States Food and Drug Administration, and the Interstate Shellfish Sanitation Conference. Finding agreement on even minor issues can be difficult. The need for new, reliable indicators and standards persists nonetheless. An alternative indicator, or perhaps a suite of indicators (combined indices), as well as new standards for classifying environmental waters, are highly desirable in situations where traditional sanitary indicators fail to reflect the actual contamination present and/or the associated risks to human health. Still, changing the ways in which we assess public health threats and environmental degradation, by using alternative indicators and new standards as new environmental and public health protection tools, has been and remains an exceptionally challenging task. What is needed to overcome the obstacles involved in

Table 3. Conventional and proposed alternative indicators.

Conventional Indicator Group	Type of Indicator
Total and fecal coliforms	Vegetative bacteria
Escherichia coli	Vegetative bacteria
Fecal *Streptococci*	Vegetative bacteria
Enterococci	Vegetative bacteria
Alternative Indicators	Type of Indicator
Clostridium perfringens	Spores (essentially)
Somatic bacteriophage	Bacterial viruses
Male-specific bacteriophage	Bacterial viruses
Polio viruses	Human viruses
Other bacterial groups and species	Vegetative bacteria
Other viruses	Human and/or nonhuman viruses
Biochemicals	Fecal sterols and fecal antibodies

establishing new indicators and standards? The answer depends upon what type of indicator is needed, and for what type of protection. Some types of indicator that are desirable are (1) a better indicator of the amounts of fecal contamination actually present; (2) an indicator indexing fecal contamination only from humans; (3) an indicator indexing fecal contamination from specific nonhuman (animal) sources; (4) an enteric viral indicator indexing human enteric viral pathogens; and, (5) a health effects indicator indexing the relative risk from the most prevalent pathogen or other hazard.

Fecal coliforms, the indicator group of bacteria most widely used today, are inherently well-suited to distinguish sanitary quality, although they do have limitations. Table 4 summarizes the relevant characteristics of this indicator group. Overall, existing indicators and standards are imperfect and have limitations. Even so, indicators of sanitation are relied upon to prevent outbreaks and epidemics of diseases transmitted by the fecal-oral route. Those characteristics of an indicator seemingly most critical to the provision of reliable public health protection, as well as characteristics postulated as embodied by ideal protective indicators, are listed in Table 5. The ideal indicator is the pathogen itself. But, as already noted, the use of any particular pathogen fails to provide protective predictability. Reasonable indications of the hazards and the levels of safety associated with various human activities are needed. And, the level of safety necessary, in turn, will depend upon the purpose for monitoring in the first place.

What can be gained by changing our current sanitary indicator system, either by replacing coliform indicators with some other indicator, or by supplementing coliform determinations with

Table 4. Characteristics of coliforms.

A. Their principal sources are fecal (human and animal), although some nonintestinal reservoirs can occur, causing some difficulty in assessing their significance.

B. They are often present in the absence of pathogens. This provides a margin of safety for established standards; it also leaves room for criticism of standards as needlessly restrictive in some instances.

C. Fecal coliforms are sometimes absent when fecal-borne pathogens are present. This leads to "lack of protection" criticisms in some instances.

D. Survival of fecal coliforms in the environment and through disinfection differs from that of viral pathogens. Longer survival of viral pathogens may compromise the effectiveness of bacterial indicators under certain circumstances and provide a false sense of safety.

E. Fecal coliforms are found in large, quantifiable numbers, and are easily measured by inexpensive enumeration methods.

Table 5. Characteristics of an ideal indicator.

A. Consistently and exclusively present where pathogens are present

B. Absent where pathogens are absent

C. Present in large enough numbers to indicate when the risk of illness is unacceptable

D. Survive in the environment as well as the most "hardy" pathogens

E. Under the same conditions, multiply at similar rate as pathogens

F. Resist the stresses and disinfection of wastewater treatment, similar to the most resistant pathogens

G. Easily measured by rapid, inexpensive, quantitative methods

measurements of other indicators? The primary reason for using an alternative indicator, or a suite (combined index) of alternative indicators, as supplements to our already imperfect system, is to provide better, more useful information. Information, which can, in general, (1) better distinguish and identify hazards; (2) better quantify the levels of hazards; (3) better distinguish the sources of hazards; (4) more accurately gauge the level of risk; (5) serve as a tool(s) to examine trends and specific conditions; (6) assist in formulating policy; and, (7) assist in design of management programs, and in determining their effectiveness. Some of the specific indicators needed and the reasons for them are as follow:

- A "True" Sanitary Indicator to determine when fecal contamination is actually present, and to clearly discern environmental situations where extra-intestinal sources of current indicators occur.
- A Human-specific Fecal Indicator to distinguish when and how much human contamination is present versus that from animals; to assist greatly toward assessing health risk in nonpoint pollution problems.
- An Enteric Virus Indicator to index potential threats from human enteric viruses when they may be present, and especially, to index when they are absent.
- A Health Effects Indicator to define a truer index of acceptable risk for a given health hazard, from both point-source-impacted and nonpoint-source-impacted waters, allowing for a health-based differentiation of animal from human wastes.
- A reliable indicator of health risk in marine benthic environments near dump sites and offshore discharge areas, and downstream areas impacted by these, where seafood harvesting has resumed or is being planned.
- An indicator to equate treated versus untreated wastewaters in terms of both relative contamination inputs and health risks.
- A scientific means to identify the most effective expenditure of limited pollution abatement dollars.
- Indicators for providing before and after databases to determine the most effective restrictions and prohibitions related to development, and differentiate these from less effective covenants.
- Differential indicators to determine relative contributions of contamination from a variety (mixture) of sources.
- A group of product quality indicators to distinguish abuse, expiration of shelf life, or inherent safety thereof.
- Indicators of naturally occurring hazards, such as pathogenic *Vibrio* species, and an index of safety.
- Indicators of marine toxins.
- Indicators of potential hazards associated with aquaculture products.

A limited number of prospective indicator microorganisms have been used to supplement determinations ordinarily made by the United States Food and Drug Administration or United States Environmental Protection Agency in selected field studies.

Materials and Methods

SEAWATER SAMPLING METHODS

Polypropylene sample bottles (500 ml) were used to collect water samples. These bottles were sterilized by autoclaving for 30 min at 121°C. For waters impacted by chlorinated effluents, 0.5 ml of a 10% solution of sodium thiosulfate ($Na_2S_2O_3$) was added to sample bottles before sterilization to neutralize any residual chlorine in the sample. Up to 15 mg l^{-1} residual could be successfully neutralized with this quantity of sodium thiosulfate.

Surface water samples were collected by hand or with the aid of a custom-made sampling device (a plastic sleeve attached to a wooden stick). At the time of collection, the lid of the sterile sample bottle was removed and the bottle held at its base to prevent accidental contamination. Subsequently the bottle was plunged below the surface of the water for filling, which was achieved by tilting the neck of the bottle slightly upward and pushing it horizontally forward in a direction away from the hand of the sampler.

Bottom water samples were collected with a Nansen type sampler (Wildlife Supply Co., Saginaw, Michigan) approximately 2-3 ft above the bottom. Collected bottom waters were carefully decanted into 500-ml bottles to minimize the possibility of extraneous contamination. After collection, all samples were placed in crushed ice in a cooler and returned to the laboratory. Analyses were initiated within 2 h of arrival in the laboratory.

Fecal coliforms and *E. coli* densities in seawater samples were determined using the mTEC procedure (Dufour et al. 1981). This method has been shown to be comparable to the APHA-MPN procedure for the enumeration of fecal coliforms and *E. coli* in saline waters (Rippey et al. 1987). Enterococci densities were determined using a modified (Dufour 1980) membrane filtration enumeration procedure (Levin et al. 1975). *Clostridium perfringens* densities in water samples were determined by the mCp procedure (Bisson and Cabelli 1979). Densities of male-specific bacteriophages were determined by a modified double-agar-overlay method (DeBartolomeis and Cabelli 1991). This method uses an *E. coli* strain (HS[pFamp]R) that is highly selective for the enumeration of these bacteriophages from municipal wastewaters and environmental waters.

SEDIMENT SAMPLING METHODS

Sediments were taken with a Smith-MacIntyre style sampler. Following the return of each sediment sample to the surface, approximately 1 cm of the upper layer of sediment was removed using a sterile, wooden tongue depressor and placed into a sterile, 150-ml polypropylene sample cup (Falcon, Lincoln Park, New Jersey). Samples were held on ice in coolers until analysis. Analyses were begun within 24 h of collection.

To prepare sediments, 15 g of sediment sample was weighed into a sterile polypropylene sample cup (Falcon) to which 135 ml of sterile phosphate-buffered saline was added. This suspension was mixed for 2 min with a sterile magnetic stir bar. A 10-ml aliquot of this mixture (this is equivalent to 1.0 g of sediment sample) was introduced into the appropriate growth medium.

Total and fecal coliforms were enumerated by the APHA-MPN procedures, using brilliant green bile and EC media as the confirmation medium, respectively. *E. coli* were enumerated using the APHA-MPN procedure modified by the addition of the fluorogenic compound 4-methylumbelliferyl β-D-glucuronide (MUG) to the EC medium (Rippey et al. 1987). *C. perfringens* densities were determined by the MPN Iron Milk method (Abeyta 1983). Indicator MPN values were determined by using Table 11 in Recommended Procedures for the Examination of Sea Water and Shellfish (American Public Health Association 1970). Densities were reported as the most probable number of organisms (MPN) per 100 g of sediment.

Results from USFDA Environmental Studies Using Alternative Indicators and New Approaches to Contamination Issues

In recent years, shellfish and pollution-related field studies conducted by the United States Food and Drug Administration have frequently employed methods for determining densities of alternative indicators as investigative tools in attempts to provide more useful information. Since about 1984 the United States Food and Drug Administration's shellfish program microbiologists have recognized that conventional determinations made for fecal coliforms simply had failed to reveal critical information in various studies of coastal waters and sediments. The abbreviated results from various studies described below are intended to show the utility of alternative indicators in detecting and quantifying contamination when traditional coliform determinations did not do so, and to provide useful information not ordinarily provided by conventional sanitation survey analyses.

RAINFALL IMPACTS ON NARRAGANSETT BAY WATER QUALITY (1988-1989)

Background

Narragansett Bay estuary, located in the state of Rhode Island, is the largest producer of hard-shelled clams (*Mercenaria mercenaria*) harvested commercially in the United States. Its waters are impacted by numerous pollution sources, and rainfall causes considerable water quality problems. Thus, a wet weather study was undertaken to more thoroughly define the magnitude of these problems, identify the principal contributing sources, and identify the target area for effective pollution abatement. The upper (northern) portion of the bay is heavily urbanized. Wastewater effluents are chlorinated to decrease the loading of microorganisms entering the estuary. Rainfalls of 0.5 inches cause closure of some shellfishing areas. Rainfalls exceeding 3.0 inches cause closure of nearly all shellfish harvesting areas.

Both United States Environmental Protection Agency and state officials have found it difficult to provide specific, effective pollution abatement measures and cost-effective remedies to improve bay water quality during precipitation events. None of the point sources have been very well characterized, particularly during precipitation events. These include many wastewater discharges: treated and disinfected wastewater from sewage treatment plants (STPs) as well as untreated wastewater (combined sewer-storm overflows [CSOs] and STP bypasses). Occasionally treatment and disinfection failures occur at STPs. Relationships between the amount of precipitation and observed impacts were not well defined or understood, especially the relative magnitude of impacts from the various sources with regard to the time and duration of storm events.

The purpose of the Wet Weather Study of the Providence watershed was identification and ranking of major pollution inputs in order to maximize the use of the limited financial resources for pollution abatement programs. The principal participants in the effort included the University of Rhode Island, the State of Rhode Island, the United States Environmental Protection Agency, the United States Food and Drug Administration, and several commercial contractors. Other co-investigators examined samples for trace metal (Cu, Cr, Cd, Ni, and Pb) contaminants (dissolved and particulate), suspended solids, dissolved nutrients (nitrate, ammonia, and orthophosphate), organic contaminants (polychlorinated biphenyls, polyaromatic hydrocarbons, and several others), a fecal sterol (coprostanol), and biological oxygen demands. The United States Food and Drug Administration supervised the determinations for microbial indicators of contamination and dye release studies to trace contamination dispersion. In addition, the hydrographic profiles for each of the three storm events studied were thoroughly characterized in and around the watershed.

The details and complexities of the study design are too large to present fully. Some of the most important pre-study factors considered were antecedent dry period; baseline data for sources and bay waters; requisite characteristics of rainfall events studied; storm hydrography for different areas of the watershed; and sampling logistics.

The microbiological goal of the study was to identify and rank major contamination sources based on indicator loading. The water quality indicators determined in this study were fecal coliforms, *Escherichia coli*, enterococci (Dufour 1980), *Clostridium perfringens*, and male-specific bacteriophage (MSB). Determinations of dry weather flows and indicator levels provided normal input profiles for each pollution source, which was calculated as Flow Rate × Indicator Density = Input.

Actual inputs may vary significantly from hour to hour due to changes in flow and large fluctuations in indicator levels. During wet weather, these variations become much more pronounced. This and other factors required that several difficulties, unique to the microbiology portion of the study, had to be addressed. First, samples had to be analyzed rapidly; they could not be archived as could samples for chemical analyses. Second, more frequent sampling (every 1-2 h, or occasionally less) was essential. Third, samples obtained could not be flow composited as they could be for other analyses. Large fluctuations anticipated for indicator levels necessitated analysis of discrete samples. The net outcome of these constraints was that over three separate wet weather events (October 1988; May 1989; and June 1989), more than 17,000 individual microbiological assays were performed on approximately 7,000 discrete samples.

Microbial indicator density data were used with flow data determined at times of sampling to calculate periodic inputs from each of the sources for each of the microbial indicators. Summations for these calculated, periodic inputs throughout the sampling periods for each storm event thus provided estimates of source strengths for each point source. Each point source then was ranked, by indicator, according to the cumulative contributions for each storm event. These total contributions were correlated with the amount of precipitation and storm duration, and the source rankings compared for each storm.

Results

Hydrographic characteristics of the storm events studied, separated by watershed areas, are shown in Table 6. Storm event two was the largest, in both rainfall amount and duration. Fecal coliform source strengths for this larger precipitation event are shown in Table 7. The contamination sources examined are ranked according to their input of fecal coliforms throughout the storm. Interestingly, the hours of input for each of the sources during the study period was not a determining factor in the overall outputs from the sources. As might be expected, sources of untreated wastewater (the STP bypasses and large CSOs) dominate as major contributors of fecal coliforms. This is, in part, due to the disinfection occurring at STPs but not at untreated sources. Ranking also points to the problems of river inputs, each receiving contamination from mixed sources.

Clostridium perfringens source strengths are shown in Table 8. *C. perfringens* spores exhibit quite a different rank order, as seen in the last column. Since spores of this species are relatively resistant to chlorination at STPs, this ranking allowed us to compare more realistically the total

Table 6. Hydrographic characteristics by watershed for all storm events.

Date (mm-dd-yy)	Tributary	Duration (h)	Rainfall (inches)	Intensity (inches h^{-1})
10-22-88[a]	Pawtuxet	11	0.91	0.20
	Blackstone	11	0.90	0.19
	Ten Mile	11	0.86	0.22
	Moshassuck	11	0.90	0.19
	Woonasquatucket	11	0.90	0.19
	Mean	11	0.89	0.20
05-10-89 thru 05-12-89[b]	Pawtuxet	33	2.45	0.20
	Blackstone	32	1.94	0.13
	Ten Mile	33	2.19	0.14
	Moshassuck	31	2.31	0.15
	Woonasquatucket	31	2.34	0.15
	Mean	32	2.25	0.15
06-13-89[c]	Pawtuxet	7	0.46	0.12
	Blackstone	9	0.37	0.08
	Ten Mile	9	0.40	0.09
	Moshassuck	8	0.44	0.11
	Woonasquatucket	7	0.46	0.15
	Mean	8	0.43	0.11

[a] Antecedent dry period, 13.5 d
[b] Antecedent dry period, 4.5 d
[c] Antecedent dry period, 3.5 d

wastewater loading (or contamination loading) from both untreated and treated sources. Such comparisons are useful when considering viruses and other, nonmicrobial hazards such as chemicals.

Source strengths determined for the viral indicator group, male-specific bacteriophage (MSB), are shown in Table 9. MSB are relatively resistant to chlorination but are somewhat more sewage-specific than *C. perfringens* spores, which can have significant inputs from runoff waters. It is significant that the BVDC Bypass in only 36 h of active flow and the NBC Bypass in only 56 h nearly equal the inputs from the other major sources of MSB after 110 h of flow. Also significant are the relatively low rankings for the BVDC and NBC STPs based on fecal coliforms, the traditional indicator group. Fecal coliforms may reveal the same information but only for untreated sources, not STPs that disinfect. These findings were supported by examining the levels determined for fecal coliforms, *C. perfringens*, and MSB in pre-chlorinated and post-chlorinated wastewaters

Table 7. Fecal coliform source strengths for storm event two (May 1989).

Rank	Point Source	Total Input[a]	Input Interval[b]
1	BVDC Bypass	6.12×10^{14}	36
2	NBC FP Bypass	4.78×10^{14}	56
3	Blackstone River	3.47×10^{14}	110
4	Moshassuck River	3.30×10^{14}	110
5	Woonasquatucket River	1.12×10^{14}	109
6	CSO D #010	9.33×10^{13}	6
7	CSO 9	8.95×10^{13}	12
8	Pawtuxet River	4.64×10^{13}	110
9	Woonsocket STP	2.33×10^{13}	106
10	BVDC STP	1.31×10^{13}	110
11	Ten Mile River	9.20×10^{12}	110
12	CSO D #007	7.67×10^{12}	2
13	CSO D #004	2.10×10^{12}	3
14	NBC FP STP	5.98×10^{11}	107
15	EP STP	1.07×10^{11}	110
Total fecal coliform input		2.16×10^{15} (100%)	

[a] Total input = flow $\times$ fecal coliform density $\times$ time.

[b] Number of hours when discrete flow determinations were actually made (tributaries and STPs) or the interval of time in which flow was continuously recorded (bypasses and CSOs).

at four STPs examined (Rippey and Watkins 1992). Fecal coliform levels were reduced about 2.4 logs by the disinfection process. The mean difference between pre- and post-chlorinated levels of *C. perfringens* was only about 0.5 log. Similar results were determined for MSB levels, with a mean difference of about 0.4 log. Interestingly, Norwalk and hepatitis A viruses also have been found to be more resistant to chlorine disinfection than fecal coliforms, and to about the same degree as are male-specific bacteriophage.

In summary, these kinds of data, together with those for chemical pollutants, greatly assisted regional officials in their pollution abatement decisions. The alternative indicators used in this study were extremely valuable for the comparisons and contrasting views they empowered.

Environmental Impacts From Offshore Wastewater Discharges

A series of studies conducted by the United States Environmental Protection Agency and supported in part by the United States Food and Drug Administration sought to assess the sanitary quality of marine environments off the mid-Atlantic United States coast. Previously it had been determined that traditional sanitary indicators, fecal coliforms and occasionally fecal *Streptococcus* species, simply did not survive well, and analyses for these indicators of contamination provided

Table 8. *Clostridium perfringens* source strengths for storm event two (May 1989).

Rank	Point Source	Total Input[a]	Fecal Coliform Rank
1	BVDC STP	2.34×10^{14}	10
2	Blackstone River	1.79×10^{14}	3
3	NBC FP STP	8.97×10^{13}	14
4	Pawtuxet River	7.76×10^{13}	8
5	BVDC Bypass	2.76×10^{13}	1
6	Woonsocket STP	2.76×10^{13}	9
7	NBC FP Bypass	2.71×10^{13}	2
8	Woonasquatucket River	1.63×10^{13}	5
9	EP STP	1.29×10^{13}	15
10	Moshassuck River	1.02×10^{13}	4
11	Ten Mile River	8.11×10^{12}	11
12	CSO 9	6.93×10^{12}	7
13	CSO D #010	2.25×10^{12}	6
14	CSO D #004	1.50×10^{11}	13
15	CSO D #007	2.47×10^{10}	12
Total *C. perfringens* input		7.21×10^{14} (100%)	

[a] Total input = flow × *C. perfringens* density × time.

very little information. Alternative approaches were implemented to assess the sanitary quality of these marine environments.

The locations for several mid-Atlantic STP outfall sites examined are shown in Fig. 1. These offshore wastewater discharges, at Bethany Beach, Delaware, Ocean City, Maryland, and Virginia Beach, Virginia, had been routinely investigated during United States Environmental Protection Agency research cruises for a number of years. Monitoring for fecal coliforms in the surface, mid-depth, and bottom waters at sampling grids located around the ocean discharge pipes for these three STPs was conducted from 1982 to 1985. The microbiological results for water samples obtained during this period are summarized in Table 10. Nearly every water sample appeared to be quite devoid of sanitary indicators, and by current fecal coliform standards these regions met the shell-fishing requirements of the National Shellfish Sanitation Program for approved status. Thus, little was gained from these costly and intensive field efforts.

The shortcomings of these studies, it was found, related to both the indicators being determined and the types of samples being examined. Using alternative approaches, it became clear that *C. perfringens* spore levels in the sediments provided a more definitive depiction of the wastewater impacts received by these areas. Microbiological results obtained for the 1991 research cruises are shown in Table 11. Total and fecal coliform indicators provided very little useful information about the sanitary quality of the sediments, and the same was true for enterococci. However, the spore

Table 9. Male-specific bacteriophage source strengths for storm event two (May 1989).

Rank	Point Source	Total Input[a]	Fecal Coliform Rank
1	NBC FP STP	1.44×10^{13}	14
2	BVDC Bypass	1.42×10^{13}	1
3	BVDC STP	1.26×10^{13}	10
4	Pawtuxet River	9.70×10^{12}	8
5	NBC FP Bypass	8.80×10^{12}	2
6	Moshassuck River	5.52×10^{12}	4
7	Blackstone River	2.04×10^{12}	3
8	Woonsocket STP	1.48×10^{12}	9
9	CSO 9	1.24×10^{12}	7
10	Woonasquatucket River	3.63×10^{11}	5
11	Ten Mile River	3.02×10^{11}	11
12	CSO D #010	2.88×10^{11}	6
13	EP STP	2.59×10^{11}	15
14	CSO D #004	1.71×10^{10}	13
15	CSO D #007	1.63×10^{9}	12
Total bacteriophage input		7.11×10^{13} (100%)	

[a] Total input = flow × male-specific bacteriophage density × time.

data revealed that these benthic areas were far from pristine. *C. perfringens* was detected in 75% of the sediment samples, and at levels greater than 100 spores g^{-1} in more than half the samples. Topography of the regions revealed that lower lying areas accounted for the highest spore levels. Fecal materials and indicators discharged apparently settle and remain stable in the benthic trenches and depressions. Similar findings have been made from studies examining the movement and impacts of sewage sludge disposal at marine dump sites (Emerson and Cabelli 1982). Thus, it was found at least there exists one reliable microbiological means to detect sewage inputs in the marine environment.

IMPACTS OF SLUDGE DISPOSAL IN THE NEW YORK BIGHT (1986-1989)

Several marine areas previously used for sewage sludge disposal have been prohibited from further dumping in an effort to restore those marine environments and, hopefully, allow for seafood harvesting. The New York Bight is one such area used for many years as a sludge disposal site (Fig. 2). Recent cessation has prompted annual assessments by the National Marine Fisheries Service and the United States Environmental Protection Agency on the recovery of the area. A summary of the United States Food and Drug Administration microbiological results for sediments taken from three sample locations in this area is given in Table 12.

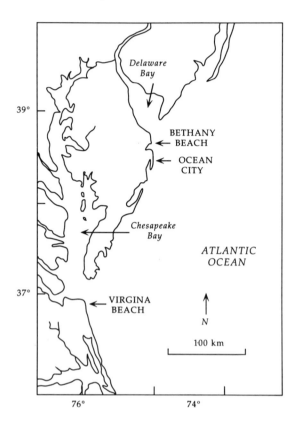

Fig. 1. Mid-Atlantic sewage outfall locations.

Again, it is evident that the total and fecal coliform groups simply do not survive well enough to provide a true assessment of the area's sanitary state. Half of the samples or more showed no detectable coliforms, total or fecal. *C. perfringens*, however, was detected in all samples, and the mean levels determined were very high. So, while the levels of vegetative indicators and other bacteria susceptible to die-off in this environment decreased steadily over the years, the more refractory indicator, spores, persist. Moreover, the amount of sludge materials, greatest at site NY6, abundant at site R2, and still evident at site NY11, may be differentiated by ranking the mean densities determined for each (n = 31). Thus, *C. perfringens* spores provided a means to gauge contamination in this marine area. However, its significance to public health protection remains unclear.

ENVIRONMENTAL IMPACTS DETERMINED DURING OCEAN SLUDGE DISPOSAL ASSESSMENT CRUISES (1990-1991)

The utility of *C. perfringens* as an indicator in the marine environment also can be seen in the United States Food and Drug Administration results from samples obtained during the National Oceanic and Atmospheric Administration's Ocean Disposal Assessment Cruises in 1990 and 1991.

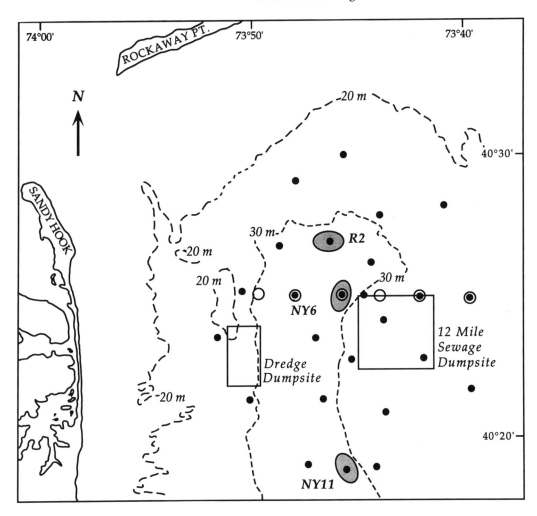

Fig. 2. New York Bight sample locations.

The sampling locations for these determinations span an area along the edge of the continental shelf from the mid-Atlantic region to Georges Bank off the coast of Maine. The impacts (Table 13) seen from ocean dumping of sewage sludge as well as those from transport of sewage sludge by the Gulf Stream are not at all reflected by fecal coliform levels determined for bottom waters. *C. perfringens* spore data, however, do provide a measure of the impacts from contaminated sludge dumped in numerous places offshore. Unfortunately, the significance of these data are not clear, other than to say that they appear to index a relative degree of the contamination present. Measures of viable infectious agents would be welcome adjuncts to these data.

Table 10. Microbiological results for mid-Atlantic receiving waters, 1982 through 1985. Fecal coliform MPNs were determined according to methods of the American Public Health Association (1970).

Sample Area	Type of Water Sample	No. of Samples Examined	No. of Fecal Coliform MPN > 9
Virginia Beach (AO stations)	Surface	45	0
	Mid depth	21	0
	Bottom	21	0
Ocean City (OC stations)	Surface	40	0
	Mid depth	18	0
	Bottom	18	1
Bethany Beach (BB stations)	Surface	36	0
	Mid depth	18	0
	Bottom	18	1
Totals		235	2

Table 11. Microbiological results for mid-Atlantic sediments, 1991.

Sample Area	No. of Samples Examined	No. of Sediment Samples Where:				
		TC MPN[a] >20	FC MPN[a] >20	Ent MPN[b] >20	Cp MPN[c] >20	Cp MPN[c] >100
Virginia Beach	12	4	1	0	11	7
Ocean City	13	0	0	0	7	5
Bethany Beach	16	0	0	0	12	11
Totals	41	4	1	0	30	23

[a] Total and fecal coliform MPNs determined using 1.0 g, 0.1 g, and 0.01 g amounts of sediments (wet weight) in a five-tube procedure according to American Public Health Association (1985).
[b] Enterococci MPNs determined using 1.0 g, 0.1 g, and 0.01 g amounts of sediments (wet weight) in a five-tube procedure using Azide dextrose broth prescribed for fecal streptococci in American Public Health Association (1985) and confirmed by membrane streaks on modified mE media (Dufour 1980).
[c] *Clostridium perfringens* MPNs determined using 1.0 g, 0.1 g, and 0.01 g amounts of sediments (wet weight) in a five-tube procedure using the Iron Milk method (Abeyta 1983).

Table 12. Microbiological results for New York Bight sediments, September 1986 through November 1989.

Sample Station	No. of Samples	Mean MPN per 100 g			No. of Samples Where MPN below detectable levels		
		TC[a]	FC[a]	Cp[b]	TC	FC	Cp
R2	31	24	12	2.6×10^6	17	25	0
NY6	31	95	26	3.3×10^6	15	18	0
NY11	31	17	8	3.8×10^5	21	31	0

[a] Total and fecal coliform MPNs determined using 1.0, 0.1, and 0.01 g amounts of sediments (wet weight) in a five-tube procedure according to the American Public Health Association (1985). In samples where MPNs were below detectable levels (< 20 per 100 g), 50% values were assigned to calculate mean MPNs.
[b] *Clostridium perfringens* MPNs determined from tenfold dilutions of 1.0 g amounts of sediments (wet weight) in a five-tube procedure using the Iron Milk method (Abeyta 1983).

Methods have been developed which allow the facile enumeration of fecal coliforms, enterococci, and *C. perfringens* from estuarine and marine sediments. But, as yet, quantitative extraction methods for MSB or any of the viruses from sediments are not reliable. Once developed, such methods will allow the establishment of a relative index with the spore data, and the survival of these spores will be of more immediate significance and utility.

COW TRAP LAKES, TEXAS

In many coastal areas of the United States, particularly those sparsely used by humans, sources of human fecal contamination are not detected, even though water quality as determined by fecal coliforms is judged to be poor, or at least unacceptable for the harvesting of shellfish. Nearly all waters are impacted in varying degrees by animal wastes, and particularly in recent years, questions have arisen frequently on the relative significance of nonpoint pollution from animal sources versus that from human wastes. In 1989 the United States Food and Drug Administration participated in a study of Cow Trap Lakes, Texas, a remote area removed from most human impacts (Fig. 3). The area is very shallow, and contains several modest oyster beds. It is flushed by runoff water during rainfall and is tidally flushed through a narrow inlet to the intercoastal waterway. A preliminary survey of the area and sampling results determined that fecal contamination entering from the intercoastal waterway was usually negligible. Large migratory bird populations and cattle pastured within the watershed appeared to be the only significant sources of contamination.

The area was studied on four occasions seasonally (February, April, June, and October). Samples of the waters, oysters, and sediments were obtained routinely during each of the 2-wk study periods. A wide array of indicator organisms and pathogens were determined, including enumeration methods for total and fecal coliforms, *Escherichia coli*, fecal streptococci, *S. bovis*, enterococci, *C. perfringens* spores (essentially), somatic coliphage, male-specific bacteriophage, *Salmonella* species, *Shigella*

Table 13. Microbiological results for continental shelf sediments, 1990-1991.

Cruise Year	Sample Site	Depth (m)	C. perfringens [a] per 100 g sediment	Fecal coliforms [b] per 100 ml bottom water
1990 [c]	Balt Cyn 1	186	220	< 1
	Balt Cyn 2	620	1,600	< 1
	Wilm Cyn	602	> 2,400	< 1
	Toms Cyn 1	664	> 2,400	< 1
	Toms Cyn 2	207	> 2,400	< 1
	Site #3	141	350	< 1
	Site #5	160	350	< 1
	Site #6	160	3,500	< 1
	Site #10	605	1,600	< 1
	Site #11	181	540	< 1
	Site #12	579	1,600	10
	Site #13	183	540	< 1
	Site #14	642	920	< 1
	Site #15	199	540	< 1
	Site #16	193	> 2,400	< 1
	New HC 1	625	1,700	< 1
	New HC 2	192	< 2,400	< 1
	Midshelf	64	79	ND [d]
1991 [c]	Noname Cyn 1	610	5,400	< 1
	Noname Cyn 2	650	3,500	< 1
	Noname Cyn 3	582	5,400	< 1
	Munson Cyn 1	653	1,300	< 1
	Munson Cyn 2	630	2,400	< 1
	Lydonia Cyn	610	1,700	< 1
	Hydrographer C	692	3,500	< 1
	Veatch Cyn 1	579	2,400	< 1
	Veatch Cyn 2	626	5,400	< 1
	Block Cyn 1	640	16,000	< 1
	Block Cyn 2	558	2,400	< 1
	Hudson Cyn 1	584	16,000	< 1
	Hudson Cyn 2	549	> 16,000	< 1
	Toms Cyn 3	579	16,000	< 1
	Toms Cyn 4	229	1,700	< 1

[a] Determined using five-tube Iron Milk MPN method (Abeyta 1983).

[b] Determined using the mTEC procedure (Dufour et al. 1981).

[c] Samples and data provided by J.L. Gaines, United States Public Health Service, Food and Drug Administration.

[d] ND = not determined.

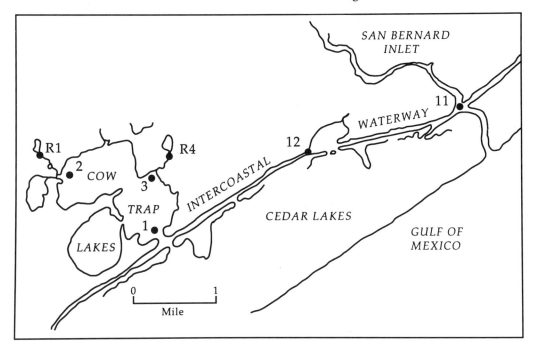

Fig. 3. Cow Trap Lakes, Texas, sample locations.

species, *Listeria* species, *Campylobacter* species, enterotoxigenic *E. coli*, *Vibrio cholera*, *Vibrio vulnificus*, *Cryptosporidium*, and *Giardia*.

The study determined the following: (1) Low numbers of most indicators were found most of the time, and appear to be from nonhuman sources. (2) The highest levels of indicators occurred during the winter study period, with both waters and oysters exceeding the acceptable levels (14 MPN per 100 ml and 230 MPN per 100 g, respectively) of fecal coliforms (United States Food and Drug Administration 1992). Highest indicator levels correlated with the most noticeable numbers of waterfowl and cattle. (3) Water quality appeared to meet the general requirements for approved status, although sampling was not strictly undertaken to occur during adverse conditions. (4) Shellfish meats frequently exceeded market guidelines (230 MPN per 100 g) for fecal coliforms (United States Food Drug Administration 1992). (5) Sediments in the area appear to be reservoirs of micro-organisms. (6) Indicator levels in waters and shellfish do not correlate well (nor are they normally expected to be so). (7) A few pathogens are present occasionally, especially during winter months when indicators were also greatest; these include a few naturally occurring *Vibrio* species in waters, low levels of enteropathogenic *E. coli* in one oyster sample, *V. cholera* found in some oysters, low levels of *Campylobacter*, *Cryptosporidium*, and *V. cholera* O-1 found in waters during the winter, There was no consistency with respect to time, place, or type of sample for those pathogens detected. Based on the levels of pathogens detected and the infectious dose information available, no signifi-cant health threats were distinguished. (8) The safety of shellfish from this area can probably be assured based on conditional criteria that take into account the winter season and rainfall. Unfortunately, the area is so remote that the State is unable to effectively regulate shellfish harvesting on a conditional basis, and the area remains closed to shellfishing.

Summary

In summary, population growth, coastal development, and the extreme variety of estuarine habitats present environmental managers with significant challenges. Land-use and wastewater disposal practices continue to adversely impact water quality throughout the United States. The degradation of many estuarine and marine environments has placed a premium on nearshore areas deemed safe by current sanitary standards for recreational and shellfish harvesting activities. Projected United States population trends, the predicted utilization of coastal areas, and the inevitable human impacts concomitant with these on water quality do not provide much optimism concerning the future status of coastal waters. It seems intuitively obvious that the ongoing struggle to preserve and reclaim nearshore water quality will place increasing demands on our scientific abilities to categorize water quality more precisely, by being able to differentiate human from nonhuman contamination, and by linking usage criteria more to potential health risks and less to merely contaminant loading.

Those attempting to more definitively assess the potential for human health threats present in our aquatic environments, and also those attempting to differentiate relative impacts for pollution abatement, need to utilize new tools and develop alternative databases for future assessments. New techniques to detect a wide variety of pathogens and an array of alternative indicators hold great promise for providing more useful information in these endeavors.

Literature Cited

Abeyta, C. 1983. Comparison of iron milk and official AOAC methods for enumeration of *Clostridium perfringens* from fresh seafoods. *Journal of the Association of Official Analytical Chemists* 66: 1175-1177.

American Public Health Association. 1970. Recommended Procedure for the Examination of Sea Water and Shellfish. 4th Ed. American Public Health Association, Washington, D.C.

American Public Health Association. 1984. Compendium of Methods for the Microbiological Examination of Foods. American Public Health Association, Washington, D.C.

American Public Health Association, American Water Works Association, and Water Environment Federation. 1985. Standard Methods for the Examination of Water and Wastewater. 16th Ed. American Public Health Association, American Water Works Association, Water Environment Federation. Washington, D.C.

American Public Health Association, American Water Works Association, and Water Environment Federation. 1992. Standard Methods for the Examination of Water and Wastewater. 18th Ed. American Public Health Association, American Water Works Association, Water Environment Federation. Washington, D.C.

Bisson, J.W. and V.J. Cabelli. 1979. Membrane filter enumeration method for *Clostridium perfringens*. *Applied and Environmental Microbiology* 37: 55-66.

Burkhardt, W., III and W.D. Watkins. 1992. *Clostridium perfringens* provided the only reliable measure of human contamination in the marine environment, p. 378. *In* Abstracts of the 92nd

General Meeting of the American Society for Microbiology. American Society for Microbiology, Washington, D.C.

Cabelli, V.J. 1983. Health effects criteria for marine recreational waters. United States Environmental Protection Agency report, EMSL, Cincinnati, Ohio. EPA-600/1-80-031.

DeBartolomeis, J. and V.J. Cabelli. 1991. Evaluation of an *Escherichia coli* host strain for enumeration of F male-specific bacteriophage. *Applied and Environmental Microbiology* 57: 1301-1305.

Dufour, A.P. 1980. A 24-hour membrane filter procedure for enumerating enterococci, p. 205. *In* Abstracts of the Annual Meeting of the American Society for Microbiology 1980. American Society for Microbiology, Washington, D.C.

Dufour, A.P. 1984. Health effects criteria for fresh recreational waters. United States Environmental Protection Agency report, EMSL, Cincinnati, Ohio. EPA-600/1/84/004.

Dufour, A.P., E.R. Strickland, and V.J. Cabelli. 1981. Membrane filter method for enumerating *Escherichia coli*. *Applied and Environmental Microbiology* 41: 1152-1158.

Emerson, D.J. and V.J. Cabelli. 1982. Extraction of *Clostridium perfringens* spores from bottom sediment samples. *Applied and Environmental Microbiology* 44: 1144-1149.

Levin, M.A., J.R. Fischer, and V.J. Cabelli. 1975. Membrane filter technique for enumeration of enterococci in marine waters. *Applied Microbiology* 30: 66-71.

Rippey, S.R. 1992. Shellfish-borne disease outbreaks. United States Food and Drug Administration report, North Kingstown, Rhode Island.

Rippey, S.R., W.N. Adams, and W.D. Watkins. 1987. Enumeration of fecal coliforms and *E. coli* in marine and estuarine waters: An alternative approach to the APHA MPN procedure. *Journal of the Water Pollution Control Federation* 59: 795-798.

Rippey, S.R., L.A. Chandler, and W.D. Watkins. 1987. Fluorometric method for enumeration of *Escherichia coli* in molluscan shellfish. *Journal of Food Protection* 50: 685-690.

Rippey, S.R. and W.D. Watkins. 1992. Comparative rates of disinfection of microbial indicator organisms in chlorinated sewage effluents. *Water Science and Technology* 26: 2185-2189.

United States Environmental Protection Agency. 1984. Water quality criteria; request for comments. *Federal Register* 49(102): 21,987.

United States Food and Drug Administration. 1992. National Shellfish Sanitation Program Manual of Operations, Parts I and II. United States Food and Drug Administration, Washington, D.C.

United States Food and Drug Administration and Texas Department of Health. 1990. Cow Trap Lakes—A Study of Pathogens, Indicators, and Classification in a Texas Shellfish Growing Area. United States Food and Drug Administration report, North Kingstown, Rhode Island.

Microbial Biotransformations of Metals:
Effects on Altering the Trophic Availability of Metals

Alan W. Decho

ABSTRACT: The availability and toxicity of metals to consumer animals is strongly influenced by the physical and chemical form of the metal. Microbial cells in natural environments are capable of transforming the physical-chemical form of metals to reduce their toxicity; this is accomplished by several mechanism: biosynthesis of intracellular metal-chelator proteins; precipitation of insoluble metal complexes (e.g., metal-sulfide granules); secretion of extracellular polymers (i.e., exopolymer slimes and capsules); binding to cell walls; energy-dependent rapid efflux systems; biomethylation; and enzymatic oxidation or reduction of metals. A potentially important side effect of microbial transformations is that the trophic availability of metals to consumer animals may be significantly altered. Some microbial transformations can result in metals having an increased bioavailability and/or toxicity to animals, while other microbial transformations may convert metals to less toxic and/or less available forms. The microbial transformation of metals commonly occurs under natural conditions, and represents a fundamental biological mechanism utilized by a wide range of organisms in dealing with metal toxicity. Microbial cells are positioned at the base of most food webs. Therefore, these metal transformation processes can have profound influences on the cycling and bioaccumulation of metals within estuarine and near-coastal food webs. How each transformation mechanism occurs and how such transformations may potentially alter the toxicity, trophic availability, and transfer of metals are discussed.

Introduction

The transformation of toxic substances is a process of considerable environmental importance since the molecular forms of these substances control their persistence, bioaccumulation, and toxicity (Ridley et al. 1977; Buhler and Williams 1988). The bioavailability of toxic metals to consumer animals is strongly influenced by the physical and chemical form of the metal. Both abiotic and biotic transformations of metals occur. Biological transformations are used by a wide range of organisms to deal with the potential toxicity of these elements (Gadd and Griffiths 1978). While many types of biological transformations are known, here they will be defined to emphasize microbial-induced changes to metals, since microorganisms often are an entry point for many toxic metals into food webs.

Microorganisms represent an important vector in the trophic transfer of metals because they can change the form of a metal from a more toxic to a less toxic form or vice versa, and are then consumed by higher trophic levels as food. While metals in aquatic environments exist in both particulate and solute form, particulate forms appear to be the major transfer vectors for at least some metals through food webs (Luoma 1983; Luoma et al. 1992). This is largely because particulates and their associated microorganisms are ingested by many animals during feeding. Microorganisms further represent a key biotic component in food webs which initially interacts with metals in solution and converts them to a particulate form. Therefore, microbial transformations occurring on particulates can have significant influences on metal availability to animals.

Microbial Metal Transformation Mechanisms and Bioavailability

Microbial flora present in estuarine and near-coastal marine environments are exposed to fluctuating, and sometimes locally high, concentrations of metals. The toxicity of metals to microorganisms is influenced by the physiochemical characteristics of its immediate environment, such as pH, Eh, presence of anionic and cationic ions, clay minerals, and organic matter (Beveridge 1989; Collins and Stotzky 1989). A property common to most microbial flora capable of growth in the presence of metals is their ability to reduce the accumulation of free intracellular metal ions (Hughes and Poole 1991). Microorganisms often accomplish this by altering the form of the metal to reduce its toxic effects (Wood and Wang 1983). Several general mechanisms (Fig. 1) are used by microorganisms to transform metals: biosynthesis of intracellular polymers that specifically bind metals (e.g., cysteine-rich proteins and peptides); precipitation of insoluble metal complexes (e.g., metal-sulfide or metal-phosphate granules at cell surfaces); secretion of extracellular polymers (i.e., exopolymer slimes and capsules); direct binding of metals to the cell wall; energy-dependent rapid efflux systems; biomethylation; and enzymatic oxidations or reductions of metals.

Microbial metal transformations, therefore, alter the micropartitioning of metals within a microbial cell, or its immediate extracellular environment. Which physiological mechanism(s) a microbial cell will use to transform a metal depends on a number of factors: the metal; the microbial strain; ambient nutrient conditions; availability of compatible plasmids; and length of exposure to the metal.

PRODUCTION OF "INTRACELLULAR" CHELATOR PROTEINS OR PEPTIDES

Transformation Mechanism

When metals are complexed to organic molecules, they are generally less toxic than the free form of the metal (Babich and Stotzky 1983). Many organisms, therefore, upon prolonged exposure to certain metals will produce specific intracellular proteins or peptides which chelate the free-ion form of a metal.

In higher organisms, metal-chelating proteins, called metallothioneins, have been well studied and show some similarities to metal-chelating proteins in bacteria. Metallothioneins are characterized by a low molecular-weight (usually < 10,000 daltons) and an unusually high cysteine content. About 20-30% of the amino acid residues are cysteine, and they have the capacity to bind 7 mol

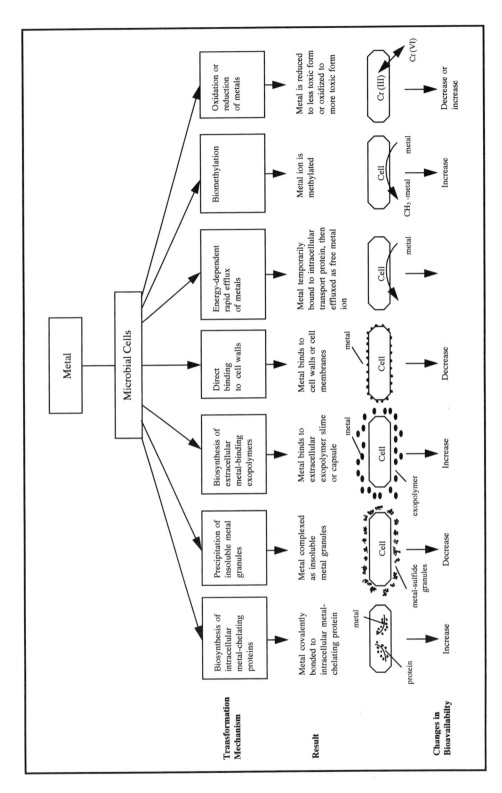

Fig. 1. The major mechanisms of metal biotransformations used by microbial flora. The probable effects on metal bioavailabilities are listed.

7 mol Cd, Zn, or Hg per mole of protein or 12 mol Cu per mole of protein (Engel and Brouwer 1989). The cysteines (Cys) are usually arranged as Cys-X-Cys sequences, where X is an amino acid other than cysteine (Norberg and Kojima 1979). Binding occurs between clusters of thiolate bonds (associated with cysteine) and the metal. The strength of metal binding can vary by over six orders of magnitude, depending on the metal ion (Hamer 1986). Metallothioneins can vary greatly in their chemical and physical properties, especially in lower (nonmammalian) organisms. Studies of the metal-thiolate clusters using [113]Cd-NMR (nuclear magnetic resonance) suggest the sulfur-metal bonds can be periodically broken and reformed, thus giving rise to a number of conformational changes in the overall structure of the protein (Vasak 1986). Within a given organism, several different metal-lothioneins may be produced. In blue crabs, two different metallothionein proteins are induced by cadmium and copper (Engel and Brouwer 1989). In lobsters, two isoforms of a single metallothionein protein have been isolated which are structurally and functionally distinct from each other. One form is thought to be used for copper detoxification, while the other is used as a Cu-donor in the synthesis of hemocyanin (Brouwer and Brouwer-Hoexum 1991).

In bacteria, a variety of intracellular proteins and peptides are produced in response to Cd, Cu, Zn, Hg, Co, Ni, Bi, and Ag (Higham et al. 1984). These proteins, though similar in function to metal-lothioneins, often show distinct compositional differences to metallothioneins. These have been reviewed by Stone and Overnell (1985). The bacterium *Pseudomonas* (Higham et al. 1984, 1986) produces three different Cd-binding proteins (4,000-7,000 daltons) depending on its growth phase (i.e., physiological state). These proteins differ from metallothioneins in having a much lower sulfhy-dral content. Therefore, much of the bound Cd is not associated with cysteine amino acids (as in metallothionein). Khazaeli and Mitra (1981) found a high molecular weight (30,000 daltons) protein was produced by *Escherichia coli* in response to cadmium. The protein chelated 60% of the total bound Cd in cells (Mitra 1984). In the alga *Eucilena gracilis*, two distinct Cd-binding proteins were found which effectively sequestered all cytosolic Cd (Gingrich et al. 1986). These proteins were distinctly different from metallothionein proteins in having a greater negative charge and a higher half-titration pH for metal displacement, and in their amino acid content (Weber et al. 1987). Of special significance in these proteins was the presence of sulfide ions, used in lieu of the cysteine thiolates that normally occur in metallothioneins. Each sulfide could potentially generate two or three times as many Cd-S bonds as does the cysteine in a metallothionein. Metal-chelating proteins have been isolated from the cyanobacterium *Synechococcus* sp. (Olafson et al. 1980), the protozoan *Tetra-hymena pyriformis* (Nakamura et al. 1981), and the bacterium *Alcaligenes eutrophus* CH34 (Remacle and Vercheval 1992). The wide variety of metal-chelating proteins isolated from microorganisms demonstrates how subtle variations in the composition and structure of the proteins can greatly affect their ability to sequester specific metals.

A second major group of intracellular metal-chelating compounds are phytochelatin peptides, which were originally isolated from higher plants (Grill et al. 1985). These peptides are synthesized in response to Cd and a wide range of other metals (Cu, Hg, Pb, Zn, Ag, Au, Sb, Sn, Ni, As, Se), and have been found in diatoms, such as *Thalassiosira*. Metal binding in these peptides occurs by reactivity with sulfhydral groups on cysteine amino acids (i.e., similar to metal binding in metallo-thioneins). Phytochelatins are small cysteine-rich cytosolic peptides and serve analogous functions to metallothioneins (Grill et al. 1987). A major and surprising difference, however, occurs in their structure. The δ-glutamyl linkages present in these peptides suggest they are not synthesized via mRNA (as are most proteins). Instead, phytochelatins are synthesized by the stepwise enzymatic condensation of δ-glutamylcysteine moieties to glutathione and a growing phytochelatin chain containing the cysteines (Grill et al. 1987). These peptides are thought to represent a degradable storage form in the homeostasis of Zn, Cu^{2+}, and Ni^{2+}, needed by plants. Metals such as Cd are extremely toxic to living organisms at low concentrations. They exert their toxic effects by complexing to sulfhydral groups of proteins and amino acids, and inhibiting cellular respiration (Trevors 1989). Therefore, synthesis of these peptides in diatoms can be induced by low levels of Cd exposure.

The application of biochemical and molecular techniques has greatly enhanced our understanding of intracellular metal-chelating proteins. Antibodies have been developed to quantitate metallothionein protein assays (Roesijadi et al. 1989). Analyses of metallothionein proteins is complicated since these proteins are being degraded over time. The metal-filled domains of metallothioneins have been shown to be much more resistant to proteases than unsaturated domains. The rates of biodegradation of metallothioneins within cells, therefore, appear to be dependent on the amount of metal bound, and degradation of unsaturated portions of these proteins may selectively occur. To more precisely quantitate metallothionein turnover rates, highly specific oligonucleotide probes have been developed to measure very accurately the levels of specific mRNA (messenger ribonucleic acid) which translates into metallothionein proteins. At present, this represents a most sensitive means by which to measure specifically metallothionein protein synthesis in response to metal exposure over short time periods.

The biological function(s) of metallothioneins and other metal-chelating proteins is not fully understood. They have been reported to occur throughout the animal, plant, and prokaryote kingdoms (Engel and Brouwer 1989 for review). At present these proteins are thought to function in metal detoxification, in donation of metals to metalloproteins or apometallo-enzymes (Brouwer et al. 1989), and as free-radical scavengers. It seems unlikely, however, that protection against metals is the primary function for such proteins, since basal levels of metallothioneins are relatively high in many organisms (Karin 1985). Hence, their usefulness as a specific biomarker for metal exposure has been questioned recently. These proteins, instead, may be involved in modulating many basic biological processes that involve Zn-requiring enzymes (e.g., replication, transcription, protein synthesis and degradation, energy metabolism).

Effects on Bioavailability

When metals are associated with the cytosolic fractions of cells, they are readily taken up by consumer animals (Reinfelder and Fisher 1991). Since metallothioneins and other metal-chelating proteins represent components of the cytosolic fraction of cells, they may serve as potentially labile vehicles for the efficient transfer of certain metals from microbial cells to consumers. This remains to be empirically tested, however. In addition, given the protection to microbial cells by intracellular metal-chelating proteins and peptides, the presence of such chelator proteins in microorganisms may result in an overall enhanced uptake of metals by microorganisms. The resultant danger would be that certain metals would be transferred with very high efficiencies through the food web (Klerks and Levinton 1988).

PRECIPITATION OF INSOLUBLE METAL GRANULES

Transformation Mechanism

Some microbial flora can precipitate metals in the form of insoluble metal-granules. This represents a strategy for reducing the concentration of free metal ions at the cell surface or within the cell. In some bacteria, this is highly dependent upon the nutrient conditions. For example, during glucose limitation, Cd-sulfide granules are precipitated on cell surfaces by *Klebsiella aerogenes* (Aiking et al. 1982) and *Clostridium thermoaceticum* (Cunningham and Lundie 1993). Cu-, Ni-, Al-, Fe-, and Cr-sulfide granules are precipitated on cell surfaces by the green alga *Cyanidium caldarium* (Wood and Wang 1983). Precipitation occurs by the activities of membrane-associated sulfate reductase enzymes or through the biosynthesis of oxidizing agents such as O_2 or H_2O_2. Toxic metals are thus prevented from entering cells through this extracellular precipitation mechanism. The reduction of sulfate to sulfide, and the diffusion of O_2 and H_2O_2 through cell membranes provides a highly reactive means by which metals can be complexed and precipitated by cells (Wood and Wang 1983). The cyanobacterium *Synechococcus* sp. precipitates Ni granules within its cells. Ni is bioconcentrated in the metal-granules to over 200 times the external concentration (Silver et al. 1981); cells can contain approximately 20% metal on the basis of dry weight. The precipitation of such granules, therefore, represents a highly efficient means to concentrate and detoxify metals.

In anoxic or near-anoxic sulfidogenic environments, geochemical conditions allow much of the Cd to be precipitated abiotically as a sulfide complex. Under other nutrient conditions such as sulfide limitation, however, polymeric cadmium-phosphate complexes are produced in some bacteria. This occurs in *Citrobacter* sp. by enzymatically cleaving the phosphate group from glycerophosphate within the cell (Macaskie and Dean 1984). The metal-phosphate complexes exist within the cell as a diffuse, finely dispersed colloidal suspension (Alking et al. 1984) or as a cell-bound precipitate (Macaskie and Dean 1984). Cd-phosphate granules have also been isolated during the early lag phase of growth in the bacterium *Pseudomonas putida*; up to 40% of the cytoplasmic Cd can be associated with phosphate granules (the remainder was bound to proteins). During the later phases of growth, the polyphosphate granules are metabolized by the bacterium and chelation of Cd occurs via specific intracellular proteins (Higham et al. 1984).

Effects on Bioavailability

The precipitation of insoluble sulfide (or phosphate) granules represents a strategy for reducing the concentration of a free metal ion within the cell or preventing entry of metal ions at the cell surfaces. The metal-complexes and granules formed by these mechanisms consist of highly concentrated forms of metals associated with cells. Owing to the insoluble nature of these granules, these metal complexes probably will not be easily hydrolyzed during enzymatic digestion by consumers. It can be predicted, therefore, that metal-sulfide and metal-phosphate granules will be relatively refractory and nontoxic forms of metals to consumers when compared with other forms of cell-associated Cd. Such a transformation mechanism will likely reduce the bioavailability of a metal.

SECRETION OF EXOPOLYMERS AS EXTRACELLULAR CHELATORS

Transformation Mechanism

Many bacteria when exposed to metals will secrete extracellular polymers (i.e., exopolymers) (Geesey and Jang 1989), which are high molecular-weight anionic molecules. Their secretion represents a strategy by which metal-binding ligands are excreted into the external environment to form relatively stable metal complexes. This reduces the concentrations of metals encountered at the cell surface (Cassity and Kolodziej 1984; Mittleman and Geesey 1985). Exopolymers may be present as a protective "capsule" that immediately surrounds the cell or as the copious, more diffuse slime found in biofilms on particle surfaces and within aggregates.

Metal binding to exopolymers can occur by several mechanisms. The first is through relatively weak ionic bonding to hydroxyl groups (Steiner et al. 1976). Most metal removal by exopolymers in the activated sludge of sewage treatment occurs via this mechanism (Brown and Lester 1979). A second mechanism involves the ionic bonding of metals to carboxyl groups. These ligands tend to select cations with larger ionic radii, such as transition metals (Cr, Mn, Cd, Ag, Fe, Co, Ni, Cu, Zn, Au, etc.). Carboxyl groups are found on the uronic acid residues and ketal-linked pyruvated sugars of exopolymers. Finally, highly-specific covalent bonding can occur via sulfhydral groups, which are present on the cysteine amino acids of exopolymer glycoproteins.

The sorption of metals to exopolymers is a relatively rapid process, taking from minutes to hours (Rudd et al. 1984; Mullen et al. 1989). Metals such as Cu^{2+} and Pb^{2+} will tend to bind faster than Cr^{3+}, Fe^{3+}, and Ni^{2+}. Also, since alkali earth metals (such as K, Ca, Mg, Na) slow the complexing capacity of transition metals (Cr, Mn, Cd, Ag, Fe, Co, Ni, Cu, Zn, Au, Pb) (Hering and Morel 1988), metal binding to exopolymers will be somewhat slower in estuarine and seawater conditions.

The production of exopolymers in response to metals has been reported for a number of bacterial strains (Corpe 1975; Bitton and Freihofer 1978; Rudd et al. 1983; Aislabie and Loutit 1986; Scott and Palmer 1988; McLean et al. 1990; Kurek et al. 1991). For example, bacterial cells protect themselves from Cr toxicity using exopolymers (Aislabie and Loutit 1986). Other bacterial cells possessing exopolymer capsules showed increased survival in 1 mM Cd when compared to non-encapsulated cells (Bitton and Freihofer 1978). Similarly, exopolymer capsules produced by the alga *Chlorella stigmatophora* reduced metal toxicity by chelation of metals to uronic acid residues (Kaplan et al. 1987).

Finally, the exopolymer capsule matrix closely surrounding microbial cells also serves as a site for microbial oxidation and reductions of metals (see below). This matrix is thought to localize the specific extracellular enzymes involved in Fe and Mn oxidation reactions (Nealson et al. 1988). Specific extracellular Cu-chelating proteins isolated from the marine bacterium *Vibrio alginolyticus* (Harwood-Sears and Gordon 1990; Schreiber et al. 1990; Gordon et al. 1993) may be localized in a similar manner. Exopolymer secretions, therefore, serve as an extracellular chelator matrix and provide a protective microenvironment for the cells enclosed within it.

Effects on Bioavailability

Production of exopolymers in response to metals has been reported for a large number of bacterial and microalgal strains. The adsorptive capacities and easily digestible nature of exopolymers predisposes these secretions to be efficient transfer vehicles for metals in lower food webs. Due to the wide range of binding affinities of many exopolymer ligands, a portion of the bound metals can be easily removed from exopolymers during gut passage. Exopolymers frequently occur as a diffuse slime on the surfaces of particles and suspended aggregates in estuarine systems. These exopolymers often represent highly labile carbon forms (Decho and Moriarty 1990), which are readily ingested by deposit-feeding and suspension-feeding animals. It has been shown experimentally that exopolymers can be potentially significant vectors for enhancing the transfer of bound metals, such as Cd, Ag, Zn, and Cr(III), to consumers (Harvey and Luoma 1985; Bremer and Loutit 1986).

CELL WALL BINDING

Transformation Mechanism

Bacterial cell walls have a high metal-binding capacity for a wide variety of metals (Beveridge and Murray 1976, 1980; Beveridge 1978, 1981; Doyle 1989). The cell walls of gram-negative and gram-positive bacteria differ with respect to their basic design, and this can affect metal binding (Ferris 1989). In gram-positive bacteria, such binding occurs via select sites such as amino, phosphate, and carboxyl groups (Doyle et al. 1980). In gram-negative bacteria a wide range of metals (Na, Ca, Mg, Sr, Ni, Mn, Pb, and Fe) have been shown to bind to the anionic phosphate groups of the cell membrane and to carboxyl groups of the cell wall (Beveridge 1981; Hoyle and Beveridge 1983; Ferris and Beveridge 1985; Ferris 1989). This occurs because these groups are negatively charged at a circumneutral pH (James 1982). The high density of electronegative sites within the cell wall allows it to form metal-precipitates under select conditions (McLean and Beveridge 1990).

At low ambient metal concentrations, cell wall binding will effectively reduce the concentration of metals reaching the intracellular portions of the cell (Beveridge and Koval 1981). However, the metabolic activity of a bacteria cell also affects its ability to complex metals to the cell walls. In actively metabolizing bacterial cells, there is a continuous pumping of H^+ protons into the cell wall, where negatively charged groups are located, and no competition occurs between H^+ and the metal ions (Urrutia-Mera et al. 1992). Therefore, less metal is bound to the cell walls of very active cells, when compared to less active or recently dead cells.

Metal binding to bacterial cell walls can be of potential importance in estuarine systems for several reasons. First, when freshwater bacteria enter metal-polluted estuarine systems, the increased salinity will decrease greatly the activity of many of these bacteria (even killing some cells). The decreased activity could potentially increase metal binding to the cell walls by the mechanism outlined above. Second, the vast majority of bacteria in estuarine and coastal marine sediments are thought to exist in a state of very low activity; a physiological state which will enhance metal binding to cell walls.

Effects on Bioavailability

How a microbial cell partitions a metal among the intracellular fluid, cell walls, and membranes can affect the absorption of that metal by a microbial consumer. Bacteria bind a wide variety of cationic metals to their cell surfaces. In studies directly examining the absorption of metals associated with cell walls, Reinfelder and Fisher (1991) found that the assimilation efficiency of copepods for a wide variety of metals was positively correlated with how much of the metal was associated with the intracellular fluid of the microbial cell. Elements associated with cell walls and membranes were not efficiently taken up by the copepods. Such data have enormous implications because they clearly demonstrate that the micropartitioning of metals within a microbial cell can differentially affect their availability to certain animals. In other animals that possess a different type of digestive system, metals associated with bacteria cell walls could be efficiently taken up. The absorption of cell-wall-bound metals will be highly dependent on the animal's digestive system.

ENERGY-DEPENDENT RAPID EFFLUX SYSTEMS

Transformation Mechanism

Another strategy used by bacteria is an energy-dependent efflux mechanism for the rapid removal of metals from within the cell. In many bacteria, this is a plasmid-mediated resistance to Cd, Zn, and Co (Tynecka et al. 1981; Laddaga et al. 1985; Nies and Silver 1989). Cd is taken up by the manganese transport system in *Staphylococcus aureus* and the Zn active transport system in *Escherichia coli* (Laddaga and Silver 1985). Arsenate enters *E. coli* via the phosphate-transport systems, even though the system has a 100 times higher affinity for phosphate than for arsenate (Silver et al. 1989). Once the metal reaches the intracellular cytoplasm, it is rapidly pumped out by a highly specific efflux system. The primary mechanism is an exchange of Cd^{2+} for $2H^+$. It derives its energy either from the pH gradient across the membrane or directly from ATP. While in the cell, Cd has been shown to be temporarily bound to the cadA polypeptide, which contains strategically positioned cysteine amino acids to bind the Cd. This peptide is a member of a group of cation translocating ATPase proteins and peptides that have been found in both gram-negative and gram-positive bacteria. In Hg-resistant bacteria, similar proteins (e.g., merA) function to transport Hg out of cells. Analogous efflux mechanisms have been found for resistance to tetracycline (an antibiotic), arsenic, cadmium, and chromate in bacteria (Silver et al. 1989). This is because the genes for heavy metal resistance, quite similar to those for antibiotic resistances, are "packaged" on the same bacteria plasmids and transposons. Such plasmids or transposons (and their associated metal-resistance mechanisms) can be rapidly transferred across competent microbial populations, an asset for cellular survival.

Effects on Bioavailability

Energy-dependent rapid efflux systems allow cells to take up toxic metal via the transport systems for essential metals. The metal ions are quickly associated with a transport protein(s) during this uptake, which weakly chelates the metal ions. While the metal ions are within the cell they will be associated with cytosolic proteins, which are potentially labile to consumer animals. Studies have shown that the transport proteins which temporarily bind metals while present in the cell, do not chelate Cd as tightly as do the metallothionein proteins (discussed earlier) (Perry and Silver 1982), and therefore may represent labile vehicles similar to other intracellular metal-chelating proteins. This should, therefore, represent a mechanism that enhances the bioavailability of the metal ions. An important point about energy-dependent efflux systems is that metal ions are quickly effluxed, at which time they regain their free-ion form. The overall effect of this mechanism is that it does not alter the form of the metal, and therefore facilitates the cycling of the free-ion form of the metal.

BIOMETHYLATION

Transformation Mechanism

The biomethylation of metals is an environmentally important transformation mechanism used by certain bacteria to detoxify metals such as Hg, Au, Sn, Pb, Pd, Pt, Tl, Cr, and metalloids such as As and Se (Thayer and Brinkman 1982; Wood and Wang 1983). Mercuric ions, for example, are extremely toxic since they bind to sulfhydral groups on proteins and inhibit enzyme activities. Therefore bacteria have evolved mechanisms to methylate Hg and other metals. While methyl mercury is more toxic than inorganic Hg to most organisms, it is less toxic to the specific bacteria responsible for the methylations. This is because biomethylation results in the synthesis of less polar organometallic compounds from polar inorganic ions. This has distinct advantages for cellular elimination by diffusion-mediated processes (Wood 1975). Even a single CH_3 group present on a metal(loid) will cause sharp changes in the metals volatility and water-lipid solubility (Thayer and Brinkman 1982).

Of the metals that may undergo microbial methylation, mercury is one of the best understood (Robinson and Tuovinen 1984). Greater than 80% of the mercury found in fish caught for human consumption is in the form of methylmercury (CH_2Hg^+) (Westoo 1973). This form is 50 to 100 times more toxic than Hg^{2+} (Bakir et al. 1973), although the latter is the primary form found in marine waters. While human activities over the last 100 years have added less than 1% of the total mercury found in oceans (Weiss et al. 1971), areas closely associated with human activities, such as estuaries and bays, can show locally high concentrations. It is within these estuarine systems where methylations most commonly occur and exert a significant trophic effect.

Studies thus far indicate that biomethylations can occur by two major mechanisms. The first mechanism involves the transfer of a methyl free-radical to a metal complexed on the corin ring of the vitamin B12 molecule (Collins and Stotzky 1989). The second mechanism involves the methyl group transfer from methyl-vitamin B12 to the heavy metal. This involves electrophilic attack by metals on the Co-C bond of the methyl B12. This latter pathway commonly occurs in bacteria living in estuarine sediments. These bacteria can carry out mercury methylation by excreting methylcobalamin, which serves as a methyl donor in vitro (Summers and Silver 1978). This process is very likely the primary route for the methylation and mobilization of mercury from sediments in polluted waters. Aerobic bacteria as well as anaerobic sediment bacteria can methylate mercury. The methylation of tin also can take place in the presence of methylcobalamin (Summers and Silver 1978).

Once methylation has occurred, the methyl mercury is released from the microbial system and enters food webs as a consequent of its rapid diffusion rate. Methyl mercury is much more bioavailable because it passes more easily through membranes, owing to its higher lipid solubility, than Hg^{2+}. Many of the plasmids having genetic antibiotic-resistance also carry resistance to Hg^{2+} (Schoftel et al. 1974). The ability for mercury methylation and resistance has been shown to be carried on special genetic elements (transposons) of plasmids (Kleckner 1977). In the simplest sense these elements are "hopping genes," which can move from plasmid to plasmid or from plasmid to chromosome, carrying the genes with them. Therefore, the physiological capability for mercury resistance can be transferred rapidly throughout certain microbial populations.

Methylations of other metals has also been demonstrated. Lead can be methylated by sediment microorganisms (Jarvie et al. 1975). Tetramethyllead is more toxic to algae than either trimethyllead or inorganic lead (Silverberg et al. 1976). Arsenic is methylated in a similar manner to mercury but using a different enzyme (McBride and Wolfe 1971). Selenium can also be methylated by bacteria (Barkes and Fleming 1974; Doran and Alexander 1977).

An important role in the biological cycling of mercury and lead is played by sulfide. H_2S is very effective at volatilization and precipitation of mercury through diproportion H_2 chemistry in aquatic environments. In estuaries and coastal zones, the mobilization of Hg from water to atmosphere occurs where *Desulfovibrio* species have access to sulfate in anaerobic ecosystems. Once in the atmosphere, volatile forms of organometallics, such as dimethylmercury, are unstable because metal-carbon bonds are susceptible to homeolytic cleavage by light (Wood and Wang 1983).

Effects on Bioavailability

Many different metals can undergo methylation. The ability of microorganisms to biomethylate metals is a plasmid-mediated process. Therefore, this ability can be transferred quickly throughout competent (i.e., capable of plasmid uptake) microbial populations. Biomethylations can significantly affect the cycling and toxicity of metals in estuaries and coastal marine systems. This is one of the few microbial transformation mechanisms for which many studies exist concerning the changes in bioavailability and toxicity of metals. In general, biomethylation processes open new pathways for metal transfer through air, water, and/or food webs. The overall higher lipid solubility of methyl mercury, compared to Hg^{2+}, accounts for its preferential incorporation into food webs. Such processes occur under both oxic and anoxic conditions (Robinson and Tuovinen 1984).

ENZYMATIC OXIDATION OR REDUCTION OF METALS

Transformation Mechanism

The oxidation or reduction of a metal is an enzymatically mediated strategy used by bacterial cells to reduce toxicity (Silver et al. 1989). Bacteria utilize intracellular and extracellular oxidases and reductases, which function as alkylating enzymes or dealkylating lyases, to add or remove covalently attached components of organometal compounds. This is a major microbial resistance mechanism used to detoxify inorganic and organic mercury compounds (Silver et al. 1989). Arsenite oxidations and chromate reductions (i.e., CR-VI to Cr-III) convert metal ions from a more toxic form into a less toxic form. For example, in the bacterium *Pseudomonas fluorescens,* the more toxic form of chromium (Cr-VI) has been shown to be enzymatically reduced to a less soluble and less toxic form (Cr-III) (Bopp and Ehrlich 1988). While it is suspected that these metabolic capabilities are plasmid-mediated, this has not been demonstrated.

Enzymatic oxidations have been well studied for the essential metal manganese (Mn). Intracellular Mn-binding and -oxidizing proteins have been isolated in a *Pseudomonas* sp. Mn oxidation involves the microbially-mediated formation of Mn oxides. This occurs outside the bacterial cell, where extracellular polymers first bind the Mn, then either autooxidation occurs because of the high Mn concentration, or Mn is oxidized by specific Mn-oxidizing proteins (Ghiorse 1984). Extracellular binding and oxidizing proteins have been isolated in *Leptothrix discophora* (Boogerd and de Vrind 1987; Adams and Ghiorse 1987). This same bacterium also secretes an iron-oxidizing protein (15,000 daltons) (Corstjens et al. 1992). The Fe-oxidizing proteins also are closely associated with an exopolymer sheath surrounding the cells. The exopolymers may serve to localize and concentrate the proteins (Nealson et al. 1988; Emerson and Ghiorse 1992).

Selenium (Se) is an example of a metal whose molecular form can greatly influence its toxicity. Optimal reduction of selenite and selenate to elemental Se occurs aerobically by *Pseudomonas stutzeri* (Lortie et al. 1992) and other bacteria (Doran and Alexander 1977; Maiers et al. 1988; Macy et al. 1989). Oxidation of elemental Se to selenite by *Bacillus meciaterium* also occurs (Sarathchandra and Watkinson 1981). Bacterial oxidations and reductions of metals are thought to occur in a wide range of bacteria under both oxic and anoxic conditions.

Effects on Bioavailability

The oxidation or reduction of a metal converts metal ions from more toxic forms into less toxic forms (although the reverse is also possible). Such a mechanism, therefore, will most often reduce the toxicity of a metal to animals consuming the bacteria. Very few studies have directly examined how specific microbial transformations change the bioavailability and toxicity of metals to consumer animals. Utilizing the limited available data and theoretical work, however, it can be predicted that certain transformation mechanisms will likely enhance the bioavailability of a metal. Such mechanisms include sequestering of metals by specific intracellular proteins or peptides, biomethylations, and the secretions of extracellular polymers. In contrast, other transformation mechanisms will likely reduce the bioavailability of a metal. These include the binding of metals to cell walls, and the precipitation of insoluble metal-granules.

Other Considerations in Assessing Microbial Transformation Effects on Metal Bioavailability

The partitioning of metals at the cellular and molecular levels may be particularly important because metals associated with cell walls, intracellular proteins, insoluble granules, or extracellular forms may have very different bioavailabilities to a consumer. Several other factors, however, can interact in affecting the bioavailability of metals from microbially altered food sources, and must be considered when assessing these effects empirically. These factors mainly relate to the digestive processing of the food and periodic changes in food concentrations. Once food material has been ingested, these factors will dictate, in part, how efficiently the metal is absorbed by a consumer animal.

An important constraint in absorption of metals from food involves the different types of digestive processing of food by the consumer. How efficiently an animal absorbs carbon and metals from a given food can be influenced greatly by the type of digestive processing, which can differ depending on the type of consumer animal (Penry and Jumars 1986). For example, some deposit-feeding polychaetes possess a "straight-tube" digestive tract that utilizes primarily "extracellular" digestion (Fig. 2A). Ingested food is passed from the stomach to the intestines, where absorption occurs. Certain forms of metals, such as Cr-III, do not readily cross the intestinal lumen, and are therefore not absorbed by this type of processing.

In contrast, other animals such as bivalves possess a two-phase digestive tract (Widdows et al. 1979) that utilizes an "intestinal digestion pathway" similar in design to the straight-tube polychaete gut and a "glandular digestion pathway", in which food is passed from the stomach to a digestive gland (Fig. 2B). Within the digestive gland, very efficient "intracellular" digestion occurs after endocytosis of the food particle. During normal food processing, a portion of the ingested food is processed by the glandular pathway, and the remainder by the intestinal pathway. It is now known that the absorption efficiency of certain metals is affected significantly by how much food is processed by either pathway (Decho and Luoma 1991). Absorption of Cr-III associated with

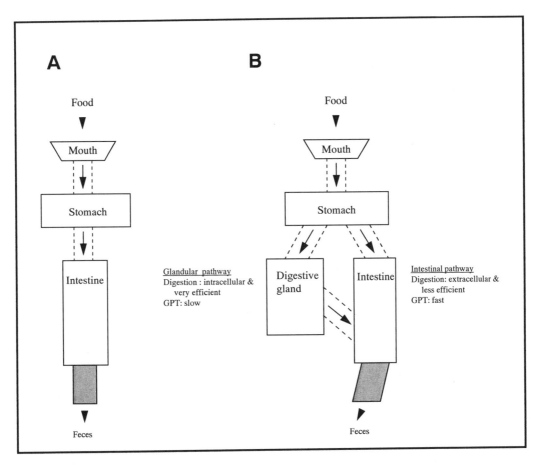

Fig. 2. Digestive tract designs: A) the "straight-tube" intestinal digestive tract, found in polychaetes and most other animals; and B) the two-phase digestive tract, found in many bivalves, which utilizes both intestinal and glandular digestion. GPT = gut-passage time.

bacterial cells does not occur by the intestinal pathway, instead, it is limited to food processed by the glandular digestion pathway. Differences in the gut architecture of an animal, therefore, can affect significantly how efficiently metals are passed from microbial food sources to consumers. In deposit-feeding worms such as *Streblospio benedicti*, sediment, cellular, and extracellular carbon (i.e., bacteria, microalgae, exopolymer secretions, etc.) and their associated metals, are all ingested and processed similarly through the straight-tube digestive tract. By contrast, in clams, exopolymers are primarily processed via the intestinal pathway, while cellular materials often are processed by either glandular or intestinal digestion, depending on food concentration. If higher proportions of the cellular materials (and their associated metals) are shunted to the digestive gland, then more efficient intracellular digestion and absorption of metals may occur. Some metal forms are not absorbed by either process in clams (e.g., Fe-oxide bound Cr-III) (Decho and Luoma 1994).

Another factor affecting absorption efficiencies of food (and metals from food) is food concentration, which can vary greatly over a tidal cycle in natural estuarine systems. The effects are especially apparent in bivalves because concentration influences how much food is processed via the glandular digestion pathway, which is more efficient in absorbing some metals than the intestinal digestion pathway. For example, at high food concentrations, smaller amounts of the total ingested food material will be processed by the glandular pathway. Instead, most of the food will be processed via intestinal digestion, which is comparatively less efficient in absorbing metals such as Cr (Decho and Luoma 1991). At lower food concentrations, a higher proportion of a given food type may be processed via glandular digestion, resulting in more efficient absorption of metals from the food. In animals such as polychaetes, which possess a straight-tube digestive tract, food concentrations can affect gut-passage rates, in turn, affecting absorption efficiencies. Food concentrations, therefore, can have potentially profound effects on the absorption of certain forms of metals (e.g., metals associated with cell walls or granules) from microbial food sources. Such processes may exert significant short-term influences on metal bioavailability and uptake in different environments (i.e., food-limited versus food-rich areas).

The bioavailability and absorption of metals that have been "transformed" by microorganisms, therefore, can vary depending on the form of the metal, the type of digestion, and the concentration of food particles. Thus, a range of animals having different gut-architectures should be utilized to examine the magnitude of such processes on the trophic transfer of metals.

Significance of Microbial Transformation Processes to Metal Bioavailability

The mechanisms regulating the transfer of metals from particulate food sources to animals are very poorly understood. Microbial metal transformations influence the micropartitioning of metals within a microbial cell or in its immediate extracellular environment, which can potentially increase or decrease the bioavailability and toxicity of metals to higher trophic levels.

Microbial flora living in sediments and on particles suspended in the water column are exposed to highly variable concentrations of metals. Specific gradients and microenvironments are created as a result of cellular activities in proximity to the cells. It is within these microenvironments that the form of a metal can be greatly altered, depending on which transformation process has occurred there. Some microbial transformations can result in metals having an increased bioavailability and toxicity, while other microbial transformations may convert metals to less toxic or less available forms. The transformations potentially change the chemistry and availability of the metal to a consumer ingesting these particles. Since microbial cells and their associated metals are readily consumed by deposit-feeding and suspension-feeding animals, these transformation processes can directly influence the cycling of metals within estuarine and near-coastal systems.

Microbial metal transformation represents a fundamental biological mechanism that has been virtually overlooked, but one that can significantly influence the bioavailability and environmental fate of metals throughout estuarine and near-coastal systems. Microorganisms are a key biotic component that initially interacts with metals, and are known to be important components in the biogeochemical cycling of metals and other toxic compounds in coastal systems. They represent an important intermediate vector in metal cycling because they create microenvironments that can change the form and availability of a metal and they are ingested by animals as food. An important aspect of microbial transformations is that they have the potential to significantly increase or decrease the bioavailability and toxicity of metals to higher trophic levels. These changes can have serious effects on the environmental fate of the metals. The transformations of metals by microorganisms, and their resulting interactions with major consumer animals will ultimately affect the dispersal and distribution of metals within estuarine and near-coastal systems.

The microbial transformation of metals is a commonly occurring process in natural environments. Similar types of transformations occur at the biochemical level in many plant and animal species. Employing first-order mechanisms to determine the bioavailability of microbially altered metals will provide insight into overall processes controlling bioavailability of metals in sediments and suspended particles. Understanding these processes will enable prediction of the bioavailability of metals in both freshwater and marine systems, in food-rich versus food-poor environments, in the mobilization (or immobilization) of metals, in food-web transfer in other systems, and in the possible bioremediation of heavily polluted sites.

LITERATURE CITED

Adams, L. and W.C. Ghiorse. 1987. Characterization of an extracellular Mn^{2+}-oxidizing activity and isolation of Mn^{2+}-oxidizing protein from *Leptothrix discophora* SS-1. *Journal of Bacteriology* 169: 1279-1285.

Aiking, H., K. Kok, H. van Heerikhuizen, and J. van T'Riet. 1982. Adaptation to cadmium by *Klebsiella aerogenes* growing in continuous culture proceeds mainly via formation of cadmium sulfide. *Applied and Environmental Microbiology* 44: 938-944.

Aiking, H., A. Stijnman, C. van Garderen, H. van Heerikhuizen, and J. van T'Riet. 1984. Inorganic phosphate accumulation and cadmium detoxification in *Klebsiella aerogenes* NCTC 418 growing in continuous culture. *Applied and Environmental Microbiology* 47: 374-377.

Aislabie, J. and M.W. Loutit. 1986. Accumulation of Cr(III) by bacteria isolated from polluted sediment. *Marine Environmental Research* 20: 221-232.

Babich, H. and G. Stotzky. 1983. Further studies on environmental factors that modify the toxicity of nickel to microbes. *Regulatory Toxicology and Pharmacology* 3: 82.

Barkes, L. and R.W. Fleming. 1974. Production of dimethylselenide gas from inorganic selenium by eleven soil fungi. *Bulletin of Environmental Contamination and Toxicology* 12: 308-311.

Bakir, F., S.F. Damluji, L. Amin-Zaki, M. Murtadha, A. Khalidi, N.Y. Al-Rawi, S. Tikriti, H.I. Dhahir, T.W. Clarkson, J.C. Smith, and R.A. Doherty. 1973. Methylmercury poisoning in Iraq. *Science* 181: 230-241.

Beveridge, T.J. 1978. The response of cell walls of *Bacillus subtilus* to metals and to electron microscope stains. *Canadian Journal of Microbiology* 24: 89-104.

Beveridge, T.J. 1981. Ultrastructure, chemistry and function of the bacterial cell wall. *International Reviews in Cytology* 72: 229-317.

Beveridge, T.J. 1989. Metal ions and bacteria, p. 1-30. *In* T.J. Beveridge and R.J. Doyle (eds.), Metal Ions and Bacteria. John Wiley and Sons, New York.

Beveridge, T.J. and R.G.E. Murray. 1976. Uptake and retention of metals by cell walls of *Bacillus subtilus*. *Journal of Bacteriology* 127: 1502-1518.

Beveridge, T.J. and R.G.E. Murray. 1980. Sites of metal deposition in the cell wall of *Bacillus subtilus*. *Journal of Bacteriology* 141: 876-887.

Beveridge, T.J. and S.F. Koval. 1981. Binding of metals to cell envelopes of *Escherichia coli* K-12. *Applied and Environmental Microbiology* 42: 325-335.

Bitton, G. and V. Freihofer. 1978. Influence of extracellular polysaccharides on the toxicity of copper and cadmium toward *Klebsiella aerogenes*. *Microbial Ecology* 4: 119-125.

Boogerd, R.C. and J.P.M. de Vrind. 1987. Manganese oxidation by *Leptothrix discophora*. *Journal of Bacteriology* 169: 489-494.

Bopp, L.H. and H.L. Ehrlich. 1988. Chromate resistance and reduction in *Pseudomonas fluorescens* strain LB300. *Archives of Microbiology* 150: 426-431.

Bremer, P.J. and M.W. Loutit. 1986. Bacterial polysaccharide as a vehicle for entry of Cr(III) to a food chain. *Marine Environmental Research* 20: 235-248.

Brouwer, M., D.R. Winge, and W.R. Gray. 1989. Structural and functional diversity of copper-metallothioneins from the American lobster, *Homarus americanus*. *Journal of Inorganic Biochemistry* 35: 289-303.

Brouwer, M. and Brouwer-Hoexum. 1991. Interaction of copper-metallothionein from the American lobster, *Homarus americanus*, with glutathione. *Archives of Biochemistry and Biophysics* 290: 207-213.

Brown, M.J. and J.N. Lester. 1979. Metal removal in activated sludge: The role of bacterial extracellular polymers. *Water Research* 13: 817-837.

Buhler, D.R. and D.E. Williams 1988. The role of biotransformations in the toxicity of chemicals. *Aquatic Toxicology* 11: 19-28.

Cassity, T.R. and B.J. Kolodziej. 1984. Role of the capsule produced by *Bacillus megaterium* ATCC 19213 in the accumulation of metallic cations. *Microbios* 41: 117-125.

Collins, Y.E. and G. Stotzky. 1989. Factors affecting the toxicity of heavy metals to microbes, p. 31-90. *In* T.J. Beveridge and R.J. Doyle (eds.), Metal Ions and Bacteria. John Wiley and Sons, New York

Corpe, W. 1975. Metal-binding properties of surface materials from marine bacteria. *Developments in Industrial Microbiology* 16: 249-255.

Corstjens, P.L.A.M., J.P.M. DeVrind, P. Westroek, and E.W. DeVrind-DeJong. 1992. Enzymatic iron oxidation by *Leptothrix discophora:* Identification of an iron-oxidizing protein. *Applied and Environmental Microbiology* 58: 450-454.

Cunningham, D.P. and L.L. Lundie. 1993. Precipitation of cadmium by *Clostridium thermoaceticum*. *Applied and Environmental Microbiology* 59: 7-14.

Decho, A.W. and S.N. Luoma. 1991. Time-courses in the retention of food material in the bivalves *Potamocorbula amurensis* and *Macoma balthica:* Significance to the absorption of carbon and chromium. *Marine Ecology Progress Series* 78: 303-314.

Decho, A.W. and S.N. Luoma. 1994. Humic and fulvic acids: Sink or source in the availability of metals to the marine bivalves *Macoma balthica* and *Potamocorbula amurensis*? *Marine Ecology Progress Series* 108: 133-145.

Decho, A.W. and D.J.W. Moriarty. 1990. Bacterial exopolymer utilization by a harpacticoid copepod: A methodology and results. *Limnology and Oceanography* 35: 1039-1049.

Doran, J.W. and M. Alexander. 1977. Microbial transformations of selenium. *Applied Environmental Microbiology* 33: 31-37.

Doyle, R.J. 1989. How cell walls of gram-positive bacteria interact with metal ions, p. 275-294. *In* T.J. Beveridge and R.J. Doyle (eds.), Metal Ions and Bacteria. John Wiley and Sons, New York.

Doyle, R.J., T.H. Matthews, and U.N. Streips. 1980. Chemical basis for selectivity of metal ions by the *Bacillus subtilis* cell wall. *Journal of Bacteriology* 143: 471-480.

Emerson, D. and W.C. Ghiorse. 1992. Isolation, cultural maintenance, and taxonomy of a sheath-forming strain of *Leptothrix discophora* and characterization of manganese-oxidizing activity associated with the sheath. *Applied and Environmental Microbiology* 58: 4001-4010.

Engel, D.W. and M. Brouwer. 1989. Metallothionein and metallothionein-like proteins: Physiological importance. *Advances in Comparative Environmental Physiology* 4: 53-75.

Ferris, F.G. 1989. Metallic ion interactions with the outer membrane of gram-negative bacteria, p. 295-324. *In* T.J. Beveridge and R.J. Doyle (eds.), Metal Ions and Bacteria. John Wiley and Sons, New York.

Ferris, F.G. and T.J. Beveridge. 1985. Functions of bacterial cell surface structures. *Bioscience* 35: 172-177.

Gadd, G.M. and A.J. Griffiths. 1978. Microorganisms and heavy metal toxicity. *Microbial Ecology* 4: 303-317.

Geesey, G.G. and L. Jang. 1989. Interactions between metal ions and capsular polymers, p. 325-357. *In* T.J. Beveridge and R.J. Doyle (eds.), Metal Ions and Bacteria. John Wiley and Sons, New York.

Ghiorse, W. C. 1984. Biology of iron- and manganese-depositing bacteria. *Annual Review of Microbiology* 38: 515-550.

Gingrich, D.J., D.N. Weber, C.F. Shaw, J.S. Garvey, and D.H. Petering. 1986. Characterization of a highly negative and labile binding protein induced in *Euglena gracilis* by cadmium. *Environmental Health Perspectives* 65: 77-85.

Gordon, A.S., V.J. Harwood, and S. Sayyar. 1993. Growth, copper-tolerant cells, and extracellular protein production in copper-stressed chemostat cultures of *Vibrio alginolyticus*. *Applied and Environmental Microbiology* 59: 60-66.

Grill, E., E.L. Winnacker, and M.H. Zenk. 1985. Phytochelatins: The principal heavy-metal complexing peptides of higher plants. *Science* 230: 674-676.

Grill, E., E.L. Winnacker, and M.H. Zenk. 1987. Phytochelatins, a class of heavy-metal-binding peptides from plants, are functionally analogous to metallothioneins. *Proceedings of the National Academy of Sciences* 84: 439-443.

Hamer, D.H. 1986. Metallothionein. *Annual Review of Biochemistry* 55: 913-951.

Harvey, R.W. and S.N. Luoma. 1985. Effect of adherent bacteria and bacterial extracellular polymers upon assimilation of *Macoma balthica* of sediment-bound Cd, Zn, and Ag. *Marine Ecology Progress Series* 22: 281-289.

Harwood-Sears, V. and A.S. Gordon. 1990. Copper-induced production of copper-binding supernatant proteins by the marine bacterium *Vibrio alginolyticus*. *Applied and Environmental Microbiology* 56: 1327-1332.

Hering, J.G. and F.M.M. Morel. 1988. Kinetics of trace metal complexation: Role of alkaline earth metals. *Environmental Science and Technology* 22: 1469-1478.

Higham, D.P., P.J. Sadler, and M.D. Scawen. 1984. Cadmium-resistant *Pseudomonas putida* synthesizes novel cadmium proteins. *Science* 225: 1043-1046.

Higham, D.P., P.J. Sadler, and M.D. Scawen. 1986. Cadmium-binding proteins in *Pseudomonas putida*: Pseudothioneins. *Environmental Health Perspectives* 65: 5-11.

Hoyle, B.D. and T.J. Beveridge. 1983. Binding of metallic ions to the outer membrane of *Escherichia coli*. *Applied and Environmental Microbiology* 46: 749-752.

Hughes, M.N. and R.K. Poole. 1991. Metal speciation and microbial growth—The hard (and soft) facts. *Journal of General Microbiology* 137: 725-734.

James, A.M. 1982. The electrical properties and topochemistry of bacterial cells. *Advances in Colloid Interface Science* 15: 171-221.

Jarvie, A.W.P., R.N. Markall, and H.R. Potter. 1975. Chemical alkylation of lead. *Nature (London)* 255: 217-218.

Kaplan, D., D. Christiaen, and S. Arad. 1987. Chelating properties of extracellular polysaccharides from *Chlorella* spp. *Applied and Environmental Microbiology* 53: 2953-2956.

Karin, M. 1985. Metallothionein: Proteins in search of function. *Cell* 41: 9-10.

Kennedy, A.F.D. and I.W. Sutherland. 1987. Analysis of bacterial exopolysaccharides. *Biotechnology and Applied Biochemistry* 9: 12-19.

Khazaeli, M.B. and R.S. Mitra. 1981. Cadmium-binding component in *Escherichia coli* during accommodation to low levels of this ion. *Applied and Environmental Microbiology* 41: 46-50.

Kleckner, N. 1977. Translocatable elements in procaryotes: Review. *Cell* 11: 11-23.

Klerks, P.L. and J. Levinton. 1988. Effects of heavy metals in a polluted aquatic environment, p. 57-84. *In* S.A. Levin, G.R. Kelly, and M.A. Harwell (eds.), Ecotoxicology: Problems and Approaches. Springer, Berlin.

Kurek, E., A.J. Francis, and J.-M. Bollag. 1991. Immobilization of Cd by microbial extracellular products. *Archives of Environmental Contamination and Toxicology* 20: 106-111.

Laddaga, R.A. and S. Silver. 1985. Cadmium uptake in *Escherichia coli* K12. *Journal of Bacteriology* 162: 1100-1105.

Laddaga, R.A., R. Bessen, and S. Silver. 1985. Cadmium-resistant mutant of *Bacillus subtilus* 168 with reduced cadmium transport. *Journal of Bacteriology* 162: 1106-1110.

Lortie, L., W.D. Gould, S. Rajan, R.G.L. McCready, and K.-J. Cheng. 1992. Reduction of selenate and selenite to elemental selenium by a *Pseudomonas stutzeri* isolate. *Applied and Environmental Microbiology* 58: 4042-4044.

Luoma, S.N. 1983. Bioavailability of trace metals to aquatic organisms—A review. *Science of the Total Environment* 28: 1-22.

Luoma, S.N., C. Johns, N.S. Fisher, N.A. Steinberg, R.S. Oremiand, and J.R. Reinfelder. 1992. Determination of selenium bioavailability to a benthic bivalve from particulate and solute pathways. *Environmental Science and Technology* 26: 485-491.

Macaskie, L.E. and A.C.R. Dean. 1984. Cadmium accumulation by a *Citrobacter* sp. *Journal of General Microbiology* 130: 53-62.

Macy, J.M., T.A. Michel, and D.G. Kirsch. 1989. Selenate reduction by a *Pseudomonas* species: A new mode of anaerobic respiration. *FEMS Microbiology Letters* 61: 195-198.

Maiers, D.T., P.L. Wichlacz, D.L Thompson, and D.F. Bruhn. 1988. Selenate reduction by bacteria from a selenium-rich environment. *Applied and Environmental Microbiology* 54: 2591-2593.

McBride, B.C. and R.S. Wolfe. 1971. Biosynthesis of dimethylarsine by methanobacterium. *Biochemistry* 10: 4312-4317.

McLean, R.J.C. and T.J. Beveridge. 1990. Metal binding capacity of bacterial surfaces and their ability to form mineralized aggregate, p. 185-222. *In* H.L. Erhlich and C.L. Brierley (eds.), Microbial Mineral Recovery. McGraw-Hill Publishing Company, New York.

McLean, R.J.C., D. Beauchemin, L. Clapham, and T.J. Beveridge. 1990. Metal-binding characteristics of the gamma-glutamyl capsular polymer of *Bacillus licheniformis* ATCC 9945. *Applied and Environmental Microbiology* 56: 3671-3677.

Mitra, R.S. 1984. Protein synthesis in *Escherichia coli* during recovery from exposure to low levels of cadmium. *Applied and Environmental Microbiology* 47: 1012-1016.

Mittleman, M.W. and G.G. Geesey. 1985. Copper-binding characteristics of exopolymers from a freshwater-sediment bacterium. *Applied and Environmental Microbiology* 49: 846-851.

Mullen, M.D., D.C. Wolf, F.G. Ferris, T.J. Beveridge, C.A. Fleming, and G.W. Bailey. 1989. Bacterial sorption of heavy metals. *Applied and Environmental Microbiology* 55: 3143-3149.

Nakamura, Y., S. Katayama, Y. Okada, F. Suuki, and Y. Nagata. 1981. The isolation and characterization of a cadmium and zinc-binding protein from *Tetrahymena pyriformis*. *Agricultural Biological Chemistry* 45: 1167-1172.

Nealson, K.H., B.M. Tebo, and R.A. Rosson. 1988. Occurrence and mechanisms of microbial oxidation of manganese. *Advances in Applied Microbiology* 33: 279-318.

Nies, D.H. and S. Silver. 1989. Plasmid-determined inducible efflux is responsible for resistance to cadmium, zinc, and cobalt in *Alcoligenes eutrophus*. *Journal of Bacteriology* 171: 896-900.

Norberg, M. and Y. Kojima. 1979. Metallothionein and other low molecular weight metal-binding proteins, p. 41-124. *In* J.H.R. Kagi and M. Norberg (eds.), Metallothionein. Pirkhouser Veriag, Basel.

Olafson, R.W., S. Loya, and R.G. Sims. 1980. Physiological parameters of prokaryote metallothionein induction. *Biochemical and Biophysical Research Communication* 95: 1495-1503.

Penry, D.L. and P.A. Jumars. 1986. Chemical reactor analysis and optimal digestion. *Bioscience* 36: 310-315.

Perry, R.D. and S. Silver. 1982. Cadmium and manganese transport in *Staphylococcus aureus* membrane vessicles. *Journal of Bacteriology* 150: 973-976.

Reinfelder, J.R. and N.S. Fisher. 1991. The assimilation of elements ingested by marine copepods. *Science* 251: 794-796.

Remacle, J. and C. Vercheval. 1992. A zinc-binding protein in a metal-resistance strain, *Alcaligenes eutrophus* CH34. *Canadian Journal of Microbiology* 37: 875-877.

Ridley, W.P., L.J. Dizikes, and J.M. Wood. 1977. Biomethylation of toxic elements in the environment. *Science* 197: 329-332.

Robinson, J.B. and O.H. Tuovinen. 1984. Mechanisms of microbial resistances and detoxification of mercury and organomercury compounds: Physiological, biochemical, and genetic analyses. *Microbiology Reviews* 48: 95-124.

Roesijadi, G., S. Kielland, and P. Klerks. 1989. Purification and properties of novel molluscan metallothioneins. *Archives of Biochemistry and Biophysics* 273: 403-413

Rudd, T., R.M. Sterritt, and J.N. Lester. 1983. Mass balances of heavy metal uptake by encapsulated cultures of *Klebsiella aerogenes*. *Microbial Ecology* 9: 261-272.

Rudd, T., R.M. Sterrift, and J.N. Lester. 1984. Formation and conditional stability constants of complexes formed between heavy metals and bacterial extracellular polymers. *Water Research* 18: 379-384.

Sarathchandra, S.U. and J.H. Watkinson. 1981. Oxidation of elemental selenium to selenite by *Bacillus megaterium*. *Science* 211: 600-611.

Schoftel, J., A. Mandal, D. Clark, S. Silver, and R.W. Hedges. 1974. Volatilisation of mercury and organomercurials determined by inducible R-factor systems in enteric bacteria. *Nature (London)* 251: 335-337.

Schreiber, D.R. F.J. Millero, and A.S. Gordon. 1990. Production of an extracellular copper-binding compound by the heterotrophic marine bacterium *Vibrio alginolyticus*. *Marine Chemistry* 28: 275-285.

Scott, J.A. and S.J. Palmer. 1988. Cadmium biosorption by bacterial exopolysaccharide. *Biotechnology Letters* 10: 21-24.

Silver, S., K. Budd, K.M. Leahy, W.V. Shaw, D. Hammond, R.P. Novick, G.R. Willsky, M.H. Malamy, and H. Rosenberg. 1981. Inducible plasmid-determined resistance to arsenate, arsenite, and antimony(III) in *Escherichia coli* and *Staphylococcus aureus*. *Journal of Bacteriology* 146: 983-986.

Silver, S., T.K. Misra, and R.A. Laddaga. 1989. Bacterial resistance to toxic heavy metals, p. 121-139. *In* T.J. Beveridge and R.J. Doyle (eds), Metal Ions and Bacteria. John Wiley and Sons, New York.

Silverberg, B.A., P.T.S. Wong, and Y.K. Chau. 1976. Ultrastructural examination of *Aeromonas* cultured in the presence of inorganic lead. *Applied and Environmental Microbiology* 32: 723-725.

Steiner, I., D.A. McLaren, and C.F. Forster. 1976. The nature of activated sludge flocs. *Water Research* 10: 25-30.

Stone, H. and J. Overnell. 1985. Non-metallothionein cadmium binding proteins. *Comparative Biochemistry and Physiology* 8OC: 9-14.

Summers, A.O. and S. Silver. 1978. Microbial transformations of metals. Annual *Review of Microbiology* 32: 637-672.

Thayer, J.S. and F.E. Brinckman. 1982. The biological methylation of metals and metalloids. *Advances in Organometallic Chemistry* 20: 313-349.

Trevors, J.T. 1989. The role of microbial resistance and detoxification in environmental bioassay research. *Hydrobiologia* 188/189: 143-147.

Tynecka, Z., Z. Gos, and J. Zajac. 1981. Reduced cadmium transport determined by a resistance plasmid in *Staphylococcus aureus*. *Journal of Bacteriology* 147: 305-312.

Urrutia-Mera, M., M. Kemper, R. Doyle, and T.J. Beveridge. 1992. The membrane-induced proton motive force influences the metal binding ability of *Bacillus subtilus* cell walls. *Applied and Environmental Microbiology* 58: 3837-3844.

Vasak, M. 1986. Dynamic metal-thiolate cluster structure of metallothioneins. *Environmental Health Perspectives* 65: 193-197.

Weber, D.N., C.F. Shaw III, and D.H. Petering. 1987. *Euglena gracilis* cadmium-binding protein II contains sulfide ion. *Journal of Biological Chemistry* 262: 6962-6964.

Weiss, H.V., M. Koide, and E.D. Goldberg. 1971. Mercury in a Greenland ice sheet: Evidence of recent input by man. *Science* 174: 692-694.

Westoo, G. 1973. Methylmercury as percentage of total mercury in flesh and viscera of salmon and sea trout of various ages. *Science* 181: 567-568.

Widdows, J., P. Fieth, and C.M. Worrall. 1979. Relationship between seston, available food and feeding activity in the common mussel *Mytilus edulis*. *Marine Biology* 50: 195-207.

Wood, J.M. 1975. Biological cycles for elements in the environment. *Naturwissenschaften* 62: 357-

Wood, J.M. and H.K. Wang. 1983. Microbial resistance to heavy metals. *Environmental Science and Technology* 17: 582A-590A.

Eutrophication in Estuaries and Coastal Systems: Relationships of Physical Alterations, Salinity Stratification, and Hypoxia

Robert J. Livingston

ABSTRACT: A comparative analysis of the relationships of depth, salinity stratification, dredging, and periodic hypoxia in a series of river-estuarine systems along the northeast coast of the Gulf of Mexico was carried out. Anthropogenous nutrient and organic carbon loading combined with physical alterations due to dredging were associated with hypoxia, anoxia, and extensive fish kills in Escambia Bay (Pensacola Bay system) during the early 1970s. Long-term databases of field conditions were used to analyze periodic chronic hypoxic conditions at depth in several estuaries of varying physiographic types. The dissolved oxygen (DO) regimes of these estuaries were influenced by the interaction of temperature, precipitation, altered water circulation patterns due to dredging, and nutrient-enhanced primary production. There were negative correlations between low dissolved oxygen and bottom salinity in the barrier lagoons. Depth and salinity stratification were often inversely related to bottom dissolved oxygen. System-specific differences in the response of the DO regime of individual estuaries were related to factors such as depth, river flow conditions, dredging, the extent and duration of salinity stratification, and anthropogenous sources of nutrients and organic carbon. Physical changes due to dredging in barrier estuaries led to major alterations in salinity distribution and hypoxia, although the physiographic structure of the subject systems determined the response of the system to such activities. Salinity stratification due to artificially created (i.e., dredged) channels to the Gulf was associated with extensive hypoxia at depth in two of the estuaries. The high mean depth and the availability of salt water via the artificial channels were important variables in the establishment of salinity stratification and accompanying hypoxia in these systems. Thus, physical and stratigraphic components tended to establish the habitat conditions for hypoxia at depth that were exacerbated by anthropogenous loading of nutrients and organic carbon. Until now, dredging (at public expense) in these systems has gone on continuously, with little effective review or regulation. Activities such as dredging that enhance salinity stratification in inshore estuaries often exacerbate existing eutrophication problems (i.e., hypoxia) in such systems. Salinity alteration due to dredging in barrier lagoons of Gulf estuaries is an important (though indirect) determinant of estuarine production: such physical alterations should be evaluated within the context of the long-term useful productivity of these coastal systems.

Introduction

Eutrophication in estuarine and coastal systems is based on the influx of nutrients and the processing of these compounds via primary production by microphytes and macrophytes. The eutrophication process involves complex trophic interactions that include both bottom-up and top-down feeding groups of consumers. Food web response to nutrient loading is often system-specific. Natural trophic processes can be altered by various anthropogenous activities, including nutrient input and physical changes in the estuarine basin. Enhanced eutrophication, or hypereutrophication, is often associated with increased loading of nutrients and organic carbon, leading to imbalances in the trophic system. Increased microphyte production can be followed by changes in estuarine food webs and periodic hypoxia and anoxia. Associated secondary effects such as reduced dissolved oxygen (DO) can then lead to massive fish kills, chronic reduction of useful habitat, and adverse impacts on important estuarine and coastal populations (Duxbury 1975; Turner et al. 1987).

Dissolved oxygen in coastal areas has considerable spatial and seasonal variability, largely because of natural fluctuations of temperature, salinity, basin stratigraphy, and changing biological conditions. The spatial and temporal patterns of dissolved oxygen levels in bay systems depend on interactions of physiographic, physical-chemical, and biological factors (Odum and Wilson 1962). The exact combination of such variables leading to hypereutrophication is often complex, and the separation of natural and anthropogenic control of a given DO regime can be difficult. This complicates the delineation of cause-and-effect relationships between nutrient and organic carbon loading and the response of the receiving bay system.

Long-term records of dissolved oxygen are often used to evaluate trends of potential anthropogenic impact on estuaries and coastal systems (Duxbury 1975). Various studies have uncovered the general conditions resulting in anoxia and/or hypoxia in estuaries and coastal systems. In some estuaries, periodic hypoxia often reflects natural conditions (Turner et al. 1987; Seliger and Boggs 1988). For example, Schroeder et al. (1990) found that river flow was the dominant control mechanism of salinity stratification in Mobile Bay; that wind stress was important to the salinity distribution only in the absence of major freshwater discharges; and that salinity changes were related to the distribution of DO. Anthropogenous activities such as increased nutrient loading, restricted water circulation through dredging, altered phytoplankton production, and associated trophic anomalies can influence the frequency and severity of hypoxic episodes (Seliger and Boggs 1988; Breitburg 1990). There are indications that anoxic and hypoxic episodes are not always related solely to anthropogenic nutrient loading and associated changes in the distribution and concentration of organic carbon in various bay systems (Jackson et al. 1987; Kuo and Neilson 1987; Kuo et al. 1991). Salinity stratification and the restriction of vertical mixing in estuaries have been associated with hypoxic conditions. Smith et al. (1992) found that the deep-water hypoxic conditions in Chesapeake Bay resulted from the cumulative effects of biochemical mechanisms that were also modified by physical stratification. Nonpoint-source nutrient inputs supported phytoplankton biomass in excess of the assimilative capacity of the bay. The exact relationship of nutrient loading (and reductions of nutrient loading) to the hypoxic condition remained undescribed due to unknown factors such as feedback loops and interannual changes in climatic factors.

The importance of dissolved oxygen to aquatic organisms is well known. Accounts of the association of extensive kills with hypoxia and/or anoxia are not uncommon in the literature (Ogren and Chess 1969). Episodes of hypoxic fish kill "jubilees" have occurred over relatively long periods in coastal areas such as Mobile Bay (Loesch 1960; May 1973) and Chesapeake Bay (Smith et al. 1992). Efforts have been made to establish appropriate criteria or standards for dissolved oxygen as part of the protection of natural systems (Doudoroff and Shumway 1967). Various field studies have been carried out to evaluate the impact of hypoxia and anoxia on estuarine populations and communities. Pearson (1980) and Pearson and Rosenberg (1978) evaluated the effects of organic enrichment and low dissolved oxygen on marine systems. A series of studies in Hillsborough Bay (Tampa Bay system) found that annual defaunation was due to hypoxia (Santos and Bloom 1980; Santos and Simon 1980a,b). A stochastic recolonization response of the soft-bottom macroinverte-brate community was demonstrated following the recurrent defaunation event. Van Es et al. (1980) demonstrated a direct response of the meiofauna and microfauna in tidal flats along distinct gradients of organic enrichment and oxygen saturation. The authors could not isolate the impact of gradients of dissolved oxygen from the effects of other natural forcing factors such as salinity (absolute value and fluctuations), sediment composition, and relative emersion time. Such interaction and covariance of important ecological features of an estuary often confound direct correlations between the oxygen regime and the biological organization of the system.

Biological response in the form of acclimatization and adaptation also complicate direct extrapolations of the impact of reduced dissolved oxygen on estuarine populations. These complications often preclude the direct designation of distinct causal relationships among the interacting physical, chemical, and biological factors associated with hypoxic and/or anoxic episodes in estuarine and coastal systems.

In this paper, I address the causal relationships of specific changes in the dissolved oxygen regime of several estuaries along the northeast Gulf Coast of Florida, with specific attention to the role of dredging in the process of salinity stratification and associated hypoxia. The relationships of these factors to biological response are analyzed.

Study Areas

The systems studied were the Perdido River-Estuary, the Pensacola River-Bay system, the Choctawhatchee River-Bay system, the Apalachicola River-Bay system, and the Apalachee Bay system (Econfina River and Fenholloway River estuaries) (Fig. 1). Specific eutrophication studies were carried out in the Pensacola Bay system, although this estuary was not included in the comparative analysis of hypoxia in the Gulf drainages.

River flow conditions of the various estuaries in this study are given in Table 1. The Apalach-icola River has the highest average daily flow rate (29,100 cfs) of the rivers in this region of the Gulf of Mexico. The combined flow (11,600 cfs) of the Escambia, Blackwater, Yellow rivers into the Pensacola Bay system is the second highest average daily flow rate of the region followed by the Choctawhatchee (8,500 cfs), and the combined flow of the Perdido, Styx, and Blackwater rivers (2,200 cfs) (no relation to the Blackwater River in the Pensacola system). The Econfina and Fen-holloway rivers have relatively low average flow rates compared to the alluvial systems mentioned above. The Econfina and Fenholloway estuaries differ from the alluvial systems in that the ratios of average flow rate to watershed area, of average flow rate to open water area, and of average flow rate to total marsh area are relatively low in the smaller river systems (Fig. 2). The Apalachicola system has a relatively high ratio of average flow rate to open water area whereas

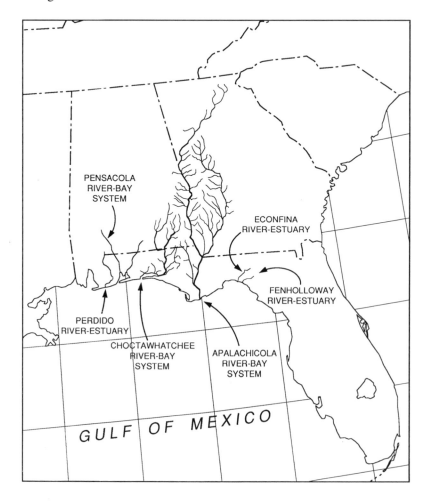

Fig. 1. Study systems along the Florida Gulf Coast: the Perdido River and estuary, the Pensacola Bay system, the Choctawhatchee River and Bay system, the Apalachicola River and Bay system, and Apalachee Bay (Econfina River and Fenholloway River estuaries).

the Choctawhatchee system has relatively high ratios of flow to watershed area and flow to marsh area. The ratio of flow to marsh area in both the Apalachicola and Choctawhatchee systems is higher than that in the Perdido system.

Drainage areas and habitat composition of the subject systems are shown in Fig. 3. The Apalachicola system has the most extensive watershed of the subject systems. The major alluvial systems (Apalachicola, Choctawhatchee, and Perdido) arise in Georgia and/or Alabama. The open water (estuarine) areas of these systems generally follow the order in Fig. 3 in terms of the extent of the respective alluvial drainages. In contrast, the Econfina and Fenholloway rivers have relatively

Table 1. Freshwater inflow data (cubic feet per second, cfs) of the major rivers of a series of estuaries in the northern Gulf of Mexico. Data are from the National Estuarine Inventory (National Oceanic and Atmospheric Administration 1985) and the United States Geological Survey (unpublished data).

River	Period of Record	Average Daily Flow (cfs)	7-d, 10-yr Low Flow (cfs)	100-yr Flood (cfs)
Apalachicola	1957-1982	29,100	8,300	242,900
Choctawhatchee	1931-1982	8,500	1,600	82,100
Escambia-Blackwater-Yellow	1934-1984	11,600	1,900	279,400
Perdido-Styx-Blackwater	1941-1983	2,200	200	32,200
Econfina	1970-1989	168	NA	NA
Fenholloway	1970-1989	144	NA	NA

restricted drainage areas, which are in Florida. These Apalachee Bay estuaries have very high ratios of wetlands to open water compared with the three alluvial estuaries. For its size, the Choctawhatchee system has relatively low development of both freshwater and saltwater marshes and a very low ratio of wetlands to open water. Comparison of the ratios of open water to watershed shows that the Apalachicola system has the lowest ratio, the Econfina and Fenholloway systems have intermediate ratios, and the Choctawhatchee and Perdido systems have the highest ratios. The relatively greater depths of the Choctawhatchee and Perdido estuaries should be taken into account. Compared with the other systems, the Choctawhatchee and Perdido systems represent intermediate conditions in terms of watershed areas with relatively low marsh development and high ratios of open water to watershed. The Econfina and Fenholloway drainage systems have relatively highly developed marsh systems and small watersheds in geographically restricted drainage basins compared with the Apalachicola system, which is a relatively shallow estuary with a major watershed and relatively well-developed freshwater and estuarine marshes. The drainage characteristics of each of these systems are important in evaluating the salinity relationships in the respective study areas.

Nearshore coastal regions in the study area are affected by both surface and groundwater runoff (Livingston 1984a). Bays and estuaries with direct freshwater runoff have highly variable salinities that are dependent on rainfall, river flow, tidal effects, and wind conditions, which interact with the local physiographic features of the respective basins. Nearshore coastal waters are often characterized by marine conditions, and have higher, temporally stable salinities. The smaller streams, such as the Econfina and Fenholloway rivers (Fig. 1), along Florida's Big Bend area, are associated with relatively limited estuarine areas that are also quite shallow (average depth 1-2 m). The barrier estuaries of Florida's Panhandle section (Fig. 1) are dominated by a series of rivers from the Perdido to the Apalachicola. Alluvial streamflow in Gulf estuarine systems, such as the Perdido (average depth 2-3 m), Pensacola (average depth 4 m), Choctawhatchee (average depth 3-8 m), and Apalachicola (average depth 2 m), dominates the respective salinity regimes (Orlando et al. 1993). River

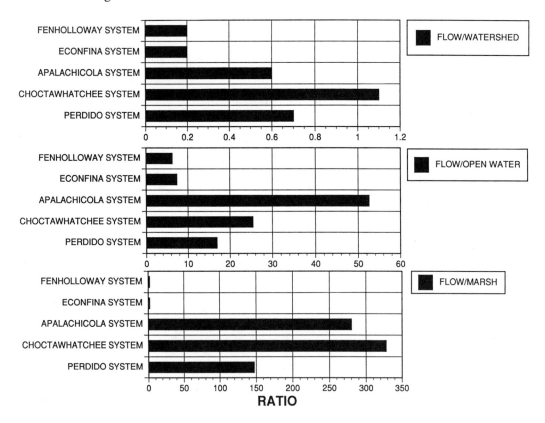

Fig. 2. Ratios of flow rate to watershed area, flow rate to open water area, and flow rate to total marsh (fresh water and estuarine) area of the five subject drainage systems. Data are taken from Orlando et al. (1993).

flow, along with the stratigraphy of the receiving basins, determines the spatial-temporal distribution of salinity stratification in these coastal areas. There is considerable variability in the freshwater flows of the various drainage areas. Peak flooding often occurs during winter and early spring months in the various north Florida drainages. The reduction in surface flows during summer periods of peak Florida rainfall is due to increased evapotranspiration throughout the region. Surface flow to the Gulf is lowest during the fall drought period.

Habitat conditions in the Gulf coastal river-estuaries in the north Florida region are determined by various factors. In the western Panhandle from the Apalachicola system to the Perdido system, astronomical tides are diurnal and have relatively small amplitudes (between 0.37 m and 0.52 m). Tides from the Fenholloway River-estuary to the Apalachicola system are mixed and semidiurnal, having two (unequal) highs and lows each tidal day (24 h, 50 min). Tides in this region range between 0.67 m and 1.16 m. Tidal effects on currents vary from one area to another, although the general effect is to enhance mixing in the nearshore waters. Wind is a major factor in the determination of water circulation and salinity in most of the shallow Gulf coastal estuaries. In areas where

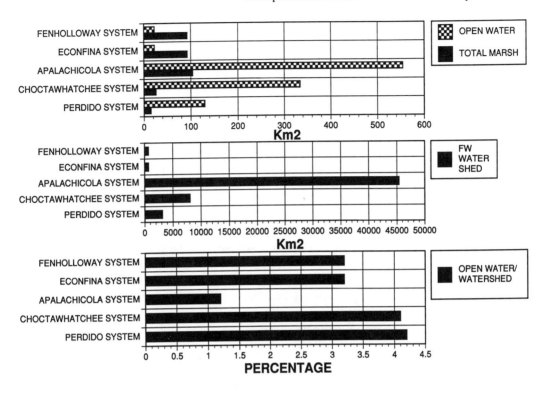

Fig. 3. Drainage areas and wetlands relationships of the major river-estuarine systems along the northeastern Gulf Coast. Data are taken from Orlando et al. (1993).

river flow is a factor, frictional effects on the salt-water regimes are combined with salt-wedge circulation and geostrophic forces to affect the estuarine salinity distribution.

The physical dimensions of a given river-estuarine basin are a key element in the determination of the distribution and nature of aquatic habitats. The size, depth, and location of passes of a system represent important determinants of the stratification potential and salinity distribution in a given estuary. The complex interactions of factors such as freshwater influxes, basin characteristics, and associated geostrophic forces thus determine spatial and temporal habitat characteristics of the Gulf coastal estuaries of North Florida.

Materials and Methods

The basis for the comparison of the various drainage systems in the northeastern Gulf of Mexico was established by conducting a review of data collected over the past 23 yr (Livingston unpublished data). Freshwater input, as a function of major river flow, was used as one of the criteria for this comparison. A review was made of the long-term river flow conditions of the Apalachicola,

Choctawhatchee, Econfina, Fenholloway, and Perdido river-estuarine systems. These data were used to establish estimates of salinity stratification and dissolved oxygen conditions in the study areas.

The various techniques used to sample the different estuaries are given in Livingston (1983, 1984a). Stations were usually sampled at biweekly to monthly intervals. Dissolved oxygen was determined with YSI oxygen meters, which were periodically standardized with Winkler determinations. In the field, the oxygen meters were routinely air-calibrated. Water samples were collected from the surface and the bottom with 1-l Kemmerer bottles. Water temperatures were measured with stick thermometers and the oxygen meters. Oxygen-meter temperature determinations were calibrated with standardized thermometers. Salinity measurements were taken with a temperature-compensated refractometer calibrated periodically with standard seawater. Oxygen anomaly data (AO2) were calculated from the field measurements as the difference between the measured oxygen content (O2) and the oxygen solubility at a given temperature and salinity ($O2_1$): $AO2 = O2 - O2_1$.

The $O2_1$ values were calculated from the equation of Weiss (1970). All computations were carried out using software developed by personnel of the Center for Aquatic Research and Resource Management on CYBER 76 computers at the FSU Computing Center and/or a series of microcomputers.

A salinity stratification classification was created through the cooperative efforts of our research group and scientists from the National Oceanic and Atmospheric Administration (C. J. Klein and S. P. Orlando, Jr.). This classification was based on the difference between surface and bottom salinity determinations from the various estuarine systems. Data were organized on an annual basis (by month, by station) for each of the subject estuaries according to the following criteria:

Highly stratified (HS):	salinity difference $\geq$ 10‰
Partially stratified, strong (PSS):	salinity difference $\geq$ 5‰ and < 10‰
Partially stratified, weak (PSW):	salinity difference $\geq$ 2‰ and < 5‰
Vertically homogeneous (VH):	salinity difference < 2‰

In addition, all salinity data were organized according to the Venice classification, as outlined below:

Limnetic (LIM):	salinity $\leq$ 0.5‰
Oligohaline (OLI):	salinity > 0.5‰ and $\leq$ 5‰
Mesohaline (MES):	salinity > 5‰ and $\leq$18‰
Polyhaline (POL):	salinity >18‰ and $\leq$ 30‰
Euhaline (EUH):	salinity > 30‰

This classification has been used traditionally as a biologically significant ordering of salinity data in estuaries, and is used here to allow generalization of the complex and extensive datasets in the interpretation of salinity distribution.

Using the long-term database and a review of selected scientific papers, the relationships of low dissolved oxygen to estuarine populations was assessed. Based on these analyses, I reordered the dissolved oxygen (DO) data taken in the each system according to the potential impact on the biological components:

Anoxic to severely hypoxic (ASH):	DO $\leq$ 2 mg l^{-1}
Hypoxic (HYP):	DO > 2 mg l^{-1} and $\leq$ 4 mg l^{-1}
Biologically "neutral" (BN):	DO > 4 mg l^{-1}

The ASH classification includes DO levels that are actively detrimental to most estuarine populations. The HYP classification includes DO levels that may be stressful to more sensitive organisms and thus can be associated with the loss of certain populations. The exact meaning of this transitional level of dissolved oxygen is, as yet, not well understood. The stress value remains relative to the stratigraphic characteristics of the area, the season, and specific biological attributes of the system in question. This model was used with the recognition that detailed determinations of the relationship between ambient DO concentrations and biotic response in Gulf Coast estuaries remains largely undocumented.

Results and Discussion

Hypereutrophication: Fish Kills in the Pensacola Bay System

The classical response of an estuary to anthropogenous nutrient loading is extreme hypoxia, and the resulting disruption of the biological relationships of the receiving system. During the late 1960s and early 1970s, Escambia Bay, part of the Pensacola Bay system (Fig. 1), was subject to nutrient loading from various point and nonpoint sources, resulting in extreme fluctuations of dissolved oxygen and fish kills (United States Environmental Protection Agency 1971). The Mulat-Mulatto Bayou was a major site of extensive kills. These multi-species fish kills occurred regularly during the summer-fall months; field estimates ranged from a few hundred to as many as 3 million fishes killed.

Mulat-Mulatto Bayou (Fig. 4) had been subjected to extensive physiographic changes due to dredging associated with the construction of a nearby highway. In 1965, the Florida Department of Transportation removed approximately 1,028,933 cubic yards of sediment from Mulatto Bayou. A dredged channel opened the south end of the bayou to the bay (Fig. 5, station 14), and deep borrow pits were created at the end of the channel (station 10a). Further dredging was carried out in the bayou in 1970; at this time, a private firm dredged finger canals in the southeastern sector of the bayou (stations 11a and 11b). Surrounding wetlands were obliterated by dredge spoils. Dye studies in Mulat-Mulatto Bayou (Livingston unpublished data) indicated the dredging created cul-de-sacs (i.e., the finger-fill canals; stations 11a and 11b) that were isolated from direct tidal current exchanges. In addition, a natural cul-de-sac (i.e., Mulat Bayou, station 7) was seasonally isolated from tidal exchanges. The low summertime DO levels in the finger-fill canals and at depth in the dredged holes (Fig. 5) were the direct result of the physiographic changes in a hypereutrophicated situation. During the study, the aquatic habitat of Escambia Bay was severely altered by the release into the bay of nutrients and toxic agents from a broad array of sources (Olinger et al. 1975).

Seasonal changes in temperature were important in the control of hypoxic conditions in the Mulat-Mulatto Bayou. The dissolved oxygen regime at depth (Fig. 5) was characterized as generally hypoxic to anoxic during warm periods. Fluctuations of surface DO in the Mulat-Mulatto Bayou over the study period (Fig. 6) indicated considerable variation on a diurnal and seasonal basis. In Mulat Bayou during early July, there was supersaturation during the day and hypoxic conditions at night. This pattern became more pronounced in August, and by September, DO was sufficiently low during early morning hours that there was a massive fish kill. In October, conditions became more stable, and by the end of November, continuous high levels of DO were noted throughout the bayou, a situation that prevailed through the following spring (April). In the finger-fill canals (station 11a), low DO at night during August was accompanied by a fish kill. Subsequent increases in DO were noted in October, with relatively high DO being maintained from November through April. This seasonal (June through October) pattern of fish kills represented a trend that was largely associated with high water temperature and periodic influxes of migrating fishes.

Fig. 4. The Mulat-Mulatto Bayou of the Pensacola Bay system showing the stations monitored during the early 1970s. The configuration of the bayous is shown before dredging (1956, top photograph) and after dredging (1968, bottom photograph) by the Florida Department of Transportation.

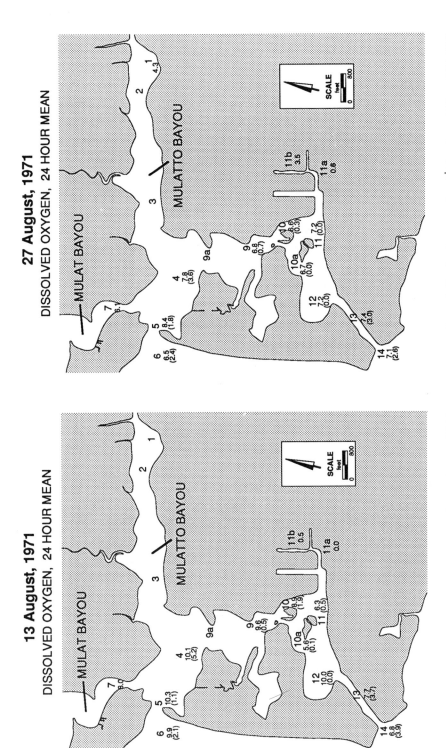

Fig. 5. The Mulat-Mulatto Bayou showing sampling stations and 24-h mean concentrations of dissolved oxygen (mg l^{-1}) for August 13 and 27, 1971. Data were taken at periods in which extensive fish kills occurred; an estimated 3 million fishes died.

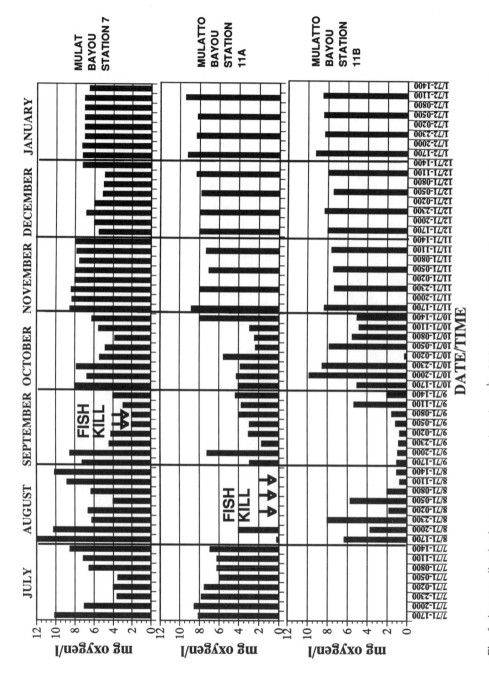

Fig. 6. Average dissolved oxygen concentrations (mg l^{-1}) of Mulat-Mulatto Bayou. Samples were taken at 3-h intervals over a 24-h period on a monthly basis from July 1971 through January 1972.

The fish kills in the Mulat-Mulatto Bayou, while directly associated with the DO regime, were actually part of a complex, interrelated series of events that was dependent on specific spatial-temporal controlling factors. These factors reflected habitat conditions associated with the dredging events described above. The extent of thermohaline stratification was also enhanced by summer rainfall, which peaked in August. Biochemical oxygen demand in the highly organic sediments (especially high in dredged holes) exacerbated the reduction of DO at depth. Vertical stratification in deeper portions of the bayou or in areas cut off from the main tidal and/or wind-driven circulation, together with nocturnally low oxygen in the water column, was thus associated with periodic hypoxia and anoxia at depth. There was an exaggerated diurnal fluctuation of DO during the summer-fall months, with surface water supersaturation during the day and hypoxic conditions during the night. Respiration of juvenile fishes could have been a contributing factor to the low levels of DO at night. Overall, however, the timing and location of the fish kills indicated that the combination of hypereutrophication and habitat alterations due to dredging were responsible for the fish kills. Dredging activities thus enhanced the effects of cultural eutrophication by inhibiting tidal and wind-produced exchanges of bay water. The fish kills—some of the most massive ever recorded—were the final consequence of a distorted DO regime, which, in turn, was influenced by sequential interactions of temperature, precipitation, altered water circulation patterns through dredging, and nutrient-enhanced primary production.

SALINITY AND DISSOLVED OXYGEN RELATIONSHIPS

The response of various other Gulf coastal systems to nutrient inputs was more complex, and the results were not as dramatic as massive (instantaneous) mortality of estuarine populations. Chronic hypoxic conditions in river-estuarine systems are often the result of complex interactions of one or more factors, including

- Thermal and/or salinity stratification of the water column
- Organic loading to an estuary that has too little hydrologic turnover to process the particulate and/or dissolved organic matter
- Nutrient-enhanced phytoplankton production leading to a disjunct food web (too few zooplankton to maintain the trophic balance), resulting in benthic loading of organics, high biochemical oxygen demand and sediment oxygen demand, and anoxia or hypoxia at depth
- A combination of the above processes, leading to time-based (seasonal, interannual) events (natural or anthropogenous) that result in nutrient and/or organic overloads and resultant low DO, usually at depth

The interaction of salinity stratification and hypereutrophication can be an important part of the eutrophication process. While it has been alluded to in various studies, it has not been addressed in a uniform manner.

The Apalachicola River and Bay System

The Apalachicola Bay system (Fig. 7) is a lagoon and barrier island complex oriented on an east-west axis parallel to the Gulf of Mexico. The boundaries of the estuary are defined from the head of tide on the Apalachicola River (40 km upstream of its terminus at East Bay, Gorsline 1963) to its southern boundary at the Gulf of Mexico. The gulfward extent of the bay is formed by three

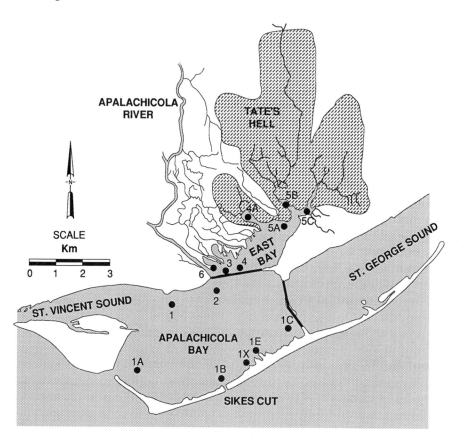

Fig. 7. The Apalachicola River and Bay system showing the various sampling stations over the 14-yr period of study.

barrier islands. There are four natural openings to the Gulf: Indian Pass, West Pass, East Pass, and a pass between Alligator Harbor and Dog Island. A manmade opening (Sikes Cut) was established in the western portion of St. George Island in 1954. An extensive delta region formed in the upper tidally-influenced reaches of the system where the Apalachicola River enters the bay through a series of major tributaries.

Apalachicola River discharge (Table 1), together with local rainfall and tidal effects, controls the salinity regime in the bay system (Livingston 1983, 1984a). Studies conducted in the Apalachicola estuary (Livingston 1984a) suggest an interaction among several dynamic physical mechanisms operating on different time scales. The functional attributes of the estuary include the seasonally fluctuating Apalachicola River, local rainfall, the physiographic structure of the receiving basin, wind speed (duration and direction), tidal currents, and exchanges between the estuary and the Gulf. Hydrodynamic processes are further complicated by bathymetric modifications due to dredging activities, including the opening and maintenance of Sikes Cut (Fig. 7) and the maintenance of the Intracoastal Waterway that extends from the mouth of the river to St. George Sound to the east.

Station 2 (Fig. 7) is on the dredged portions of the Intracoastal Waterway. The degree of interaction among these variables produces salinity profiles in the primary estuary ranging from nearly fresh water at the mouth to saline Gulf waters in the passes. Discharge from the Apalachicola River system appears to dominate the salinity structure. Studies by Meeter and Livingston (1978) and Meeter et al. (1979) showed a strong correlation of Apalachicola River flow with the spatial and temporal distribution of salinity throughout the bay.

Although Apalachicola river flow is the primary controlling feature of the estuarine salinity regime, various factors combine to modify this influence. These factors affect both the vertical and horizontal distribution of salinity in space and time. Salinity in the estuary showed distinct latitudinal gradients. Mean salinity values are lowest at the mouth of the river and in East Bay. The lower reaches of the Apalachicola River generally constitute the tidal fresh zone (riverine or limnetic, 0-0.5‰). During the high flow season, this zone is expanded to include East Bay and upper portions of Apalachicola Bay. The lower river and upper East Bay, located northeast of the Apalachicola river head, are oligohaline (0.5-5‰) during most of the year. Middle-to-lower East Bay and upper-to-middle Apalachicola Bay are usually mesohaline (5-19‰), although these areas do undergo rapid changes, especially during summer-early fall rainfall, periods of increased river flow, and episodic events such as hurricanes. Mid-portions of Apalachicola Bay, St. Vincent Sound, and western portions of St. George Sound vary between mesohaline (5-18‰) and polyhaline (18-30‰) depending on river flow. Areas near the passes and in the eastern section of St. George Sound vary from polyhaline to euhaline (> 30‰) conditions. The highest salinities with the least temporal variation can be found just inside Sikes Cut, with some extensions of high-salinity water into Apalachicola Bay (Livingston 1984a).

The Apalachicola system is relatively shallow compared to other estuaries along the northeast Gulf coast (Fig. 8). The deepest areas were in the dredged opening to the bay at Sikes Cut (station 1B) (Fig. 7) and in the dredged canal leading from the upper bay to the river mouth (station 2). Early studies (Dawson 1955; Gorsline 1963) did not mention salinity stratification in the Apalachicola Bay system. However, my analyses indicate that the estuary is periodically stratified (Fig. 9). The highest level of stratification in the bay occurred at Sikes Cut (station 1B). At West Pass (station 1A), tidal variability was predominant: bottom salinities were often less than those in the vicinity of Sikes Cut. Stratification was high at the various passes to the bay but was especially pronounced at the dredged pass. It should be noted that Sikes Cut, an "artificial" pass, opens onto the primary basin of Apalachicola Bay whereas the natural West Pass has restricted access due to oyster bar development. Stratification was generally less well developed in western sections of the bay (St. Vincent Sound) where tidal and subtidal variations were prominent.

The lowest levels of stratification in the Apalachicola system were noted in East Bay (Fig. 9, stations 4A, 5A, 5B, and 5C). These areas had shallow depths and generally low salinities. Eastern portions of East Bay were not directly affected by Apalachicola river flow and were more affected by drainage from Tate's Hell Swamp (Fig. 7). Areas directly affected by Apalachicola river flow (stations 1, 2, 3, 4, and 5) were characterized by low salinities during late winter-spring periods of high river flow and increased vertical salinity stratification. Compared with areas of the bay that are not directly influenced by the flooding river, the salinity of areas affected by river flow had greater ranges and greater standard deviations both at the surface and at the bottom.

During periods of high river flow, there is an increased salinity gradient in all directions, and the Apalachicola estuary remains generally stratified, with the range of salinity gradients dependent

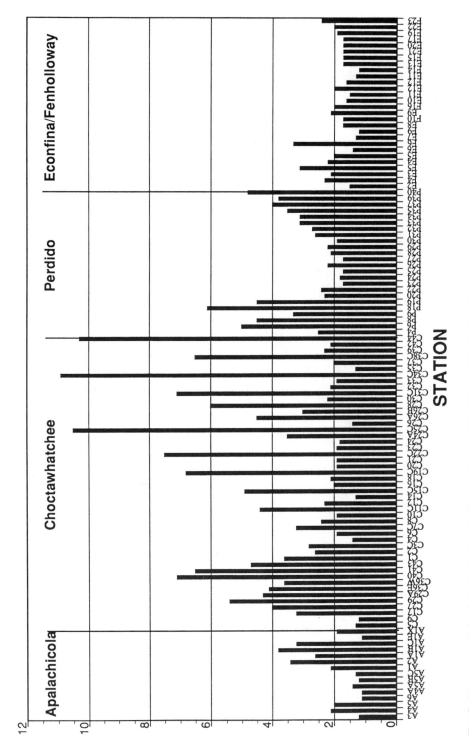

Fig. 8. Mean depth (m) of the Apalachicola, Choctawhatchee, Perdido, and Apalachee Bay systems.

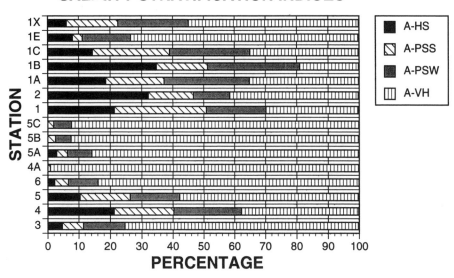

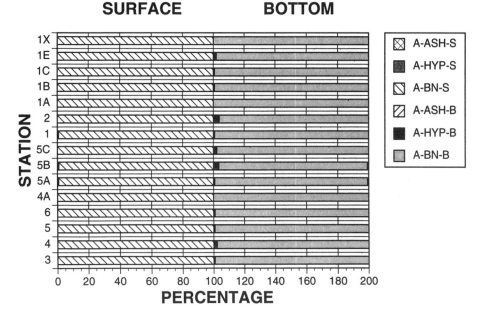

Fig. 9. Salinity stratification and dissolved oxygen indices in the Apalachicola Bay system computed from monthly measurements of salinity and dissolved oxygen at the surface and bottom, March 1972 through July 1984.

on season and location. Using a combination of regression and analysis of variance with the long-term database, Livingston (1984b) showed that surface to bottom salinity-by-month interactions were significant at Sikes Cut and in the Intracoastal Waterway at the mouth of the river. The combination of river flow and depth (dredging) are thus important variables in the long-term trends of stratification in the bay. Thus, stratification in Apalachicola Bay can be significant over prolonged periods in the two areas directly affected by dredging: Sikes Cut and the Intracoastal Waterway.

The magnitude, spatial extent, and temporal characteristics of vertical stratification within the Apalachicola system are complex. Despite its shallow depths, the bay is moderately stratified throughout the year. Stratification-destratification events fluctuate on time scales ranging from days to months as a result of freshets, wind events, tidal cycles, and frontal movements. Wind events of sufficient magnitude and direction (such as Hurricane Elena in September 1985) resulted in near-homogeneous conditions throughout the estuary (Livingston unpublished data). On average, there is an inflow of high-salinity water through Sikes Cut, which is opposite of the mean flow out of the bay through West Pass at the surface and bottom (Weisberg 1976, 1989). The distribution of DO indices in the Apalachicola estuary (Fig. 9) indicates that dissolved oxygen exceeded 4 mg l^{-1} at all of the sampling stations during most months over the period of analysis. Hypoxic conditions were noted at stations 5B and 2 and lesser periods of hypoxia were also evident at stations 5B and 5C. Dredged areas showed the highest incidence of hypoxia in the bay. Areas that were over 2 m deep (stations 2, 1A, 1B, and 1C) showed the highest levels of salinity stratification. A correlation matrix and regression analysis indicated no significant correlation of hypoxic conditions with any of the stratification indices or salinity coefficients. The data indicate that the general shallowness of the estuary could have been associated with the general lack of hypoxic conditions at depth in this system.

The Choctawhatchee River and Bay System

The Choctawhatchee Bay system (Fig. 10) is a west-sloping drowned river plain surrounded by shallow shelf-slopes and inshore bayous. Several physiographic and geomorphological features contribute to observed ecological characteristics of the Choctawhatchee system. This bay is aligned along an east-west axis with a major alluvial river basin to the east and a limited but important Gulf pass (East Pass) to the west. Freshwater input is primarily associated with the Choctawhatchee River; secondary inflows are from a series of bayous located primarily in the northern sections of the bay. Salt-water input from the Gulf comes through East Pass, a "created" pass. In 1929, a group of people dug a channel through the barrier island in a region now known as East Pass (Fig. 10). The "blow-out" of East Pass during the particularly heavy flooding at this time was followed by increased salinity throughout Choctawhatchee Bay. Local observers associated this increased salinity with the losses of emergent (marsh, swamp) and submergent (seagrass) vegetation. The Choctawhatchee system currently has one of the least well-developed fringing (emergent) vegetation zones of the various Gulf estuaries in the region (Fig. 3). Existing emergent vegetation is limited to a few peripheral areas bordering several bayous, Live Oak Point, and the river delta.

Choctawhatchee Bay has shallow shelf areas with relatively steep slopes that eventually level out to average depths of 3 m in eastern sections and 8 m in western sections of the central portions of the estuary (Fig. 8). Over the past 30-35 yr, there has been a major increase in coastal land use within the Garnier Bayou complex, the Boggy Bayou basin, and the Rocky Bayou basin (Fig. 10).

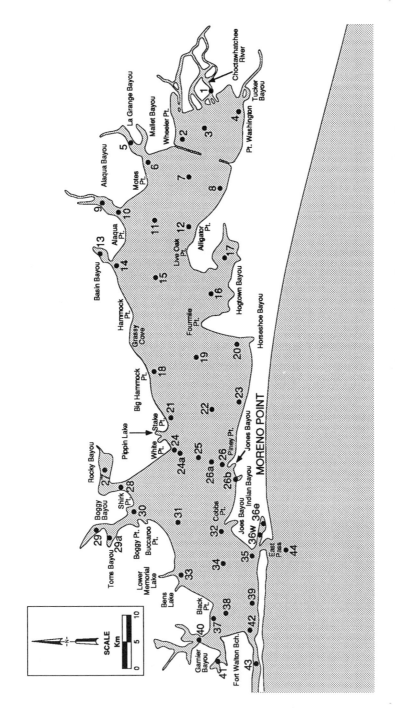

Fig. 10. Chart of the Choctawhatchee Bay system showing the various sampling stations over the 1.5-yr period of study.

High rates of development have also occurred in the White Point and Moreno Point (Destin) drainages, with major population increases in Fort Walton Beach. Relatively little increase in usage and development was noted in the Walton County (eastern bay) regional drainage basins. Thus, coastal land use has undergone major changes in the western bay drainages, with major increases in population and urbanization in the primary cities, whereas in Walton County to the east, growth in population and urbanization has been slow.

Salinity stratification indices for the bayous of the Choctawhatchee Bay system are given in Fig. 11. Highly stratified (HS) and strong partially stratified (PSS) conditions were noted at all bayou stations with the exception of Hogtown Bayou. Dissolved oxygen at the surface was consistently above 4 mg l^{-1} at all stations; however, bottom levels of dissolved oxygen were lower among the westernmost bayous. These trends followed depth relationships (Fig. 8) and increased urban development. Overall, salinity stratification was generally associated with spatial trends of hypoxia at depth. However, other factors were also associated with these trends. Station 36e was located in a deadend canal surrounded by high levels of urbanization and marina development. In associated areas, where there was more exchange with the open Gulf (station 36w), hypoxic conditions at depth were minimal. These data indicate reduced tidal exchanges, increased depth and salinity stratification, and increased urbanization have led to hypoxic conditions at depth in bayou areas.

Along the primary axis of Choctawhatchee Bay, mid-bay areas tend to be the deepest of those analyzed in the comparative study (Fig. 8). There is a general east-west gradient of increasing depth. The shallow shelf of the bay is generally less than 2 m deep. The deepest portions of the bay are positively correlated with high stratification (Fig. 12; correlation coefficients: HS = 0.335; PSS = 0.465). Extreme hypoxia (ASH) is highly correlated (correlation coefficient = 0.605) with highly stratified conditions, and there is a decrease in correlation with decreasing stratification (correlation coefficients: PSS = 0.322; PSW = -0.294; VH = -0.553). Hypoxic conditions (HYP) show a similar trend (correlation coefficients: HS = 0.451; PSS = 0.702; PSW = -0.384; VH = -0.552). Areas characterized by DO concentrations > 4.0 mg l^{-1} show an opposite trend as a function of the stratification (correlation coefficients: HS = -0.562; PSS = -0.672; PSW = 0.407; VH = 0.627). A regression of subhalocline hypoxic conditions (HYP) with mean depths in the Choctawhatchee system gives a relatively high value ($r^2 = 0.636$, p = 0.003) as does the regression of such hypoxia with high levels of stratification ($r^2 = 0.562$; p = 0.0001). The data indicate there is a direct association of depth, salinity stratification, and the extent of hypoxia in Choctawhatchee Bay. Depth is a leading variable in the distribution of hypoxia in the Choctawhatchee system, with salinity stratification as a necessary prerequisite for such conditions. The primary difference between this system and Apalachicola Bay is the shallow depths of the Apalachicola system and the lack of hypoxia despite stratification at the passes, which are subject to some of the highest levels of active mixing in the bay.

The Perdido River and Bay System

The Perdido Bay system (Fig. 13) is a shallow to moderately deep inshore body of water (Fig. 8) oriented along a northeast-southwest axis, approximately perpendicular to the Gulf of Mexico. The estuary is about 35 km long (mouth to head of tide) and is bounded by the Perdido River to the north and a dredged inlet, Perdido Pass, to the south. The mean width is 4.18 km. The Gulf Intracoastal Waterway runs through the lower end of Perdido Bay, about 5.6 km northeast of Perdido Pass. The Perdido Pass channel is kept at a depth of about 4 m as part of the maintained Intracoastal Waterway (United States Army Corps of Engineers 1976).

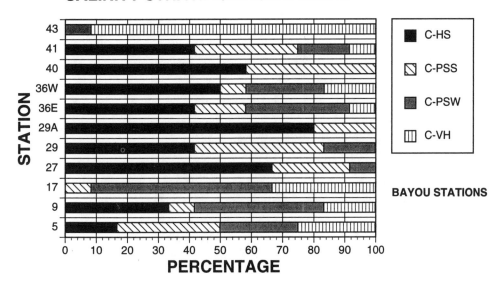

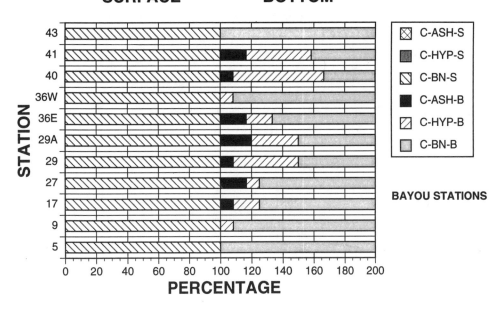

Fig. 11. Salinity stratification and dissolved oxygen indices in the bayous of the Choctawhatchee Bay system computed from monthly measurements of salinity and dissolved oxygen at the surface and bottom.

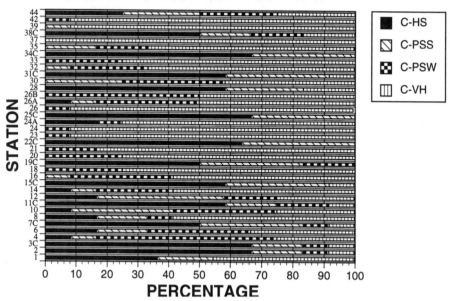

SALINITY STRATIFICATION INDICES

Legend:
- C-HS
- C-PSS
- C-PSW
- C-VH

STATION / PERCENTAGE

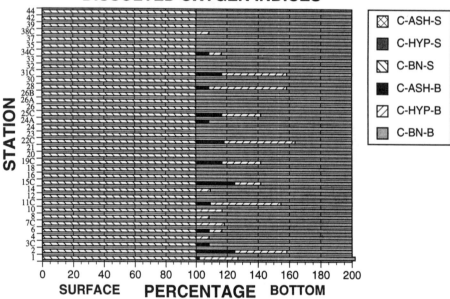

DISSOLVED OXYGEN INDICES

Legend:
- C-ASH-S
- C-HYP-S
- C-BN-S
- C-ASH-B
- C-HYP-B
- C-BN-B

STATION / SURFACE PERCENTAGE BOTTOM

Fig. 12. Salinity stratification and dissolved oxygen indices in the Choctawhatchee Bay system computed from monthly measurements of salinity and dissolved oxygen at the surface and bottom.

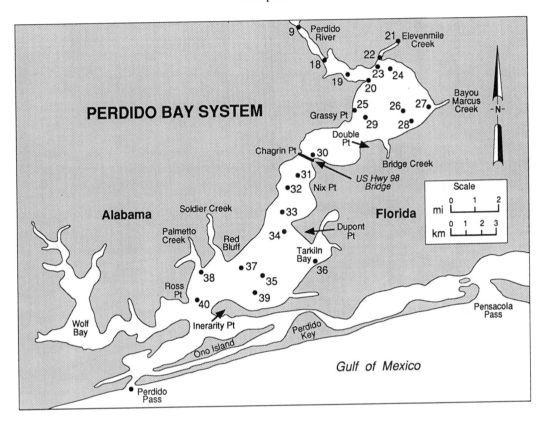

Fig. 13. Chart of the Perdido Bay system showing the various sampling stations over the 3-yr period of study.

The bay can be divided into four distinct geographic regions: the lower Perdido River, upper Perdido Bay (north of the Route 98 bridge), lower Perdido Bay (bounded to the south by a line between Ross Point and Inerarity Point), and the Perdido Pass complex (Fig. 13). Communication among the various portions of the estuary is determined largely by bathymetric conditions (Fig. 8). Like the Choctawhatchee Bay system, there is a shelf around the periphery of the Perdido estuary; this shelf usually does not exceed 1-1.5 m in depth and can extend up to 400 m in width. The upper bay is relatively shallow, and depth tends to increase southward. The deepest portions of the Perdido estuary are located at the mouth of the Perdido River and in southern areas. The greatest depths occur in the basin of the southern bay off Ross Point. Freshwater inflow to the estuary is dominated by the Perdido River. Relatively steep gradients and a high incidence of flash flooding (due to regional rainfall events) contribute to very rapid responses of the estuarine salinity regime (Livingston unpublished data). During a recent summer period of flooding, nearly the entire bay was characterized as fresh water.

Various parts of Perdido Bay are among the most stratified areas noted in the overall survey (Fig. 14). Depth is inversely correlated with vertically homogeneous areas ($r^2 = 0.406$) and weakly stratified areas ($r^2 = 0.479$). High-salinity water moves northward along the bottom of the bay to fill the deeper holes at the mouth of the Perdido River. During periods of extreme flooding, these areas are well flushed; within a few weeks of reduced freshwater input, the salinity increases.

Spatial-temporal trends of salinity in Perdido Bay follow seasonal and interannual patterns of freshwater runoff. Winter to early spring periods represent the low-salinity period whereas the fall months of drought usually are characterized by the highest salinities of the year. Salinity stratification of the estuary essentially creates two very different habitats that are depth-related (Fig. 14). The estuarine portions of the Perdido River and Elevenmile Creek showed the highest levels of salinity stratification, with such stratification evident in over 80% of the samples (Fig. 14). These areas represent the highest levels of stratification of all of the bays surveyed. Most areas of the upper bay (stations 24-30) are characterized by low levels of vertical stratification; these are the shallowest stations in the bay. Overall, mean depth in Perdido Bay is highly correlated with high salinity stratification (correlation coefficient = 0.688) and is inversely correlated with vertical homogeneity (correlation coefficient = -0.468).

Elevenmile Creek has been affected by pulp mill effluents, which contribute high nutrients (P and N) and organic carbon to the Perdido Bay system. With the exception of the lower portion of Elevenmile Creek (station 22, Fig. 13), shallow waters above the halocline in Perdido Bay are characterized by DO levels above 4 mg l^{-1} (Fig. 14). The highest levels of severe to moderate hypoxia at depth are located in Elevenmile Creek. The DO regime of Elevenmile Creek is affected by the high level of dissolved organic carbon (and thus high BOD) released from the pulp mill located at the head of the creek (Livingston unpublished data).

High levels of severe to moderate hypoxia are found in estuarine portions of the Perdido River system. Lower levels of hypoxia occur at depth in upper portions of the estuary. In the lower estuary, subhalocline hypoxic conditions are found in just over 40% of the samples taken. These levels are comparable to those conditions found in deeper portions of Choctawhatchee Bay. Extreme hypoxia in the bottom waters of Perdido Bay is highly correlated with high stratification (correlation coefficient = 0.749). There are inverse correlations of bottom hypoxia with decreasing levels of stratification (correlation coefficients: PSS = -0.210; PSW = -0.521; VH = -0.418). Vertically homogeneous salinity conditions show an opposite trend (correlation coefficients: HS = -0.787; PSS = 0.275; PSW = 0.521; VH = 0.406). Regressions of severe hypoxia have relatively strong associations with mean depth ($r^2 = 0.255$, p = 0.01) and high salinity stratification ($r^2 = 0.562$, p = 0.0001). There is a negative association of severe hypoxia with surface salinity ($r^2 = 0.248$, p = 0.007), and hypoxia is positively associated with depth ($r^2 = 0.255$, p = 0.01). These trends are similar to those noted in the Choctawhatchee Bay system. Salinity stratification due to dredging at Perdido Pass is thus a factor in the generally hypoxic conditions at depth in Perdido Bay during warm periods of the year.

The Econfina River and Fenholloway River Estuaries

The Econfina and Fenholloway systems of Apalachee Bay (Fig. 15) are part of one of the most extensive series of seagrass beds in the northern hemisphere (Iverson and Bittaker 1986; Zieman and Zieman 1989). In general, the Econfina and Fenholloway drainages and associated offshore areas are relatively shallow (Fig. 8). Although this coastal system remains in pristine condition due to a lack of development and population in the primary drainage areas, there is pulp mill discharge into the Fenholloway River at station F01F (Fig. 15). The release of pulp mill effluents has caused adverse effects in the receiving Gulf waters due to increased color and turbidity (Livingston 1984b). Zimmerman and Livingston (1976a,b, 1979) found the area off the Fenholloway

SALINITY STRATIFICATION INDICES

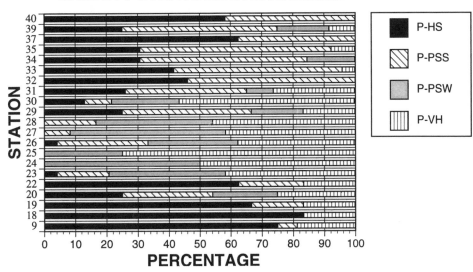

DISSOLVED OXYGEN INDICES
SURFACE   BOTTOM

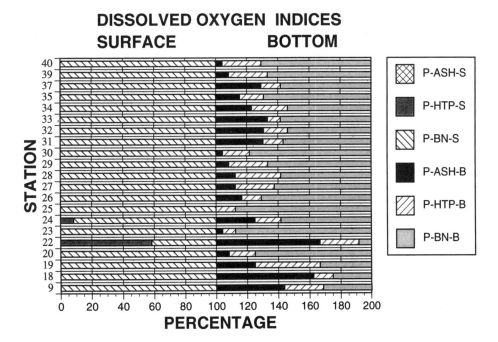

Fig. 14. Salinity stratification and dissolved oxygen indices of the Perdido Bay system computed from monthly measurements of salinity and dissolved oxygen at the surface and bottom.

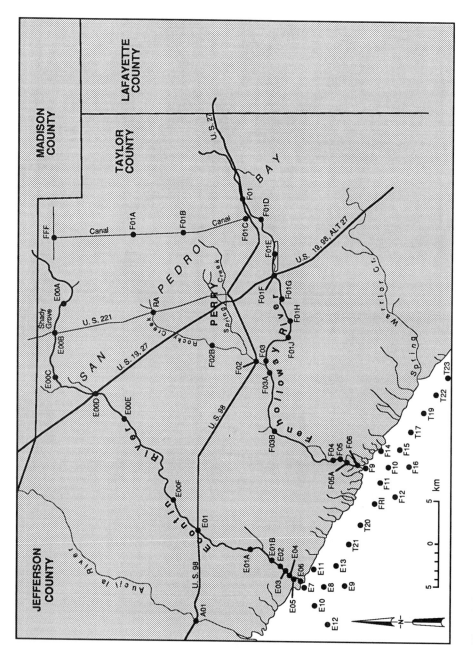

Fig. 15. Chart of the Apalachee Bay system showing the various sampling stations in the Econfina and Fenholloway systems over the 10-yr period of study.

River was characterized by reduced seagrass cover compared with similar areas in the reference Econfina system (Fig. 15). The dissolved oxygen regime of the Fenholloway River and its associated estuary has been adversely affected by pulp mill effluents (Livingston 1982, 1984b).

Data for the two river systems indicate that river flow of both tends to peak during February, March, April, and August (United States Geological Survey, Tallahassee, Florida, unpublished data). The primary difference between the two river flows over the study period (Table 1) is the increased flows of the Ecofina during winter and early spring periods (January-April). During the other periods of the year, the Fenholloway flows have been either comparable to or greater than the Econfina flows. The overall variance in river flow of the Fenholloway is less relative to the Econfina. This situation is due, in part, to the paper mill contribution to the Fenholloway River flow levels.

In the Fenholloway system, the highest levels of salinity stratification have been noted at the mouth of the river (Fig. 16). The nearest offshore station (station F9) is also highly stratified, although such stratification is not as pronounced as that in the river-estuary. Offshore areas of the Fenholloway drainage system are not strongly stratified; most of the measurements made monthly over the 10-yr period of observation showed a strong level of vertical homogeneity. Data from the Econfina system show a similar pattern of stratification (Fig. 16): the estuary is salinity-stratified compared to offshore stations, which remain vertically homogeneous most of the time. The overall level of stratification is somewhat less in the Econfina system than that in the Fenholloway system. In terms of the general salinity distribution, the two drainages are comparable. The lower estuaries have a regular seasonal progression: limnetic to oligohaline to mesohaline. The offshore systems are largely mesohaline to polyhaline, with specific periods of euhaline waters in the outermost stations. Overall, the salinities are comparable at the matched stations of the two systems (Livingston 1975, 1982, 1984b). The salinity stratification of the two river-estuaries is maximal in the lower portions of the respective drainage areas (Fig. 16, stations E3, F5; E6, F6; and E7, F9). The relatively higher stratification of the Fenholloway stations may be due to their greater depths (Fig. 8) relative to comparable stations in the Econfina estuary.

Dissolved oxygen is low in the Fenholloway River-estuary at the surface and the bottom (Fig. 16). Those areas of the Fenholloway estuary characterized by high stratification and the presence of pulp mill effluents (stations F4, F5, and F6) have severe to moderate hypoxic conditions in surface and bottom waters relative to conditions in comparable areas of the Econfina estuary. The increased BOD from the pulp mill effluents appears to be responsible for these conditions in the Fenholloway system (Livingston 1975), which is similar to the Perdido estuary (Elevenmile Creek). In offshore areas of the Gulf, the mean dissolved oxygen levels in the Fenholloway drainage are slightly lower than those in the Econfina areas. However, such levels are generally higher than 7 mg l^{-1} at all offshore stations (Livingston 1984b) and minima do not go below 4 mg l^{-1} (Fig. 16). In most instances, the DO minima are comparable in the two offshore systems. There is thus evidence of severely hypoxic conditions in the highly (salinity) stratified portions of the lower Fenholloway estuary but not in the Econfina estuary. Such hypoxia does not usually extend to the open Gulf areas.

Severely hypoxic conditions (ASH) in the Econfina and Fenholloway systems are not strongly correlated with stratification, although those areas characterized by hypoxic conditions (HYP) show trends similar to those in the Choctawhatchee and Perdido Bay systems (correlation coefficients: HS = 0.474; PSS = 0.156; PSW = -0.270; VH = -0.301). Hypoxic conditions at depth (HYP) are directly associated with mean depth (r^2 = 0.402, p = 0.0003), mean bottom salinity (r^2 = 0.425, p = 0.0002), and vertical stratification (r^2 = 0.225, p = 0.01), and are inversely related to mean surface salinity (r^2 = 0.441, p = 0.0001). Thus, despite considerable differences in physiography and river

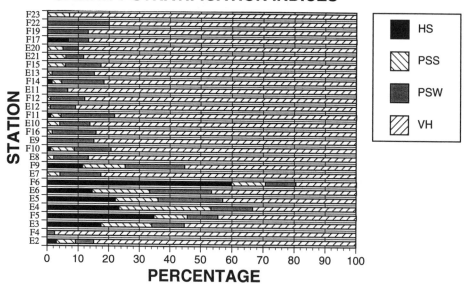

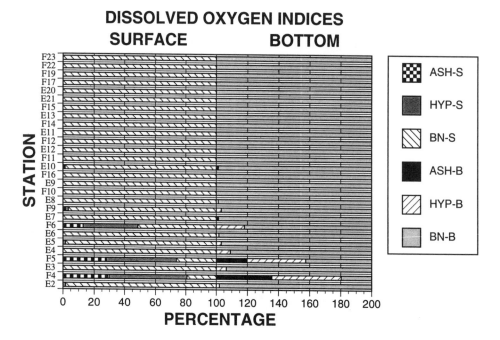

Fig. 16. Salinity stratification and dissolved oxygen indices in the Econfina and Fenholloway systems computed from monthly measurements of salinity and dissolved oxygen at the surface and bottom over the 10-yr period of study.

flow, the general relationships of depth, salinity stratification, and hypoxia at depth in the Econfina and Fenholloway systems are similar to those in the Perdido and Choctawhatchee systems. Increased dissolved organic carbon and nutrients due to anthropogenous activity, such as pulp mill discharges, enhance the hypoxia in the entire water column in the lower portions of the receiving rivers. However, in the open water portions of the Gulf receiving flow from the Fenholloway River, hypoxia at depth does not follow an exact pattern of response to pulp mill effluents due to enhanced vertical mixing and dilution of the high levels of river-borne DOC.

PHYSICAL CONTROL OF HYPOXIC CONDITIONS AT DEPTH

The basis for further statistical comparison of the subject systems was established by comparing long-term changes in the river flows of the various drainages. A 2-yr series of data on each system was chosen based on comparable levels of drought and river-flow conditions. A combined database of the various physical-chemical variables and stratification indices was constructed and bottom dissolved oxygen was regressed on the chief habitat variables of temperature, salinity, and stratification potential. The results showed similar relationships to those described in the individual bay analyses. Negative, statistically significant ($p < 0.05$) correlations were found between dissolved oxygen and bottom salinity. Increased salinity at depth usually was significantly ($p = 0.05$) associated with low dissolved oxygen. Depth and bottom-surface salinity differences were inversely related to the bottom dissolved oxygen. Depth was thus a major determinant of hypoxia in the inshore portions of the various estuaries. The data indicated depth, season, and salinity stratification were related to the observed hypoxia in the Perdido, Choctawhatchee, and Fenholloway estuaries, but these factors did not result in similar hypoxic conditions in the Apalachicola and Econfina estuaries. The implicit difference between the Econfina and Fenholloway systems was the paper mill, which was associated with the lowered dissolved oxygen of the Fenholloway River estuary relative to the reference (Ecofina) sites. However, there is no paper mill within the Choctawhatchee system, indicating that factors other than nutrient and organic carbon loading from pulp mills are operational here.

Seasonal differences in hypoxia at depth have been noted among the various subject systems. During the winter in the Perdido estuary, there is a relatively high level of hypoxia (DO < 4.0 mg l^{-1}), and such hypoxic conditions are directly related to the difference between bottom and surface salinity. This same condition is apparent in the Choctawhatchee Bay system but not in the shallow Apalachicola system. In the Apalachicola estuary, there is no obvious relationship between the stratification of the estuary and the concentration of dissolved oxygen. During the winter, there is some hypoxia in the Fenholloway estuary relative to the Econfina estuary. In the spring, there is recurring direct correspondence of hypoxic conditions with the level of salinity stratification in both the Perdido and Choctawhatchee Bay systems. Although there is a shift to lower dissolved oxygen in the Apalachicola estuary (in part attributed to temperature effects), hypoxia is not pronounced. Hypoxic conditions in the Fenholloway estuary intensify during the spring, indicating temperature is a contributing factor to low oxygen in the Fenholloway River estuary. By contrast, there is no spring hypoxia in the Econfina estuary, although natural changes in the hypoxic conditions at depth in the Econfina system cannot be ruled out. The hypoxia in the Fenholloway estuary is largely restricted to stations F4, F5, and F6 (i.e., the lower estuary), and DO concentrations appear to be inversely related to depth during most of the study. During the summer, hypoxic conditions intensify in the Perdido and Choctawhatchee systems, again as a function of increased temperature. The relationship with salinity stratification remains, however. In the Apalachicola estuary, although there is some evidence of an increase in hypoxia during the warmer summer months, there is no clear relationship between salinity stratification and hypoxia. The above-described summer conditions in the various estuaries are also apparent during the fall months.

A principal components analysis (Table 2) of the combined physical-chemical database by season in the subject estuaries was performed. In spring, there was a relationship of low bottom DO and increased depth combined with considerable differences between the surface and bottom salinities. Summer months were characterized by major differences in the surface and bottom DO when surface and bottom salinities showed maximal differences. During the fall, increased depth and increased salinity differences were accompanied by low bottom DO. Winter months were associated with reduced DO at depth as a function of high bottom salinity and considerable differences between the surface and bottom salinities.

The estuarine systems also were analyzed individually. The direct relationship of low dissolved oxygen and depth was apparent during all seasons in the Perdido system. This effect was also apparent in the Choctawhatchee and Fenholloway systems but not in the Econfina and Apalachicola systems. Thus, depth and salinity stratification were important qualifying agents in the incidence of hypoxia in the various Gulf estuaries, with the presence of a pulp mill a likely contributor to such effects at the mouths of Elevenmile Creek and the Fenholloway River. Hypoxic conditions in the Choctawhatchee estuary, where there is no pulp mill, indicate that, given the right conditions of depth, stratification, temperature, and sediment oxygen demand, hypoxia can occur naturally in the open portions of a given inshore bay system but not in the open Gulf. Thus, the vertical mixing function remains an important determinant of hypoxia below the halocline in the various estuaries.

The relationship between nutrient and organic carbon loading and hypoxia is complex and is not as clearly delineated as that between salinity stratification and hypoxia. The direct connection between nutrient loading and phytoplankton production is often modified by other factors such as temperature, salinity, and physiographic features of the receiving system. Spatial-temporal trends of nutrient limitation of phytoplankton production also play a role in these relationships. Kuo et al. (1991) showed that vertical mixing controls the longitudinal position of the minimum DO in a Virginia estuary. Portnoy (1991) found that channelization contributed to oxygen stress by substituting deep organic sinks for what were originally shallow habitats. Reyes and Merino (1991) found that sewage releases and dredging adversely affected the dissolved oxygen in a lagoon in the Mexican Caribbean. Breitburg (1990) indicated that wind-driven salinity alterations were associated with severe hypoxia at depth. Stanley and Nixon (1992), working in the Pamlico River Estuary, found that hypoxia developed only under conditions of vertical water-column stratification and warm temperatures. Stratification and low DO events were associated with freshwater discharge and wind stress. Over the 15-yr period of observation, there was no trend toward lower bottom water DO, and there were no demonstrated cause-and-effect relationships between nutrients, algal abundance, and bottom water DO levels. Proposed reductions of nitrogen were not expected to change the natural hypoxia and anoxia in the Pamlico system. Parker and O'Reilly (1991) reviewed long-term DO concentrations in Long Island Sound. They found that there was a spatial extension of the subpycnoclinal hypoxia eastward in terms of severity and frequency of hypoxia. Improvements in parts of the system were associated with upgrades in several sewage treatment plants in the drainage area. Welsh and Eller (1991) found that the ultimate control of the hypoxic conditions in Long Island Sound was salinity stratification; even a weak pycnocline was effective in maintaining low oxygen at depth.

Table 2. Eigenvalues of a principal components analysis of the comparative data of the Econfina, Fenholloway, Apalachicola, Choctawhatchee, and Perdido drainage systems. The data are 24 monthly measurements of depth, surface temperature, surface and bottom salinity, salinity difference (bottom minus surface), surface and bottom dissolved oxygen (DO), and dissolved oxygen (DO) difference (surface minus bottom).

Loading Component	Spring		Summer		Fall		Winter	
Depth	0.509	0.081	-0.385	0.288	0.509	0.081	0.463	0.192
Surface Temperature	0.371	-0.225	0.148	0.386	0.371	0.225	0.672	0.399
Surface Salinity	-0.058	0.875	0.488	0.601	-0.058	0.875	0.390	0.804
Bottom Salinity	0.338	0.847	0.122	0.830	0.338	0.847	0.694	0.587
Salinity Difference	0.820	0.036	-0.683	0.560	0.591	-0.002	0.801	-0.223
Surface DO	0.105	0.788	0.254	0.716	0.105	0.788	-0.389	0.325
Bottom DO	-0.791	0.367	-0.888	-0.870	-0.791	0.367	-0.791	0.482
DO Difference	0.923	0.054	-0.783	0.470	0.923	0.054	0.876	0.063
% Total Variance	36.5	21.6	29.8	28.6	36.5	21.6	39.6	24.1

There is considerable (and legitimate) concern regarding the adverse impacts of anthropogenous loading of nutrients and organic carbon into estuarine and coastal systems. However, little regard has been expressed concerning habitat alterations and resulting changes in salinity stratification due to dredging in such areas. Regardless of the effects of nutrients and organic carbon loading, hypoxic conditions can be directly related to extensive changes in the salinity stratification of an inshore estuary due to the opening of a barrier island and subsequent inflow of high-salinity Gulf waters. The resulting enhancement of salinity stratification can be directly responsible for the periodic establishment of hypoxic conditions below the pycnocline. Physical and stratigraphic components tend to establish the habitat conditions for hypoxia at depth regardless of anthropogenous loading of nutrients and organic carbon. Dredging of waterways also exacerbates salinity stratification in inshore estuaries, thus contributing to potential eutrophication problems in such coastal systems. Where dredging activities are accompanied by municipal development and industrial discharges of organic carbon and nutrients, the dissolved oxygen regimes can be further adversely affected. Whereas point-source pollution is being controlled in a generally effective manner, currently there is virtually no control concerning dredging activities in barrier estuaries along the northeast Gulf Coast. The results of the long-term analyses presented here suggest salinity alteration due to dredging in such areas requires further inquiry and possible regulation if the useful productivity of these coastal systems is to be maintained.

ACKNOWLEDGMENTS

   Much of the research that has been carried out to generate the field databases for this paper involved the unpaid support of undergraduate students, graduate students, staff, and scientists of the Department of Biological Science and the Center for Aquatic Research and Resource Management of Florida State University. Analytical help was also rendered through a series of grants, administered by S.P. Orlando, Jr. and C.J. Klein of the National Oceanic and Atmospheric Administration, Office of Ocean Resources Conservation and Assessment. Analytical support also was given by the Northwest Florida Water Management District through a series of grants, administered by F.G. Lewis, III, for analyses of the Apalachicola system.

LITERATURE CITED

Breitburg, D.L. 1990. Near-shore hypoxia in the Chesapeake Bay: Patterns and relationships among physical factors. *Estuarine, Coastal and Shelf Science* 30: 593-609.

Dawson, C.E. 1955. A contribution to the hydrography of Apalachicola Bay. *Publications of the Texas Institute of Marine Science* 4: 15-35.

Doudoroff, P. and D.L. Shumway. 1967. Dissolved oxygen criteria for the protection of fish. *American Fisheries Society Special Publication* 4: 13-19.

Duxbury, A.C. 1975. Orthophosphate and dissolved oxygen in Puget Sound. *Limnology and Oceanography* 20: 270-274.

Gorsline, D.S. 1963. Oceanography of Apalachicola Bay, Florida, p. 67-96. *In* T. Clements (ed.), Essays in Marine Geology in Honor of K.O. Emery. University of Southern California Press, Los Angeles.

Iverson, R.L. and H.F. Bittaker. 1986. Seagrass distribution and abundance in eastern Gulf of Mexico coastal waters. *Estuarine Coastal and Shelf Science* 22: 577-602.

Jackson, R.H.P., P.J. LeB. Williams, and I.R. Point. 1987. Freshwater phytoplankton in the low salinity region of the River Tamar estuary. *Estuarine and Coastal Marine Science* 25: 299-311.

Kuo, A.Y. and B.J. Neilson. 1987. Hypoxia and salinity in Virginia estuaries. *Estuaries* 10: 277-283.

Kuo, A.Y., K. Park, and M.Z. Moustafa. 1991. Spatial and temporal variability of hypoxia in the Rappanannock River, Virginia. *Estuaries* 14: 113-121.

Livingston, R.J. 1975. Impact of kraft pulp-mill effluents on estuarine and coastal fishes in Apalachee Bay, Florida, USA. *Marine Biology* 32: 19-48.

Livingston, R.J. 1982. Trophic organization of fishes in a coastal seagrass system. *Marine Ecology Progress Series* 7: 1-12.

Livingston, R.J. 1983. Resource Atlas of the Apalachicola Estuary. Florida Sea Grant College, Gainesville, Florida. Report No. 55.

Livingston, R.J. 1984a. The Ecology of the Apalachicola Bay system: An Estuarine Profile. United States Fish and Wildlife Service FWS/PBS 82/05. Washington, D.C.

Livingston, R.J. 1984b. Trophic response of fishes to habitat variability in coastal seagrass systems. *Ecology* 65: 1258-1275.

Loesch, H. 1960. Sporadic mass shoreward migrations of demersal fish and crustaceans in Mobile Bay, Alabama. *Ecology* 41: 292-298.

May, E.B. 1973. Extensive oxygen depletion in Mobile Bay, Alabama. *Limnology and Oceanography* 18: 353-366.

Meeter, D.A. and R.J. Livingston. 1978. Statistical methods applied to a four-year multivariate study of a Florida estuarine system, p. 53-67. *In* J. Cairns, Jr., K. Dickson, and R.J. Livingston (eds.), Biological Data in Water Pollution Assessment: Quantitative and Statistical Analyses. American Society of Testing and Materials, Philadelphia. Special Technical Publication 652.

Meeter, D.A., R.J. Livingston, and G.C. Woodsum. 1979. Short- and long-term hydrological cycles of the Apalachicola drainage system with application to Gulf coastal populations, p. 315-338. *In* R. J. Livingston (ed.), Ecological Processes in Coastal and Marine Systems. Plenum Press, New York.

National Oceanic and Atmospheric Administration. 1985. National Estuarine Inventory, Data Atlas. National Oceanic and Atmospheric Administration, Rockville, Maryland.

Odum, H.T. and R.F. Wilson. 1962. Further studies on reaeration and metabolism of Texas bays, 1958-1960. *Publications of the Institute of Marine Science, University of Texas* 8: 23-55.

Ogren, L. and J. Chess. 1969. A marine kill on New Jersey wrecks. *Underwater Naturalist* 3: 4-12.

Olinger, L.W. 1975. Environmental and recovery studies of Escambia Bay and the Pensacola Bay system, Florida. United States Environmental Protection Agency, Region IV, Atlanta, Georgia.

Orlando, S.P. Jr., L.P. Rozas, G.H. Ward, and C.J. Klein. 1993. Salinity characteristics of Gulf of Mexico estuaries. National Oceanic and Atmospheric Administration, Office of Ocean Resources Conservation and Assessment. Silver Spring, Maryland.

Parker, C.A. and J.E. O'Reilly. 1991. Oxygen depletion in Long Island Sound: A historical perspective. *Estuaries* 14: 248-264.

Pearson, T.H. 1980. Marine pollution effects of pulp and paper industry wastes. *Helgolander Wissenshaftliche Meeresuntersuchungen* 33: 340-365.

Pearson, T.H. and R. Rosenberg. 1978. Macrobenthic succession in relation to organic enrichment and pollution of the marine environment. *Oceanography and Marine Biology Annual Reviews* 16: 229-331.

Portnoy, J.W. 1991. Summer oxygen depletion in a diked New England estuary. *Estuaries* 14: 122-129.

Reyes, E. and M. Merino. 1991. Diel dissolved oxygen dynamics and eutrophication in a shallow well-mixed tropical lagoon. *Estuaries* 14: 372-381.

Santos, S.L. and S.A. Bloom. 1980. Stability in an annually defaunated estuarine soft-bottom community. *Oecologia* 46: 290-294.

Santos, S.L. and J.L. Simon. 1980a. Marine soft-bottom community-establishment following annual defaunation: Larval or adult recruitment? *Marine Ecology* 2: 235-241.

Santos, S.L. and J.L. Simon. 1980b. Response of soft-bottom benthos to annual catastrophic disturbance in a south Florida estuary. *Marine Ecology* 3: 347-355.

Schroeder, W.W., S.P. Dinnel, and W.J. Wiseman, Jr. 1990. Salinity stratification in a river-dominated estuary. *Estuaries* 213: 145-154.

Seliger, H.H. and J.A. Boggs. 1988. Long-term pattern of anoxia in the Chesapeake Bay, p. 570-583. *In* M.P. Lynch and E.C. Krome (eds.), Understanding the Estuary: Advances in Chesapeake Bay Research. Chesapeake Research Consortium, Solomons, Maryland.

Smith, D.E., M. Leffler, and G. Mackierman. 1992. Oxygen Dynamics in the Chesapeake Bay. Maryland Sea Grant, College Park, Maryland.

Stanley, D.W. and S.W. Nixon. 1992. Stratification and bottom-water hypoxia in the Pamlico River Estuary. *Estuaries* 15: 270-281.

Turner, R.W., W.W. Schroeder, and W.J. Wiseman, Jr. 1987. The role of stratification in the deoxygenation of Mobile Bay and adjacent shelf bottom waters. *Estuaries* 10: 13-20.

United States Army Corps of Engineers. 1976. Final Environmental Statement: Apalachicola, Chattahoochee, and Flint rivers, Alabama, Florida, and Georgia (Operation and Maintenance). United States Army Corps of Engineers, Mobile, Alabama.

United States Environmental Protection Agency. 1971. Conference in the matter of pollution of the interstate waters of the Escambia River basin (Alabama-Florida) and the intrastate portions of the Escambia basin within the state of Florida. United States Environmental Protection Agency, Pensacola, Florida.

Van Es, F.B., M.A. Van Arkel, L.A. Bowman, and H.G.J. Schroder. 1980. Influence of organic pollution on bacterial, macrobenthic, and meiobenthic populations in intertidal flats of the Dollard. *Netherlands Journal of Sea Research* 14: 288-304.

Weisberg, R.H. 1976. A note on estuarine mean flow estimation. *Journal of Marine Research* 34: 387-394.

Weisberg, R.H. 1989. Sikes Cut—A review of data and physical model studies by the COE on the salinity effects for Apalachicola Bay. Final report for the Florida Department of Environmental Regulation. Tallahassee, Florida.

Welsh, B.L. and F.C. Eller. 1991. Mechanisms controlling summertime oxygen depletion in Western Long Island Sound. *Estuaries* 14: 265-278.

Weiss, R.F. 1970. Helium isotope effect in solution in water and seawater. *Science* 168: 247-248.

Zieman, J.C. and R.T. Zieman. 1989. The ecology of the seagrass meadows of the west coast of Florida: A community profile. United States Fish and Wildlife Service Biological Report 85(7.25), Washington, D.C.

Zimmerman, M.S. and R.J. Livingston. 1976. Effects of kraft mill effluents on benthic macrophyte assemblages in a shallow-bay system (Apalachee Bay, North Florida, USA). *Marine Biology* 34: 297-312.

Zimmerman, M.S. and R.J. Livingston. 1976a. The effects of kraft mill effluents on benthic macrophyte assemblages in a shallow bay system (Apalachee Bay, north Florida, U.S.A.). *Marine Biology* 34: 297-312.

Zimmerman, M.S. and R.J. Livingston. 1976b. Seasonality and physico-chemical ranges of benthic macrophytes from a north Florida estuary (Apalachee Bay). *Contributions in Marine Science* 20: 34-45.

Zimmerman, M.S. and R.J. Livingston. 1979. Dominance and distribution of benthic macrophyte assemblages in a north Florida estuary (Apalachee Bay, Florida). *Bulletin of Marine Science* 29: 27-40.

Long-term Trends in Nutrient Generation by Point and Nonpoint Sources in the Albemarle-Pamlico Estuarine Basin

Donald W. Stanley

ABSTRACT: This paper summarizes the results of a study of long-term trends in annual rates of nutrient generation in the watershed of the Albemarle-Pamlico Sound system, a major estuary in North Carolina, USA. The primary goal of the study was to determine whether or not the historic record supports the contention that the estuary is receiving increasing nutrient loadings. A secondary goal was to learn whether or not trends, or lack of trends, in water quality in the estuary could be explained by the historic pattern of nutrient generation in the watershed. The watershed's annual generation of nitrogen and phosphorus is estimated to have increased twofold to threefold between 1880 and 1970 but appears to have stabilized after 1970, due primarily to decreased application of fertilizer on croplands, which offset increases in municipal loading and farm animals nutrient generation. This finding is paralleled by the lack of increases since 1970 in ammonia nitrogen, nitrate nitrogen, phosphate phosphorus, or chlorophyll *a* concentrations in the Pamlico River, one of the subestuaries of the Albemarle-Pamlico system. The weight of the evidence is that the Albemarle-Pamlico estuaries have not become more eutrophic during the past two decades.

Introduction

There is a growing perception that coastal environments in the United States and elsewhere are deteriorating, in part due to nitrogen (N) and phosphorus (P) pollution. Increases in population density, fertilizer use, and conversion of forest land to agriculture are thought to be the primary sources of excess nutrients leading to eutrophication in estuaries. Despite great interest in—and large expenditures for—estuarine water quality management during recent decades, evaluations of long- term trends have been made infrequently (e.g., Officer et al. 1984; Jordan et al. 1991). Consequently, little is known about the effectiveness of past and present management programs for most of our estuaries (National Research Council 1990). The problem is compounded by 1) the scarcity of quantitative information on historical trends in N and P generation in the watersheds of estuaries, and 2) a lack of quantitative understanding of how changes in inputs are related to conditions in the estuaries. Scores of snapshot estuarine nutrient loading computations have been made in recent times. The few available long-term studies of nutrient flux include an estimate of historical P loading trends to the Great Lakes (Chapra 1977) and analyses of water quality trends in rivers and streams in the United States (Smith et al. 1987; Lettenmaier et al. 1991), including the Mississippi River (Turner and Rabalais 1991).

This paper summarizes the results of a study of long-term trends in annual rates of nutrient generation by point and nonpoint sources in the Albemarle-Pamlico estuarine drainage basin in North Carolina and Virginia. The primary goal of the study was to determine whether or not the historic record supports the contention that the estuary is becoming more eutrophic (North Carolina Department of Natural Resources and Community Development 1989). A secondary goal was to learn whether or not trends, or lack of trends, in water quality in the estuary could be explained by the historic pattern of nutrient generation in the watershed.

There can be a large difference between nutrient generation within a watershed and nutrient loading to an estuary. Here, nutrient generation refers to the sum of 1) point source nutrient discharges, 2) five percent of the nutrients contained in farm animal wastes, 3) nutrients contained in surface runoff from all land areas except harvested cropland, and 4) nutrient yield from harvested cropland, estimated by means of a mass balance model. Loading, on the other hand, refers to the quantities of nutrient actually reaching the estuary. The generation rate normally exceeds the loading rate because of losses between the sources and the estuary, such as sedimentation of phosphorus and denitrification which are likely to occur as cropland runoff moves through swamp-forests (Kuenzler 1989; Jaworski et al. 1992). Loading can be computed by multiplying stream discharges times nutrient concentrations at the head of the estuary. However, the technique could not be used in this study because N and P concentrations at the mouths of the streams and rivers emptying into the estuary have not been monitored long term.

North Carolina's Albemarle-Pamlico estuarine system dominates the state's coastline and is the second largest estuary in the United States (7,765 km^2) and the third largest in North America. The two largest components of the system, Albemarle and Pamlico sounds, are bounded on the east by a chain of barrier islands (the Outer Banks) broken only by narrow inlets through which oceanic and estuarine waters are exchanged. On the west side, the Chowan and Roanoke rivers empty into Albemarle Sound, and the Tar and Neuse rivers discharge into Pamlico Sound (Fig. 1). Three of these rivers form the major tributary estuaries in the system, each of which is named after the river that feeds it (i.e., the Chowan River estuary, Tar-Pamlico River estuary, and Neuse River estuary). The sounds and river estuaries are shallow, low-to-mid salinity systems with a low lunar tidal amplitude. Their circulation is driven primarily by wind and freshwater inflow. Water depths in the tributary river estuaries average 2-4 m; the deepest areas of Pamlico Sound are only about 7-10 m. Salinities are very low throughout the Albemarle Sound region, ranging from fresh water in the Chowan River estuary to around 2-4‰ at the eastern end of Albemarle Sound. The two Pamlico Sound subestuaries, the Tar-Pamlico River and the Neuse River, have similar salinity patterns with ranges from 0‰ to about 15‰; Pamlico Sound has salinities in the 15-25‰ range. Intermittent salinity stratification is common in the Neuse and Tar-Pamlico, but normally persists for no more than a few days before being broken up by wind mixing associated with passing weather fronts.

The land near the sounds is low-lying and is mostly agricultural and wetlands. Urban and industrial uses are minimal, although there is a large phosphate mine on the shores of the Pamlico River estuary. Overall, the Albemarle-Pamlico drainage basin is about 60% forested, about 20%

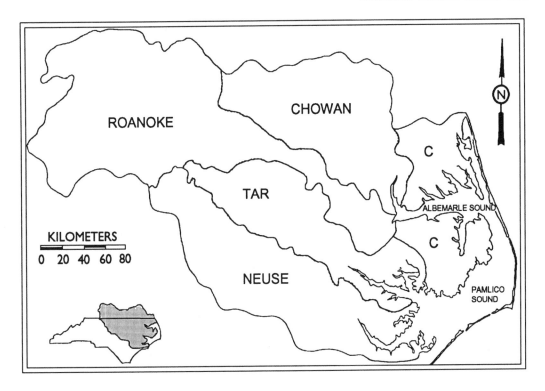

Fig. 1. Map showing boundaries of the Albemarle-Pamlico sub-basins. C refers to the Coastal sub-basin.

cropland, 18% other rural land, and only 2% urban. Most of the human population lives in the western regions of the basin away from the estuaries, although present growth rates in three of the coastal counties on the barrier islands are among the highest in the state. The Albemarle-Pamlico system is the major contributor to North Carolina's $1 billion-a-year commercial fishing industry as well as to a large recreational fishery. Details of the hydrography and basin characteristics for the Albemarle-Pamlico estuaries are given in Giese et al. (1979), Copeland et al. (1984), and Stanley (1992), and in the literature cited in these three publications.

Methods

Trends in annual total N and total P generation in the Albemarle-Pamlico basin were estimated for the period 1880-1987 at 4-yr to 10-yr intervals, depending on the availability of data. The procedure, which was based on those used by Chapra (1977), Thomas and Gilliam (1978), Kuenzler and Craig (1986), Lowrance et al. (1985), and Jaworski et al. (1992), involved computing point and nonpoint source nutrient generation on a county-by-county basis, and summing the county estimates to give an estimate for the whole watershed. For border counties the nonpoint data were weighted by the percentage of the county within the basin. Nonpoint sources included 1) harvested agricultural cropland, 2) other nonforested farmland (mostly idle cropland), 3) forested land, 4) pastureland, 5) urban land, 6) all other land areas, and 7) farm animals. Point sources included municipal and industrial discharges. In this paper, results are presented for the whole Albemarle-Pamlico watershed; results for the individual major sub-basins (Chowan River, Roanoke River, Tar-Pamlico River, Neuse River, and Coastal) are given in Stanley (1992, 1993). The Coastal sub-basin includes all land area downstream from the mouths of the river estuaries.

Nutrient generation by harvested agricultural lands was computed using a mass-balance model, similar to those of Kuenzler and Craig (1986), Lowrance et al. (1985), and Jaworski et al. (1992). It accounts for fertilizer application, nitrogen fixation, precipitation, crop harvest, and denitrification. Estimation of generation from other land uses was based on export coefficients. The primary data sources are listed in Table 1. Here, urban land use refers to areas within the limits of towns and cities with populations greater than 2,500. The other land use category was calculated by difference. It consists primarily of nonforested, nonagricultural lands outside the boundaries of urban areas (i.e., business properties, house lots, roads, cleared power line right-of-ways, etc.).

For each crop type (e.g., corn, tobacco), the "gross" generation of N and P was calculated as:

$$\text{kg N ha}^{-1}\text{ yr}^{-1} = (\text{fertilizer N} + \text{precipitation N} + \text{symbiotic N-fixation})$$
$$- (\text{harvest N} + \text{denitrification})$$

$$\text{kg P ha}^{-1}\text{ yr}^{-1} = (\text{fertilizer P} + \text{precipitation P}) - (\text{harvest P})$$

These estimates are referred to as "gross" generation because, as will be discussed below, there is evidence that significant quantities of N and P are lost—by mechanisms not accounted for in the above calculations—before runoff reaches the receiving streams.

The total amount of fertilizer applied annually to cropland in a county was assumed to be equal to the amount sold in or shipped to the county. Most of the fertilizer data were reported as tons of mixed fertilizer and fertilizer materials. To convert these data into tons of elemental N and P, the tonnage of fertilizer was multiplied by the percentages of the elements in each type of material sold. Total fertilizer application was apportioned to individual crop types on the basis of recommended fertilizer application rates. The symbiotic nitrogen fixation term was included only in the soybean and peanut calculations (105 kg N ha^{-1} yr^{-1} and 112 kg N ha^{-1} yr^{-1}, respectively) (Frissel 1978; Kuenzler and Craig 1986). Quantities of N and P in the harvest were determined by multiplying annual yields by the nutrient content per unit of harvest (Romaine 1965; Gilbertson et al. 1978). Denitrification rates were assumed to be 15% of the applied fertilizer nitrogen (Thomas and Gilliam 1978).

Estimates of wet and dry N and P deposition onto cropland during the 1980s were based on National Atmospheric Deposition Program wet precipitation measurements at stations in the basin. Total N deposition (wet and dry) was assumed to be twice the wet precipitation deposition (Stansland et al. 1986). The historical trend in N deposition was estimated by assuming that 1880 deposition was 20% of the current deposition (8.64 kg ha^{-1} yr^{-1}), and that the rate of change has been roughly exponential (Gschwandtner et al. 1985; Husar 1986). No information on historical trends in atmospheric P deposition were available; therefore, a constant rate of 0.5 kg ha^{-1} yr^{-1} was assumed, based on recent measurements in the region.

Nutrient generation for each other land use category was calculated by multiplying an export coefficient (kg N and P ha^{-1} yr^{-1}, taken from the literature, Table 2) times the land area (ha). Animal nutrient generation, here defined as the N and P contained in surface runoff, was assumed to be

Table 1. Sources for land use, fertilizer sales, point source discharges, and atmospheric deposition data.

Agricultural Land Use, Crop Harvests, and Farm Animals Inventory

United States Bureau of the Census (1880-1987); Virginia Department of Agriculture (1920-1988); North Carolina Department of Agriculture (1923-1988)

Forest Data

Cruikshank (1940); United States Forest Service (1943); Cruikshank and Evans (1945); Larson (1957); Larson and Bryan (1959); Knight and McClure (1966); Cost (1974, 1976); Welch and Knight (1974); Welch (1975); Sheffield (1976, 1977a, 1977b); Bechtold (1985); Brown (1985, 1986); Brown and Carver (1985)

Fertilizer Sales

United States Bureau of the Census (1954, 1959, 1964); Virginia Department of Agriculture (1956-1988); Hargett and Berry (1985); Mehring et al. (1985); North Carolina Department of Agriculture (various dates between 1956 and 1988)

Population and Urban Land Areas

United States Bureau of the Census (1880-1987)

Municipal and Industrial Discharges

United States Public Health Service (1944, 1951, 1958, 1963); North Carolina Stream Sanitation Committee (1946, 1957, 1959, 1961); Hall (1970); United States Environmental Protection Agency (1971); Virginia State Water Control Board (1975); North Carolina Division of Environmental Management (1986); North Carolina Division of Environmental Management, unpublished NPDES Self Monitoring Data (1986-1989)

Atmospheric Deposition

Junge (1958); Wells et al. (1972); Wells and Jorgensen (1975); Holmes (1977); Kuenzler et al. (1980); Galloway et al. (1984); Olsen and Slavich (1986); Olsen and Watson (1986)

---

equal to 5% of the nutrients in animal wastes. Numbers of animals were multiplied by the per animal waste generation rates (Table 2).

Point source nutrient generation was calculated for all municipal and industrial discharges in the basin. For industrial sources, the annual generation was calculated by multiplying daily data available for most of the industrial sources, but many of the municipal sewage systems were in operation long before effluent flow and nutrient concentration data collection began. Thus, N and

Table 2. Coefficients used to compute nitrogen and phosphorus generation by five different land use categories and by different types of farm animals. Values for forest are from Loehr (1974); values for other land uses are from Beaulac and Reckhow (1982); values for animals are from Barker (1987) and Robbins et al. (1972).

Land Use Category	Nitrogen (kg yr^{-1} ha^{-1})	Phosphorus (kg yr^{-1} ha^{-1})
Other Farmland	3.00	0.40
Other Land	3.00	0.40
Forest	1.50	0.20
Pastureland	4.00	0.60
Urban Land	6.00	1.10

Animal Type	Nitrogen (kg yr^{-1} animal^{-1})	Phosphorus (kg yr^{-1} animal^{-1})
Cattle		
Dairy	121.00	22.00
Beef	48.10	13.10
Swine	11.90	4.20
Horses	46.40	11.00
Poultry		
Broilers	0.40	0.10
Layers	0.56	0.20
Turkeys	1.36	0.52

Table 3. Total per capita nitrogen and phosphorus loads (kg yr^{-1}) in wastewater effluents as a function of treatment type (Gakstatter et al. 1978). Treatment factors are equal to the load for a given treatment type divided by the load for no treatment.

Treatment Type	Nitrogen		Phosphorus	
	kg yr^{-1}	Factor	kg yr^{-1}	Factor
None	4.6	1.00	1.2	1.00
Primary	4.2	0.90	1.1	0.90
Secondary				
Trickling filter	2.9	0.62	1.0	0.82
Activated sludge	2.2	0.47	1.0	0.82
Stabilization pond	1.9	0.42	0.9	0.74

P generation by municipal sources had to be estimated by a less direct method, involving the sewered population, the type of treatment in effect, and the efficiency of N and P removal expected from that treatment. The calculation was as follows:

kg N or P yr^{-1} = (sewered population) (per capita annual N or P generation) (treatment factor)

The per capita annual N and P generation was taken as 4.6 kg N and 1.2 kg P (Gakstatter et al. 1978), and the N treatment factors ranged from 1 (untreated) to 0.47 (secondary treatment), depending on the type of wastewater treatment practiced by the municipal treatment plant. Phosphorus treatment factors ranged from 1.0 to 0. 74 (Table 3). National Pollution Discharge Elimination System (NPDES) compliance monitoring data files were searched to provide lists of all current discharges, as well as historical information on discharges. The most difficult parameters to estimate were the treatment factors to be applied to each municipal discharge. Fortunately, there were periodic inventories of municipal wastewater facilities from 1942 through 1986 (see Table 1) that included detailed information on the levels of treatment provided by each facility and the size of the sewered population. For years before 1942, the sewered population was assumed to be equal to the city population, back to the time when the first sewage collection system for the town was constructed.

Results

Land use has changed little in the Albemarle-Pamlico basin over the past 60 yr (Fig. 2). Forest has been the most prevalent land use, ranging between 58% and 64% of the total basin area (4.02 - 4.43 × 10^6 ha). There was a peak in forest acreage in the 1960s. Cropland, the second most prevalent land use, peaked around 1940 at 21% of basin area (1.45 × 10^6 ha) and has generally declined since then, to 14% in 1987 (0.97 × 10^6 ha). Thus, forest and cropland together have constituted 74-81% of basin area since 1925. Before 1925, there are good data only for the cropland category; thus 1880-1920 values for other categories were estimated. For example, based on data available for the period (number of cattle on farms, cropland acreages, and the total land in farms) and the assumption that urban land was much less than 1% of the total, it can be calculated that forested areas must have been about the same in the late 1800s as in 1925. Today, urban areas account for about 2% of basin area (0.12 × 10^6 ha).

Some crops are much more important in the Albemarle-Pamlico region now than in the past, while others have diminished greatly in importance over the years (Fig. 3). Corn has been dominant for most of the past century, averaging 38% of total harvested cropland. The second most widely planted crop today, soybeans, has risen steadily in importance since it was introduced around 1910. On the other hand, tobacco and cotton plantings have declined since 1930. At its peak in the 1920s, cotton was the second most widely planted crop. Peanuts, a relatively minor crop, increased in acreage during the early part of this century up until the 1940s but have decreased slowly since then. Wheat and other small grains have never been dominant in this area.

Chemical fertilizer application to agricultural lands has had a great impact on cropland nutrient mass balances over the past century (Fig. 4). Average phosphorus application rates rose to a peak of 40 kg ha^{-1} yr^{-1} in the 1960s but has declined since then to around 25 kg ha^{-1} in 1987. Nitrogen fertilizer use increased about sevenfold between 1940 and 1978, when on average 110 kg N ha^{-1} was applied. Since then, N fertilizer use has declined slightly. Atmospheric N deposition onto cropland in the basin is estimated to have increased fivefold over the past century, but it is still

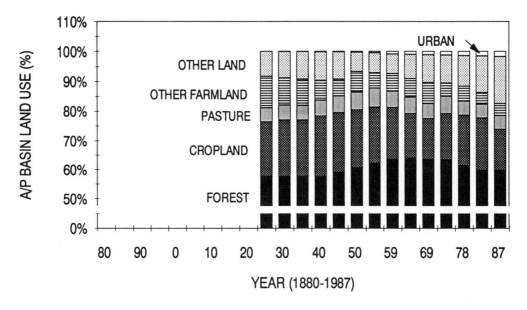

Fig. 2. Land uses, as percentages of total land area, in the Albemarle-Pamlico basin, 1925-1987. Note that the vertical axis is broken.

very small (4.3 kg ha^{-1} in 1987) in comparison to fertilizer N input and N fixation. As a result of increased fertilizer use, and more productive varieties, increases in yields (and hence nutrient output in harvest) for some crops have been very impressive. For example, corn yield per ha increased about fivefold, and the soybean yield approximately doubled over the past 40 yr. There have been impressive increases in the tobacco and peanut yields also (see Stanley 1992 for details).

Cropland gross N generation increased gradually from near zero in the late 1800s to around 57 × 10^6 kg N yr^{-1} by 1974 (54.9 kg N ha^{-1} yr^{-1}) but has not changed much since then (Fig. 4). Phosphorus generation increased most rapidly in the early 1900s. It reached a peak in 1974 of about 34 × 10^6 kg P (32.9 kg P ha^{-1} yr^{-1}), since then, basin cropland gross P generation has decreased substantially, to about 16 × 10^6 kg P yr^{-1} (14.5 kg P ha^{-1} yr^{-1}).

When converted to areal rates, the gross cropland nutrient generation values are high (48.5 kg N ha^{-1} and 15.3 kg P ha^{-1} for 1987) in comparison to literature values for measured edge-of-field nutrient fluxes (15-30 kg N ha^{-1} and 1-5 kg P ha^{-1}) (Frink 1991). I suspect that the problem lies in the output side of the cropland nutrient mass balances. There are probably significant unaccounted losses before the nutrients have reached the field's edge. For example, Lowrance et al. (1985) concluded that on upland agricultural areas of coastal Georgia, most of the 50 kg N ha^{-1} yr^{-1} of the N input (precipitation, fertilizer, and N fixation) unaccounted for in the harvest probably left the field via subsurface flow and denitrification. For this reason, I reduced the gross cropland nutrient generation by 66.6% (N) and 80% (P) to give what I call estimated "net" cropland nutrient generation. These net values were in turn used in the calculation of total basin nutrient generation (see below).

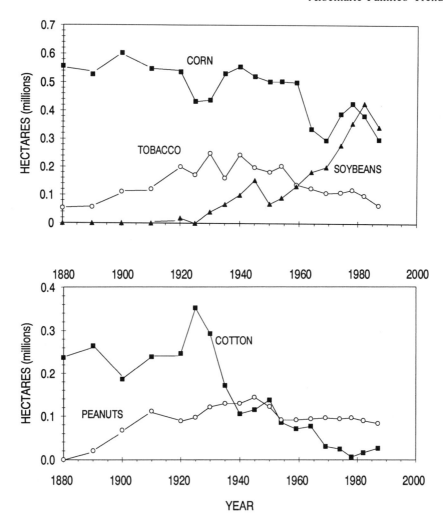

Fig. 3. Trends in plantings of major crops in the Pamlico River estuary watershed, 1880-1987.

During the past two decades, swine and poultry generation have expanded significantly in the central coastal plain of North Carolina. Growth of the poultry industry has been one of the most notable developments in Southern agriculture since World War II. Total poultry inventories (broilers, layers, and turkeys) in the Albemarle-Pamlico basin grew slowly from around 0.3×10^6 in 1880 to approximately 1.1×10^6 in 1959, since then the numbers have increased at an amazing rate such that in 1987 there were over 10×10^6. In addition, swine inventories have approximately doubled in the past two decades.

The rapid uptrend in farm animal nutrient generation in recent years reflects the growth in swine and poultry production (Fig. 5). Nitrogen generation by this source showed no long-term trend before 1969, fluctuating between 1.7×10^6 kg N yr^{-1} and 2.6×10^6 kg N yr^{-1}. However, by

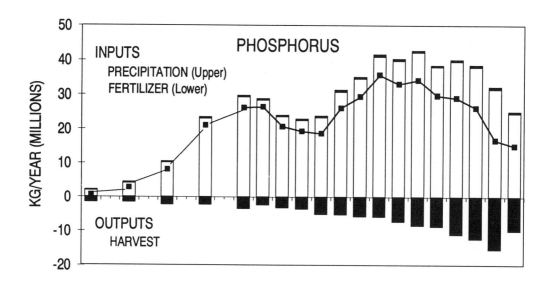

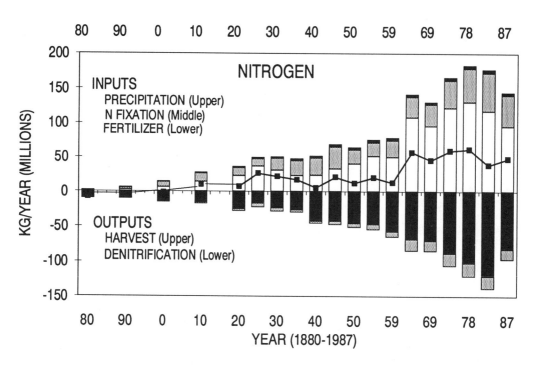

Fig. 4. Cropland N and P balances, 1880-1987. "Gross" annual N and P generation (inputs minus outputs) are indicated by the solid lines with symbols.

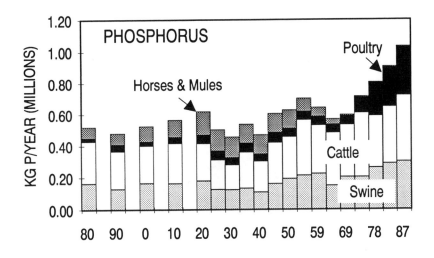

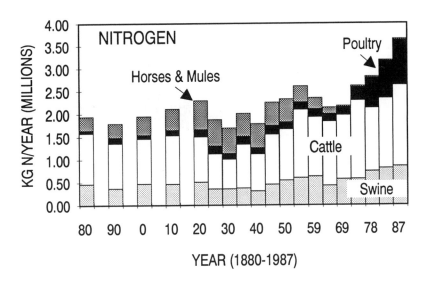

Fig. 5. N and P generation by farm animals in the Albemarle-Pamlico basin, 1880-1987.

1987 it had risen to 3.6×10^6 kg yr^{-1}, a 65% increase compared to the 1969 generation rate. Similarly, farm animal P generation rose 67% between 1969 and 1987, from 0.6×10^6 kg yr^{-1} to 1.0×10^6 kg yr^{-1}. Before 1969, cattle typically contributed 40%-60% of the total N and P, with most of the remainder divided between horses and mules. In recent years the percentages have shifted toward dominance by swine and poultry. Poultry have accounted for most of the long-term increases in total generation of N and P by farm animals.

The urban population, and hence the estimated sewered population, in the Albemarle-Pamlico, has risen rapidly in recent years. Although sewage collection systems had been constructed for

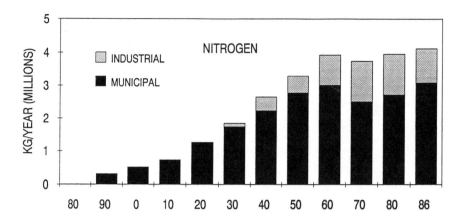

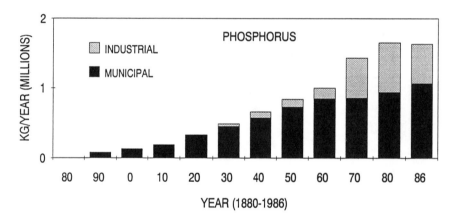

Fig. 6. Trends in point source nitrogen (N) and phosphorus (P) generation in the Albemarle-Pamlico basin, 1880-1987.

most of the larger towns in the early 1900s, as late as 1945 about two-thirds of the sewered population were on systems that provided no treatment (North Carolina Stream Sanitation Committee 1946). About half of the sewage that was treated received only primary treatment, which removes, at best, only about 10% of the N and P. Thus, N and P generation were growing at about the same rate as the sewered population (Fig. 6). As secondary treatment came into widespread use in the 1950s and 1960s, the nutrient removal efficiencies increased and the rate of increase in point source N and P generation slowed. But, there was little additional improvement until a North Carolina statewide phosphate detergent ban went into effect January 1, 1988. Thus, nutrient generation by municipal sources continued to increase approximately in proportion to population growth through 1987, when the annual rates were 3.1×10^6 kg N and 1.1×10^6 kg P. A high percentage of the total municipal loading comes from a small number of the largest cities.

Although the Albemarle-Pamlico basin is relatively unindustrialized, there are a few major industrial N and P sources. Two types of industries—pulp and paper mills and phosphate mining—are dominant in terms of N and P generation. In 1987 all industries were estimated to have discharged a total of 1.0×10^6 kg N and 0.6×10^6 kg P into the estuary. This amounts to about one-fourth and one-third the total point source N and P, respectively.

Trends in N and P generation by all sources are summarized in Fig. 7. Note that cropland N and P generation rates plotted are net values that are one-third and one-fifth, respectively, the gross generation rates calculated from the input-output mass balances (see above for rationale). Total annual N generation is estimated to have nearly doubled over the past century, from 31×10^6 kg in 1880 to 55×10^6 kg in 1987. Most of the increases occurred between 1950 and 1970, due in part to the rapid increase in cropland generation in the 1960s, and to increases in farm animals and point source generation. Since 1964, there has been little change in the estimated annual N generation; however, the relative importance of some N sources has changed greatly in recent times. For example, in 1880, the most important sources were runoff from forest, pasture, and other lands (>90% of total). Today, the N generation by forest and other lands is about the same as in 1880, in absolute terms, but their relative importance is greatly diminished. The most important new nitrogen source is cropland N. Farm animals and point sources have also become more important.

Nonpoint source P generation began to increase earlier in this century than nonpoint N generation, primarily because of the earlier use of P fertilizers on cropland. Between 1880 and 1920, total P generation increased about 250%, from 4.3×10^6 kg yr^{-1} to around 10×10^6 kg yr^{-1}. Since then, there have been both increases and decreases. The most notable change in recent times is the apparent downtrend in total basin P generation since about 1969, due primarily to reduced net cropland P generation resulting from decreased P fertilizer application rates.

Discussion

UNCERTAINTIES IN THE NUTRIENT PRODUCTION ESTIMATES

Nutrient export coefficients are notoriously variable (see reviews by Beaulac and Reckhow 1982 and Frink 1991). For example, the range of measured N export coefficients for forests spans at least an order of magnitude (0.10-12.0 kg ha^{-1} yr^{-1}, as reported in Frink 1991). Beaulac and Reckhow (1982) discussed factors affecting the coefficients and urged that for application to a particular geographic area, only those coefficients from studies in similar areas be considered. Following their advice, I chose, when possible, values derived from studies made in the coastal plain region of the southeastern United States.

Soil scientists are much more certain about what factors affect rates of denitrification than they are about the actual rates in the field. Studies in North Carolina and elsewhere have shown rates of denitrification to be inversely related to drainage and directly related to the presence of some soil horizons that restrict water movement. Gambrell et al. (1975) measured essentially no denitrification on one moderately well-drained soil and as much as 60 kg N ha^{-1} denitrified in a poorly-drained soil; both sites were in the Tar River basin. The figure of 15% applied N lost by denitrification that I used is frequently used in computations of N balances. Thomas and Gilliam (1978) concluded that the 15% figure is generally accepted as being as accurate as any.

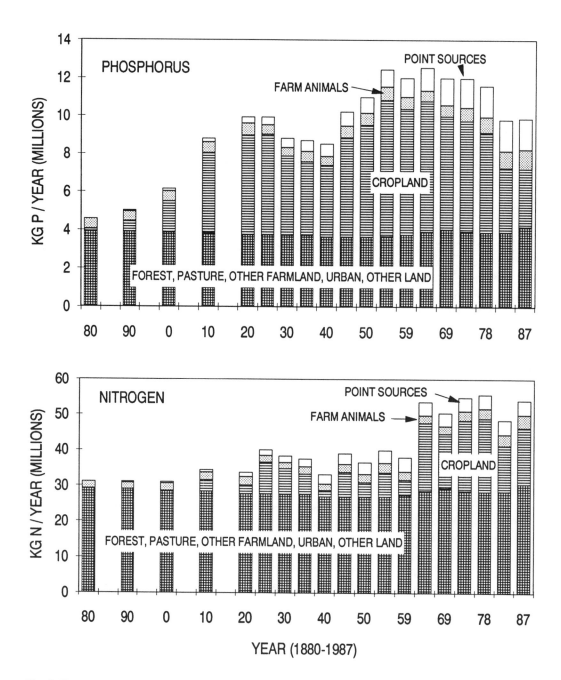

Fig. 7. Trends in estimated total nitrogen and phosphorus generation in the Albemarle-Pamlico basin, 1880-1987.

Estimating trends in atmospheric N and P deposition onto cropland is difficult because of the weak historical database for precipitation chemistry. Before 1955 there were only sporadic measurements (none in the Albemarle-Pamlico basin); Stansland et al. (1986) concluded that their reliability is so questionable that they should not be used for trend analysis. Thus, my indirect estimates of the trends are based on three assumptions: 1) 1880 N concentrations in basin precipitation were the same as those measured today in remote areas unaffected by anthropogenic NO_x emissions, 2) N deposition since 1880 has increased monotonically, and 3) there has been no trend in P deposition. The present-day N deposition rate used in the calculations (8.64 kg ha^{-1} yr^{-1}) is well within the range of recent measurements for the Southeastern United States (Jaworski et al. 1992). Since atmospheric deposition accounts for only about 5% of the calculated N input and 2% of the P input to cropland, modest errors in estimating this source would not appreciably affect cropland nutrient generation calculations.

The 5% value used as an estimate of the fraction of animal waste in surface runoff is highly uncertain. It is based solely on the report of Robbins et al. (1972). This value may be increasing, which, in combination with recent dramatic increases in swine and poultry production, could have a significant impact on total nutrient generation in the Pamlico basin. Modern animal operations involve the use of feedlots or buildings in which hundreds (swine) to tens-of-thousands (poultry) of animals are confined in very small areas. These operations become essentially point-source discharges, and indeed the wastes are now often treated by aeration lagoons or other techniques similar to those employed by conventional municipal treatment plants. Unfortunately, however, the animal waste treatment facilities are not nearly as strongly regulated as municipal point sources (North Carolina Department of Natural Resources and Community Development 1986).

Potential sources of error in the municipal nutrient generation estimates include the sewered population values and the treatment factors. For the years prior to 1942—the year the first municipal treatment plant inventory was conducted—the sewered populations were assumed to be equal to the populations of the cities and towns. This caused an overestimation of the nutrient generation. However, this error makes an insignificant difference in total nutrient generation since the urban population was so small. The problem with using treatment factors is that the facilities in a given city often do not perform at the expected efficiencies, for a number of reasons, including storm-related bypassing of raw sewage in combined systems, wastewater flows exceeding the design capacity of the systems, and poor maintenance of the equipment. The latter was reported to be a serious problem in many cities and towns in North Carolina during the 1950s (North Carolina Stream Sanitation Committee 1961). This problem would result in an underestimation of the actual municipal generation of N and P by the technique I used. However, a comparison calculation I made did show that, for recent times at least, results from the treatment-factors method are comparable to those obtained by a more direct method; that is, summing the products of measured effluent flows and multiplying that value times the measured N and P concentrations in effluent for all cities and towns in the basin (Stanley 1992).

There is evidence that, as expected, total basin nutrient generation is higher than nutrient loading to the estuaries of the Albemarle-Pamlico system. For recent times, there are estimates of the annual nutrient loading rates for all the Albemarle-Pamlico sub-basins except what I have referred to as the Coastal sub-basin (see Fig. 1). The loading calculations were made by the North Carolina Department of Natural Resources and Community Development (1982, 1983, 1987) and are based primarily on instream flow multiplied times nutrient concentration calculations, and summed point source loadings. These loading estimates (summarized in Table 4) are approximately one-third the

1987 total nutrient generation estimates (compare Table 4 with Fig. 7). Only a small part of the discrepancy can be accounted for by the omission of the Coastal sub-basin from the loading estimates, since this sub-basin constitutes only about 10% of the total basin area. Also, there is little difference between my point source nutrient generation estimates and the North Carolina Department of Natural Resources and Community Development point source loadings. Rather, most of the difference is associated with the nonpoint source category. Evidently, there are significant nutrient losses between the sources and the estuary due to groundwater infiltration and sedimentation of P and N, and volatilization and denitrification of N. In particular, lowland swamp forests along coastal rivers (like the Tar, Neuse, Chowan, and Roanoke) probably are major sinks for nutrients. Kuenzler and Craig (1986) estimated that in eastern North Carolina these systems are capable of removing 83% of the total nitrogen and 51% of the total phosphorus from water draining through them.

ESTUARINE WATER QUALITY TRENDS

One obvious question that arises from this exercise is whether or not the estimated long-term nutrient generation trends are related to trends in water quality conditions in the estuaries. Unfortunately, there is practically no direct evidence of trophic condition (e.g., nutrient concentrations, algal biomass, dissolved oxygen) available for the Albemarle-Pamlico system prior to the mid-1960s. Also, data collection since then has been very uneven. No studies have been made in the open waters of Pamlico Sound, and there are very little data for Albemarle Sound.

The Pamlico River is the only estuary in the Albemarle-Pamlico system for which there is a sufficient record of water quality to permit trend analysis. It is, in fact, one of the most thoroughly monitored estuaries in the Southeast United States region. Since the late 1960s there has been a Pamlico monitoring program in operation nearly continuously, funded primarily by PCS Phosphate (formerly Texasgulf, Inc.), which operates a phosphate mine on the south shore of the estuary. The monitoring study was carried out by scientists at North Carolina State University (1967-1973) and at East Carolina University (1975-present). Nitrogen, phosphorus, chlorophyll a, salinity, and dissolved oxygen are monitored every other week at approximately 20 stations in the estuary. Using the Seasonal Kendall-Tau test, Stanley (1993) analyzed trends in nutrient data gathered over the past 20-24 yr. Also, Stanley and Nixon (1992) reported on trends in bottom water oxygen in the estuary and investigated the relationship between stratification and hypoxia in the Pamlico. The findings of these studies can be summarized as follows:

Nitrate nitrogen (NO_3^{-1}) decreased in the upper and middle regions of the estuary by 2.8% yr^{-1} and 6.5% yr^{-1}, respectively, between 1969 and 1991. There was no decrease in NO_3^{-1} in the increased about 2% yr^{-1} in the lower two-thirds of the estuary below the PCS Phosphate mine discharge. Upstream from the phosphate mine, there was no trend in PO_4^{+2}. In the upper estuary, chlorophyll a (CHLa) showed an uptrend between 1970 and 1991 while bottom water dissolved oxygen (DO) showed a downtrend (1968-1991). The CHLa levels increased 0.7 μg l^{-1} yr^{-1} (6.6% yr^{-1}), and the DO decreased very slowly at a rate of 0.01 mg l^{-1} yr^{-1} (0.17% yr^{-1}, or less than 5% total over the past two decades). There were no trends in CHLa and bottom water DO in the middle and lower estuary regions. Finally, the trend analysis showed that neither Tar River flow or salinity and stratification patterns in the estuary changed between 1967 and 1991 (Stanley and Nixon 1992; Stanley 1993).

The PO_4^{+2} increase in the lower two-thirds of the Pamlico is almost certainly related to the discharge of large quantities of P from the phosphate mine. The increased PO_4^{+2} levels resulting

Table 4. Nutrient loading estimates for sub-basins of the Albemarle-Pamlico Sound system.

Basin	Land Area (km^2)	N Annual Loading Rate (kg km^{-2})	N Annual Loading (kg 10^{-3})	P Annual Loading Rate (kg km^{-2})	P Annual Loading (kg 10^{-3})
Chowan	12,673		4,197		443
Point			881		165
Nonpoint		261	3,316	21	278
Roanoke	25,063		5,436		486
R.R. Res.	21,780		3,845		279
Bel. Res.	3,283				
Point			593		133
Nonpoint		303	998	22	73
Tar-Pamlico	11,650		3,223		933
Point			625		201
Nonpoint		216	2,522	26	312
Texasgulf			76		419
Neuse	15,979		7,358		962
Point			1,513		430
Nonpoint		365	5,845	33	532
TOTAL	65,365		20,214		2,824
Point					
Nonpoint		290		27	

Notes:
1. Chowan and Roanoke data from North Carolina Department of Natural Resources and Community Development (1982)
2. Tar-Pamlico data from North Carolina Department of Natural Resources and Community Development (1987)
3. Neuse data from North Carolina Department of Natural Resources and Community Development (1983)
4. R.R. Res. refers to the Roanoke River Reservoir; Bel. Res. refers to the land area downstream from the reservoir
5. Texasgulf refers to discharge from the Texasgulf phosphate mining facility

from the mine discharge have not promoted eutrophication, as evidenced by the lack of trends in CHL*a* or bottom water DO in the lower two-thirds of the estuary. This finding lends support to the notion that this element is often not a factor limiting estuarine primary production (Ryther and

Dunstan 1971; Hecky and Kilham 1988). In addition, more than 95% of measurements made between 1980 and 1991 gave water column $DIN:PO_4^{+2}$ ratios ($DIN = NO_3^{-1} + NH_4^{+1}$) less than $16:1$. This is also indicative of a lack of P limitation in the estuary. Nevertheless, PCS Phosphate recently has upgraded its wastewater treatment process so as to reduce its P release by 90%, which is equivalent to approximately a 50% reduction in total P loading to the estuary. The consequences of this large reduction are being monitored.

Factors other than N, P, or the quantity of fresh water flowing into the Pamlico (and hence salinity patterns) must be responsible for the trend toward increasing phytoplankton biomass in the upper estuary. Although the average annual CHLa concentration (20 μg l^{-1}) is comparable to averages for other river-dominated estuaries in the region (Boynton et al. 1982), it is nearly three-fold higher now than two decades ago. Harned and Davenport (1990) analyzed trends in suspended solids concentrations throughout the Albemarle-Pamlico estuarine system, and found that since the early 1970s they have decreased in almost all areas, including the Pamlico River estuary. One possible explanation for this decline is improved agricultural practices; the construction of reservoirs also may have played a role. Thus, light limitation in the upper estuary may not be as severe now as in the past, which could help explain the increase in CHLa. Unfortunately, there is no long-term record of light extinction for the estuary.

The weight of the evidence is that the Pamlico River estuary has not become more eutrophic over the past two decades. This conclusion parallels the finding that while nutrient generation in the Albemarle-Pamlico basin is estimated to have increased significantly during the past century, it has changed little since 1969.

In addition to the Pamlico River estuary monitoring program, there have been research projects that focused on eutrophication in the Chowan and Neuse estuaries. The impetus for this research was the occurrence of blooms of blue-green algae in the upper regions of these estuaries during some, but not all, summers in the late 1970s and early 1980s. The blooms were restricted to the riverine and freshwater tidal portions of the estuaries because the blue-green algal species comprising them cannot tolerate salt water (Paerl et al. 1984). The blooms extended for 10-30 km stretches and lasted from a few days to several weeks. Chlorophyll a levels were typically several hundred μg l^{-1} (North Carolina Department of Natural Resources and Community Development 1982; Paerl 1982, 1987; Christian et al. 1986, 1988). It has been speculated that the blue-green algal blooms are more prevalent in these estuaries now than in past decades (North Carolina Department of Natural Resources and Community Development 1987), but there is no historical systematic sampling record to confirm the speculation. It is also possible that blooms were just as common earlier, but like most other symptoms of eutrophication, were paid little attention.

Research has improved our knowledge of several factors other than nutrients that contribute to the blooms. For example, the relationship between nitrogen and phosphorus and bloom occurrence is difficult to understand, in part because variations in the N and P loading rates and instream concentrations do not appear to correlate well with bloom occurrence. Blooms developed in the lower Neuse River during two of the four summers of the period 1979-1982, even though there was very little year-to-year variability in the instream nutrient levels (Stanley 1983). An analysis of chlorophyll a data taken during this period suggested an inverse relationship between bloom intensity and river flow rate. This observation led to an experimental study to test the following two-part hypothesis: a) summer algal blooms are prevented from developing by intermediate-to-high flows because nutrient-rich water is carried to the estuary before algal densities can reach bloom proportions; and b) summer blooms do develop during sustained low-flow periods because the algae grow at a more rapid rate than when flow is high (due to reduced light limitation and water turbulence), and because water parcels remain in the river long enough for bloom densities to develop. The outcome of this research was a mathematical model which, given historical river flow as input, accurately predicted the occurrence or non-occurrence of blooms during the preceding decade (Christian et al. 1986).

However, this finding does not resolve the issue of the relationship between the blooms and nutrient loading; in particular, whether or not reducing loading would reduce or eliminate the problem. The North Carolina Department of Environment, Health, and Natural Resources has made a commitment to pursue a goal of reducing nutrient loading, based on the assumption that less nutrient input would not only reduce the threat of blue-green algal blooms but also improve bottom water oxygen conditions, and even reduce the severity of fish kills in the estuaries. The State is currently developing a mathematical model to predict how much loading reduction will be required. Based on previous research, Paerl (1987) estimated that quite large reductions, on the order of 30% for nitrogen and 50% for phosphorus, will be needed to meet the goal. Recall, however, that the estimates I have presented above suggest that during the past century total N and P generation in the Albemarle-Pamlico basin have increased by a factor of only 2 for N and a factor of 2.5 for P. Thus, it may be very difficult to achieve the proposed loading reductions.

ACKNOWLEDGMENTS

PCS Phosphate (formerly Texasgulf, Inc.) has generously supported the Pamlico River estuary water quality monitoring program since 1966. Primary funding for this trend analysis of the historical data was also provided by PCS Phosphate. Additional support for the historical nutrient generation calculations was provided by a grant from the National Ocean Pollution Program Office of the National Oceanic and Atmospheric Administration, United States Department of Commerce. The grant (NA86AA-D-SG046) was administered through the University of North Carolina Sea Grant College Program at North Carolina State University (as project R/SF-2). I thank William Schimming and Jeff Furness of PCS Phosphate for providing additional data. East Carolina University students and staff involved in transcribing data from printed records into computer files included Ray Taft, Jeff Taft, Sharon Reid, Colleen Reid, Deborah Daniel, and Anne Anderson. Kay Evans and Mark Hollingsworth provided assistance in the preparation of the report.

LITERATURE CITED

Barker, J.C. 1987. North Carolina Agricultural Chemicals Manual. North Carolina State University, Raleigh, North Carolina.

Beaulac, M.N. and K.H. Reckhow. 1982. An examination of land use-nutrient export relationships. *Water Resources Bulletin* 18: 1013-1024.

Bechtold, W.A. 1985. Forest statistics for North Carolina, 1984. Resource Bulletin SE-78. United States Forest Service, Southeastern Forest Experiment Station, Asheville, North Carolina.

Boynton, W.R., W.M. Kemp, and C.W. Keefe. 1982. A comparative analysis of nutrients and other factors influencing estuarine productivity, p. 69-90. *In* V. S. Kennedy (ed.), Estuarine Comparisons. Academic Press, New York.

Brown, M.J. 1985. Forest statistics for the southern piedmont of Virginia, 1985. Resource Bulletin SE-81. United States Department of Agriculture, Forest Service, Southeastern Forest Experiment Station, Asheville, North Carolina.

Brown, M.J. 1986. Forest statistics for the northern mountains of Virginia, 1986. Resource Bulletin SE-85. United States Department of Agriculture, Forest Service, Southeastern Forest Experiment Station, Asheville, North Carolina.

Brown, M.J. and G.C. Carver. 1985. Forest statistics for the coastal plain of Virginia, 1985. Resource Bulletin SE-80. United States Department of Agriculture, Forest Service, Southeastern Forest Experiment Station, Asheville, North Carolina.

Chapra, S.C. 1977. Total phosphorus model for the Great Lakes. *Journal of the Environmental Engineering Division, American Society of Civil Engineers* 103: 147-161.

Christian, R.R., W.L. Bryant, Jr., and D.W. Stanley. 1986. The relationship between river flow and *Microcystis aeruginosa* blooms in the Neuse River, North Carolina. Report No. 223, University of North Carolina Water Resources Research Institute. Raleigh, North Carolina.

Christian, R.R., D.W. Stanley, and D.A. Daniel. 1988. Characteristics of a blue-green algal bloom in the Neuse River, North Carolina. Working Paper 87-2, University of North Carolina Sea Grant College Program, North Carolina State University, Raleigh, North Carolina.

Copeland, B.J., R.G. Hodson, and S.R. Riggs. 1984. The Ecology of the Pamlico River Estuary: An Estuarine Profile, United States Fish and Wildlife Service, Washington, D.C.

Cost, N.D. 1974. Forest statistics for the coastal plain of Virginia, 1976. Resource Bulletin SE-34, United States Forest Service, Southeastern Forest Experiment Station. Asheville, North Carolina.

Cost, N.D. 1976. Forest statistics for the southern coastal plain of North Carolina, 1973. Resource Bulletin SE-26, United States Forest Service, Southeastern Forest Experiment Station. Asheville, North Carolina.

Cruikshank, J.W. 1940. Forest resources of the southern coastal plain of North Carolina. Forest Survey Release No. 4. United States Forest Service, Appalachian Forest Experiment Station, Asheville, North Carolina.

Cruikshank, J.W. and T.C. Evans. 1945. Approximate forest area and timber volume by county in the Carolinas and Virginia. Forest Service Release No. 19. United States Forest Service, Appalachian Forest Experiment Station, Asheville, North Carolina.

Frink, C.R. 1991. Estimating nutrient exports to estuaries. *Journal of Environmental Quality* 20: 17-724.

Frissel, M.J. 1978. Cycling of Mineral Nutrients in Agricultural Systems. Elsevier, New York.

Galloway, J.N., G.E. Likens, and M.E. Hawley. 1984. Acid precipitation: Natural versus anthropogenic components. *Science* 226: 29-831.

Gambrell, R.P., J.W. Gilliam, and S.B. Weed. 1975. Denitrification in subsoils of the North Carolina coastal plain as affected by soil drainage. *Journal of Environmental Quality* 4: 11-316.

Gakstatter, J.H., M.O. Allum, S.E. Dominguez, and M.R. Crouse. 1978. A survey of phosphorus and nitrogen levels in treated municipal wastewater. *Journal of the Water Pollution Control Federation* 50: 718-722.

Giese, G.L., H.B. Wilder, and G.G. Parker, Jr. 1979. Hydrology of major estuaries and sounds in North Carolina. United States Geological Survey Water Resources Investigation Report 79-46.

Gilbertson, C.B., F.A. Norstadt, A.C. Matthews, R.F. Holt, A.P. Barnett, T.M. McCalla, C.A. Onstad, R.A. Young, L.R. Shuyler, L.A. Christensen, and D.L. van Dyne. 1978. Animal waste utilization on crops and pastureland. United States Environmental Protection Agency, Washington, D.C. EPA-600/2-79-059.

Gschwandtner, G., K.C. Gschwandtner, and E. Eldridge. 1985. Historic emissions of sulfur and nitrogen oxides in the United States from 1900 to 1980, Vol. I, Results. Report EPA-600/7-85-009a, United States Environmental Protection Agency, Washington, D.C.

Hall, W.T. 1970. Municipal water and sewer systems, an inventory in eastern North Carolina. East Carolina, University Regional Development Institute, Greenville, North Carolina.

Hargett, N.L. and J.T. Berry. 1985. 1984 fertilizer summary data report. National Fertilizer Development Center, Tennessee Valley Authority, Muscle Shoals, Alabama.

Harned, D.A. and M.S. Davenport. 1990. Water-quality trends and basin activities and characteristics for the Albemarle-Pamlico estuarine system, North Carolina and Virginia. United States Geological Survey Open File Report 90-398. Raleigh, North Carolina.

Hecky, R.E. and P. Kilham. 1988. Nutrient limitation of phytoplankton in freshwater and marine environments: A review of recent evidence on the effects of enrichment. *Limnology and Oceanography* 33: 796-822.

Holmes, R.N. 1977. Phosphorus cycling in an alluvial swamp forest in the North Carolina coastal plain. M.S. thesis, East Carolina University, Greenville, North Carolina.

Husar, R.B. 1986. Emissions of sulfur dioxide and nitrogen oxides and trends for eastern North America, p. 48-92. *In* National Research Council, Acid Deposition, Long-Term Trends. National Academy Press, Washington, D.C.

Jaworski, N.A., P.M. Groffman, A.A. Keller, and J.C. Prager. 1992. A watershed nitrogen and phosphorus balance: The upper Potomac River basin. *Estuaries* 15: 83-95.

Jordan, T.E., D.L. Correll, J. Miklas, and D.E. Weller. 1991. Long-term trends in estuarine nutrients and chlorophyll, and short-term effects of variation in watershed discharge. *Marine Ecology Progress Series* 75: 121-132.

Junge, C.E. 1958. Atmospheric chemistry. *Advances in Geophysics* 4: 1-108.

Knight, H.A. and J.P. McClure. 1966. North Carolina's timber, 1961-1964. Resource Bulletin SE-5, United States Forest Service, Southeastern Forest Experiment Station. Asheville, North Carolina.

Kuenzler, E.J. 1989. Value of forested wetlands as filters for sediments and nutrients, p. 85-96. *In* D.L. Hook and L. Russ (eds.), The Forested Wetlands of the Southeastern United States. Technical Report SE-50, United States Department of Agriculture, Forest Service, Southeastern Forest Experiment Station, Asheville, North Carolina.

Kuenzler, E.J., P.J. Mulholland, L.A. Yarbro, and L. Smook. 1980. Distributions and budgets of carbon, phosphorus, iron, and manganese in a floodplain swamp ecosystem. Report 157, University of North Carolina Water Resources Research Institute, North Carolina State University, Raleigh, North Carolina.

Kuenzler, E.J. and N.J. Craig. 1986. Land use and nutrient yields of the Chowan River watershed, p. 77-107. *In* D.L. Correll (ed.), Watershed Research Perspectives. Smithsonian Institution Press, Washington, D.C.

Larson, R.W. 1957. North Carolina's timber supply, 1955. Forest Service Release No. 49, United States Forest Service, Appalachian Forest Experiment Station. Asheville, North Carolina.

Larson, R.W. and M.B. Bryan. 1959. Virginia's timber. Forest Survey Release No. 54. United States Department of Agriculture, Forest Service, Appalachian Forest Experiment Station, Asheville, North Carolina.

Lettenmaier, D.P., E.R. Hooper, C. Wagoner, and K.B. Faris. 1991. Trends in stream quality in the continental United States, 1978-1987. *Water Resources Research* 27: 327-339.

Loehr, R.C. 1974. Characteristics and comparative magnitude of non-point sources. *Journal of the Water Pollution Control Federation* 46: 1849-1872.

Lowrance, R.R., R.A. Leonard, and L.E. Asmussen. 1985. Nutrient budgets for agricultural watersheds in the southeastern coastal plain. *Ecology* 66: 287-296.

Mehring, A.L., J.R. Adams, and K.D. Jacob. 1985. Statistics on fertilizers and liming materials in the United States. Statistical Bulletin 191, United States Department of Agriculture, Washington, D.C.

National Research Council. 1990. Managing Troubled Waters, The Role of Marine Environmental Monitoring. National Academy Press, Washington, D.C.

North Carolina Department of Agriculture. 1923-1988. North Carolina Agricultural Statistics (Annual Bulletins and Reports). Raleigh, North Carolina.

North Carolina Department of Natural Resources and Community Development. 1982. Chowan River Water Quality Management Plan. Raleigh, North Carolina.

North Carolina Department of Natural Resources and Community Development. 1983. Nutrient management strategy for the Neuse River basin. Raleigh, North Carolina.

North Carolina Department of Natural Resources and Community Development. 1986. Animal operations and water quality in North Carolina. Raleigh, North Carolina.

North Carolina Department of Natural Resources and Community Development. 1987. Surface water quality concerns in the Tar-Pamlico River basin. Raleigh, North Carolina.

North Carolina Department of Natural Resources and Community Development. 1989. Tar-Pamlico River Basin Nutrient Sensitive Waters Designation and Nutrient Management Strategy. Raleigh, North Carolina.

North Carolina Division of Environmental Management. 1986. Nutrient Management in the Lower Neuse Basin. Raleigh, North Carolina.

North Carolina Stream Sanitation Committee. 1946. North Carolina Stream Pollution Survey. Raleigh, North Carolina.

North Carolina Stream Sanitation Committee. 1957. The Pasquotank River basin. Pollution Survey Report 8, Raleigh, North Carolina.

North Carolina Stream Sanitation Committee. 1959. The Neuse River basin. Pollution Survey Report 7. Raleigh, North Carolina.

North Carolina Stream Sanitation Committee. 1961. The Tar-Pamlico River basin. Pollution Survey Report 12. Raleigh, North Carolina.

Officer, C.B., R.B. Biggs, J. Taft, L.E. Cronin, M.A. Tyler, and W.R. Boynton. 1984. Chesapeake Bay anoxia: Origin, development, and significance. *Science* 223: 23-27.

Olsen, A.R. and A.L. Slavich. 1986. Acid precipitation in North America: 1983 annual data summary from atmospheric deposition system data base. Report EPA-600/4-85-061, United States Environmental Protection Agency, Research Triangle Park, North Carolina.

Olsen, A.R. and C.R. Watson. 1986. Acid precipitation in North America: 1980, 1981, and 1982 annual data summaries based on atmospheric deposition system data base. EPA-600/7-84-097, United States Environmental Protection Agency, Research Triangle Park, North Carolina.

Paerl, H.W. 1982. Environmental factors promoting and regulating N_2 fixing blue-green algal blooms in the Chowan River. Report No. 176, University of North Carolina Water Resources Research Institute, Raleigh, North Carolina.

Paerl, H.W. 1987. Dynamics of blue-green algal blooms in the lower Neuse River, North Carolina: Causative factors and potential controls. Report No. 229, University of North Carolina Water Resources Research Institute. Raleigh, North Carolina.

Paerl, H.W., P.T. Bland, J.H. Blackwell, and N.D. Bowles. 1984. The effects of salinity on the potential of a blue-green algal bloom in the Neuse River estuary, North Carolina Working Paper 84-1, University of North Carolina Sea Grant College Program, Raleigh, North Carolina.

Robbins, J.W.P., D.H. Howell, and G.J. Kriz. 1972. Stream pollution from animal production units. *Journal of the Water Pollution Control Federation* 44: 1536-1544.

Romaine, J.D. 1965. When fertilizing, consider plant food content of your crops. *Better Crops Plant Food* May-June: 1-8.

Ryther, J.H. and W.M. Dunstan. 1971. Nitrogen, phosphorus, and eutrophication in the coastal marine environment. *Science* 171: 1008-1013.

Sheffield, R.M. 1976. Forest statistics for the southern piedmont of Virginia, 1976. Resource Bulletin SE-35. United States Department of Agriculture, Forest Service, Southeastern Forest Experiment Station, Asheville, North Carolina.

Sheffield, R.M. 1977a. Forest statistics for the northern mountain region of Virginia, 1977. Resource Bulletin SE-41. United States Department of Agriculture, Forest Service, Southeastern Forest Experiment Station, Asheville, North Carolina.

Sheffield, R.M. 1977b. Forest statistics for the southern mountain region of Virginia, 1977. Resource Bulletin SE-42. United States Department of Agriculture, Forest Service, Southeastern Forest Experiment Station, Asheville, North Carolina.

Smith, R.A., R.B. Alexander, and M.G. Wolman. 1987. Water quality trends in the nation's rivers. *Science* 235: 1607-1615.

Stanley, D.W. 1983. Nitrogen cycling and phytoplankton growth in the Neuse River. Report No. 204. University of North Carolina Water Resources Research Institute. Raleigh, North Carolina.

Stanley, D.W. 1992. Historical trends: Water quality and fisheries, Albemarle-Pamlico Sounds, with emphasis on the Pamlico River estuary. Publication UNC-SG-94-04, UNC Sea Grant College Program, North Carolina State University, Raleigh, North Carolina.

Stanley, D.W. 1993. Long-term trends in Pamlico River estuary nutrients, chlorophyll, dissolved oxygen, and watershed nutrient production. *Water Resources Research* 29: 2651-2662.

Stanley, D.W. and S.W. Nixon. 1992. Stratification and hypoxia in the Pamlico River estuary. *Estuaries* 15: 270-281.

Stansland, G.J., D.M. Whelpdale, and G. Oehlert. 1986. Precipitation chemistry, p. 128-199. *In* National Research Council, Acid Deposition, Long-Term Trends, National Academy Press, Washington, D.C.

Thomas, G.W. and J.W. Gilliam. 1978. Agroecosystems in the USA., p. 182-243. *In* M.J. Frissel (ed.), Cycling of Mineral Nutrients in Agricultural Ecosystems. Elsevier, New York.

Turner, R.E. and N.N. Rabalais. 1991. Changes in Mississippi River water quality this century, *BioScience* 41: 140-147.

United States Bureau of the Census. 1880, 1890, 1900, 1910, 1920, 1925, 1930, 1935, 1940, 1945, 1950, 1954, 1959, 1964, 1969, 1974, 1978, 1982, 1987. Census of Agriculture. Washington, D.C.

United States Environmental Protection Agency. 1971. 1968 inventory of municipal waste facilities. Vol. 3-4, Report EPA OWP-1. Washington, D.C.

United States Forest Service. 1943. Preliminary estimate of 1942 lumber production in the Carolinas, Virginia, West Virginia, Kentucky, and Tennessee. Southeastern Forest Experiment Station, Asheville, North Carolina.

United States Public Health Service. 1944. National inventory of needs for sanitation facilities: III sewerage and water pollution abatement. *Public Health Reports* 59: 857-882.

United States Public Health Service. 1951. Southeast drainage basins: Summary report on water pollution. Publication 153, Washington, D.C.

United States Public Health Service. 1958. Municipal and industrial waste facilities, 1957 inventory. Publication 622, vol. 3. Washington, D.C.

United States Public Health Service. 1963. Municipal and industrial waste facilities, 1962 inventory. Publication 1065, vol. 3. Washington, D.C.

Virginia Department of Agriculture. 1920-1988. Virginia agricultural statistics (annual reports and bulletins). Richmond, Virginia.

Virginia Department of Agriculture. 1956-1988. Fertilizer used and results of inspections (annual reports). Richmond, Virginia.

Virginia State Water Control Board. 1975. Roanoke River Basin, comprehensive water resources plan. Planning Bulletin 247A, part 4. Richmond, Virginia.

Welch, R.L. 1975. Forest statistics for the piedmont of North Carolina. Resource Bulletin SE-32, United States Forest Service, Southeastern Forest Experiment Station. Asheville, North Carolina.

Welch, R.L. and H.A. Knight. 1974. Forest statistics for the northern coastal plain of North Carolina. Resource Bulletin SE-30, United States Forest Service, Southeastern Forest Experiment Station. Asheville, North Carolina.

Wells, C.A., D. Whigham, and H. Leith. 1972. Investigation of mineral nutrient cycling in a upland Piedmont forest. *Journal of the Elisha Mitchell Scientific Society* 88: 66-78.

Wells, C.G. and J.R. Jorgensen. 1975. Nutrient cycling in loblolly pine plantations, p. 137-158. *In* B. Bernier and C.H. Winget (eds.), Forest Soils and Forest Land Management. Les Presses de l'Université Laval, Quebec, Canada.

Geographic Information Systems for Sustainable Development: South Carolina's Edisto River Basin Project

William D. Marshall

ABSTRACT: Sustainable development will require a complex integration of many economic, ecological, social, and political factors affecting large areas of land—a situation in which the management and output of information will be critical for sound decision-making. Computer geographic information systems show great potential for effectively managing, integrating, and conveying the information required to deal with many of the complexities of achieving sustainable development. A research and demonstration project conducted by the South Carolina Department of Natural Resources, Water Resources Division, in the Edisto River Basin of South Carolina is developing geographic information systems (GIS) and a public policy process to improve environmental decision-making. Specifically, its goal is to address the problems of inadequate information and increasing conflicts that revolve around economic development and environmental protection. Application of the project's GIS has focused on the analysis of natural landscape units, specifically watersheds. GIS was used to assess cumulative impacts and ecological conditions in the Edisto River Basin and it was also used to identify potential wetland mitigation sites within the region. The most challenging application is using GIS as a tool for planning and decision-making within a citizen-based resource assessment and planning process for the entire Edisto River Basin. The process, directed by a citizen task force, involves 15 expert committees in the development of evaluation criteria to distinguish areas of relative significance for 15 categories of resource use (such as forestry, wildlife habitat, industrial development, etc.). GIS spatial models are used to automate the evaluation criteria for a series of basinwide analyses that assess the suitability and relative significance of areas for different resource uses. GIS is used to synthesize all the assessment results to facilitate the task force's development of goals and plans for improved resource management. Information from this process will help local decision-makers better understand the suitability and significance of the basin's land and natural resources for many different uses and can lead to more ecologically and economically sound development decisions.

Introduction

The concept of "sustainable development" is comparable to a stewardship ethic that is based on living off the interest while leaving the principle intact. As defined by the 1987 World Commission on Environment and Development, sustainable development is development that meets the needs of the present without compromising the ability of future generations to meet their own needs (Brundtland Commission 1987). However one defines it, sustainable development will ultimately require a complex integration of many economic, ecological, social, and political factors affecting large areas of land—a situation in which the management and output of information will be critical for sound decision-making within democratic social processes. The developing technology of computer geographic information systems has great potential for effectively managing, integrating, and conveying the information that will be required to deal with many of the technical and sociopolitical complexities of achieving sustainable development (Levinsohn and Brown 1991).

South Carolina's Edisto River Basin Project

Being motivated by goals akin to sustainable development, the South Carolina Department of Natural Resources, Water Resources Division, in cooperation with the National Oceanic and Atmospheric Administration is conducting a multi-year research and demonstration project to develop an information system and public policy process to bring about more informed decisions and fewer conflicts regarding resource conservation and development. The project has taken two tracks: (1) development of a geographic information system (GIS) for natural resources management applications in the Edisto River Basin of South Carolina, and (2) development of public policy procedures to identify public interests and values in natural resources and provide alternative, more equitable approaches to environmental management. The goal of the project is to integrate these two tracks: to use GIS technology as a tool to facilitate a public policy process that will yield better decision-making and more comprehensive management of natural resources as well as cultural and economic resources.

In order to bring the project goal to life, a citizen-based resource assessment and planning process focused on the entire Edisto River Basin was begun in 1992. This process, which has become known simply as the "Edisto River Basin Project," incorporates the following:

1. Baseline studies of ecology, socioeconomics, and public opinion;
2. Classification of resources into categories of use and relative value by various committees of local resource experts;
3. Recommendation of goals, priorities, and plans for resource management by a regionally representative Edisto Basin Task Force.

Components of the baseline studies and the classification of resources (1 and 2 above) involve the use of GIS analyses and modeling techniques for a number of applications that are described in greater detail below. The information derived from these efforts is to be used by the primary decision-makers in the process, the Edisto Basin Task Force, which is composed of local citizens representing interests from throughout the region. The Task Force will use the information to gain a greater understanding of the basin's resources and the problems and opportunities facing the region. Finally, through an open and structured public process, they will use the information to discuss issues and develop goals and recommendations for future management of the basin and its resources—goals that may be consistent with achieving sustainable development in the region.

In 1993, the Water Resources Division established a partnership with the South Carolina Department of Commerce and the South Carolina Department of Parks, Recreation, and Tourism to implement the Edisto River Basin Project. This partnership broadened the base of support for the project and added an extremely valuable asset—a GIS database designed for economic development applications—from the South Carolina Infrastructure/Economic Development Program at the South Carolina Department of Commerce.

The Edisto River Basin Project Area

The Edisto River Basin (see Fig. 1) encompasses portions of 12 South Carolina counties and spans the entire width of the Coastal Plain. From its headwaters in the eastern portions of Saluda and Edgefield counties to the Atlantic Ocean, the Edisto Basin is approximately 3,120 square miles, an area equal to 10% of the state.

The 1990 population of the basin was estimated at 240,514, which represented 6.9% of South Carolina's population. The basin is primarily rural in character with a number of small towns and cities dispersed through the region. Forestry and agriculture are the dominant land uses in the basin, but these activities employ less than 5% of the work force. Manufacturing and service sector jobs provide most of the employment (South Carolina Water Resources Commission 1993).

The Edisto River Basin is drained by four major river systems: the South Fork Edisto River, North Fork Edisto River, Four Hole Swamp, and the main stem of the Edisto River. The approximately 250 unobstructed river miles from the Atlantic Ocean to its headwaters distinguish the Edisto as one of the longest undisturbed blackwater rivers in the United States.

What is GIS?

GIS—an acronym for Geographic Information Systems—can be defined as an organized collection of computer hardware, software, and skilled personnel capable of capturing, storing, updating, manipulating, analyzing, and displaying all forms of data that describe places on the earth's surface. A GIS will store and manage spatial (locational) information such as points, lines, polygons, or grids that represent geographic features commonly displayed on hardcopy maps and it will automatically generate customized digital representations of maps from its database. A GIS also links spatial information with relevant data (facts, figures, and statistics) about those features.

The integration of different themes or layers of information (layers such as soils, land use, roads, etc.) to create new information through processes referred to as overlays is the most powerful and significant operation of a GIS. While computerized mapping functions are provided by many types of systems, a true GIS provides the tools to synthesize different sources of spatial information. It has been suggested that a GIS is best defined as "a decision support system involving the integration of spatially referenced data in a problem solving environment," and the most important part of this definition is its emphasis on integration (Cowen 1988). The ability of GIS to overlay and integrate multiple layers of data allows the user to design spatial models that systematically combine information to address real world problems. Spatial models may lead to the development of new information that subsequently may be incorporated into existing databases

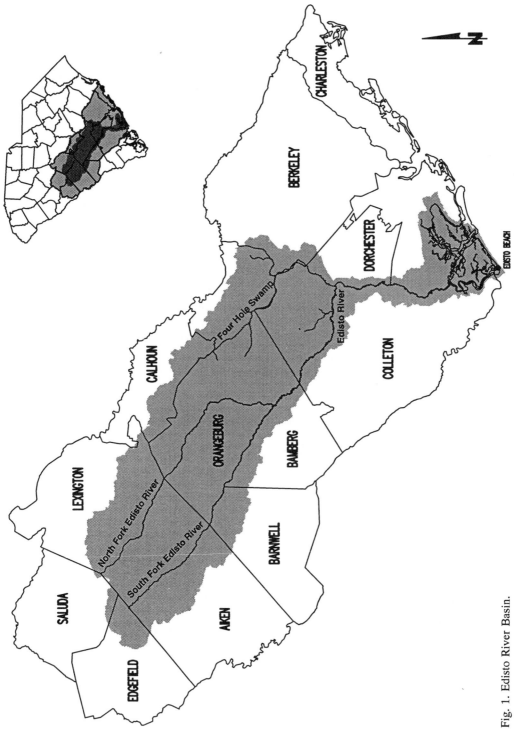

Fig. 1. Edisto River Basin.

or be used in further modeling procedures. When combined with statistical analyses, spatial modeling provides the opportunity to assemble data through time and predict future scenarios.

With continuous advances in computer technology coupled with declines in costs, the versatile functions of GIS, in particular the analytical and synthesizing capabilities, have quickly made these computing tools a necessity for many organizations responsible for complex planning and management of geographically distributed markets, resources, or infrastructure. Examples include commercial delivery services, military bases, timber industries, and local governments.

GIS DATABASES

The utility of a GIS depends on the design and limits of its database. As mentioned in the introduction, the Water Resources Division has developed a comprehensive natural resources and environmental database for the Edisto River Basin. The information in this system was mapped at a 1:24,000 scale and includes the following types of data: land use, land cover, and National Wetlands Inventory (from 1:40,000 scale color-infrared photography); soils (from United States Department of Agriculture); hydrography, transportation, and political boundaries (from United States Geological Survey Digital Line Graphs); environmental permits for air quality, water quality, water use, hazardous and solid wastes, mining, wetlands, and navigable waters; historical and archaeological sites; sensitive species and communities (from the State Heritage database); and the State Rivers Assessment and the Edisto River Basin Natural Area Inventory (both from South Carolina Department of Natural Resources).

The South Carolina Department of Commerce has developed a statewide GIS database known as the South Carolina Infrastructure/Economic Development Program. The information in this system was mapped at a 1:100,000 scale and includes the following types of data: roads, airports, railroads, water systems, wastewater systems, solid waste disposal facilities, utilities, existing industries, industrial buildings, industrial parks, business data, census and demographics, labor data, hydrography, land use and land cover.

GIS Applications

The potential uses of a GIS for natural resource management range from resource inventory and monitoring to complex spatial modeling. Applications can address site-specific, regional, or even global problems.

Sometimes a simple geographic display of a resource inventory can convey important information to decision-makers as illustrated by the state's inventory of sensitive species and communities in the Edisto River Basin. After using GIS to plot this inventory and to produce a map for the first time, the map revealed an interesting pattern. The distribution and concentration of features is not as one would expect; in fact, the data for these natural features show minimal occurrences in or adjacent to the riverine wetland corridors of the basin. The explanation is *not* that the species and habitats are not there; rather, the inventory is incomplete primarily due to limitations on funding and manpower—a common situation for many state natural resource programs. The encouraging side to this story is that when the Water Resources Division began presenting this map to citizens and government officials, it provided awareness and a unique insight into a particular problem, which many of these people expressed was important and should be addressed.

Site-specific GIS applications conducted by the Water Resources Division have included projects such as an impact assessment of alternative transmission line routes for the South Carolina Electric and Gas Company's Cope Power Plant in Orangeburg County (Marshall 1991). This project involved state and federal regulators in a cooperative planning effort prior to any permit applications. A hypothetical hurricane flood analysis for Charleston, South Carolina, was developed (by Jim Scurry, GIS manager, South Carolina Department of Natural Resources) using results from a SLOSH Model. SLOSH refers to the computer model Sea, Lake, and Overland Surge from an Hurricane that estimates the height and extent of storm surge at sea level. To see the potential height of flood waters over Charleston, the surge-level data were overlayed with land elevation data to produce a map of flood potential.

Another application was a methodology for identifying potential wetland mitigation sites using GIS (Brown et al. 1993). This was a GIS model developed by the Water Resources Division with funding from the Unites States Environmental Protection Agency and was applied in the Four Hole Swamp watershed within the Edisto Basin. Wetland losses that are permitted under Section 404 of the Federal Clean Water Act require compensation (i.e., mitigation) through either wetland protection, enhancement, or restoration activities. This methodology identifies potential mitigation sites on the basis of physical factors (soils, hydrology, land use, and vegetative cover) and according to characteristics that indicate ecological functions. GIS was used to analyze soils, hydrology, land use, and vegetative cover data to identify the following wetland characteristics:

- habitat fragmentation
- contiguity with other wetlands, and thus existence of large complexes
- the presence of interior habitat for wildlife
- adjacency to water bodies, and thus opportunity to provide floodflow storage and water quality improvement
- presence of potential threats to the ecological integrity of the site
- opportunities to provide habitat for sensitive species and communities

Finally, GIS was used to integrate these analyses through composite overlays of the resulting information. Based on their physical suitability and opportunity to serve ecological functions, selected wetland areas were identified and categorized as potential mitigation sites.

A Resource Assessment and Planning Process

The most significant application of GIS in the Edisto River Basin Project involves using it as a tool for planning and decision-making within a basinwide resource assessment and planning process. Within this process, a landscape-level ecological characterization study was conducted to assess the cumulative effects of development activities on the region. In addition, committees of resource experts will develop criteria to distinguish the relative significance of different resources and then GIS models will be used to automate the criteria for a comparative resource assessment of all types of resource uses and interests within the region.

As mentioned in the introduction, the information derived from these efforts is to be used by the Edisto Basin Task Force to gain a greater understanding of the basin's resources and the problems and opportunities facing the region. Ultimately the information is to be used for developing goals and plans for future management of the basin and its resources.

LANDSCAPE ECOLOGICAL CHARACTERIZATION

One of the project's baseline studies, referred to as the ecological characterization of the Edisto River Basin, applies principles of landscape ecology and biogeography to evaluate available information on landscape structure (patterns of land use and land cover), water quality, hydrology, and indigenous animal populations. This study assesses the ecological conditions of the Edisto Basin using a cumulative impact assessment methodology developed by Gosselink and Lee (1989). The information analyzed includes long-term datasets, repeated survey data, and/or indicators of landscape ecological conditions. The indices used to determine the Edisto Basin's ecosystem health, or ecological integrity, were forest and native vegetation loss, forest patch pattern, stream-edge habitat condition, water quality changes in the streams, stability of stream hydrology, and the presence of balanced indigenous wildlife populations and natural areas. Three of these—forest and native vegetation loss, forest patch pattern, and stream-edge habitat condition—were used to characterize landscape structure and required the spatial analysis capabilities provided by GIS. The other indices—water quality, hydrology, and wildlife diversity—described environmental conditions related to landscape functions or ecological processes. These functional indices were critically related to the structure of the landscape but were evaluated without extensive GIS support. The Edisto Basin landscape structure analyses and related results are described below. For a full description of methods and results refer to Marshall (1993).

Forest and Native Vegetation Loss

GIS analyses of temporal changes in land use/land cover data and soils data were used to evaluate forest and native vegetation losses. Prior to European settlement, greater than 90% the land of the Edisto River Basin was covered with forest and open woodland, as estimated from Kuchler (1964). Based on an analysis of soils data, approximately 70% of the region was covered in native upland habitats (natural vegetative communities) and about 30% was in native wetland habitats. Historically, about three-quarters of the native upland habitats and over one-third of the native wetland habitats were converted to other land uses and vegetative cover types. Land use data from 1989, overlayed on the soils data, show that most of the conversions were to agriculture and pine plantation forests.

Forest Patch Pattern

GIS analysis to identify contiguous forest patches showed that most of the forest area (56% of the basin) is found in a few large patches. These patches extend through most of the landscape via the bottomlands of the rivers and streams, linking upland and wetland forests into an irregular, or in some cases dendritic (branching), pattern of forested corridors. The total area of forest was 1,112,600 acres, distributed among many (4,025) patches. The large patches found in the Edisto Basin result from many narrow connections in a mosaic of forested tracts that create the irregular, dendritic pattern of forested corridors, described above. A substantial portion of the habitats associated with these large patches are relatively exposed forest corridors and forest edges; therefore, the forest pattern does not seem highly favorable for sensitive forest-interior species. Forest patch characteristics indicate that the basin's forest pattern, though far from being in pristine condition, remains favorable for supporting many indigenous wildlife species because of extensive forest connectivity throughout the basin. These conditions, in particular the largely intact bottomland forest system, indicate that the Edisto landscape remains favorable for supporting very good water quality.

Stream-edge Habitat Condition

Evaluation of stream-edge condition involved a GIS "buffer" analysis that tallied the land use and land cover types within two stream-edge zones of different widths: 60 meters and 125 meters from either side of the basin's streams. The analysis showed that a minor proportion (15-25%) of the stream edges are under intensive land uses: urban 2%, agriculture 9-15%, and pine plantation 4-8% of the basin's stream edges. The remaining 75-85% of the stream-edge habitats are in natural cover: 33% as forested wetland, 14-19% as mixed upland forest, 14-27% as palustrine non-forested wetland, and 9-11% as estuarine wetland. Because the Edisto Basin's stream edges are largely in natural cover, they likely support good riparian wildlife habitat corridors and improve water quality by reducing sediment, nutrients, and other contaminants coming into the rivers and streams.

COMPARATIVE RESOURCE ASSESSMENT

A comparative resource assessment is a procedure for classifying resource types into categories that reflect their level of significance, sensitivity, or suitability for particular uses or purposes. Comparative resource assessment is a variation of land suitability analysis. Land suitability analysis represents a class of expert judgment planning techniques used to evaluate alternative sites for a specific use (such as power plants, highways, or a regional recreation facility). It is also used to prepare a complete land use plan for a region by evaluating the suitability of all sites for each of several land use options (McAllister 1980). Land suitability analysis is based on the concept that the extent and intensity of development depends largely upon the natural capacity of the land for development in addition to the available infrastructure. Land suitability analysis using a GIS enables the user to delineate areas suitable or unsuitable for proposed development by spatially relating land characteristics that represent constraints or opportunities for development such as soils, hydrology, existing land use, or available infrastructure. Suitable land for development may be delineated by overlaying data layers of known environmental constraints (e.g., slopes, wetlands, poor soils, aquifer recharge areas, and so on) in order to locate areas with an absence of constraints. Buffers can be generated around sensitive resources where special land management or regulation may be desired. Areas determined to be less suitable for development but highly valued for wildlife or recreation may be identified for a greater level of protection through regulation or zoning. Ian McHarg's notable work, Design with Nature, showed how suitability analysis could be performed for a development project by manually overlaying and comparing mylar maps. The maps display areas with varying levels of constraint for construction and varying levels of significance for natural or social values (McHarg 1969). McHarg's system of using mylar overlays to perform his suitability analysis was, in essence, a *manual* GIS in which he combined spatial information to make development decisions.

The comparative resource assessment being conducted as part of the Edisto River Basin Project will develop an information base that provides an evaluation of both the suitability and the significance of areas for each of 15 different resource uses. The process employs committees of experts in combination with GIS analyses and modeling techniques to evaluate resources and classify them into categories that reflect their level of significance for particular uses and interests. The Edisto River Basin Task Force will synthesize the information, with the aid of GIS, to consider potential future resource demands, areas of conflict, and alternatives for protection and development of the region's resources. Components of the comparative resource evaluation and its application to planning for resource management in the Edisto River Basin are described below.

Expert Committees and Resource Use Categories

Expert committees consist of individuals with specialized knowledge and experience in particular "resource use categories" (described below). These individuals include local citizens, scientists, knowledgeable resource users, and representatives of relevant interest groups and government agencies. The chairperson from each expert committee serves on the Basin Task Force. These committees are responsible for classifying their respective resources into categories of relative significance (i.e., ranking the resources) and providing recommendations to the Basin Task Force. A final product from the expert committees is a series of maps of the Edisto River Basin that show areas of relative importance to many different resource users (such as foresters, farmers, fishermen, developers, etc.).

The "resource use categories" reflect the region's overall natural, cultural, and economic resource values and the interests. Categories are based on relevant uses of the region's resources, focusing on human interests relative to the resources. The 15 resource use categories for the Edisto River Basin Project are recreational hunting, recreational boating, recreational fishing, wetlands, fisheries habitat, wildlife habitat, commercial development, residential development, industrial development, tourism, water resources, agriculture, cultural resources, natural areas and sensitive species, and forestry.

Resource Evaluation Criteria and Value Classes

Each expert committee's charge is to develop criteria and a systematic method (methodology) for evaluating the areas that are relevant to their respective resource use category. The evaluations for each category are conducted independently. However, all criteria are used to rank areas according to a standard scale of relative value classes. The value classes represent the ranking scheme used by each committee.

The standard scale for value classification (ranking) follows: Value Class 1 = a resource of high significance for the basin or beyond; Value Class 2 = a resource of moderate significance for the basin; and Value Class 3 = a resource of low (typical) significance for the basin.

GIS Support

The Water Resources Division's GIS database, including maps and tabular data, are made available to support the work of each expert committee. The South Carolina Department of Commerce has developed a statewide GIS database to support economic development. These agencies work in partnership to provide support for those committees focused on economic development uses. The agencies' staff help each committee make maximum use of the available data and provide GIS computer services as is practically possible. Using the evaluation methodology and criteria developed by each committee, the staff seek to create a GIS spatial model for each evaluation. The results of each committee are then automated to generate basinwide maps showing the spatial distribution and relationships of the various resource use categories and their relative values.

The GIS-generated maps and statistical output are used to synthesize the results of all the expert committees. This synthesis (overlay) of results creates various composite maps that reveal several types of areas: (1) areas valuable to single resource uses; (2) areas valuable to several different resource uses (multiple, conflicting, and compatible uses); and (3) areas with low attributed value for the resource use categories.

Task Force Recommendations for Resource Management

Upon satisfactory completion of their respective resource evaluation methods, each committee assesses the resulting maps and output from the GIS. They assess the implications for their particular resource use category, based on the GIS map results. Finally, each committee develops recommendations regarding resource management issues and alternative actions to be considered by the Basin Task Force.

In the final phase of the process, the Basin Task Force convenes to develop a series of recommendations focusing on goals and priorities relevant to regional problems. The Task Force has access to all information from the baseline studies and from the expert committees' evaluations. The process of synthesizing the results from each expert committee and the baseline studies provides the foundation for developing recommendations and setting goals and priorities for resource management. Goals and priorities for management can be based on an analysis of the multiple, conflicting, and compatible resource use values attributed to areas in the basin. Goals and priorities can emphasize specific objectives to address resource management problems and opportunities illuminated through the overlay of classifications and from baseline studies.

The process for setting goals and priorities may, depending upon the wishes of the Basin Task Force, involve the following: (1) The most important resource management issues and resources of concern may be identified; (2) The focus should be on the broader regional issues of concern -- not local issues; (3) The priorities for resource management can be a series of recommendations specifying voluntary actions that could yield desired future results; (4) The priorities and relevant objectives should address specified issues of concern such as (a) management of the overall ecological conditions of the basin; (b) management of the areas of multiple conflicting and compatible resource use values; (c) management of the areas with an assessment of Value Class 1, the most significant resources.

The work of developing Task Force recommendations is conducted in an open and structured consensus-building process. Strategies for achieving the established goals and priorities are developed by identifying local initiatives and targeting existing programs, agencies, and funding sources that can provide assistance and/or implementation. When completed, the final results, recommendations, and strategies from the project are published and made available for use in planning and management decisions for public agencies and private landowners.

Final products that result from the project include (1) a set of recommendations and a report from the Basin Task Force that addresses goals and priorities for the future use and conservation of the basin's resources; (2) an atlas showing results from the expert committees' resource assessments, including a series of comparative maps showing areas of compatible and conflicting resource values and uses; and (3) a plan that addresses strategies and guidelines for implementing project recommendations.

In the end, citizens of the Edisto Basin will have more information that will help them better understand the suitability and significance of the basin's land and natural resources for different uses. Related problems and opportunities will be better understood and thus enable citizens to make more informed decisions regarding future economic development and resource conservation in the basin.

Conclusions

Developing information and public policy procedures to build consensus and reduce conflicts regarding goals and priorities for resource conservation and development has been this project's goal and challenge. Documented experiences from other states and regions in America suggest that the most effective means to this goal is via a citizen-based planning process designed to establish resource management priorities and objectives for a specific geographic area using a reliable and accepted information base.

The tools of GIS, supported by the disciplines of biogeography and landscape ecology, offer a new and broader perspective to natural resource management and evaluation. GIS databases and modeling techniques can be used to evaluate broad geographic areas to determine priority areas and management strategies for maintaining the general environmental health of natural systems, including the maintenance of wildlife diversity and the protection of wetlands. Methods to determine the suitability or sensitivity of areas to particular types of development also may be employed. Coupling this type of information with the regional patterns and distribution of productive areas for agriculture, forestry, and commercial and/or industrial development can enable proactive resource management and decision-making, and ultimately, conflict avoidance.

The information and utility of a comprehensive GIS, such as the ones being used in the Edisto River Basin Project, have great value to analysts and decision-makers. Employing these systems in a citizen-based resource assessment and planning process, as described here, can yield a synthesis of information, expertise, and public input that can be of even greater value to society through more proactive stewardship of our natural resources.

Literature Cited

Brown, C.R., F.O. Stayner, C.L. Page, and C.A. Aulbach-Smith. 1993. Toward no net loss: A methodology for identifying potential mitigation sites using a geographic information system. South Carolina Water Resources Commission, Report No. 178 (United States Environmental Protection Agency Report No. EPA904-R-94-001) Columbia, South Carolina.

Brundtland Commission. 1987. Our Common Future. Oxford University Press, London.

Cowen, D.J. 1988. GIS versus CAD versus DBMS: What are the differences? *Photogrammetric Engineering and Remote Sensing* 54(11): 1551-1555.

Gosselink, J.G. and L.C. Lee. 1989. Cumulative Impact Assessment in Bottomland Hardwood Forests. *Wetlands: The Journal of the Society of Wetland Scientists* Vol. 9 (special issue)

Kuchler, A.W. 1964. Potential natural vegetation of the conterminous United States. Manual to accompany the map. American Geographic Society, Special Publication No. 36. New York.

Levinsohn, A.G. and S.J. Brown. 1991. GIS and sustainable development in natural resource management, p. . *In* M. Heit and A. Shortreid (eds.), GIS Applications in Natural Resources. GIS World Inc., Fort Collins, Colorado.

Marshall, W.D. 1991. Using GIS to facilitate multi-agency environmental planning for routing power transmission lines. Open file report of the Natural Resources Decision Support System Project, South Carolina Water Resources Commission, Columbia, South Carolina.

Marshall, W.D. 1993. Assessing change in the Edisto River Basin: An ecological characterization. South Carolina Water Resources Commission, Report No. 177. Columbia, South Carolina.

McAllister, D.M. 1980. Evaluation in environmental planning. The Massachusetts Institute of Technology Press, Cambridge, Massachusetts.

McHarg, I. 1969. Design with Nature. Natural History Press. New York.

South Carolina Water Resources Commission. 1993. Socioeconomic conditions in the Edisto River Basin. Open file report of the Natural Resources Decision Support System Project, South Carolina Water Resources Commission, Columbia, South Carolina.

Geographic Information Processing Assessment of the Impacts of Urbanization on Localized Coastal Estuaries: A Multidisciplinary Approach

Dwayne E. Porter, William K. Michener, Tom Siewicki,
Don Edwards, and Christopher Corbett

ABSTRACT: Increasing urbanization of coastal areas is an important concern in the Southeastern United States where small, high-salinity, sensitive estuaries have been targeted for development over the next two decades. This is a particularly acute problem in coastal South Carolina which is dependent on tourism and traditional fishing and shellfish harvesting activities. Accelerated coastal development and the continued influx of people into the coastal zone of South Carolina have increased the pressures on the limited coastal resources. These continuing pressures threaten the salt marsh estuaries, which are highly vulnerable to commercial, industrial, and residential activities in addition to physiographic changes brought on by tides, winds and storms. The complexity and severity of environmental problems associated with coastal growth have been the impetus for many agencies and organizations to explore the use of new spatial analytical techniques as a means of obtaining timely and valid information which will aid problem solving and assist with effective coastal zone management. In response to these environmental concerns and the need for better databases and integrated spatial models for supporting sustainable coastal development in the Southeastern United States, a six-year study of the impacts of urbanization on small, high-salinity estuaries was initiated in 1990. An overall goal of the Urbanization and Southeastern Estuarine Systems (USES) project is utilizing Geographic Information Processing (GIP) to integrate data and scientific expertise for the identification, assessment, and modeling of relationships within coastal estuaries and impacts associated with urbanization and natural activities. This goal is being achieved through the continued development and utilization of the multi-agency Coastal Geographic Information System (C-GIS) and the development and validation of spatially explicit models. These models can be used to develop and apply a vulnerability index to coastal areas that, based on such factors as land use and land cover characteristics, receiving waters, and socioeconomic conditions, suggest different vulnerabilities to natural and anthropogenic influences.

Introduction

Increasing development in the coastal zone has placed a high demand on limited coastal resources. Every year the population, and consequential development, along the coast continues unabated. With this growth comes elevated demands on the coastal environment for commercial, industrial, recreational and residential facilities. By the year 2000, it has been estimated that 75% of the population of the United States will be living within a one-hour drive of the shore (Vernberg et al. 1992). In many places, development has been uncontrolled, resulting in the degradation and destruction of the coastal environment. Eroding or physically altered shorelines, impacted wetland and wildlife habitats, and degraded water quality are just a few examples of improper or inadequate coastal zone management.

Increased urbanization of coastal areas is an important concern in the Southeastern United States where estuarine watersheds remain relatively undeveloped. More than 320 nonriverine estuaries are located between Cape Fear, North Carolina, and Cape Canaveral, Florida, and approximately half of these are located in South Carolina. Most of the estuaries of the Southeastern United States are small, high-salinity, sensitive ecosystems, many of which have been targeted for significant developmental pressures over the next two decades (Vernberg et al. 1992). Yet, estuarine urbanization studies have been almost exclusively confined to very large, riverine systems such as Chesapeake Bay.

The complexity and severity of environmental problems associated with coastal growth have been the impetus for many agencies and organizations to explore the use of new spatial analytical techniques as a means of obtaining timely and valid information which will aid problem solving and assist with effective coastal zone management. In response to these environmental concerns and the need for better databases and integrated spatial models for supporting sustainable coastal development in the Southeastern United States, a six-year study of the impacts of urbanization on small, high-salinity estuaries of the Southeast was initiated in 1990. An overall goal of the Urbanization and Southeastern Estuarine Systems (USES) project is utilizing Geographic Information Processing (GIP) to integrate the data and scientific expertise for the identification, assessment, and modeling of relationships within coastal estuaries and impacts associated with urbanization and natural activities. This goal is being achieved through the continued development and utilization of the multi-agency Coastal Geographic Information System (C-GIS) and the development and validation of spatially explicit models. This paper discusses the role of GIP in coastal zone management as well as issues related to the development of data layers. Two primary study sites are described and GIP analyses are presented related to vegetation community distribution, modeling wetland alterations and nonpoint source pollution (NPS) within the two estuaries, and relationships between observed pollution levels, water quality and shellfish recruitment in the more urbanized estuary.

Use of GIP for Coastal Resource Management

Geographic Information Processing (GIP) is an integration of the technologies of remote sensing, Global Positioning Systems (GPS), Geographic Information Systems (GIS), and computer cartography (Dunlap and Porter 1993). The utilization of GIP is being tested and adopted by estuarine researchers and resource managers to address ecosystem, landscape, and global issues important to estuarine resource management (Michener et al. 1989; Haddad and Michener 1991;

Jefferson et al. 1991; Michener et al. 1992; Dunlap and Porter 1993; Holland et al. 1993). In 1989, the International Geographical Union established the Commission on the Coastal Environment to investigate and promote the utility and application of GIS as a tool for coastal management. Advancements in telecommunications have also opened up a new avenue for those using GIS for coastal zone management. An electronic discussion list on the Internet computer network focusing on coastal issues and GIS applications provides a readily accessible forum for the exchange of ideas. Bartlett (1993) surveyed refereed journals and gray literature and identified over 150 references to the use of GIS for coastal zone management GIS provide proven valuable tools for resource managers, administrators, and lawmakers because their potential for information analysis and presentation far exceeds previous capabilities (Porter and Eiser 1991). GIS support the integration of historical and recently acquired data from disparate sources into an analytical system that provides powerful tools for examining and evaluating various resource management issues (Haddad and Harris 1986; Haddad and Hoffman 1987; Haddad and McGarry 1989; Haddad and Michener 1991; Jefferson et al. 1991; Somers et al. 1991; Hunsaker et al. 1993).

The GIS provides powerful tools for examining and evaluating a multitude of estuarine resource issues. This is accomplished by integrating biological, chemical, physical and socioeconomic data related to a specific issue. This integration provides for more rapid and precise assessment of existing conditions and relationships. The use of remotely sensed data for coastal resource research and management is increased and enhanced with the acquisition of satellite images, aerial photographs and adequate image processing equipment. Digital image processing techniques in conjunction with GIS provide tools for the identification and assessment of land use and land cover (LU/LC) and oceanographic characteristics while requiring less in situ observations and providing extensive spatial coverage. When combined with in situ sampling, the GIS provide tools for the study of relationships among land use and land cover and environmental conditions as well as ecological modeling. The inclusion of socioeconomic data provides valuable information on how lifestyle characteristics may affect an estuary, as well as the impact a degraded estuary may have on the surrounding population.

Study Sites

To gain a better understanding of the potential impacts of urbanization on localized coastal estuaries, comparative studies have been established at both a relatively pristine estuary (North Inlet, South Carolina) and a nearby urbanized estuary (Murrells Inlet, South Carolina) (Fig. 1).

NORTH INLET, SOUTH CAROLINA

North Inlet, located 90 km northeast of Charleston, South Carolina, covers about 80 km^2 and consists of barrier islands, intertidal salt marsh, and low-lying coastal forest (Fig. 2). Most of the wetlands and uplands of North Inlet are undeveloped and are managed in their natural state by the Belle W. Baruch Foundation. The North Inlet study site, home of the North Inlet–Winyah Bay National Estuarine Research Reserve, is representative of an undeveloped estuary. For over 20 years the site has been the focus of studies by the Belle W. Baruch Institute for Marine Biology and Coastal Research, University of South Carolina, and the Belle W. Baruch Forest Science Institute, Clemson University (Miller et al. 1989). An extensive long-term database (>10 years) containing hundreds of biological, chemical, and physical variables has been developed (Michener et al. 1990).

Primary research areas include a 2,630 ha high-salinity *Spartina alterniflora* marsh and 715 ha of tidal creeks and intertidal flats that are separated from the Atlantic Ocean by sandy barrier islands. The estuary is bordered on the west by loblolly and longleaf pine forests. Hydrographic characteristics of the North Inlet estuary include an annual seasonal salinity range of 30-34‰ (monthly mean salinities average 19-36‰), an average channel depth of 3 m, and a seasonal water temperature range of 3-33°C. Wetland habitats include exposed and sheltered sandy beaches; marsh; intertidal flats and oyster beds; submerged macroalgal mats; sand, shell, and mud benthic habitats; shell middens; and bird rookery islands. At mean tide, *Spartina alterniflora* marsh comprises 73.0%, tidal creeks 20.6%, oyster reefs 1.0%, and exposed mud flats 5.4% of the marsh-estuarine zone (Dame et al. 1986). More than 1,200 ha of brackish and freshwater marshes border the Winyah Bay side of the North Inlet estuary.

The forest ecosystem at North Inlet has developed on sandy Pleistocene beach ridges and swales, which trend northeast-southwest (Gardner and Bohn 1980). The highest ridges lie about 6 m above mean sea level (MSL). The forest system primarily consists of variable-age pine forest growing on the ridges. The swales between ridges typically contain intermittent blackwater streams, support stands of cypress and gum, and have fringes of mixed bottomland hardwoods.

MURRELLS INLET, SOUTH CAROLINA

Murrells Inlet is the comparison study site for assessing the impacts of urbanization. Located approximately 32 km north of North Inlet, Murrells Inlet is also a localized estuary with a bar-built inlet. The Murrells Inlet site comprises approximately 2,670 ha of wetlands, open water, and residential and commercial development. There is no riverine input and the estuary is characterized by vertically homogenous high-salinity water. Hydrographic characteristics of the Murrells Inlet estuary include an average annual salinity of 31.4‰ and an average water temperature of 20°C (Jefferson et al. 1991). Like North Inlet, freshwater dilution is the result of rainfall and runoff. *Spartina alterniflora* is the dominant marsh vegetative species. Tides are semidiurnal, approximately equal in magnitude, and have a mean tidal range of 1.37 m with a maximum at 1.62 m during spring tides (United States Department of Commerce 1995).

Unlike North Inlet, Murrells Inlet has been highly developed to accommodate an increasing influx of residents and tourists. The Murrells Inlet study site is surrounded by, and encompasses, development on all sides with the exception of the Atlantic Ocean to the east and Huntington Beach State Park to the southeast (Fig. 3). Six marinas are located throughout the estuary and periodic dredging takes place to maintain navigability of the open water channels (Jefferson et al. 1991). The population density of permanent residents is 236 km^{-2} as compared to the average population of 44 residents km^{-2} in South Carolina (South Carolina State Data Center 1991). Population density peaks during summer vacation periods leading to increased pressures on the coastal resources.

The primary difference between the North Inlet and Murrells Inlet study sites is that Murrells Inlet has been subjected to anthropogenic alterations resulting from extensive upland and shoreline development associated with urbanization and the dredging of waterways. The distribution and magnitude of these anthropogenic influences make the Murrells Inlet area an ideal study site to assess the impacts of urbanization.

GIS Database Development

An initial step of any GIP related activity is the determination of the data layers necessary to perform the required analyses and the availability and reliability of the needed data layers. Following the determination of the necessary data layers, the acquisition of the GIS data layers is initiated. This may be as simple as ordering a data layer from a government or private agency or as complex as developing a data layer from in-house data collection activities. Overall, this process of identifying and acquiring data and developing metadata is very time consuming. Metadata are the accompanying documentation describing the data (for a discussion of metadata, refer to Michener et al. 1996).

Spatial scale is related to the amount and accuracy of information that can be derived from a data layer. Scale is also directly related to storage requirements and costs to maintain data layers within a GIS. Scales of the various source data range from GPS-derived point data to 1:4,800 scale aerial photographs to 1:250,000 scale databases developed by the federal government. In some cases, multiple data layers exist for a specific land cover theme (e.g., wetlands), but each may be compiled from a different source at a different scale. The use of the appropriate data layer is determined by the application or research problem to be addressed.

For the USES project, small-scale data layers (scale < 1:24,000) are appropriate for general characterization of resource features, for identification of some spatial relationships, and for use in information portrayal. They may not be adequate for addressing site specific research and resource management issues because they may not provide the necessary spatial accuracy or detail. The development of GIS data layers from large-scale source data does not guarantee accuracy; however, when combined with appropriate ground truthing procedures, more accurate and detailed information can be obtained. Large-scale data layers (scale ≥ 1:24,000) are necessary for use in addressing the research and management issues associated with the USES project. In most cases, these large-scale data layers cost more to develop and maintain but are required to provide the spatial accuracy and information needed by the USES researchers. Primary GIS data layers, and their corresponding source and scale, input into the C-GIS to date are listed in Table 1.

GIP Analyses

For the USES project, multidisciplinary studies were designed to utilize GIS, digital image processing, and GPS technology, as well as innovative sampling strategies, and spatio-statistical algorithms (kriging) to characterize the relationships among land use patterns, nutrient loading, water quality, chemical contaminants, bacteriology, toxicology, hydrodynamics, and primary and secondary production (Vernberg et al. 1992). GIS-based analyses proved essential for (1) characterizing salt marsh plant communities and their distribution throughout the North Inlet and Murrells Inlet estuaries and determining if and to what extent adjacent land use restricts development and maintenance of high-marsh plant communities; (2) modeling the rate of wetland alterations; (3) modeling nonpoint source pollution in an estuarine environment; (4) examining oyster recruitment patterns throughout the two estuaries and relating oyster population dynamics within Murrells Inlet estuary to adjacent land use, water quality, and point and nonpoint source pollution; and (5) modeling the distribution of pollution levels within the Murrells Inlet estuary.

Table 1. C-GIS data layers available for Murrells Inlet and North Inlet, SC.

Layer	Source	Scale
Administrative boundaries	federal government	1:100,000
Base map	USES	1:4,800
GPS survey	USES	point data
Hydrography		
Detailed	USES	1:4,800
DLG	federal government	1:100,000
Infrastructure		
Roads	federal government & SDNR	1:100,000
Sewer lines	SC Department of Commerce	1:100,000
Wastewater sites	SC Department of Commerce	1:100,000
Water lines	SC Department of Commerce	1:100,000
Land use / land cover		
FLUCCS	USES	1:40,000 / 1:24,000
General 10 category	SCDNR	20 meter
GIRAS	federal government	1:250,000
Regulatory permitted activities		
SCCC	SCDHEC, SCDNR, USC	point data
USACOE	SCDNR and USACOE	point data
Shellfish		
Bacteria levels	USES	point data
Oyster reefs	SCDNR and USES	1:24,000
Socioeconomic		
Census survey	federal government	Census
USES survey	USES	point data
Soils	federal government	1:20,000
Threatened & endangered species	federal government	point data
Water quality		
Bacteria levels	USES	point data
Chemistry	USES	point data
Concentration dynamics	USES	point data
Sediment composition	USES	point data
Wetlands		
Detailed	USES	1:6,000
FLUCCS	USES	1:40,000 / 1:24,000
NWI	federal government & SCDNR	1:58,000 / 1:24,000

Distribution of Salt Marsh Plant Communities Within North Inlet and Murrells Inlet Estuaries

Low altitude, 1:6,000 scale, color infrared photography of the two estuaries during leaf-off conditions was acquired to be used as source data for vegetation mapping. Individual 9.5 × 9.5 inch frames were registered to 1:4,800 scale base maps of both Murrells Inlet and North Inlet. Coupled with extensive vegetation ground surveys of grids and selected points, the photographs were manually interpreted and digitized to create GIS data layers representing vegetation associations.

Analysis of the vegetation GIS layers indicated the North Inlet salt marsh-estuarine system contains extensive stands of *Spartina alterniflora* that are bordered on terrestrial margins by a complex mixture of high-marsh species, a scrub-shrub zone, and loblolly and longleaf pine forest (Fig. 4). Composition of the salt marsh vegetation community varies across the elevation gradient from the creeks to the forest border. Tall-form *Spartina* borders the salt marsh creeks and may extend several meters inland. At slightly higher elevations (above MSL), medium-form *Spartina* dominates. With increasing elevation, the vegetation shifts to a monotypic short-form *Spartina* zone followed by mixed stands that include short-form *Spartina*, *Limonium carolinianum*, and *Salicornia*. Monotypic stands of *Salicornia* and *Juncus* generally occur at the highest salt marsh elevations. The high-marsh community occupies a broad zone which can be on the order of 10s of meters wide. A narrow shrub zone (predominantly *Iva*) demarcates the transition between marsh and forest.

The Murrells Inlet salt marsh also contains extensive stands of *Spartina alterniflora* (Fig. 5). Whereas the extensive high-marsh zone in North Inlet consists of numerous plant species including a variety of shrub species, the high-marsh zone in Murrells Inlet is very restricted or absent due to upland development and bulkheading, which extends to the edge of the *Spartina* marsh and typically define the marsh perimeter. *Juncus* and *Borrichia* may be present in a very narrow high-marsh zone in developed portions of Murrells Inlet. The high-marsh community in Murrells Inlet, when present, occupies a narrow band only a few meters wide, except at the southern end near Huntington Beach State Park where development is minimal.

Modeling Impacts of Regulatory Permitted Activities on Coastal Wetlands

Accelerated coastal development and the continued influx of people into the coastal zone of South Carolina have increased the pressures on coastal wetlands (Vernberg et al. 1992). These continuing pressures threaten salt marsh estuaries, which are sensitive to commercial, industrial, and residential activities as well as physiographic changes brought on by tides, winds, and storms. In view of this, the need was evident for a procedure to estimate the overall spatial and temporal impacts of these alterations to coastal wetlands using currently available data and knowledge (United States Environmental Protection Agency 1988; Kiraly et al. 1990). A GIS model for cumulative impact assessment was developed that accounted for both physiographic-induced changes as well as physical alterations to wetlands as permitted under state and federal regulatory permitting programs.

C-GIS land cover data layers representing conditions in 1983 and 1989 were analyzed using GIS overlay techniques to determine the extent and magnitude of change in acreage of wetlands in both North Inlet and Murrells Inlet. The temporal component of this study was determined based on the availability of source data for the development of GIS data layers and the impact of Hurricane Hugo in September 1989. Based on work by Jensen et al. (1993) and Porter (1995), front beach areas seaward of the primary sand dunes were excluded from the analyses to minimize potential impacts of tidal stage on photointerpretation of land cover. Using a 45 acre (18.2 ha) grid overlay (Field et al. 1990), the results of a paired comparison t-test showed that the mean acreage of wetlands in 1983 was not significantly different (p > 0.05) than the mean acreage of wetlands in 1989 for the North Inlet study site (Fig. 6). The results of a paired comparison t-test of change in mean acreage of wetlands in Murrells Inlet between 1983 and 1989 suggested there was a difference (p < 0.05) (Fig. 7). Both parametric and nonparametric statistical tests were performed to determine whether the Murrells Inlet site experienced a greater rate of wetlands change than the relatively pristine North Inlet site. The results of the intersite comparisons showed (p < 0.05) that the rate of wetlands alteration was greater in the Murrells Inlet estuary than the North Inlet estuary.

Physiographic forces were considered the prime agent of land cover change in North Inlet since no activities requiring permit approval for the alteration of wetlands took place in the study area between 1983 and 1989. A regression model of physiographic alteration was developed from the analysis of change in the distribution and quantity of the wetlands, open water, and uplands composing North Inlet between 1983 and 1989. The model results were subjected to an analysis to determine the strength of the relationship between actual wetlands acreage in 1989 and predicted acreage in 1989; the r^2 of 0.974 was significant.

When applied to Murrells Inlet, the model of physiographic alteration only accounted for 44.9% of the measured change in wetlands acreage between 1983 and 1989. When the estimated impact of the 150 wetlands-altering activities approved by the United States Army Corps of Engineers (USACOE) and South Carolina Department of Health and Environmental Control's Office of Ocean and Coastal Resource Management (SCDHEC-OCRM) were input as model parameters, the cumulative impact assessment model accounted for nearly 95.0% of the measured wetlands alterations in Murrells Inlet between 1983 and 1989. The model results were subjected to an analysis to determine the strength of the relationship between actual wetlands acreage in 1989 and predicted acreage in 1989; the r^2 of 0.970 was significant (Porter 1995).

MODELING NONPOINT SOURCE POLLUTION IN AN ESTUARINE ENVIRONMENT

The objectives of this study were to compare single-storm yield of surface water, sediment, and dissolved nutrients in an undeveloped and urbanized coastal watershed, to investigate the seasonal variation in single-storm yield, and to develop a method to simulate the effect of hypothetical land cover changes (e.g., the addition of impervious surface) on watershed yield. The Agricultural Non-point Source Pollution (AGNPS) model was applied to an undeveloped 37-ha watershed in North Inlet (Oyster Creek) and a developed 12-ha watershed in Murrells Inlet (Dog Creek). AGNPS was selected because of its distributed parameter or grid cell structure, which can be integrated with a GIS to generate spatially explicit output. The model simulates surface-water runoff, sediment erosion and transport, and nutrient (dissolved and sediment-associated N and P) loading of user-defined single storm events. Although intended for agricultural watersheds, the model equations are applicable to a wider range of land use given adequate empirical calibration data (Young et al. 1987). The Soil Conservation Service TR-55 method (United States Department of Agriculture 1972) determines model hydrology; sediment processes are simulated with the Modified Universal Soil Loss Equation (Wischmeier and Smith 1978); and the nutrient component is adapted from the USDA field-scale model CREAMS (Frere et al. 1980). These three submodels are not spatial in nature. When used alone, model inputs (which may vary spatially) are averaged over some known area and average output is calculated per unit area. The approach of AGNPS is to partition a watershed into square cells, calculate the equations in every cell, and add the output to the next downstream cell. Model output can be examined in any cell, group of cells, or as a whole.

Variability in the chemical behavior and spatial distribution of different pollutants limits the development of a general mechanistic nonpoint-source pollution model. Watershed pollution models abound but usually only address one or a few specific pollutants. In this study, it was decided to first concentrate on storm surface-runoff volumes and sediment production. Water and sediment are the main transport mechanisms of pollutants in Murrells Inlet. Identifying areas of surface water and sediment production along with estimates of surface-water volume and sediment mass yield provides a basis for measuring dissolved or sediment adsorbed pollutant concentrations to calculate loading rates.

The undeveloped Oyster Creek system was the control watershed. The land cover is mixed second-growth hardwood and pine forest with interspersed cypress wetland, sandy soils, and very low elevational gradients (< 1.0%). Over 100 years ago, the land was cleared and used for agricultural purposes. A ditch and dike drainage control system still remains, forming the topographic water-shed boundary and drainage network. The rectangular watershed is aligned between two ancient beach ridges with the main channel in the swale. The main channel is intersected by straight tributary channels oriented normal to the main channel. The urban Dog Creek watershed contains residential and commercial land cover and a segment of major highway. The creek was created in the 1930s and, like many other artificial drainage channels in the area, intercepts the groundwater table, thereby altering physical and chemical characteristics of the stream.

AGNPS, when applied to the urban setting at the scale used in this study, required detailed land use and hydrography information. For compatibility with the spatial resolution of current remote-sensing platforms and to capture the spatial variability of urban land cover, a cell size of 10 m^2 was used in the urban model. The best available large-scale aerial photographs were scanned into digital format, rectified using GPS control, and on-screen digitized to create vector data layers of land use and hydrography which were in turn rasterized for use in the model. Other C-GIS data layers used to generate model input included soil information (type and erodibility), slope, and aspect (direction of steepest descent).

An effect of urbanization, which became obvious after mapping the hydrography, was the unnatural, forced flow routing. In the urban setting, the drainage pattern is mostly straight lines and right angles. Often, drainage channels are immediately adjacent to or cross roadways and lack any form of riparian vegetative buffer. In addition, some channels do not connect with the drainage network and merely hold water until it evaporates or infiltrates. The coastal watersheds in this study have a microtopographic boundary that could easily be altered during development projects. For example, an existing drainage channel was designed to flow north following the land slope into Dog Creek but, in fact, drained south because a culvert was blocked with sediment. Proactive land use planning relative to the drainage network may be a method of reducing stream pollutant loading.

Watershed delineation and flow routing are important for application of the AGNPS model and for distributed-parameter hydrological models in general. Low elevational gradients in coastal South Carolina make watershed delineation difficult. It was impractical and unrealistic to measure the elevation in every 10 m^2 cell of the model. Traditional surveying techniques in conjunction with GPS were used to locate ground points in and around each watershed for horizontal (longitude and latitude) and vertical (elevation) positions to delineate the topographic watershed. Survey points were obtained at topographic inflection points and connected in a triangular irregular network (TIN) to capture the general lay of the land most efficiently (Fig. 8). These data were used in a GIS to construct digital elevation models (DEM) of each watershed, thus generating slope and aspect data required for each 10 m^2 grid cell of the model.

Initially it was believed a high quality DEM of the terrain surface would be sufficient to define flow routing, but existing hydrography must also be considered. Many urban drainage channels are cut across slope, so that water does not always flow down the steepest line of descent. Another issue became evident when defining the urban model flow routing: surface water flows around buildings and not over them. The urban model flow routing was manually edited to correct the cells that received surface flow according to the DEM but in reality were cells where a house or other structure stood. Manual editing was also required to eliminate flow loops and sinkholes generated by the DEM which are not permitted in the model.

For a 12-month period, field data were collected for use in various USES study components in addition to calibrating the AGNPS model output. Ideally, many points should be sampled to calibrate a spatial model, but logistic constraints limited field data collection to one site at Oyster Creek and two sites at Dog Creek. Field sample collection points were located at the watershed outfalls of both study sites, and a second site at Dog Creek to isolate the influence of residential land use. Field data used for calibration of AGNPS included rainfall amount and duration, peak flow rate, runoff volume, sediment and dissolved nutrient concentrations.

AGNPS requires input data in a specific format. The model runs within a menu-driven shell and, when used without a GIS, all data are manually input and edited in a spreadsheet. Although AGNPS can be used without a GIS, separate model input datasets are required to simulate each watershed scenario and since each cell may require 20 or more input parameters, manual input is impractical when cells number in the thousands. This approach used database management software to merge and format GIS data layers for import to the model.

SPATIAL AND TEMPORAL PATTERNS OF OYSTER RECRUITMENT

A series of experiments were performed in both the North Inlet and Murrells Inlet estuaries to examine recruitment variability across several spatial and temporal scales, and to develop new sampling strategies that could be applied at broader scales in conjunction with GIS and other analytical tools to assess landscape patterns and processes (Michener and Kenny 1991). Both biological (gregarious settlement behavior, competition, predation, etc.) and physical (tide and substrata characteristics, sedimentation, light, etc.) factors accounted for the variability that was observed at different scales.

New oyster recruitment sampling techniques (Michener and Kenny 1991), GPS surveys (Michener 1992), kriging of point data, and analyses of oyster reef distribution were utilized in mapping oyster recruitment throughout Murrells Inlet estuary. GIS-based analyses of observed recruitment patterns, water quality (based on maps and surveys by the SCDHEC), as well as water and oyster tissue samples collected throughout the estuary enabled researchers to relate oyster recruitment to adjacent land use, water quality, and point and nonpoint source pollution within Murrells Inlet (Michener et al. 1992). Figure 9 illustrates the overlay techniques utilized in conjunction with the various data sources. Oyster recruitment was observed to be related to reef characteristics (oyster density, shell matrix characteristics, and substrate), harvesting (high recruitment in protected commercial lease lots and low recruitment in public fishing grounds, which are subject to overharvesting of oysters and substrate disturbance), and water quality (high recruitment in less

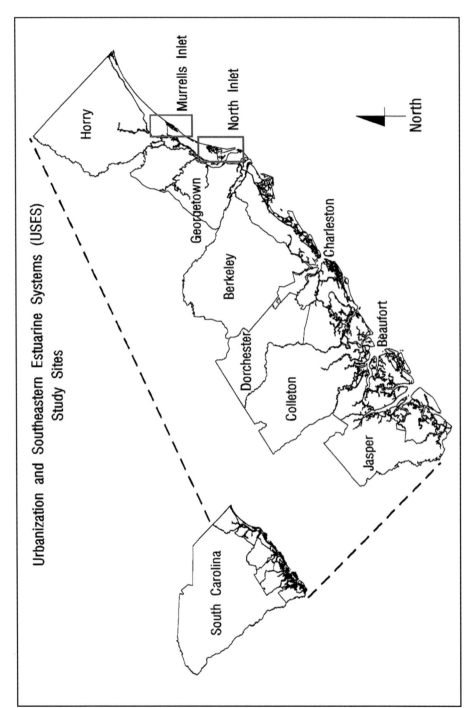

Urbanization and Southeastern Estuarine Systems (USES)
Study Sites

Fig. 1. Map of North Inlet and Murrells Inlet, South Carolina, study sites.

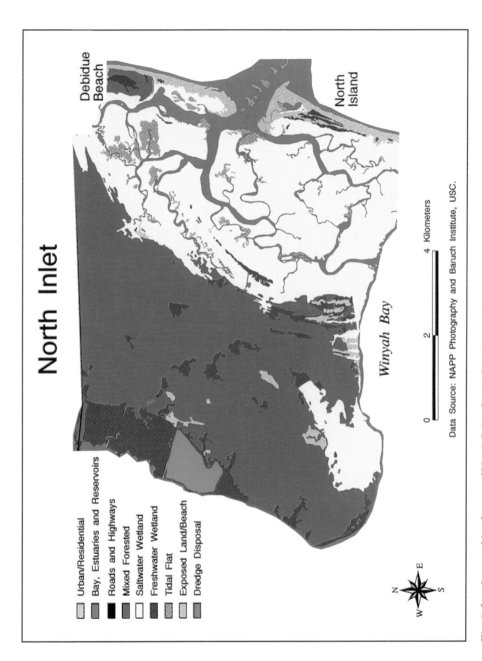

Fig. 2. Land use and land cover of North Inlet, South Carolina, study site.

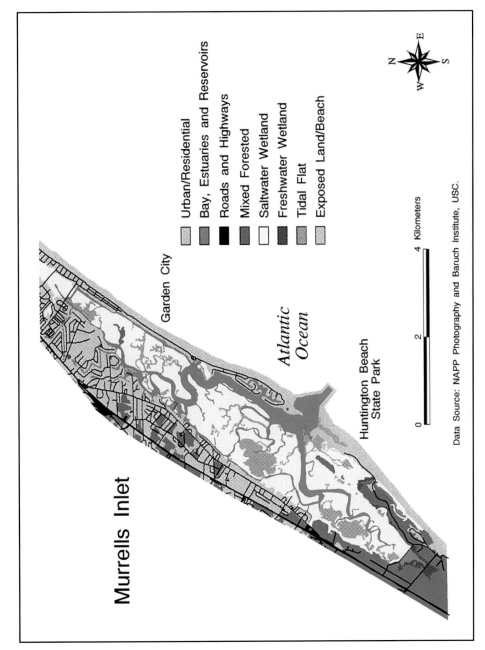

Fig. 3. Land use and land cover of the Murrells Inlet, South Carolina, study site.

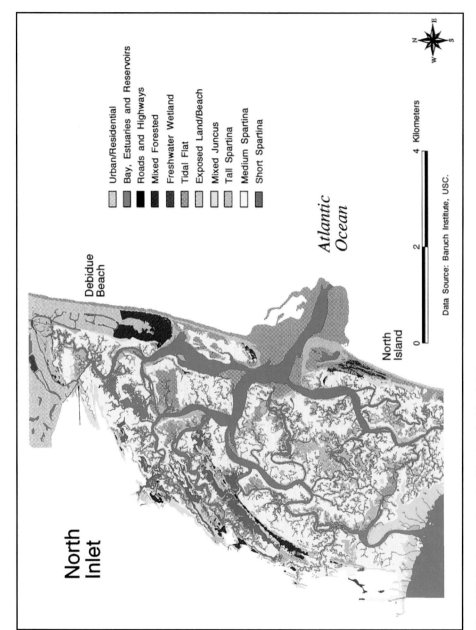

Fig. 4. Wetland vegetation classification for North Inlet estuary.

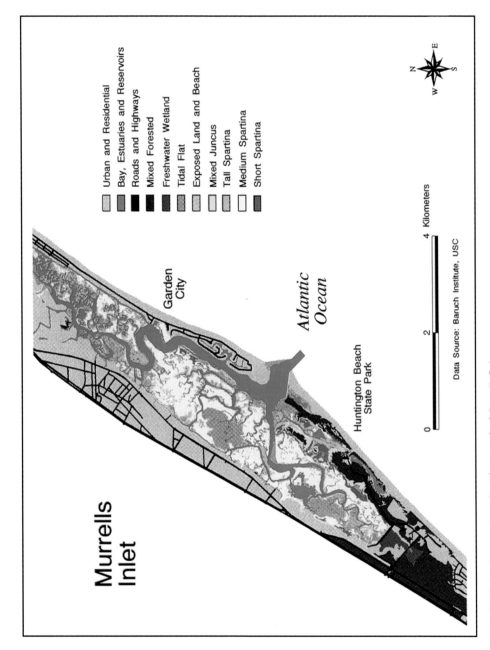

Fig. 5. Wetland vegetation classification for Murrells Inlet estuary.

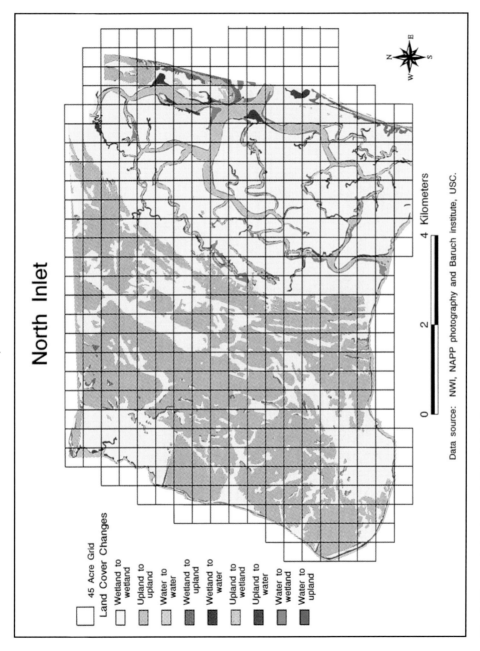

Fig. 6. Changes in land cover in North Inlet between 1983 and 1989.

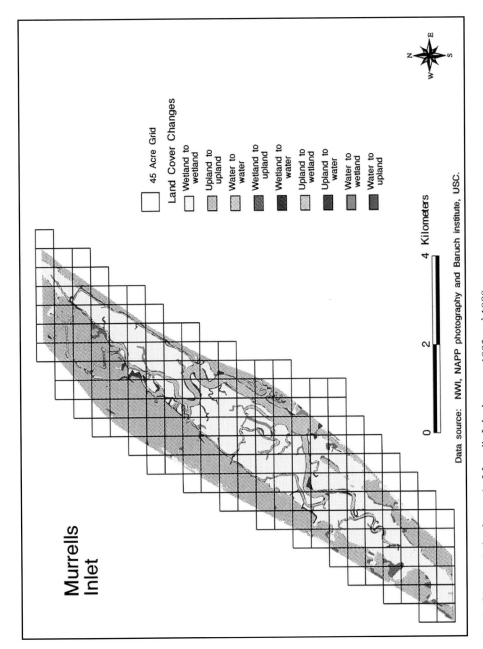

Fig. 7. Changes in land cover in Murrells Inlet between 1983 and 1989.

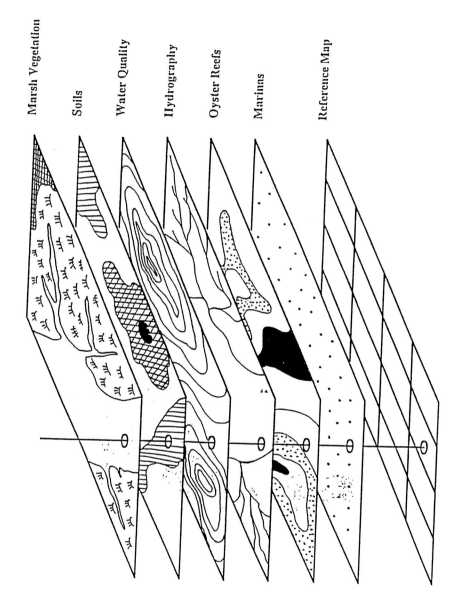

Marsh Vegetation

Soils

Water Quality

Hydrography

Oyster Reefs

Marinas

Reference Map

Fig. 8. Digital elevation model developed for Oyster Creek watershed.

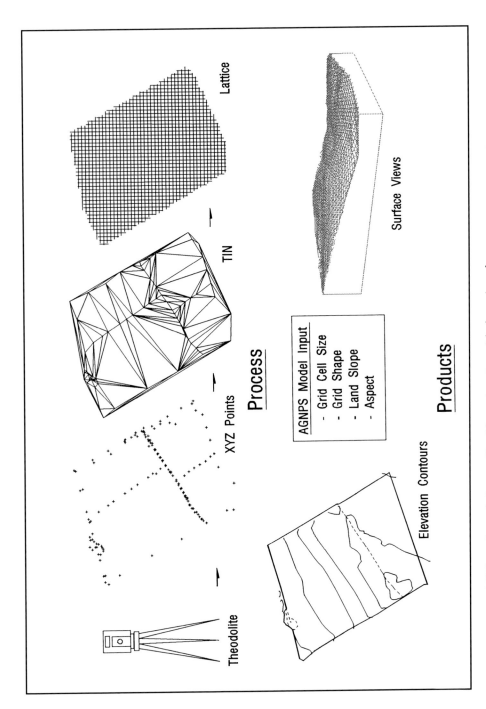

Fig. 9. Illustration of GIS overlay techniques utilized in conjunction with the various data sources to assess oyster population dynamics.

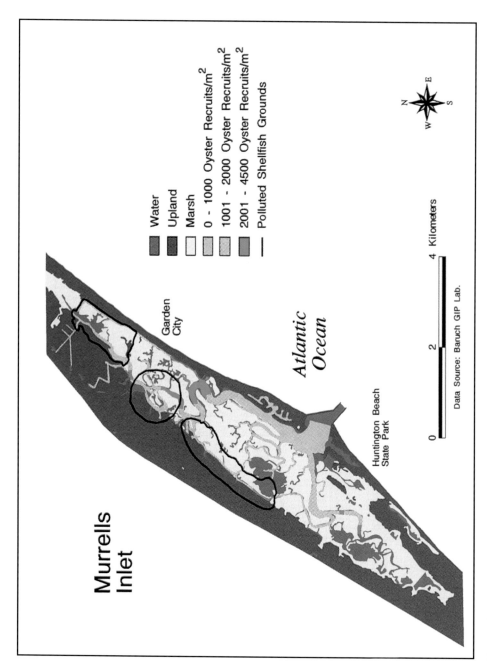

Fig. 10. Pollution zones and contours of oyster recruitment in Murrells Inlet estuary.

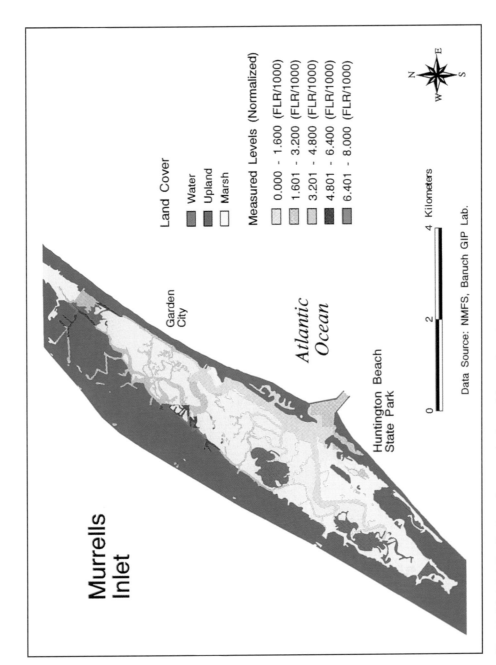

Fig. 11. Modeled distribution of measured values of fluoranthene in oysters.

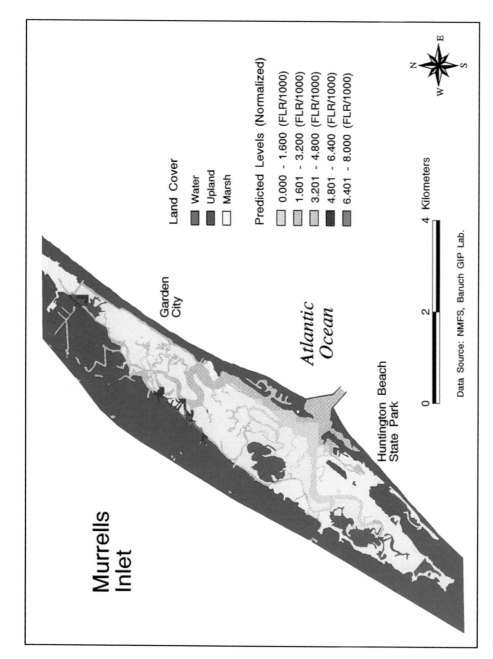

Fig. 12. Modeled distribution of predicted values of fluoranthene in oysters.

developed portions of the estuary near Huntington Beach State Park, low recruitment near a densely populated trailer park at the northern end of the estuary) (Fig. 10). Vernberg et al. (1992) found higher concentrations of polycyclic aromatic hydrocarbons (PAH), copper, and fecal coliforms in oysters collected within Murrells Inlet than in those collected at North Inlet; distributions of copper and fecal coliforms, especially, were closely related to degree of urbanization.

MODELING THE DISTRIBUTION OF POLLUTION LEVELS WITHIN THE MURRELLS INLET ESTUARY

Many environmental parameters were measured that relate to anthropogenic chemical contamination, primary and secondary productivity, ecological and organism toxicology, eutrophication and nutrient loading, and bacterial contamination. Along with these parameters, detailed characterization of land use and land cover, hydrography, and socioeconomics of the town of Murrells Inlet are being incorporated into the C-GIS. Using a subset of these data, the utility of multivariate and regression analysis techniques and kriging for discriminating key variables necessary for predicting impacts of urbanization was demonstrated.

Toxicological examination of the chemical contaminants data revealed that fluoranthene is accumulated in oysters and sediments and approaches minimal threshold levels for expected toxic effects at some sites. Therefore, the level of fluoranthene in oyster tissues was selected as the model measure of impact of urbanization in Murrells Inlet. Urban fluoranthene comes from combustion of fossil fuels, is classified as a possible carcinogen (United States Environmental Protection Agency 1990), is on the priority list of toxic substances (Agency for Toxic Substances and Disease Registry 1992), and is ranked as the fourth highest chemical contaminant of concern in the Gulf of Mexico (Brecken-Folse et al. 1993). Fluoranthene concentrations were the highest of polycyclic aromatic hydrocarbons measured in oysters in Murrells Inlet. The chemical has a high affinity for carbonaceous particulate material in the water column; the same materials that are selectively filtered by oysters. It was postulated that fluoranthene levels in oysters would be related to their proximity to sources of PAH as well as other factors affecting exposure and absorption.

Several variables were measured at 30 sites (chosen by a randomized grid approach) throughout Murrells Inlet and evaluated as measures of polycyclic aromatic hydrocarbon impacts (Table 2). Concentrations of chemicals in oysters and sediments were normalized, as routinely done in ecological assessments, by dividing by the percent fraction of lipid and total organic carbon (TOC), respectively. Reciprocal transformations were used to normalize distances to nearest docks or paved roadways. Dock density within 305 meters of each sampling site was evaluated as another measure of PAH impact because of the common prohibition for public health purposes of shellfish harvests within this range (United States Food and Drug Administration 1991). Concentrations of hydrogen and nitrogen, and clay and silt particle sizes filtered by oysters were used as measures of sediment characteristics potentially affecting exposure and absorption of fluoranthene by oysters. Water and sediment fecal coliform concentrations were chosen because they are routinely measured by public health agencies to classify shellfish harvest areas (United States Food and Drug Administration 1991) and are indicative of nearby pollution discharges such as sewers and runoff. Additional variables tested and eliminated because of high correlation with retained variables included non-normalized fluoranthene concentrations in oysters and sediments, non-normalized distances to docks and roads, and apparent and actual oyster fluoranthene accumulation factors.

Table 2. Variables used in predicting oyster fluoranthene concentrations.

Variable	Fluoranthene ($\bar{x} \pm$ SEM)		
oyster fluoranthene lipid^{-1} (ng 100 g^{-1})	2620	±	370
sediment fluoranthene TOC^{-1} (ng 100 g^{-1})	4810	±	610
meters to road (× 100)	0.182	±	0.032
meters to dock (× 100)	0.587	±	0.172
docks within 305 meters	8.67	±	1.61
percent sediment hydrogen	0.407	±	0.070
percent sediment nitrogen	0.129	±	0.021
percent sediment clay and silt	23.1	±	2.70
water fecal coliform (MPN)	354	±	106
oyster fecal coliform (MPN)	136	±	29

Fluoranthene levels in oyster tissue and sediment were measured by extraction in methylene chloride then partitioned by gel permeation high-performance liquid chromatography and cyano-propyl solid-phase extraction. Samples were tested for individual polycyclic aromatic hydrocarbons on a Waters high performance liquid chromatograph with a Perkin Elmer fluorescence detector (Krahn et al. 1988; Wise et al. 1988). Lipid concentrations were determined as total weights of methylene chloride extracted substances. Total organic carbon, hydrogen, and nitrogen were measured on a Perkin Elmer 2400 CHN Elemental Analyzer (Kuehl et al. 1993). Particle sizes were determined by differential sieving. Fecal coliform bacteria in water and oysters were measured by the Most Probable Number method (American Public Health Association 1970). Measures of distances from sampling sites to docks and roads as well as counting of docks within 305 meters were done from low altitude orthophotographs and confirmed by ground-truthing.

Principal factor analysis (Mulaik 1972; SAS Institute, Inc. 1987) was used to identify a linear combination of a subset of variables that explain most of the variance in the original set of variables. The SAS procedure Proc Factor was used on the 10 variables in Table 2. Approximately 79% of the system variance was explained by just three combinations of these variables. Similar results (77%) were obtained when the variable for distance to docks (a redundant measure of dock density) was eliminated. Strong loadings on one factor by measures of sediment characteristics (hydrogen, nitrogen, and clay-silt content) accounted for 34% of the system variance. Another latent factor having heavy loadings from variables representing proximity to fluoranthene source and level (oyster concentration, dock density, and distance to road) and bacterial pollution (oyster fecal coliform concentration) accounted for an additional 32% of the total variance. Interestingly, sediment fluoranthene and water fecal coliform levels, frequently used to assess estuarine water quality, contributed only slightly to the explanation of the total variance. Thus, just two factors (loading heavily on seven variables) explain 66% of the variance, and approximately equal amounts pertain to sediment quality and pollution sources. Promax rotation was also used to develop a rotation matrix providing maximal loadings of each variable on single factors; little change in interpretation resulted.

Nine variables (with fluoranthene in oysters as the dependent variable) were included in multiple regression modeling to determine a compact and efficient model for fluoranthene prediction using the SAS stepwise, forward, and backward procedures (SAS Institute, Inc. 1987; Neter et al. 1990).

The forward procedure resulted in the following fitted prediction model:

ppb fluoranthene lipid^{-1} = 398 + (749,000 / no. meters to road) + (3.89 × oyster fecal coliform)
+ (0.0685 × (ppb sediment fluoranthene / TOC))

p > 0.10
MSE = 1,070,000
adjusted r^2 = 0.740
cp/p+1 = 0.667
Press Statistic = 35,500,000

The stepwise and backward procedures resulted in the same model:

ppb fluoranthene lipid^{-1} = 687 + (785,000 / no. meters to road) + (3.70 × oyster fecal coliform)

p > 0.10
MSE = 1,080,000
adjusted r^2 = 0.737
cp/p+1 = 0.648
Press Statistic = 35,400,000

The adjusted r^2 values for both models are high by environmental research standards, indicating both are useful for prediction. Given that two procedures yielded the last model, that the cp/p+1 and Press Statistic favor this model and that the MSE and adjusted r^2 are nearly identical, the simpler latter model was used for prediction (Table 3). This model has the additional advantage of relying upon relatively low-cost parameters. Table 3 shows actual and predicted values were very similar at higher fluoranthene levels. Twice the square root of the model MSE approximates the accuracy of prediction; in this case, predictions using this model are accurate to +2.1 ppm normalized fluoranthene (or about one-third of the mean at the higher concentrations) in approximately 95% of predictions.

To relate actual and predicted concentrations of fluoranthene in oysters to land use, it was necessary to develop continuous surface models from the point data. Kriging was the spatio-statistical technique used to develop the GIS data layers from point measures of fluoranthene. Kriging, in its simplest form, predicts the value a variable would have at a given unsampled location, using the observed values of the variable at other locations. Once predictions have been computed for many unsampled locations, usually on a regular grid, these can then be contoured and examined for meaningful pattern and/or integrated into a GIS analysis as a new data layer to compare the spatial pattern of the kriged variable to other key variables.

A kriged value (prediction) is a weighted average of the observations, typically with weights dropping off with increasing distance from the location being predicted. In actuality, every spatial interpolation scheme can be described in this way; what sets kriging apart from other methods is that (1) the weighting scheme is not arbitrarily chosen; it is optimized according to the results of a semivariogram analysis, an intermediate step quantifying the spatial correlation structure in the data; and (2) a measure of accuracy of the predictions can be obtained.

Table 3. Predicted and normalized actual fluoranthene values of oysters from Murrells Inlet.

Actual	Predicted
7920	7960
6620	5400
6140	4400
5780	6150
4610	4460
4280	4810
3650	1380
3500	3470
3570	2330
3460	2010
3090	4240
3030	2600
2910	1210
2820	1860
2010	1840
1700	3200
1600	1020
1550	2320
1500	2920
1030	1560
1020	1160
919	1170
874	1260
774	1010
738	1340
726	1520
726	1020
681	2030
635	1490
495	1350

The semivariogram analysis is critical to kriging and can also provide useful information to aid in designing efficient future sampling plans. A semivariogram analysis examines the rate at which half the squared difference between variable values at two locations increases with the distance between the locations. Typically, these squared distances are plotted versus distance for each pair of sampling sites, and a curve with a convenient functional form fit through the points. After some experimentation, the spherical semivariogram was selected as the functional form for these analyses, fit by ordinary least squares with a standard nonlinear minimization routine (all kriging-related analysis were carried out using modifications of the S-plus functions in Rao [1992]; for a discussion of S-plus, see Venables and Ripley [1994] who also discuss spatial analyses). The final spherical semivariogram used for kriging is defined by three parameter values estimated from the data: the

Table 4. Estimated spherical semivariogram parameters.

Variable	Nugget	Sill	Scale (m)
Normalized fluoranthene / 1000	0.4156	3.6507	1904
$\log_{10}$ sediment fluoranthene	0.1549	> 0.2*	> 4000*
$\log_{10}$ fecal coliform, Feb. 92	0.1388	> 0.1*	> 4000*
$\log_{10}$ total coliform, Feb. 92	0.2873	0.1331	2182
$\log_{10}$ total PAH	0.0981	> 0.2*	> 4000*

* Scale value lies outside the data range.

nugget, which represents variability between measurements taken "at the same location"; the sill, which is the curve asymptote, and which when added to the nugget gives the variance between values taken at well-separated variable sites; and the scale, which represents the smallest distance sampling points need to be separated in order for there to be no spatial autocorrelation. The nugget, sill, and scale characterize the spatial structure of the data. Table 4 contains the estimated values for these three parameters for some representative variables that have been kriged in this study. As an example interpretation, a future study of normalized fluoranthene in oysters in Murrells Inlet with sampling sites separated by at least 1900 m should observe little or no spatial autocorrelation, since this variable is apparently not correlated at distances beyond this, its scale value. For several variables the actual scale parameter value was apparently outside the range of the data, in which cases neither it nor the sill could be estimated uniquely. The final fitted curve is still useful in that (in the range of distances found in the data) it well approximates the pattern of spatial correlation.

A critical assumption of the ordinary kriging analyses is the assumption of isotropy: the spatial autocorrelation between two points depends only on the distance between them and not on their relative orientation in space. Intuition suggests this assumption would be violated in an estuary because points at a given distance in the same creek should be more similar than points separated by the same distance but in different creeks. However, the Murrells Inlet estuary is completely flooded at certain high tides, which may have a homogenizing effect that would validate the isotropic assumption. As a check, kriging analyses using distance between sampled points measured both "as the crow flies" (Euclidean distance) and "as the boat floats" (in-water distance) are currently being conducted. The accuracy of predictions by the two methods will be compared via cross-validation. In an independent study on the larger, more riverine Charleston Harbor system, Rathbun (1995) had mixed results using in-water distances. Some of his models showed improved predictions using in-water distances and in these cases only slight improvement was observed. Work continues to investigate alternative approaches for more efficient use of spatially-explicit data for kriging small estuaries. Some avenues of exploration currently in progress include the incorporation of covariates (e.g., distance to nearest dock and/or the ocean inlet) in both universal kriging and co-kriging.

Both multivariate and linear regression modeling techniques were effective in reducing the number of variables necessary to predict fluoranthene contamination of Murrells Inlet. Factor analyses indicated that two underlying factors related to 1) characteristics of the sediment and

2) sources and impacts of fluoranthene, account for the majority of the variance in the 10 selected variables. This suggests two phenomena govern most of the oyster fluoranthene distribution in Murrells Inlet: transport and exposure of particulate-bound fluoranthene to oysters, and proximate sources of pollution discharge. These findings are not surprising. Fluoranthene and other polycyclic aromatic hydrocarbons readily bind to small, carbonaceous particles and can be transported long distances if the particles remain suspended (Butler and Crossley 1981). Hoffman et al. (1982) and Takada et al. (1991) have shown that urban runoff contains high levels of small particles that are enriched with polycyclic aromatic hydrocarbons. These small particles contribute greatly to environmental diffusion of organic chemical contaminants. Bivalve mollusks have been shown to bioconcentrate polycyclic aromatic hydrocarbons (Dobroski and Epifanio 1980; Augenfield et al. 1982). Ferraro et al. (1990) showed that *Macoma nasuto* will bioconcentrate polycyclic aromatic hydrocarbons bound to recently deposited sediments. Newell and Jordan (1983) showed that oysters (*Crassostrea virginica*) preferentially filter small particles (between 4 μm and 100 μm). Gardner et al. (1991) exposed oysters, mussels, and winter flounder to polycyclic aromatic hydrocarbons and other organic contaminants associated with sediments. They found high concentrations of contaminants and high numbers of neoplastic disorders; both of which resulted from contaminant exposure either directly from the sediments or through food-chain transfer. These studies underscore the importance of understanding environmental fate and effects of anthropogenic chemicals and the need for cost-effective management tools.

The linear regression modeling techniques suggest that just two variables—proximity to roads and oyster fecal coliform—are sufficient to predict oyster tissue burdens of fluoranthene. Kriging of the spatial data show that these parameters are highly predictive of elevated levels and that the areas adjacent to certain types of land use are most susceptible to fluoranthene accumulation. Figures 12 and 13 show the actual and predicted results, respectively. They are very similar, indicating that the highest levels of normalized fluoranthene in oysters occur near water-upland interfaces proximate to both paved roads and boat dockage and passageways. These two variables are relatively inexpensive to measure. Oysters comprise a significant food source for a wide variety of estuarine organisms, are harvested for human consumption, and serve as nonmotile sentinels of environmental insults. Quantitative predictions of effects on oysters may be used by regulatory officials to compare alternative plans for roads, marinas, and other structures in order to minimize the impacts to coastal ecosystem health. Studies are underway to confirm the utility of this approach and to evaluate additional variables for predicting anthropogenic impacts.

Conclusions

Models developed to estimate the impacts of urbanization on localized coastal estuaries are no better than the data and scientific principles used for model development and calibration. When coupled with the best available data and scientific reasoning, Geographic Information Processing provides tools to study the relationships between the natural environment and human activities. This provides the opportunity to assess the impacts of both ongoing and proposed ecosystem changes on the health and welfare of humans and the environment. Whether these changes are the result of normal day-to-day activities, proposed development, new legislation, or a catastrophic event, proper resource management requires that resource managers have the data and scientific means to understand and predict the potential ramifications.

The USES project has shown that Geographic Information Processing, when combined with appropriate data and scientific knowledge, can be used to develop practical tools for predicting impacts to the health of highly productive and sensitive localized coastal estuaries. It is believed that the results of this research will provide an improved understanding of the impact of increasing urbanization in coastal areas. As important coastal resources continue to be stressed and thus decline, coastal resource managers and researchers need to take advantage of the spatial analytical tools provided by the emerging technology of GIP.

According to Vernberg et al. (1992), the estimated acreage of the nearly 160 small estuaries in coastal South Carolina exceeds the total combined acreage of South Carolina's largest estuarine systems, including Charleston Harbor, Port Royal Sound, Santee Delta, and Winyah Bay. Many of these estuaries are within the water-quality gradient between the pristine North Inlet and the urbanized Murrells Inlet, and all will require effective proactive coastal zone management. Since there are over 320 localized creeks, inlets, and estuaries in the southeastern United States similar in size and natural characteristics to North Inlet and Murrells Inlet, many opportunities exist for the application and refinement of these spatial analyses and models.

ACKNOWLEDGMENTS

Funding for portions of the research described in this chapter was provided by National Oceanic and Atmospheric Administration grant NA90AA-D-SG672 (awarded to Drs. John Vernberg and Winona Vernberg). The SCDHEC-OCRM provided funding for the intertidal oyster survey. William Jefferson, David Karinshak, Ben Jones, Danny Taylor, Derrick Kuhl, Kara Hastings, Catherine Coleman, Sharon Lawrie, and Danny Spoon participated in GIS and field research activities. Jim Monck, Mike Yianopoulos, and Ray Haggerty completed the intertidal oyster resource assessment in the study areas. The authors wish to thank Scott Sivertsen, Marion Sanders, and Alan Fortner for PAH analyses; Marty Levison for sediment particle analyses; John Bemiss and David Carter for coliform analyses; and Eric Tappa for sediment carbon, nitrogen, and hydrogen analyses. The authors would also like to thank Laurie S. Little for conducting many of the kriging analyses, and Anne B. Miller for her editorial comments. S-plus is a trademark of MathSoft, Inc. SAS is a trademark of SAS Institute, Inc.

LITERATURE CITED

American Public Health Association. 1970. Recommended Procedures for the Examination of Seawater and Shellfish. 4th ed. American Public Health Association, Inc., Washington, D.C.

Agency for Toxic Substances and Disease Registry. 1992. Fiscal Year 1992 Agency Profile and Annual Report. United States Department of Health and Human Services, Agency for Toxic Substances and Disease Registry, Atlanta, Georgia.

Augenfield, J.M., J.W. Anderson, R.G. Riley, and B.L. Thomas. 1982. The fate of polyaromatic hydrocarbons in an intertidal sediment exposure system: Bioavailability to *Macoma inquiata* and *Aberenciola pacifica*. *Marine Environmental Research* 7: 31-50.

Bartlett, D.J. 1993. GIS and the coastal zone: An annotated bibliography. Technical Report 93-9. National Center for Geographic Information and Analysis. Santa Barbara, California.

Brecken-Folse, J., M.G. Babikow, and T.W. Duke. 1993. Draft evaluation of the Gulf of Mexico sediment inventory. United States Environmental Protection Agency, contract no. 9315-013, United States Environmental Protection Agency, Washington, D.C.

Burrough, P.A. 1987. Spatial aspects of ecological data, p. 213-251. *In* R.H.G. Jongman, C.J.F. ter Braak, and O.F.R. van Tongeren (eds.), Data Analysis in Community and Landscape Ecology. Pudoc, Wageningen, The Netherlands.

Butler, J.D. and P. Crossley. 1981. Reactivity of polycyclic aromatic hydrocarbons adsorbed on soot particles. *Atmospheric Environment* 15: 91-94.

Cressie, N. 1993. Statistics for Spatial Data. Wiley, New York.

Dame, R. F., T. Chrzanowski, K. Bildstein, B. Kjerfve, H. McKellar, D. Nelson, J. Spurrier, S. Stancyk, H. Stevenson, J. Vernberg, and R. Zingmark. 1986. The outwelling hypothesis and North Inlet, South Carolina. *Marine Ecology Progress Series* 33: 217-229.

Dobroski, C.J. and C.E. Epifanio. 1980. Accumulation of benzopyrene in larval bivalves via trophic transfer. *Canadian Journal of Fisheries and Aquatic Sciences* 37: 2318-2322.

Dunlap, R.E. and D.E. Porter. 1993. Use of geographic information processing for the identification of 'indirect' impacts associated with regulatory permitting programs: For now, a conceptual model. Proceedings, Coastal Zone '93. Vol. 1. p. 79-93.

Ferraro, S.P., H. Lee II, R.J. Ozerich, and D.T. Specht. 1990. Predicting bioaccumulation potential: A test of a fugacity-based model. *Archives of Environmental Contamination and Toxicology* 19: 386-394.

Field, D.W., A.J. Reyer, C.E. Alexander, B.D. Shearer, and P.V. Genovese. 1990. National Oceanic and Atmospheric Administration's National Coastal Wetlands Inventory. *In* S.J. Kiraly, F.A. Cross, and J.D. Buffington (eds.), Federal Coastal Wetland Mapping Programs. United States Department of the Interior, Washington, D.C. *Biological Report* 90(18): 39-49.

Frere, M.H., J.D. Ross, and L.J. Lane. 1980. The nutrient submodel CREAMS, a field scale model for chemicals, runoff, and erosion from agricultural management systems. Conservation Research Report 26. Agricultural Research Service, United States Department of Agriculture. Washington D.C.

Gardner, L. R. and M. Bohn. 1980. Geomorphic and hydraulic evolution of tidal creeks on a slowly subsiding beach ridge plain, North Inlet, South Carolina. *Marine Geology* 34: 91-97.

Gardner, G.R., P.P. Yevich, J.C. Harshbarger, and A.R. Malcolm. 1991. Carcinogenicity of Black Rock Harbor sediment to the eastern oyster and trophic transfer of Black Rock Harbor carcinogens from the blue mussel to the winter flounder. *Environmental Health Perspectives* 90: 53-66.

Haddad, K.D. 1990. Marine wetland mapping and monitoring in Florida. *In* S.J. Kiraly, F.A. Cross, and J.D. Buffington (eds.), Federal Coastal Wetland Mapping Programs. United States Department of the Interior, Washington, D.C. *Biological Report* 90(18):145-150.

Haddad, K.D. and B.A. Harris. 1986. A Florida GIS for estuarine management. Technical Papers, American Congress on Surveying and Mapping–American Society for Photogrammetry and Remote Sensing. Vol. 3. p. 2-11.

Haddad, K.D. and B.A. Hoffman. 1987. The role of Geographic Information Systems in managing Florida's coastal wetland resource. Proceedings, Coastal Zone '87. p. 5812-5195.

Haddad, K.D. and G.A. McGarry. 1989. Basin-wide management: A remote sensing/GIS approach. Proceedings, Coastal Zone '89. Vol. 2. p. 1822-1836.

Haddad, K.D. and W.K. Michener. 1991. Design and implementation of a coastal resource Geographic Information System: administrative considerations. Proceedings, Coastal Zone '91. Vol. 3. p. 1958-1967.

Hoffman E.J., J.S. Latimer, G.L. Mills, and J.G. Quinn. 1982. Petroleum hydrocarbons in urban runoff from a commercial land use area. *Journal of Water Pollution Control* 54:1517-1525.

Holland, A.F., D.E. Porter, R.F. Van Dolah, R.H. Dunlap, G.H. Steele, and S.M. Upchurch. 1993. Environmental assessment for alternative dredged material disposal sites in Charleston Harbor. Technical Report Number 82. Marine Resources Division, South Carolina Wildlife and Marine Resources Department, Charleston, South Carolina.

Hunsaker, C.T., R.A. Nisbet, D.C.L. Lam, J.A. Browder, W.L. Baker, M.G. Turner, and D.B. Botkin. 1993. Spatial models of ecological systems and processes: The role of GIS, p. 248-264. *In* M. Goodchild, B. Parks, and L. Steyaert (eds.) Environmental Modeling with GIS. Oxford University Press, New York.

Jefferson, W.H., W.K. Michener, D.A. Karinshak, W. Anderson, and D.E. Porter. 1991. Developing GIS data layers for estuarine resource management. Proceedings, GIS/LIS 91. Vol. 1. p. 331-342.

Jensen, J.R., D.J. Cowen, J.D. Althausen, S. Narumalani, and O. Weatherbee. 1993. An evaluation of the CoastWatch change detection protocol in South Carolina. *Photogrammetric Engineering and Remote Sensing* 59(6):1039-1046.

Kiraly, S.J., F.A. Cross, and J.D. Buffington. 1990. Overview and recommendation. *In* S.J. Kiraly, F.A. Cross, and J.D. Buffington (eds.), Federal Coastal Wetland Mapping Programs. United States Department of the Interior, Washington, D.C. *Biological Report* 90(18):1-7.

Krahn, M.M., C.A. Wigran, and R.W. Pearce. 1988. New HPLC cleanup and revised extraction procedures for organic contaminants. National Oceanic and Atmospheric Administration, Technical Memorandum NMFS F/NWC-153, 23-47.

Krige, D.G. 1951. A statistical approach to some basic mine valuation problems on the Witwaterstrand. *Journal of the Chemical, Metallurgical, and Mining Society of South Africa* 52: 119-139.

Kuehl, S.A., T.J. Fuglseth, and R.C. Thunell. 1993. Sediment mixing and accumulation rates in the Sulu and South China seas: Implications for organic carbon preservation in deep-sea environments. *Marine Geology* 111: 14-35.

Matheron, G. 1963. Principles of geostatistics. *Economic Geology* 58: 1246-1266.

Michener, W. 1992. GPS support vital to long-term ecological research program. *GIS World* February: 58-63.

Michener, W.K., D.J. Cowen, and W.L. Shirley. 1989. Geographic Information Systems for coastal research, p. 4791-4805. *In* Proceedings, Sixth Symposium on Coastal and Ocean Management/ American Society of Civil Engineers.

Michener, W.K., D.P. Lanter, and P.F. Houhoulis. 1996. Geographic Information Systems for Sustainable Development in the Southeastern United States: A Review of Applications and Research Needs, p. 89-110. *In* F.J. Vernberg, W.B. Vernberg, and T. Siewicki (eds.), Sustainable Development in the Southeastern Coastal Zone. University of South Carolina Press, Columbia, South Carolina.

Michener, W.K., W.H. Jefferson, D.A. Karinshak, and D. Edwards. 1992. An integrated geographic information system, global positioning system, and spatio-statistical approach for analyzing ecological patterns at landscape scales. Proceedings, GIS/LIS '92 1: 564-575.

Michener, W.K. and P.D. Kenny. 1991. Spatial and temporal patterns of *Crassostrea virginica* (Gmelin) recruitment: Relationship to scale and substratum. *Journal of Experimental Marine Biology and Ecology* 154: 97-121.

Michener, W.K., A.B. Miller, and R. Nottrott. 1990. Long-Term Ecological Research Core Data Set Catalog. Belle W. Baruch Institute for Marine Biology and Coastal Research, University of South Carolina, Columbia, South Carolina.

Miller A.B., W.K. Michener, A. Barnard, and F.J. Vernberg. 1989. Publications of the Belle W. Baruch Institute for Marine Biology and Coastal Research 1969-1989. Research Bibliography of the Baruch Institute. Technical Report 89-02, Belle W. Baruch Institute, University of South Carolina, Columbia, South Carolina.

Mulaik, S.A. 1972. The Foundation of Factor Analysis. McGraw-Hill Book Co., New York.

Neter, J., W. Wasserman, and M.H. Kutner. 1990. Applied Linear Statistical Models. Richard D. Irwin, Inc., Boston, Massachusetts.

Newell, R.I.E. and S.J. Jordan. 1983. Preferential ingestion of organic material by the American oyster *Crassostrea virginica*. *Marine Ecology Progress Series* 13:47-53.

Porter, D.E. 1995. Use of geographic information processing to model the cumulative impact of regulatory permitting programs on coastal wetlands: A South Carolina perspective. Ph.D. dissertation. University of South Carolina, Columbia, South Carolina.

Porter, D.E. and W.C. Eiser. 1991. Using GIS technology in assessing the impact of the South Carolina Beachfront Management Act following Hurricane Hugo. Proceedings, Coastal Zone '91. Vol. 2. p. 1213-1219.

Rao, G.R. 1992. Programs for kriging in Matlab and S-plus. M.S. Thesis, Department of Statistics, University of South Carolina, Columbia, South Carolina.

Rathbun, S.L. 1995. Spatial modeling in irregularly shaped regions: Kriging estuaries. Department of Statistics Technical Report #95-1, University of Georgia, Athens, Georgia.

SAS Institute, Inc. 1987. SAS/STAT Guide for Personal Computers, Version 6 Edition. SAS Institute, Inc., Cary, North Carolina.

Somers, R., B. Jones, and S. Snyder. 1989. Managing and disseminating data necessary for coastal wetland management in South Carolina. Proceedings, Coastal Zone '89. Vol. 5, p. 4125-4128.

South Carolina State Data Center. 1991. Selected demographic data for South Carolina. Division of Research Services, South Carolina Budget and Control Board, Columbia, South Carolina.

Takada, H., O. Tomoko, H. Mamoru, and N. Ogura. 1991. Distribution and sources of polycyclic aromatic hydrocarbons (PAHs) in street dust from the Tokyo Metropolitan area. *Science of the Total Environment* 107: 45-69.

United States Department of Agriculture, Soil Conservation Service. 1972. Hydrology. *In* National Engineering Handbook. United States Department of Agriculture, Washington D.C.

United States Department of Commerce. 1995. Tide Tables 1995 - East Coast of North and South America including Greenland. National Oceanic and Atmospheric Administration National Ocean Service, Silver Spring, Maryland.

United States Environmental Protection Agency. 1988. America's Wetlands: Our Vital Link Between Land and Water. United States Environmental Protection Agency Public Information Center, Washington, D.C.

United States Environmental Protection Agency. 1990. Ambient Water Quality Criteria Document Addendum for Fluoranthene. Document no. PB91-161430. United States Environmental Protection Agency, Cincinnati, Ohio.

United States Food and Drug Administration. 1991. National Shellfish Sanitation Program Manual of Operations. Part I. United States Department of Health and Human Services Food and Drug Administration, Washington, D.C.

Venables, W.N. and B.D. Ripley. 1994. Modern Applied Statistics with S-plus. Springer-Verlag, New York.

Vernberg, F. J., W. B. Vernberg, E. Blood, A. Fortner, M. Fulton, H. McKellar, W. Michener, G. Scott, T. Siewicki, and K. El-Figi. 1992. Impact of urbanization on high-salinity estuaries in the southeastern United States. *Netherlands Journal of Sea Research* 30: 239-248.

Wischmeier, W.H. and D.D. Smith. 1978. Predicting rainfall erosion losses. Agricultural Handbook 537. United States Department of Agriculture, Washington, D.C.

Wise, S.A., B.A. Brenner, and G.D. Byrd. 1988. Determination of polycyclic aromatic hydrocarbons in a coal tar standard reference material. *Analytical Chemistry* 60: 887-895.

Young, R.A., C.A. Onstad, D.D. Bosch, and W.P. Anderson. 1987. AGNPS, Agricultural Nonpoint Source Pollution Model: A large watershed analysis tool. Conservation Research Report 35. Agricultural Research Service, United States Department of Agriculture, Washington, D.C.

The Effects of Coastal Development on Watershed Hydrography and the Transport of Organic Carbon

Matthew Wahl, H.N. McKellar, Jr., and Thomas M. Williams

ABSTRACT: The effect of coastal development on watershed loading of organic carbon was examined at three first-order blackwater streams. Two streams represent suburban-residential drainage areas (310 acres and 30 acres) near Murrells Inlet, South Carolina, and the other represents drainage from an undeveloped forested watershed (92 acres) near North Inlet, South Carolina. Results for a 3-yr period (September 1990 through October 1993) indicate lower mean concentrations of dissolved organic carbon (DOC) in runoff from suburbanized watersheds (12.5 mg l^{-1} ± 0.3 se and 15.9 mg l^{-1} ± 0.2 se) than in runoff from the forested watershed (25.6 mg l^{-1} ± 0.7 se). This reflects both reduced carbon availability and lower water retention at the suburbanized sites. Of the suburbanized watersheds, higher DOC concentrations were observed from the nonimpounded creek (versus the impounded creek, which flows through two serial 0.5-acre ponds), suggesting carbon processing within the impoundment system. Runoff patterns at all three watersheds indicate rapid stormflow response to rainfall events, with lag times from 2 h to 6 h after peak rainfall intensity. Hydrograph recession, however, was more rapid at the suburbanized watershed. At the impounded, suburbanized stream, a 50% reduction in peak stormflow occurred within 6-7 h, versus 20 h at the forested stream. The nonimpounded stream exhibited a 50% reduction of stormflow peak within 5.5 h. Rapid hydrograph recession may reflect the impervious surfaces and reduced infiltration capacities at the Murrells Inlet watersheds. At the forested site, trends in DOC concentration may provide a method for developing a deterministic model for predicting watershed loading of organic carbon. A consistent pattern of DOC reduction in concentration during peak stormflow (36%) suggested dilution resulted from rising groundwater that had a lower DOC concentration.

Introduction

Freshwater inputs to high-salinity marsh estuaries of the Southeast are often dominated by discharge from small, low-gradient, blackwater streams. These streams typically have high concentrations of dissolved organic matter (DOM), due largely to low retention of DOM by sandy soils, and extended contact between water and organic debris in the low-gradient streams and floodplain areas (Mulholland and Kuenzler 1979). This contact and leaching varies with frequency, duration, and extent of inundation (Mulholland 1981; Williams et al. 1992; McCarthy et al. 1993), which respond directly to local patterns of rainfall, evapotranspiration, and resultant water table fluctuations (Williams 1979).

Organic carbon transport by these blackwater streams may represent an important energy source to downstream aquatic ecosystems. Labile fractions of DOM are assimilated by bacteria, forming an important link in aquatic food webs (Meyer et al. 1987). Recalcitrant fractions of dissolved humic and fulvic acids are important because of interactions with trace metals, hydrocarbons, and colloidal surfaces (McKnight et al. 1990). These streams may provide areas that are ecologically important to downstream energy transfer, as well as to the transport and fate of certain pollutants.

Watershed changes associated with coastal urbanization (commercial and residential development) may significantly alter the quality, quantity, and timing of organic carbon flux in small blackwater streams. Forested watersheds have high rates of carbon fixation. Storage of terrestrial organic carbon occurs in the form of leaf litter (much of which is leachable and labile) and in recalcitrant forms of litter, woody material, soil humus, and humate sands. This carbon undergoes slow mineralization during water surplus due to the presence of a high water table in the upper soil strata. When it rains, the infiltration capacity is greater than the rainfall rate in a forested watershed unless the soil is saturated. Once saturated, natural (irregular) microtopography provides for depressional storage of water in contact with leachable organic matter. The resultant runoff is composed in part by organic carbon release from this storage, serving to both moderate the runoff volume and enrich it with organic carbon.

In a developed watershed, unsaturated areas are created that have limited production and storage of organic carbon. These areas often have truncated soils where the upper organic horizons have been removed during grading, and shallower root systems where turfgrass was added over compacted ground. Saturated areas are reduced to small areas inside the drainage ditch or detention pond areas. These morphological alterations change the local hydrological cycle due to reduced interception, infiltration, retention or detention, and evapotranspiration of water (Soil Conservation Service 1986). Consequently, changes in watershed hydrology may also affect the concentration and transport of organic carbon in impacted watersheds. Subsequent changes to carbon dynamics and transport could have important implications to the structure and functioning of downstream estuarine ecosystems, as well as to the fugacity of environmental pollutants (McCarthy et al. 1991).

At present, little is known about the effects of coastal development on local watershed dynamics and the implications to organic carbon inputs to estuarine ecosystems. As part of a larger investigation of the effects of coastal urbanization on southeastern, high-salinity estuaries, we studied the hydrology and carbon dynamics of several small coastal watersheds (92-310 acre catchments). The main objectives were to quantify basic differences between forested and suburbanized catchments in terms of base flow and storm runoff hydrology and corresponding levels of organic carbon concentration. As part of a longer term study, this initial examination was used to design a more comprehensive study of annual patterns of stream discharge and carbon loading.

Study Sites

Three watersheds were investigated to assess loading differences between forested and suburban land uses (Table 1). The Oyster Creek site at North Inlet, South Carolina, was selected to represent runoff from an undeveloped, forested watershed. The study site is on the property of the Belle W. Baruch Foundation; these lands—both the salt marsh estuary and the adjacent forested uplands—are protected in perpetuity from development and are maintained in a relatively natural state for research and education (Vernberg et al. 1992). The Oyster Creek catchment was formed over 100 yr ago when an earthen dike and ditch network was hand-constructed in an 92-acre agricultural field (Fig. 1). The watershed is now dominated by a 30-yr-old stand of loblolly pines *(Pinus taeda)*, with some mature loblolly pine, live oak *(Quercus virginiana)*, water oak *(Quercus nigra)*, sweet gum *(Liquidambar styraciflua)*, American elm *(Ulmus americana)*, and an understory of wax myrtle *(Myrica cerifera)* and other herbaceous vegetation. The watershed is further characterized by poorly drained spodic soils (such as Leon; aeric haplaquods), low elevation, and very low stream gradients. A more detailed description is provided by Williams (1979) and Blood (1991). The first-order stream is largely intermittant, with extended discharge typically during the winter and early spring. The lower reaches of the stream are periodically affected by tidal intrusions, especially during low flows on autumn spring tides (Blood 1990).

The Gasque Creek and Dog Creek watersheds near Murrells Inlet, South Carolina, were selected to represent suburban-residential drainage areas ($\approx$ 310 acres and 30 acres, respectively). The Murrells Inlet estuary (20 miles north of North Inlet) is similar to North Inlet estuary in many respects, being particularly representative of the numerous high-salinity salt-marsh estuaries along the southeastern coast of the United States. However, the uplands surrounding Murrells Inlet are largely characterized by suburban development dominated by residential housing and infrastructures supporting an intense summer tourist industry (roads, restaurants, and condominiums). The Gasque Creek catchment (Fig. 2) includes two 0.5-acre serial impoundments that resulted from coquina mining in 1945. Discharge from the downstream impoundment is controlled by a broad-crested spillway structure that directs water through a culvert and into the tidal waters of Murrells Inlet. Discharge from the pond is not affected by tidal action. The Dog Creek watershed (Fig. 3) is not impounded and experiences some tidal influence at its lower reaches. Drainage areas for both sites at Murrells Inlet have been altered as a result of suburban development and construction of the US Route 17 bypass. Both streams originate on higher beach ridge topography than Oyster Creek at North Inlet (Fig. 4), and subsequently have more well-drained soils (Lakeland; typic quartzipamments).

Methodology

Stream hydrology was examined through a combination of stream stage monitoring and direct measures of stream discharge. Forested Oyster Creek and suburbanized Gasque Creek were both monitored continuously in the first year (1990-1991) using a float and stilling well arrangement where stage was recorded at 15-min intervals on digital tape (Carter and Davidian 1968). This work was contracted to the United States Geological Survey; the Survey maintained the recorders and the resulting database. A stage-discharge rating was developed from on-site measurements of instantaneous stream depth and velocity within a 3-ft flume. These measurements were taken monthly and during selected storm events. Velocity profiles were constructed using a calibrated wading rod and hand-held electromagnetic velocity meter (Marsh-McBirney 201M). For Gasque

Table 1. Watershed characteristics of the forested and suburban streams.

Name	Type	Watershed Area (acres)	Low Elevation (ft above MSL)	High Elevation (ft above MSL)	Average Slope (%)	% Hydrologic Soil Group*					
						A	B	C	D	A/D	B/D
Oyster Creek	Forested	92	2.5	6.9	0.3					22	78
Gasque Creek	Suburban, impounded	310	11.0	27.0	0.667	26	57		8	9	
Dog Creek	Suburban, not impounded	30	3.5	24.0	1.100	55	45				

* The percent of watershed area by hydrological soil group is a measure of average soil infiltration. This is based on a minimum infiltration rate for a particular soil (bare) after prolonged wetting. Soils in group A have the highest infiltration rate (0.30-0.45 inches h^{-1}) and soils in group D have the lowest infiltration rate (0.00-0.05 inches h^{-1}). Soils classified as A/D or B/D are permeable soils that have periods of low surface intake (low infiltration) due to high water table conditions.

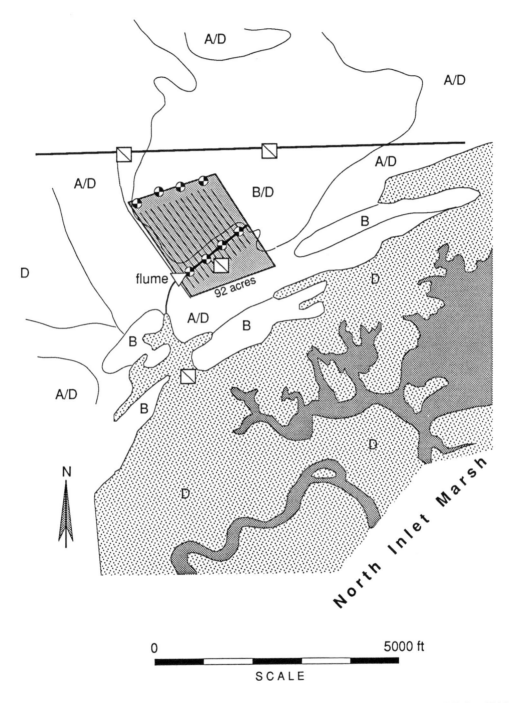

Fig. 1. The Oyster Creek watershed of North Inlet. Hydrologic soil groups are B, D, A/D, and B/D (see Table 1 for description). Stream discharge sites are indicated by ∇, well sites by ◐, and rain gauge sites by ▨.

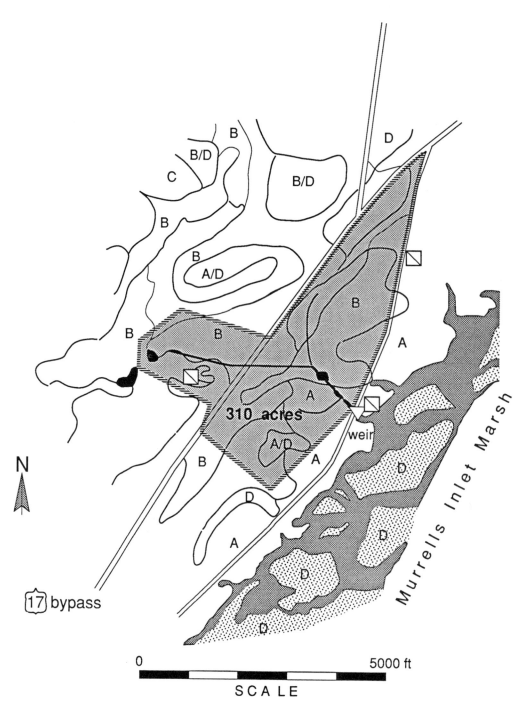

Fig. 2. The Gasque Creek watershed of Murrells Inlet. Hydrologic soil groups are A, B, C, A/D, and B/D (see Table 1 for description). Stream discharge sites are indicated by ∇ and rain gauge sites by $\boxslash$.

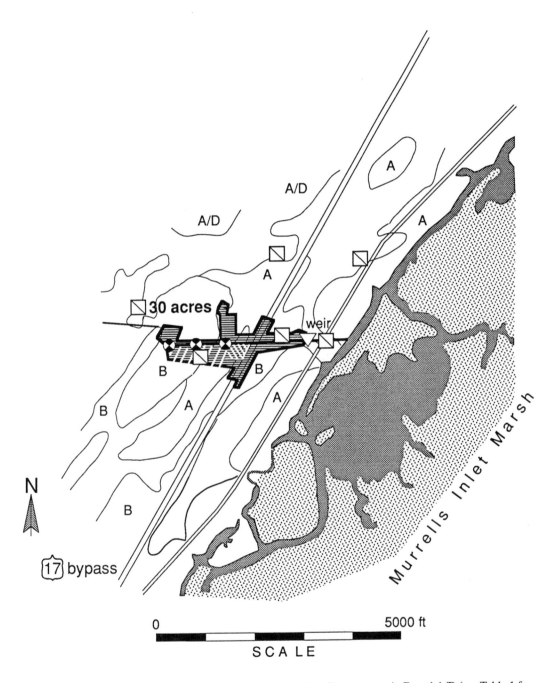

Fig. 3. The Dog Creek watershed of Murrells Inlet. Hydrologic soil groups are A, B, and A/D (see Table 1 for description). Stream discharge sites are indicated by ▽ and rain gauge sites by ▨.

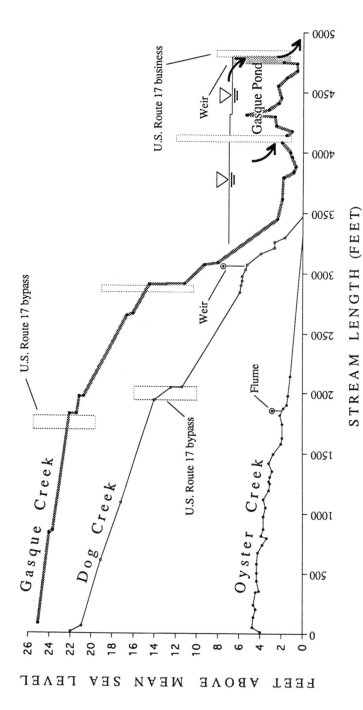

Fig. 4. Streambed elevation versus stream length for forested Oyster Creek (North Inlet) and suburbanized Gasque and Dog creeks (Murrells Inlet).

Pond, discharge (Q, in cubic feet per second, cfs) was computed directly from pond stage using standard relationships established for a broad-crested weir (Hulsing 1967):

$$Q = CbH^{2/3}$$

where C is a coefficient determined as a function of head (H) and b is the length of the spillway crest (1.24 ft for the lower spillway and 10.92 ft for the upper spillway).

The Oyster Creek stream record was interrupted for a 7-mo period (January-July 1992) during installation of a V-bottomed parshall flume (2 ft) and a roadway culvert, and during a dry period (only intermittant flow). Discharges during the interim were estimated from direct stream measurements along the storm hydrograph. At suburbanized Dog Creek, a sharp-crested weir (90° V-notch and 6-ft Cippoletti combination) was also built and installed (July 1992).

Water sampling focused on water quality trends during storm events, and sequential automatic samplers (ISCO, model 1000) were used to collect stream water samples during major phases of a storm hydrograph (pre-storm conditions, rising limb, and recession). As part of a longer term study, stormflow water quality was sampled during nine different storm events at both forested Oyster Creek and suburbanized Gasque Creek, and seven different storm events at suburbanized Dog Creek (1991-1993). Ultimately, this data will allow us to extrapolate our results over a full range of hydrographic conditions and estimate patterns of annual loading of organic carbon.

Water samples (900 ml) were collected at mid-channel locations in acid-washed plastic bottles. The samples were labeled and covered in ice, filtered within 12 h of collection through a combusted glass-fiber filter (2.5 cm Whatman GF/F), acidified to pH < 2 with concentrated H_3PO_4, and stored at 4°C. Dissolved organic carbon (DOC) was defined as the organic carbon in solute and particles < 0.45 μm. Concentrations of DOC were analyzed using a Dohrman DC-190 carbon analyzer. The filtrate was sparged for 6 min with ultra-high purity O_2 gas, and triplicate 200-μl aliquots were injected into a 680°C combustion chamber. The resulting CO_2 concentrations were determined using nondispersive infrared (NDIR) analysis.

Results and Discussion

GENERAL HYDROGRAPHY

The comparison between Oyster and Gasque Creeks for year 1 (September 1, 1990 through August 31, 1991) indicates that discharge at Oyster Creek was perennial (sustained by baseflow), while Gasque Pond underwent significant periods of no outflow (Fig. 5). Total annual rainfall at Oyster Creek was 54 inches, and the estimated area-weighted depth of runoff was 22 inches (or 40% of rainfall). Runoff estimated at Gasque Creek during this same period was considerably less (14 inches; ≈ 26% of rainfall), suggesting less water exited the Gasque Creek basin as surface water. Another explanation is that the watershed area was less than the 310 acres. Baseflow composed a greater portion of the surface runoff at Gasque Creek, and this may reflect differences in regional groundwater dynamics. Although tropical storms Klaus and Marco (October 10 and 23, 1990) resulted in similar hydrographs for both streams, less agreement was exhibited in the hydrographs during early and mid summer (1991). Particularly after dry conditions, Oyster Creek

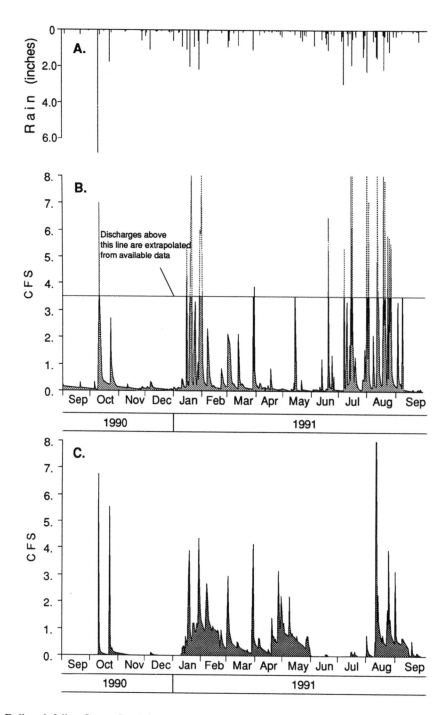

Fig. 5. Daily rainfall at Oyster Creek (A), and discharge hydrographs of Oyster Creek (B) and Gasque Creek (C). Discharge at Oyster Creek was perennial (sustained by baseflow). Gasque Creek had significant periods of no outflow.

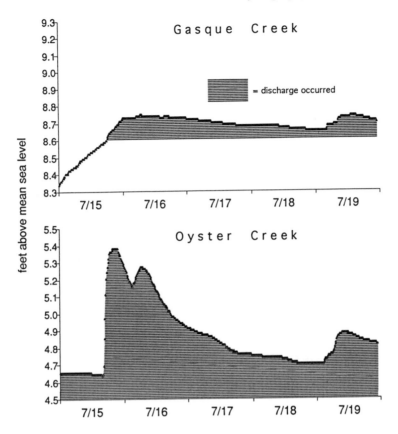

Fig. 6. Stage hydrograph response following ≈ 2 inches of rainfall at both Gasque Creek and Oyster Creek on July 15-16, 1991. The stormflow at Gasque Creek filled pond retention before discharge occurred. Once pond retention had been satisfied, however, the creeks responded similarly following 0.5 inches of rainfall on July 19.

exhibited stronger initial responses to storm events than Gasque Creek. For example, stage hydrographs resulting from a 2-inch rain on July 15-16, 1991, reflected the rapid response at Oyster Creek (indicating immediate discharge), and the initial retention of stormflow at Gasque Creek before stage exceeded spillway elevation (Fig. 6). This pond retention resulted when outflows from leaks (in the riser-crossdrain connection) exceeded inflows. Once retention volume within the impoundment had been satisfied, however, similar responses between streams were observed (July 19, 1991, Fig. 6). Drawdown of the impoundment stage during a period of low potential evapotranspiration (in December 1991) demonstrates the importance of this water loss and its effect on retention (Fig. 7).

An important factor influencing stream hydrology at Oyster Creek was the extremely low streambed gradient (see Fig. 4), and the resultant shifts in the stage-discharge relationship due to the growth and senescence of stream and riparian macrophytes (Fig. 8). Direct measurements of discharge were compared with a continuous record of stream stage, and three overall stage-discharge

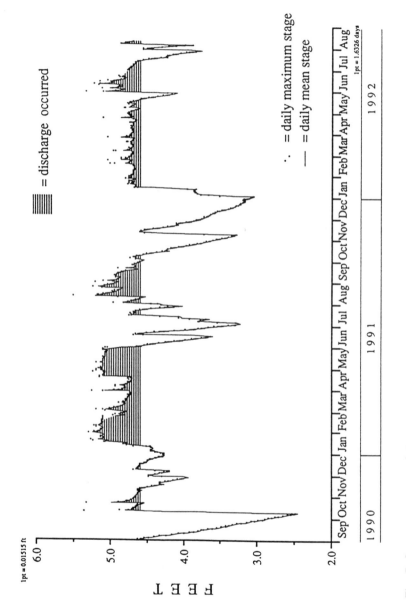

Fig. 7. Stage hydrograph of Gasque Creek (Murrells Inlet). Drawdown of the impoundment during a period of low evapotranspiration (December 1991) suggests that outflows from leaks exceeded inflows, resulting in retention volume.

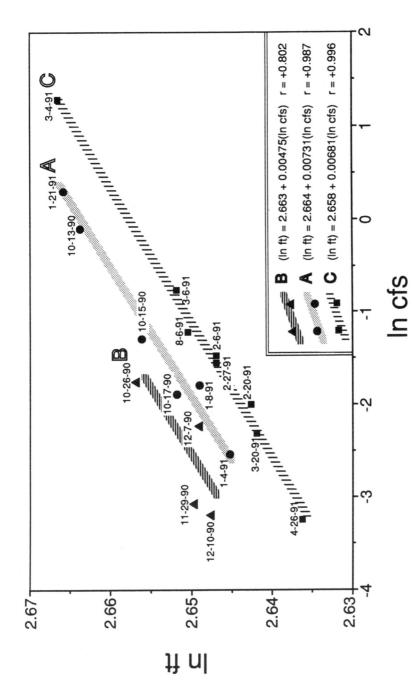

Fig. 8. Stage-discharge rating curves for Oyster Creek. Due to the extremely low streambed gradient (0.13%) , growth and senescence of stream and riparian macrophytes resulted in variable control of stream hydrology. Peak vegetative resistance occurred in November and December of 1990 (rating B). As these plants senesced during early winter (January 1991), decreased hydraulic resistance resulted in a lower stage per unit discharge. Stormflow then cleared away debris dams of this material, resulting in the lowest stage for a given discharge (rating C).

relationships were observed. Peak vegetative resistance occurred in November and December of 1990 (Fig. 8, rating B), resulting in the greatest stage for a given discharge. As these plants senesced during early winter (January) decreased hydraulic resistance resulted in a lower stage per unit discharge (Fig. 8, rating A). Stormflow (2.2 inch rainfall on January 29, 1991) may then have cleared away resultant debris dams of this material, resulting in further decrease in channel roughness and a lower stage for a given discharge (Fig. 8, rating C).

STORMFLOW RUNOFF

Stormflow at forested Oyster Creek was characterized by a rapid response time and a gradual hydrograph recession. During a 0.9-inch, 5-h rain event under moderate baseflow conditions (0.28 cfs), ≈ 10% of the runoff volume was discharged prior to peak flow (3-h lag to peak), with only 50% reduction in stormflow occurring after ≈ 20 h (Fig. 9a.). This is a typical response for a lower coastal plain watershed in South Carolina (Williams personal communication). Stormflow at Gasque Creek delivered a relatively sharp response during a 1.3-inch, 9-h rainfall event (Fig. 9b) under moderate baseflow conditions (0.28 cfs). Although lag time at Gasque Creek (6 h) was twice that of Oyster Creek, it exhibited a more rapid hydrograph recession, with 50% reduction in peak stormflow occurring after only 6-7 h. More rapid hydrograph recession observed at Gasque Creek may have reflected the impervious surfaces and reduced infiltration capacities of the Murrells Inlet watershed. This occurred despite attenuation and detention of stormflow by the impoundment. Given extensive aquatic macrophyte beds within the impoundment, the extent to which stormflow was moderated is beyond the scope of this preliminary study.

Preliminary hydrographs from Dog Creek appear similar to hydrographs of impounded Gasque Creek in terms of overall shape. This similarity can be seen when compared with a 1.4-inch, 4-h rainfall event that resulted in 1.5 cfs (Fig. 10), with a 50% reduction in peak stormflow occurring after only 5.5 h. Addition of impervious surfaces generally result in quicker stormflow responses as well as an overall increases in stormflow volume (Soil Conservation Service 1986). It may suffice to note that stormflow moderation by the impoundment would tend to make the observed effects of development more conservative. Because of the characteristically fast responses in "natural" (pervious) coastal systems (such as by Oyster Creek), the contribution of water from a paved (developed) source may occur during peak discharge on a "natural" hydrograph. This hydrographic assumption will be important when considering concentration trends of dissolved organic carbon (DOC) and the effects of coastal development.

DOC CONCENTRATION DYNAMICS

Preliminary results indicate lower mean concentrations of dissolved organic carbon (DOC) in runoff from the suburbanized watersheds (Fig. 11). Mean DOC concentrations of Gasque Creek and Dog Creek at Murrells Inlet (12.5 mg l^{-1} and 15.9 mg l^{-1} respectively) were lower than those of Oyster Creek at North Inlet (30.1 mg l^{-1}). The suburbanized watersheds' lower level of organic carbon may reflect reduced availability of organic carbon and/or reduced water retention due to steeper stream gradients (see Fig. 4).

Reduced availability of organic carbon results from the removal of forest vegetation and upper soil horizons, land filling, and the ditching and draining of connected wetland areas with saturated

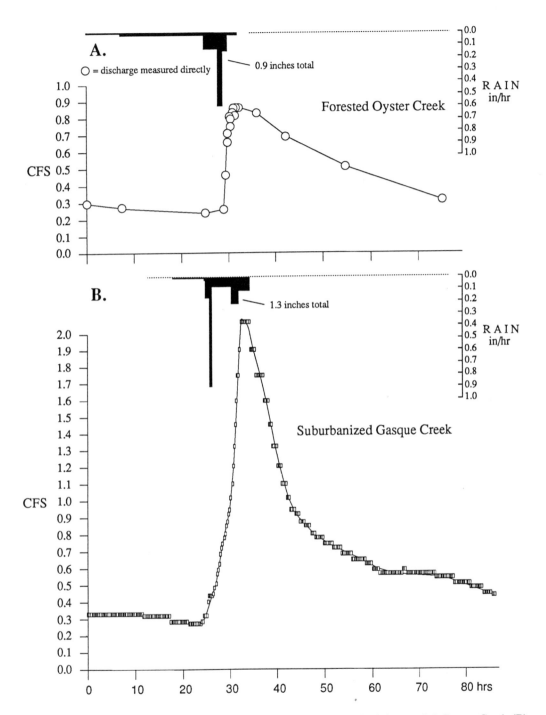

Fig. 9. Discharge hydrographs of forested Oyster Creek (A) and urbanized, impounded Gasque Creek (B). Note the rapid recession at Gasque Creek.

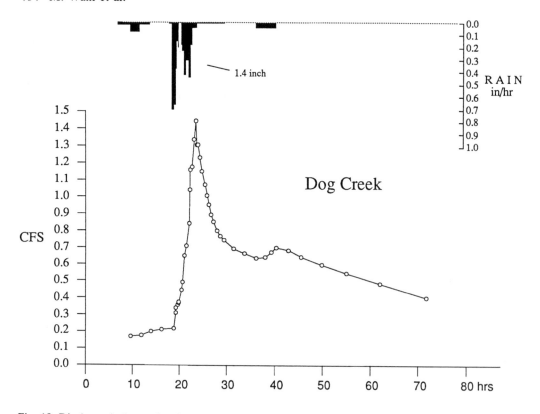

Fig. 10. Discharge hydrographs of urbanized Dog Creek.

soils and fluctuating water tables. Less water retention results from steeper stream gradients, as well as the loss of connected wetland areas. Steeper stream gradients at the suburbanized sites reflect both the higher beach ridge topography, and the orientation of the streams (perpendicular to the coast). Deeply excavated, coast-perpendicular ditches across the topographic beach ridges of the Murrells Inlet sites increases the rate of water movement toward the marsh, and more effectively reduces areas of saturated soil. In contrast, Oyster Creek occupies the natural topographic low between a single beach ridge and swale feature and is parallel to the coast. When the DOC concentrations of the two Murrells Inlet streams are compared, lower DOC levels are evident in runoff from impounded Gasque Creek, which may indicate carbon processing within the pond.

During periods of storm runoff, there were differences in the timing of organic carbon transport between watersheds. The concentration dynamics may reflect the overall flowpaths involved in storm runoff. Assuming the greatest sources for organic carbon enrichment at the Oyster Creek watershed are in the upper soil horizons and in depressional storage, the concentration history of DOC after 1.8 inches of rainfall suggests early channel connection to these carbon-rich sources on the rising limb (during moderately high baseflow conditions $\approx$ 0.26 cfs). The peak runoff concentration of DOC (a 37% increase) occurred prior to peak discharge (Fig. 12); by peak discharge, DOC concentration was decreasing, and it continued to decrease rapidly to below pre-storm levels. This

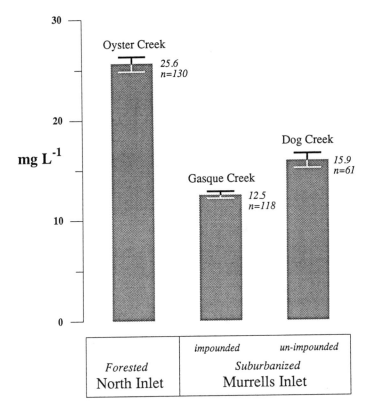

Fig. 11. Mean annual dissolved organic carbon concentration (± se) for each creek. Note the higher concentrations of the forested stream, Oyster Creek.

dilution may have resulted from the predominance of less concentrated rainwater, or may reflect the displacement of less concentrated groundwaters. Groundwater with a lower concentration of DOC (coming from deeper and less organically rich source areas) was likely being displaced into streamflow by newly infiltrated DOC-enriched water. Such a mechanism is supported by gradual increase in DOC concentration during hydrograph recession, as new water proceeded old water into streamflow.

In contrast to the dynamics observed at Oyster Creek, stormflow at Gasque Creek (from 1.3 inches of rain, June 3-4, 1992) exhibited relatively constant DOC concentrations under similar antecedent baseflow conditions (Fig. 13). This constancy may reflect the displacement of impoundment waters by inflowing stormwaters. Such a mechanism is supported by measurements of specific conductance (232-310 mhos), water temperature (19.1-19.3°C), and dissolved oxygen (0.2-0.5 mg l^{-1}) that were within a constant, narrow range.

Gradual increases in DOC concentration at Oyster Creek were observed after a larger 2.4-inch, 6-h rainfall, which was followed 9 h later by a 2.6-inch, 5-h rainfall (September 5-6, 1992, Fig. 14). The DOC concentration exhibited a period of dilution occurring approximately around the

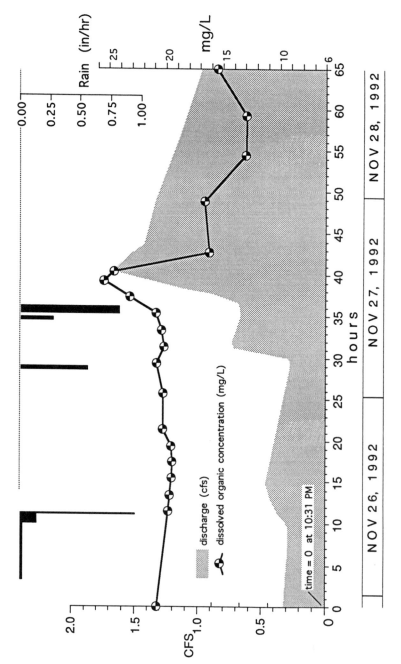

Fig. 12. Oyster Creek discharge, dissolved organic carbon (DOC), and rainfall (1.8 inches) on November 26-28, 1992. Dramatic reduction in DOC concentration (50%) is associated with peak discharge. This dilution may have resulted from the predominance of less concentrated rainwater, or reflect the displacement of less concentrated groundwaters.

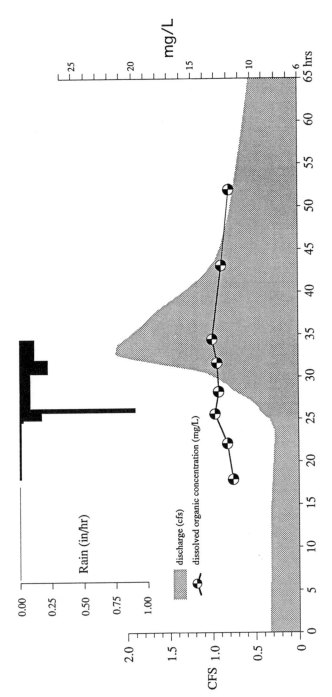

Fig. 13. Gasque Creek discharge, dissolved organic carbon (DOC), and rainfall (1.3 inches) on June 3-4, 1992 (time = 0 at 1700 h). The relatively constant DOC concentration suggests displacement of impoundment waters. This is consistent with measurements of specific conductance (232-310 mhos), water temperature (19.1-19.3°C), and dissolved oxygen (0.2-0.5 mg l^{-1}), which are within constant, narrow ranges.

peak discharges of both events. This again may reflect input of rainwater with a lower DOC concentration, or a greater occurrence of rising groundwater that has a lower DOC concentration. Groundwater seepage may be less concentrated in DOC because of its longer residence time in the aquifer, and resultant removal of DOC due to processes that include degradation, sorption, complexation, and mobilization (Thurman 1985). Sustained, gradual increases in DOC concentration during larger rain events may reflect the continuous input of newly infiltrated carbon-enriched water. This enrichment results when DOC adsorption by soils reaches a steady state, and forms of DOC that are normally retarded became mobile (McCarthy et al. 1993). This hypothesis may work well with earlier hydrologic investigations by Williams (1979) at Oyster Creek, assuming the confining layer is sufficiently nonconductive, most of the water is exiting the watershed as channel flow, and the water table is functioning as both a storage reservoir and flow medium.

Conversely, constant, lower levels of DOC were observed out of Gasque Creek during the same time period (from 2.32 inches of rainfall). This may reflect either displacement of less concentrated impoundment waters by stormflow, or a more systematic moderation of DOC due to reduced carbon availability and/or the predominance of regional groundwater flow.

Comparison of particulate organic carbon (POC) concentration for this rain event show trends similar to those observed for DOC: strong storm dynamics at Oyster Creek, and constant low POC levels out of Gasque Creek (Fig. 13c). Oyster Creek concentrations were closely associated with the approximate stream discharge, and Gasque Creek concentrations exhibited initial dilution (80%) to constant low POC levels. This reduction may reflect both the effective trapping efficiency of POC at Gasque Pond and displacement of less concentrated impoundment waters by stormflow.

Retention ponds are an increasingly common alteration to small blackwater streams in coastal areas. Used in the remediation of urbanization effects, they capture the first flush of suburban runoff. However, these impoundments may also serve to reduce the energy input (in the form of organic matter) to the receiving marsh ecosystem through retention storage and/or the displacement of more dilute impoundment waters (Wahl 1991).

Summary and Recommendations

Differences between forested and suburbanized watersheds were observed in terms of their hydrography and carbon dynamics. Lower mean DOC concentrations at the Murrells Inlet sites may reflect reduced carbon availability resulting from suburban development. Lower DOC from impounded Gasque Creek may reflect carbon processing within the impoundment. In Gasque Pond, stormwater retention and displacement of impoundment waters are important mechanisms influencing organic carbon transport. Since impoundments represent a common alteration to coastal streams in developed areas, an additional sampling station at the inflow would help established the differences between autochthonous and allochthonous processes.

Hydrologic responses to rainfall events in coastal watersheds are often dominated by the presence of a high water table. Williams (1979) observed a threshold water table level at Oyster Creek below which the streambed was dry and rainfall input went into storage with little or no discharge. In addition, a close association was observed between the change of storage (fall in water table) and stream runoff, suggesting that most of the water leaving the watershed in liquid form was channelized (Williams 1979).

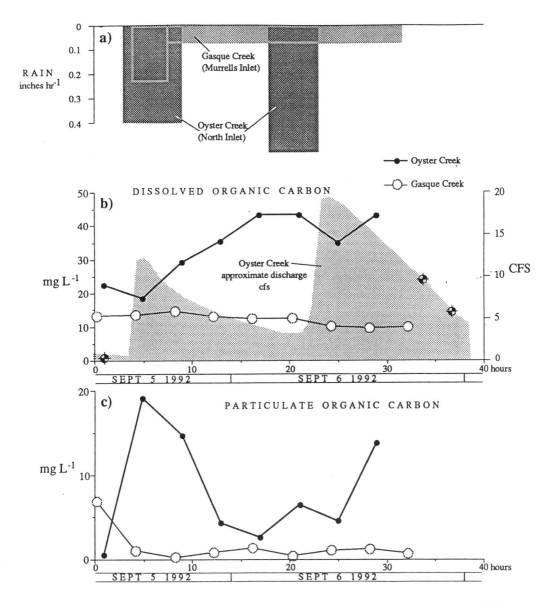

Fig. 14. (A) Rainfall (5 inches), (B) dissolved organic carbon, and (C) particulate organic carbon of forested Oyster Creek (North Inlet) and suburbanized Gasque Creek (Murrells Inlet).

Concentration histories of DOC during storm events at Oyster Creek suggest a simple way to model overall stormflow, with early connection to carbon-rich tributary channels, and subsequent predominance of less concentrated groundwater. To better understand groundwater contributions and observed transformations, responses in piezometric surface should be estimated for each storm event (by measuring water levels in wells at different depths along a transect at each watershed). Water levels should be measured prior to, during, and subsequent to peak rainfall intensity. Combined with estimates of hydraulic conductivity at each piezometer, this would offer a way of testing if the dilution effect of DOC during stormflow resulted from less concentrated groundwater seepage. Well samples could be bailed prior to and during stormflow response, and DOC analysis of molecular size fractions could be performed (< 3000 MW, McCarthy et al. 1993) on both groundwater and runoff. If groundwater contributions resulted in dilution of DOC in stormflow, then there would be a change in DOC size fractions from larger (more hydrophobic) molecules to smaller (more hydrophilic), more mobile molecules.

Understanding stream hydrology (stage and discharge; rainfall and runoff) remains a major component of evaluating watershed loading. For Oyster Creek, the frequent shifts in the stage-discharge relationship increased the difficulty of computations of continuous discharge. To improve discharge estimates at Oyster Creek, a V-bottomed parshall flume flow-control structure was installed (April 1992). At Dog Creek, adequate streambed gradient at the sampling location allowed for streamflow to be controlled by a simpler V-notch weir, and installation of this structure was completed in June 1992 (see Fig. 11).

Potential transformations at the saltwater-freshwater interface could be investigated quarterly where freshwater stormflow mixes with tidal water near the outlet of both Oyster Creek and Dog Creek. The stormflow hydrographs could be compared with tidal stage hydrographs and constituent concentrations over a complete tidal cycle. These boundary measurements could be combined with a survey of basin topography of the stream segment and trends in water temperature, specific conductance, and suspended solids to yield information on both tidal restriction to freshwater discharge and other related physical and chemical processes affecting transport.

LITERATURE CITED

Carter, R.W., and J. Davidian. 1968. General procedure for gaging streams, p. 1-13. *In* Techniques of Water Resource Investigation of the United States Geological Survey, Book 3. Application of Hydraulics, United States Geological Survey, Arlington, Virginia.

Hulsing, H. 1967. Measurements of peak discharge at dams by indirect method, p. 14-24. *In* Techniques of Water Resources Investigations of the United States Geological Survey. Book 3. Application of Hydraulics. United States Geological Survey, Alexandria, Virginia.

McCarthy, J.F., T.M. Williams, L. Liang, P.M. Jardine, L.W. Jolley, D.L. Taylor, A.V. Palumbo, and L.W. Cooper. 1993. Mobility of natural organic matter in a sandy aquifer. *Environmental Science Technology* 27(4): 667-676.

McKnight, D.M., P. Behmel, D.A. Franko, E.T. Gjessing, U. Munster, R.C. Petersen, Jr., O.M. Skulberg, C.E.W. Steinberg, E. Tipping, S.A. Visser, P.W. Werner, and R.G. Wetzel. 1990. Group report, how do organic acids interact with solutes, surfaces, and organisms? p. 223-243. *In* E.M. Perdue and E.T. Gjessing (eds.), Organic Acids in Aquatic Ecosystems. John Wiley & Sons Ltd., New York.

Meyer, J.L., R.T. Edwards, and R. Risley. 1987. Bacterial growth on dissolved organic carbon from a blackwater river. *Microbial Ecology* 13: 13-29.

Mulholland, P.J. and E.J. Kuenzler. 1979. Organic carbon export from upland and forested wetland watersheds. *Limnology and Oceanography* 24(5): 960-966.

Soil Conservation Service. 1986. Urban hydrology for small watersheds. Technical Release 55. Soil Conservation Service. United States Department of Agriculture.

Thurman, E.M. 1985. Organic Geochemistry of Natural Waters. Klewers Academic Publishers. Hingham, Massachusetts.

Vernberg, F.J., W.B. Vernberg, E. Blood, A. Fortner, M. Fulton, H.N. McKellar, Jr., W.K. Michener, G. Scott, T. Siewicki, and K. El-Figi. 1992. Impact of urbanization of high-salinity estuaries in the southeastern United States. *Netherlands Journal of Sea Research* 30: 239-248.

Wahl, M. H. 1992. Carbon transport in low-order low-gradient streams; the effects of storm events and stream impoundment. M.S. Thesis. University of South Carolina, Columbia, South Carolina.

Williams, T.M. 1979. Implications of hydrologic response to the practice of forestry on coastal forests. *In* W. H. Smith (ed.), Proceedings: Forest Practice and Water. 1979 Annual Meeting, Florida Section of Southeastern Association of Fisheries. Jacksonville, Florida.

Williams, T.M., T.G. Wolaver, R.F. Dame, and J.D. Spurrier. 1992. The Bly Creek ecosystem study—Organic carbon transport within a euhaline salt marsh basin, North Inlet, South Carolina. *Journal of Experimental Biology and Ecology* 163: 125-139.

Water Quality in Two High-salinity Estuaries: Effects of Watershed Alteration

Elizabeth R. Blood and Pauley A. Smith

ABSTRACT: Throughout the world, 70% of the human population resides on coastal plains, and the number will increase in the future. Concurrent with these population shifts will be an increase in point-source and nonpoint-source runoff into coastal waters. Watershed alterations resulting from development and the associated increased runoff alter the spatial and temporal patterns of nutrients and water quality in estuarine systems. A number of estuarine studies have reported substantial nutrient enrichment and a shift to eutrophic conditions associated with human-related activities. Municipal discharges have been a major cause of eutrophic conditions in urbanized estuaries. In recent years, nonpoint-source inputs have gained increasing attention as sources of water quality problems in estuarine systems. In South Carolina's coastal counties, the major shift in land use will be from forest to urban. The South Carolina coast has numerous estuaries, limited in riverine influence with average annual salinities ranging from 30‰ to 34‰. These estuaries are relatively shallow and generally characterized by tidal exchange through a single inlet, which accounts for greater than 90% of the water exchange. Much of the undeveloped coast lies adjacent to these small high-salinity estuaries. As urbanization occurs, assessment of its effects on spatial and temporal water quality and nutrient distributions is problematic because of the lack of pre-existing information from which effects can be quantified. Water quality and nutrients were measured seasonally in two high-salinity estuaries: North Inlet Estuary and Murrells Inlet Estuary. Less than 6% of the North Inlet watershed is developed while over 50% of the Murrells Inlet watershed is in urban development. Thirty locations within each estuary were sampled. For each estuary, locations were grouped into land-influenced regions and ocean-influenced regions; for North Inlet there was also a bay-influenced region. In North Inlet Estuary, salinities are affected by exchange with a mesohaline bay (Winyah Bay) and intermittent surface water and groundwater runoff from the watershed. Surface water impoundments in Murrells Inlet Estuary resulted in higher salinities than those in North Inlet Estuary. Salinities in the land regions of both estuaries were lower and more variable. The lowest salinities were detected within the bay region of North Inlet Estuary. Urbanization in Murrells Inlet Estuary had little effect on dissolved oxygen concentrations. High oxygen demand within the two estuaries resulted in no significant differences in dissolved oxygen concentrations between the estuaries or with estuarine region. Lowest dissolved oxygen occurred at low tide during the summer season. No significant differences in average nutrient (ammonium, nitrate, and orthophosphate) concentrations were observed between estuaries. Spatial differences within each estuary and between estuaries varied with tidal stage and seasonally. Generally, highest inorganic nutrient concentrations occurred at low tide and during the summer or fall season. Ammonium concentrations were highest in the land region of both estuaries and higher in the land region of North Inlet Estuary than the land region of Murrells Inlet Estuary. Nitrate and orthophosphate concentrations did not differ between estuaries or between the land and ocean regions within a given estuary. However, during the summer and fall season, nitrate and orthophosphate concentrations were higher in Murrells Inlet Estuary than North Inlet Estuary, with the highest concentrations occurring adjacent to a trailer park. The bay region of North Inlet Estuary had higher nitrate concentrations than other regions of both estuaries. The highest nitrate concentrations occurred at high tide and during the summer season. The processes controlling oxygen and nutrient distributions and dynamics in estuaries are driven by water budget characteristics. In shallow, high-salinity estuaries with relatively small watersheds, water quality may have greater internal controls or nonpoint-source loads may be diluted and dispersed rapidly within the estuary via tidal exchange. Internal processes are amplified particularly when freshwater flow is limited, as when upland creeks are impounded (Murrells Inlet Estuary), and/or when hydrologic conditions prevent freshwater inputs. Differences in tidal exchange rates and estuarine turnover also could have contributed to differences between the two estuaries and could have minimized the differences in water quality attributable to urbanization.

Introduction

Throughout the world, 70% of the human population resides on coastal plains (Cherfas 1990), and the numbers will increase in the future. By the year 2000, it is estimated that 80% of the United States population will live within 59 miles of the Great Lakes or an ocean (Bohlen 1990). In the eight coastal counties of South Carolina, the population is expected to increase by 50% in the next 20 years.

In South Carolina's coastal counties, the major shift in land use will be from forest to urban (Blood and Vernberg 1992). These shifts will result in an increase in point-source and nonpoint-source runoff into our coastal waters. Nonpoint-source inputs from urban areas have higher surface runoff, nutrients, and sediment loads, and oxygen-demanding substances than runoff from forested areas (Loehr 1974). Municipal treatment is the primary point-source input associated with urbanization. Typical concentrations of total nitrogen and total phosphorus in secondarily treated municipal sewage are 30 mg l^{-1} and 5 mg l^{-1}, respectively (Novotny and Chester 1981), and concentrations in untreated sewage are 40 mg l^{-1} and 10 mg l^{-1}, respectively. Jaworski (1981) suggested 5.4 g N m^{-2} yr^{-1} and 0.75 g P m^{-2} yr^{-1} as levels of nitrogen and phosphorus loading to estuaries that would not result in excessive eutrophic conditions. In storm drain systems, with combined storm and sewer drains, sewer overflow associated with rainstorms discharged over 6 times more ammonium and 3 times more total phosphorus (as orthophosphate) than systems with a separate storm and sewer drains (Straub 1989). In areas where septic tanks are the primary municipal treatment, nutrients and oxygen-demanding substances are transported to estuarine systems by shallow groundwater. Weiskel and Howes (1991) reported that 99% of the flux of groundwater-dissolved nitrogen through the coastal watershed to Buzzards Bay, Massachusetts, was anthropogenic. While only 20% of the nitrate generated in the residential portion of the sub-basin was removed, the undisturbed woodland was highly efficient at retaining nitrate.

Point-source and nonpoint-source inputs have been altering the water quality patterns of estuarine ecosystems for hundreds of years. As early as 1885, nutrient (total nitrogen and ammonium) levels were being studied in conjunction with sewage outfalls on the Thames River, England (Nixon and Pilson 1983). A number of estuarine studies have reported substantial nutrient enrichment and a shift to eutrophic conditions associated with human-related activities (Jaworski 1981; D'Elia et al. 1986; Hecky and Kilham 1988). Nixon et al. (1986) have concluded that estuarine systems are the most heavily fertilized ecosystems because of increasing anthropogenic inputs of nitrogen and phosphorus. Municipal discharges have been a major cause of eutrophic conditions in urbanized estuaries (Ryther and Dunstan 1977; Karydis et al. 1983; Lee and Olsen 1985; D'Elia et al. 1986; Hecky and Kilham 1988).

In recent years, nonpoint-source inputs have gained increasing attention as sources of water quality problems in estuarine systems. It is estimated that nonpoint sources alone contribute 79-88% of the nitrogen and 74-87% of the phosphorus entering estuarine systems (Gilliland and Baxter-Porter 1987; Alm 1990). Terrestrial loading via surface water and groundwater flows (Valiela et al. 1978, 1990; DeLaune et al. 1989; Dame et al. 1991; Stern et al. 1991), exchange with open water systems such as bays or oceans (Valiela and Teal 1979; Kjerfve and McKellar 1980; Dame et al. 1986; Whiting et al. 1987), rainfall (Jordan et al. 1983), and biota (Bildstein et al. 1992) are important nonpoint-source inputs to estuaries. Studies have investigated nutrient runoff from agricultural fields (United States Environmental Protection Agency 1980, 1983; Gilliam et al. 1986; Kuenzler and Craig 1986), from activities related to forest clearing (Douglas and Swift 1977), and from various land-use patterns (Omernik 1976; Straub 1989). A comprehensive evaluation of urban nonpoint-source runoff, which includes analysis of urban land uses, impervious surface coverage, and nutrient loadings, may be found in Lazaro (1990).

In addition to external point-source and nonpoint-source inputs, there are many sources and sinks of nutrients in the estuarine ecosystem that affect nutrient distributions and forms available to support primary production (Valiela et al. 1978; DeLaune and Patrick 1980; Pritchard and Schubel 1981; Wolaver et al. 1984; Whiting et al. 1989; Dame et al. 1989). Areal extent of tidal inundation, duration of flooding, and direction (ebb versus flood) and velocity of tidal flow (Jordan et al. 1983; Wolaver et al. 1984) affect the quantity and form of nutrients present in tidal surface waters. Exchanges between the estuary and atmosphere via estuarine microbial processes (i.e., nitrogen fixation and denitrification) can be larger than the hydrologically mediated inputs and outputs (e.g., river inflow, tidal outflow) from estuarine systems (Kaplan et al. 1979; Smith et al. 1985; Howarth et al. 1988; Seitzinger 1988; DeLaune et al. 1989). Other important biotic controls include nutrient depletion by phytoplankton (D'Elia et al. 1986; Pennock and Sharp 1986), uptake and release by oyster reefs (Dame et al. 1989), and nutrient translocation and release by macrophytes (DeLaune and Patrick 1980). Benthic remineralization may be the primary factor controlling relative quantity and availability of nutrients in surface tidal waters of some estuaries (Nixon et al. 1976; Boynton et al. 1980; Hammond et al. 1985). Bioturbation can greatly enhance benthic flux of mineralized nutrients and particulate resuspension (Gardner et al. 1989). Therefore, nutrients (bound to sediments or as organic material) entering tidal surface waters from point and nonpoint sources may be released later through benthic or water-column remineralization.

High-salinity (average annual salinities 30-34‰) estuaries with limited riverine influence dominate the coastline of the Southeast United States. Over 320 such estuaries occur between Cape Fear, North Carolina, and Cape Canaveral, Florida, and nearly half are in South Carolina (Vernberg et al. 1992). These estuaries are relatively shallow and generally characterized by tidal exchange through a single inlet, which accounts for greater than 90% of the water exchange. Relatively few studies of these estuarine ecosystems (Vernberg et al. 1989, 1992; Blood and Vernberg 1992) or the effects that urbanization will have on these systems have been conducted. The purpose of this study is to quantify salinity, oxygen, inorganic nitrogen and phosphorus temporal and spatial distribution patterns in a relatively undisturbed high-salinity estuary and quantify the alteration in these distribution patterns as a result of urbanization. An undisturbed estuary (North Inlet Estuary, South Carolina) was selected to evaluate the effect of nonpoint-source inputs from a forested system having a watershed with less than 6% urban development. An urbanized estuarine system (Murrells Inlet Estuary, South Carolina) with greater than 50% urban development located approximately 20 km north was selected for comparison.

Study Sites

NORTH INLET

North Inlet Estuary is a bar-built, class C estuary (dominated by tidal flushing, with no salinity stratification) (Pritchard 1955) located 70 km northeast of Charleston, South Carolina (Fig. 1). The watershed is 24.8 km^2; 60% of the land area is to the north and drains into the upper portion of North Inlet Estuary and 40% is to the west (Blood and Vernberg 1992). Residential development, including a golf course, is less than 6% of the land area and located in the northern portion of the watershed (Waccamaw Regional Planning and Development Council 1985, personal communication 1995). The watershed topography is flat (< 0.1% slope), soils are sandy, and the groundwater table ranges from 0 m to 5 m below the surface. Freshwater inputs to the system from the watershed are less than 2% of the tidal prism and occur primarily from November to May. Thus the estuary has an average annual salinity of 30-34‰ and little variation in mean monthly salinities (29.5‰ to 34.4‰).

The estuarine system consists of *Spartina alterniflora* marsh (75.2%), exposed mudflats (2.5%), and tidal creeks (22.0%). The marsh is bounded to the east by sandy barrier islands, to the north and west by forested uplands, and to the southwest and south by Winyah Bay. North Inlet connects with the coastal ocean via a tidal inlet (Town Creek) on the eastern boundary, and connects with Winyah Bay through three creeks: South Jones, No Man's Friend, and Haulover. The primary water exchange occurs through Town Creek (79%) (Kjerfve 1982). Water exchange between North Inlet Estuary and Winyah Bay is restricted to the lower third of the estuary; a nodal zone (Fig. 1) is located approximately 0.5 km to 1.5 km from the Winyah Bay entrance (Schwing et al. 1983). Only during high freshwater discharge into Winyah Bay or with dominant southwesterly winds is the nodal zone overridden and net flows traverse from Winyah Bay to North Inlet Estuary (Michener et al. 1990).

The North Inlet system has numerous tidal creeks, with an average channel depth of 3 m. The deepest point (7.4 m) is in Town Creek adjacent to the inlet (Kjerfve 1989). The estuary has a semidiurnal tide with a mean tidal range of 1.4 m, and a tidally-driven circulation. The large tidal volume and shallow depth result in a residence time for tidal water in the estuary of 5 d to 7 d. Because approximately 40% of the water is exchanged on each tide, there is no significant vertical stratification of salinity or density (Kjerfve 1989).

MURRELLS INLET

Murrells Inlet is located midway along the South Carolina coast and is approximately 20 km north of North Inlet (Fig. 2). The 24.0 km^2 estuary has a 26 km^2 watershed of forested and urban land. The inlet has been developed to meet the needs of permanent residents and seasonal tourists. Over half (14.1 km^2) of the watershed is urban, with a permanent resident population of 3,334. Population density is 6 times greater during the tourist season (South Carolina Data Center 1990). Bordering the inlet to the north is Garden City, an area of beach homes, condominiums, and hotels, and to the south is Huntington Beach State Park. The Waccamaw Neck Region, which is to the west, is dominated by homes and restaurants. The estuary has six boat marinas and substantial water traffic.

Murrells Inlet is a bar-built estuary with shallow tidal creeks draining marshes dominated by *Spartina alterniflora*. The inlet has a single opening to the ocean and a semidiurnal tide with a range of 1.5 m. The waterways have been modified by dredging, filling, and jetty construction (Marcus 1985). The inlet's waters are vertically well-mixed and salinities are typically greater than 30‰ but may drop to 20‰ during storms (South Carolina Department of Health and Environmental Control 1990).

Climate

The climate of North Inlet and Winyah Bay estuaries is temperate to subtropical; the average temperature is 18°C and the range 8-27°C. Two major factors affecting southeastern coastal environments are the recurrence of large rainfall deficits (droughts) and excesses (tropical storms and hurricanes). Droughts have occurred in the Southeast 17 times in the past 100 years (Guttman and Plantico 1987). Precipitation in the study area averages 130 cm yr^{-1} (National Oceanic and Atmospheric Administration 1985), but annual precipitation patterns are highly variable. Summer is the wettest season, with 35% of annual precipitation; fall (24%), winter (20%), and spring (21%) are drier. Tropical storms or hurricanes impact the South Carolina coast approximately once every 2.6 years (Gentry 1971). They contribute 10-15% of the average total annual precipitation at North Inlet Estuary and may account for up to 25% of the annual rainfall (Blood et al. 1991). Storm size and frequency for a given season is quite variable. Northeasterly (fall and winter) and southwesterly (summer) winds are the most common. Spring winds are the most variable but are predominately from the southwest (Michener et al. 1990).

Sampling and Analyses

Thirty locations were sampled in each estuary (Figs. 1 and 2). Stations were located at the most landward extent of major tidal creeks to assess terrestrial nonpoint-source runoff and at approximately 1-km intervals along the main axis of these tidal creeks to the inlets. Because of the large tidal exchange and range within both estuaries, stations were sampled at high tide and low tide to maximize information on land and ocean influences. Sampling was conducted in December 1990 (winter season), April 1991 (spring), July 1991 (summer), and October 1991 (fall). Temperature and dissolved oxygen were measured with a YSI model 55 oxygen meter. Conductivity was measured with a YSI model TCS conductivity meter.

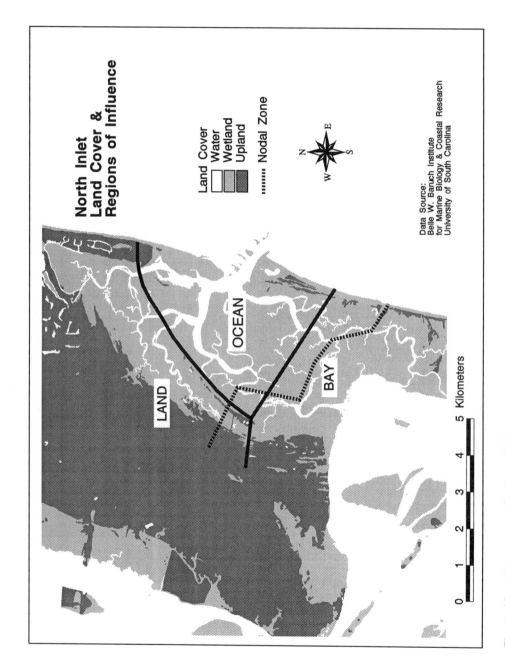

Fig. 1a. North Inlet estuary. Regions of influence, land cover, and nodal zone.

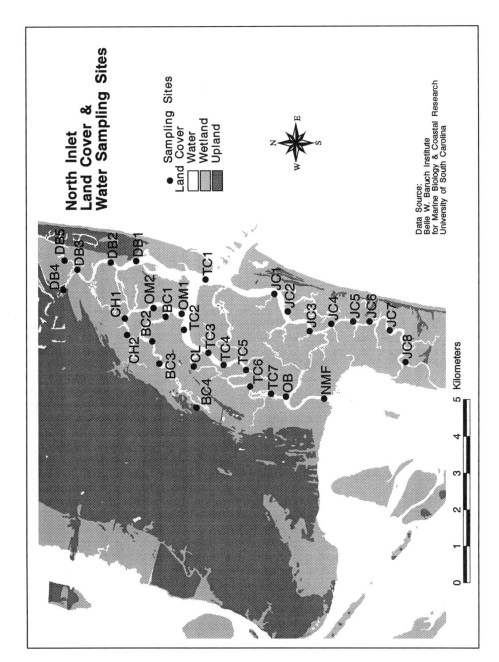

Fig. 1b. North Inlet Estuary. Sampling sites and land cover. DB = Debidue Creek, CH = Crab Haul Creek, BC = Bly Creek, OM = Old Man Creek, TC = Town Creek, CL = Clambank Creek, JC = Jones Creek, OB = Oyster Bay, NMF = No Man's Friend.

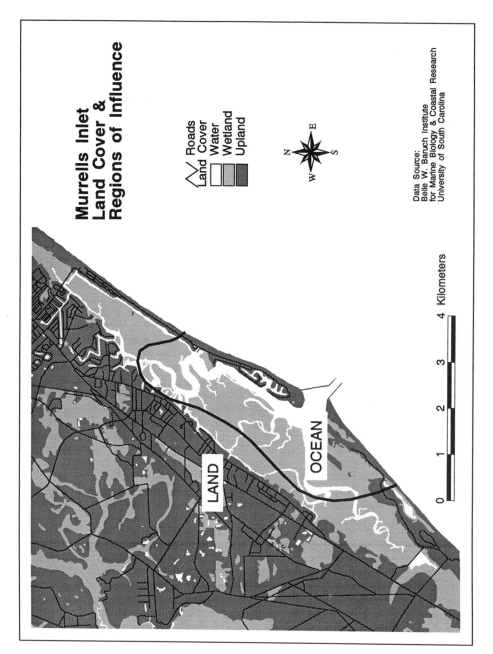

Fig. 2a. Murrells Inlet Estuary. Regions of influence, land cover, and nodal zone.

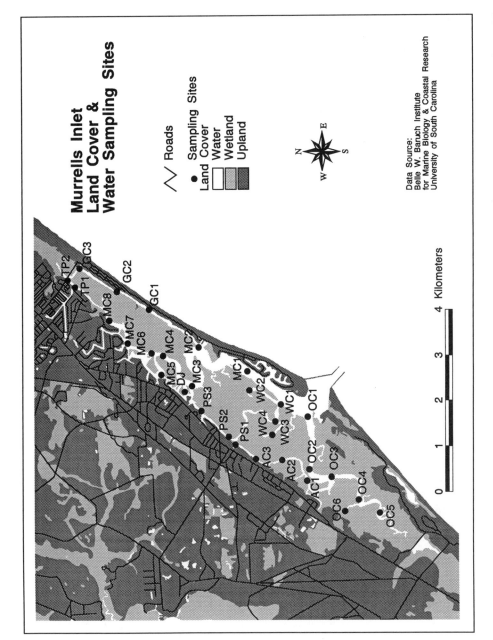

Fig. 2b. Murrells Inlet Estuary. Sampling sites and land cover. TP = Trailer Park, GC = Garden City, MC = Main Creek, PS = Parsonage Creek, WC = Woodland Creek, DJ = Drunken Jacks, AC = Allston Creek, OC = Oaks Creek.

Samples were transported immediately to the Baruch Marine Field Laboratory (adjacent to North Inlet Estuary). Approximately 200 ml of each sample was filtered through a precombusted Whatman GF/F glass-fiber filter. Aliquots for ammonium and for nitrate plus nitrite were preserved with phenol and mercuric chloride, respectively, stored below 4°C, and analyzed within 2 wk to minimize loss due to storage. Water samples for orthophosphate determinations were not preserved but were analyzed within 24 h of returning to Columbia, South Carolina. Nutrients were measured by automated colorimetric tests using either a Technicon Autoanalyzer II or Orion Scientific Auto-analyzer System. Ammonium was determined by the phenate method (Technicon Industrial method no. 154-71W) and nitrate plus nitrite by cadmium reduction (Technicon Industrial method no. 158-71W) (American Public Health Association 1985). In oxidized surface waters, nitrogen is primarily nitrate and, therefore, nitrate plus nitrite will be expressed as nitrate. Orthophosphate was determined by ascorbic acid reduction (Technicon Industrial method no. 155-71W) (American Public Health Association 1985).

Data were initially analyzed for normality using univariate analyses (SAS 1985). All nutrient concentrations were logarithmically transformed to obtain a normal distribution prior to statistical analyses. For the purposes of this study, stations were grouped into regions to evaluate the effect of nonpoint-source runoff versus oceanic exchange on surface water quality (Figs. 1 and 2). In Murrells Inlet, stations were grouped into a land region and an ocean region. The North Inlet stations were grouped into three regions: land, ocean, and Winyah Bay. Preliminary analyses of the North Inlet Estuary individual stations indicated that Winyah Bay affected the observed water quality and therefore, may bias an evaluation of nonpoint-source runoff effects if those stations were grouped with land or ocean regions. A general linear model was used to evaluate main and interaction effects of inlet, season, region, and tide on water quality and nutrients. The data were partitioned by inlet, season, region, and tide, and contrasts were performed to evaluate differences within each partition. Only the main effects and contrasts within main effects will be discussed in this study.

Results

SALINITY

Salinity varied significantly with region, season, tidal stage, and between estuaries (significance level for each main effect was $p < 0.0001$) (Fig. 3). The average salinity (over tide, region, and season) for North Inlet Estuary was 26‰ and for Murrells Inlet Estuary was 31‰. North Inlet Estuary salinities ranged from 10‰ to 35‰ while Murrells Inlet Estuary salinities ranged from 23‰ to 37‰. Salinity variability was influenced by oceanic exchanges and terrestrial runoff. In Murrells Inlet Estuary, salinities were significantly lower and more variable in the land region compared with the ocean region. Upland freshwater inflow was greater into North Inlet Estuary than Murrells Inlet Estuary and resulted in significantly lower (3-5‰) estuarine and regional salinities in North Inlet Estuary than Murrells Inlet Estuary. This additional inflow, however, did not result in significantly lower land region salinities than ocean region salinities in North Inlet Estuary. The greatest variability and the lowest salinities in North Inlet Estuary were from stations adjacent to the mesohaline Winyah Bay. The average salinity of the Winyah Bay region was significantly lower (4‰ lower; $p < 0.05$) than the land or ocean regions of North Inlet Estuary. In general, for each estuary, the spatial variability within a given tidal stage was greater than the differences between tides. Salinities were

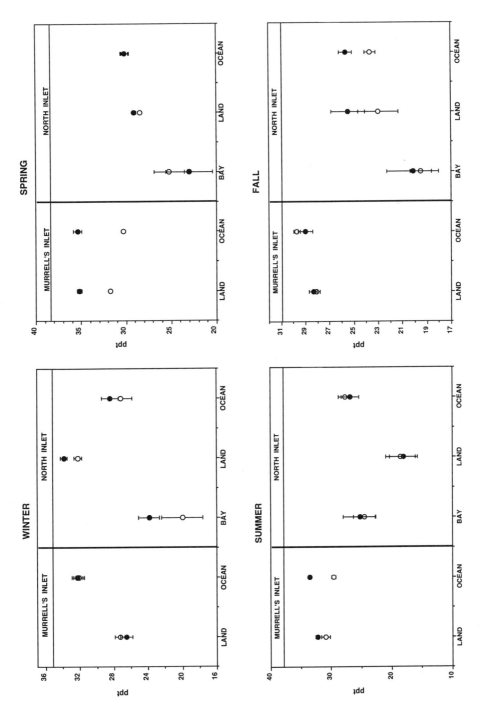

Fig. 3. Seasonal mean salinity concentration and standard error by region within each estuary. Winter season is December 1990, spring is April 1991, summer is July 1991, and fall is October 1991. ● represents high tide samples, ○ represents low tide samples.

lower at low tide than high tide in each estuary, reflecting surface water and groundwater contributions from the adjacent terrestrial systems. Salinity differences between high and low tide were significantly ($p < 0.05$) greater in Murrells Inlet Estuary than North Inlet Estuary while spatial variability in salinity was significantly ($p < 0.05$) greater in North Inlet Estuary than Murrells Inlet Estuary.

Significant ($p < 0.0001$) seasonal differences in mean salinities (averaging region, tide, and estuary) were found. Lowest salinities occurred in the fall and highest salinities in the spring in both estuarine systems. Fall mean salinities were 4‰ lower than in the spring for both estuaries. Significant ($p < 0.05$) estuarine and regional differences in salinity occurred within a given season. For example, in the land region of North Inlet Estuary, salinities were significantly lower during the summer season while the Murrells Inlet Estuary land region had significantly lower seasonal salinities in the winter. Also, North Inlet Estuary salinities during the summer season were significantly lower in the land region than in the ocean region, but no differences between land region and ocean region summer salinities were observed in Murrells Inlet Estuary.

DISSOLVED OXYGEN

Dissolved oxygen concentrations were not a good indicator of urban influences on estuarine processes as no significant differences were found between estuaries or between regions within a given estuary. Both estuaries averaged 6.2 ± 1.8 mg l^{-1} dissolved oxygen. Concentrations varied significantly ($p < 0.0001$) with season and tidal stage (Fig. 4). Dissolved oxygen concentrations were significantly higher during the winter and significantly lower during the summer. The lowest concentrations were detected in July, dropping to less than 2 mg l^{-1}, in both estuaries. Dissolved oxygen was significantly ($p < 0.0001$) higher at high tide than low tide. Low tide concentrations averaged 1 mg l^{-1} to 2 mg l^{-1} less than those at high tide. The relationship between tidal stage and dissolved oxygen concentration was likely accentuated by sampling time as low tide samples were consistently collected in the morning and high tide samples in the mid to late afternoon.

Regional variation in dissolved oxygen differed with tidal stage, but there were no patterns clearly attributable to upland runoff. Tidal differences in dissolved oxygen varied significantly ($p < 0.05$) by season between estuaries and within a region. At high tide in July and December, the dissolved oxygen concentration of the Murrells Inlet ocean region was significantly greater ($p < 0.05$) than that of the North Inlet Estuary ocean region. The opposite pattern was observed in October. At low tide, lower dissolved oxygen concentrations were detected in North Inlet Estuary adjacent to the Winyah Bay region and at stations receiving drainage from the upland forest. In Murrells Inlet Estuary, the lowest dissolved oxygen concentrations were detected adjacent to the land in the spring; no significant regional differences were found during the summer.

NUTRIENTS

No significant differences in average nutrient (ammonium, nitrate, and orthophosphate) concentrations were observed between estuaries when averaged over seasons and tides (Table 1). Ammonium averaged 2.7 μg-at N l^{-1}, nitrate 1.2 μg-at N l^{-1}, and orthophosphate 3.9 μg-at P l^{-1}. There were regional differences in nutrient patterns, which were not the same for the two estuaries. Ammonium concentrations in both estuaries were higher in the land region than the ocean region, but the differences were not significant ($p > 0.05$). Ammonium in the land region of Murrells Inlet

Table 1. Average water quality constituents for Murrells Inlet Estuary and North Inlet Estuary. Mean concentration and standard deviation are averaged over station, tide, and season.

Region	Salinity (‰)		Dissolved oxygen (mg l⁻¹)		Nitrate (µg-at l⁻¹)		Phosphate (µg-at l⁻¹)		Ammonium (µg-at l⁻¹)		N : P
	mean	sd	mean	sd	mean	sd	mean	sd	mean	sd	
MURRELLS INLET ESTUARY											
Estuary	30.7	3.1	6.2	1.6	1.3	2.7	4.0	1.3	2.8	1.8	1.0
Land	30.0	3.4	6.2	1.6	1.5	2.4	4.0	1.3	3.0	1.7	1.1
Ocean	31.5	2.6	6.3	1.6	1.2	3.2	4.0	1.2	2.5	1.9	0.9
NORTH INLET ESTUARY											
Estuary	26.1	5.1	6.3	1.8	1.4	2.1	3.8	1.3	2.7	1.7	1.1
Land	27.1	4.9	6.2	1.8	1.3	1.7	3.8	1.3	2.9	1.7	1.1
Ocean	27.4	3.9	6.3	1.7	1.2	1.8	3.9	1.2	2.6	1.7	1.0
Winyah Bay	22.9	5.8	6.2	1.9	2.0	2.5	3.5	1.3	2.6	1.6	1.3

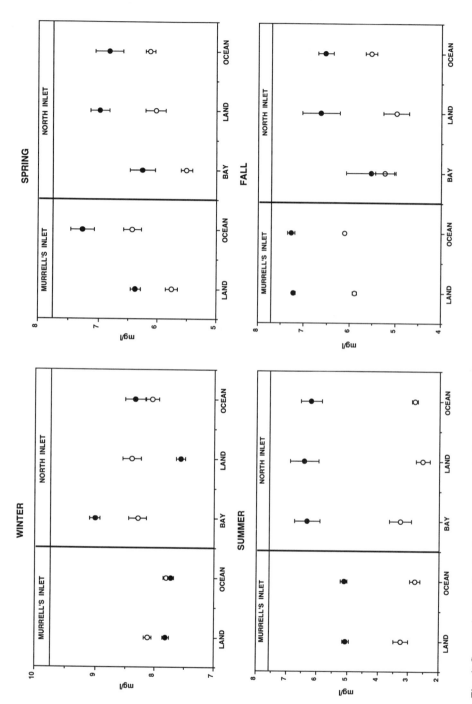

Fig. 4. Seasonal mean dissolved oxygen concentration and standard error by region within each estuary. Winter season is December 1990, spring is April 1991, summer is July 1991, and fall is October 1991. ● represents high tide samples, ○ represents low tide samples.

was 0.5 μg-at N l^{-1} higher than in the ocean region. The highest ammonium concentration (7.8 μg-at N l^{-1}) in Murrells Inlet Estuary was detected adjacent to a trailer park and a marina. In North Inlet Estuary, the highest concentrations were detected at low tide and at the shallowest stations adjacent to upland areas. Ammonium concentrations in waters draining from the upland forest into North Inlet were 3 to 4 times greater than concentrations detected within the estuary. In fact, the highest concentration detected during the study period (> 60 μg-at N l^{-1}) was in drainage from the North Inlet Estuary upland watershed. This concentration exceeded levels detected at any location in Murrells Inlet Estuary. The variability in ammonium observed in both estuaries may have contributed to the lack of statistical differences in means between the land and ocean regions. Greater spatial variation occurred for ammonium at low tide in both estuaries (Fig. 5).

No significant differences in average nitrate concentration were detected between the ocean and land regions within either North Inlet Estuary or Murrells Inlet Estuary, neither were any found when comparing regions between estuaries. Nitrate concentrations averaged 1.4 μg-at N l^{-1} in Murrells Inlet Estuary and 1.2 μg-at N l^{-1} in North Inlet Estuary. Nitrate concentrations in North Inlet Estuary were influenced by intrusions from the mesohaline bay, with significantly higher concentrations ($p < 0.05$) in the Winyah Bay region than either the ocean or land region (Fig. 5). Average nitrate concentrations in the Winyah Bay region were 0.7 μg-at N l^{-1} higher than the land and ocean regions in North Inlet. The highest mean nitrate concentration (6.3 μg-at N l^{-1}) occurred in July at high tide in the Winyah Bay region. Some regional differences in nitrate were found between the estuaries when the data were partitioned by tide and season. Nitrate concentrations were 50% higher in the land region at low tide in Murrells Inlet Estuary than North Inlet Estuary. In the spring and summer seasons, Murrells Inlet Estuary land and ocean regions had significantly higher ($p < 0.05$) nitrate concentrations than the respective North Inlet Estuary regions. Murrells Inlet Estuary nitrate concentrations averaged 70% higher ($p < 0.05$) than North Inlet Estuary during these months even when the Winyah Bay region is included in the analysis. However, in the winter season at high tide, nitrate concentrations were 4.5 times higher ($p < 0.05$) in North Inlet Estuary than Murrells Inlet Estuary due in part to intrusions from Winyah Bay.

No significant regional differences were observed for orthophosphate in either estuary (Fig. 6). Both the land and ocean regions of Murrells Inlet Estuary averaged 4.0 μg-at P l^{-1} while the land and ocean regions of North Inlet Estuary averaged 3.9 μg-at P l^{-1}. The Winyah Bay region was lower (by 0.4 μg-at P l^{-1}) than either the ocean or land region of North Inlet Estuary. Significant regional differences ($p < 0.05$) were found when the data were examined by tide and season. For example, mean orthophosphate concentrations in the land and ocean regions of Murrells Inlet Estuary were significantly greater than mean concentrations in the respective regions of North Inlet Estuary during the spring at both high and low tide and in the summer at low tide. The opposite difference occurred during the winter, with significantly higher ($p < 0.05$) mean orthophosphate concentrations in North Inlet Estuary land and ocean regions than in the respective regions of Murrells Inlet Estuary (Fig. 7).

Only ammonium concentrations varied significantly ($p < 0.0001$) with tidal stage. Ammonium was higher at low tide in both estuaries. When comparing land and ocean regions, nitrate concentrations in Murrells Inlet Estuary were generally higher at low tide. The lack of difference in overall estuary or regional tidal nitrate concentrations in North Inlet Estuary may be due to the significantly higher concentrations of nitrate entering the estuary through Winyah Bay. Nitrate concentrations in the Winyah Bay region were significantly higher at high tide than the ocean region of North

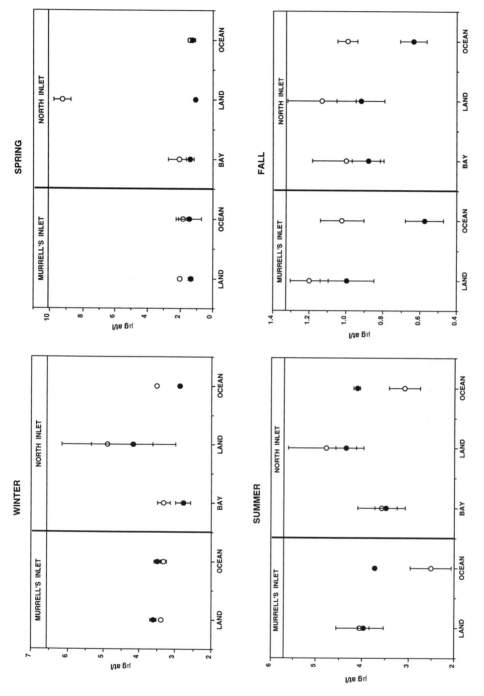

Fig. 5. Seasonal mean ammonium concentration and standard error by region within each estuary. Winter season is December 1990, spring is April 1991, summer is July 1991, and fall is October 1991. ● represents high tide samples, ○ represents low tide samples.

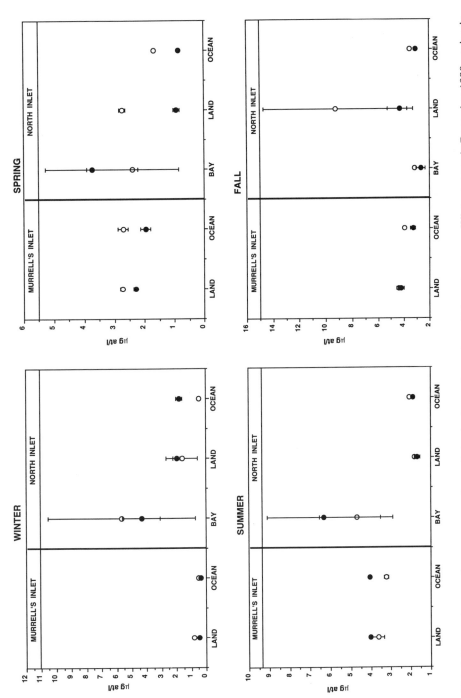

Fig. 6. Seasonal mean nitrate concentration and standard error by region within each estuary. Winter season is December 1990, spring is April 1991, summer is July 1991, and fall is October 1991. ● represents high tide samples, ○ represents low tide samples.

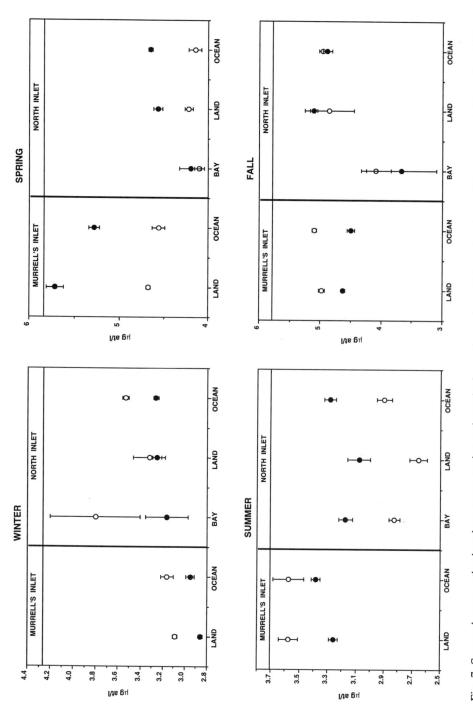

Fig. 7. Seasonal mean orthophosphate concentration and standard error by region within each estuary. Winter season is December 1990, spring is April 1991, summer is July 1991, and fall is October 1991. ● represents high tide samples, ○ represents low tide samples.

Inlet Estuary. Few tidal differences in orthophosphate concentrations were observed for either estuary even when separated by region within an estuary.

Nutrients varied significantly ($p < 0.05$) with season. Seasonal patterns in nitrate and phosphate concentrations were similar between estuaries; highest concentrations occurred during the summer. Murrells Inlet Estuary orthophosphate and nitrate concentrations were significantly higher ($p < 0.05$) than North Inlet Estuary concentrations during the spring and summer. Ammonium seasonal patterns differed between estuaries, with significantly higher ($p < 0.05$) concentrations occurring during the summer in North Inlet Estuary and during the fall in Murrells Inlet Estuary.

Discussion

Inter-estuary and intra-estuary salinity variation was influenced by tidal exchange and watershed runoff characteristics. Although watershed runoff contributed to the overall lower salinities observed in North Inlet Estuary, it was not a primary determinant. Runoff is less than 1% of the water entering the North Inlet Estuary; over 98% enters the through tidal exchange (Kjerfve et al. 1982). The mean salinities of the land and ocean regions of North Inlet Estuary were not significantly different. Salinities of the Winyah Bay region were much lower than those of the land and ocean regions in North Inlet Estuary. The mean salinity in the bay region was significantly lower than (and had a larger standard error than) that of either the land or ocean region of North Inlet Estuary. For the Winyah Bay region of North Inlet Estuary, freshwater input from the bay is probably more important than local watershed inputs in determining salinity. The Winyah Bay Estuary varies from essentially fresh water to oceanic salinities. Salinities at a long-term sampling station maintained by the South Carolina Department of Health and Environmental Control at the US Highway 17 bridge (MD080) ranged from 3.5‰ to 15‰, with a mean salinity of 7.4‰ ($\pm$ 2.0‰) (Blood and Vernberg 1992). Fresh-water inputs from Winyah Bay contribute over 20% of the tidal exchange in North Inlet Estuary (Kjerfve et al. 1982). Schwing and Kjerfve (1980) measured salinities below 5‰ in North Inlet Estuary near Winyah Bay and observed increasing salinities as distance inland from Winyah Bay increased. Long-term data for North Inlet Estuary show a similar salinity gradient (Blood and Vernberg 1992). Exchange with Winyah Bay is enhanced at high tide, after rain events, and with winds from the westerly direction (Michener et al. 1990). The strongest relationship with tidal intrusion was with winds from the southwest. Wind direction averaged westerly to northwesterly for the week prior to each of the four sampling trips, which may have aided in the exchange of fresher waters from Winyah Bay with the more saline waters of North Inlet Estuary.

The lack of significant differences between the land and ocean stations could have resulted from limited watershed runoff or rapid mixing of estuarine waters in North Inlet Estuary. North Inlet Estuary receives surface water input via two first-order streams draining into the western portion of the marsh and through diffuse inputs from groundwater and upland runoff. Runoff rate from the first-order stream draining into Oyster Creek is generally low (0.003 m^3 s^{-1}) but averages 41% of the annual rainfall input to the upland watershed (Garner 1991; Blood and Vernberg 1992). As with the Bly Creek basin runoff reported by Dame et al. (1991), total runoff amount from the Oyster Landing watershed is small in comparison to the tidal prism. Previous studies have shown a significant relationship between upland runoff and salinity variation at a long-term study site located adjacent to the landward portion of the estuary (Blood and Vernberg 1992). The runoff is highly seasonal and dependent on groundwater table elevation. Only during July were salinities significantly lower at the landward region of North Inlet Estuary. Runoff was minimal prior to all but the July sampling (Wahl unpublished data). Generally, the greatest rainfall inputs occur during summer months; however, low groundwater levels inhibit surface water runoff. If storms exceed 6.9 cm within a two-week period, runoff will result (Blood unpublished data). During the two weeks prior to the July sampling, sufficient rain occurred to generate runoff and the observed depressions in salinity in the land region. In addition, the differences between the land and ocean regions may have been reduced by a mixing of lower salinity bay water with tidal waters in the ocean region. Mixing of tidal waters in North Inlet Estuary is rapid—a 5 d to 7 d turnover (Kjerfve et al. 1982).

Spatial and seasonal salinities in Murrells Inlet Estuary differed from the patterns observed for North Inlet Estuary. While salinities overall were higher in Murrells Inlet Estuary than North Inlet Estuary, salinities in the land regions were significantly lower than in the ocean-influenced regions. The lowest salinities in the land region occurred in December and were lower in Murrells Inlet Estuary than North Inlet Estuary. These differences indicated that stream flow and/or groundwater flow may occur to a notable degree in Murrells Inlet Estuary but may be limited in effect on the entire estuary. We speculate that the lower salinities observed in the land region are influenced by groundwater inflow. In Murrells Inlet Estuary, stream input is derived from five creeks draining the watershed. Four of the five creeks are impounded, likely resulting in limited stream flow.

Both estuaries receive direct rainfall input to the tidal creeks. For the week prior to each of the four sampling trips, precipitation averaged 0.5 cm d^{-1}. This quantity was insufficient to affect surface water salinities. In North Inlet Estuary, summer thunderstorms may lower surface salinities several parts per thousand (Blood unpublished data). However, although 6.4 cm of rain fell 2 d prior to the summer sampling, it did not suppress the overall salinities in either estuary. Rainfall data for the week prior to the sampling reflects the average seasonal patterns: spring having the highest salinity, with a small rainfall input of 0.12 cm (Taylor unpublished data). The lowest average salinity in both Murrells Inlet Estuary and North Inlet Estuary occurred during the fall. Two days prior to the fall sampling, 0.5 cm of rain was measured and this rainfall may have been sufficient with the elevated water table to generate surface water or groundwater inflow to the estuaries and thus contributing to the lower salinities.

The effects of urbanization on dissolved oxygen concentrations in Murrells Inlet Estuary tidal waters were limited in space and time. No broad scale (mean estuary, mean region) significant differences were detected. Dissolved oxygen concentrations and variation in both estuaries were similar to previous studies of North Inlet Estuary in which dissolved oxygen varied from 1.5 mg l^{-1} to 7.4 mg l^{-1} (Gardner and Gorman 1984). A significant tidal difference occurred in both estuaries, as was noted by Gardner and Gorman (1984). Dissolved oxygen concentrations were lower at low tide than at high tide for both Murrells Inlet Estuary and North Inlet Estuary.

Differences between dissolved oxygen at high tide and low tide were not greater for the land region than ocean region. Larger differences in dissolved oxygen between tidal stage and regions were measured in the undeveloped estuary (North Inlet Estuary). The extent of the tidal difference may have been enhanced by the time of sampling: low tides were sampled just after dawn. The lowest dissolved oxygen concentrations generally occur at prior to dawn and are lower when that coincides with low tide (Gardner and Gorman 1984). The tidal dissolved oxygen patterns reflect the diel respiration-production patterns typical of estuaries.

Terrestrial runoff affected dissolved oxygen concentrations of the land region, but no consistently lower concentrations could be attributed to urbanization. The largest reduction in dissolved oxygen occurred in the land region of North Inlet Estuary and was correlated with runoff from the coastal forest. In the land region, the lowest dissolved oxygen concentrations varied with season and estuary. In the spring in Murrells Inlet Estuary and summer and fall in North Inlet Estuary, the dissolved oxygen concentration of the land region was lower than the ocean region at low tide. In addition, no such relationship was observed in the other estuary during the same period such that the regional differences could be attributed to higher benthic processes in the shallower creeks of the land margin. As an example, in the summer at low tide, land margin dissolved oxygen concentration was 0.4 mg l^{-1} lower than the ocean region in North Inlet Estuary but was 0.4 mg l^{-1} higher in the land region of Murrells Inlet Estuary than the ocean region. Therefore, terrestrial runoff containing oxygen-demanding substances must have contributed to the decline in oxygen concentrations observed in North Inlet Estuary. Freshwater inflow to estuaries from undeveloped watersheds and freshwater wetlands have high BOD, which result from decomposition products (Loehr 1974). These substances are capable of reducing oxygen levels once they enter estuarine systems. Generally nonpoint-source runoff from urbanized areas have higher levels of BOD and COD than undeveloped watersheds (United States Environmental Protection Agency 1983). Based on the Nationwide Urban Runoff Program (United States Environmental Protection Agency 1983), mean COD concentrations in residential runoff is 102 mg l^{-1} and mean BOD 13 mg l^{-1}. Impoundments on the streams draining into the Murrells Inlet Estuary may have had sufficient retention times to reduce the BOD and COD. Impoundments can be up to 90% efficient at removing oxygen-demanding substances from urban runoff (United States Environmental Protection Agency 1993). The lack of consistently lower dissolved oxygen concentrations in Murrells Inlet Estuary may be due to the effectiveness of impoundments on the streams draining into Murrells Inlet Estuary.

Dissolved oxygen exhibited a distinct seasonal pattern, with highs during the winter and lows during the summer, which was consistent between both estuaries. The seasonal pattern is consistent with the temperature-oxygen solubility relationships and was supported by a strong negative correlation between dissolved oxygen and temperature. Percent oxygen saturation for the estuaries was similar, around 76% in winter and only 55% in summer, supporting the idea that internal biological processes control dissolved oxygen concentrations. Dissolved oxygen was significantly inversely correlated with temperature ($r^2 = -0.73$, combining both estuaries). Temperature correlations were greater ($r^2 = -0.85$) in Murrells Inlet Estuary than North Inlet Estuary ($r^2 = -0.65$). The lower correlation coefficient for North Inlet Estuary suggests that other factors such as watershed runoff may affect dissolved oxygen concentrations in this estuary. Similar temperature-dependent relationships with dissolved oxygen have been noted for other small estuaries that have minimal watershed development (Portnoy 1991). In highly developed watersheds (e.g., Charleston Harbor, South Carolina; Narragansett Bay, Rhode Island; Chesapeake Bay; Pamlico Sound, North Carolina; San Francisco Bay, California), low dissolved oxygen concentrations in the summer were attributed to a combination of benthic respiration and increased water column stratification and additional BOD loads from point-source and nonpoint-source runoff (Officer et al. 1984; Kemp et al. 1992; Stanley and Nixon 1992).

The spatial and temporal variation in ammonium concentration of both estuaries were similar. The concentrations were a function of watershed runoff and internal estuarine processes. In both estuaries, ammonium concentrations were significantly higher at low tide than high tide (p < 0.0001), higher during the summer months (p < 0.0001), and higher in the land region than ocean region (p < 0.0001). The estuarine mean ammonium concentrations were not significantly different from each other. While watershed runoff was important in both estuaries, given the current level of urbanization, ammonium concentrations in tidal creeks were likely dominated by recycled ammonium.

The importance of terrestrial loading via surface water and groundwater flows varies among estuarine systems (Valiela et al. 1978; DeLaune et al. 1989), with riverine inputs providing 12% (Apalachicola Bay, Estabrook 1973; Barataria Bay, Day et al. 1973; Smith et al. 1985) to 525% (Lower New York Bay, O'Reilly et al. 1976) of the nitrogen. No detailed studies of estuarine processes have been conducted in Murrells Inlet Estuary; however, several empirical and modeling studies have been conducted in North Inlet Estuary that could provide some generalizations about the relative importance of new and recycled ammonium (Dame et al. 1986; Childers and McKellar 1987; Whiting et al. 1987, 1989; Dame et al. 1991; Childers et al. 1993). Input-output budgets constructed by Dame et al. (1986, 1991) for a sub-basin in the land region of the estuary and for the entire estuary reported tidal creek exports that exceeded new inputs and these exports were greater during the summer months when watershed runoff was minimal. Both studies showed higher ammonium concentrations in ebbing tidal waters, the highest concentrations at low tide, and higher concentrations in the summer months when no forest runoff occurred (Wolaver et al. 1984; Wolaver and Williams 1986; Whiting et al. 1987; Blood and Vernberg 1992). Measurements of daily ammonium concentrations in the tidal creeks of North Inlet Estuary have shown similar variation over several years, which was attributed to internal recycling (Wolaver et al. 1984; Blood and Vernberg 1992). Detailed empirical studies of subsystem contributions identified oyster reefs, low tide drainage, and benthic advection from the tidal creeks as sources for the ammonium exported from the basin (Whiting et al. 1989; Dame et al. 1991). Forest runoff and precipitation contributed 11%, oyster reef 17%, and low tide drainage 16% of ammonium imports to the tidal creek. Advection from the bottom of the tidal creek was 54% of the total input to the tidal creek. The measurement of tidal creek benthic advection did not discriminate between return flow from the basin and flux from the mineralization of in situ organic material. Given the measured groundwater flows for the basin, return flow is likely much less than that from in situ mineralization. Subtidal benthic fluxes from the creek bottom quantitatively exceeded ammonium in low tide drainage (Whiting and Childers 1989). Benthic fluxes into tidal creeks have been shown to be important in the release of ammonium in estuarine systems (Boynton et al. 1980; Hammond et al. 1985; Kasper et al. 1985). These benthic ammonium releases have been attributed to diffusion from pore waters, advection from marsh soils via groundwater, and biologically-mediated mineralization of organic matter on the marsh surface and subsequent release with flooding tidal waters (Chambers 1992). No empirical subsystem studies have been conducted in the ocean region of North Inlet Estuary. Childers et al. (1993) developed a dynamic nutrient budget for the entire estuary based on the major estuarine subsystems and processes measured in the Bly Creek basin study. When results from this model were compared with the measured fluxes from the entire estuary, net exports of ammonium were partially accounted for by recycled ammonium associated with benthic fluxes, oyster reefs, and low tide drainage. These processes are temperature-dependent and would have resulted in the higher concentrations during the summer (Scudlark and Church 1989; Chambers et al. 1992). Childers et al. (1993) attributed the difference in computed and measured ammonium fluxes to water column nutrient mineralization, which was not included in the model. Childers and McKellar's (1987) simulation of North Inlet Estuary water-column dynamics clearly showed water column processes were important, with summertime ammonium turnover times as short as 1.8 d.

Urbanization may have contributed to higher average ammonium concentrations in the land and ocean regions of Murrells Inlet Estuary than the respective regions of North Inlet Estuary during the winter and the fall. Winter and fall are normally periods of higher surface water and groundwater flows. Specific sources of ammonium were not identified; however, Murrells Inlet Estuary sources are potentially influenced by urban runoff and perhaps septic tank leaching. Septic tanks leak substantial quantities of ammonium into shallow groundwater. Waymer (1990) studied ammonium concentrations below septic fields in the coastal zone of South Carolina and found concentrations ranging from 26 μg-at N l^{-1} to 1,900 μg-at N l^{-1}. Murrells Inlet Estuary homes have only recently converted to sewer and numerous active and abandoned septic tank systems exist. Normally, ammonium does not migrate far from the septic fields because it is oxidized to nitrate or bound to clays in the soil. Groundwater and stream water draining from the forest surrounding the North Inlet Estuary has higher ammonium than nitrate concentrations, suggesting that the low clay, sandy soils characterizing this portion of the South Carolina coast permit migration of ammonium (Dame et al. 1991). Waymer's (1990) study of septic fields found ammonium migration away from the septic field was greater at residential sites having soils with low clay content than sites with clay soils. The highly permeable sandy soils of Murrells Inlet Estuary would facilitate the rapid transport of ammonium to the tidal creeks. Additional support for septic drain field leakage is provided by bacteriological analyses of samples collected concurrently with those of Waymer. The results of those analyses showed high fecal coliform levels (Wolfe 1995).

Nitrate concentrations in tidal waters of North Inlet Estuary were affected more by exchanges with Winyah Bay than by watershed runoff. Unlike ammonium, there were no statistically significant differences between the land or ocean regions or between high and low tides. The Winyah Bay region had significantly higher concentrations than the ocean or land regions, with the significantly greater differences at high tide and during the winter season. Previous flux studies in the Bly Creek basin and the entire watershed noted that net nitrate exports from the North Inlet Estuary and net imports to the Bly Creek basin could not be accounted for by new inputs from precipitation, groundwater, or stream water (Dame et al. 1986, 1991; Whiting et al. 1987). Nitrate input to the Bly Creek basin of North Inlet Estuary was less than 25% of the ammonium input (Dame et al. 1991). Nitrate input to the basin from the lower estuary was 10-fold greater than new inputs from the watershed. When Childers et al. (1993) extrapolated the Bly Creek basin study to the entire estuary using the dynamic nutrient budget, new nitrate from groundwater, stream water, and precipitation were not sufficient to support the export from the entire estuary. Whiting et al. (1987) reported a net import of nitrate from Winyah Bay and, when this import was included in the Childers et al. dynamic nutrient budget, 50% of the net nitrate export from North Inlet Estuary was accounted for. Nitrate inputs from the forest and precipitation were approximately 3% of the nitrate entering from Winyah Bay. The importance of the Winyah Bay nitrate source is consistent with results from this study. The highest nitrate concentrations occurred in the Winyah Bay region and, during the winter, high tide nitrate concentrations were significantly higher than low tide concentrations. Rapid mixing of high nitrate concentrations in tidal waters from Winyah Bay may have contributed to the lack of differences in the land and ocean regions. The turnover time for water in North Inlet Estuary is 5 d to 7 d (Kjerfve et al. 1982).

Recycled nitrate also was important in controlling the observed spatial and temporal patterns in North Inlet Estuary and Murrells Inlet Estuary (Whiting et al. 1987; Childers et al. 1993). Within the Bly Creek basin, the marsh surface was a net nitrate sink and during the study period removed more nitrate from the tidal waters than was imported to the basin. Although little nitrate was measured in low tide drainage or advecting from the bottom of the tidal creek, nitrate concentrations were higher in ebbing water and highest at low tide. The authors suggested that the nitrate resulted from nitrification of ammonium in low tide drainage and advection from the bottom of the tidal creek. Given that the Bly Creek basin is representative of the land region of North Inlet Estuary, additional benthic or water-column mineralization and nitrification in the ocean region would be required to account for the exports from the land region and from the estuary. Benthic algal production, *Spartina* primary production, and nitrogen fixation measured in the ocean region of North Inlet Estuary could provide sufficient nitrogen for mineralization and nitrification to support phytoplankton uptake, removal by microbes or benthic algae, or denitrification (Coutinho 1987; Pennock 1987; Whiting et al. 1987; Seitzinger 1988; Morris and Haskin 1990; Blood and Vernberg 1992). Rapid removal of nitrate by phytoplankton or retention by biota on the marsh surface may have minimized spatial differences in nitrate. It is generally believed that phytoplankton prefer ammonium over nitrate; however, several studies have shown that phytoplankton can acquire nitrate in the presence of ammonium concentrations of up to 40 μg-at l^{-1} (Jordan et al. 1983; Pennock 1987; Correll et al. 1992). Since ammonium concentrations only reached 4.1 μg-at l^{-1} during the summer months, nitrate uptake seems possible. Daily chlorophyll concentrations in North Inlet Estuary were statistically related to ammonium concentrations measured on the previous day and nitrate measured 5 d prior (Zingmark unpublished data).

Nitrate concentrations did not differ between Murrells Inlet Estuary and North Inlet Estuary when averaged over the four seasons. However, seasonal analyses showed distinct spatial differences in mean nitrate concentrations. The effect of urbanization on oxidized nitrogen was limited to the spring and summer, with higher average nitrate concentrations in Murrells Inlet Estuary than in North Inlet Estuary. During the summer, average concentrations in the land and ocean regions of Murrells Inlet Estuary were higher than the averages in the respective regions of North Inlet Estuary. The elevated concentrations in Murrells Inlet Estuary may result from both residential storm runoff and septic tank drainage. Nitrate in residential runoff averages 53 μg-at N l^{-1}, which is over 35 times higher than concentrations in the estuary (United States Environmental Protection Agency 1983). As with ammonium, the source is likely groundwater affected by leaking septic systems associated with the resident and tourist populations in the Murrells Inlet Estuary watershed. Nitrate in septic drain fields studied by Waymer (1990) averaged 487 μg-at N l^{-1} (1 μg-at N l^{-1} to 1,182 μg-at N l^{-1}). Valiela et al. (1990) and Lee and Olsen (1985) reported elevated groundwater nitrate concentrations in urbanized areas and attributed this to the disposal of wastewater via septic tanks and the use of fertilizers. Nitrate is highly mobile in soils and would be rapidly transported through the sandy coastal soils of Murrells Inlet to the estuary.

Orthophosphate concentrations did not exhibited any spatial differences, between estuaries or between regions within an estuary, when averaged over the four seasons. In North Inlet Estuary, orthophosphate concentrations were greater in the land and ocean regions than the Winyah Bay region during the spring and fall. Unlike nitrate, Winyah Bay was not the source of orthophosphate. Concentrations in Winyah Bay average 0.55 μg-at P l^{-1} and range spatially from 0.74 μg-at P l^{-1} in the fresher portions of the bay to 0.24 μg-at P l^{-1} in the ocean areas of Winyah Bay (Allen et al. 1984). Wolaver et al. (1984) did not find that orthophosphate was draining from the upland forested watershed. Concentrations in streams and groundwater draining the upland forest were lower than tidal water concentrations (Blood unpublished data). Upland imports to the Bly Creek basin were less than 10% of the exports from the basin (Dame et al. 1991).

The source of orthophosphate in tidal waters of North Inlet Estuary is internal recycling and release from the sediments. Similar internal sources of orthophosphate have been found in other estuaries (Callender and Hammond 1982; Jordan et al. 1983; Boynton and Kemp 1985; Rizzo 1990). Several studies and modeling activities in North Inlet Estuary support the importance of recycled phosphorus. Gardner (1975) reported exports of orthophosphate from the marsh surface and attributed these exports to release from pore waters through diffusion. Wolaver et al. (1984) determined that in North Inlet Estuary, orthophosphate enters marsh waters through diffusion from tidal creek sediments and/or from seepage from the vegetated marsh surface. Seepage from the marsh surface (0.6 kg P ha^{-1}) in the Bly Creek basin was 10 times greater than the total quantities entering from the uplands (Dame et al. 1991). However, retention of orthophosphate by the marsh surface was approximately 5 times greater than the quantity released with low tide drainage, suggesting tight recycling within the North Inlet Estuary. Whiting and Childers (1989) measured 1.3 times greater advective flux from the creek bottoms than accounted for by low tide drainage. When this flux was included in the dynamic nutrient budget, a net phosphorus export from the basin was calculated (Childers et al. 1993). Dame et al. (1991) reported a net export of orthophosphate from the North Inlet Estuary; this export could not be accounted for in the Childers et al. (1991) nutrient budget by additional exports from the land region of the estuary or release from tidal creek bottoms. The authors suggested that water-column nutrient remineralization in the ocean region of the estuary was the plausible source.

As with inorganic nitrogen, orthophosphate concentrations in Murrells Inlet Estuary were influenced by runoff associated with the residential community. The residential influence varied with season. When the tourist population was low, mean orthophosphate concentrations in the land and ocean regions of North Inlet Estuary were greater than in the land and ocean regions of Murrells Inlet Estuary. During the spring and summer (peak tourist season), average orthophosphate concentrations in the land and ocean regions of Murrells Inlet Estuary were greater than in the respective regions of North Inlet Estuary. In addition, July and October concentrations were higher in Murrells Inlet Estuary than North Inlet Estuary at low tide. Observed concentrations probably were not a result of nonpoint-source surface runoff from the urbanized watershed. Concentrations in storm runoff from residential communities average 4.5 μg-at P l^{-1} (United States Environmental Protection Agency 1983), which is similar to the concentrations measured in Murrells Inlet Estuary. Subsurface inputs from septic tanks may be an important source of orthophosphate. Concentrations of orthophosphate in septic wastewater can range from 23 μg-at P l^{-1} to 213 μg-at P l^{-1} (Straub 1989). Although Valiela et al. (1990) reported orthophosphate concentration in groundwater of an urbanized watershed to be low due to adsorption by sediment surfaces, in the sandy soils of Murrells Inlet Estuary, little retention is likely.

Based on the ratios of inorganic nitrogen and phosphorus measured in the tidal creeks during this study, both Murrells Inlet Estuary and North Inlet Estuary were nitrogen limited. The N:P ratios were 5 to 10 times lower than the average 16:1 N:P ratio needed to maintain optimal phytoplankton production (Table 1). The ratios calculated from this study were within the range previously reported for North Inlet Estuary but were 4 times lower than the average monthly ratio obtained over 5 years (Blood and Vernberg 1992; Blood unpublished data). Limited watershed inputs of inorganic nitrogen and rapid recycling of internally generated inorganic nitrogen by phytoplankton in North Inlet Estuary and Murrells Inlet Estuary may have left little residual inorganic nitrogen in tidal waters (Stanley and Hobbie 1981; Childers and McKellar 1987).

If watershed inputs to Murrells Inlet Estuary were to increase as a result of further urbanization or the removal of the detention ponds, nitrogen limitation would be reduced and increased phytoplankton production would be expected. Such a response is suggested from the observations of the Winyah Bay region of North Inlet Estuary. Nitrate concentrations were significantly higher in this region of North Inlet Estuary. At high tide, nitrate concentrations were 2.5 times greater in the Winyah Bay region than the land or ocean regions of North Inlet Estuary. The higher nitrates originated from point-source and nonpoint-source inputs to Winyah Bay (Blood and Vernberg 1992), which entered the Winyah Bay region of North Inlet Estuary through tidal exchange. The N: P ratios and phytoplankton production in the Winyah Bay region were significantly (p < 0.05) higher than the ocean or land regions at high tide (Smith 1992).

Conclusions

Water quality in estuarine ecosystems is a function of watershed and estuarine hydrology, geomorphology, and biotic structure and function. In estuaries where watershed hydrologic inflows are less than 10% of the water entering the estuary by tidal exchange, internal estuarine processes exert important controls over water quality. The spatial and temporal patterns observed in North Inlet Estuary water quality during this study were consistent with previous detailed empirical and modeling studies. Watershed contributions to salinity, dissolved oxygen, and nutrient variability were not as important as internal estuarine processes. Dissolved oxygen was lower and nutrients higher at low tide and during the summer. No significant differences between the land and ocean regions occurred for dissolved oxygen, nutrients, or salinity.

The effects of urbanization on estuarine water quality will depend on the degree and type of watershed alteration, the relative importance of watershed inputs versus tidal exchange, and the capacity of the estuarine system to process increased inputs of nutrients and oxygen-demanding substances. Salinities were generally lower in North Inlet Estuary than Murrells Inlet Estuary, suggesting the impoundments were limiting freshwater input to Murrells Inlet Estuary. The lower surface water inflows may have reduced the potential effects of urban stormwater runoff. Impounding surface water streams may have reduced the nutrient loads to Murrells Inlet Estuary during the winter and spring. Highest inorganic nutrient concentrations in the tidal creeks of Murrells Inlet Estuary were detected during the summer and fall, which are the periods with the lowest surface water runoff. Higher nitrate, ammonium, and orthophosphate concentrations were detected in the land region, which is consistent with peak tourist population in the Murrells Inlet Estuary watershed. Previous studies in North Inlet Estuary indicated that diffusion and advection from the bottoms of tidal creeks were important mechanisms of nutrient transport to tidal creeks. Rapid infiltration of surface runoff, seepage below the impoundments, and leaking of septic tanks may be sources of inorganic nutrients, which are then transported to Murrells Inlet Estuary by subsurface flow and by advection from the bottoms of tidal creeks. Temperature and dissolved oxygen concentrations were generally similar for both estuaries, suggesting control by internal mechanisms rather than by processes associated with urbanization. No differences in dissolved oxygen between the estuaries or between regions within Murrells Inlet Estuary were observed. Impoundments constructed on the Murrells Inlet Estuary streams are effective in reducing both chemical and biological oxygen-demanding substances. In addition, anoxic sediments and mineralization of estuarine organic matter are effective in reducing dissolved oxygen concentrations, which is consistent with the variation observed in this study. The rapid mixing of tidal waters in these two estuaries may have minimized the development of anoxic zones within the tidal waters.

The processes that control nutrient distributions and dynamics in estuaries are driven by water budget characteristics. In shallow, high-salinity estuaries with relatively small watersheds, water quality may have greater internal controls or nonpoint-source loads may be diluted and dispersed rapidly within the estuary from tidal exchange. Internal processes are amplified particularly when freshwater flow is limited, as when upland creeks are impounded (Murrells Inlet Estuary), and/or when hydrologic conditions prevent freshwater inputs. Differences in tidal exchange rates and estuarine turnover also could contribute to differences between the two estuaries and could have minimized the differences in water quality attributable to urbanization. In North Inlet Estuary, the effects of terrestrial runoff were spatially restricted. Rapid mixing of oceanic waters within expansive tidal marshes quickly dilutes or processes incoming nutrients. Murrells Inlet Estuary and North Inlet Estuary are dominated by oceanic exchange, thus the effects of runoff from the urbanized watershed are spatially restricted and limited to periods of high tourist populations. Both estuaries are nitrogen limited (based on N:P ratios) and it appears that Murrells Inlet Estuary is capable of assimilating nutrients to a greater degree than they are being contributed presently from urbanization. The Winyah Bay region of North Inlet Estuary had higher inorganic nitrogen, higher N:P ratios, and higher chlorophyll *a* concentrations than other regions in North Inlet Estuary, demonstrating that increased nutrient loading will result in increased primary production.

LITERATURE CITED

Allen, D.M., W.K. Michener, and S. E. Stancyk (eds.). 1984. Pollution Ecology of Winyah Bay, South Carolina: Characterization of the Estuary and Potential Impacts of Petroleum. Technical publication no. 84-1. Belle W. Baruch Institute for Marine Biology and Coastal Research, University of South Carolina, Columbia, South Carolina.

Alm, A.L. 1990. Nonpoint sources of water pollution. *Environmental Science and Technology* 24(7): 967.

American Public Health Association. 1985. Standard Methods for the Examination of Water and Wastewater. American Public Health Association,Washington, D.C.

Bildstein, K.L., E.R. Blood, and P. Frederick. 1992. The relative importance of biotic and abiotic vectors in nutrient processing in a South Carolina estuarine system. *Estuaries* 15(2): 147-157.

Blood, E.R., P. Anderson, P.A. Smith, K.A. Ginsberg, and C. Nybro. 1991. The effects of Hurricane Hugo on coastal soil processes. *Biotropica* 23(4): 348-355.

Blood, E.R. and F.J. Vernberg. 1992. Characterization of the Physical, Chemical, and Biological Conditions and Trends in Three South Carolina Estuaries: 1970-1985, Volume II. Winyah Bay and North Inlet Estuaries. South Carolina Sea Grant Consortium, Charleston, South Carolina.

Bohlen, C. 1990. Protecting the coast. *Bioscience* 40(8): 243.

Boynton, W.R. and W.M. Kemp. 1985. Nutrient regeneration and oxygen consumption by sediments along as estuarine salinity gradient. *Marine Ecology Progress Series* 23: 45-55.

Boynton, W.R., W.M. Kemp, and C.G. Osborne. 1980. Nutrient fluxes across the sediment-water interface in the turbid zone of a coastal plain estuary, p. 69-90. *In* V. S. Kennedy (ed.), Estuarine Perspectives. New York, Academic Press, New York.

Callender, E. and D.E. Hammond. 1982. Nutrient exchange across the sediment-water interface in the Potomac River estuary. *Estuarine, Coastal and Shelf Science* 15: 395-413.

Chambers, R.M., J.W. Harvey, and W.E. Odum. 1992. Ammonium and phosphate dynamics in a Virginia salt marsh. *Estuaries* 15(3): 349-359.

Cherfas, J. 1990. The fringe of the ocean—Under siege from the land. *Science* 248: 163-165.

Childers, D.L. and H.N. McKellar, Jr. 1987. A simulation of saltmarsh water column dynamics. *Ecological Modelling* 36: 211-238.

Childers, D.L., H.N. McKellar, Jr., R.F. Dame, F.H. Sklar, and E.R. Blood. 1993. A dynamic nutrient budget of subsystem interactions in a salt-marsh estuary. *Estuarine Coastal and Shelf Science* 36(2): 105-131.

Correll, D.L., T.E. Jordan, and D.E. Weller. 1992. Cross media inputs to eastern United States watersheds and their significance to estuarine water quality. *Water Science and Technology* 26(12): 2675-2683.

Coutinho, R. 1987. Ecology of macroalgae in North Inlet Estuary, South Carolina. Ph.D. dissertation, University of South Carolina, Columbia, South Carolina.

D'Elia, C.F., J.G. Sanders, and W.R. Boynton. 1986. Nutrient enrichment studies in a coastal plain estuary: Phytoplankton growth in large-scale, continuous cultures. *Canadian Journal of Fisheries and Aquatic Science* 43: 397-406.

Dame, R.F, T. Chrzanowski, K. Bildstein, B. Kjerfve, H.N. McKellar, Jr., D. Nelson, J. Spurrier, S. Stancyk, H. Stevenson, F.J. Vernberg, and R. Zingmark, 1986. The outwelling hypothesis in North Inlet, South Carolina. *Marine Ecology Progress Series* 33: 217-229.

Dame, R.F., J.D. Spurrier, T.M. Williams, B. Kjerfve, R.G. Zingmark, T.G. Wolaver, T.H. Chrzanowski, H.N. McKellar, Jr., and F.J. Vernberg. 1991. Annual material processing by a salt-marsh estuarine basin in South Carolina, USA. *Marine Ecology Progress Series* 72(1-2): 153-166.

Dame, R.F., J.D. Spurrier, and T.G. Wolaver. 1989. Carbon, nitrogen, and phosphorus processing by a oyster reef. *Marine Ecology Progress Series* 54: 249-256.

Day, J.W., W.G. Smith, P.R. Wagner, and W.C. Stone. 1973. Community structure and carbon budget of a salt marsh and shallow bay estuarine system in Louisiana. Publ. no. LSU-SG72-04, Center for Wetlands Resources, Louisiana State University, Baton Rouge, Louisiana.

DeLaune, R.D., T. Feijte, and W.H. Patrick, Jr. 1989. Nitrogen flows in a Louisiana Gulf Coast salt marsh: Spatial considerations. *Biogeochemistry* 8: 25-37.

DeLaune, R.D. and J.W.H. Patrick. 1980. Nitrogen and phosphorus cycling in a Gulf Coast salt marsh, p. 143-151. *In* V. S. Kennedy (ed.), Estuarine Perspectives. Academic Press, New York.

Douglas, J.E. and L.W. Swift, Jr. 1977. Forest Service studies of soil and nutrient losses caused by roads, logging, mechanical site preparation, and prescribed burning in the southeast, p. 489-504. *In* D.L. Correll (ed.), Watershed Research in North America. Chesapeake Bay Center for Environmental Studies, Smithsonian Institution, Edgewater, Maryland.

Estabrook, R.H. 1973. Phytoplankton ecology and hydrography of Apalachicola Bay. M.S. thesis, Florida State University, Tallahassee, Florida.

Gardner, L.R. 1975. Chemical and sediment budgets for a small tidal creek, Charleston Harbor. South Carolina Water Resources Research Institute, Report No. 57. Clemson University, Clemson, South Carolina.

Gardner, L.R. and C. Gorman. 1984. Summertime net transport of dissolved oxygen, salt, and heat in a salt marsh basin, North Inlet, SC. *Estuarine Coastal and Shelf Science* 19: 331-339.

Gardner, L.R., L. Thombs, D. Edwards, and D. Nelson. 1989. Time series analyses of suspended sediment concentrations at North Inlet, South Carolina. *Estuaries* 12(4): 211-221.

Garner, E.C. 1991. The effect of salt water interaction on nutrient transport in the hyporheic zone of coastal streams. M.S. thesis, University of South Carolina, Columbia, South Carolina.

Gentry, R.C. 1971. Hurricanes, one of the major features of air-sea interaction in the Caribbean Sea, p. 80-87. *In* Symposium on Investigations and Resources of the Caribbean and Adjacent Regions. UNESCO and FAO, Paris, France.

Gilliam, J.W., R.W. Skaggs, and C.W. Doty. 1986. Controlled agricultural drainage: An alternative to riparian vegetation. *In* D.L. Correll (ed.), Watershed Research Perspectives. Smithsonian Institution Press, Washington, D.C.

Gilliland, M.W. and W. Baxter-Porter. 1987. A geographical information system to predict nonpoint source pollution potential. *Water Resources Bulletin* 23(2): 281-291.

Guttman, N.B. and M.S. Plantico. 1987. Drought history and chances of recurrence, p. 4-7. *In* J.C. Purvis, S.F. Sidlow, and W. Tyler (eds.), Southeastern Drought Symposium. South Carolina Climatology Office, Columbia, South Carolina.

Hammond, C.F., D. Harmon, B. Harmena, M. Korosec, L.G. Miller, R. Rea, S. Warren, W. Berelson, and S.W. Hager. 1985. Benthic fluxes in San Francisco Bay. *Hydrobiologia* 129: 69-90.

Hecky, R.E. and P. Kilham. 1988. Nutrient limitation of phytoplankton in freshwater and marine environments: A review of recent evidence on the effects of enrichment. *Limnology and Oceanography* 33: 796-822.

Howarth, R.W., R. Marino, and J. Lane. 1988. Nitrogen fixation in freshwater, estuarine, and marine ecosystems. 1. Rates and importance. *Limnology and Oceanography* 433: 688-701.

Jaworski, N.A. 1981. Sources of nutrients and scale of eutrophication problems in estuaries, p. 83-110. *In* B.J. Neilson and L.E. Cronin (eds.), Estuaries and Nutrients. Humana Press, Clifton, New Jersey.

Jordan, T.E., D.L. Correll, and D.F. Whigham. 1983. Nutrient flux in the Rhode River. *Estuarine Coastal and Shelf Science* 17: 651-667.

Kaplan, W., I. Valiela, and J.M. Teal. 1979. Denitrification in a salt marsh ecosystem. *Limnology and Oceanography* 24: 726-734.

Kardydis, M., L. Ignatiades, and N. Moschopoulou, 1983. An index associated with nutrient eutrophication in the marine environment. *Estuarine Coastal and Shelf Science* 16: 339-344.

Kasper, H.F., R.A. Asher, and I.C. Boyer. 1985. Microbial nitrogen transformations in sediments and inorganic nitrogen fluxes across the sediment-water interface on the South Island West Coast, New Zealand. *Estuarine Coastal and Shelf Science* 21: 245-255.

Kemp, W.M., P.A. Sampou, J. Garber, J. Tuttle, and W.R. Boynton. 1992. Seasonal depletion of oxygen from bottom waters of Chesapeake Bay—Roles of benthic and planktonic respiration and physical exchange processes. *Marine Ecology Progress Series* 85(1-2): 137-152.

Kjerfve, B. 1989. Estuarine geomorphology and physical oceanography, p. 47-78. *In* J.W. Day, Jr., C.A.S. Hall, W.M. Kemp, and A. Yanez-Arancibia, (eds.), Estuarine Ecology. John Wiley & Sons, Inc. New York.

Kjerfve, B. and H.N. McKellar, Jr. 1980. Time series measurements of estuarine material fluxes, p. 341-357. *In* V. S. Kennedy (ed.), Estuarine Perspectives. Academic Press, New York.

Kjerfve, B., A. Proehl, F.B. Schwing, H.E. Seim, and M. Marozas. 1982. Temporal and spatial considerations in measuring estuarine water fluxes, p. 37-51. *In* V.S. Kennedy (ed.), Estuarine Comparisons. Academic Press, New York.

Kuenzler, E.J. and N.J. Craig. 1986. Land use and nutrient yields of the Chowan River Watershed. *In* D.L. Correll (ed.), Watershed Research Perspectives. Smithsonian Institution Press, Washington, D.C.

Lazaro, T.R. 1990. Urban Hydrology - A Multidisciplinary Perspective. Technomic Publishing Company, Lancaster, Pennsylvania.

Lee, V. and S. Olsen. 1985. Eutrophication and management initiatives for the control of nutrient inputs to Rhode Island Coastal Lagoons. *Estuaries* 8: 191-202.

Loehr, R.C. 1974. Characteristics and comparative magnitude of non-point sources. *Journal of the Water Pollution Control Federation* 46(8): 1849-1872..

Marcus, J.M. 1985. A hydrological reconnaissance of Murrells Inlet, Georgetown County, South Carolina. Technical Report No. 001-85. South Carolina Department of Health and Environmental Control, Columbia, South Carolina.

Michener, W.K., D.M. Allen, E.R. Blood, T.A. Hiltz, B. Kjerfve, and F.H. Sklar. 1990. Climatic variability and salt marsh ecosystem response: Relationship to scale, p. 27-37. *In* D. Greenland and J.L.W. Swift (eds.), Climate Variability and Ecosystem Response. Proceedings of the LTER Workshop. United States Department of Agriculture, Forest Service, Asheville, North Carolina.

Morris, J.T. and B. Haskin 1990. A 5-year record of aerial primary production and stand characteristics of *Spartina alterniflora*. *Ecology* 716: 2209-2217.

Nixon, S.W., C.A. Oviat, and S.S. Hale. 1976. Nitrogen regeneration and the metabolism of coastal marine bottom communities, p. 269-283. *In* J.M. Anderson and A. Macfadyen (eds.), The Role of Terrestrial and Aquatic Organisms in Decomposition Processes. Blackwell, Oxford,

Nixon, S.W., C.A. Oviatt, J. Frithesen, and B. Sullivan. 1986. Nutrients and productivity of estuarine and coastal marine systems. *Journal of the Limnological Society of South Africa* 12: 43-71.

Nixon, S.W. and M.Q. Pilson 1983. Nitrogen in estuarine and coastal marine ecosystems, p. 565-646. *In* E.J. Carpenter and D.G. Capone (eds.), Nitrogen in the Marine Environment. Academic Press, New York.

National Oceanic and Atmospheric Administration. 1985. Local climatological data for Georgetown, South Carolina. 30-year summary, 1951-1981. National Climatic Data Center, Asheville, North Carolina.

Novotny, V. and G. Chesters. 1981. Handbook of Nonpoint Pollution—Sources and Management. Van Nostrand Reinhold Company, New York.

O'Reilly, J.E., J.P. Thomas, and C. Evans. 1976. Annual primary production nannoplankton, net plankton, dissolved organic matter in the Lower New York Bay. Fourth Symposium on Hudson River Ecology. Hudson River Environmental Society, Inc., New York.

Officer, C.B., R.B. Biggs, J.L. Taft, L.E. Cronin, M.A. Tyler, and W.R. Boynton. 1984. Chesapeake Bay anoxia: Origin, development, and significance. *Science* 222: 22-27.

Omernik, J.M. 1976. The influence of land use on stream nutrient levels. EPA-600-76-014. United States Environmental Protection Agency, Corvallis, Oregon, p 46. *In* V. Novotny and G. Chesters (eds.), 1981 Handbook of Nonpoint Pollution—Sources and Management. Van Nostrand Reinhold Company, New York.

Pennock, J.R. 1987. Temporal and spatial variability in phytoplankton ammonium and nitrate uptake in the Delaware Estuary. *Estuarine, Coastal, and Shelf Science* 24: 841-857..

Pennock, J.R. and J.H. Sharp. 1986. Phytoplankton production in the Delaware estuary: Temporal and spatial variability. *Marine Ecology Progress Series* 34: 143-155.

Portnoy, J.W. 1991. Summer oxygen depletion in a diked New England estuary. *Estuaries* 14(2): 122-129.

Pritchard, D.W. 1955. Estuarine circulation patterns. *Proceedings of the American Society of Civil Engineering* 81(717): 1-11.

Pritchard, D.W. and J.R. Schubel. 1981. Physical and geological processes controlling nutrient levels in estuaries, p. 47-70. *In* B.J. Neilson and L.E. Cronin (eds.), Estuaries and Nutrients. Humana Press, Clifton, New Jersey.

Rizzo, W.M. 1990. Nutrient exchanges between the water column and a subtidal benthic microalgal community. *Estuaries* 13(3): 219-226.

Ryther, J.H. and W.M. Dunstan. 1977. Nitrogen, phosphorus, and eutrophication in the marine environment. *Science* 171: 1008-1013.

SAS Institute, Inc. 1985. SAS Users Guide: Statistics, version 5 edition. SAS Institute, Cary, North Carolina.

Schwing, F.B. and B. Kjerfve. 1980. Longitudinal characterization of a tidal marsh creek separating two hydrographically distinct estuaries. *Estuaries* 3(4): 236-241.

Schwing, F.B., B. Kjerfve, and J.E. Sneed. 1983. Nearshore coastal currents on the South Carolina continental shelf. *Journal of Geophysical Research* 88: 4719-4729.

Scudlark, J.R. and T.M. Church. 1989. The sedimentary flux of nutrients at a Delaware salt marsh site: A geochemical perspective. *Biogeochemistry* 7: 55-75.

Seitzinger, S.P. 1988. Denitrification in freshwater and coastal marine ecosystems: Ecological and geochemical significance. *Limnology and Oceanography* 33: 702-723.

Smith, C.J., R.D. DeLaune, and W.H. Patrick, Jr. 1985. Fate of riverine nitrate entering an estuary: I. Denitrification and nitrogen burial. *Estuaries* 8: 15-21

Smith, P.A. 1992. The effects of urbanization on spatial and temporal nutrient distributions in two southeastern estuaries. M.S. thesis, University of South Carolina, Columbia, South Carolina.

South Carolina Department of Health and Environmental Control. 1990. Area IV Study Sanitary Survey. Shellfish Sanitation Program, Waccamaw District. South Carolina Department of Health and Environmental Control, Columbia, South Carolina.

South Carolina State Data Center, Division of Research and Statistical Services. 1990. Demographic Data for Murrells Inlet, South Carolina from Census Tape STF1A. South Carolina State Data Center, Columbia, South Carolina.

Stanley, D.W. and J.E. Hobbie 1981. Nitrogen recycling in a North Carolina coastal river. *Limnology and Oceanography* 261: 30-42.

Stanley, D.W. and S.W. Nixon. 1992. Stratification and Bottom Water Hypoxia in the Pamlico River Estuary. *Estuaries* 15(3): 270-281.

Stern, M.K., J.W. Day, Jr., and K.G. Teague. 1991. Nutrient transport in a riverine-influenced tidal freshwater bayou in Louisiana. *Estuaries* 14:382-394.

Straub, C.P., 1989. Practical Handbook of Environmental Control. CRC Press, Inc., Boca Raton, Florida.

United States Environmental Protection Agency. 1980. Urban Storm Water and Combined Sewer Overflow Impact on Receiving Water Bodies. Proceedings of National Conference. United States Environmental Protection Agency, Orlando, Florida. EPA-600/9-80-056.

United States Environmental Protection Agency. 1983. Results of the nationwide urban runoff program. Executive summary. United States Environmental Protection Agency, Washington, D.C. PB84-185545.

Valiela, I., J. Costa, K. Foreman, J.M. Teal, B. Howes, and D. Aubrey. 1990. Transport of groundwater-borne nutrients from watersheds and their effects on coastal waters. *Biogeochemistry* 10: 177-197.

Valiela, I. and J.M. Teal 1979. The nitrogen budget of a salt marsh ecosystem. *Nature* 280: 652-656.

Valiela, I., J.M. Teal, S. Volkoman, D. Shafer, and E.J. Carpenter. 1978. Nutrient and particulate fluxes in salt marsh ecosystems: Tidal exchanges and inputs by precipitation and groundwater. *Limnology and Oceanography* 23: 798-812.

Vernberg, F.J., W.B. Vernberg, E. Blood, A. Fortner, M. Fulton, H.N. McKellar, Jr., W.K. Michener, G. Scott, T. Siewicki, and K. El-Figi. 1992. Impact of urbanization on high-salinity estuaries in the southeastern United States. *Netherlands Journal of Sea Research* 30: 239-248.

Vernberg, F.J., R.G. Zingmark, R. Dame, S.E. Stancyk, B.C. Coull, R. Feller, D.M. Allen, K. Bildstein, E.R. Blood, L.R. Gardner, T. Williams, F. Sklar, H.N. McKellar, Jr., D. Childers, and W.K. Michener. 1989. Long-term Ecological Research on the North Inlet Forest–Wetlands–Marine Landscape, Georgetown, South Carolina. NOAA Estuary-of-the-Month Seminar Series: Barrier Island/Salt Marsh Estuaries, Southeast Atlantic Coast: Issues, Resources, Status and Management. National Oceanic and Atmospheric Administration, Washington, D.C.

Waccamaw Regional Planning and Development Council. 1985. Land use update for the Waccamaw Neck. Report. Waccamaw Regional Planning and Development Council, Georgetown, South Carolina.

Waymer, K. 1990. An Examination of soil leachate for nutrient contamination in septic fields on the coastal plain of South Carolina. M.S. thesis. University of South Carolina, Columbia, South Carolina.

Weiskel, P.K. and B.L. Howes. 1991. Quantifying dissolved nitrogen flux through a coastal watershed. *Water Resources Research* 27: 2929-2939.

Whiting, G.J. and D.L. Childers. 1989. Subtidal advective water flux as a potentially important nutrient input to southeastern USA saltmarsh estuaries. *Estuarine Coastal and Shelf Science* 28: 417-431.

Whiting, G.J., H.N. McKellar, Jr., B. Kjerfve, and J.D. Spurrier. 1987. Nitrogen exchange between a southeastern USA salt marsh ecosystem and the coastal ocean. *Marine Biology* 95: 173-182.

Whiting, G.J., H.N. McKellar, Jr., J.D. Spurrier, and T.G. Wolaver. 1989. Nitrogen exchange between a portion of vegetated salt marsh and the adjoining creek. *Limnology Oceanography* 34(2): 463-473.

Wolaver, T.G., W.V. Johnson, and M. Marozas. 1984. Nitrogen and phosphorus concentrations with North Inlet, South Carolina: Speculation as to sources and sinks. *Estuarine Coastal and Shelf Science* 19: 243-255.

Wolaver, T.G. and T.M. Williams. 1986. Stream water chemistry of a small forested watershed on the South Carolina coast. *Southeastern Geology* 27 (1): 45-52.

Wolfe, T. 1995. A comparison of fecal coliform densities and fluorescent intensities in Murrells Inlet, a highly urbanized estuary, and North Inlet, a pristine forested estuary. M.S. thesis, University of South Carolina, Columbia, South Carolina.

Polynuclear Aromatic Hydrocarbon and Trace Metal Burdens in Sediment and the Oyster, *Crassostrea virginica* Gmelin, From Two High-salinity Estuaries in South Carolina

Alan R. Fortner, Marion Sanders, and Sharon W. Lemire

ABSTRACT: The southeast coast of the United States has experienced an extraordinarily high rate of urban development in recent years. Although previous studies (Hungspreugs et al. 1984; Merrill and Wade 1985; Martel et al. 1986; Bryan et al. 1987; Paulson et al. 1989) have examined environmental impacts in heavily developed, industrialized riverine estuaries, little is known concerning the potential effects of moderate urbanization (i.e., housing and service industries), without concurrent industrialization, on small nonriverine estuaries. The two estuaries selected for study were Murrells Inlet, South Carolina, an urbanized estuary, and North Inlet, South Carolina, which is largely pristine. Levels of selected PAHs (polynuclear aromatic hydrocarbons) and trace metals in sediment and oysters are compared between estuaries and within each estuary. Stations were grouped according to the level of urban development within estuaries and statistically analyzed. Examination of results indicated considerable variation in total PAHs and trace metals for stations within each estuary, with as much as an 180-fold difference. When comparing estuaries, average total PAHs in sediment and oysters from Murrells Inlet were significantly ($p \leq 0.05$) higher than those from North Inlet; this was also the case for the average total trace metal concentrations in oysters. However, total trace metal levels in sediment were significantly higher ($p \leq 0.05$) at North Inlet. Analysis of the data from both sites relative to the degree of urban development indicated significantly higher ($p \leq 0.05$) levels of PAHs in sediment and of PAHs and metals in oysters in the most urbanized areas of Murrells Inlet. Total trace metals in sediment were similar for both urbanized and relatively pristine stations at Murrells Inlet and North Inlet, suggesting that trace metals per se were an inadequate indicator of urban stress. At North Inlet, only metals in oysters were significantly higher ($p \leq 0.05$) at developed versus undeveloped stations. This study suggests increased urbanization in an estuary like Murrells Inlet results in higher levels of certain chemical contaminants.

Introduction

Coastal areas in the Southeast United States have experienced an increased rate of residential and other urban development in recent years. Continued development of the Southeast coast will likely be in the form of urbanization rather than industrialization. Urbanization as used here includes residential, commercial, and recreational tourism development, whereas industrialization is characterized by standard industrial-code-type manufacturing and related transportation. Prevailing urbanization occurring in the numerous high-salinity estuaries in the Southeast is primarily characterized by residential and service industry development. These estuaries have limited adjacent upland and are generally unsuitable, as deep water ports. Therefore they are unlikely to become industrialized. Specific chemical pollution of the adjacent estuarine environment from human activity has been documented in other areas of the United States and the world (Hoffman et al. 1982; Brown et al. 1985; Liston and Maher 1986).

Nonpoint source runoff from urban areas has been shown to be a source of petroleum hydrocarbon (Hunter et al. 1979; Brown et al. 1985) and heavy metal pollution (Whipple and Hunter 1977). Hoffman et al. (1985) also found that stormwater runoff could convey polynuclear aromatic hydrocarbons (PAHs), lead, and zinc to adjacent waters. An additional source of chemical contamination for urbanized, high-salinity estuaries in the Southeast is recreational boating and related marinas. Voudrias and Smith (1986) found elevated PAHs in sediments proximal to marinas. Marcus and Thompson (1986) also determined an intimate association between copper and zinc in oyster tissue and recreational marinas, and Swearingen and Marcus (1983) reported elevated levels of metals and PAHs in sediments dredged from a marina basin.

Although previous studies have focused on heavily developed coastal areas or marinas, little is known concerning effects in toto of urbanization on the small, less developed, high-salinity, nonriverine estuaries of the coastal Southeast United States. The purpose of this study was to determine whether an urbanized estuarine area in coastal South Carolina contains higher levels of selected PAHs and metals than one having little or no urban influences. In addition, efforts were made to examine the relationship between in situ chemical contaminant levels and upland anthropogenic sources.

Materials and Methods

Two estuaries located on the northern coast of South Carolina were selected for study. The first, Murrells Inlet is adjacent to an urban area characterized as residential, transient and commercial, while the second, North Inlet is a relatively pristine estuary receiving minimal input from anthropogenic sources, except for limited tidal intrusion from Winyah Bay, which is influenced by the city of Georgetown, South Carolina. The two sites are approximately 20 km apart and are similar in geology, biology, and hydrography.

Samples were collected from 31 stations within Murrells Inlet (Fig. 1). Stations along the shoreline are typically adjacent to human activity, such as permanent residences and summer homes (primarily single family), trailer parks, restaurants, retail stores, and marinas. The barrier island known as Garden City Beach is also extensively developed, having single and multiple family seasonal and year-round homes, restaurants, retail stores, and a marina. The southern

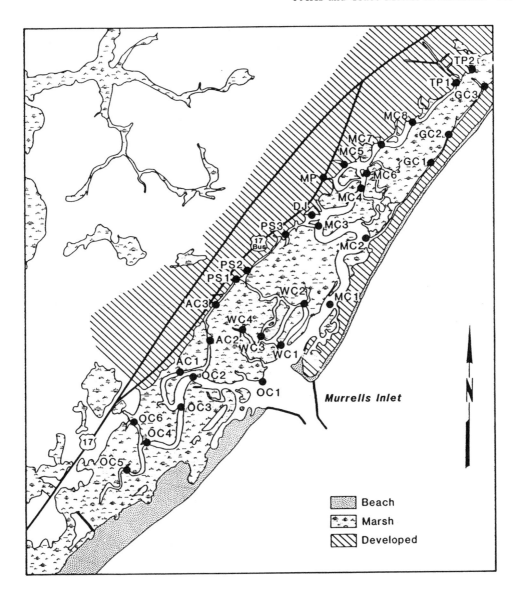

Fig. 1. Map of Murrells Inlet and sampling stations.

portion of the estuary is less developed and abuts Huntington Beach State Park. Water-related recreational activities are prominent throughout Murrells Inlet.

The location of the 32 sample stations in North Inlet are indicated in Fig. 2. Most of the upland and marsh adjacent to the estuary is owned by the Belle W. Baruch Foundation or by other private foundations and has suffered little negative anthropogenic influence in recent decades. The northern end of the estuary borders DeBordieu, a small subdivision of single family homes.

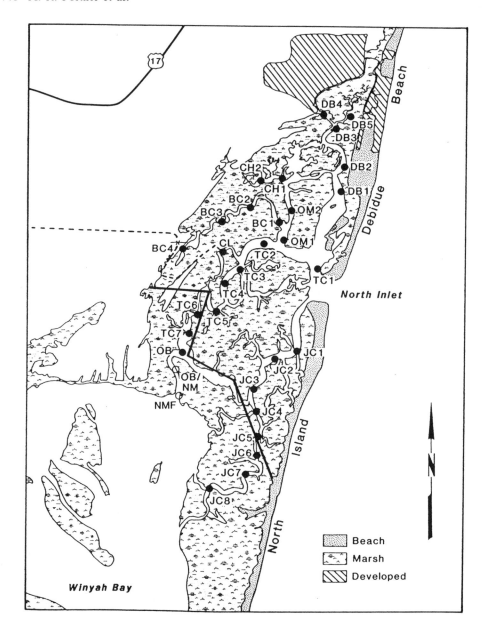

Fig. 2. Map of North Inlet and sampling stations.

Residents have access to the inlet through Debidue Creek. Stations influenced by Winyah Bay are in the southern section of the estuary. The irregular black line in Fig. 2 indicates the tidal node point that separates North Inlet from Winyah Bay and ocean influences.

Two environmental matrices were selected for study. The first, oyster tissue, was selected because these animals are capable of bioaccumulating a wide variety of chemical contaminants (Goldberg 1980) and are frequently used as sentinels of contamination. Sediment was the second matrix chosen because elevated levels of chemical contaminants are frequently found in sediments associated with anthropogenic pollution sources (Brown et al. 1985; Huggett et al. 1988). This matrix is the primary repository of many hydrophobic and lipophilic chemicals and is analyzed in estuarine monitoring programs such as the National Status and Trends Program (National Oceanic and Atmospheric Administration 1989).

Oysters were collected in November 1990. Thirty-one stations in Murrells Inlet and 30 stations in North Inlet were sampled. Thirty to 60 oysters were collected from each station. Oysters were stored at 3°C and shucked within 2 d of collection. Shucked oysters were homogenized with an Omni Model 17105 titanium probe. The comminuted sample was transferred to polypropylene cups for trace metal analysis and glass jars for PAH analyses. Both sets of samples were stored at -70°C. Average oyster size at Murrells Inlet and North Inlet were 5.24 ± 1.25 g and 5.43 ± 1.21 g respectively. Sediments adjacent to these oyster reefs were sampled in November 1991. Thirty stations from Murrells Inlet and 31 stations from North Inlet were sampled. The top 3 cm of sediment was collected in polypropylene cups for trace metals analysis and glass jars for PAH analyses. Approximately 100 ml were collected for each. Sediment samples were iced in transit, then stored at -70°C. Sediments analyzed for metals were dried according to a procedure of the United States Environmental Protection Agency (1982) and stored in a desiccator prior to analyses. All other analyses were performed on wet samples.

The same suite of chemical contaminants was selected for determination in oysters and sediments where possible. The following PAHs were measured in oyster and sediment samples: phenanthrene (Phn), anthracene (Ant), fluoranthene (Flr), pyrene (Pyr), benzo(a)anthracene (BaA), chrysene (Cry), benzo(b)fluoranthene (BbF), benzo(k)fluoranthene (BkF), benzo(a)pyrene (BaP), and benzo(ghi)perylene (ghi). PAH selection is based on their association with fuel use and represents variation in volatility and water solubility in the environment with increasing molecular mass and ring configuration (Mackay et al. 1992). The trace metals selected for both oyster and sediment analyses: cadmium, chromium, copper, nickel, lead, and zinc, are commonly found in many estuarine ecological compartments. Levels of one or more of these trace metals above the norm may indicate anthropogenically induced pollution and may be toxic to biota (Mance 1987). Tin was determined only in oysters. Note that arsenic causes a minor interference in the determination of cadmium in the sediments analyzed. Thus cadmium levels may be even lower than reported if arsenic is present. In general, data reported is from a single sample analysis for each station. However, about 10% of the samples were analyzed in duplicate. Duplicate results were averaged.

Analytical Methodology

PAH analyses were conducted using modifications of the methods of Krahn et al. (1985) and Wise et al. (1988), which consisted of Soxhlet extraction with methylene chloride, cleanup with gel permeation chromatography, and cyanopropyl solid phase extraction. High performance liquid chromatography with fluorescence detection (Perkin-Elmer) was used to analyze the purified extract.

Samples for metal analyses were microwave-digested (CEM 1988) in closed Teflon vessels with nitric acid. Hydrochloric acid was added after digestion to enhance tin dissolution in oyster residues. The digestate was analyzed on a Perkin-Elmer Inductively Coupled Plasma Sequential Spectrometer (United States Environmental Protection Agency 1982; Perkin-Elmer 1990).

Quality assurance (QA) consisted of control charts, reference materials, duplicate analyses, and blank and spiked blank determinations (Horwitz 1978; Taylor 1985; Ouchi 1987). Only data that passed QA criteria based on analyses of QA materials are reported. All PAH (ng g^{-1}) and trace metal (μg g^{-1}) sediment and oyster data are reported on a dry weight basis, except where noted.

Stations at Murrells Inlet and North Inlet were grouped according to possible adverse anthropogenic impacts. Station data were assigned to developed and undeveloped categories for Murrells Inlet, and developed, undeveloped, and Winyah Bay for North Inlet. A "developed" station is adjacent to human activity (commercial businesses, roads, and residences). Murrells Inlet (Fig. 1) developed stations (n = 14 for sediments, n = 15 for oysters) are along the high-ground estuarine interface on the mainland and the northern barrier island. Undeveloped stations (n = 16 for sediments, n = 16 for oysters) are in the marsh and at the southern end of Murrells Inlet. The developed category for North Inlet (Fig. 2) comprises two stations, DB4 and DB5, adjacent to the only residential area at the inlet (Fig. 2, top of map). The area below the tidal node at North Inlet was categorized separately (Winyah Bay, n = 7 for sediments and oysters) due to its hydrologic influence from Winyah Bay and anthropogenic input related to the city of Georgetown, South Carolina (Georgetown has developed and industrial components). The remainder of the North Inlet stations (n = 21 for sediments and oysters) are assigned to the undeveloped category.

Kruskal-Wallis nonparametric ANOVA was performed using SAS software to determine differences in means. The level of significance used was p = 0.05.

Results and Discussion

PAH LEVELS IN SEDIMENT

Total PAH levels in sediments from Murrells Inlet stations (Fig. 3) varied 180-fold, from 14 ng g^{-1} at OC1 to 2,580 ng g^{-1} at TP2. Individual PAHs were found more consistently in sediment than in oysters from Murrells Inlet. All 10 individual PAHs were found at 87% of the stations; the exceptions were MC1, OC1, OC2, and WC1. Anthracene, fluoranthene, benzo(a)-pyrene, and benzo(ghi)perylene were not detected at one or more of these four stations. The mean PAH level for Murrells Inlet was 518 ng g^{-1}.

Total PAH levels in sediments from North Inlet stations (Fig. 4) had a 34-fold range, from 9 ng g^{-1} at TC4 to 308 ng g^{-1} at OM1. Individual PAHs were found with comparable frequency at North Inlet and Murrells Inlet. Phenanthrene, anthracene, and fluoranthene were not found at one or more of the following North Inlet stations: JC2, JC7, JC8, and TC4. The remaining PAHs were detected at all North Inlet stations, and an extremely high level of PAHs was found at station BC4. When the North Inlet dataset was tested for outliers using the method described in Li (1964), the resulting sum of squares ratio was lower than the theoretical value. Thus, the data for stations BC4 were eliminated from the mean because the data were not representative of the

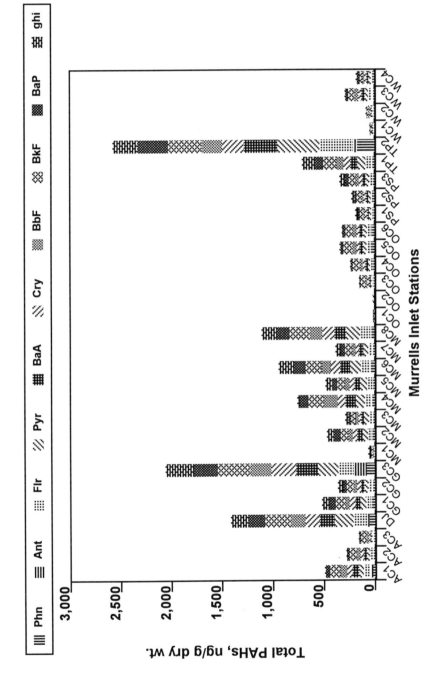

Fig. 3. Total and individual PAHs in sediments from the Murrells Inlet stations. Stacked bars represent the levels of individual PAHs; the sequence reads from the X-axis upward. Phn = phenanthrene, Ant = anthracene, Flr = fluoranthene, Pyr = pyrene, BaA = benzo(a)anthracene, Cry = chrysene, BbF = benzo(b)fluoranthene, BkF = benzo(k)fluoranthene, BaP = benzo(a)pyrene, and ghi = benzo(ghi)perylene.

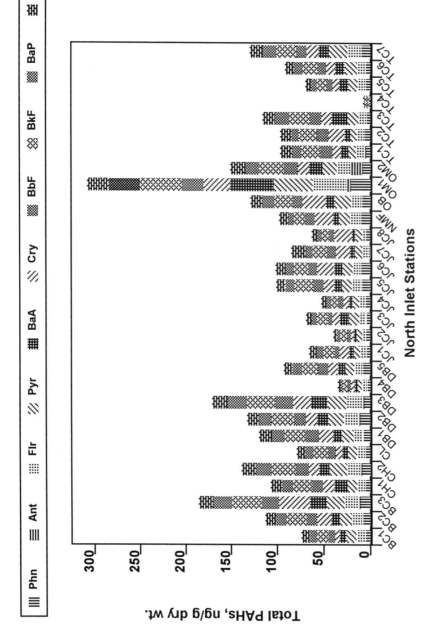

Fig. 4. Total and individual PAHs in sediments from the North Inlet stations. Stacked bars represent the levels of individual PAHs; the sequence reads from the X-axis upward. Phn = phenanthrene, Ant = anthracene, Flr = fluoranthene, Pyr = pyrene, BaA = benzo(a)anthracene, Cry = chrysene, BbF = benzo(b)fluoranthene, BkF = benzo(k)fluoranthene, BaP = benzo(a)pyrene, and ghi = benzo(ghi)perylene.

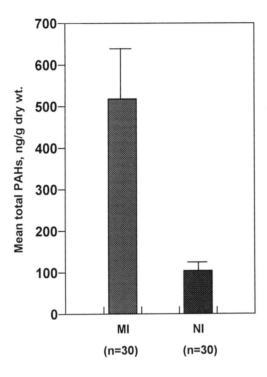

Fig. 5. Mean total PAHs in sediments from Murrells Inlet (MI) and North Inlet (NI). The mean of total PAHs at Murrells Inlet was significantly higher than at North Inlet ($p \leq 0.05$).

North Inlet sample population. The high PAH levels at BC4 may be due to a creosote-treated-wood bridge adjacent to the station. The relation of BC4 sediment PAHs with the bridge will be examined further. The resulting adjusted mean concentration of total PAHs in North Inlet was 104 ng g^{-1}. Statistical comparison (Fig. 5) indicates that concentrations of PAHs were significantly higher ($p \leq 0.05$) at Murrells Inlet than North Inlet.

For comparative purposes, sediment PAHs from Murrells Inlet, North Inlet, and several other South Carolina estuaries are shown in Fig. 6. Total mean sediment PAH levels in Murrells Inlet (518 ng g^{-1}) and North Inlet (104 ng g^{-1}) were lower than the mean total levels of 948 ng g^{-1} in industrialized Charleston Harbor (CHS) in 1986 and 1987 (National Marine Fisheries Service unpublished data). Studies by Marcus and Stokes (1985) and Marcus et al. (1988) showed that sediments from selected South Carolina marinas varied with the number of boats berthed. As shown in Fig. 6, Marcus and Stokes (1985) found PAH levels of 207 ng g^{-1}, 552 ng g^{-1}, and 36 ng g^{-1}, respectively, for the Palmetto Bay Marina (PALM-1), Outdoor Resorts Marina (OUTDR-1), and Fripp Island Marina (FRIP-1). A later study of the same marinas by Marcus et al. (1988) found PAH levels of 140 ng g^{-1}, 352 ng g^{-1}, and 36 ng g^{-1}, respectively, for PALM-2, OUTDR-2, and FRIP-2. Murrells Inlet data are similar to those from OUTDR-1 and OUTDR-2, and North Inlet data are bracketed by PALM and FRIP results.

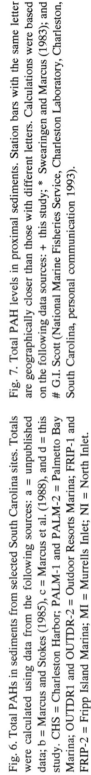

Fig. 7. Total PAH levels in proximal sediments. Station bars with the same letter are geographically closer than those with different letters. Calculations were based on the following data sources: + this study; * Swearingen and Marcus (1983); and # G.I. Scott (National Marine Fisheries Service, Charleston Laboratory, Charleston, South Carolina, personal communication 1993).

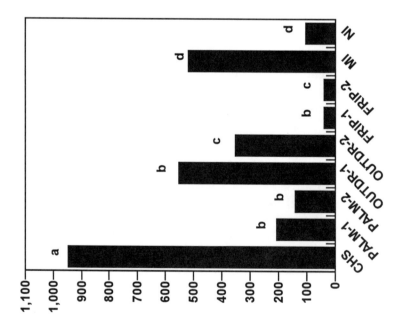

Fig. 6. Total PAHs in sediments from selected South Carolina sites. Totals were calculated using data from the following sources: a = unpublished data; b = Marcus and Stokes (1985); c = Marcus et al. (1988), and d = this study. CHS = Charleston Harbor; PALM-1 and PALM-2 = Palmetto Bay Marina; OUTDR1 and OUTDR-2 = Outdoor Resorts Marina; FRIP-1 and FRIP-2 = Fripp Island Marina; MI = Murrells Inlet; NI = North Inlet.

Swearingen and Marcus (1983) reported on sediment PAHs in their study of a marina contiguous to Main Creek in Murrells Inlet. Their sampling stations correspond to our stations DJ, MC1, MC2, MC3, MC4, MC5, and PS3 (Fig. 7). The FLO'S station is near MC5 (G.I. Scott, National Marine Fisheries Service, Charleston Laboratory, Charleston, South Carolina, personal communication 1993).

PAH levels (ng g^{-1}, wet weight) among adjacent stations are similar except for higher PAH levels at MD-716, which may have been because it is further inside the marina basin than other stations, and at MD-719, which may have resulted from a fossil fuel spill, as suggested by Swearingen and Marcus (1983).

PAH LEVELS IN OYSTERS

Total PAH concentrations (Fig. 8) in oysters from Murrells Inlet varied 20-fold, from 95 ng g^{-1} at AC2 to 1,970 ng g^{-1} at MP. The number as well as concentration of individual PAHs varied among stations at Murrells Inlet. Fluoranthene and pyrene, on average, contributed to more than one half of the total PAHs found at Murrells Inlet stations. And, only fluoranthene was detected in all samples. Anthracene, benzo(k)fluoranthene, chrysene, phenanthrene, and pyrene were found at 84% of stations tested. The remaining five analytes were detected at less than 65% of the stations sampled. The number of stations at which each PAH was found also varied. All 10 PAHs were found at five stations. Fourteen stations had eight to nine PAHS, and 12 stations had four to seven PAHS.

Total PAH concentrations (Fig. 9) in oysters collected from North Inlet were lower than in oysters from Murrells Inlet, and varied 15-fold, from 11 ng g^{-1} at JC4 to 170 ng g^{-1} at TC7. Detection of individual PAHs among North Inlet stations was less frequent than at Murrells Inlet. Fluoranthene and benzo(a)pyrene were detected at 33% of the North Inlet stations. Anthracene, benzo(k)fluoranthene, and phenanthrene were found at 40%, 47%, and 87% of stations, respectively. All other analytes were found at 0% to 20% of the North Inlet stations. Three stations had only phenanthrene present. The number of North Inlet stations at which each PAH was found was much lower than at Murrells Inlet. In fact, no station within North Inlet had all of the individual PAHs present.

The mean total PAH level (452 ng g^{-1}) in oysters from Murrells Inlet (Fig. 10) was significantly higher ($p \leq 0.05$) than that in North Inlet oysters (71 ng g^{-1}). Many stations in Murrells Inlet are close to marinas and other boating activities. Data on oysters (sampled for the same PAHs) from several South Carolina marinas are compared with Murrells Inlet and North Inlet oyster data in Fig. 11. Marcus and Stokes (1985) reported on South Carolina oysters proximal to selected marinas. PALM-1, OUTDR-1, and FRIP-1 oysters had mean total PAH levels of 390 ng g^{-1}, 239 ng g^{-1}, and 105 ng g^{-1}, respectively (their data was converted to dry weight basis for comparison). These values are comparable to our station totals from Murrells Inlet and are generally higher than stations in North Inlet. PAH levels in oysters from Murrells Inlet and North Inlet are lower than levels in oysters from Charleston Harbor (National Oceanic and Atmospheric Administration 1989). CHFJ and CHSF had mean total PAH concentrations of 430 ng g^{-1} and 952 ng g^{-1}, respectively.

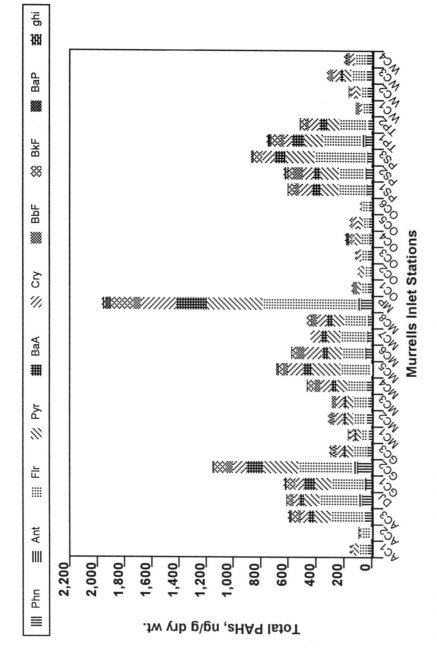

Fig. 8. Total and individual PAHs in oysters from the Murrells Inlet stations. Stacked bars represent the levels of individual PAHs; the sequence reads from the X-axis upward. Phn = phenanthrene, Ant = anthracene, Flr = fluoranthene, Pyr = pyrene, BaA = benzo(a)anthracene, Cry = chrysene, BbF = benzo(b)fluoranthene, BkF = benzo(k)fluoranthene, BaP = benzo(a)pyrene, and ghi = benzo(ghi)perylene.

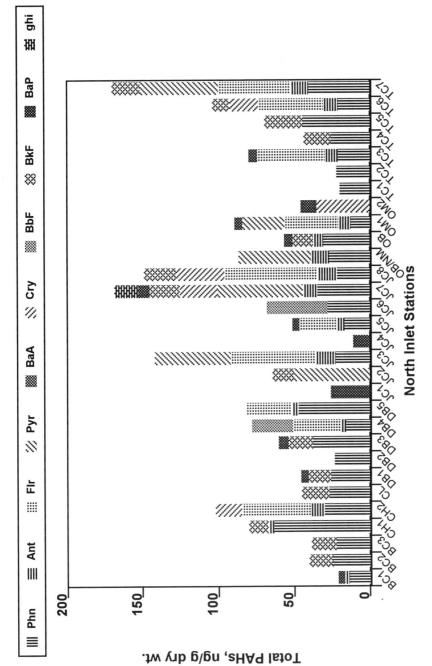

Fig. 9. Total and individual PAHs in oysters from the North Inlet stations. Stacked bars represent the levels of individual PAHs; the sequence reads from the X-axis upward. Phn = phenanthrene, Ant = anthracene, Flr = fluoranthene, Pyr = pyrene, BaA = benzo(a)anthracene, Cry = chrysene, BbF = benzo(b)fluoranthene, BkF = benzo(k)fluoranthene, BaP = benzo(a)pyrene, and ghi = benzo(ghi)perylene.

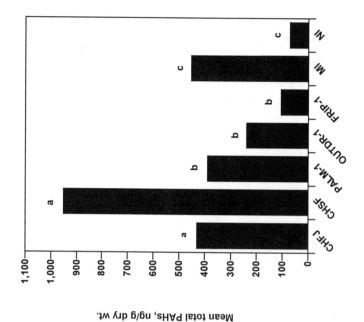

Fig. 11. Comparison of total PAHs in oysters from selected South Carolina sites. Totals were calculated using data from the following sources: a = National Oceanic and Atmospheric Administration (1989); b. Marcus and Stokes (1985); c. this study. CHFJ = Fort Johnson, Charleston Harbor; CHSF = Shutes Folly, Charleston Harbor; PALM-1 = Palmetto Bay Marina; OUTDR-1 = Outdoor Resorts Marina; FRIP-1 = Fripp Island Marina; MI = Murrells Inlet; NI = North Inlet.

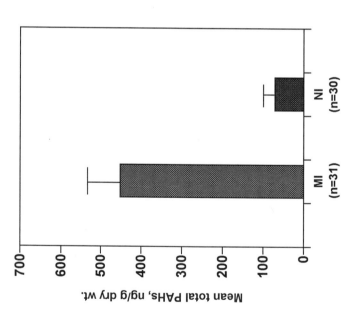

Fig. 10. Mean total PAHs in oysters from Murrells Inlet (MI) and North Inlet (NI). The mean of total PAHs at Murrells Inlet was significantly higher than at North Inlet (p ≤ 0.05).

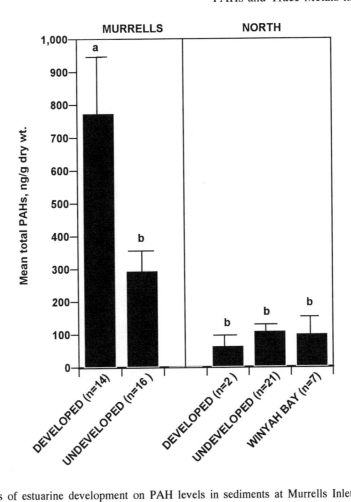

MURRELLS   NORTH

Fig. 12. Effects of estuarine development on PAH levels in sediments at Murrells Inlet and North Inlet. Stations have been grouped according to their proximity to development. Winyah Bay stations were grouped separately, reflecting possible influence by the nearby city of Georgetown, South Carolina. Bars with the same letter represent means that were not significantly different (p > 0.05).

Effects of Human Activity on PAH Levels

SPATIAL DISTRIBUTION OF PAH LEVELS IN SEDIMENT— DEVELOPED VERSUS UNDEVELOPED AREAS

Mean total PAH levels in sediment (Fig. 12) from developed areas in Murrells Inlet were significantly higher ($p \leq 0.05$) than from undeveloped stations, 774 ng g^{-1} versus 294 ng g^{-1}. Total PAH means at North Inlet were 64 ng g^{-1}, 109 ng g^{-1}, and 100 ng g^{-1} in developed, undeveloped, and Winyah Bay stations, respectively, and were not significantly different ($p > 0.05$). Sediments from developed Murrells Inlet stations had significantly higher (p ≤ 0.05) PAH levels than those from all North Inlet categories. Sediment PAH levels at undeveloped stations in Murrells Inlet were not significantly different (p > 0.05) than those from all categories at North Inlet. Clearly, PAH contamination of sediments is more extensive at Murrells Inlet than at North Inlet.

SPATIAL DISTRIBUTION OF PAH LEVELS IN OYSTERS— DEVELOPED VERSUS UNDEVELOPED AREAS

Murrells Inlet oysters from developed areas had significantly higher mean total PAHs than those from undeveloped areas (704 ng g^{-1} versus 215 ng g^{-1}, p ≤ 0.05), and also had significantly higher concentrations than North Inlet oysters (mean concentrations for developed, undeveloped, and Winyah Bay of 80 ng g^{-1}, 53 ng g^{-1}, and 115 ng g^{-1}, respectively, p ≤ 0.05) (Fig. 13). Winyah Bay oysters had PAH levels significantly higher than undeveloped stations at North Inlet. Oysters from undeveloped Murrells Inlet stations, like their sediment counterparts, have higher PAHs (although not significantly different at p = 0.05) than all North Inlet groups, suggesting that they are contaminated with PAHs transported from anthropogenic sources.

Trace Metal Levels in Sediment

Total trace metal concentrations in Murrells Inlet sediments (Fig. 14) varied 30-fold, from 7 μg g^{-1} at MC1 to 211 μg g^{-1} at TP2. Cadmium was below detection limits at 13 of 30 stations. Zinc and chromium were generally the most highly concentrated. All six metals, with the exception of zinc, were found at all stations. Surprisingly, zinc (an ubiquitous element) was not found at MC1 and WC1.

Total trace metals in North Inlet sediments (Fig. 15) varied 10-fold, from 20 μg g^{-1} at DB4 to 200 μg g^{-1} at JC7. Each metal was found at all stations, except cadmium, which was not detected at JC2. As observed at Murrells Inlet, zinc and chromium levels at North Inlet were generally higher than other metals.

The sums of trace metals in sediments were compared between sites. The station means for Murrells Inlet and North Inlet (Fig. 16) were 77 μg g^{-1} and 117 μg g^{-1}, respectively. Levels of metals were significantly (p ≤ 0.05) different between sites. Higher metal levels at North Inlet as compared with Murrells Inlet imply little or no metal input from anthropogenic sources at Murrells Inlet. However, trace metals may differ naturally between sites.

Trace metal levels in sediments from several South Carolina sites are compared in Fig. 17. Metal levels reported here are similar to those reported for Charleston Harbor sediments (National Oceanic and Atmospheric Administration 1988). The total mean level of cadmium, chromium, copper, lead, nickel, and zinc for samples collected between 1984 and 1987 from two sites in Charleston Harbor, CHSF and CHS, were 151 μg g^{-1} and 230 μg g^{-1}, respectively. Contrary to PAH concentrations, metal concentrations are lower in Murrells Inlet than in unpolluted North Inlet and also lower than in Charleston Harbor. Although higher than Murrells Inlet, North Inlet metal levels are lower than those reported in Charleston Harbor. Marcus and Thompson (1986) analyzed sediments for metals at three marinas in coastal South Carolina: Palmetto Bay (PALM-1), Outdoor Resorts (OUTDR-1), and Fripp Island (FRIP-1). PALM-1, OUTDR-1, and

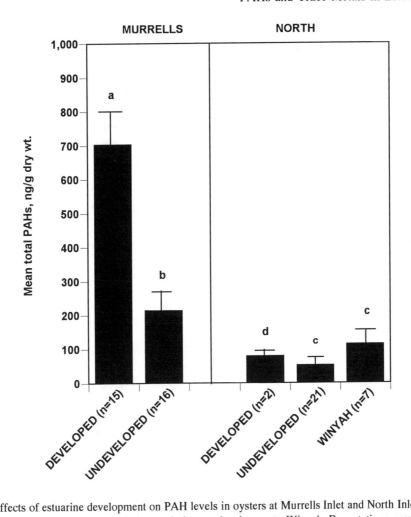

Fig. 13. Effects of estuarine development on PAH levels in oysters at Murrells Inlet and North Inlet. Stations have been grouped according to their proximity to development. Winyah Bay stations were grouped separately, reflecting possible influence by the nearby city of Georgetown, South Carolina. Bars with the same letter represent means that were not significantly different (p > 0.05).

FRIP-1 had mean total trace metal concentrations in sediments of 227 μg g^{-1}, 233 μg g^{-1}, and 280 μg g^{-1}, respectively. Marcus et al. (1988) reported total trace metal levels in sediments from these same marinas of 72 μg g^{-1} (PALM-2), 76 μg g^{-1} (OUTDR-2), and 93 μg g^{-1} (FRIP-2). Trace metal levels in sediments from Murrells Inlet and North Inlet were generally lower than in Charleston Harbor or these marinas.

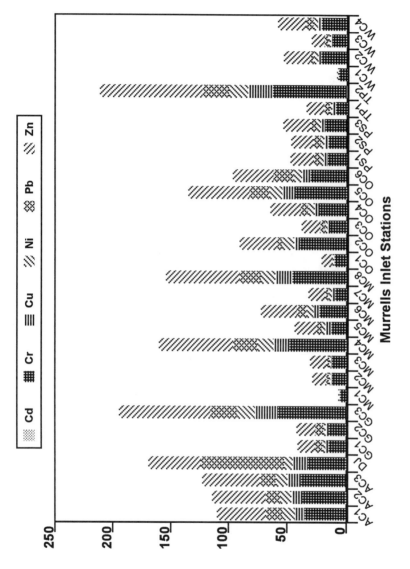

Fig. 14. Total and individual trace metals in sediments from the Murrells Inlet stations. Stacked bars represent the levels of individual trace metals; the sequence reads from the X-axis upward. Cd = cadmium, Cr = chromium, Cu = copper, Ni = Nickel, Pb = lead, Zn = zinc.

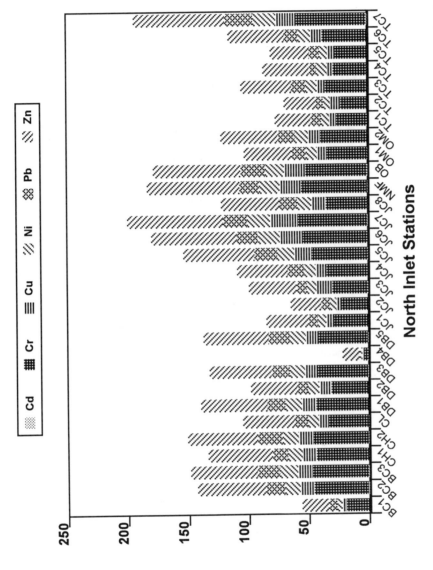

Fig. 15. Total and individual trace metals in sediments from the North Inlet stations. Stacked bars represent individual trace metals; the sequence reads from the X-axis upward. Cd = cadmium, Cr = chromium, Cu = copper, Ni = Nickel, Pb = lead, Zn = zinc.

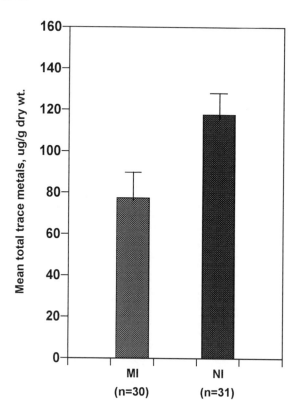

Fig. 16. Mean total metals in sediments from Murrells Inlet (MI) and North Inlet (NI). North Inlet metals were significantly higher than those at Murrells Inlet (p ≤ 0.05).

In a study of the pollution effects of a marina on the environment, Swearingen and Marcus (1983) analyzed sediment samples in the vicinity of Main Creek in Murrells Inlet. Their sample sites are geographically close to our stations: DJ, MC1, MC2, MC3, MC4, MC5, and PS3. Their station FLO'S is near our MC5 station (G.I. Scott, National Marine Fisheries Service, Charleston Laboratory, Charleston, South Carolina, personal communication 1993). Sediment total mean metal levels (Fig. 18) were similar for these spatially associated stations, regardless of when studied, except for MC4 and MD-717. No explanation has been discovered for the high total metal level at MC4. Stations MD-717, MD-716, and DJ are within areas of high recreational boating and sediments from these stations have similar total mean metal levels. Although PS3 is adjacent to MD-717, it does not appear to be influenced by the same inputs of metal contaminants.

Trace Metal Levels in Oysters

Total trace metal concentrations (Fig. 19) in oysters collected from Murrells Inlet varied 5-fold, from 560 μg g^{-1} at OC3 to 3,100 μg g^{-1} at MP. Five metals, cadmium, chromium, copper, nickel, and zinc, were detected at all stations. Lead was found only at MC2 and OC4, and tin was

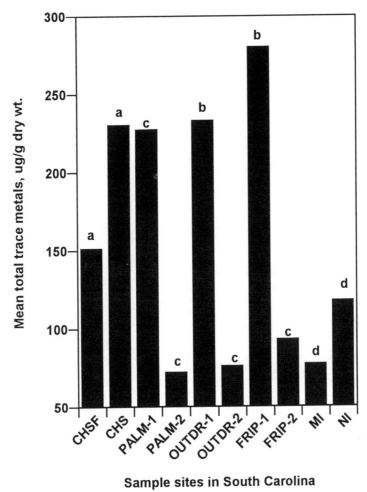

Fig. 17. Comparison of total trace metals in sediments from selected South Carolina sites. Totals were calculated using data from the following sources: a = National Oceanic and Atmospheric Administration (1988); b = Marcus and Thompson (1986); c = Marcus et al. (1988) and d = this study. CHSF = Shutes Folly, Charleston Harbor; CHS= Fort Johnson, Charleston Harbor; PALM-1 and PALM-2 = Palmetto Bay Marina; OUTDR-1 and OUTDR-2 = Outdoor Resorts Marina; FRIP-1 and FRIP-2 = Fripp Island Marina; MI = Murrells Inlet; NI = North Inlet.

found only at MC5. Zinc made up most of the metal total and varied 5-fold, from 530 μg g^{-1} (OC2) to 2,600 μg g^{-1} (MC5). Copper concentrations varied 10-fold among stations, ranging from 22 μg g^{-1} (ACl) to 220 μg g^{-1} (DJ).

Total trace metal concentrations (Fig. 20) in oysters collected from North Inlet varied 5-fold, from 450 μg g^{-1} (TC4) to 2,500 μg g^{-1} (JC7). Cadmium, chromium, copper, nickel, and zinc were found in oysters from all stations. Lead and tin were not found at any North Inlet stations. Zinc

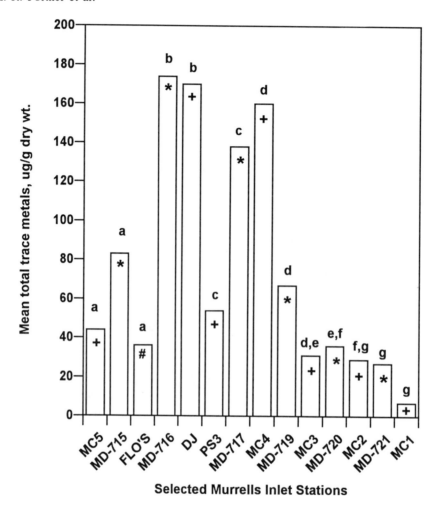

Fig. 18. Comparison of total trace metals in proximal sediments. Bars with the same letter are geographically closer than those with different letters. Calculations were based on the following data sources: + this study; * Swearingen and Marcus (1983); and # G.I. Scott (National Marine Fisheries Service, Charleston Laboratory, Charleston, South Carolina, personal communication 1993).

composed most of the total trace metal concentrations determined; and varied 6-fold from 420 μg g^{-1} (TC4) to 2,500 μg g^{-1} (JC7); copper varied 8-fold among stations, ranging from 22 μg g^{-1} (TC4) to 85 μg g^{-1} (JC8).

Total trace metal concentrations at Murrells Inlet (1,350 μg g^{-1}) were significantly higher (p $\leq$ 0.05) than at North Inlet (835 μg g^{-1}) (Fig. 21). For comparison to the data from the present study, selected total metal levels in oysters from three marinas and an industrialized estuary in South Carolina are given in Fig. 22. Levels in oysters from Murrells Inlet and North Inlet are lower compared to Charleston Harbor (1,820 μg g^{-1} at CHFJ and 2340 μg g^{-1} at CHSF; National

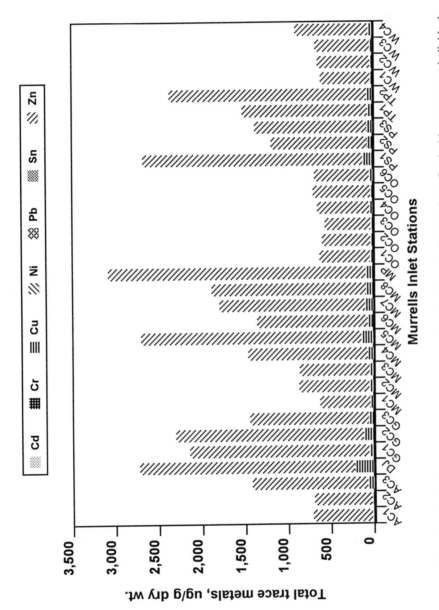

Fig. 19. Total and individual trace metals in oysters from the Murrells Inlet stations. Stacked bars represent individual trace metals; the sequence reads from the X-axis upward. Cd = cadmium, Cr = chromium, Cu = copper, Ni = Nickel, Pb = lead, Sn = tin, Zn = zinc.

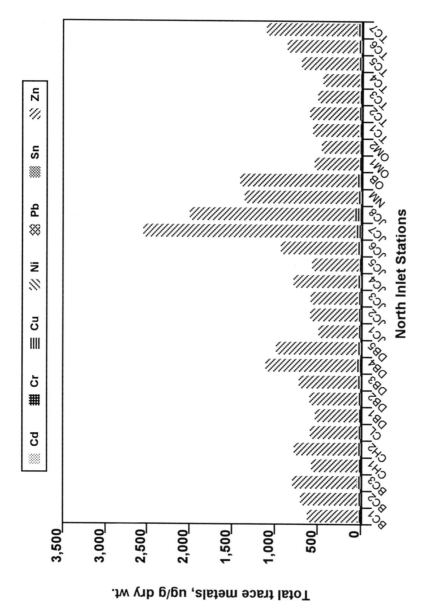

Fig. 20. Total and individual trace metals in oysters from the North Inlet stations. Stacked bars represent individual trace metals; the sequence reads from the X-axis upward. Cd = cadmium, Cr = chromium, Ni = Nickel, Pb = lead, Sn = tin, Zn = zinc.

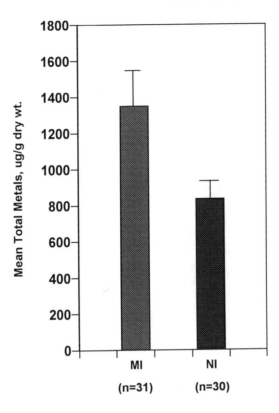

Fig. 21. Mean total metals in oysters from Murrells Inlet (MI) and North Inlet (NI). Murrells Inlet metal levels were significantly higher than those at North Inlet (p ≤ 0.05).

Oceanic and Atmospheric Administration 1989). Oysters from three South Carolina marinas (Palmetto Bay, Outdoor Resorts, and Fripp Island) had mean total metal levels (tin was not determined) of 402 μg g^{-1} (PALM-1), 434 μg g^{-1} (OUTDR-1), and 307 μg g^{-1} (FRIP-1) (Marcus and Thompson 1986). These values are lower than mean totals (tin detected in only one sample) found in Murrells Inlet and North Inlet.

Effect of Human Activity on Trace Metal Levels

SPATIAL DISTRIBUTION OF TRACE METAL LEVELS IN SEDIMENTS— DEVELOPED VERSUS UNDEVELOPED AREAS

A comparison of mean total trace metals in sediment from developed (88 μg g^{-1}) and undeveloped (68 μg g^{-1}) areas of Murrells Inlet found no significant difference (p > 0.05) (Fig. 23). Similarly, means were not significantly different (p > 0.05) for oysters from developed and

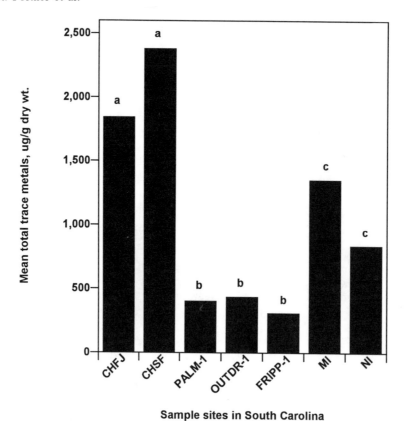

Fig. 22. Comparison of total trace metals in oysters from selected South Carolina sites. Totals were calculated using data from the following sources: a = National Oceanic and Atmospheric Administration (1989); b. Marcus and Thompson (1986); c. this study. CHFJ = Fort Johnson, Charleston Harbor; CHSF = Shutes Folly, Charleston Harbor; PALM-1 = Palmetto Bay Marina; OUTDR-1 = Outdoor Resorts Marina; FRIP-1 = Fripp Island Marina; MI = Murrells Inlet; NI = North Inlet.

undeveloped areas of North Inlet. These results indicate that there is no increase in the total metal burden to sediments at Murrells Inlet due to anthropogenic influences. However, the mean of Winyah Bay stations was significantly higher ($p \leq 0.05$) than that for undeveloped Murrells Inlet stations. Winyah Bay's mean total metal level of 167 μg g^{-1} suggests anthropogenic input, possibly from nearby Georgetown where there is a steel mill and a paper pulp mill.

SPATIAL DISTRIBUTION OF TRACE METAL LEVELS IN OYSTERS— DEVELOPED VERSUS UNDEVELOPED AREAS

Contrary to sediment trace metal comparisons, mean total metals in oysters from developed and undeveloped areas of Murrells Inlet were found to be significantly different ($p \leq 0.05$) (Fig. 24). A mean trace metal level of 1,970 μg g^{-1} for developed stations compared with 770 μg g^{-1}

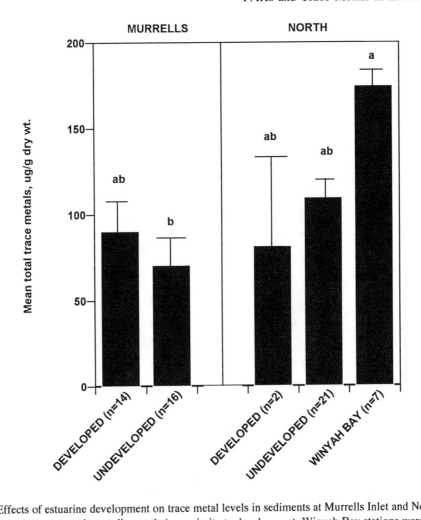

Fig. 23. Effects of estuarine development on trace metal levels in sediments at Murrells Inlet and North Inlet. Stations have been grouped according to their proximity to development. Winyah Bay stations were grouped separately, reflecting possible influence by the nearby city of Georgetown, South Carolina. Bars with the same letter represent means that were not significantly different (p > 0.05).

for undeveloped stations may signify considerable metal contaminant input from human activity. Similarly, means were significantly different (p ≤ 0.05) for oysters from developed and undeveloped areas of North Inlet. Note that there are two developed stations in North Inlet. Oysters from developed Murrells Inlet stations were similar to Winyah Bay oysters (mean total metals of 1,970 μg g^{-1} and 1,460 μg g^{-1}, respectively, p > 0.05), suggesting that both urban development (Murrells Inlet) and industry (Winyah Bay) may contribute to increased oyster trace metal levels in their related estuaries.

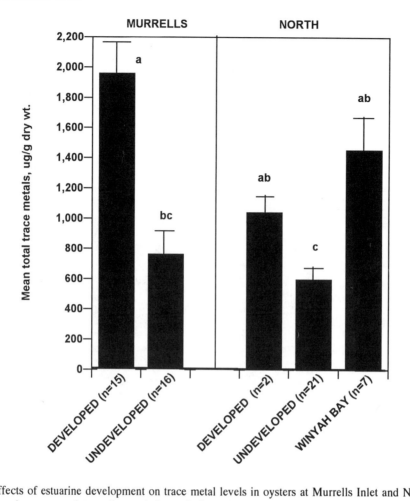

Fig. 24. Effects of estuarine development on trace metal levels in oysters at Murrells Inlet and North Inlet. Stations have been grouped according to their proximity to development. Winyah Bay stations were grouped separately, reflecting possible influence by the nearby city of Georgetown, South Carolina. Bars with the same letter represent means that were not significantly different (p > 0.05).

Conclusions

The ranges of sediment and oyster PAH levels from stations within Murrells Inlet and North Inlet were similar to PAH levels from sites along the coast of South Carolina. Our data, as well as data from these other sources, appear to vary according to proximity to anthropogenic input. PAH burdens in sediments and oysters at Murrells Inlet were significantly higher (p ≤ 0.05) than those in North Inlet. Not only were total PAH levels lower in oysters at North Inlet, but the number of individual PAHs found at each station was lower. In addition, spatial analysis indicated that the most contaminated Murrells Inlet oysters were from stations influenced by development of the adjacent uplands. Clearly, the presence of human activity in or near the creeks within

Murrells Inlet affects the PAH burden of Murrells Inlet sediments and oysters. Environmental monitoring, which has demonstrated PAH contamination of an urbanized estuary, provides land-use managers with the basis to better regulate upland development and require appropriate water treatment systems to reduce PAHs in stormwater runoff from roads, parking lots, etc.

Trace metal levels determined in sediments and oysters in the present study are comparable to levels at other South Carolina sites. Trace metal levels as an indicator of a cause-and-effect relationship (upland development with contamination) is not as obvious as is indicated by total PAH levels. Sediment trace metal concentrations at pristine North Inlet were higher than at urbanized Murrells Inlet. Also, there were no trace metal differences between developed and undeveloped sediments at both Murrells Inlet and North Inlet. Notwithstanding, oyster trace metal levels in Murrells Inlet were significantly higher ($p \leq 0.05$) than in North Inlet. Furthermore, oysters show significantly higher ($p \leq 0.05$) total trace metal concentrations in developed than undeveloped stations at Murrells Inlet. Thus, in Murrells Inlet oyster trace metal concentrations suggest a cause-and-effect relationship between land use and metal level.

PAH concentrations are more responsive to development and, therefore, are better measures of anthropogenic contaminant inputs than trace metals. Studies of an urbanized estuary, such as Murrells Inlet, having no source of industrial pollution are uncommon. The work reported here is additionally unique because it utilizes intensive sampling to identify chemical contaminant differences within the estuary studied. Most chemical contaminant study designs sample an estuary at a broader spatial scale than the present work. For example, the area represented by each sample from Murrells Inlet or North Inlet is approximately 0.2×10^6 m^2. However, the area represented by each sample collected for each of two sites in the National Status and Trends Program (National Oceanic and Atmospheric Administration 1989) was 4.0×10^6 m^2 in Charleston Harbor and 420×10^6 m^2 in Chesapeake Bay. Thus, data from these locations describe 20 times and 2,000 times the spatial scale sampled in Murrells Inlet and North Inlet. The consequence of the more intensive spatial sample collection is a body of data that more completely describe the status of chemical contamination from urban sources in the Murrells Inlet estuary. Furthermore, in the present study, incidence of chemical contamination is relatable to development of the land adjacent to the estuary.

ACKNOWLEDGMENTS

We gratefully acknowledge Erich D. Strozier and Jeffery F. Seel for sample analysis and Wendell L. Richardson for statistical analysis of data. Use of brand names does not constitute endorsement by the National Marine Fisheries Service, National Oceanic and Atmospheric Administration.

LITERATURE CITED

Brown, R.C., R.H. Pierce, and S.A. Rice. 1985. Hydrocarbon contamination in sediments from urban stormwater runoff. *Marine Pollution Bulletin* 16: 236-240.

Bryan, G.W., P.E. Gibbs, L.G. Hummerstone, and G.R. Burt. 1987. Copper, zinc, and organotin as long-term factors governing the distribution of organisms in the Fal estuary in Southwest England. *Estuaries* 10: 208-219

CEM. 1988. Microwave application note for acid digestion. Note AM-3 CEM Corporation, Matthews, North Carolina.

Goldberg, E.D. 1980. The surveillance of coastal marine waters with bivalves—The Mussel Watch Program, p. 373-386. *In* J. Albaiges (ed.), Analytical Techniques in Environmental Chemistry. Pergamon, New York.

Hoffman EJ, J.S. Latimer, C.D. Hunt, G.L. Mills, and J.G. Quinn. 1985. Stormwater runoff from highways. *Water, Air, and Soil Pollution* 25: 349-364.

Hoffman E.J., J.S. Latimer, G.L. Mills, and J.G. Quinn. 1982. Petroleum hydrocarbons in urban runoff from a commercial land use area. *Journal of the Water Pollution Control Federation* 54: 1517-1515.

Horwitz, W. 1978. Good laboratory practices in analytical chemistry. *Analytical Chemistry* 50: 521-524.

Huggett R.J., P.O. deFur, and R.H. Beiri. 1988. Organic compounds in Chesapeake Bay sediments. *Marine Pollution Bulletin* 19: 454-458.

Hungspreugs, M., S. Silpipat, C. Tonapong, R.F. Lee, H.L. Windom, and K. R. Tenore. 1984. Heavy metals and polycyclic hydrocarbon compounds in benthic organisms of the Upper Gulf of Thailand. *Marine Pollution Bulletin* 15: 213-218.

Hunter J.V., T. Sabatino, R. Gomperts, and M.J. MacKinzie. 1979. Contribution of urban runoff to hydrocarbon pollution. *Journal of Water Pollution Control Federation* 51: 2129-2138.

Li, J.C.R. 1964. Statistical Inference. Edwards Brothers, Inc., Ann Arbor, Michigan.

Liston, P. and W. Maher. 1986. Trace metal export in urban runoff and its biological significance. *Bulletin of Environmental Contamination and Toxicology* 36: 900-905.

Krahn M.M., C.A. Wigren, R.W. Pearce, L.K. Moore, R.G. Bogar, W.D. MacLeod, Jr., S.L. Chan, and D.W. Brown. 1985. New HPLC cleanup and revised extraction procedures for organic contaminants. National Oceanic and Atmospheric Administration Technical Memorandum NMFS F/NWC-153.

Mackay, D., W.A. Shiu, and K.C. Ma. 1992. Illustrated Handbook of Physical-Chemical Properties and Environmental Fate for Organic Chemicals. Volume II. Lewis Publishers, Boca Raton, Florida.

Mance, G. 1987. Pollution threat of heavy metals in aquatic environments. Elsevier Applied Science, London.

Marcus, J.M. and T.P. Stokes. 1985. Polynuclear aromatic hydrocarbons in oyster tissue around three coastal marinas. *Bulletin of Environmental Contamination and Toxicology* 35: 835-844.

Marcus, J.M., G.R. Swearingen, A.D. Williams, and D.D. Heizer. 1988. Polynuclear aromatic hydrocarbons and heavy metal concentrations in sediments at coastal South Carolina marinas. *Archives of Environmental Contamination and Toxicology* 17: 103-113.

Marcus J.M. and A.M. Thompson. 1986. Heavy metals in oyster tissue around three coastal marinas. *Bulletin of Environmental Contamination* and *Toxicology* 36: 587-594.

Martel, L., M.J. Gagnon, R. Massé, A. Leclerc, and L. Tremblay. 1986. Polycyclic aromatic hydro-carbons in sediments from the Saguenay Fjord, Canada. *Bulletin of Environmental Contam-ination and Toxicology* 37: 133-140.

Merrill, E.G. and T.L. Wade. 1985. Carbonized coal products as a source of aromatic hydrocar-bons to sediments from a highly industrialized estuary. *Environmental Science and Technology* 19: 597-603.

National Oceanic and Atmospheric Administration. 1988. A summary of selected data on chemical contaminants in sediments collected during 1984, 1985, 1986, and 1987. National Oceanic and Atmospheric Administration Technical Memorandum NOS OMA 44. Washington, D.C.

National Oceanic and Atmospheric Administration. 1989. A summary of data on tissue contamination from the first three years, 1986–1988, of the Mussel Watch Program. National Oceanic and Atmospheric Administration Technical Memorandum NOS OMA 49. Washington, D.C.

Ouchi, G.I. 1987. Control charting with Lotus 1-2-3. *American Laboratory* 2: 82-95.

Paulson, A.J., H.C. Curl, and R.A. Feely. 1989. Estimates of trace metal inputs from non-point sources discharged into estuaries. *Marine Pollution Bulletin* 20: 549-555.

Perkin-Elmer. 1990. Reference manual for Plasma 1000/2000 Emission Spectrometer. Perkin-Elmer, Norwalk, Connecticut.

Swearingen G.R. and J.M. Marcus. 1983. A water quality assessment of marina activities at Murrells Inlet, Georgetown County, South Carolina. Technical Report No. 027-83, South Carolina Department of Health and Environmental Control, Columbia, South Carolina.

Taylor, J.K. 1985. Principles of Quality Assurance of Chemical Measurements, National Bureau of Standards, Washington, D.C. NBSIR 85-3105.

United States Environmental Protection Agency. 1982. Inductively coupled plasma-atomic emission spectrometric method for trace element analysis of water and wastes. Method 200.7. United States Environmental Protection Agency, Washington, D.C.

Voudrias, E.A. and C.L. Smith. 1986. Hydrocarbon pollution from marinas in estuarine sediments. *Estuarine, Coastal* and *Shelf Science* 22: 271-284.

Whipple, W., Jr. and J.V. Hunter. 1977. Nonpoint sources and planning for water pollution control. *Journal of Water Pollution Control Federation* 49: 15-23.

Wise, S.A, B.A. Brenner, G.D. Byrd, S.N. Chesler R.E. Rebbert, and M.M. Schantz. 1988. Determination of polycyclic aromatic hydrocarbons in a coal tar standard reference material. *Analytical Chemistry* 60: 887-895A.

Urbanization Effects on the Fauna of a Southeastern U.S.A. Bar-built Estuary

Michael H. Fulton, G. Thomas Chandler, and Geoffrey I. Scott

ABSTRACT: Studies from estuaries throughout the United States indicate that urbanization may result in significant runoff of pesticides, fertilizers, polycyclic aromatic hydrocarbons (PAHs), and trace metals from lawns, road surfaces, parking lots, junkyards, and dumps. Additionally, activities associated with urbanization (dredging, road construction, and bulkheading) lead to physical modifications of the estuarine habitat. The goal of this study was to use a variety of toxicological and ecological research techniques to evaluate the impacts of urbanization on an estuary (Murrells Inlet, South Carolina, USA) with solely urban influences. An unimpacted estuary (North Inlet, South Carolina, USA) was used for comparative purposes. The results of this study have indicated the following: 1) no site-related effects on the survival of grass shrimp and mummichogs deployed in in situ bioassays; 2) more static physicochemical environmental conditions at the urbanized, Murrells Inlet site; 3) increased bioaccumulation of PAHs in oysters deployed at the urbanized site; 4) negative effects on growth in juvenile sheepshead minnows deployed at the urbanized site; 5) reduced molting efficiency in copepods exposed to sediments from the urbanized site, and 6) reduced numbers of grass shrimp in a tidal creek at the urbanized site. The environmental effects observed in this study were most probably the result of the combined effects of physical habitat modification and increased chemical contaminant loading. Additional work is needed to better define the contribution of each of these factors to the observed effects.

Introduction

Studies from estuaries throughout the United States clearly indicate that urbanization may result in significant runoff of pesticides, fertilizers, polycyclic aromatic hydrocarbons (PAHs), and trace metals from lawns, road surfaces, parking lots, junk yards, and dumps. Inputs of household groundwater-associated products and microbial pathogens (from septic tanks) are also possible. Additionally, activities associated with urbanization (dredging, road construction, and bulkheading) lead to physical modifications of the estuarine habitat that may disrupt physicochemical and ecological processes.

To effectively assess impacts of urbanization, study sites must be selected which have solely urban sources (e.g., roadways and housing, and service industries) of inputs rather than sites with inputs from multiple land uses (e.g., industry, agriculture, and silviculture). This assures that effects due solely to urbanization can be identified.

The goal of this study was to use a variety of toxicological and ecological research techniques to evaluate the impacts of urbanization on an estuary (Murrells Inlet, South Carolina, United States) with solely urban influences. As a reference, an unimpacted, pristine estuary (North Inlet, South Carolina, United States) was used for comparative purposes. This study had the following specific objectives:

1) To assess the acute effects of nonpoint source (NPS) runoff on both pelagic and benthic organisms in pristine and urbanized estuarine ecosystems.
2) To assess the sublethal and/or chronic effects of NPS runoff on both benthic and pelagic organisms in pristine and urbanized estuarine ecosystems.
3) To measure the bioaccumulation of chemical contaminants in the dominant filter-feeding organism in both systems, *Crassostrea virginica*, during runoff events from combined water and sediment exposure.
4) To determine population responses of natant fauna to urbanization (contaminants, habitat alteration) and compare these with population responses in pristine North Inlet.

Materials and Methods

STUDY SITES

The two estuaries, Murrells Inlet and North Inlet, and sites selected for study are shown in Fig. 1. Murrells Inlet, a bar-built estuary on the northern South Carolina coast, encompasses 49 $\times 10^6$ m^2 of marsh and 5.76×10^6 m^2 of open water (Mathews et al. 1980). It receives relatively little freshwater inflow, with the dominant inputs consisting of rainfall and runoff. Murrells Inlet has been highly developed to meet residential and tourism demands. The resident population density is 611 persons mi^2; in the summer months, the population density increases dramatically (South Carolina State Data Center 1991). Human-induced stressors in Murrells Inlet include extensive upland development, dredging, and jetty construction.

North Inlet is also a bar-built estuary. Located approximately 20 mi to the south of Murrells Inlet, this estuary envelops 19.9×10^6 m^2 of marsh and 7.33×10^6 m^2 of open water. In contrast to Murrells Inlet, most of the marshlands and highlands in North Inlet are owned by private foundations and are undeveloped. Consequently, this estuary has not been heavily impacted by anthropogenic influences.

IN SITU BIOASSAYS

In situ, 96-h bioassays were conducted during the fall of 1990 and the spring of 1991 at sites in Murrells Inlet and North Inlet. The Murrells Inlet deployment site was located in a small tidal creek that receives runoff from a restaurant parking lot, road surfaces, and a condominium complex. The North Inlet deployment site was located in a similar small tidal creek that receives runoff

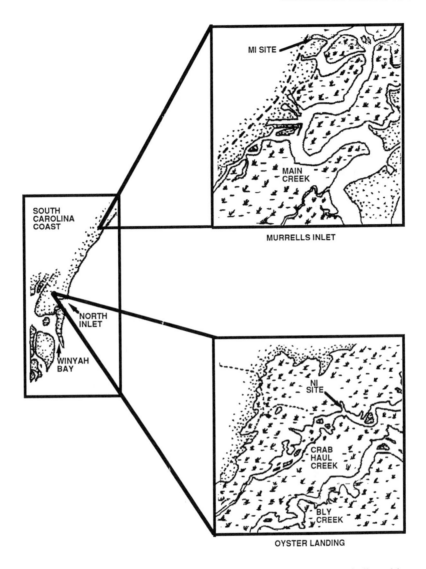

Fig. 1. Map showing North Inlet and Murrells Inlet study sites. Site locations are indicated by arrows.

predominantly from undisturbed forested uplands. Nine bioassays were conducted during 1990 and 1991. Two estuarine species, the mummichog, *Fundulus heteroclitus* (adults > 35 mm), and the grass shrimp, *Palaemonetes pugio* (adults 15-35 mm), were utilized in these bioassays. Animals were deployed in plexiglas cages with Nitex screening (10 individuals cage^{-1}, 3 cages site^{-1} = 30 individuals species^{-1} site^{-1}). Bioassays were conducted during periods of fair weather and times of precipitation so that potential urban NPS runoff effects could be assessed. The endpoints for each toxicity test were discrete (24-h bioassay) and continuous (96-h bioassay) mortality.

Physicochemical water quality parameters (temperature, pH, salinity, dissolved oxygen, and depth) were monitored continuously during both fall 1990 and spring 1991 field studies using a Datasonde™3 Hydrolab data logger. Additionally, rainfall amounts at each of the field sites were measured daily.

CHEMICAL CONTAMINANT BIOACCUMULATION IN OYSTERS

Adult American oysters *(Crassostrea virginica)* were deployed at the same field sites to allow for the assessment of organic and inorganic chemical contaminant uptake. Adult oysters of legally harvestable size ($\geq$ 7.5 cm in height) were collected by hand from the mid-intertidal zone of a reef near the mouth of Leadenwah Creek, Wadmalaw Island, South Carolina. This site has been extensively investigated in earlier studies (Scott 1979; Scott et al. 1989) and found to contain a healthy well-established population of oysters. Immediately following collection, a subsample of these oysters was taken for chemical analysis to provide baseline values for PAH and metal contaminant levels in this oyster population. The remaining oysters were separated into two groups for deployment at the Murrells Inlet and North Inlet sites. Plastic trays were used as cages (91.5 cm length × 61 cm width × 15.4 cm height). During the fall 1990 studies, oysters were deployed at the Murrells Inlet and North Inlet sites from October 23 to November 13. During the spring 1991 studies, oysters were deployed from May 22 to June 7. Following the deployment period, oysters were removed from the field and transported to the laboratory where they were shucked and prepared for analysis.

Analysis of polycyclic aromatic hydrocarbons was performed using modifications of the methods of Wise et al. (1988) and Krahn et al. (1988), which consisted of Soxhlet extraction with $MeCl_2$, cleanup by gel permeation chromatography, and cyanopropyl solid phase extraction. HPLC (waters) with fluorescence detection (Perkin-Elmer) was used to analyze for PAHs. Samples for metal analyses were microwave-digested (CEM Corporation 1988) in closed Teflon vessels with nitric acid. Hydrochloric acid was added after digestion to enhance tin dissolution in the analysis of oyster samples. The digestate was analyzed on a Perkin-Elmer Inductively Coupled Plasma Sequential Spectrometer (United States Environmental Protection Agency 1982). Detection limits for PAHs and metals in oyster tissues are shown in Tables 1 and 2.

SHEEPSHEAD MINNOW SURVIVAL AND GROWTH STUDIES

In situ exposures were conducted May 16-28, 1992, with juvenile sheepshead minnows, *Cyprinodon variegatus* (10-20 mm total length, ~ 75 d old), in an effort to address Objective 2. Fish were deployed at the field sites located in North Inlet and Murrells Inlet in 1-mm meshed Plexiglas cages (20 cm length × 4 cm width × 4 cm height) containing 10 individual compartments. A total of three cages containing 10 fish cage^{-1} were deployed at each site (n = 30). Plexiglas cages were placed in a larger exclusion cage to prevent predation. Physicochemical water quality was monitored continuously at each site using a Datasonde™3 Hydrolab data logger. To control for cage effects on feeding and growth, two additional groups of 30 fish were placed in identical cages and held in the laboratory for the duration of the field deployments. One group of these fish was fed Tetramin™ flakes daily and served as a fed control; the other group was not fed and served as a starved control. Prior to placement in the cages for deployment, each fish was assigned a unique number, placed in a tared beaker containing seawater, and weighed.

Table 1. Polycyclic aromatic hydrocarbons (PAHs) selected for analysis in oyster tissue.

Selected PAHs	Limit of Detection (ng g^{-1})
Anthracene	0.3
Benzo(a)anthracene	2.1
Benzo(a)pyrene	0.5
Benzo(b)fluoranthene	1.9
Benzo(k)fluoranthene	1.5
Benzo(ghi)perylene	1.1
Chrysene	1.8
Fluorene	2.9
Phenanthrene	0.6
Pyrene	3.6

Upon termination of the 16-d deployments, all surviving fish were removed from the field sites and control aquaria, measured (total length, cm), and reweighed. Length and weight measurements were used to calculate an initial and final condition index (CI) for each fish using the following formula (Busacker et al. 1990):

$$CI = weight / (length)^3$$

where weight is in mg and length in cm. The initial and final condition index values were then compared (ANOVA, Fisher's PLSD test) to determine if there were differences in condition index that were related to the deployment site.

COPEPOD BIOASSAYS OF MURRELLS INLET AND NORTH INLET SEDIMENTS

Cultured meiobenthic copepods were used as model benthic infauna to bioassay whole sediments and pore waters from seven Murrells Inlet urbanized sites and one North Inlet nonurbanized site (Table 3). Initial 96-h acute toxicity screenings of pore waters were used to delineate the three Murrells Inlet sites with the largest potential to impair copepod survival, reproduction, and/or population growth. In July 1992, oxic-zone field sediments were collected within 1 h of low tide from seven sites in Murrells Inlet, placed on ice, and transported to the laboratory for immediate porewater extraction. Three 20-g aliquots of sediment from each site were centrifuged at 3,000 g for 10 min to separate the porewater and sediment fractions. Five milliliters of pore water were pipetted into three, HNO_3–cleaned, 7-ml quartz crystallizing dishes and loaded randomly with 25

Table 2. Metals selected for analysis in oyster tissue.

Selected Metals	Limit of Detection (μg g^{-1})
Cd	0.02
Cr	0.03
Cu	0.03
Ni	0.07
Pb	0.11
Sn	0.09
Zn	0.36

infaunal benthic copepods, *Amphiascus tenuiremis*. All stock copepods were cultured on phyto-plankton detritus (*Isochrysis galbana* and *Dunaliela tertiolecta*) in clean sediments from North Inlet (hence the North Inlet control reference) and were fed up to the day of test onset. Copepods were exposed statically without food for 96 h to obtain acute percent mortality values based on number of live individuals recovered from pore waters of treatment versus control sediments (Chandler 1990; Chandler and Scott 1991; DiPinto et al. 1993; Green et al. 1993). After 96 h, all copepods were collected, counted twice for living and dead individuals, and the counts analyzed statistically by SAS ANOVA/GLM (Kruskal-Wallis, Dunnet's Multiple Comparison Test) for significant mortality effects.

Copepod full life-cycle tests (i.e., 14 d) were begun September 29, 1992, using the two most contaminated Murrells Inlet sites (Trailer Park and Drunken Jack's Marina) to determine if these sediments would generate significant chronic effects on survival, clutch size, and larval survival and/or production. For each contaminated and uncontaminated (control) field sediment sample the following procedures were followed: 1) all meiofauna and particles > 0.125 mm were press-sieved from 150 g of sediments; 2) 5 g wet weight, sieved sediments were extruded onto the bottoms of triplicate 150 ml beakers filled with clean sterile-filtered (0.2 μm) artificial seawater, and 3) exactly 35 barren females and 15 male *Amphiascus tenuiremis* were loaded into each bioassay beaker and connected to a recirculating seawater culture system (1 ml min^{-1} exchange rate; Chandler 1986). Fifteen males can easily stud 35 virgin copepods in less than 24 h (Chandler unpublished data). On days 3, 6, 9, and 12, 2-ml of heat-shocked phytoplankton detritus was fed to each sediment culture. After 14 d, all males, females, egg masses, and cultured offspring were counted and com-pared across sediment treatments by SAS ANOVA/GLM (Kruskal-Wallis, Dunnett's Multiple Comparison Test). In our flow-through tests, loss of copepods by passive flushing from treatment dishes was completely prevented by 0.045-mm mesh traps. During all acute and chronic bioassays, dissolved oxygen, salinity or osmolality, temperature, and pH were measured every 48 h. All tests

Table 3. Sediment collection sites utilized in benthic copepod bioassays.

Site	Site Characteristics
Garden City (GC2)	Adjacent to high density housing in Murrells Inlet
Trailer Park (TP)	Adjacent to trailer park in Murrells Inlet
Marina Pipe (MP)	Adjacent to marina in Murrells Inlet
Main Creek 5 (MC5)	Adjacent to marina in Murrells Inlet
Drunken Jack's (DJ)	Adjacent to marina in Murrells Inlet
Main Creek 3 (MC3)	Adjacent to marina in Murrells Inlet
Control	Pristine site in North Inlet

were conducted within digital environmental chambers at 21°C, 30‰ salinity, and a 12 h : 12 h light : dark cycle.

ECOLOGICAL FIELD POPULATION STUDIES

To address Objective 4, ecotoxicological field population sampling was initiated at sites located within Murrells Inlet and North Inlet in August 1990. These sites were the same as those used for the in situ bioassays. The following two sampling protocols were utilized at each site:

1) Block seining. At each site, three consecutive 16.3-m stretches of stream were permanently marked with metal stakes. During monthly sampling, a total of four seine nets (12 m × 1.5 m × 4 mm mesh, with 2-m long poles) were anchored into the sediments for each 16.3-m interval. Another net was then pulled between each set of block nets and the contents of each seine placed into a plastic bucket, preserved in 10% buffered formalin, and stored for subsequent taxonomic identification and enumeration.

2) Push netting. At each site, three consecutive 25-m stretches of stream were permanently marked with metal stakes. During monthly sampling, two tows (by hand) were made using a push net (31 cm length × 30 cm width × 5 mm mesh); one tow along each bank in each stream reach at or near low tide. Tows were made against the tide. The contents of the two tows were pooled, placed in 10% formalin, and stored for subsequent taxonomic identification and enumeration. This procedure was a modification of the method described by Welsh (1975) as a rapid screening tool for assessing grass shrimp population dynamics.

The following parameters were calculated for each sample collected using either the block seine or push net method: total density, total biomass, grass shrimp density, and grass shrimp biomass. These ecological parameters at each sampling site were statistically compared using a nonparametric procedure (Mann Whitney, Wilcoxon Rank Sums, and Kruskal-Wallis) (Wilcoxon

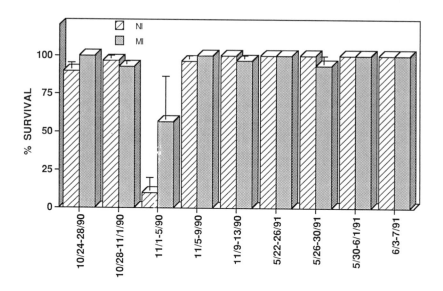

Fig. 2. Survival of grass shrimp deployed during 1990 and 1991 field studies at Murrells Inlet (MI) and North Inlet (NI).

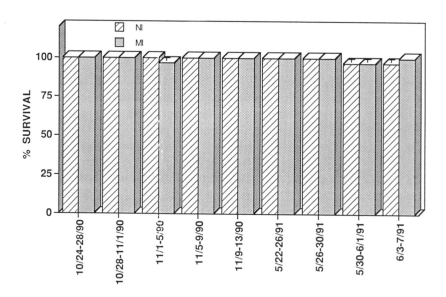

Fig. 3. Survival of mummichogs deployed during 1990 and 1991 field studies at Murrells Inlet (MI) and North Inlet (NI).

and Wilcox 1964; Zar 1974). An alpha level of 0.05 was chosen as a minimum for significance when comparing samples between sites.

Results and Discussion

IN SITU BIOASSAYS

The summarized results of the in situ bioassays conducted during 1990 and 1991 are shown in Figs. 2 and 3. Survival among grass shrimp at each of the sites during the 1990 field study was generally high (90-100%) during four of the five bioassays (Fig. 2). However, reduced survival (10-57%) was observed during the bioassay of November 1-5, 1990 at each of the field sites. Unusually low tides during this bioassay allowed grass shrimp cages to be stranded above water, resulting in reduced survival. Exclusion cages were redesigned to prevent this from occurring in future toxicity tests. Survival was high (97-100%) among mummichogs (Fig. 3) at each of the sites in all bioassays conducted during 1990. Survival was uniformly high among both grass shrimp (100%) and mummichogs (97-100%) in all bioassays conducted during 1991 (Figs. 2 and 3).

Plots of physicochemical water quality parameter data measured using the Hydrolabs deployed at the field sites from October 23 to November 13, 1990, are shown in Fig. 4 (North Inlet) and Fig. 5 (Murrells Inlet). Mean values for salinity (‰), temperature (°C), DO (mg l^{-1}), and pH were significantly (p ≤ 0.0001) lower at the North Inlet site than at the Murrells Inlet site.

Over the course of the study, salinity at the North Inlet site fluctuated with the tidal cycle to a much greater extent than at the Murrells Inlet site. Lowest salinities were typically recorded at low tide. Salinity at the North Inlet site ranged from 3.8‰ to 36.4 ‰ compared to a range of 30.4‰ to 37.5‰ at the Murrells Inlet site. A similar pattern was observed with pH—fluctuations with the tidal cycle were much greater at the North Inlet site and lowest pH values were recorded at low tide. Measured pH values ranged from 6.97 to 8.08 at the North Inlet site and from 7.56 to 8.00 at the Murrells Inlet site. DO levels showed considerable fluctuation with the tidal cycle and time of day at each of the sites; however, once again fluctuations were more extreme at the North Inlet site. Lowest DO concentrations at each of the sites were typically measured at early morning low tides. DO levels were generally higher at high tide and afternoon low tides. Daily maximum DO concentrations were generally only slightly higher at the Murrells Inlet site and daily lows were considerably lower at the North Inlet site. Measured DO concentrations ranged from 2.53 mg l^{-1} to 7.68 mg l^{-1} at the North Inlet site and from 4.56 mg l^{-1} to 8.27 mg l^{-1} at the Murrells Inlet site. Water temperature at each of the sites was influenced by the tidal stage and the ambient air temperature. Fluctuations with the tidal cycle were slightly more pronounced at the North Inlet site. Water temperature ranged from 13.37°C to 24.04°C at the North Inlet site and from 14.73°C to 24.51°C at the Murrells Inlet site.

Plots of physicochemical water quality measured using the Hydrolabs deployed at the field sites from May 22 to June 7, 1991, are shown in Fig. 6 (North Inlet) and Fig. 7 (Murrells Inlet). Mean values for salinity (‰), pH, and DO (mg l^{-1}) were significantly (p ≤ 0.0001) lower at the North Inlet site than at the Murrells Inlet site.

Again, salinity at the North Inlet site again fluctuated with the tidal cycle to a greater extent than that at Murrells Inlet. Lowest salinities were typically observed at low tide. Salinity measured at the North Inlet site over the course of this study ranged from 19.6‰ to 34.9‰. The range at

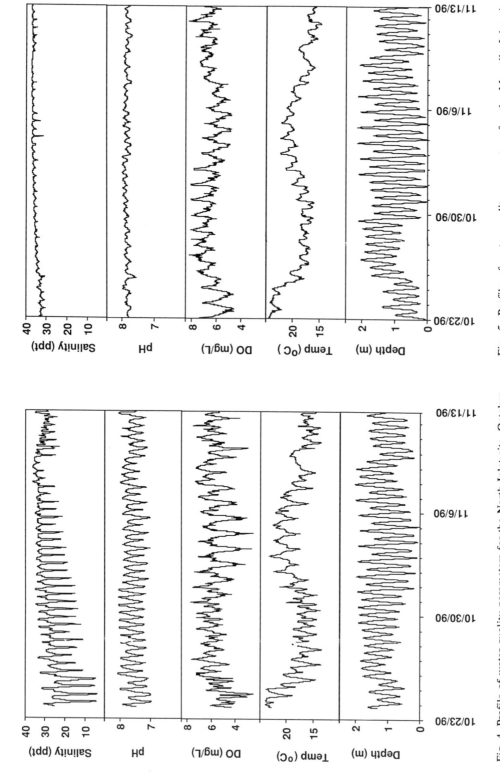

Fig. 4. Profile of water quality parameters for the North Inlet site, October 23-November 13, 1990.

Fig. 5. Profile of water quality parameters for the Murrells Inlet site, October 23-November 13, 1990.

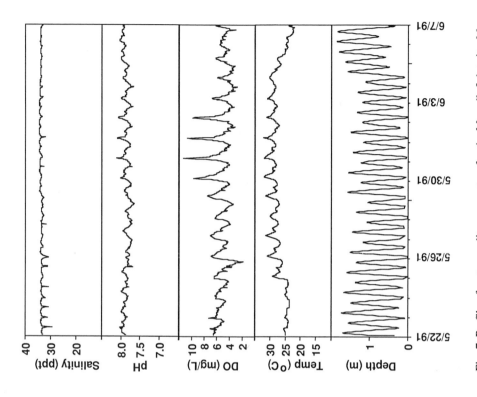

Fig. 6. Profile of water quality parameters for the North Inlet site, May 22-June 7, 1991.

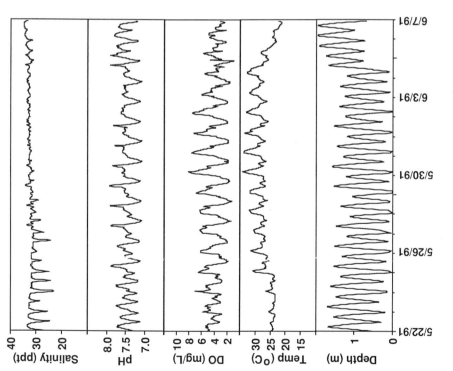

Fig. 7. Profile of water quality parameters for the Murrells Inlet site, May 22-June 7, 1991.

the Murrells Inlet site was 29.5‰ to 34.6‰. A similar pattern was noted with pH, as fluctuations with the tidal cycle were greater at the North Inlet site and lowest pH values were recorded at low tide. Measured pH values ranged from 7.09 to 7.93 at the North Inlet site and from 7.66 to 8.11 at the Murrells Inlet site. DO levels showed considerable fluctuations with the tidal cycle and time of day at each of the sites. Measured DO concentrations ranged from 1.03 mg l^{-1} to 8.10 mg l^{-1} at the North Inlet site and from 1.77 mg l^{-1} to 11.28 mg l^{-1} at the Murrells Inlet site. Water temperature at each of the sites was influenced by ambient air temperature and tidal stage. Fluctuations with the tidal cycle were slightly more pronounced at the North Inlet site. Water temperature ranged from 21.38°C to 34.13°C at the North Inlet site and from 22.08°C to 32.21°C at the Murrells Inlet site.

Two relatively minor rain events were monitored at each of the field sites during the 1990 field study. During the first rain event which occurred on October 25-26, 0.29 cm of rain fell at the North Inlet site while 0.51 cm of rain was measured at the Murrells Inlet site. Little impact on any of the water quality parameters attributable to this rain event were observed at either of the field sites (Figs. 4 and 5). The salinity at the North Inlet site was already depressed as a result of rainfall that had occurred prior to the initiation of the field study. The only effect on salinity observed at the North Inlet site was a slightly delayed increase in salinity with the incoming tide on the morning of October 26. The only effect on salinity observed at the Murrells Inlet site was a very slight drop in salinity (≈ 1‰) at low tide. A second rain event occurred November 9-10, resulting in 0.51 cm of rain at the Murrells Inlet site and 0.56 cm at the North Inlet site. Salinity at the North Inlet site declined by ≈ 7.0‰; however, a similar decline was not observed at the Murrells Inlet site (Figs. 4 and 5).

A number of rainfall events were monitored at the field sites during 1991 field study. Several periods of fairly light rainfall occurred at each of the field sites May 22-29. Cumulative amounts for this time period were 2.03 cm at North Inlet and 2.54 cm at Murrells Inlet. Reductions in salinity at low tide were observed at each of the sites as a result of these rainfall events (Figs. 6 and 7). Salinity at the North Inlet site was influenced to a greater extent than that at the Murrells Inlet site. An additional period of rainfall (2.24 cm) occurred at the North Inlet site on June 4, resulting in a slight drop in salinity at this site (Fig. 6). No additional rainfall occurred at the Murrells Inlet site during this time period.

OYSTER CONTAMINANT UPTAKE STUDIES

Figure 8 shows the mean total PAH level in oysters deployed at the Murrells Inlet and North Inlet estuarine sites; also shown are the baseline level of these contaminants in the oysters from Leadenwah Creek prior to deployment. Mean PAH levels ranged from 3.6 ng g^{-1} in oysters deployed at the relatively pristine North Inlet site to 84.8 ng g^{-1} in oysters deployed at the urbanized Murrells Inlet site. The PAH levels measured in the oysters deployed at the Murrells Inlet site were significantly ($p < 0.05$) higher than those in oysters deployed at North Inlet. Mean baseline total PAH levels in the Leadenwah Creek oysters were intermediate between the levels in the oysters deployed at the two field sites and were not significantly ($p > 0.05$) different from the levels in either of these two groups. These results suggest that the oysters deployed at Murrells Inlet tended to bioaccumulate PAHs while those at North Inlet depurated PAHs from their tissues.

Mean total metal levels in oysters deployed at each of the field sites and in the Leadenwah Creek oysters prior to deployment are shown in Fig. 9. Mean total metal levels ranged from 137.2

μg g^{-1} in the oysters deployed at North Inlet to 152.3 μg g^{-1} in the oysters from Leadenwah Creek prior to deployment. There was no significant (p > 0.05) difference in total metal levels between the three groups.

SHEEPSHEAD MINNOW (CYPRINODON VARIEGATUS) GROWTH AND SURVIVAL

Survival among the fish deployed at each of the field sites and survival of the fed and starved laboratory controls is shown in Fig. 10. Survival was 90% in each of the deployed groups. Survival ranged from 53% in the starved controls to 100% in the fed controls. Although there was no statistically significant (p > 0.05) difference in survival among any of the four groups due to the high variability among the individual replicates, there was, as would be expected, an apparent trend toward reduced survival in the starved laboratory control. Figure 11 shows the initial and final condition indexes calculated for the four groups; values ranged from 12.49 in the fed control to 17.71 in the starved control. The relatively high initial condition index for the starved control group was the due to the analytical protocol used: initial condition indexes were calculated only for animals that survived until the end of the test. Thus, the animals in this group that survived the period of food deprivation were more likely to have had high initial condition indexes. As a result of this effect as well as other differences observed among the various treatment groups, all subsequent group comparisons were based on the percent change in condition index observed in each of the groups from the beginning of the study to that measured at the end of the study. Figure 12 shows the percent change in condition indexes observed in the four treatment groups. As might be expected, the condition index of the starved control group showed a decline by the end of the study. Each of the other three experimental groups had a higher condition index at the end of the study. It should be noted, however, that all initial condition indexes were somewhat artificially low due to the experimental protocol employed. Length measurements were not taken at the beginning of the study to avoid additional stress to the animals. Thus, the initial condition indexes were based on an initial weight measurement and a final length measurement.

Animals deployed at the urbanized Murrells Inlet site showed slightly less (p ≤ 0.05) improvement in condition indexes than those deployed at North Inlet. This suggests that conditions for *Cyprinodon* growth were slightly poorer at the Murrells Inlet site. A number of factors may have contributed to this phenomenon, including reduced food availability; decreased assimilative efficiency, or increased metabolic demands due to environmental stressors (PAHs, metals, etc.).

Differences in physicochemical water quality were observed at the two sites over the course of this study (Figs. 13 and 14, Murrells Inlet and North Inlet, respectively). These figures clearly indicate that the physicochemical environment at Murrells Inlet was much more static than that at North Inlet. These differences in physicochemical water quality may have influenced the observed differences in growth among the deployed *Cyprinodon*.

SEDIMENT CONTAMINANT STUDIES WITH MEIOBENTHIC COPEPODS

No porewater exposures from any of the seven Murrells Inlet urbanized test sites caused mortality significantly different from clean seawater controls (Fig. 15). This was surprising given the moderately high metal and PAH contamination found at several sites (Figs. 16 and 17). Dissolved organic carbon (DOC) concentrations in our porewater samples were at normal field values and extremely consistent (range: 62–64 μg ml^{-1}). DOC likely made metals and PAHs in

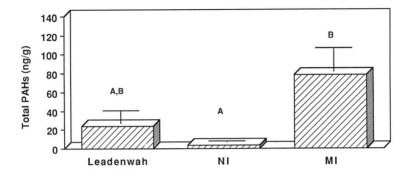

Fig. 8. Mean total tissue PAH levels in oysters collected from Leadenwah Creek and those deployed at the North Inlet and Murrells Inlet sites. Groups with different letter are significantly different at p ≤ 0.05.

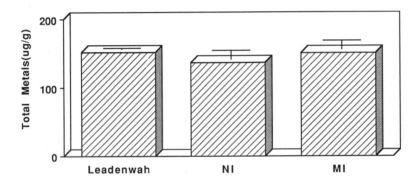

Fig. 9. Mean total tissue metal levels in oysters collected from Leadenwah Creek and those deployed at the North Inlet and Murrells Inlet sites.

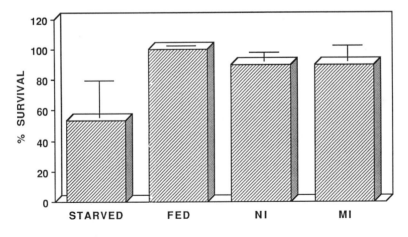

Fig. 10. Survival of *Cyprinodon* deployed at field sites and of both fed and starved laboratory controls, May 12-28, 1992.

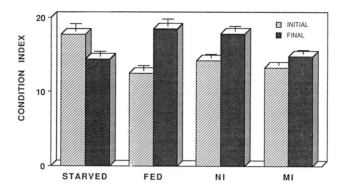

Fig. 11. Condition index of *Cyprinodon* deployed at field sites and of both fed and starved laboratory controls, May 12-28, 1992.

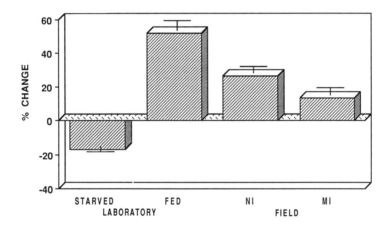

Fig. 12. Percent change in condition index of *Cyprinodon* in the four treatment groups.

pore water much less bioavailable due to contaminant: organic-ligand complexing (e.g., see DiToro et al. 1991).

Based on sediment chemical constituents and loadings and the trends in the porewater bioassays, three of the most contaminated sediment sites in Murrells Inlet were chosen and bioassayed for full life-cycle effects on the benthic copepod *Amphiascus tenuiremis*. Survival of parental males and females, as well as numbers of females successfully producing clutches, were not significantly different among sediment treatments (Fig. 18). On average, >10 of 15 males and >30 of 35 females survived and were recovered after 14 d of treatment, and from 60% to 65% of females mated and produced clutches (Fig. 18). Surprisingly, mean clutch sizes from both contaminated sediment types were significantly larger than those from control sediments (Fig. 19; 7.1 eggs for Drunken

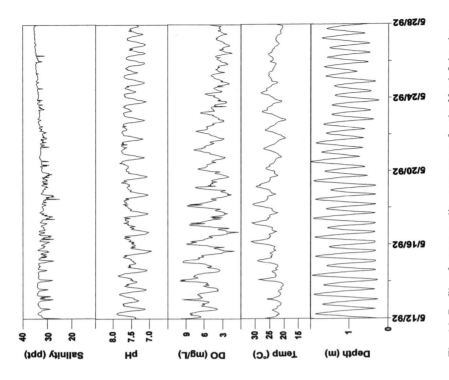

Fig. 14. Profile of water quality parameters for the North Inlet site, May 28, 1992.

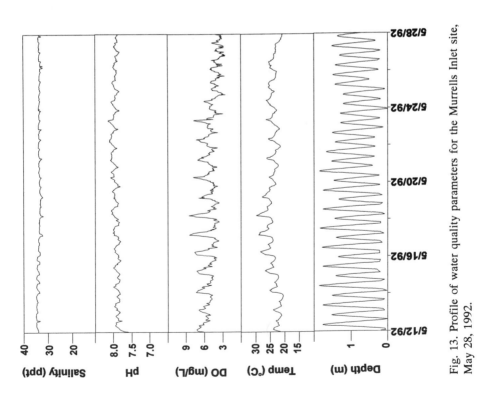

Fig. 13. Profile of water quality parameters for the Murrells Inlet site, May 28, 1992.

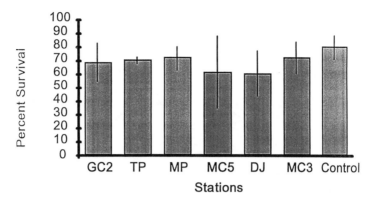

Fig. 15. Mean survival of *Amphiascus tenuiremis* after 96-h exposures to pore water from six sediment sites in Murrells Inlet and clean control sediments from North Inlet. Highest acute mortality occurred in pore water from Drunken Jack's Marina, but no values were significantly different from controls ($p < 0.05$).

Jack's Marina, 7.5 eggs for Trailer Park, and 5.6 eggs for control). The mean numbers of nauplii hatching per surviving female (Fig. 20) were almost identical for control sediments and Trailer Park sediments but were significantly ($p \leq 0.05$) greater in sediments from Drunken Jack's Marina. Since Trailer Park females produced larger clutches than controls but female survival and fertility rates were equivalent (Fig. 18), then clearly larval survival or hatching success (or both) was lower in Trailer Park sediments than in control sediments. If hatching success and survival rates were equivalent, one would expect a mean nauplii : female statistic approximately two units larger than seen here. Sediments from the Drunken Jack's Marina site were very stimulatory to copepod reproduction, yielding total naupliar production three times larger than that from control and Trailer Park sediments (Fig. 21). For control and Trailer Park sediments, mean total naupliar densities were identical.

The most dramatic chronic adverse effect occurred for the most contaminated sediments —those impacted by a residential trailer park—and manifested itself in the third copepod life-stage transition (i.e., nauplius to copepodite). In this transition a dramatic metamorphosis changes the body form from an elliptical discoid "mouth with legs" to a miniature adult morph developing rapidly toward sexual maturity. For sediments from control and Drunken Jack's Marina, the mean numbers of nauplii that successfully metamorphosed into copepodites after 14 d were not significantly different (21 versus 27 copepodites) (Fig. 22). However, for Trailer Park sediments, the mean number of nauplii making the transition and surviving was strongly and significantly depressed by greater than 900% (Fig. 23; Kruskal-Wallis ANOVA, $p < 0.02$). This depressed response was also very consistent among Trailer Park replicates (range = 0 to 5 successful transitions). If one compares the ratios of copepodites to nauplii as a measure of transition success in each sediment type, sediments from Drunken Jack's Marina yielded fewer copepodites from the available naupliar pool than did control sediments (6.2% less than controls, 9% greater than Trailer Park, Fig. 24; not significant, Kruskal-Wallis ANOVA, $p < 0.1$). The Trailer Park sediments yielded the lowest transition percentage, 1.9% ± 1.6, which was highly significant compared with the control rate of 17.1%. The Trailer Park site has exhibited relatively high metal and PAH

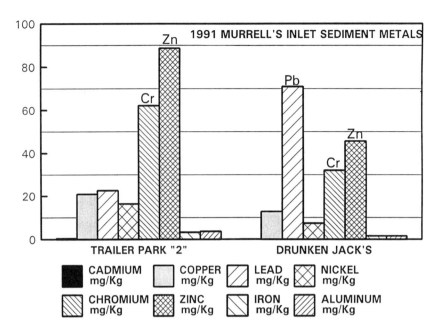

Fig. 16. Sediment metal concentrations at the two most contaminated sites in Murrells Inlet (1991 values).

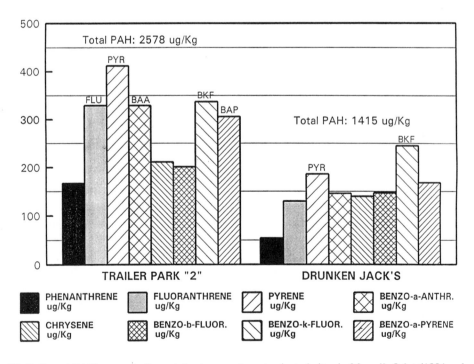

Fig. 17. Sediment PAH concentrations at the two most contaminated sites in Murrells Inlet (1991 values).

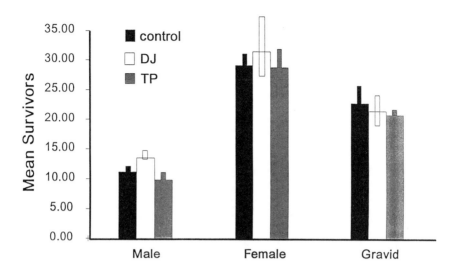

Fig. 18. Chronic mean survival (± 1 sd) of adult male and female *Amphiascus tenuiremis* after 14 d in each sediment type. Gravid columns represent females carrying eggsacs. No significant difference in adult mortality was found among treatments (p < 0.05).

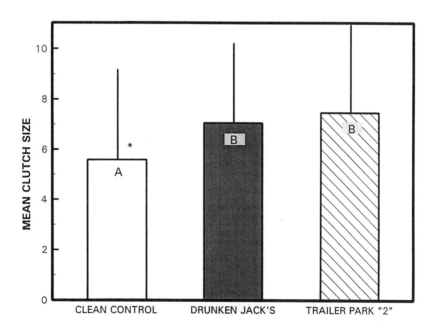

Fig. 19. Mean clutch size (± 1 sd) per gravid *Amphiascus tenuiremis* after 14 d in each sediment type. Columns sharing identical letters are not significantly different (Kruskal-Wallis one-way ANOVA, p < 0.05).

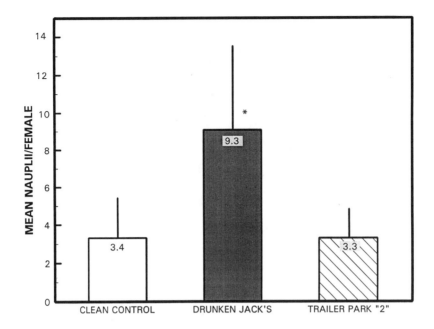

Fig. 20. Mean number (± 1 sd) of surviving *Amphiascus* nauplii per surviving female after 14 d in each sediment type. The mean number for Drunken Jack's Marina was significantly different from the control and Trailer Park (Kruskal-Wallis ANOVA, p < 0.05).

concentrations (Al Fortner personal communication) and these contaminants may have interfered with the molting process.

ECOLOGICAL FIELD POPULATION STUDIES

Results from block-seining surveys conducted from September 1990 through December 1991 are shown in Fig. 25 through Fig. 28. Significantly (p ≤ 0.05) higher total densities were observed in 44% of the monthly samples from North Inlet (Fig. 25). These differences were due primarily to higher densities of grass shrimp and mummichogs at the North Inlet site.

Total biomass was significantly (p ≤ 0.05) higher at North Inlet in 25% of the monthly samples (Fig. 26). These differences were observed primarily during periods of significant grass shrimp recruitment (October 1990, December 1990, August 1991, and November 1991). Cumulative total biomass for the period from August 1990 to December 1991 was 16,779 g per 16.3 m of stream at Murrells Inlet versus 31,735 g per 16.3 m of stream at North Inlet. This represented a 47.1% reduction in biomass for this sampling period.

Mean grass shrimp densities and biomass were significantly (p ≤ 0.05) higher at North Inlet in 69% of the monthly samples (Figs. 27 and 28). Cumulative mean grass shrimp densities for the 16 mo sampled ranged from 2,611 per 16.3 m of stream at Murrells Inlet to 75,157 per 16.3 m of stream at North Inlet. This represented a 97% reduction in grass shrimp densities at Murrells Inlet.

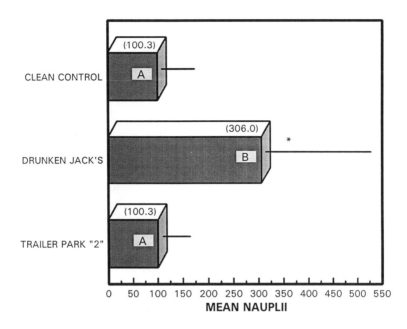

Fig. 21. *Amphiascus*. Mean (± 1 sd) naupliar production after 14 d in each sediment type. Bars sharing identical letters are not significantly different (Kruskal-Wallis one-way ANOVA, p < 0.05).

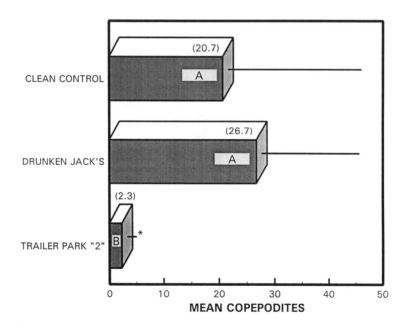

Fig. 22. *Amphiascus*. Mean (± 1 sd) copepodite production after 14 d in each sediment type. Bars sharing any identical letters are not different (Kruskal-Wallis one-way ANOVA, p < 0.02).

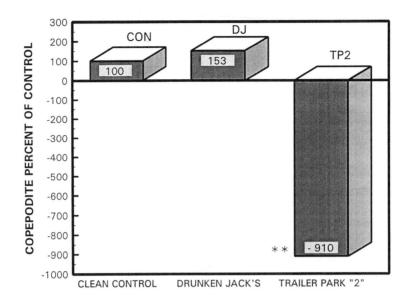

Fig. 23. *Amphiascus*. Mean copepodite production expressed as percent of production in control sediment (14-d exposure; p < 0.02).

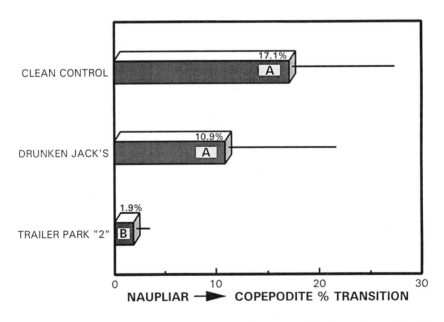

Fig. 24. *Amphiascus*. Percent life-stage transition from nauplii to copepodite after 14 d in each sediment type. Bars sharing identical letters are not significantly different (p < 0.05).

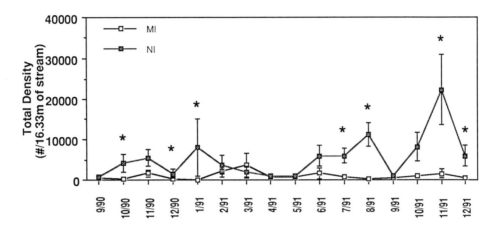

Fig. 25. Total density measured by block seining at Murrells Inlet and North Inlet sites. Asterisks indicate significant site differences (p ≤ 0.05).

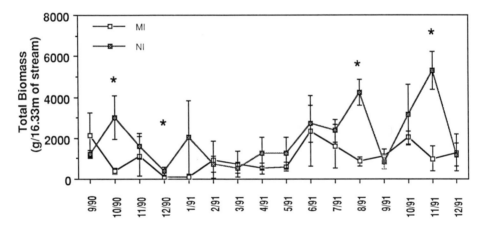

Fig. 26. Total biomass measured by block seining at Murrells Inlet and North Inlet sites. Asterisks indicate significant site differences (p ≤ 0.05).

Cumulative mean grass shrimp biomass for the 16-mo period at Murrells Inlet was 447 g per 16.3 m of stream while that at North Inlet was 14,458 g per 16.3 m of stream. This represented a 97% reduction of grass shrimp biomass at the Murrells Inlet site relative to North Inlet.

Results from push-netting surveys conducted from August 1990 through December 1991 are shown in Figs. 29-32. Mean total densities at North Inlet were significantly (p ≤ 0.05) higher than those at Murrells Inlet in 65% of monthly samples. Likewise, grass shrimp densities at North Inlet were significantly (p ≤ 0.05) higher than those at Murrells Inlet in 65% of the samples collected. Mean total biomass at the North Inlet site was significantly (p ≤ 0.05) higher than that at Murrells

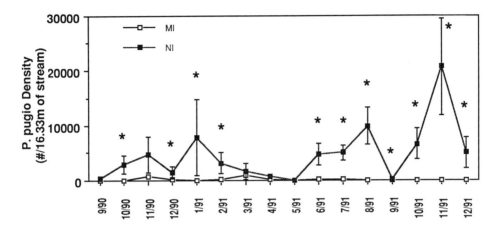

Fig. 27. Grass shrimp density measured by block seining at Murrells Inlet and North Inlet sites. Asterisks indicate significant site differences ($p \leq 0.05$).

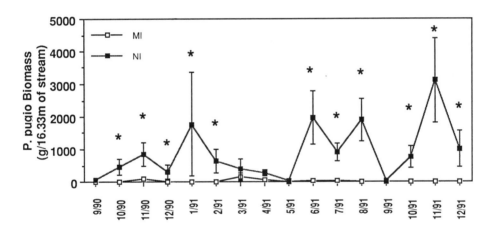

Fig. 28. Grass shrimp biomass measured by block seining at Murrells Inlet and North Inlet sites. Asterisks indicate significant site differences ($p \leq 0.05$).

Inlet in 59% of the monthly samples while grass shrimp biomass was significantly ($p \leq 0.05$) higher in 65% of the samples.

The results from each of the sampling protocols utilized, clearly indicate that there were lower total densities and biomass at the urbanized Murrells Inlet site relative to the more pristine North Inlet site. Most of these differences can be explained by the very pronounced reduction in grass shrimp numbers at the Murrells Inlet site, which may be related to a variety of factors. First, the physioco-chemical environment at the Murrells Inlet site is much less dynamic than that at North Inlet. The extreme fluctuations in dissolved oxygen and salinity at North Inlet may actually be

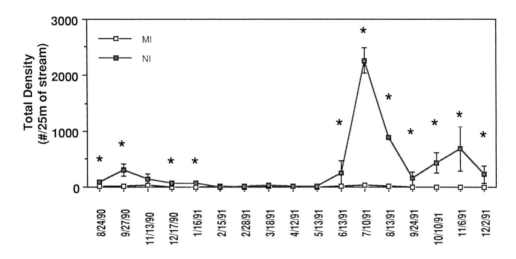

Fig. 29. Total density measured by push netting at Murrells Inlet and North Inlet sites. Asterisks indicate significant site differences (p ≤ 0.05).

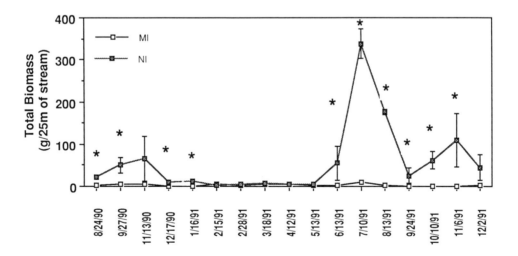

Fig. 30. Total biomass measured by push netting at Murrells Inlet and North Inlet sites. Asterisks indicate significant site differences (p ≤ 0.05).

protective for the grass shrimp by excluding many potential predatory species that lack the tolerance of grass shrimp to reduced dissolved oxygen and salinity (Buikema et al. 1980). Additionally, the Murrells Inlet site has reduced stands of marsh grass, *Spartina alterniflora,* which may make

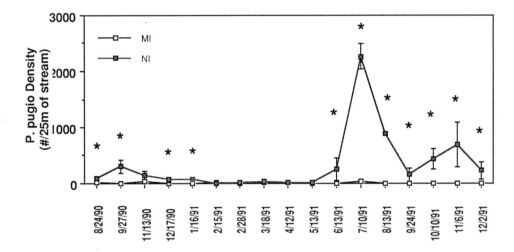

Fig. 31. Grass shrimp density measured by push netting at Murrells Inlet and North Inlet sites. Asterisks indicate significant site differences (p ≤ 0.05).

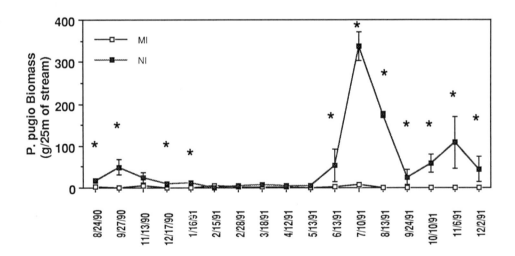

Fig. 32. Grass shrimp biomass measured by push netting at Murrells Inlet and North Inlet sites. Asterisks indicate significant site differences (p ≤ 0.05).

this site less suitable for grass shrimp populations. Finally, the previously described oyster bio-accumulation studies suggested higher levels of PAHs at the Murrells Inlet site. Thus, chemical contaminants may be exerting subtle negative influences on some aspect of the grass shrimp life cycle. Scott et al. (1989) have shown reduced grass shrimp densities at estuarine sites impacted by nonpoint source agricultural runoff.

Summary and Conclusions

Urban inputs into the estuarine waters of the Murrells Inlet site resulted in significantly higher levels of PAH bioaccumulation in oysters than was observed in oysters from pristine North Inlet. These findings suggest the presence of higher levels of these contaminants in the estuarine environment at this site. However, the levels of these contaminants were not high enough to produce mortality in the grass shrimp and mummichogs deployed at the Murrells Inlet site.

Hydrolab monitoring at the two sites indicated that there were significant differences in several physicochemical parameters at the two study sites. The physicochemical environment at the North Inlet site was much more dynamic than that at the urbanized Murrells Inlet site. The tidal creek at the Murrells Inlet site has been affected by anthropogenic influences (dredge and fill activities) and may have contributed to the less dynamic nature of the environment at this site.

Several subtle differences were observed in the quality of the environment at the Murrells Inlet site relative to pristine North Inlet. First, the *Cyprinodon* deployment experiments suggested that growth conditions for this species at the Murrells Inlet site were poorer than those at North Inlet. Whole life-cycle bioassays of benthic copepods showed that some constituent present in the sediment from the Murrells Inlet site had a negative effect on the molting efficiency of larval copepods. Finally, block-seining and push-netting surveys indicated that grass shrimp densities at the urbanized Murrells Inlet site were markedly reduced relative to North Inlet.

The effects observed in this study were most probably the result of the combined effects of physical habitat modification and increased chemical contaminant loading. Additional work is needed to better define the relative contribution of each of these factors to the observed effects.

LITERATURE CITED

Buikema, A.L., Jr., B.R. Niderlehner, and J. Cairns, Jr. 1980. Use of grass shrimp in toxicity tests, p. 155-173. *In* A.L. Buikema Jr. and J. Cairns, Jr. (eds.), Aquatic Invertebrate Bioassays, PCN 04-715000-16 American Society for Testing Materials, Philadelphia.

Busacker, G., I. Adelman, and E. Goolish. 1990. Growth, p. 363-387. *In* C. Shreck and P. Moyle (eds.), Methods for Fish Biology. American Fisheries Society, Bethesda, Maryland.

CEM Corporation. 1988. Microwave application note for acid digestion. Note AM-3. CEM Corporation

Chandler, G.T. 1986. High density culture of meiobenthic harpacticoid copepods within a muddy sediment substrate. *Canadian Journal of Fisheries and Aquatic Sciences* 43: 53-59.

Chandler, G.T. 1990. Effects of sediment-bound residues of the pyrethoid insecticide fenvalerate on survival and reproduction of meiobenthic copepods. *Marine Environmental Research* 29: 65-76.

Chandler, G.T. and G.I. Scott. 1991. Effects of sediment-bound endosulfan on survival, reproduction and larval settlement of meiobenthic polychaetes and copepods. *Environmental Toxicology and Chemistry* 10: 375-382.

DiPinto, L.M., B.C. Coull, and G.T. Chandler. 1993. Lethal and sublethal effects of the sediment-associated PCB Aroclor 1254 on a meiobenthic copepod. *Environmental Toxicology and Chemistry* 12: 1909-1918.

DiToro, D.M., C.S. Zarba, D.J. Hansen, W.J. Berry, R.C. Swartz, C.E. Cowan, S.P. Pavlou, H.E. Allen, N.A. Thomas, and P.R. Paquin. 1991. Technical basis for establishing sediment quality criteria for nonionic organic chemicals using equilibrium partitioning. *Environmental Toxicology and Chemistry* 10: 1541-1587.

Green, A.S., G.T. Chandler, and E.R. Blood. 1993. Aqueous-, pore-water, and sediment-phase toxicity relationships for a meiobenthic copepod. *Environmental Toxicology and Chemistry* 12: 1497-1506.

Krahn, M.M., C.A. Wigren, R.W. Pearce, L.K. Moore, R.G. Boger, W.D. MacLeod, Jr., S.L. Chan, and D.W. Brown. 1988. New HPLC cleanup and revised extraction procedures for organic contaminants. National Oceanic and Atmospheric Administration Technical Memorandum, NMFS F/NWC-153:23-47.

Mathews, T.D., F.W. Stapor, and C.R. Richter. 1980. Ecological characterization of the sea island coastal region of SC and GA, Vol. I: Physical features of the characterization areas. FWS/OBS 79/40. United States Fish and Wildlife Service, Washington, D.C.

Scott, G.I. 1979. The effects of seasonal chronic chlorination on the growth, survival and physiology of the American oyster, *Crassostrea virginica* (Gmelin). Ph.D. dissertation, University of South Carolina, Columbia, South Carolina.

Scott, G.I., D.W. Moore, M.H. Fulton, T.W. Hampton, J.M. Marcus, G.T. Chandler, K.L. Jackson, D.S. Baughman, A.H. Trim, C.J. Louden, and E.R. Patterson. 1989. Agricultural Insecticide Runoff Effects on Estuarine Organisms: Correlating Laboratory and Field Toxicity Testing with Ecotoxicology and Biomonitoring. Volumes I and II, 2nd Annual Report, United States Environmental Protection Agency, Gulf Breeze, Florida.

South Carolina State Data Center. 1991. Selected demographic data for South Carolina, Division of Research and Statistical Services, Columbia, South Carolina.

United States Environmental Protection Agency. 1982. Inductively coupled plasma-atomic emission spectrometric method for trace element analysis of water and wastes. EPA Method 200.7. United States Environmental Protection Agency, Washington, D.C.

Welsh, B.L. 1975. The role of grass shrimp, *Palaemonetes pugio*, in the Galveston Bay Estuarine System. *Contributions in Marine Science* (University of Texas) 12: 54-79.

Wilcoxon, F. and R. Wilcox. 1964. Some rapid approximate statistical procedures. Lederle Laboratories, New York.

Wise, S.A., B.A Brenner, G.D. Byrd, S.N. Chesler, R.E. Rebbert, and M.M. Schantz. 1988. Determination of polycyclic aromatic hydrocarbons in a coal tar standard reference material. *Analytical Chemistry* 60: 887-895.

Zar, J. 1974. Biostatistical Analysis. Prentice Hall, Inc. Englewood Cliffs, New Jersey.

Achieving Sustainable Development in the Southeastern Coastal Zone: Roundtable Discussion of Science in Support of Resource Management

Donald Scavia, Robert Boyles, Jr., and Isobel C. Sheifer

ABSTRACT: At the conclusion of the symposium, a discussion was held to focus on the current status and trends of coastal resources and on what actions are likely to be needed to achieve sustainable development in the coastal zone. This paper summarizes that discussion. Comments underscored the fact that while other regions of the country have experienced significant degradation of estuaries and other coastal resources, the resources of the Southeastern coastal zone appear to be at a crossroads. Although unambiguous signs of significant degradation are not evident, there is a growing consensus that resources are at risk and, unless new approaches are begun soon, the prospects for sustaining healthy ecosystems and economies will diminish. To bring about sustainable development, there was agreement that natural, social, and economic systems must be managed in an integrated fashion.

Introduction

The coastal zone of the Southeastern United States has undergone major population growth over the past 30 years and is expected to extend that growth through the year 2010. Statistics for the coastal counties of the Southeastern states indicate the period of greatest growth of the coastal population occurred between 1970 and 1980 when the population increased by 36%. Between 1988 and 2010 almost one-third of the coastal counties are projected to have population increases of 35-75% (Culliton et al. 1990). Along with this growing population has come, and will continue to come, escalating pressure on natural resources stemming from increased demands for clean water, roads, homes, waste treatment, and other goods and services.

Until recently, natural resource agencies, regional planning agencies, and local governments have addressed these "growing pains" and subsequent impacts on natural resources on a single-issue basis. Many managers realize this traditional approach can lead to inefficient, conflicting, and often ineffective results. The cumulative impacts from many simple stresses on an ecosystem can cause serious degradation. Planners and resource managers in the Southeast will increasingly be called upon to find ways to allow development without overusing natural resources or damaging the environment. The dichotomy between economic growth and environmental conservation should be relegated to the past.

To foster a new awareness of the issues surrounding sustainable development along the coast of the Southeast and to develop a framework for achieving sustainable development, the following questions were used to guide a roundtable discussion at the end of the symposium:

- Are the resources of the Southeast degraded? If not, how are those resources at risk?
- What are the primary sustainable development issues related to natural systems? social systems? economic systems?
- What types of scientific information are needed to support sustainable development?
- What social, economic, and environmental policy changes are needed to support sustainable development?

Status of Coastal Resources in the Southeastern United States

Resource managers interested in promoting sustainable development policies require accurate assessments of the status of diverse resources both to ascertain their current state and to evaluate the potential impacts of alternative management scenarios. To date, these data for the Southeast appear to be available only in isolated sectors. Some good data on fisheries are available, but such single-sector statistics are not capable of supporting multiple-resource decisions.

Some early signs of deteriorating resources, such as fish kills, shellfish bed closures, and water quality degradation, have prompted calls to action. However, other indicators of resource degradation, such as sublethal effects of water pollution on fish, are more difficult to measure. Most assessments are based on anecdotal information or some combination of single-issue studies and have not provided the comprehensive scientific information needed for development and implementation of policy.

Although the status of resources in the Southeast has not been determined with a significant degree of certainty, there is a growing consensus that environmental quality and resources are being degraded, albeit at an unknown rate.

Natural, Social, and Economic Systems and Their Management

Human population growth has historically produced adverse effects on natural resources because "progress" (i.e., an increase in facilities and amenities having social and economic value) threatens environmental quality and natural resources. Reversing or preventing degraded natural systems may be viewed more appropriately as an exercise in solving human problems rather than managing natural resources. The challenge is to manage economic development within the context of the sustainability of natural systems.

Sustainable development has been defined as development "which meets the needs of the present without compromising the ability of future generations to meet their own needs" (World Commission on Environment and Development 1987). Although this definition has been modified through the addition of other concepts or enhancements by those who feel the need for a more detailed insight into the problem, this definition is generally accepted as a sound statement of the tenets of sustainable development.

To move toward sustainable development, our natural, social, and economic systems must be managed in an integrated fashion. The concepts of "Ocean Governance" and "Integrated Coastal Management" explicitly recognize the interconnectedness of not only the different natural systems of the coasts and oceans but also of the natural systems with the social and economic institutions, which shape the use of natural systems. Strong intergovernmental relations are also a basic need for sustainable development. Nearly all major federal legislation dealing with marine resources involves a direct role for state or regional officials and carrying out this responsibility requires cooperative policymaking within and between multiple government agencies (King 1992).

Directions for Scientific Research, Assessment, and Prediction

The consensus of resource managers in the Southeast is that the prevention of further degradation in the Southeast is feasible. However, to stem the perceived degradation of natural systems and their natural resources and diminished biological diversity and to provide for sustainable development in the Southeast, new scientific approaches are needed. These approaches must acknowledge the region or the watershed as a critical entity for scientific investigation. Such efforts must be supported by greater interagency cooperation in conducting coastal ocean research (National Oceanic and Atmospheric Administration 1992)

The needs to be fuller development of scientific information on both a regional and local scale to assist with policy guidance. Both current and new data and information must be compiled in relational and accessible databases. Scientists must work with policymakers to ask the right questions. For example, managers need to know how to mitigate damage to a marsh; but, it is equally important to develop methods of evaluating the success of the "restoration." It is also important to understand the complex and subtle interactions among human activity and the resources. For example, indirect, sublethal effects of a given development project on fisheries resources may, in some cases, be as important as the direct impact of harvesting.

The ability to understand and confidently predict the impacts of development is a fundamental precursor to sustainable development. Scientists must move away from single-focused efforts and toward programs designed to ultimately provide predictive capabilities for alternative courses of action. Multidisciplinary research is a key to developing these predictive tools.

Integrating Social Science and Economics into Management Decisions

Just as development has economic and social values, so too does a healthy environment has economic and social values. To negotiate the bridge that allows the nation to have both sets of values, the public seeks solutions from science and technology. Yet the public must be a partner in finding solutions as they have been in bringing on the problems. Science and technology will not resolve the parts of problems that require both understanding the human dimension in development pressures and conceiving of ways to manage this pressure. In the Southeast, where degradation, which is difficult to reverse, has not occurred, there is an unparalleled opportunity to employ new strategies to good advantage. New approaches must be developed and used, for example, economic incentives to developers to prevent degradation.

As a complement to these new approaches, natural and social scientists must improve their communication with the public. They must take on the role of explaining what they know in terms that nonscientists can understand. For example, results of environmental valuation studies must be presented by economists in a comprehensive and comprehensible form to the public; scientists need to explain such things as the functions of wetlands and how they relate to the public good. In this way, the public can be informed about the principles and practices underlying the concept of sustainable development and how these relate to the environmental issues that must be resolved. From this informed public can come the political will to move ahead on assuring sustainable development in the Southeast.

Conclusions

Sustainable development is as much about altering society's behavior as it is about determining the carrying capacity of a watershed. To achieve sustainable development in the Southeast, there is a developing consensus that there needs to be (1) improved, integrated scientific information for both regional and local areas; (2) assessment and prediction tools that give resource managers the answers to the appropriate questions; (3) economic incentives to prevent damage to environmental resources from development (i.e., incentives for prevention of degradation); and (4) an informed public capable of setting the environmental and economic agenda for policymakers and resource managers. Focusing on these objectives will go a long way in helping manage resources on a sustainable basis.

LITERATURE CITED

Culliton, Thomas J., T.J. Culliton, M.A. Warren, T.R. Goodspeed, D.G. Remer, C.M. Blackwell, and J.J. McDonough, III. 1990. 50 Years of Population Change along the Nation's Coasts, 1960-2010. Coastal Trends Series. Strategic Assessment Branch, National Oceanic and Atmospheric Administration, United States Department of Commerce, Rockville, Maryland.

King, Lauriston R. 1992. Ocean and coastal management in the United States: The need to incorporate local, state, and regional perspectives, p. 34-35. *In* B. Cicin (ed.), Ocean Governance: A New Vision. Ocean Governance Study Group, Center for the Study of Marine Policy, Graduate College of Marine Studies, University of Delaware.

Ludwig, D., R. Hilborn, and C. Walters. 1993. Uncertainty, resource exploitation, and conservation: lessons from history. *Science* 260: 17- 36.

National Oceanic and Atmospheric Administration.1992. Southeast United States Coast Workshop to Improve Coordination of Coastal Ocean Research. Coastal Ocean Program, National Oceanic and Atmospheric Administration, United States Department of Commerce, Washington, D.C.

World Commission on Environment and Development. 1987. Our Common Future. Oxford University Press, Oxford.

Sustainable Development in the Southeastern Coastal Zone: A Summary

Carl J. Sindermann

Introduction

As a preface to this summary of the Symposium on Sustainable Development in the Southeastern Coastal Zone, I would like to comment on the logical, effective structure of the meeting. It began with a series of well-selected overview papers stating policies and problems associated with the always uneasy wedding of development and ecology, moved to overviews of more specific areas of environmental impacts (eutrophication, contaminants, wetlands, fisheries, water resources, public health, and economics), and then in the technical sessions elaborated on some of these areas (eutrophication, water quality, toxicology) and gave consideration to coastal geographic information systems. This sequence proved to be an admirable framework for consideration of many issues involved in sustainable development of the southeastern coastline of the United States.

My general plan for this summation of two days of presentations and discussions is to approach the task from four perspectives:

(1) to review definitions of sustainable development and the concepts encompassed by the terms;
(2) to explore the reasons for increasing public concern about sustainable development (especially apparent since the Stockholm Conference on the Environment held in 1972);
(3) to summarize some of the insights gained during this symposium that are relevant to sustainable development; and
(4) to offer some ideas on how sustainable development in the coastal zone can be achieved in the Southeast and elsewhere.

These perspectives are of course highly subjective, but they seem to encompass at least a reasonable portion of the meeting content.

Definitions and Concepts Included in the Term Sustainable Development

The World Commission on Environment and Development (1987) proposed a remarkably simple definition of sustainable development: "Sustainable development is development that meets

510   C. J. Sindermann

the needs of the present without compromising the ability of future generations to meet their own needs." The concept of sustainable development has gained remarkable favor, especially during the past decade—to the point where an extensive literature now exists and books with that title have appeared (Redclift 1987; Tolba 1987). But the World Commission definition of sustainable development is too simple for any insecure person; it needs dissection and amplification and mastication—a task to which many authors have addressed themselves. As an example, a useful augmentation of the definition was proposed by Carpenter and Harper (1989): "To be sustainable the rate of regeneration, maintenance or repair must, over time, equal or exceed the rate of harvest, consumption or degradation."

The terms development, sustainable development, and ecologically sustainable development are used freely, with the assumption that some common understanding of them exists. But it can be instructive to examine how the terms are being used by other people. For example, the term development—to some people the word is immediately translated into *economic* development, which is the improvement of social well-being through the production and acquisition of economic goods and services. Others have a broader view: development is not seen exclusively as the growth rate of national per capita income or capital formation but includes more qualitative aspects, such as improvements in income distribution, employment, health, housing, and education (Tolba 1987).

If we introduce the modifier sustainable to the term development, the level of ambiguity increases; however, the World Resources Institute has a good definition: "sustainable development is a development strategy that manages all assets—natural and human resources, as well as financial and physical assets—to increase wealth and well being." Two very important provisos are included, as was pointed out by Brown et al. (1987): 1) sustainable economic development depends on *sound environmental management*; and 2) current decisions should not damage prospects for maintaining or improving living standards in the *future*. This second proviso—of not taking actions that would compromise the well-being of future generations—leads to the third term. After development and sustainable development, we come at last to what we are really talking about in this symposium: ecologically sustainable development. There are three principal contexts in which sustainability can be used: social, economic, and ecological (Fig. 1). The social includes the continued satisfaction of basic human needs (the Maslow pyramid). The economic perspective is confused, since continued growth rather than sustainability with limits is an important consideration. (One economist tried to reduce my confusion by pointing out that economics is always concerned with maximizing strategies, which are subject to constraints. If some of the constraints are natural resources, then it is not a maximizing strategy to loot them for short-term gain. The economics lesson went on to explain that the weight assigned to future generations rather than the present generation in making economic decisions is determined by the "discount rate"—in which the value of an estuary would be the current year's fishing harvest plus all future harvests discounted by some rate reflecting our preference for current rather than future consumption.) The ecological perspective, which has been of particular concern to us at this symposium, focuses on natural biological processes and the continued productivity and functioning of ecosystems. Long-term ecological sustainability requires protection of genetic resources and conservation of biological diversity (Brown et al. 1987). It requires understanding of factors responsible for short-term variability, and its role in long-term sustainability of ecosystems (Holling 1978).

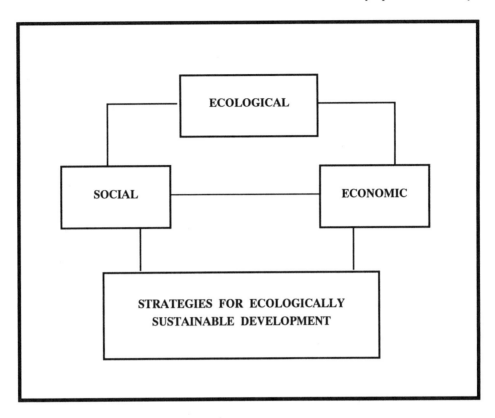

Fig. 1. The relationships between perspectives addressing ecologically sustainable development (modified from Shearman 1990).

Reasons for Increasing Concerns About
Sustainable Development

The overriding concern of thinking people—and the fear that leads to the convening of symposia such as this one—is that "our current organization of society and modes of production and consumption are not sustainable, and that we as a species need to undergo a transformation so we can meet the needs of the present without compromising the ability of future generations to meet their own needs" (a rough quote from the World Commission on Environment and Development 1987).

The major concerns with respect to sustainability—all of which have been expressed in some form during this symposium—were well summarized by Dovers (1990):

• "Resources are being used or degraded at such a rate as to significantly compromise their availability to future human generations (e.g., fossil fuels, timber, soils)."

• "Humanity's wastes are accumulating to such an extent as to also severely compromise future use of the biosphere (e.g., ocean pollution, nutrification of waterways, greenhouse effect)."

• "The earth's biological diversity is being reduced at an unacceptable rate, threatening both a significant proportion of nonhuman life and the future use of the biosphere by humans (e.g., tropical forests, genetic diversity in crops)."

• "Present societal arrangements and the existing models of growth and development create many goods, services, and situations that are not necessarily socially or humanly desirable (e.g., crowding, stress, some drugs, overconsumption)."

• "Existing models of development are fundamentally inequitable, particularly between what are known as the developed and developing worlds, but also within nation states."

Some of these concerns are of course more relevant than others to coastal zone development in the Southeastern United States, but in aggregate they indicate an unprecedented dissatisfaction with the abusive behavior of the human species, insofar as environmental management practices are involved.

Some Insights Derived from Symposium Discussions

Each participant in a symposium brings a suite of background, attitudes, and perceptions to the meeting, and sometimes hears or does not hear statements that agree with or disagree with elements of that suite. This is, of course, not a problem for designated meeting summarizers; and with that firm assurance, here is just a small selection of valuable elements that emerged for me during the sessions:

Regional or whole watershed programs seem to be the most efficient. Extremely local problems need to be addressed as well, but they should be approached from a broader perspective and as components of broader programs. A critical mass of competencies to address sustainable development issues is more apt to be available regionally than locally. But—and this is a large but—*in the pursuit of regional cooperation it is important not to lose sight of the fact that the region is part of a greater whole.* A geographically well-defined coastal region such as the Southeast Atlantic still experiences problems whose boundaries extend beyond the region and therefore are not easily manageable by the coastal states alone. Examples would be air pollution or the management of large gamefish and other highly migratory species. The obverse of this would of course be the ability of a broad policy to be applicable to a specific local area.

*There exist at present **extensive** as well as **intensive** programs examining and monitoring human-mediated environmental changes.* On a large geographic scale, for example, is the National Oceanic and Atmospheric Administration's Status and Trends Program—a nationwide monitoring effort to measure the biological significance of contaminants. Elements of the program examine sediments, bivalves, and demersal fish for toxics. This is a multi-laboratory program, designed to be long term. It uses an array of indicators; it continues to explore new approaches; and it is flexible enough to change when advisable. At the other end of the spectrum are the intensive studies of localized areas, such as the multidisciplinary work in two South Carolina estuaries—Murrells Inlet and North Inlet. Nutrients, sediment chemistry, hydrography, oyster contaminant levels, and microbiology are all part of the research effort.

We need more of these extensive as well as intensive examinations of environmental status and changes in status, since the quality of management decisions can be improved by data from them. Programs need to be long term and in multiple systems, as emphasized by several of the meeting participants.

We need to separate, with consistency, the concept of sustainable development from the obsolescent concept of continued economic growth. Continued economic growth would require long-term management of resources, but developers, fishermen, and other commercial interests may not be willing to accept some of the strictures that might be needed to ensure long-term sustainable use of resources. The role of government in promoting an "economically efficient" use of resources is too limited, since it focuses on commercial value and may ignore or minimize the "quality of life" kinds of values that are increasingly important to this generation and will be to succeeding generations. Even the most basic of strategies for sustainable economic growth should consider all external costs, which include costs imposed on future generations as a consequence of pollution or overexploitation of resources.

Sustainable development may actually dictate *reductions* rather than growth. Examples mentioned during the symposium included a beach management program that emphasizes retreat from the erosion zone—or opposition to the national flood insurance program, to discourage further development in vulnerable coastal areas.

Ecologically sustainable development should consider in its planning stages new or emerging concepts in ecology. Some concepts to be included might be the proper valuation of nonmarket goods and services; the false perception of a steady state in nature (the pulsing paradigm); differentiating growth (quantitative) from development (qualitative); differential energy flow in young and mature systems (growth versus maintenance); and hierarchies of ecological systems. Critical questions to be answered include: "How are these newer concepts to be translated and then transmitted to the general public, developers, and industry representatives?" and "Are some 'environmental experts' and managers operating on occasion with outmoded concepts?"

Although relationships are not well understood, *development may be the greatest single factor (except possibly for overfishing) affecting fisheries of the United States.* Estuarine dependency of young fish occurs in 95% of species in the coastal states of the Southeast. Problems impacting fisheries include freshwater diversion, eutrophication, chemical contamination, and physical modification of habitats. But, effects at the population level have not been determined with any degree of precision. Until they are, impacts on abundance will remain matters of conjecture.

Another (and final) element in this very selective listing of insights gained from the symposium is that *ensuring sustainable development is a major and difficult responsibility of government regulatory agencies at all levels—federal, state, and local—and can be best accomplished with support and participation of an informed public.* Although much has already been accomplished, there is a continuing need in the southeastern coastal states (as well as elsewhere) to further develop constituencies—private citizens (including tourists) and organizations —that know about regional arrangements to support sustainable development. These are "environmental consumers" who must be ready to pay (tax increases, use taxes) to solve some of the environmental problems that they help create. Awareness of environmental problems must be increased, with the assumption that the more informed the taxpayers are, the more they will value their natural resources, and the more they should be willing to pay in taxes and costs of goods to protect those resources.

This listing of only six insights or generalizations seems just a tad inadequate. Some other topics mentioned during the sessions that should be explored (but not here) include these:

• Efforts should be made to provide better linkages between scientists and policy makers.

• Today's (and tomorrow's) emphasis in sustainable development is often at the interfaces of disciplines (economics and ecology, for example). Consideration of the scope and intensity of the action is especially important (Carpenter and Dixon 1985).

• Prevention of further degradation in the coastal zone of the Southeast is feasible; whereas, in many other coastal areas costly restoration is the route that must be followed. Preservation is cheaper.

How Sustainable Development Can Be Achieved

Fortunately, a consensus is emerging on some possible approaches to achieving sustainable development, although perspectives and priorities will vary on a global basis, and the developing nations will have their own agendas. Some generally accepted means of achieving sustainable development include the following (all of them have been discussed or alluded to during this symposium, and many have been examined from a global perspective by Tolba [1987]):

• Ensure that environmental considerations are not left out in developmental planning
• Gather sufficient environmental data to enable the implementation of sound development planning (a point stressed repeatedly during this meeting).
• Inform the public about what is at stake, and develop public constituencies; concentrate on ecologically valuable systems particularly at risk. In the Southeast where such coastal systems are threatened by rapid urban expansion, an approach of choice might be to buy "remote and useless" areas now, before developers find them and bid up prices.
• Learn from mistakes that have been made in other areas; capitalize on existing environmental and natural resource management capabilities; don't exclude anyone; and integrate planning within a regional framework, including all legal entities with concerns and involvements; then develop scenarios to assess the impact of alternative development strategies (possibly modeled on the Mediterranean Action Plan).

Requirements for achieving sustainable development have been listed from a global perspective by the World Commission on Environment and Development (1987). Their list, as summarized by Shearman (1990), includes the needs for

• "A political system that secures effective citizen participation in decision making;
• An economic system that is able to generate surpluses and technical knowledge on a self-reliant and sustained basis;
• A social system that provides for solutions for the tensions arising from disharmonious development;
• A production system that respects the obligation to preserve the ecological base for development;
• A technological system that can search continuously for new solutions;
• An international system that fosters sustainable patterns of trade and finance; and
• An administrative system that is flexible and has the capacity for self-correction."

We are fortunate in the United States to have ingredients of most of these systems already in place. Once we have concluded that sustainability is a desirable goal and have selected the circumstances under which it is desirable, we need action and commitment.

Conclusions

I feel at this point in the symposium summary that at least some of the essence of the meeting has been captured. Obviously, most of the vital interactions among participants disappear when they leave, and while the published record is at best only a limited portrayal of the event, fortunately the papers constituting the symposium volume do have an independent and less transient existence.

This summary has tried to relate thinking, planning, and research in the southeastern United States with comparable activities on a global scale—a task that is not too difficult since issues concerned with sustainable development have universal elements, regardless of variations in the level of industrial development. It seems that, when compared with other coastal areas of the United States, the southeastern coast is not yet severely degraded, so research and management efforts accompanied by policy changes, can help to prevent further damage. The concept of sustainable development offers an excellent guideline for future actions by those in positions of authority.

I would like to close this report with an affirmation by one of my favorite authors, René Dubos, from his 1981 book *Celebrations of Life*.

> *...it is possible for human beings to modify the surface of the earth in such a way as to create environments that are ecologically viable, esthetically pleasurable and economically profitable....*

To this I would only add that we have much of the necessary technology at hand; we need the will and the resolve to proceed.

LITERATURE CITED

Brown, B., M.E. Hanson, D.M. Liverman, and R.W. Merideth, Jr. 1987. Global sustainability: toward definition. *Environmental Management* 11: 713-719.

Carpenter, R.A. and J.A. Dixon. 1985. Ecology meets economics: A guide to sustainable development. *Environment* 27: 6-11, 27-32.

Carpenter, R.A. and D.E. Harper. 1989. Towards a science of sustainable upland management in developing countries. *Environmental Management* 13: 43-54.

Dovers, S.R. 1990. Sustainability in content: An Australian perspective. *Environmental Management* 14: 297-305.

Dubos, R. 1981. Celebrations of Life. McGraw-Hill, New York.

Holling, C.S. (ed.). 1978. Adaptive Environmental Assessment and Management. John Wiley and Sons, New York.

Redclift, M. 1987. Sustainable Development: Exploring the Contradictions. Methuen, London.

Shearman, R. 1990. The meaning and ethics of sustainability. *Environmental Management* 14: 1-8.

Tolba, M.K. 1987. Sustainable Development: Constraints and Opportunities. Butterworths, London.

World Commission on Environment and Development. 1987. Our Common Future. Oxford University Press, Oxford.

Index

The page number refers to the first page of the chapter in which the index word or phrase occurs.

Albemarle Sound 319
alteration of freshwater flow 171
ammonium 413
anoxia 285
anthropogenic impacts 135
aromatic hydrocarbons 445

biogeochemical cycling 117
biological factors 117
biomarkers 187
biomethylation 265
bivalve molluscs 187

carbon 285, 389
census data 55
chemical factors 117
chemical contaminants 445
chemical loading 171
chlorophyll *a* 319
coastal dredging 285
coastal eutrophication 171
coastal pollution 171
coastal resource management 505
coastal wetlands 111
coastal zone 75
coastal zone management 25
  federal provisions 25
  South Carolina provisions 25
coliform bacteria 241
contaminant effects 135
  on primary production 135
  on salt marsh meiofauna 135
  on salt marsh microbes 135

contaminants 135, 477
copepod 477
Crassostrea virginica 445

data 89
data lineage 89
database management 355
demographics 55
development 171
dissolved organic carbon 389
dissolved oxygen 285, 413
dredging 135, 285

ecology 117
economics 1, 31
enteric pathogens 241
error 89
estuaries 445
eutrophication 135, 221, 285, 319

fecal coliform bacteria 221
fish kills 285
fisheries 81, 285

Geographic Information Systems (GIS)
  89, 343, 355
Geographic Information Processing
  (GIP) 355
geological factors 117
geospatial data 89
golf course management 31
grass shrimp 477
growth forms 75

habitat 477
habitat modification 171
heavy metals 445
hierarchical organization 75
human health effects 221
hydrology 389
hypoxia 285

impacts on fisheries 171

land settlement 7
land use 319
land use planning 7
local growth control policies 31

mapping, maps 89
marina and recreational boating impacts
   135
marine bacterial pathogens 221
marine debris 171
marine fish 187
metadata 89
metal bioaccumulation 265
metal bioavailability 265
metal toxicity 265
microbial indicators of contamination 241
microbial transformation of metals 265
mitigation techniques 171
modeling 117
models 343
mollusks 445
mummichog 477
Murrells Inlet Estuary 413
Murrells Inlet, South Carolina 221, 389

network principle 75
nitrate 413
nitrogen 285, 319, 413
nonmarket values 75
nonpoint source pollution (NPS) 355
North Inlet Estuary 413
North Inlet, South Carolina 221, 389
nutrients 221, 285, 319, 413

oil impacts 135
   mitigation 135
   effects on biota 135
orthophosphate 413
oyster 445, 477

PAHs 445
Pamlico Sound 319
pathogen contamination 135
pathogens in shellfish 171
phosphorus 285, 319
physical alterations 285
population trends 55
primary production 117
productivity 285
public health 221
public policy 7
public policy process 343
pulsing paradigm 75

resource allocation 1

salinity 413
salinity stratification 285
salt marsh creation, restoration,
   mitigation 135
salt marsh(es) 117, 135
sanitation standards 241
secondary production 117
sediment 445
sediment toxicity 187
sheepshead minnow 477
spatial modeling 355
stormwater management 31
sustainability 75
sustainable development 355
sustainable development 505, 509
   approaches to achieving 509
   concepts and definitions 509

toxicants 187
trace metals 445
transformation mechanisms 265
transportation 31

uncertainity 89

Waccamaw region, South Carolina 31
wastewater discharges 241
water quality 31, 221, 413
watershed 389, 413
   alteration 413
   characteristics 389
   nutrient loading 389